RORSCHACH
PSYCHOLOGY

RORSCHACH PSYCHOLOGY

edited by

MARIA A. RICKERS-OVSIANKINA

ROBERT E. KRIEGER PUBLISHING COMPANY
HUNTINGTON, NEW YORK
1977

Original Edition 1960
Second Edition 1977

Printed and Published by
ROBERT E. KRIEGER PUBLISHING CO., INC.
645 NEW YORK AVENUE
HUNTINGTON, NEW YORK 11743

Original Work © Copyright 1960 by
JOHN WILEY & SONS, INC.
New Material © Copyright 1977
ROBERT E. KRIEGER PUBLISHING CO., INC.

Library of Congress Catalog Card Number 74-266
ISBN Number 0-88275-168-9

Printed in the U.S.A. by
Noble Offset Printers Inc.
New York, N. Y. 10003

PREFACE TO
THE SECOND EDITION

During its presence on the American psychological scene the Rorschach has lived through a rather stormy course of identity formation. At first there was a phase of rapid accumulation of impressive successes in exploring heretofore inaccessible areas of personality functioning. Encouraged by these accomplishments, occasionally magnified by enthusiastic promoters, the Rorschach enterprise took on a somewhat manic tinge, ready to tackle any and all personality problems and confident in the method's ability to supply the answers.

Understandably, an inflated self image of this kind was not likely to survive, especially in the severe climate of a psychometrically dominated assessment world. Voices of critical doubt, frequently based on epistomologically misapplied research models, became audible. Rather than succumb to such an atmosphere of pessimism, however, the Rorschach underwent a period of healthy self-appraisal, from which in due course it emerged with new vigor, realistic in scope and sound in methodology. These developments, so fortunate for the future of personality study, owe their strength to the conceptual nature of the psychological premises underlying this unique assessment device. Any systematically thinking psychologist has no difficulty in recognizing how the interpretative significance that Rorschach assigned to the various perceptual-cognitive components of his test is implicitly rooted in a well thought-out, broadly integrated personality theory.

Guided by this scientific asset of the method, discerning Rorschach workers have recently been able to bring forth a substantial number of informative findings, covering a wide range of personality problems, problems that in one form or another derive from the basic premises of the instrument. As a result of such methodologically constructive research activity the Rorschach's role among projective techniques is now firmly established. It is one of unrivaled potential for portraying human individuality in all its richness: the patterned interaction among cognitive, emotional, conative, and attitudinal dimensions, and likewise, the longitudinal unfolding of levels and hierarchies.

The importance of a conceptual framework for any meaningful application of the Rorschach was actually foreshadowed in the first edition of *Rorschach Psychology* by its explicit orientation toward theoretical concerns. Hence the present edition re-states and develops further the basic goals of its predecessor. It is not a handbook, nor an instructional manual on the mechanics of employing the method. Rather it aims at exploring systematically the various components of the Rorschach with respect to their usefulness for conceptually founded personality study.

Accordingly, the plan of the book, built upon the individual treatment of each of the Rorschach components, is kept intact. Within this general framework, however, there is a good deal that is new. Chapters that were developed around a conceptual position of continuing significance for Rorschach theorizing are left relatively unchanged, except for minor commentaries, addenda, etc. Where, on the other hand, the previous treatment of the topic was chiefly in the form of a survey of research findings, the availability of new material led to complete re-writing of the particular chapter. Over and above this up-dating of the earlier material, the present volume is enriched by the addition of five new chapters, prepared especially for it. These new contributions were chosen to reflect recent creative developments in the employment of the Rorschach for the tapping of ever broader and deeper aspects of a person's inner being.

Among the individual components of a Rorschach analysis innovative thinking has centered primarily around the movement determinant and the content interpretation. Hence, an additional chapter on the *M* response is included, that scrutinizes systematically the spectrum of explanatory hypotheses stimulated by this intriguing perceptual phenomenon. Similarly the section of the book dealing with the content category contains two new chapters. The first presents a novel method for uncovering hidden symbolic meaning beyond the surface representational implications of a response, that traditionally have served as basis for content interpretation. The second views the over-all manner and style of a subject's verbalizations during a Rorschach performance as sample reflections of the person's interpersonal communicative stance, an area relatively neglected in standard Rorschach personality pictures.

A much overdue avenue of Rorschach theorizing grows out of the profound affinity between Rorschach's conceptions of personality patterning and those of Carl G. Jung. To explore this avenue the part of the book devoted to matters of the total test pattern has been augmented by the addition of a chapter that applies Jung's theory of archetypal energy to Rorschach analysis. By following the course of image formation during a Rorschach experience the author endeavors to demonstrate how such an approach can extend our grasp of the range and nature of psychic processes, of the Self as it is "becoming." Finally, in the last section of the book the chapter on reliability was written for the first edition by the late Jules Holzberg. Since this thorny problem was handled by him in a manner still very basic and timely, the chapter appears in its original form. The chapter on validity, on the other hand, was a product of the gloom-and-doom period, alluded to above, that by now is fortunately a matter of the past. For these reasons the chapter is replaced by a new presentation of the topic that reflects contemporary sophistication in research design and thereby highlights effectively what can and what cannot reasonably be expected of the Rorschach.

The epigraphs to Chapters 4, 6, 7, 8, 9, 11 through 16 were provided by the respective authors of the chapters; the remaining seven epigraphs were chosen by the editor.

I wish to thank all the authors of the chapters for their expert handling of their respective topics. I am especially grateful to Sheldon J. Korchin and Margaret Thaler Singer who contributed in many more ways to the completion of this volume. Thanks are also due to Marguerite R. Hertz, Robert R. Holt, Walter G. Klopfer, and Zygmunt

A. Piotrowski for checking the accuracy of scoring systems, listed in the Appendix. Many more persons have contributed to the completion of this book. Special mention should be made of the competent and conscientious work of Allan Warrern in translating Chapter 9 and of Hilde Bernstein and Alexander Nemeth in translating Chapter 14. The ultimate responsibility for the translations, however, is my own. Both translations were authorized by the authors.

This updated and expanded edition is offered in the hope that it will stimulate renewed impetus toward conceptually oriented Rorschach research and thus contribute to the integration of Rorschach psychology into the broader body of the psychology of normal and abnormal personality.

MARIA A. RICKERS-OVSIANKINA
Berkeley, California, November, 1976

PREFACE TO
THE FIRST EDITION

The function envisioned for this book might best be expressed by stating first what it is not. The book is not planned to furnish another instructional manual on the use of the Rorschach method. It does not intend to teach the standard mechanics of administering, scoring, and interpreting the test. Rather, it is directed to theory-minded readers from the ranks of clinicians and general psychologists alike.

It is no exaggeration to say that the majority of contemporary clinicians would find it difficult even to contemplate their field of specialization without Rorschach's contribution to it. In fact, for no small number, personality assessment and the Rorschach are practically synonymous. And yet, paradoxically enough, despite the prominence accorded to the Rorschach test in their daily work, these psychologists would be hard pressed if asked to spell out the place of their method within the theoretical framework of psychology at large and within the psychology of personality in particular. Conversely, many general psychologists, active in the area of personality, motivation, emotion, and cognition, are rarely aware of what a mine of wealth for their own domain can be found within the diversified pattern of a Rorschach protocol.

This lack of contact between two groups equally devoted to the study of personality problems becomes at least partially understandable when the nature of the test and its history are considered. In the spirit of traditional faculty-symptom-oriented psychology and psychiatry of the second decade of our century, Hermann Rorschach set out to devise a method for the measurement of a particular psychological function, one that in its extreme manifestations serves as a differential symptom in psychiatric classification: the function of imagination. The choice of ink blots for such a purpose also has its precedent. However, in the course of his experimentations, with conventional methods on a conventional topic, clinical insight, supported by the then very new ideas of Freudian-Jungian psychoanalysis, soon extended the scope of his research beyond the traditions of his time. Keenly cognizant of the individuality of the particular person in whom he was observing the imaginative processes, Rorschach became impressed with the evidence that the subject's perceptual reactions, while yielding information about imagination, were at the same time telling a great deal more about the person. He began to see the imaginative processes as closely interacting with other psychological functions. Recognition of this interaction, in turn, meant orientation to a fundamental principle of personality organization, and with this step he found himself right in the midst of the broad and complex problems of total-personality functioning.

We are told that grasping the inner workings of man was a life-long concern of Rorschach's. It is understandable, therefore, how exciting the prospect must have been to him that his experimentations with ink blots might provide a workable method for attaining this goal. Inspired by such perspectives, he threw his full efforts into the task: the skills of artist and of scientist blended by the zeal of a sensitive, highly gifted man. The result, as we all know, was both a comprehensive schema for the representation of the total personality and a concrete procedure for measuring individual differences among personalities. Rorschach thus discovered a fundamental organismic principle independently and in advance of his scientific milieu, and, in addition, laid the groundwork for the quantitative study of these intricate patterns of personality organization.

It is hardly surprising that a revolutionary achievement of such magnitude and singularity could not be readily incorporated into the framework of conventional psychology of his time. Although Rorschach's discovery remained apart from the main stream of academic psychology over the following decades, this did not mean stagnation. The exceptional usefulness of the method for personality assessment was soon recognized and realized in clinical settings. From this basic field of application it has been spreading rapidly into an ever-widening circle of psychodiagnostic investigations.

The extensive and varied use of the method has resulted in the accumulation of a vast amount of information about it. The bulk of this material is in the form of statistical studies on a broad range of populations tested for every conceivable purpose. The chief value of this impressive storehouse of empirical data lies in providing not only confirmation but also some modifications and extensions to the clinical validity of Rorschach's original interpretative hypotheses.

In addition to this dominant, primarily solidifying type of development, some noteworthy inroads are being made along frankly exploratory and qualitative rather than quantitative lines. The challenge of probing for further and further understanding of a person's personality, so characteristic of intensive clinical work, is particularly stimulated by test material as complex in nature as the Rorschach. In this manner, over the years, a good many new ways of looking at one aspect or another of the test have been evolved by perceptive clinicians, explicitly or implicitly guided by theoretical assumptions and principles inherent in their particular philosophy of psychopathology.

Finally, there are the relative newcomers, the system-oriented Rorschach workers. Centering their interest on the theoretical underpinnings of the instrument, these researchers attempt to relate the psychological interpretation of the test variables to ideas and findings from other areas of psychology, to evolve hypotheses around these relationships, and to subject them to experimental scrutiny.

The present volume was prompted by the feeling that the time was ripe for sorting out and formulating systematically from among these different sources the material that appeared promising for fostering our understanding of the psychological foundations of the method. Guided by these considerations, Rorschach issues that have stimulated basic research were selected for exploration in individual chapters. Each chapter is handled by an author for whom the particular topic constitutes a major research interest. An introductory chapter supplies a brief over-all view of the method and assigns the place of every chapter topic within this framework.

Although intended primarily as contributions toward a theoretical basis for the Rorschach, these presentations are not shaped to conform to one specific theoretical model. In his writings, Rorschach left us neither a complete nor a neat or consistent theory for the conceptualization of the problems involved in his instrument. He was quite emphatic, however, in stressing certain basic premises that are absolutely indispensable for the comprehension of the psychological essence of his method: the utilization of primarily formal features of the test responses as indicators of personality dimensions and the adherence to the principle of interaction among the test variables. These general premises would seem to provide a favorable climate for present-day attempts to re-evaluate theoretically its major psychological properties. It is in the nature of formally conceived variables to be adaptable to the schemes of varying theoretical models. Without essential changes in the diagnostic procedure of the test, its theoretical foundation is, hence, capable of effectively participating in the growth process of contemporary psychological thinking.

Psychology of personality has hardly reached a level of scientific maturity that would permit meaningful conceptualization within one tight unitary system. At the same time it is evident that during the last decades some common trends have become dominant in the broad area of personality theory: a realization that, in order to contribute fruitfully to this branch of inquiry, the conceptual system employed must operate within a holistic, "molar" frame of thinking and, furthermore, must gear its hypothetical constructs to formal or functional categories. Consequently, in this book, a variety of holistically oriented modes of theorizing (including some European work) will be given expression, each author choosing the conceptual system that in his eyes holds the greatest promise for enriching insight into the Rorschach issues under consideration in that particular chapter. Although the level of generality of the constructs utilized in these presentations naturally will vary, the orientation is toward greater formalization than heretofore common in the Rorschach literature.

Similarly, the aim of this book also led to considerable freedom in choice of method for dealing with the assigned topic. Thus some authors depend heavily on experimental data, others base their reasoning primarily on clinical evidence. Some emphasize coverage of available research, others subordinate research citation to theory building. Some favor discursive speculation, others dwell on matters as concrete as the inauguration of a new scoring schema. Whatever the methodological approach and whatever the conceptual tools, the main criterion of selection remains throughout usability for a systematic formulation in the particular branch of inquiry. Occasional discrepancies in hypotheses advanced by different authors may then not only be expected but should actually be welcomed for throwing the issue into sharper focus. By the same token, scattered spots of overlap from chapter to chapter were allowed to stay lest the cogency within an author's message might suffer.

It is hoped that this collation will have the effect of enhancing the conceptual precision of the basic test variables, of detecting and delineating gaps in our knowledge, and of pointing up pertinent research areas. The groundwork then would have been laid for further fruitful interaction between theory and practice in the complex task of developing this most challenging area of Rorschach psychology.

MARIA A. RICKERS-OVSIANKINA
Storrs, Connecticut, July, 1960

CONTRIBUTORS

EWALD BOHM, Ph.D.
Clinical Psychologist
Waedenswil, Switzerland

SERENA-LYNN BROWN, M.A.
graduate student
Yale University

CHARLES FONDA, Ph.D.
Clinical Psychologist
Cranbury, New Jersey

LAURENCE HEMMENDINGER, Ph.D.
Chief Clinical Psychologist
West Haven Mental Hygiene Clinic
Veterans Administration

MARGUERITE R. HERTZ, Ph.D.
Professor emeritus
Case Western Reserve University

ROBERT R. HOLT, Ph.D.
Professor
New York University

JULES D. HOLZBERG, Ph.D.
deceased, formerly professor
Wesleyan University

SHELDON J. KORCHIN, Ph.D.
Professor
University of California, Berkeley

ROLAND KUHN, M.D.
Kantonale Heil-und-Pflegeanstalt
Muensterlingen, Switzerland

DALE G. LARSON, M.A.
graduate student
University of California, Berkeley

MARTIN MAYMAN, Ph.D.
Professor
University of Michigan

ROBERT S. McCULLY, Ph.D.
Professor
Medical University of South Carolina

FLORENCE R. MIALE, Ph.D.
Clinical Psychologist
New York City

GARDNER MURPHY, Ph.D.
Director of research, retired
Menninger Foundation

LOIS B. MURPHY, Ph.D.
Member of Academic Advisory Staff
Children's Hospital, Washington, D.C.

ZYGMUNT A. PIOTROWSKI, Ph.D.
Professor, retired
Thomas Jefferson University

MARIA A. RICKERS-OVSIANKINA, Ph.D.
Professor emeritus
University of Connecticut

DAVID SHAPIRO, Ph.D.
Private Practice of Psychotherapy
Los Angeles

DAVID SCHULTZ, M.S.
graduate student
Yale University

JEROME L. SINGER, Ph.D.
Professor
Yale University

MARGARET THALER SINGER, Ph.D.
Lecturer
University of California, Berkeley

LAURA C. TOOMEY, Ph.D.
Coordinator of Clinical Psychology Training
Connecticut Valley Hospital

IRVING B. WEINER, Ph.D.
Professor
Case Western Reserve University

CONTENTS

INTRODUCTION

1   Synopsis of psychological premises underlying the Rorschach   3
    Maria A. Rickers-Ovsiankina

CATEGORIES OF ANALYSIS: LOCATION

2   The organization activity   29
    Marguerite R. Hertz

3   Developmental theory and the Rorschach method   83
    Laurence Hemmendinger and K. David Schultz

4   The white-space response   113
    Charles P. Fonda

CATEGORIES OF ANALYSIS: DETERMINANTS

5   Form perception and ego functioning   159
    Sheldon J. Korchin and Dale G. Larson

6   The movement responses   189
    Zygmunt A. Piotrowski

7   A multi-dimensional view of the Rorschach movement response   229
    Martin Mayman

8   A perceptual understanding of color response   251
    David Shapiro

9   The Binder chiaroscuro system and its theoretical basis   303
    Ewald Bohm

10 The experience type: Some behavioral correlates and theoretical
    implications   325
    Jerome L. Singer and Serena-Lynn Brown

CATEGORIES OF ANALYSIS: CONTENT

11   A method for assessing primary process manifestations and their
     control in Rorschach responses   375
     Robert R. Holt

12   Symbolic imagery in Rorschach material   421
     Florence R. Miale

13   The Rorschach as a transaction   455
     Margaret Thaler Singer

THE TEST PATTERN

14   Some problems concerning the psychological implications of
     Rorschach's form interpretation test   489
     Roland Kuhn

15   Jung's depth psychology and Rorschach patterning   513
     Robert S. McCully

16   Hermann Rorschach and personality research   535
     Lois and Gardner Murphy

METHODOLOGICAL CONSIDERATIONS

17   Reliability re-examined   555
     Jules D. Holzberg

18   Approaches to Rorschach validation   575
     Irving B. Weiner

APPENDIX

Tabular comparison of scoring systems   609
     Laura C. Toomey and Maria A. Rickers-Ovsiankina

NAME INDEX   633

SUBJECT INDEX   643

ACKNOWLEDGMENTS   649

INTRODUCTION

To proceed beyond the limitations of a given level of knowledge the researcher, as a rule, has to break down methodological taboos which condemn as "unscientific" or "illogical" the very methods or concepts which later on prove to be basic for the next major progress.

KURT LEWIN

1

by M. A. Rickers-Ovsiankina

Synopsis of Psychological Premises Underlying the Rorschach

To engage profitably in explorations of the theoretical and research potential of the Rorschach method, it is essential to keep in mind the psychological tenets inherent in this highly valued, yet inadequately understood, diagnostic instrument. In this chapter these issues are put into focus by reviewing briefly the Rorschach's chief working principles, and by examining these principles in the light of contemporary psychological knowledge.

The outstanding feature of the Rorschach method is generally recognized to lie in its power to provide an integrated pattern of the total personality, while simultaneously articulating this pattern in specific quantitative ways into a manifold of personality dimensions. This accomplishment, still unique among assessment procedures, was made possible to a considerable degree by the way in which Rorschach defined his task from a systematic point of view. His primary interest was in getting at the nature of the basic modes of functioning, underlying all of an individual's psychic activity. He was quite explicit in emphasizing that his goal was to uncover *how*, rather than *what*, the person experiences. This meant looking, e.g., not so much for the particular content of a subject's preoccupations, hopes, and fears as for the modes by which these psychic

3

events come about: whether they are experienced as impulsive upsurges, as all pervading emotional states, as lively resonances to the surrounding atmosphere, or as rationally controlled reactions. The concern is more with the formal or functional than with the contentual, substantive aspects of the personality.

It was Rorschach's conviction that a person's perceptual responses to the ink blots were capable of serving as clues to such basic tendencies so long as the responses were viewed consistently in the frame of this systematic orientation. Accordingly, when abstracting from the complex test performance certain components for analysis, he concentrated primarily on formal categories and only secondarily on content categories. With the formal test dimensions thus providing the basic structure or scaffolding of the equally formal personality configuration, the actual content of day-to-day experiences then, but only then, becomes important in lending individuality and concreteness to the formal representation. The outcome is a formalized, yet alive, picture of the complete personality.

Besides Rorschach's choice of categories of analysis, his manner of employing these variables is of equal importance for a full appreciation of what Rorschach has given psychology with his instrument. While taking full advantage of the amenability of these categories of analysis to precise identification and measurement, he never interpreted any one of the categories by itself, but always as dependent upon the others, thus adhering to his basic principle of interaction among psychological functions right at the level of their correlates within the test data.

Over and over again Rorschach impresses upon the reader the importance of observing this principle. Each scoring category is viewed in relation to the other extant categories—whether the numerical pattern of the whole protocol or a single test response is under consideration. An individual response acquires its true meaning only when perceived against the background of the total cross-sectional psychogram, and when considered in terms of its place in the longitudinal sequence of the test performance. It is a matter of wholes and subwholes of a horizontal-structural and of a temporal nature. This emphasis on the pattern or configuration, however, never leads to vague globality, since each component scoring category is given a great deal of attention *per se*, each being recorded and evaluated in careful and very specific detail. The Rorschach worker has to be constantly attuned to handling the subunits now as dependent parts and now as gestalten in their own right. In other words, the test as envisioned by its founder constitutes a true *unitas multiplex*.

For an understanding of how such unified, formalized, yet richly individual personality pictures derive from a set of responses to ink blots, we must turn our attention to the psychological meaning of the test components, both singly and in their interplay. Inasmuch as these components constitute the cornerstones of the method, it is only through an illumination of their respective roles in the test pattern that this pattern in its deeper personality implications will acquire full significance. The manner in which Rorschach relates specific aspects of percepts, represented by the scoring categories, to those basic personality dimensions that were of major concern to him, reflects well the origin of the test; empirical generalizations, rational deductions, artistic intuition, hunches, and flashes of ideas intermingle in providing the foundation for this multifaceted system of interrelated functioning. Unraveling this isomorphism of percept and personality is complicated by the fact that the correspondences do not constitute simple one-to-one equivalents. Every category of test performance taps more than one psychological function and, conversely, a psychological characteristic is derived from a combination of several test categories.

In the following chapters, these links will be recast by utilizing contemporary theories, relevant research data, and accumulated clinical experience to explore, first, the major test categories individually and then, in the last chapters, the method in its totality. For purposes of unity in this multiauthored endeavor, the problems involved in the various chapter topics are here anticipated by means of a bird's eye view of the Rorschach procedure and its basic psychological postulates.

CATEGORIES OF ANALYSIS

A response to the ink blots is classified under four major headings:

Location refers to the area of the plate chosen, to whether the area is whole or part, and to what kind of part.

Determinant comprises the specific properties of the blot that according to the testee prompted the response, such as the form of the blot, its color, shading, kinesthetic features.

Content identifies the subject matter of the response in broad categories; e.g., human, animal, landscape.

Popularity-originality represents the opposite poles of frequency in the identification of a certain blot area with a certain content.

Under each of these four major classes Rorschach employed a set of differential scoring categories. In essence, his classification system is still followed in contemporary practice. Since the test has been used so widely, a considerable number of modifications have naturally evolved around certain aspects of the scoring system, resulting in additional scores, in subdivisions, and in reformulations. Inasmuch as these particularities of scoring lie outside the focal orientation of this book, they will not be discussed in the present synopsis. For the convenience of the reader, however, the Appendix contains in tabular form a schematic comparison of the main scoring systems appearing in English language publications.

Location

The location scores deal with such configurational properties of a percept as extension, connectedness, and segregation in visual space. The main distinctions derived from these features rest on the question as to whether the response pertains to the whole blot (W), to a readily isolated, frequently apprehended blot detail (D), to a less obvious blot detail (Dd), or whether the subject reverses figure and ground, selecting the white space for an interpretation (S). Within these classifications a good deal of attention is paid to such qualitative considerations as to whether a certain whole response is aimed at embracing the totality of the given material to the neglect of details, or whether the response constitutes an effort to combine into a meaningful whole as many of the details as possible.

The numerical constellation of location scores, supplemented by these kinds of qualitative elaborations, is considered to reveal the fundamental orientation of a person's mental functioning. This orientation refers to the relative weight of organization versus articulation, of synthesis versus analysis in the subject's cognitive activities, and to the degree of generality, complexity, and specificity that characterizes the activities. Although primarily indicative of such variations in intellectual ability, the psychological significance of the location scores is not limited to the cognitive area. In a way typical of Rorschach's thinking, the location measures reflect also some volitional factors of effort or intent toward cognitive display.

Here, then, essential psychological functions are identified effectively for diagnostic purposes on the basis of structural characteristics of a person's perceptual behavior. Quite independently, such properties of the perceptual process have been studied and conceptualized by the laboratory psychologist. The challenge of following up this parallel between the Rorschach and perception psychology is close at hand. It has been met in this book along several lines.

Chapter 2 reviews the work that has grown up around an interest in isolating numerically the organizational activity in Rorschach responses through a statistically established score. By citing norms for this "organization score," relating it to standard Rorschach factors, correlating it with functionally corresponding variables from other psychological tests, and comparing clinical groups on this measure, an empirical foundation for the psychological significance of the "organization score" is mapped out.

In Chapter 3, Werner's (1948 and 1956) developmental sensory-tonic theory is utilized as a model for subdividing the location scores in terms of the type of organizational activity involved. According to this experimentally and genetically-observationally grounded theory, differences in perceptual behavior are to be viewed as indicative of differences in organismic levels of development. By applying the major criteria that differentiate such levels to the varieties of perceptual structuring observable among the location scores, it becomes possible to order the various types of perceptual structuring into a logical continuum. A quantifiable means is thus supplied for relating a certain aspect of test behavior to a broader orbit of theoretically founded conceptions regarding differences in mental functioning.

Chapter 4 is devoted to the problem of figure-ground reversal, a gestalt phenomenon that has intrigued the laboratory worker for some time, and that has been much investigated with respect to general laws governing its occurrence. It is through the Rorschach test, however, that research interest has turned to individual differences in this form of perceptual behavior, known in the context of the test as the space response (S). The emphasis here is not just on a subject's tendency for perceptual structuring, but on restructuring, i.e., on the shifting from the initially conceived configuration to the production of a new one and, moreover, achieving this by means of a figural reversal. Since ease and efficiency of restructuring is, nowadays, understood to be based on some very fundamental forces in a person's psychological make-up, the diagnostic implications of restructuring through figure-ground reversal would appear to be of particular significance. These implications are highlighted by employing contemporary personality theory for closer integration of the space response into the broader Rorschach pattern than heretofore customary. While lending to the space response greater clarity and weight as a test factor *per se*, such theoretical reformulation brings, in turn, new perspectives and new cohesion to the over-all potential of the Rorschach.

Determinants

The test is introduced by the examiner's question, "What might this be?" The subject's task is thus formulated as one of recognition. We know from psychology of memory that the occurrence of an experience of recognition presupposes the existence of a certain degree of similarity between the incoming stimulus complex and a system of memory traces left behind by an earlier perceptual process. According to gestalt theory (Koffka, 1935) this correspondence does not imply absolute similarity, or similarity based on identity of elements, but rather similarity of gestalt character.

Instruction to the subjects to draw their percepts results in a considerable range of variations in apparently the same responses to the same blot or blot detail (Levine, K. and Grassi, J., 1942). As Brosin has pointed out, a response like "bat" is given with high frequency to several of the cards, which are neither identical in their perceptual features, nor does any one of them represent an accurate image of a real bat. What seems to elicit this response is that "these cards have a batlike character, . . . the gestalt quality of a bat" (1942, p. 4). The question arises as to what it is that conveys to one subject a batlike character in a certain ink blot, or that makes another subject see the same blot as a crouching giant?

In Rorschach's thinking these problems occupy a central position. In the analysis of a person's perceptual performance he considers them under a separate classificational grouping called *determinants*, subdivided into *form, color, chiaroscuro (shading), movement*. In the following, these categories will be identified, first, in terms of the perceptual processes involved in each determinant and, second, in terms of the psychodiagnostic implications accorded to a determinant within the test procedure.

Perceptual processes. The description of the perceptual processes underlying the respective determinant will begin with the auto-chthonous properties of these processes and will then evolve from these properties the type of person-environment interplay and the activity level characteristic of the particular perceptual process.

FORM (*F*). When the interpretation given by the subject is based primarily on the shape or form of the chosen blot area, as "bat" or "aeroplane" for all of card I, the determinant is indicated by the *Form* score (*F*). The perceptual process involved in this type of reaction can be readily represented as an instance of proficiency in perceptual organization. Structural gestalt principles of symmetry, contour, and closure operate in producing the figural quality that is perceived by the testee as a certain object. Individual parts are utilized according to their place within the over-all percept. The emerging gestalt character of the perceived figure is viewed in relation to another organized pattern, that of a memory trace complex; or, to state it a little differently, a "hypothesis" is checked against the input information (Bruner, J.S., 1951). The more accurately these organizational principles are applied in bringing about the particular interpretation, i.e., the greater the figural "goodness" or the *prägnanz* of the percept, the higher, in Rorschach terminology, the form level of the subject's functioning.

In achieving such a *prägnant* percept, the subject has to exert a certain amount of effort. We know from the psychology of perception that the activation of organizational processes consumes energy. In establishing gestalt similarity between the visual figure before him and an appropriate memory image, the person has to apply himself actively and deliberately. He has to select, weigh, and evaluate. His reactions are controlled and guided by objective features of the given material. They are stimulusbound. In keeping with this nature of the task, the observer's activity level may be characterized as relatively high, and the prevailing subject-environment relation as object-determined, detached, and impersonal.

MOVEMENT (M). There is a type of response in which the gestalt character does not follow strictly from the forms of the two-dimensional card but implies, as it were, a third dimension. The perceived configuration is no longer static for the subject, as in form-determined responses, but has a dynamic character, direction, figural incompleteness, tension. As Arnheim has demonstrated, such occurrences follow logically from the basic principle of gestalt theory that all perception is dynamic in nature: "Visual forms are striving in certain directions, they contain directed tension. They represent a happening, rather than a being." The phenomenon of experiencing locomotion when viewing certain Rorschach cards is thus "not an illusion or an imagination, but an inherent feature of visual perception." Experiencially it is enhanced beyond the threshold of awareness by "gradients of perceptual qualities . . . oblique forms, shadings" (1969, p. 269f.). On the Rorschach test such dynamic effect, when apprehended by a person, usually leads to an interpretation of a human or animal figure seen in motion. Accordingly, the determinant for this group of reactions is designated as *Movement* or *kinesthetic response*. Rorschach maintained that some kind of kinesthetic element actually enters into the experience of a genuine movement percept. From a theoretical point of view this assumption is noteworthy. If one interprets it not in the narrow connotation of sensory awareness of muscular stimulation, but rather in a broader meaning of somatic participation in a perceptual experience, then Rorschach here actually anticipated in an interesting way present-day organismic, field-theoretical models of perception.[1]

In the movement response we have a situation where the subject

[1] Goldstein has asserted "to every sense stimulation there is a corresponding specific response pattern of the entire organism . . . a certain muscle tension corresponds to every sense impression" (1963, p. 263f.). Similarly Werner and Wapner state that "perception is defined as a total dynamic process that can be analyzed empirically into its contributing factors that are tonic and sensory . . . The potency of tonic factors for perception would

interacts with the structural features of the stimulus manifold freely and autonomously in the course of his perceptual production. He is less stimulusbound and less closely dependent on the objectively given than in the case of a form response. In contrast to the latter, when bringing about the relatively complex movement response, the testee puts more of himself into the task, drawing on broader and deeper personal resources. Correspondingly the subject-environment relation is no longer detached and object-controlled, but is marked by spontaneity and ego involvement, while the activity level of the observer remains as high as in form perception.

COLOR (C). When the gestalt character of the percept is evoked either solely or in conjunction with form by the hue of the blot ("flowers, fire") the determinant of *Color* (C) is used in the scoring of the respective response. Whereas, with both form and movement interpretations, the subject is actively at work on an organizational process consuming energy, when color serves as the carrier of the gestalt character the situation is quite different in this respect. As the author has pointed out elsewhere (Rickers-Ovsiankina, 1943), apart from the circumstance that color differences might demarcate different regions within the visual field and thereby bring into play the factor of form with its organizational properties, color perception as such does not involve complex processes of articulation and organization. Characteristically, the experience of color is of un-differentiated nature. It is a much more direct sense datum than is either form or movement. The person becomes aware of color at once, without an intermediate step of reflecting, organizing, or evaluating processes. Colors, particularly the warm or hard hues, impress themselves in an immediate, one might say personal, manner. They affect us, speak to us, in a simple, rather primitive, fashion (Rickers-Ovsiankina, 1955). This impact is rarely experienced as neutral. Colors strike us as pleasing, displeasing, exciting, or soothing. They attract or repel us. Because of this vivid, emotionally toned quality, the author has referred to color experience as physiognomic (1943). Similarly, Bash (1957) has pointed out that color perception

---

be obscure without appreciating that the state of the organism is part and parcel of per-ceptual events" (1949, p. 191, 192).

fits Metzger's identification of an entity's gestalt character in terms of its intrinsic nature or essence (*Wesen*).[2]

The object's physiognomy or essence is thrust upon the observer in a specific, universally compelling fashion.[3] The direction of the action goes from object to subject. This latter aspect of the interplay, together with its immediacy and forcefulness has led to characterizing the subject's position in color perception as receptive, passive (Schachtel, 1966; Shapiro, 1956), or as a state of surrender (Goldstein, 1963). The perceptual process that underlies the color determinant, then, may be characterized as a state of passivity regarding the activity level, and as a condition of being subjectively affected by the essence of a particular outside object with respect to the person-environment relation.

CHIAROSCURO (*Ch.*). Akin to the color is the *Chiaroscuro* or *Shading* determinant. It is used when the gestalt character of the percept is brought about exclusively, or in combination with form, by transitions within the achromatic light-dark continuum. Unlike the chromatic response, however, the chiaroscuro interpretation is not evoked by single intensities. A shading reaction is rather produced by a diffuse total impression of the manifold of lightness nuances blurring into each other. The darkness, or haziness, or fluffiness of this impression typically leads to percepts of a synesthetic nature, such as "fur," "storm clouds," "rocks." Following Bash's application of Metzger's classifications one might, therefore, identify the gestalt character of the chiaroscuro determinant as based chiefly on the substance or fabric of the perceived material (see footnote 2), or one might say with Koffka (1935) and Gibson (1950) that the response derives from the microstructure (grain, texture) of the stimulus constellation. Although the subject is in the case of the shading response equally, if not more than in the case of the color response, at the mercy of the environment, the components of the

---

[2] Metzger (1932) differentiates the following three modes by which the gestalt character of an entity may become apparent: (a) Structure (*Struktur*) or organization (*Gefüge*), referring to all types of spatial-temporal formation and patterning; (b) global quality (*Ganzqualität*) or substance (*Ganzbeschaffenheit*), comprising all characteristics of material or fabric; (c) essence or intrinsic nature (*Wesen*), including all expressive, physiognomic features.

[3] The phenomenon is reflected in the symbolic meaning that colors play in religious art, as in Russian icons (Trubetskoi, 1973) and in the imagery of Tibetan mysticism (A. Govinda, 1967).

interaction stand out less, no part of the field acquires figure character, there is only ground. The situation is not experienced as one of
being affected by the essence of an individual object in the environment, but rather as a generalized state of finding oneself in the
atmosphere or the mood emanated by the material substance of the
environmental setting. The diffuseness and lack of clear-cut articulation within the setting has an overpowering, frequently disquieting
or threatening, effect upon the observer. Because of the pervading
quality of this effect, the subject feels submerged, enveloped by
its atmosphere. Similarly to color experience, the person feels passively affected, acted upon by the environment, with the important
difference, however, that now there is no one particular environmental object affecting the observer. Instead, there is a general
blurring of boundaries, not only in the visual field but also in the
person-versus-environment differentiation.

Psychodiagnostic implications. By thinking of the response
determinants in the light of the perceptual processes underlying
these determinants, it becomes psychologically meaningful, if not
actually compelling, how these determinants can be understood
as being functionally dependent on certain personality characteristics.

FORM. Rorschach saw in the form level not only a measure of the
directly observable ability for appropriate structuring of visual
stimulus material but, moreover, an index of the person's total
rational equipment for comprehending and grasping relations. Such
a generalization should make sense to those students of psychology
who view all modes of cognitive functioning as governed by the
same fundamental organizational laws, and who consider precision
and versatility in structuring a crucial factor in evaluating any intellectual performance.

When, furthermore, the subject-environment relation described
above for the F determinant is taken into consideration, it becomes
clear that possession of a certain level of intellectual ability is not
likely by itself to result in a corresponding level of form perception on
the test. To adhere to the given reality of the test material throughout the examination, there has to be not only ability for accurate
perception but also the power to apply oneself consistently to the
task in a critical and objective manner. The exercising of such a

power requires control over interference from internal pressures of an emotional-motivational nature, a constellation of forces dynamically referred to as ego strength. In Chapter 5 the role of the F determinant will be discussed within this broader framework of personality, rather than of mental ability alone.

MOVEMENT. Rorschach contended that the ability to employ the movement factor in interpreting the ink-blots implies mental productivity, a creative potential and, in a more extended sense, a tendency toward inner living. Viewing M as an indicator of creativity falls in line with gestalt psychological principles since structuring activity that depends for its completion on components not exlicitly given (the type of structuring found in the movement response) is in gestalt literature equated cognitively with creativity and inventiveness rather than with mere comprehension (Koehler, 1930). If, in addition, we accept the organismic dictum that no cognitive behavior is without supporting conative-emotional components (Sheerer, 1953), then it is to be expected that these components would be particularly evident in as complex a cognitive process as the movement response; and the spontaneous, ego-involving character of the subject-environment relation, prevailing in the "creating" of an M response, will further the participation of relatively central inner-personal regions. It is, then, inherent in the specific fashion by which the M determinant comes about that the study of such responses should be capable of providing clues not only regarding the subject's creative potential but also of supplying insights into the general realm of his inner living. In Chapters 6 and 7 the implications that follow from this role of the M determinant are examined, interpreted, and developed further.

COLOR. In Rorschach practice the color determinant is related specifically to the emotional sphere and, more generally, to a person's environmental reactivity. The isomorphism of chromatic color perception and emotionality has been forecast by our earlier description of the perceptual properties of the color determinant. In a situation where an environmental object impresses its physiognomy or essence upon the observer in an immediate and impelling fashion, allowing for no emancipative distance, there can be no place for active reflection or sober evaluation, so fundamental in the exercise of purely intellectual functions of the human mind; the behavior will tend rather toward receptive and relatively direct, primitive forms. If, furthermore, one wanted to identify these forms of behavior in terms of a conventionally known psychological function, the dimension of emotionality naturally suggests itself. As pointed out above, chromatic colors affect us with quite individualized, directed, and provocative qualities, and we know from general psychology that being affected in such ways by an environmental event is considered to be falling into the broader realm of experiencing emotion (Arnold, 1960).

Although matters of person-environment interaction play a cardinal role in most field-theoretical personality systems, Lewin's (1936) treatment of the problem seems most appropriate to this discussion. In his conceptual model, both the extent of accessibility of inner personal regions to outside influences and the facility of outward expression of these regions depend on the degree of permeability of the individual's outside boundary. The greater the functional permeability of the outer boundary, the freer the interplay between the person and his immediate environment. Applying this line of thinking to our discussion of color perception, one could say that the freedom of interplay is manifested equally in the subject's being easily impressed, affected, provoked by the essence of outside objects, and in his reacting to such "intrusions" in a spontaneous, immediate, and more or less uncontrolled fashion. Among the latter reactions, emotionality is but one mode, yet the clearest. From this point of view, color responses on the Rorschach become indicators of a very basic personality variable—the degree of permeability of the subject's outside boundary.

It would thus appear that the diagnostic role assigned by Rorschach to the color determinant readily lends itself to fruitful treatment within contemporary theoretical frames. In Chapter 8 an attempt of this kind is offered in the form of a set of formulations on the psychology of color perception that has been stimulated by Freud's ideas on capacity for delay of tension discharge, and that is based on a scrutiny of developmental and clinical Rorschach and non-Rorschach research data.

CHIAROSCURO. The diffuse total impression of shading on the Rorschach finds its laboratory parallel in the total homogeneous field. The latter, when produced under controlled "pure" conditions, is experienced phenomenologically as moving toward the subject and as oppressing him (Metzger, 1930). This finding corresponds well to the earlier cited observations, emphasizing the depressive, discomfort- and anxiety-arousing states that seem to overpower the perceiver of the achromatic light-dark continuum. Psychiatrically, the emotional state of anxiety has been frequently likened to a condition of being lost in a world that has no discernible organization or, in a phrase of the existentialists, that engulfs the person by its nothingness. Correspondingly it has become Rorschach practice to interpret the chiaroscuro responses as signs of generalized emotional states or moods (chiefly of a dysphoric nature) in contradistinction to the specifically object-oriented emotions that are associated with the chromatic color determinants.

In his original volume Rorschach did not consider the shading of the ink blots as a separate test variable, and in his posthumous publication he merely introduced one score for it. Here was, then, a natural area for further development. In view of the extensive usage of the test, it is not surprising that such developments have proceeded through the years along a diversity of lines, both in classificational criteria applied to the shading element and in the interpretative significance coordinated to these criteria.

For purposes of this book, rather than survey all of the scoring systems, it seemed more appropriate to concentrate on one system, of which the research and theoretical potentialities are relatively unknown in the United States: the method of Hans Binder, a student and co-worker of Rorschach (Chapter 9). The distinguishing feature of this classificational system lies in the fact that it is consistently based on the methodological principles of psychological phenomenology, and that it is linked to a theory of emotions, also phenomenological.[4]

---

[4] Phenomenology is an orientation that emphasizes less the conceptualization of data than a way of approaching them. It stresses the importance of viewing psychological phenomena at their own face value. When dealing with new material, the psychologist is urged to cast aside any previously acquired frame of reference and to contemplate his task with a fresh and unbiased attitude. By observing carefully and recording with meticulous accuracy what is before him, he is taking the first, indispensable step toward his ultimate goal of discovering the intrinsic psychological nature of the phenomenon under consideration. "It [phenomenology] reveals meaning as the very stuff of experience, and it invites the psychologist to turn his attention to the meaningful aspects of the world" (Macleod, 1951, p. 228). The approach has been developed most fruitfully in Western continental Europe where its application to the cognitive areas of thinking and perception has yielded rich and penetrating descriptive insights.

Binder's treatment of the shading determinant shows the phenomenological procedure on two levels. Through painstaking qualitative analysis of a large number of subjects' responses and introspections to the shaded areas of the blots, he endeavored to discern the intrinsic personal meanings inherent in this material. After casting the salient trends of his analysis into a set of classificational categories, he was able to spell out the diagnostic significance of the different categories by relating them to the concepts of the Munich phenomenological theory of emotions. In addition to providing a demonstration of psychological phenomenology in Rorschach usage, the exposition of Binder's ideas on the chiaroscuro determinant acquaints the reader with a scheme for conceptualizing emotive phenomena in a somewhat more differentiated and subtle manner than is habitual in standard clinical practice.

American commentaries on the phenomenological approach in psychology (MacLeod, 1951) usually point to the desirability for phenomenology to parallel its contributions to the cognitive field by similar accomplishments in the emotional-motivational realm, and to the advisability of strengthening its scientific respectability by some form of quantification. It is the writer's opinion that Binder's chiaroscuro system constitutes a positive step in both these directions, particularly since some of his hypotheses would appear quite amenable to experimental manipulation.

EXPERIENCE TYPE ($M:C$). Besides the interpretative significance accorded the M and the C determinants separately, even greater significance is ascribed to their interrelationship. This interrelationship is represented by a variable, called the experience type (*Erlebnistypus*). It is expressed numerically as the ratio of the M to the sum C scores. When viewed in the frame of this configuration, the impact of the two determinants, their qualitative nuances, and, primarily, their broader personality implications, all undergo reciprocal modifications. Since M and C represent opposite forms of the subject-environment relation, Rorschach looked upon their numerical constellation as an expression of the fundamental polarity of an individual's stance to his surrounding world: his inwardly determined strivings versus his outwardly stimulated reactions. Depending on whether the balance in the ratio is tipped toward the movement or toward the color side, the experience type is designated as "introversive" or "extratensive" respectively. When the two sides approximate each other, either in abundance or in impoverishment, the experience type becomes "dilated" in the first place and "coartated" in the second. Considering how many intermediary combinations are possible, it is clear that this schema provides for a wide range of individualized patterns of basic orientations.

For Rorschach these patterns do not correspond to mutually exclusive personality types. Their poles are universal psychological functions, present in varying degrees in every person. He felt that the totality of a person's enduring features is most pertinently conceived when organized around this nuclear pattern, "the inmost, intimate capacity of resonance to life experiences", as Ellenberger (1954, p. 203) has aptly defined the experience type. In evolving the ultimate personality picture from the test, all other variables are viewed in the light of this catalytic factor, or the "axis" as Rorschach liked to call it.

Because of the psychologically challenging problems that are entailed in the far-reaching significance attached to the experience type, a good deal of thinking has revolved around it. In Chapter 10 these activities are reviewed, emphasizing research findings, and culminating in some tentative theoretical prepositions that draw eclectically on several contemporary personality models.

Content

The last category of analysis to be sketched here deals with the ideational content of the subject's responses in contrast to the foregoing categories, which derive from formal aspects of the perceptual process. As noted earlier, Rorschach was explicit in ascribing to the formal features the primary power in his diagnostic method: "The actual content of the interpretations comes into consideration only secondarily" (Rorschach, 1951, p. 181), and "the content of the interpretations offers little indication as to the content of the psyche until it is considered in relation to the psychogram" (tabulation of all scores) (p. 122). These two quotations convey succinctly Rorschach's position: Although unquestionably subordinated to the formal components, the content factor plays an integral role, provided that it is treated as closely embedded into the total test analysis.

In spite of the usual recognition of the desirability of taking into account both the formal (function) and the substantive (content) aspects in personality representation, contemporary theories have been relatively unsuccessful in attaining an intrinsic synthesis of these two conceptually divergent avenues of personality exploration. In contrast, Rorschach's psychodiagnosis stands out by genuinely integrating both approaches, not in the loosely additive manner of an afterthought, but in a sense that takes seriously the implications of such synthesis at every level of test interpretation. Thus the evaluation of an individual response always incorporates along with the formal characteristics the respective content as an essential factor that is not only modified in its significance by the formal categories but also, in turn, can influence the meaning of these categories. To give just one example, the color determinant is interpreted quite differently according to whether it serves as basis for the content "fire" or for "rose water."

Since the particular blots used in the Rorschach test lend themselves to the production of a great many percepts, over the years a substantial number of systems for the classification of the content score have been inaugurated. And a corresponding broad variety of psychodiagnostic interpretations have been assigned to the respective categories. Several procedures were chosen from this range of possibilities for inclusion in the present volume that, in keeping with our principal orientation, are noteworthy for such features as conceptualization, research potential, and originality.

Besides adhering to the principle of embedded handling of the content variable, the method presented in Chapter 11 endeavors to enhance the formalization of content analysis by introducing a scoring system that is rooted theoretically in the psychoanalytic distinction between primary and secondary process. A review of studies stimulated by this conceptual framework bares witness to its fruitfulness in enriching our understanding of personality processes.

Another extension of standard Rorschach procedure is the practice of going in the interpretation of the content of a response beyond its representationally given identification by endowing it with symbolic meaning. Although the inferential nature of such an approach has met with criticism from psychometrically minded researchers (see Chapter 18, p. 602 f.), the potentiality of opening up dimensions of personality not amenable to the more conventional means of investigation, continues to challenge many clinicians. Hence in Chapter 12 a procedure is described that aims at minimizing the degree of uncertainty of symbolic inferences by casting them into a consistent framework of self-reference and furthermore by viewing the process of symbol formation as an integral aspect of the total longitudinal pattern of the subject's Rorschach performance.

The last chapter in the section on content (Chapter 13) does not fit readily into any category of Rorschach analysis, since it does not concern itself with particular aspects (ideational or otherwise) of the response per se, but rather with the style of the person's over-all verbalizations during the test performance—a medium largely neglected by projective techniques. More specifically, the object of study is the identification, formalization, and interpretation of the impact of a person's verbal communications upon other people, demonstrated on verbatim Rorschach records of various types of subjects. Here then, in a novel way, Rorschach's dictum of the psychodiagnostic primacy of the "how" over the "what" is given full expression. By operating on this level of abstraction, the method becomes equally adaptable to a broad variety of verbal communication samples. Furthermore, by its focus on the transactional aspect of a person's behavior, this type of assessment provides insights into the interpersonal dimension of personality and thereby supplements cogently the intrapersonal emphasis of standard Rorschach personality pictures.

The location, determinant, and content categories, introduced so far in this chapter and taken up in detail in their respective places in the book, cover Rorschach's major test components with the exception of the popularity-originality dimension. The latter is omitted from discussion because, in addition to constituting the least novel aspect of Rorschach's psychodiagnostic method, it has failed to stimulate a notable amount of either research or fruitful theorizing.

THE TEST PATTERN

Our presentation of the psychological tenets of the Rorschach method moves now to a higher level of generality by focusing on the over-all pattern that results from the interplay of the test components.

At the outset of this chapter, emphasis was placed on the point that the test interpretation involves a complex process of integration, of handling the part processes at times as relatively independent units and in other contexts as dependent parts. An idea of how these interpretative principles operate in reality can be gleaned from the implications of the *M* and the *C* determinants, when considered separately and when viewed within the experience type. As described earlier, by virtue of the particular perceptual features underlying each of these determinants, their individual roles as representatives of certain personality dimensions are accrued to them. The treatment, on the other hand, of the same determinants as juxtaposed in the experience type cogently brings out the power of organizational principles in the Rorschach.

The observation that the respective weights of either *M* or *C* are reciprocally accentuated, dampened, or blocked reflects the principle of interdependence of subwholes within a larger whole. The fact that the new whole—the experience type—carries new, broader psychological implications than either of its constituent components did by themselves, illustrates the principle that the whole is greater than the sum of its parts. Finally, the circumstance that this integrated whole —the experience type—emerges as the catalytic factor of the superordinate whole—the total personality configuration—impressively exemplifies the principle of organization of a larger whole around a nuclear subunit or strong part, to use a gestalt term.

Full appreciation of how this complex method of interpretation shifts back and forth from one level of organization to another would perhaps best be conveyed by following a Rorschach worker through the elaborate procedure of studying a test record on all levels and in all detail: Viewing the combination of scores on an individual response as a unit in its own right; analyzing the temporal pattern of these responses in the sequence of the entire record and in relation to accompanying behavioral data; scrutinizing the cross-sectional configuration (psychogram) of all the scoring categories; and, after all this sorting, weighing, relating, arranging, and rearranging has been done, observing the evolution of the final *unitas multiplex* of the Rorschach personality picture.

As important as it is for a proper understanding of the nature of the Rorschach method to witness this multifaceted process of test interpretation concretely and in full, no such demonstration will be attempted here. There are numerous publications which very adequately meet this need. Instead, it would appear closer to the intent of this book to consider a few creative developments that center around the crucial theme of the test pattern.

In Chapter 14 a phenomenological-existential model[5] is applied first to an analysis of the process of change among three temporally spaced protocols of the same subject, and then to a reexamination of the conventional meaning of certain test categories. In Chapter 15 the problem of patterning is approached by focusing on the intrinsic nature of the processes underlying the shaping of Rorschach images. For the exploration of these, less accessible dimensions of the personality, C. Jung's conceptual framework of archetypal energy is introduced. The psychological value of this type of language for Rorschach analysis is demonstrated on some samples of Rorschach material. Chapter 16 is devoted to a cardinal problem of the Rorschach, the conceptualization of organization within the over-all personality constellation. A theoretical model of levels and interdependencies is proposed, and its applicability to Rorschach's implicit conceptual frame of reference is indicated.

METHODOLOGICAL CONSIDERATIONS

An enterprise dealing with the place of the Rorschach within the broader orbit of psychology would be incomplete without consideration of an issue that has aroused a vast amount of argumentation: the dependability and trustworthiness of the Rorschach method as a diagnostic tool. The problem itself is certainly a legitimate one, recognized by every serious psychologist with respect for scientific stan-

[5] Phenomenological existentialism, presently exerting a profound influence upon European psychology and psychiatry, is an extension and adaptation of phenomenology (see footnote 4). In its major objectives this movement may be likened, in the United States, to the systems of ideas dominant in humanistic psychology and centering around the concepts of becoming, growth, self-actualization. Applied to a clinical setting phenomenological existentialism emphasizes that, "Knowing means knowing in the context of the same world. The world of this particular patient must be grasped from the inside, be known and seen so far as possible from the angle of the one who exists in it" (May, et al, 1958, p. 12). This phenomenal universe is the totality of 'evaluated' people and things which play potential or

dards. The controversy centers not around the need for such demonstration of worth, but around the question as to just what means of demonstration may be accepted as scientifically irreproachable.

Psychometric practice, influenced in its basic philosophy by behavioristic tradition, relies for such purposes on the two time-honored indicators—reliability and validity. For the readily isolatable and accurately measurable variables of psychometric assessment, these indicators constitute an entirely appropriate means of establishing in correspondingly dissective and quantitative fashion the respectability of a test. As the reader realizes by now, the Rorschach, and for that matter any projective technique, having grown up in a distinctly different theoretical climate has very little in common with psychometric tests either in objectives or in actual test composition, or in underlying premises. It hardly can be surprising, therefore, that its organismically integrated configuration of variables does not yield smoothly to evaluation by the traditional procedures of reliability-validity probing.

The recognition of this difficulty, however, should in no sense be interpreted as denial of the problem. The implication is rather a quest for recasting the criteria for establishment of the scientific worth of a projective method in a way that is syntonic to the intrinsic nature of the diagnostic tool. To the same extent to which a truly scientific spirit requires us to stand ready constantly to revise our knowledge, so this spirit compels us to modify correspondingly our means of evaluating the growing and changing body of knowledge. One might say that what should remain unquestioned with projective as with any other assessment techniques is the genotype of scientific standards, whereas the phenotype of carrying out these standards has to resonate with the contemporary state of developments in psychology in general, and, more specifically, in the area under investigation —in this case the area of personality exploration.

In the light of these principles the complex problem of assessing the Rorschach's status as a psychodiagnostic instrument is discussed

---

actual roles in his [the patient's] existence" (van Kaam, 1960, p. 12). Inasmuch as existence is a dynamic process of becoming, the understanding of a person in an existential sense is aided by directing the clinician's attention to crucial events in the individual's life, as crises, decisions, encounters of tragedy, and by attempting to grasp the extent and character of the person's consciousness of his own self, of fulfillment of his existence, and of finality of his life.

in the final two chapters of this book. Chapter 17 identifies in detail the issues involved in attempting to determine the reliability of the method, examines critically various standard and newer approaches employed for this purpose, and leads up to constructive suggestions for further research. Chapter 18 presents a comprehensive perspective on the topic of Rorschach validation. First, the conceptual and methodological limitations of several types of validational studies are pointed out. In contrast to such failures at validation, it is then demonstrated how a conceptually based research design will consistently yield positive findings. Thus, if meaningfully used, the Rorschach may be understood to "rest on solid empirical grounds".

BIBLIOGRAPHY

Arnheim, R. *Art and visual perception.* Berkeley: Univ. Calif. Press, 1969.

Arnold, M. Emotion and personality. New York: Columbia Univ. Press, 1960.

Bash, K. W. Ganzeigenschaften als Determinantenträger im Rorschach Versuch. *Schw. Z. f. Psychol. und ihre Anw.*, 1957, **16**, 121-126.

Brosin, H. W., and Fromm, E. Some principles of gestalt psychology in the Rorschach experiment. *Rorschach Res. Exch.*, 1942, **6**, 1-15.

Bruner, J. S. Personality and the process of perceiving. In: R. R. Blake and G. V. Ramsey (eds.). *Perception—an approach to personality.* New York: Ronald Press, 1951.

Ellenberger, H. Hermann Rorschach, M.D., 1884-1922: A biographical study. *Bull. Menn. Clin.*, 1954, **18**, 173-219.

Gibson, J. J. The perception of visual surfaces. *Amer. J. Psychol.*, 1950, **63**, 367-384.

Goldstein, K. *The organism.* New York: Am. Book Co., 1963.

Govinda, A., Lama. *Foundations of Tibetan Mysticism.* London: Rider, 1967.

Koehler, W. Das Wesen der Intelligenz. In: A. Keller (ed.). *Kind und Umwelt, Anlage und Erziehung.* Leipzig: Deuticke, 1930.

Koffka, K. *Principles of gestalt psychology.* New York: Harcourt Brace, 1935.

Levine, M. and Grassi, J. The relation between blot and concept in graphic Rorschach responses. *Rorschach Res. Exch.*, 1942, **6**, 71-73.

Lewin, K. *Principles of topological psychology.* New York and London: McGraw-Hill, 1936.

Macleod, R. B. Some new tasks for psychological phenomenology. *Proceedings, 15th Intern. Congress Psychol.*, Brussels, 1957.

Macleod, R. B. The place of phenomenological analysis in social psychological theory. In: J. H. Rohrer and M. Sherif (eds.). *Social psychology at the crossroads.* New York: Harper, 1951.

May, R., Angel, E., Ellenberger, H. F. (eds.). *Existence: A new dimension in psychiatry and psychology.* New York: Basic Books, 1958.

Metzger, W. Optische Untersuchungen am Ganzfeld. II. Zur Phänomenologie des homogenen Ganzfelds. *Psych. Forsch.*, 1930, **13**, 6-29.

Metzger, W. *Psychologie.* 2nd ed. Darmstadt: Steinkopf, 1954.

Rickers-Ovsiankina, M. Prognostic Rorschach indices in schizophrenia. *Review of Diagn. Psychol. and Personal. Explor.*, 1955, **3**, 246-255.

Rickers-Ovsiankina, M. Some theoretical considerations regarding the Rorschach method. *Rorschach Res. Exch.*, 1943, **7**, 41-53.

Rorschach, H. *Psychodiagnostics,* 5th ed. Bern: Huber, 1951 (orig. publ. 1921).

Schachtel, E. *Experiential foundations of Rorschach's test*. New York: Basic Books, 1966.

Shapiro, D. Color-response and perceptual passivity. *J. Proj. Techn.*, 1956, **20**, 52-69.

Sheerer, M. Personality functioning and cognitive psychology. *J. Personal.*, 1953, **22**, 1-16.

Trubetskoi, E. N. *Icons: Theology in color*. New York: St. Vladimir's Seminary Press, 1973, (translated from the Russian by G. Vakar).

van Kaam, A. L. The third force in European psychology: Its expression in a theory of psychotherapy. Psychosynthesis Research Foundation, 1960.

Werner, H., and Wapner, S. The non-projective aspects of the Rorschach experiment: II. Organismic theory and perceptual response. *J. Soc. Psychol.*, 1956, **44**, 193-198.

Werner, H. *Comparative psychology of mental development*. Chicago: Follett, 1948.

Werner, H., and Wapner, S. Sensory-tonic field theory of perception. *J. Personal.*, 1949, **18**, 88-107.

CATEGORIES OF ANALYSIS: LOCATION

With each part, irrespective of the amount of study it may itself require, we must not lose sight of the fact that it is only a part of the whole.

PAUL KLEE

2

by Marguerite R. Hertz

THE

ORGANIZATION ACTIVITY

Rorschach (1942) did not refer directly to organizational activity as such in his original monograph. He considered it indirectly, however, in reference to the whole factor or W^1. This factor represented for Rorschach the capacity of the individual to analyze the blots into parts, to combine and to integrate them into meaningful wholes. The W revealed, then, analytic-synthetic ability and the ability for abstraction and generalization. It also reflected drive and need for achievement. As Rorschach said, the W indicated "conscious or unconscious 'willing' in the direction of achieving complicated performance, such as abstractions or combinations in interpretations" (1942, p. 59).

Rorschach recognized that there were different kinds of whole responses, depending on the degree of articulation and organization and on the clarity achieved. Thus some simple global W's such as those involving popular forms were relatively easy to give, requiring little organizing ability. Others, however, more complex and well constructed, involved considerable effort and ability. He also distinguished several varieties of W, such as the simple immediate W, the successively-combined W, the confabulated W, and the contaminated W, each of which had different significance for him.

Rorschach likewise recognized that the W's reflected organiza-

[1] For explanation of Hertz scoring symbols, see Appendix, p. 609 ff.

tional activity in varying degrees, that such activity depended on the mental set of the individual and his drive toward complicated performance. He included W in his battery of factors which reflect level of intellectual functioning.

APPROACHES IN
EVALUATING ORGANIZATIONAL ABILITY

In the course of the years, those who worked with the Rorschach observed that the ease with which W's are achieved varies in the respective blots, that the capacity to analyze the blots into their component elements and to combine and to integrate them, is revealed in varying degrees in responses to other areas of the blots besides the whole. An organization factor called "Z" was systematically developed by Beck (1933) in his study of configurational tendencies in Rorschach responses. Vernon (1933) utilized a "g" which he combined with location categories (Wg, Dg) to reflect combinatory and integrative activity. Guirdham (1935) identified "incorporation responses" in the attempt to evaluate capacity for abstractive organization. Ford (1946) worked with "organizational links" ($O L$) representing the number of logical connections within a response. Hertz (1938, 1942) experimented with a similar organization factor called "g".

Approaching the problem from another point of view, Janoff (1951) constructed a form-level rating scale which permitted evaluation of organizational activity in terms of reality testing and the degree of complexity of a response.

Klopfer and his colleagues (1944, 1954) also constructed a form-level rating scale distinguishing accuracy (the fit or match of a concept to the blot area), specification (the use of specific elements within a chosen blot), and organizational activity (where two or more areas of the blot are perceived as separate concepts but in relation to each other), all of which furnish the basis for a quantifiable evaluation of the form level of each Rorschach response. This system is reviewed by Korchin (Chapter 5 of this volume) in his summary of form perception and ego functioning.

In the early 1940's Meili-Dworetzki (1956), in research on the genetic aspects of Rorschach categories, recognized the need to analyze Rorschach responses in terms of form level and to consider the degree of differentiation and complexity by some score which ought to compliment the traditional scoring. While she did not identify an organization score as such, she did develop subcategories for the mental approach factors qualitatively evaluated in the developmental sequence.

Rapaport et al. (1946) was one of the first to sense the potentialities in the Rorschach response for reflecting combinatory, abstracting, and integrative abilities of an individual. He identified combination and construction responses, fabulized responses, fabulized combinations, and confabulations. His influence, as well as that of Beck (1933) and Werner (1948), is discernible in the subsequent developments with the location categories as evolved at Clarke University by Becker (1956), Friedman (1952, 1953), Hemmendinger (Chapter 3 of this volume), Phillips and his colleagues (1953, 1959) and Siegal (1953), all of whom dealt with the structural aspects of Rorschach location scores.

Friedman, for example, analyzed location scores in terms of level of organization of the response, whether undifferentiated and diffused, or differentiated or integrated. He introduced form level scores based on tables published by Beck (1949, 1961) or Hertz (1936-1961, 1970). He presented evidence that his system could evaluate not only the individual's level of development but also the adequacy of his cognitive functioning.

Friedman's system was revised and further developed by Phillips and his colleagues (1959) who included not only location categories but determinants as well. Their developmental level scoring was based on the adequacy and specificity of form, form determinants in combination (form dominance, subordination, or absence), the perception of activity (movement), and the organization of blot elements (adequate organizing giving an "integration score", or inadequate, as in confabulation, contamination, and fabulized combination). They too report evidence from experimental and normative studies of the relationship between their location choice and genetic development, intelligence, and diagnostic grouping.

The developmental level scoring systems are discussed in detail by Hemmendinger in this volume (Chapter 3) and Phillips and Smith

(1953), and are critically reviewed in the recent book by Goldfried, Stricker and Weiner (1971).

Recently Zubin, Eron and Schumer (1965), who adopt a rigid psychometric orientation, have developed 75 different scales for the Rorschach categories, including scales for organization, based in part on Beck's Z. Three aspects of organization are distinguished—mode, type, and figure-ground relationships. For mode, they drew on Beck's Z scale, reducing his values to scores running from 0 to 4 to make them conform to the scales used for other Rorschach categories. Their transformed values are presented in tabular form in their book (1965, p. 346). The organization scale evaluates confabulatory or pseudo-organization (DW, DrW, DrD), combinatory organization and immediate or instant organization. The figure-ground relationships scale evaluates the degree to which white spaces are incorporated in the responses.

Mention should be made of the new psychometric system of scoring inkblots similar to the Rorschach blots, developed by Holtzman and his colleagues (1961) since, according to their research, the Rorschach and the Holtzman systems have much in common in terms of the underlying meaning of the respective scores utilized. Their scoring involves several variables, one of which is "integration" which indicates the presence or absence of the organization of adequately perceived inkblot elements into a unified response. This variable is evaluated in conjunction with three other variables —form appropriateness or F.A., defined as goodness of fit of the concept to the form of the blot area; form definiteness or F.D., i.e., definiteness in form as opposed to formlessness or lack of specificity; and pathognomic verbalization or V. This system was further extended by Thorpe (1966) who introduced the genetic pattern scores of Phillips et al., (1959) and Becker (1956). His revised system linked integration with location, movement, and human and animal forms.

Thus it may be seen that throughout the years many investigators recognized the need to evaluate organizational activity in the Rorschach response and to introduce some score to compliment the traditional scoring. In addition, many workers in the field sought some means of analyzing organizational activity qualitatively, in terms of other Rorschach patterns, to indicate degree of differentiation and complexity.

Since Beck's (1933, 1950, 1961) approach to the problem of

organization is probably among the best known, it will be considered in detail.

Beck's Z Score

According to Beck, a response is scored organization or "Z" when two or more portions of the figures are seen in relation to one another, and when the meaning perceived in the combination, or in any of the component portions obtains only from the fact of this organization (1950, p. 59). A weighted score is assigned to the organized response, based on an early study (1933) in which he analyzed the records of 35 very superior adults for the ways they organized wholes and diverse areas of the blots. He identified six modes of organization—(1) wholes (w), (2) adjacent details (j), (3) distant details seen in combination (t), (4) white spaces organized with filled-in elements, (5) simultaneous organization involving both w and j (wj), and (6) simultaneous organization involving both w and t (wt). Assuming that the type of organization which was least frequent in a blot was the most difficult to perform, he computed the organizational difficulties that each card presented in terms of frequency of occurrence, which he viewed as an index of difficulty. Because of gross infrequency, the last two types of organization which he set out to study were dropped. He computed the sigma values of each kind of organizational activity in each card, transforming them into Z weights. The Z values therefore represent differing degrees of difficulty in achieving each type of organization in each of the ten cards. These numerical values ranging from 1 to 6, are listed in tabular form in his books (1950, 1961).

In the Beck system, each response in a record is scrutinized and, where organization as defined has taken place, the kind of organization is identified, the table consulted, and the appropriate Z value introduced in the scoring formula. Thus a response to Card I—"Two witches flying on brooms" for the side figures—receives a weight of 4.0 according to the table because this is the value given to adjacent details seen in combination for this card. Again a response to Card II —"Dogs facing about to fight"—is weighted 5.5 because this is the Z value for the organization of distant details in Card II. Finally a sum organization weight is computed for each individual record, consisting of the sum of all the Z values.

There has been much critical comment on Beck's rationale for the scoring of Z. Sarason (1950) and Kropp (1955) question Beck's assumption that frequency of organizational acts implies degree of difficulty. Furthermore, Z values were developed from the records of a small and selected sample of superior adults. Such a sample may not be adequate to serve as a basis for determining order of difficulty of any type of responses. Kropp also demonstrates by reviewing norms published for Z values, that the Z activity is not distributed normally in the general population. Beck has, of course, indicated several times that the distributions for several of the Rorschach categories, including Z, are markedly skewed.

Kropp (1955) developed another set of sigma values for each of the five organizational acts identified by Beck, based on 53 records found in Beck's volumes II (1945) and III (1952). Despite Kropp's criticisms, however, in his cross validation of the Z weights originally developed by Beck, his set relates highly to Beck's set of weights.

Several studies also question the value of the weighting system as devised by Beck in relation to the various types of organizational activity. On the basis of a study of the records of five different normal and abnormal groups, 104 subjects in all, Wilson and Blake (1950) show a high correlation between Beck's total weighted Z score and the frequency of occurrence of organizational acts. They therefore conclude that the total number of times organization takes place, i.e., when Z appears, may be substituted for total weighted Z score. A table is presented for predicting total weighted Z scores when the number of Z responses is known.

Sisson and Taulbee (1955) present further evidence of the high relationship between the frequency of Z scores and the weighted Z scores on the basis of an analysis of the records of five groups of subjects, 285 in all, consisting of schizophrenic, neurotic and organic male patients and normal male and female children. Employing the table of Wilson and Blake for the total weighted Z prediction when the total number of Z responses is known, they correctly identify from 71% to 100% of the cases within one and two standard errors.

In Beck's revised editions (1961, 1967), he accepts the frequency of organizational acts (Zf) as a short-cut for the over-all evaluation of organizational activity as suggested by Wilson and Blake. He presents their table which converts his Sum Z into frequency of organizational acts (1961, p. 232).

,Norms for Beck's Z. Since Beck's original study, norms have been reported for "normal" children (Beck, 1954; Beck et al., 1961; Sisson and Taulbee, 1955; Thetford et al., 1951), high school students (Beck, 1954; Beck et al., 1961), college students and constricted subjects (Varvel, 1941), "normal" adults (Beck et al., 1961, 1950), mentally defective children (Jolles, 1947), neurotic and schizophrenic children (Beck, 1954; Wishner, 1948), neurotic adult patients

TABLE 2.1

Weighted Z Values

Investigator	Group	N	Mean	S.D.	Median
Beck et al., (1954, 1961, 1950)	Adults, employees of Spiegel Mail Order House	157	22.48	14.91	
	Vocational Group I*	36	28.60	15.70	
	Vocational Group II	49	24.70	13.66	
	Vocational Group III	48	20.60	14.00	
	Vocational Group IV	24	16.20	15.40	
Beck (1954)	High school students 14-17 yrs.	48	25.54	19.60	
Thetford et al., (1951)	Children 6-9 yrs.	69	7.15	7.40	4.88
	10-13 yrs.	62	8.45	10.10	5.61
	14-17 yrs.	24	28.90	23.00	24.50
	Total	155	11.05	14.45	6.10
Sisson and Taulbee (1955)	Adults, "normal" 20-52 yrs.	60	24.03	18.32	
	Children, "normal" 8-18 yrs.	70	23.22	19.40	
Varvel (1941)	College students	144	43.10		25.60
	Constricted subjects	20	20.70		10.26
Jolles (1947)†	Children, feeble-minded	65	19.09	15.24	
Wishner (1948)	Adults, "neurotic"	42	21.31	15.39	
Sisson and Taulbee (1955)	Neurotics, 20-46 yrs.	35	26.87	19.59	
Beck (1954)	Neurotic children	50	20.30		
	Neurotic adults	60	24.90		
	Schizophrenic children	50	20.65		
	Schizophrenic adults	60	18.90		
Sisson and Taulbee (1955)	Schizophrenics 20-46 yrs.	60	27.38	17.30	
	Organics	10	27.50	15.11	
Molish (1965)	Orthogenic school children 6-9 yrs.	27	22.00		
	10-13 yrs.	23	27.00		
	Total	50	25.00		

*Refers to vocational groups described, p. 9.
† As reported by Kropp

(Beck, 1954; Wishner, 1948), schizophrenic adult patients (Beck, 1954; Sisson and Taulbee, 1955), and organic patients (Sisson and Taulbee, 1955). Table 2.1 summarizes these norms.

The study by Beck and his colleagues (1950) is probably one of the most ambitious attempts to understand the normal personality by means of the Rorschach Test. On the basis of 157 subjects, age range 17 to 69, mean age 30.5, all employees of the Spiegal Mail Order House in Chicago, normal central tendencies, the ranges, and the indices of variability were computed for all the Rorschach categories including the Z score, for the group as a whole and for subgroups, divided on the basis of occupational level: I. executives and junior executives; II. skilled; III. semi-skilled; and IV. unskilled workers. Since this sample was considered a fair representation of the "average" man in the City of Chicago and "presumably of the United States generally," these norms were presented as general norms for adults, and are utilized today for "normal" populations. The scorer is cautioned, however, that the norms are not valid for persons of very high intelligence (Beck et al., 1961, p. 230).

The norms used today for children are based on the study (Thetford et al., 1951) of 155 children and adolescents from the Chicago Public Schools, ages 6 to 17 years, divided into three age groups, picked by teachers as overly free from personality difficulties and of average intelligence and achievement. They were considered fairly representative of children out of the middle to lower middle class sectors, with the exception of the 14 to 17 year high school students who were in the above average population range. Since this group involved only 24 students, it was later increased to 48 and new norms computed which are used for an adolescent population today (Beck et al., 1961, p. 230).

The studies by Beck and his colleagues will be discussed later in this chapter in the section on validity.

Hertz' g Score

In 1933, an organization score or "g" (the g taken from the word "organization") was first introduced at the Brush Foundation, the Cleveland School of Medicine, in conjunction with the analyses of other Rorschach factors which were gradually developed (Hertz,

1938, 1942). It was recognized that there was need to develop some pattern which would identify organization in different areas of the blots as well as in the whole areas. Furthermore, it was thought that some means should be devised to study organizational activity qualitatively, to determine the accuracy of the forms organized and the extent to which the combinations and integrations themselves were realistic and constructive, or irrealistic, arbitrary and far-fetched.

An organization score was therefore developed which took in more than the location scores. It embraced form quality $(F+, F-)$, vagueness (v), popularity (P), and originality (O), the complexity of this activity, and the adequacy and appropriateness of the relationships seen. Organization was defined in the following manner. Organization is said to take place where: (a) a blot area is analyzed into one or more component parts, (b) different forms are projected in those parts, (c) these forms are seen in relationship to each other, and (d) the final response given to the combination or integration depends entirely on the fact of their being seen in relationship. These criteria for the organization score hold today.

Thus organization may take place in areas other than the whole (D, Dr, S, s), and the areas may be adjacent, distant, one within the other, or spaces combined with spaces or with filled-in areas.

In our system, organization by definition always involves form. Again, organization may be instant or immediate, the percept given at once (Card I. "a bat", "an acrobat act"), or it may be built up by successive associations and elaborations to different elements of the blot area (Card I. "Two men on the sides . . . this here a person in the middle . . . they are holding on to this person . . . they are doing an acrobat stunt").

Again organization may take place by a kind of collective grouping of elements of the blot, such as responses in terms of "a marine scene," "a garden scene of flowers," "an exhibition of insects." This kind of organization must of course be distinguished from mere enumeration of objects, such as "a bunch of animals here, here, and here," "lots of flowers." In the former collective integration, the grouping reflects a conceptualizing or classifying process. In the latter, there is no such process at work. No organization has taken place, hence no g score is applied.

It should further be emphasized that organization as herein defined applies only to independent contents seen in combination, not to parts of one form. For example, a response "a person . . . because this is the head, the body, and feet" is not scored for organization. Although it is true that analysis of the blot area has taken place, this is mere enumeration or specification of parts of one form. The response is not scored for organization. The organization score is reserved for different contents given to different elements of the blot area and seen in meaningful connection so that the final response gives a new meaning.

There is one exception to this rule. All whole responses which involve form are automatically assigned an organization score whether or not one or more independent forms are projected. The rationale is that the individual, to give a whole, must analyze the blot into its component parts and synthesize the elements into a meaningful larger unit.

Scoring scale for g. After considerable experimentation with various schemes of weighting in order to evaluate qualitative differentiations of this score, a simple scale was devised for weighting organization, ranging from .0 to 1.5. This scheme is used today.

1. A score of 1.5 is assigned to the organization of blot elements where the forms seen in relationship are adequately perceived and acceptably combined or integrated, resulting in a meaningful percept which is highly different and original (g O+).[2]

2. A score of 1.0 is assigned to the organization of blot elements where the forms seen in relationship are fitting ($F+$) and adequately combined into meaningful percepts which, however, are not original, popular, or vague ($g+$).

3. A weighting of .5 is assigned to simple or inadequate organizations of blot elements, specifically where

　　a. there is minimal differentiation and integration of the blot

---

[2] In our system, adequacy of form is determined by consultation with published Frequency Tables (Hertz, 1936-1961, 1970), which are based on frequency of occurrence in a large adolescent population, supplemented by subjective judgments of three to five judges where infrequent responses occur.

Original responses (O) are those which are given least frequently in a group, determined by the frequency of one in one hundred responses and checked by three to five judges.

Frequency Tables list $F+$, $F-$, $O+$, $O-$, and P and should be consulted for further directions.

elements, and where content involved tends to be vague and un-specific (g $v+$, g $v-$ by the criterion of frequency);[3]

b. the forms involved are easy and popular (g P);

c. the forms involved are poor and inaccurate resulting in a percept which is irrealistic, but not too infrequent or unusual ($g-$);

d. the forms involved are poor and inaccurate and combined unrealistically or illogically, resulting in highly infrequent and/or absurd or bizarre percepts (g $O-$).

Thus with this weighting scheme, the organization of the blot elements, the adequacy of reality testing, the complexity, originality and conventionality of the forms and of the combinations, are taken into consideration. The percepts which reflect a fine degree of articulation and integration, where the forms and relationships are clear, logical, and fitting, and where the resulting percepts are highly different and original, receive the highest weighting. Those in the medium range which show adequate organization of elements and forms which are logical and fitting get less weight. Those where there is little articulation of the blots or where the organization is minimal or deficient or inappropriate, receive the lowest weighting.

At first, lower figures (.25, .10, .05) were used for weighting organization in responses with poorly perceived forms and inade-quate relationships. After many trials, however, it was discovered that too little was added to the significance of the score to warrant the use of a more detailed weighting system. Therefore the weighting of .5 was applied to all responses where organization was minimal or deficient.

Scoring organization in combinatory responses. Combinatory re-sponses are those where (a) two or more responses take separate scoring formulae but are tightly linked, and (b) a single response involves two or more independent percepts which are tightly com-bined and integrated into a complex unit. In the latter case, though only one response is given, the contents involved are highly different

[3] Vague forms (v) are those based on a general impression of the blot. They involve little analysis and synthesis. Some form element is present but it is unspecific. They in-clude maps, charts, islands, x-rays, etc. On the basis of frequency of occurrence, they receive plus or minus form level, as indicated in the Frequency Tables (Hertz, 1936-1961, 1970).

and require determinants which are radically different in type or in form quality. Taking two or more scoring formulae which are bracketed to indicate linkage, the response is then fragmented and weighted for organization.[4]

The same scheme of weighting organization is applied to combinatory responses.

1. An organization score of 1.5 is assigned where the combinations involve blot elements which are well differentiated and combined in a well organized manner, the forms involved are fitting and appropriate, the relationships realistic, logical, and acceptable, and, in addition, the combination is highly different and original (g O+ comb).

2. An organization score of 1.0 is given where the forms in the combination are fitting and acceptable and the combinations realistic and appropriate, but not especially different (g+ comb).

3. A weighting of .5 is assigned where:

a. the combination involves one or more scores where form quality is poor or form is entirely missing, or the relationships themselves are inappropriate, but the combination is not especially different or original (g− comb);

b. the combination involves relationships which themselves are highly different, unrealistic, illogical, even arbitrary or absurd, whether the forms involved are fitting or not g O− comb). Here the elements of the blot are related because of some common quality, spatial relationship or incidental feature of the blot structure, or because of the meanings given to one of the parts. At times, the objects combined are well perceived and acceptable but the relationship is improbable and far-fetched. This pattern is so often indicative of severe impairment that often an exclamation mark is placed after it (g O− comb!) to suggest it may be an indicator of pathology.

Examples of scoring organization

g O+: weight 1.5
    Card II. "Oriental figures back to back (projection top middle)." $\underline{\text{D}}$ M+   H   O+
                             1.5

[4] Other Rorschach scorers follow this procedure of fragmentation (Klopfer et al., 1954). Beck says he disapproves of fragmentation but examination of the scoring of his published records reveals frequent fragmentation and application of his organization values as we recommend (Beck et al., 1961, 1967).

Card	Loc	Det	Content	Spec
Card X. "Hooded figures holding up a post as in a Disney production (gray top center)."	$\dfrac{D}{1.5}$	M+	(H) obj	O+
Card V. "An imaginary picture of a rabbit in the center with wings, surrealist art."	$\dfrac{W}{1.5}$	F+	(A)	O+

g+: weight 1.0

Card	Loc	Det	Content	Spec
Card I. "Witch (side figure) with cloak flying out (side projection)."	$\dfrac{D}{1.0}$	F+ Fm+	(H) App	
Card VIII. "Emblem with two bears."	$\dfrac{W}{1.0}$	F+	Emb (A)	(P)
Card X. "Cliffs (red) and some kind of structure (blue) joining them."	$\dfrac{D}{1.0}$	F(C)+	Mt Str	

g v+: weight .5

Card	Loc	Det	Content	Spec
Card VII. "A group of islands but they are joined."	$\dfrac{Wv}{.5}$	F+	Map	
Card VIII. "Anatomical chart (lower red-orange) showing one organ next to another . . . that's why it is colored that way."	$\dfrac{Wv}{.5}$	C/F+	Anat- obj	

g v−: weight .5

Card	Loc	Det	Content	Spec
Card IX. "A map of Russia (green) with land and a body of water inside."	$\dfrac{D(s)v}{.5}$	F−	Map	
Card I. "Chart of the inside of the body."	$\dfrac{Wv}{.5}$	F−	Anat- obj	

g P: weight .5

Card	Loc	Det	Content	Spec
Card VII. "Women's faces (top third), as if arguing with each other."	$\dfrac{D}{.5}$	M+	Hd	P
Card II. "Animals . . . dogs looking at each other."	$\dfrac{D}{.5}$	FM+	A	P
Card III. "Two people bowing to each other."	$\dfrac{W}{.5}$	M+	H	P

g−: weight .5

Card	Loc	Det	Content	Spec
Card II. "A bug."	$\dfrac{W}{.5}$	F−	A	
Card VIII. "Two insects joined together (top green)."	$\dfrac{D}{.5}$	F−	A	
Card IX. "Some kind of a bug, I don't know why."	$\dfrac{W}{.5}$	F−	A	

g O—: weight .5

Card VIII. "Wolves bunched together (top green)... here are the tails sticking out... they are sort of climbing up."	D .5	FM—	A	O—
Card IX. "This is all a colored butter-fly."	W .5	CF—	A	O—
Card IV. "part of the throat (lower part of middle projection) with tonsils sticking out."	Dr .5	F—	Anat	O—

As illustrated, the organization score is written under the location category.

On rare occasions, the scorer may be tempted to give an organization score to a response where different areas are perceived and parts of *one* form projected into each area and seen in relationship, with the resultant response depending clearly upon something new by virtue of the relationship. Here a *single object* results from the connection between two or more areas.

Examples

Card II (red areas at top seen together "andirons."	D .5	F—	Hh	O—
Card II. (tiny lines, upper part of middle space) "electric current... going across."	Dr 1.5	F+	Current	O+
Card X. (green middle bottom) "lyre but strings are missing."	D .5	F—	Music	O—

The organization score is applied only once in any given response. When the organization takes place more than once, i.e., at different qualitative levels, the highest score is applied.

Card II. "Two bears in a vaudeville act, dancing together, with red hats on their heads."	W 1.5	FM+ FC+	A (P) App	O+

In this response, the organization score for the popular forms in interaction would be .5; for the animals with red hats on, 1.0. The organized response as a whole is highly original, however, hence the highest weighting, 1.5. Thus the highest level of organization determines the weighted score.

Examples of organization scores in combinatory responses.

g O+ comb

    a. Two or more responses linked

Card III. "Two people dancing."

D	M+	H	P

    +

"Torches on the side here (red."

D	CF+	Fire	

    +

"here is red fire (red bottom)."

D	C	Fire

"The people are dancing at a carnival, maybe the torches are there to throw off light on the scene, adding to the gaiety and the carnival atmosphere."

$\overline{W}$

g comb 1.5. . . . . O+

Card VIII. "Animals on the sides."

D	F+	A	P

    +

"This in the middle, a shield."

D	CF+	Emb

"It might be a coat-of-arms with animals on each side . . . like a family crest . . . painted in colors."

$\overline{W}$

g comb 1.5. . . . . O+

    b. Single response fragmented

Card IX. "Fantastic figure (top orange) emerging from a heavy billowy cloud (green)."

D	M+	(H)

    +

D	ChF+	Cl.

g comb 1.5. . . . . O+

Card II. "A wooly toy dog (side) with a red hat on him (top) . . . a fancy toy, like a Christmas gift."

D	Fc+	(A)	P

    +

D	FC+	App

g comb 1.5. . . . . O+

These combinations generally include richly imaginative elaborations which involve forms which maintain their separate identity and which are combined in a well organized and original manner.

g+ comb: weight 1.0

    a. Two or more responses linked

Card II. "Two men at the sides."

D	M+	H

"Here are candles . . . rough because of the dripping wax (conelike projections, top middle)."

    +

D	Fc+	Hh

"These men are holding the candles."

g comb 1.0

Card VIII. "Two animals climbing."   D+   FM+   A   P

"These could be painted rocks, because of the colors."   D   C/F+   Sc

"It's a scene, animals climbing painted rocks."   g comb 1.0

b. *A single response which is fragmented*

Card VIII. "Two little bears feeding off a pine tree (grey-green top middle) ... the tree is greenish."   { D+   FM+   A   P
{ D   FC+   Bo   P

g comb 1.0

Card VII. "Clouds in formation with this part (top third) taking the form of a lady's head."   { W+   ChF+   Cl
{ D   F+   Hd   P

g comb 1.0

g— comb: weighting .5

a. *Two or more responses linked*

Card II. "Two bears dancing (side black)."   D+   FM+   A   P

"This is a red balloon, (top red)."   D   CF—   Toy

"Maybe the balloon is on the bear's head."   g com .5

Card VII. "Land and water scene."   W(S)+   F+   Sc

"A canal down here (lower axial figure) going through."   D+   F(C)+   Sc

"This darker part is a boat."   Dr   F—   Str

"The boat is probably coming into a lake which is surrounded by this land."   g comb .5

b. *A single response which is fragmented*

Card VIII. "Some animals walking on some grass (top green)."   { D+   FM+   A   P
{ D   C   Bo

g comb .5

Card X. "Two worms (green bottom) biting this leaf in the center" (Inquiry: "Worms are wiggling, and this green leaf is between them.")

D	FM+	A	P
+			
D	CF−	Bo	

g comb .5

g O− comb: weight .5

a. Two or more responses linked

Card VIII. "Two men fighting."

D	M+	H	P

.5
+

"These red spots are blood."

D	C	Blood	

"Maybe the blood is coming out of their bodies."

g comb! .5 . . . . O−

Card X. "A green insect (upper green)."

Dr	FC−	A	O−

+

"This could be a crab (side blue)."

D	F+	A	P

"The insect is trying to hold on to the crab."

g comb! .5 . . . . O−

b. Responses which are fragmented

Card VIII. "Animals at the sides holding onto a piece of torn skin."
(Inquiry: "The skin because it has these marks in them, like folds.")

D	FM+	A	P
+			
D	Fc−	Ad-obj	O−

g comb! .05 . . . . O−

Card VIII. "An animal climbing up from a colored butterfly (red-orange) up to a green tree (top center)."

D	FM+	A	P
+			
D	CF+	A	
+			
D	FC+	Bo	P

g comb! .5 . . . . O−

These g O− combinations are sometimes called "fabulized combinations" (Phillips and Smith, 1953, Rapaport, 1946). The structural elements are inappropriately combined and integrated in sharp contradiction to reality possibilities, and the contents are inappropriately elaborated. Often parts of the combinations are fitting and accurate and alone would receive plus form quality, but the relationships are irrealistic, far-fetched, sometimes absurd.

A peculiar kind of organization which is also scored g O− comb! sometimes occurs where the response on one card is related to the response on a previous card. This corresponds to the "relationship verbalization" of Rapaport and his colleagues (Rapaport, 1946).

Example:

> Card V. "Butterfly, . . . this is the one I saw in the other card (Card I) but now he is flying or resting."

+			
W	*FM+*	*A*	*P*
g comb! .5.			*O—*

In our scoring column, we place the plus sign above the *W* and the organization score below.

In our system, confabulatory responses are not scored for organization. Here the meaning is generalized to a larger unit on the basis of what is seen in one part of it. Nothing is really combined or integrated. Thus in the following, responses are determined from the interpretation of a smaller area.

> Card VI. "A cat because of the whiskers."

Dr W	*F—*	*A*
conf		

> Card IV inverted. "A dog . . . it must be because of these large ears (side areas)."

DW	*F—*	*A*
conf		

Contaminations, however, involve organization in the sense of fusion or merging of impressions. In the contamination, independent impressions given to the same area are fused without regard for their realistic separateness, into a single percept. Organization score is therefore assigned. It is of course grossly inadequate organization and always involves poor form level or fusion of form and formless determinants.

> Card VIII. "Flags flying in the sky (middle blue)."
> Inquiry: "They are blue flags, blowing in the breeze . . . you can see the ripples. Well the sky is often blue in color."

D	*FC+*	*Emb*	*O+*
+	*Fcm+*		
D	*C*	*Nat*	
g comb! .5.			*O—*
contam.			

> Card IX. "A grass-bear (green)" Inquiry: "It has the shape of a big bear and grass is green."

D	*F+*	*A*	
+			
D	*C*	*Bo*	
g comb! .5.			*O—*
contam.			

The organization scores are recorded on our psychogram (Hertz, 1942, 1969), both the summary scores (Sum g wt, sum org. acts) and the sum of the various qualitatively differentiated scores.

g O+	+	g O—	=	Sum g O	
g O+ comb	+	g O— comb	=	Sum g O comb	⎫
g+ comb	+	g— comb	=	Sum g comb	⎬ Sum g comb
g+	+	g—			⎭
g v+	+	g v—	=	Sum g v	
g P					

Sum g + wt	+	Sum g — wt	=	Sum g wt
Sum org. acts +	+	Sum org. acts—	=	Sum org. acts

In this way, we evaluate the frequency of organizational activity (Sum org. acts, Sum g wt), representing the total organizational ability manifested, and the adequacy and appropriateness of the organizational activity (Sum g+ wt, Sum g— wt, Sum org. acts +, Sum org. acts—). We also assess the combinatory responses which are fitting and integrated in a well organized manner (Sum g+ comb) or unrealistic, poorly organized and integrated (Sum g— comb).

Comparison with other systems of scoring for organization. It may be noted that the g score is applied within the same framework and according to the same criterion adopted by Beck (1933, 1961). It is simplified as to the weights assigned, and extended to include the qualitative differentiations of organization.

The sum Z correlates highly with sum g. The records of several groups of adolescents in the Brush series were scored for organization utilizing Beck's Z and Hertz' g. In all of them, high correspondence was observed as can be seen from the correlations presented below for two groups of children, 12 and 15 years of age respectively.

			Sum g wt	Sum g+ wt
	75	12-year old children 41 boys, 34 girls	.953 ± .011	.881 ± .026
Beck's Z wt				
	57	15-year old children 29 boys, 28 girls	.958 ± .011	.936 ± .016
Beck's Z+ wt	75	12-year old children 41 boys, 34 girls	.890 ± .024	.937 ± .014

It appears that for "normal" groups at least, there is a close relationship between Sum Z wt and Sum g wt. Since the g score is so easily learned and applied, and since it correlates so highly with the Z score, it seems unnecessary to use the more complicated Z system.

It may be noted that the g score also involves many of the criteria utilized in the developmental level scores (Friedman, 1952; Hemmendinger, 1953, Chapter 3 this volume; Phillips et al., 1959) since it takes into account the level of organization of the blot elements, the adequacy and specificity of the forms, and the complexity of the relationships involved. Our Sum $g+$ wt roughly corresponds to the developmentally high or mature classification and our Sum $g-$ wt to the developmentally low or immature category. Our g score also considers certain aspects of Klopfer's Form Level Rating Scale (1954), since it includes accuracy of fit of the concept to the blot area and to some extent "specifications". It involves the items in the scales recommended by Zubin, et al. (1965) such as mode and type or organization and figure-ground relationships. Finally, it corresponds in large measure to "integration" as defined by Holtzman et al. (1961).

Norms for Hertz' g score. Normative data taken from the original Brush studies are presented in Table 2.2, which gives means and medians for the summary scores and for the qualitative differentiations of the organization score for children 12, 14, and 15 years old, for groups of high and low intelligence, for college women, and for neurotic, depressed and delusional schizophrenic patients. Included also are norms for a brain-injured and an old-age group.

Table 2.3 shows the proportions of the groups giving a certain number of organizational acts where originality, form level and appropriateness of combinatory responses are considered.

The children, 12 and 15 years of age were taken from the Brush series. They were generally average to superior in intelligence and of high social status and income group. The 14-year-old group were tested in the public schools of Cleveland. The high Otis group, 12 years of age, showed I.Q.'s of over 120, the low Otis group, I.Q.'s 86-100, which represented the upper and lower 20% of a larger 12-year-old group. The superior children, ages 11 to 16 years, were selected at random from a larger group of superior children who participated in a contest sponsored by a Cleveland newspaper to

TABLE 2.3

**Proportions of the Groups Showing Appropriate
and/or Inappropriate Organizational Acts (in Percentages)**

		Scores						
		g O+		g+	g−			g− O− comb!
		Number of Occurrences						
N	Groups	0−1	2 or more	8 or more	0−1	4 or more	1	2 or more
50	14-year-old group	52	48	56	58	18	−	−
50	Very superior group, ages 11-16 yrs.	18	82	74	54	8	10	2
40	College women (young adults)	33	68	90	43	33	13	−
25	Subnormal group, ages 10-13 yrs.	96	4	−	72	8	16	4
25	Depressed patients (adults)	88	12	32	64	12	12	−
35	Delusional schizophrenics (adults)	80	20	9	14	51	34	31

select "the most superior child" in that age range in the public schools. They were selected in the schools on the basis of school achievement scores, teachers' estimates, rating scales by supervisors and peers, and other test data. They were sent to the Brush Foundation for physical measurements and additional mental and personality tests.

The subnormal group consisted of boys and girls, age range 10 to 13 years, who scored between 50 and 65 I.Q. on the Binet 1937 Scale. The college group of women were students in an elementary psychology class. Patients in a state mental hospital and Veterans Administration hospital made up the clinical groups and the brain-injured group, studied by Loehrke (1952). Finally, the old-age group were institutionalized old people, subjects in the study by Hertz et al. (1951).

Included also are the norms from a more recent study by Hertz and Paolino (1961) based on the records of two groups of male patients, 35 delusional paranoid schizophrenics and 35 neurotic

TABLE 2.2
Norms for Organizational Scores Based on g

| | | Organizational Acts | | | | | | | | | | | Sum g Weighted | | | |
| | | R | | | gO+ | | Sum g− | | Total Sum Org. Acts | | Sum g+ wt | | Total Sum g wt | | | |
N	Groups	M	Md	Q	Md	Q	Md	Q	Md	Q	Md	Q	Md	Q	M	S.D.
	1. 12-year old children															
41	boys	34.25													12.01	6.35
34	girls	38.71													12.44	5.56
75	Total group	36.43													12.22	5.98
	2. 15-year-old children															
29	boys	33.87													10.80	6.02
28	girls	41.37													11.87	6.14
57	Total group	37.54													11.33	6.11
	3. 14-year-old children															
25	boys				9.0	2.8			10.0	3.7	9.0	2.8	8.0	2.8	9.82	
25	girls				8.6	2.8			10.0	3.7	8.6	2.8	8.0	2.9	10.62	
50	Total group		30.1	13.9	8.9	2.8			10.0	3.6	8.9	2.8	8.0	2.9	10.22	
	4. Very superior, ages 11-16 yrs.															
25	boys								11.3	3.5			11.7	2.8	12.52	
25	girls								10.1	2.9			9.4	4.0	12.54	
50	Total group		31.1	4.3	9.5	2.9	1.4	.9	10.8	3.5	9.7	3.4	10.5	3.2	12.53	
	5. Extreme groups on Otis I.Q., age 12 yrs.															
28	High boys												15.8	5.2		
28	High girls												15.5	3.6		
56	Total high												15.1	3.3		

Group	n													
Low boys	28										8.5	3.2		
Low girls	28										9.8	3.1		
Total low	56										9.2	3.0		
6. College women (young adults)	40	14.3		12.5	5.4			14.0	6.3	12.5	6.6	13.0	5.5	16.67
7. Subnormal, ages 10-13 yrs. (boys and girls)	25	3.1		1.2	1.5			1.9	1.7	1.1	.9	1.3	1.0	1.86
8. Depressed patients (adults)	25	24.0	6.4	4.9	2.3			7.7	4.0	3.4	1.7	5.6	2.9	5.36
9. Delusional schizophrenics (adults)	35	22.5	6.2	4.3	1.4	3.6	1.3	7.6	2.8	3.4	1.9	6.1	2.3	6.07
10. Delusional schizophrenics (adults)	35	26.7						16.0				11.0		
Neurotics (adults)	35	25.5						11.0				9.0		
11. Brain-injured male patients (adults)	50	17.7	5.1									5.1	1.7	
12. Old-age group, age range 60-74 yrs.	28	23.5										4.8		
75-90 yrs.	22	17.7										4.8		
Total	50	20.8	6.2									4.8		2.6

TABLE 2.4

Means and Medians of the Qualitatively Different
Kinds of Organizational Acts for the Contrasting Groups

| | Paranoid Schizophrenic (N = 35) | | Neurotic (N = 35) | | Diff |
	M	Mdn	M	Mdn	Z^b
g O+ wt	1.93	1.50	2.57	1.50	.48
g+ wt	3.94	4.0	4.80	4.0	1.02
g P wt	1.07	1.00	1.19	1.0	.66
g v+ wt	. . .	0 (65.7)a	. . .	0 (51.4)	. . .
g v− wt	. . .	0 (94.3)	. . .	0 (100)	. . .
g− wt	. . .	0 (77.1)	. . .	0 (80)	. . .
g O− wt	1.86	1.5	.50	.5	5.43***
g+ comb wt	. . .	0 (65.7)	. . .	0 (71.4)	. . .
g+ O+ comb wt	. . .	0 (94.3)	. . .	0 (74.3)	. . .
g− comb wt	. . .	0 (94.3)	. . .	0 (100)	. . .
g O− comb wt	1.49	1.0	.07	0 (88.6)	6.25***
Σg+ wt	7.74	7.0	9.76	8.5	1.35
Σg− wt	3.61	3.5	.66	.5	6.42***
Total Σ g wt	11.35	11.0	10.42	9.0	1.19
Σ org acts+	8.49	8.0	10.4	9.0	1.63
Σ org acts−	7.29	7.0	1.34	1.0	6.40***
Total Σ org acts	15.78	16.0	11.74	11.0	1.30

*, **, *** = Significant at the .05, .01, and .001 levels respectively.

aZero medians indicate that more than 50% of the group have not shown the pattern. Where this occurs, parenthetical figures indicate the percentage of the cases in the group which do not show the pattern.

bComparison by means of Mann-Whitney U-Test.

patients, matched for age, I.Q., socio-economic status, and for productivity or R in the Rorschach records. Since these are the only detailed norms so far reported for all the qualitatively different organization patterns weighted and unweighted, they are reproduced in Tables 2.4 and 2.5.

Viewing the so called "normal" children in the Brush series, the range for Sum g wt for the 12-year-old group is 6 to 18, for the 15-year-old group, 5 to 17. Other groups studied above the age of 11 years showed approximately the same range. The normative range tentatively adopted then for adolescents of average intelligence is 5 to 18 Sum g wt.

TABLE 2.5

Proportions of the Groups giving Qualitatively Different
Kinds of Organizational Acts showing Differences based on Chi-square Test

	Paranoid Schizophrenics	Neurotics	Chi-square	P
g O +	65.7	68.6	0	—
g +	97.1	100	0	—
g P	91.4	100	.019	—
g v +	34.3	48.6	.013	—
g v −	5.7	0	.52	—
g −	22.8	20.0	0	—
g O −	94.3	57.1	11.11	⟨.001***
g + comb	34.3	28.6	0	
g + O + comb	5.7	25.7	3.88	⟨.05*
g − comb	11.4	0	2.38	
g − O − comb	85.7	11.4	35.74	⟨.001***

These studies will be discussed further in this chapter in the section on validity (supra p. 54 f.).

Reliability. To the writer's knowledge, there has been no serious attempts to deal with the question of reliability of either Beck's Z or Hertz' g. No information is available on interscorer or retest reliability, reliability of the organization score over time, or reliability of the interpretive hypotheses among scorers.

Reliability of the scoring of organization depends on the identification of the organizing activity and the application of the appropriate weights. It is not difficult to establish the presence of organization in a response or to apply either the Z weights or the g weights. It probably has been assumed that both systems are sufficiently objective so that systematic study of reliability is not needed, especially if there is sufficient practice with respect to a specific system of scoring. In classroom training and in clinical practice, consistency in the mechanical aspects of scoring organization has been demonstrated again and again.

For those who find the qualitatively differentiated scores more meaningful, however, reliability cannot be assumed. Once organizational activity has been established in a response, scoring the qualitative differentiations depends upon the scorer's interpretation of what constitutes a response, the mere verbalization or the total psychological reaction to the blot (Hertz, 1963, 1970). Further, scoring of organization is influenced by the manner of scoring complex and combinative responses—with one scoring formula, multiple scores, or fragmentation of response into separate scoring formulae.

Reliability therefore cannot be taken for granted with any system of scoring. It must be systematically studied.

VALIDITY OF THE ORGANIZATION FACTOR IN THE RORSCHACH

The organization score is utilized today rather widely in the clinical evaluation of Rorschach records and in research. To a great extent, reliance has been placed on theoretical assumptions and "clinical validity," or better the pattern's pragmatic and clinical utility. Rorschach clinicians have demonstrated through case studies that the organizational pattern in global context offers interpretations congruent with data based on case material, interpretations which have been confirmed in subsequent case studies. While such procedure does not constitute scientific evidence for the validity of the hypotheses assigned to the organization score in the traditional sense, it certainly furnishes many hypotheses which may be subjected to more systematic verification.

Research studies are available with the Z score and to a lesser extent with the g score, especially in relation to hypotheses pertaining to level and quality of intellectual functioning, motivation and drive, impact of affect, and differential diagnosis. For the most part, attempts have been made to establish the scientific validity of the organization score according to traditional psychometric criteria.

The Z Score

Through the years, Beck and his colleagues (1945, 1952, 1960, 1967, Molish, 1967), relied on the case study method for validating interpretive hypotheses for Rorschach patterns, including the Z score.

In case after case of normal and pathological subjects they have compared their interpretations of Z as reflecting intelligence level, drive, and achievement potential, with psychometric and educational data, and their hypotheses concerning degree of pathology with case material and psychiatric data.

According to Beck and his colleagues, Z reveals the ability to grasp relationships, to conceptualize and to abstract. It is "an index of intellectual energy as such . . . the intellectual functioning per se" (1945, p. 12). It is an index of the amount of energy available for intellectual activity, of energy which can be converted into intellectual achievement, irrespective of the kind of intelligence. Hence Z is an index of intellectual effort, drive, and initiative (Beck and Molish, 1967, p. 130). Beck generalizes further, Z reflects the capacity of the individual to see relations between various aspects of his experience and to organize the stimuli of his world meaningfully (Beck, 1960, p. 189).

Comparing W and Z, both show the extent to which the individual synthesizes, W telling more of his conceptual activity, and Z, of his grasp of relations between the stimuli in his perceptual field (Beck, 1952, p. 23). The higher the Sum Z, the more able the individual to perform work which requires difficult and complex intellectual effort. Thus in pictures of superior intelligence, Beck anticipates high W and high Z. On the other hand, where analytic, synthetic, and abstracting ability is low, as in subnormal pictures and in some cases of organic brain damage, W and Z will be low (Beck, 1952, Beck and Molish, 1967).

Interpretive hypotheses for the organization score are advanced also for the various clinical groups by Beck and his colleagues, based on extensive clinical experience (Beck, 1952, 1960, Beck and Molish, 1967; Molish, 1967). They anticipate low Z in clinical pictures characterized by inhibition, constriction, depressed states, repression of affects, and loss of intellectual drive. On the other hand organization will be high in pictures characterized by strong intellectual drive, overambitiousness, emotional expansiveness, elation, excitability. In manic conditions, the Z may be high but qualitatively poor or very low, due to erratic and disrupted attention. In obsessive-compulsive pictures, the Z may be high "not only because of their intellectual drive, but also because the command forces them to look for connections." On the other hand, Z may be low because "the frantic search for the minute prevents grasping relations of which they are capable" or "as a direct consequence of the rigorous pattern, the defense which constricts the functioning along all dimensions of personality" (Beck, 1952, p. 30).

As with every other factor in the Rorschach, the interpretation of Z varies with the total personality picture. Thus Z is discussed for the most part in terms of other factors and patterns. Z with R, and content for example, reflects the ego's initiative and energy (Beck, 1952, p. 19). Again high Z with low $F+\%$ and with many personal $F-$, and with high S, represents a cluster suggesting the sick paranoid (Beck, 1952, p. 22).

Some of the above interpretations based on case studies have been subjected to systematic study. Thus research dealing directly with Beck's Z score as it relates to intelligence have been reported, some showing a positive relationship while others fail to find any relationship.

Goldfarb (1945) interpreted Beck's Z as reflecting the individual's "ability to organize his experience and to generalize from it, and his will or drive to think along the lines of abstraction and generalization" (1945, p. 525). He therefore hypothesized a relationship between the Z score and various scores on other tests of concept formation and categorical behavior (the Block Design and the Similarities Test in the Wechsler-Bellevue Intelligence Scale, the Weigl Color Form Test, the Vigotsky Test of Abstraction). Studying the records of 30 normal adolescents, mean age 12 years 3 months, he could find no reliable relationship between Z and scores on these tests. Since Beck's Z does not make qualitative differentiations in terms of form level or adequacy of organizational activity, Goldfarb studied in his subjects only that Z activity which was $F+$, and also a score based on the form-level rating of Klopfer et al. (1944). Beck's Sum $Z+$ did not relate to the scores of the other tests either. The form-level rating scores, however, were reliably related to the scores on the other tests.

The writer was similarly unsuccessful in obtaining significant relationships between Z and either M.A. or I.Q. based on the Higher Otis Test or the Stanford-Binet. On the basis of scores of 75 twelve-year-old children in the Brush series, Pearson correlations were obtained as follows:

Z : M.A. .156 ± .113 Z : I.Q.   .174 ± .112

Other studies considered only the $F+$ in the responses rated organization, with the following results:

$Z+$: M.A. .182 ± .112 $Z+$: I.Q.   .198 ± .111

Again for 57 fifteen-year-old children, results were similar:

$Z+$: M.A. .205 ± .127 Z : I.Q.   .213 ± .126

Similarly, Sarason (1950) could find no relationship between M.A. and Z values when studying the records of two groups of mental defectives. Using the measure $Z-\%$, however, consisting of the number of minus responses scored Z over the total number of Z responses, he obtained correlations of $-.55$ and $-.63$ between the $Z-$ score and M.A. for the two groups. The $Z-$ score appeared to be associated with lower intelligence.

Kropp (1955) reported that Jolles (1947) found insignificant correlations between total Z scores and Binet and Wechsler-Bellevue I.Q.'s in a group of 66 mental defectives. Similarly, on the basis of a large college population, Wilson (1952) could find no relation between intelligence and specific Rorschach factors including Z.

On the other hand, there is considerable evidence of a positive relationship between weighted Z scores and intelligence. Wishner (1948), for example, obtained a correlation of .536 between Z and full weighted scale on the Wechsler-Bellevue Intelligence Test, in his study of intellectual factors in the Rorschach records of 42 neurotic subjects, 16 to 42 years of age, I.Q. 79 to 130. For his neurotic group, then, he could conclude that Z measures intellectual capacity as reflected in this scale. Similarly, Sisson and Taulbee (1955), working with the records of 50 psychiatric patients, randomly selected, obtained a correlation of .428 between the weighted Z score and the full scale Wechsler I.Q., and .52 between unweighted Z responses and the full scale Wechsler I.Q.

Two other studies corroborate this positive relationship between Z and intelligence. Batt (1953) obtained statistically significant correlations of .49 and .46 between weighted Z score and the verbal and reasoning parts of the Primary Mental Abilities Test in a study of 32 high school students. Accordingly, the Z score was assumed to reflect the capacity to understand ideas expressed in words, to solve logical problems, and to foresee and to plan.

Taulbee (1955) was interested in applying the Rorschach to evaluate levels of intellectual functioning of a group of 60 hospitalized schizophrenic patients. In this study, Z along with R, W, M, and $F+$, showed a positive relationship with the full-scale Wechsler-Bellevue I.Q. The W and Z correlations, although low, were significantly reliable. Studying the Z scores in relation to the subtest scores, he obtained especially high correlations with digit span, similarities, and vocabulary. He concluded that the Z score in the records of schizophrenic patients could be said to relate to the ability to engage in verbal abstraction, the ability for concept formation, and freedom from distractibility.

In like manner, Sinnett and Roberts (1956) set out to study the relationships between the organization of Rorschach stimuli represented by the Mental Approach and the Z score, and the organization of cognitive material represented by a structured task (a Reading Comprehension Test) and an unstructured task (Free recall of stories). According to their results, Z score was related to the selection of more highly organized responses in the structured cognitive task when intelligence and speed were controlled.

The organization score was involved in the study of the developmental aspects of personality structure in normal children by Thetford et al. (1951), who compared the norms for three groups, 6 to 9 years, 10 to 13 years, and 14 to 17 years of age (Table 2.2). The Z activity increased from 4.88 in the youngest group to 5.61 in the middle group, to 24.50 in the oldest group. Significantly reliable differences were obtained between the weighted Z scores of the youngest group and the oldest group, and also between the middle group and the oldest group. The investigators concluded that if there is no interference with the level of functioning, there is an increase in the ability to organize relationships with age, and that this ability manifests itself to a pronounced degree during the adolescent years. These findings, they suggest, may be "interpreted in relation to our knowledge of the normal growth curve emphasizing the freedom of mental energy which accompanies the maximum release of intellectual capacity during adolescence" (Thetford et al., 1951, p. 76).

The organization score was also analyzed in connection with

prediction of academic success in the study of McCandless (1949) on the basis of Rorschach records of two matched groups of officer candidates in the U.S. Maritime Service, differing in academic achievement. Rorschach patterns failed to differentiate reliably between the "high-grade group" and the "low-grade group". Similarly, Thompson (1941) failed to show that Z relates uniformly to academic success.

Beck and his colleagues (1950) demonstrate a relationship between Z scores and skilled and unskilled occupations. As may be observed in the table of norms (Table 2.1), the higher the skilled vocational group, the higher the Z values. They conclude there is a relationship between Z and occupational level.

Their findings were only partially substantiated by Otis (1959) who compared Z scores of a group of executives with those of lower occupation groups. While the Z scores distinguished between executive and junior executive groups, they failed to differentiate between skilled, semi-skilled, and unskilled groups.

A few studies of mentally defective children show the organization score helpful in differentiating groups. Sloan (1947) matched a defective group of 26 children, I.Q. ranging from 44 to 79, with a similar number of nondefective children, I.Q. 80 to 100, this latter group having been considered defective prior to institutionalization. The purpose of the study was to determine whether certain personality disturbances may be mistaken for mental deficiency. The Rorschach records were studied for ten "signs" of mental deficiency, one of which was Beck's Z (normative range 5 to 31). The deviation of each subject on each sign was computed. Total Z score was one of five factors on which the defective subjects deviated most frequently, the others being A%, F+%, F%, and R. It was concluded that these patterns would help diagnose mental deficiency.

Jolles (1947) was interested in a similar problem, namely, the importance of personality adjustment as a factor in the etiology of mental deficiency. The 66 children utilized in case studies, ages 10 to 15, I.Q.'s 65 to 79, were divided into three groups according to Rorschach patterns: (1) normal mental ability; (2) at least one indication of normal ability in an otherwise abnormal picture; and (3) no indication of normal mental ability. Certain inferences were made as to the influence of emotional disturbances on intellectual development and functioning. For the present purpose, it is sufficient to point out that high Z in conjunction with qualitatively good W and M, adequate range of content, and adequate $F+$ would contraindicate mental deficiency.

The Z score also appears in research studies as part of clusters or batteries of Rorschach factors characterizing clinical groups. The Z score for example, figures in one of the five patterns developed by Thiesen (1952), which discriminated Beck's normal group of adults from 60 schizophrenic adults. In his Pattern B, an $F+\%$ lower than 69% with a Z score less than 8.0, was reliably associated with the schizophrenic group, reflecting, according to him, perceptual inaccuracy with low mental drive. This was not, however, confirmed in a subsequent study by Rubin and Lonstein (1963) who compared 42 hospitalized male schizophrenics with Beck's normal group, or by Taulbee and Sisson (1954) who compared 52 hospitalized male schizophrenic patients with Beck's normal group.

In Beck's study of the six schizophrenias (1954), results are reported for the comparisons of Rorschach norms for normal children, and neurotic and schizophrenic children. These are reproduced in Table 2.1. Of the six variables in which the schizophrenic children and the neurotic children exceeded the norms, the high W and high Z were conspicuous, suggesting greater application of energy. According to Beck, intellectual drive appeared to be released more by the neurotic and the schizophrenic children than by the normal group (1954, p. 215). When norms for the normal neurotic and schizophrenic adults (Table 2.1) were compared, no significant differences were found for W or Z (1954, p. 212).

In this study, the Z score played an important part in many of the configurations which differentiated the six "reaction patterns." For example, Z score was involved in Rorschach correlates of "rigid hold on self," defense of isolation, synthesis of ideas, spontaneity, social adaptation, limitation of achievement, obsessive-compulsive thoughts, expressed anxiety, and depression. In his group $S-1$, "projection" was reflected by the triad, high Z, low $F+\%$, and high $S\%$. Many of his other clinical observations were confirmed.

Molish (1965) compared an orthogenic school group of children with behavior disorders with the "normal" group of Thetford et al. (1951) and the 60 neurotic and 60 schizophrenic children studied by Beck (1954). Among other patterns, reliable differences were obtained for W and Z, the orthogenic group showing higher scores. Despite the evidence of greater potential for intellectual drive, however, when the Z and W were studied in context, in relation to other Rorschach patterns, especially in terms of productivity or R, the mean Z score fell below expectancy. Molish concluded that the orthogenic children did not grasp relations commensurate with their mental ability; they appeared to direct their intellectual drive into concern over details. While having ability, they made less constructive and less effective use of their intellectual drive and energy.

The Z score also figures in a study by Schmidt and Fonda (1954) in the analysis of the records of 42 manic patients compared with those of a similar number of schizophrenic patients, the groups matched on the basis of age, sex, and number of response. Comparing the Z values (Table 2.1), the manic patients gave Z scores reliably higher than the schizophrenic group. They exceeded Beck's normals in Z score. This higher output was also reflected in their stronger tendency to generalize (W). Although the investigators did not study the Z score qualitatively, their figures showed that the $F+\%$ and the number of P were much lower as compared with Beck's normal subjects. Thus while the Z score tended to be high, no doubt it involved more poor forms and fewer P.

In a study of the relation of Rorschach test to brain injury, Reitan (1955) compared 65 patients with verified brain damage with 127 hospitalized control subjects on a variety of ratios made up of traditional Rorschach scores, including Z. Of interest to us are his results for the following patterns—Z (organizing activity), T/R (time per response), $Z: T/R$ (organizing activity in relation to the amount of time taken per response reflecting speed or facility with which organization occurs), and Z/R (percentage of organizing activity in terms of total output). Significant differences were reported between the means of the control group and those of the brain-injured group with respect to the time per response (T/R) and the speed of organizing (ratio $Z: T/R$). The latter ratio, however was no more effective than the Z score alone and not quite as effective as T/R. Correlations were computed between the Halstead Impairment Index and the ratios for a separate group of 100 persons, heterogenous in respect to diagnosis. The ratio $Z: T/R$ was especially significant. When that ratio was low, the Halstead Index of Impairment tended to be high. Two patterns, then, Z and T/R contribute to the detection of organic condition of the brain.

Two intercorrelational studies have been reported between Z and other Rorschach factors. According to Varvel's (1941) statistics based on a study of the records of 144 normal college students, Z correlated with $F+\%$, $-.29\pm .05$; with $A\%+ P\%+ F+\%$, $-.46\pm .04$; and with $M+$, $.79\pm .02$. He concluded that "constricted stereotyped individuals show rigidity of personality structure, lack of that perceptual-cognitive 'fluidity' which in combination with attentiveness and intellectual precision $(F+)$ is associated with productive, differentiated intellectual and easy adaptability" (1941, p. 12).

Kropp (1955) computed intercorrelations on the basis of the 53 records given by Beck (1952). Z correlated with W, $.843$; with M, $.581$; and with R, $.565$. He also obtained multiple correlations of Z with W and M, $.93$; and Z with W and M and F, $.95$. On the basis of these correlations he concluded that a Z score might be estimated from W and M scores, and, hence, he found it unnecessary to evaluate weighted Z scores.

It is of interest to note that in the Holtzman system (1961) to which we have referred (supra p. 32) research based on factor analysis revealed gross factors, two of which, Factor I (defined by integration, Form definiteness, M, H, and P), and Factor IV (defined by Location and Form definiteness) were interpreted as reflecting well organized ideational activity and differentiated accurate form perception respectively (Holtzman et al., 1961, p. 177). Low but significant correlations were obtained between general intelligence and scores which identify Factors I and IV.

Subsequent research by Thorpe (1965) revealed significant age differences in five groups ranging from preschool children, 5 years of age to college students from 18 to 21 years of age, in many of the Holtzman variables, including form appropriateness, form definiteness and integration. These scores were viewed as valid indices of level of perceptual development.

The Hertz g score

An investigation of the organizational factor was included in the preliminary research which was conducted at the Brush Foundation.

The research involved exploratory studies of normal children in the Brush series and in the Cleveland Public Schools and adult patients from psychiatric institutions and V.A. hospitals.

From the beginning, the Rorschach Test was viewed primarily as a perceptual-cognitive task. Since the individual was requested not only to perceive the blots but to give meaning to them, he had to impose some structure and organization on the blots. To do this he had to exercise perceptual and cognitive abilities. Thus his responses involved a series of cognitive activities including perception, association, memories, even feelings. In addition, the task required verbal communication. Hence, perceptual-cognitive theory furnished the basis for our early research.

For the organization factor, the following hypotheses were originally formulated.

1. Since the organization pattern by definition refers to the analysis of the blot areas into component parts, projecting objects into them, seeing them in relationships, and combining and integrating them into meaningful units, it reflects analytic and synthetic processes.

2. Since the organization pattern involves selection of certain qualities and relations of objects from the whole blot, evaluating them, apprehending their properties as belonging to a whole class of objects (abstraction) and deciding upon the "appropriate" concept (generalization), the organization pattern may be said to reflect the ability to abstract, to conceptualize and to generalize.

3. Since these aspects of cognitive functioning are essential features of intelligence, the summary score for organization is an indication of intelligence. The g score should be high for individuals of high intelligence and low for those of inferior intelligence and for those where there is some impairment of intellectual functioning.

4. Since the individual must persist if he analyzes the blots into their component parts, see relationships, and reintegrate parts into meaningful units, he must persevere and be motivated. Hence the g reveals intellectual drive and effort.

5. The qualitative differentiations of the organization score reflect the adequacy, the appropriateness, and the complexity of the thought processes of an individual.

6. Since cognitive functions may be impaired by emotional

disturbance and by pathological conditions, the organization score is likewise affected by these conditions and hence should reflect them.

In general then, the Rorschach organization score should be able to reflect certain aspects of cognitive functioning and personality characteristics.

To a considerable extent Hertz, like Beck and his colleagues, relied for her interpretation of the organizational factor on these theoretical assumptions, cumulative clinical experience with normal and pathological groups using case histories, clinical data, and other test data to verify the interpretive hypotheses given to the g score (Hertz, 1969). Some of these clinical hypotheses were subjected to empirical studies, however. A few of the fragmentary studies may be reviewed. Unfortunately, termination of the Brush research program prevented more systematic exploration of some of the promising preliminary results.[5] In the light of the very high correlation between Z and g, it is likely that results reported for Beck's Z whether positive, negative or equivocal, carry meaning for g as well.

The total number of responses were significantly related to both weighted g score and sum organizational acts. On the basis of an analysis of the organizing ability of 50 fourteen-year-old boys and girls, correlations were obtained of .396 between R and sum organizing acts and .283 between R and sum g wt. There was a low positive correlation then between productivity and the organization score as herein defined. While the g score is no doubt affected by the number of responses in a record, this does not mean, as has been interpreted, that increase or decrease in g is to be explained exclusively in terms of the variation in the number of responses. The low but positive correlation may also reflect the involvement of other factors.

As reported for Beck's Z, there is a high correlation between sum g wt and sum organizational acts which involve mere frequency of occurrence of organization. In a recent study (Hertz and Paolino, 1960) based on 35 delusional paranoid schizophrenic and 35 neurotic

[5] Even more unfortunate, a book in preparation based on research studies of hundreds of records of school children, adolescents and adults of varying intelligence and from different clinical groups, together with statistical material, other test data, and physical and social histories, all of which had been stored at the Medical School, were burnt by mistake. The data herein reported are all that were salvaged.

patients, the Spearman *rho* correlation between these variables was .896 for the schizophrenic group and .942 for the neurotics. However, as we will note in discussing Table 2.4, there were marked differences between the groups in the qualitatively differentiated organizational patterns.

Relationship of g scores and intelligence. Equivocal results were obtained in studies relating g scores to general tests of intelligence. Studying the records of 75 twelve-year-old children, Otis I.Q.'s ranging from 86 to 140, Pearson correlations were obtained for M.A. with g and $g+$ of .209± .110 and .226± .110, reflecting a very low but positive relationship. Again, correlations based on a study of the records of 57 children, 15 years old, revealed very low correlations: M.A. with g and $g+$ respectively: .249± .124 and .243± .125; I.Q. with g and $g+$ respectively: .256± .124 and .250± .124. Thus for these groups, g did not measure the intellectual level which was reflected by either Otis or Binet scores. This was also demonstrated with Z.

The contradictory results obtained in the attempt to demonstrate that the organization score is linked with intellectual ability as measured by standard intelligence tests can be explained in part by the fact that too often, the qualitative differentiations of the organization score are ignored. Further sum organization may tap only limited aspects of intelligence, while the I.Q. is a summary score made up of different aspects of intellectual functioning. It may well be that they do not coincide with the abilities hypothesized for Z or g. It therefore appears futile to rely on the gross I.Q. as the criterion of intelligence against which to correlate Z or g. No doubt it would be more profitable to use more refined intelligence criteria. Some of the studies reported with Z indicate that a better design would involve utilization of separate cognitive abilities as criteria, and to conceptualize Z or g in terms of its qualities.

This problem has been attacked by comparing groups of varying intellectual levels. While some of the groups referred to in Tables 2.2 and 2.3 are not comparable because they represent differing populations, it is possible to trace some general trends in the organizing activity.

It may be noted that 48% of the 14-year-old group gave two or more g O+ and 56% gave eight or more $g+$ as compared to only 18%

which gave inferior organization $(g-)$. Not one in this group gave the highly negative pattern, g $O-$ $comb!$. Again, while the superior group did not show on an average a higher organization score than expectancy, 82% gave two or more $g+$ and only 8% gave four or more $g-$. Similarly a high proportion of the college women, 68%, showed two or more g $O+$, and 90% showed eight or more $g+$. Thus more of the groups of high intelligence gave organizing acts involving realistic forms and combinations than inferior organizations.

It should be noted, however, that a small proportion of both the superior group and the college women also gave some g $O-$ combinations. As has been hypothesized, emotional and personal factors influence reality testing and other cognitive abilities which are reflected in the quality of the organizational activity in all groups, whatever the level of intelligence.

The subnormal group shows on an average a very low median compared with the norm adapted. In the group studied, there was hardly any distribution of scores. Over half of the group, 56% fell below 1.5 sum g wt. Of course it is generally observed that mental defectives have very low capacity to analyze and synthesize. They are not capable of much conceptual thinking, especially the kind that is in tune with reality. It may be viewed from Table 2.3 that very few of the group gave four or more $g+$, and 16% gave different and strange combinations (g $O-$ $comb!$). Although the groups are not comparable, there is a marked difference between the average number and quality of the organizational scores of the subnormal group and the groups of higher intelligence.

This may be seen in a study comparing the medians of high Otis group with those of the low Otis group of 12-year-old boys and girls. The following results show statistically reliable differences at the 5% level of confidence or less.

	Diff	C.R.
High Otis boys with low Otis boys	6.8	3.33
High Otis boys with low Otis girls	5.5	2.68
High Otis girls with low Otis girls	5.7	3.11
High Otis girls with low Otis boys	7.0	3.87
Total high group with total low group	5.9	4.37

Thus 12-year-old children at the higher levels of intelligence, as determined by the Otis test, show higher sum g wt than those at the lower levels.

Pertinent to this discussion is a study (Hertz and Kennedy, 1940) of the human movement in the records of 137 children, 69 boys and 70 girls, 14 and 15 years of age, the I.Q. range from 95 to 159 based on the revised Stanford-Binet. The group was divided into average and superior levels based on I.Q. Among the patterns studied in conjunction with the M score, was M in combination with g, i.e., $W M g$, $D M g$, $S M g$ and sum $M g$. It was found that reliably more of the superior group than the average group gave sum $M g$, and more gave $D M g$ and $D M O+ g$. Thus more children of superior intelligence gave human movement responses scored for organization than those of average intelligence. It was concluded that responses which involved the organization of elements in normal detail areas, with well perceived forms experienced in movement, were prone to reflect superior mental functioning.

In summarizing the studies of children in the second decade of life, Hertz (1965) reported that while there were divergences in the statistical norms reported by various investigators, there appeared to be a definite increase in organizational activity with age. In Hertz' study of children, 10 to 16 years, while she did not find an increase in overall organization scores, qualitative analysis of the patterns showed increase in complex differentiated perception, ability to analyze, see relationships, and achieve an integrated view of situations. The results reported appeared to be in agreement with Meili-Dworetzki's (1956) studies on the perceptual development of children 2 to 16 years of age, based on the qualitative analysis of mental approach categories. Development occurred from "primitive Wholes" which represented the most rudimentary forms of perceptual structuralization and which were the products of superficial perception and superficial conceptualization, to superior differentiation and globalization and superior combinatorial whole processes (1956, p. 140).

The g score in clinical groups. As may be noted in Table 2.2, the depressed group gave very low sum g wt of 5.6. Clinically we know that individuals who are tense, anxious, and constrained give low g. They appear unable to analyze situations and see relationships. They are "stimulus-bound." They lack verve. Varvel (1941) showed this close relationship between limited perceptual organization and the constricted personality.

Thus in depressed conditions, intrapsychic constriction impairs cognitive functioning and reduces drive and initiative. With the present depressed group, the reduced organizational score no doubt reflects this intellectual impairment and lowered drive.

From Table 2.3 it may be observed that almost a third of the depressed group gave eight or more $g+$ and a very large proportion (65%) gave no or only one $g-$. Those who have had experience with the depressed know that this $F+$ reflects chiefly a rigid adherence to reality, to the easy and the commonplace, due to extreme cautiousness, guardedness, and repression.

A few of the depressed group (12%) gave one g O$-$ combination. They saw relations between elements of the blots, projecting forms which were unrealistic and peculiar. This would appear to point to gross misinterpretation or distortion of reality which we know may occur in some depressed conditions.

The schizophrenic group characterized by delusions, studied by Loehrke (1952) had a low median sum g wt (6.1). About half of the group gave four or more $g-$, and 31% gave four or more g O$-$ combinations, suggesting considerable distortion of reality and the possibility of thought disorders.

In the more recent study by Hertz and Paolino (1960), of the thinking processes of the two groups of delusional paranoid schizophrenics and neurotic patients (Table 2.4), the investigators set out (1) to study the nature and the quality of the perceptual and conceptual processes of two groups representing varying levels of psychological disorganization and (2) to investigate the power of the organization score to detect impaired thinking, primary thought disorders, and delusional states. Perceptual-cognitive theory and ego psychoanalytic psychology formed the conceptual basis for their approach and suggested several hypotheses as to the potential of the various organizational patterns to reveal perceptual and conceptual disorganization.

The investigators adopted a configurational approach, studying each record as a whole in global fashion but concentrating on one dimension, organizational activity. Specifically the organization pattern was studied in terms of (1) the blot elements which were organized (Mental Approach), (2) the extent to which determinants were integrated in the combinations and integrations (M, FM, m, F

Crude, *F* Prim, varieties of shading and color), (3) the adequacy of the form level, (4) the various kinds of content involved in the organizational acts (traditional categories), (5) the extent to which content was fabulized and/or influenced by the inroads of primary process thinking, and (6) styles in communication, in vocabulary and in choice of language. The fabulized content categories and the stylistic features of the responses were taken from the qualitative features of responses identified in previous studies (Hertz 1951, 1963) and from those suggested in the literature (Phillips and Smith, 1953; Rapaport, 1946).

Results based on a comparison of the two groups in each of the six areas of inquiry may be summarized as follows:[6]

1. The schizophrenic group appeared capable of approximately as much organizational activity as the neurotic group (Table 2.4), since no significant difference was obtained between sum *g wt* and sum org. acts in the two groups, but on an average, the schizophrenic group gave reliable evidence of more sum org. acts— and sum *g— wt* and *g O— comb.* Further highly significant differences were obtained between the proportions of the groups showing these patterns (Table 2.5). Thus the schizophrenics showed more evidence of thinking involving unrealistic, distorted, and/or personalized thinking and more evidence of thinking involving incongruent and inappropriate relationships, suggesting different and /or bizarre thinking, and in general, less mature integrated thinking. Further the *g O—* combinations pointed to thought disorders.

2. When the areas involved in the organizational acts were analyzed, the schizophrenics reliably showed greater proneness to organize details and details with spaces (*Dg, D+S(S)g, Dr+s(s)g,*[7] a larger proportion showing distortion of the usual or normal details (*Dg—, D+S(S)g—*). Thus even the usual and obvious aspects of the blots were prone to be misinterpreted or distorted. In addition, the schizophrenic group showed marked perceptual articulation of the rare areas (*Dr + s(s)g*) and greater proness to misinterpret them (*Dr + s (s)g—*), suggesting an overresponsiveness and overalertness to the rare

---

[6] Reference must be made to the original reports (Hertz and Paolino, 1960, 1961) for tables and for the statistical data, other than those reproduced in the present study.

[7] In the Hertz system, the scores with parentheses refer to multiple scores. Those in parentheses are "tendencies," "additionals" or "blends."

and the unusual in a situation. Again, the highest incidence of organized spaces occurred with the schizophrenic group $(S(S) + s(s)$ g, $s(s)g)$, with more showing unrealistic integrations of rare space areas $(s(s)g-)$. Further analysis of the organized space responses, revealed schizophrenic proneness to project solids into spaces suggesting the oppositionalism and stubborn adherence to ideas often encountered in paranoid schizophrenic conditions.

3. Viewing results for the determinants involved in the organizational acts, a significantly greater proportion of the schizophrenic group showed organized responses involving imaginative and fantasy activity out of touch with reality $(Mg-)$ reflecting greater breakdown in reality testing and greater proneness to regressive and/or autistic thinking. In addition, more schizophrenics appeared to be influenced and disrupted by their impulses (FMg). A tendency was likewise noted for more of the schizophrenics to infuse their organizational activity with chaotic and diffuse primitive emotions $(C+CF\ g)$. On the other hand, the schizophrenic group also reliably showed on an average more F crude g suggesting more crude and impersonal kind of thinking, stripped of emotional and imaginative qualities.

4. No significant differences were reported for the number of content categories as traditionally defined. A significantly larger proportion of the schizophrenics, however, gave specific themes including imaginary animals, anatomy and sex, specific body parts, articles of clothing, other "covering" concepts (such as "emblems," "shrouds," "blankets"), and more gave fabulized content, enlivening their percepts with affective enrichment beyond what the blot areas could evoke, reflecting body, sexual and/or homosexual and sado-masochistic preoccupations.

5. Again significantly more schizophrenics showed "negative" stylistic features of their organized responses, such as contamination, autistic logic, fluidity, incompatible alternatives, nonsequitur reasoning, and reference relationships, reflecting severely deviant thought processes.

6. Finally, in their style of communication, more schizophrenics reliably displayed peculiarities in speech style and language usage.

The results of the study were consistent with theoretical expectations and clinical experiences with similar clinical groups.

According to the investigators, the study demonstrated that the organization score, quantitatively and qualitatively analyzed in terms of other formal scores, thematic analysis, stylistic features of the responses, and mode of communication could distinguish between groups of varying levels of psychological organization. It showed that the weighted scheme of scoring organization in terms of form quality, and the nature and the complexity of the combinations and the integrations, was more effective for diagnostic purposes than the mere frequency of organizational acts.

In a subsequent study of the distribution of the organizational patterns (Hertz and Paolino, 1961) based on the records of the same schizophrenic and neurotic groups, it was found that the variability of the qualitatively evaluated organizational patterns was an additional differentiating factor. Three kinds of variability were identified: (1) extreme variability where within a card the patterns g $O+$ or g $O+$ *comb* occurred with g $O-$ or g $O-$ *comb*, (2) moderate variability where (a) g $O+$ or g $O+$ *comb* occurred with $g-$, or (b) g $O-$ or g $O-$ *comb* occurred with $g+$, and (3) tendency to variability, where $g+$ occurred with $g-$.

The paranoid schizophrenic group in contrast with the neurotic showed significantly more extreme variability and more variability when all patterns of variability were combined. Thus the schizophrenics showed a marked imbalance and unevenness in the pacing of their organizational patterns. They exercised their organizational ability more unevenly and more inefficiently, reflecting greater variability and lability in their intellectual functioning. Since abruptness of shift in any cognitive dimension may be related to unstable and unpredictable behavior, the g score may aid in assessing unstable and unpredictable behavior.

Unfortunately data with patients showing predominantly obsessive compulsive features or excitable, manic features are no longer available. Abstracting from our clinical notes on patients showing obsessive compulsive defensive operations, some show surprisingly high sum g *wt*. We can account for this at least in part in terms of the meticulous approach, the drive to perform, the striving to see as many things in as many relationships as possible, all of which inflate the g score, sometimes out of proportion to actual intellectual capacity. On the other hand, sum g *wt* is often low, even zero. Some obsessive-compulsive individuals select detail after detail, giving each in unadorned and unelaborated fashion, without attempting any combinations and without seeing any relationships.

Similarly with the records of excitable, impulsive, and manic patients, sum g wt is either high or low. Where high, qualitative analysis reveals predominance of sum $g-$ reflecting inferior organizations, many in the form of distorted and illogical combinations and vague abstractions. Where low, the Rorschach record is either sparse or erratic, unconnected, and disorganized.

The sparse data on the brain injured suggest a low sum g wt. In the studies by Loehrke (1952) and Hertz and Loehrke (1955) the organizational score was not studied in isolation but within configurations which were quantitatively and qualitatively described in terms of Rorschach patterns. In certain of the configurations however, such as intellectual deterioration, vagueness of perception, intellectual confusion, intellectual inconsistencies, and defect in analytic-synthetic ability, which were found to differentiate the brain damaged from contrasting groups, the organizational patterns figured prominently.

The results of the old age group (Table 2.2) showed very low organization scores. The group as a whole showed considerable intellectual deterioration and constriction by other criteria. Analysis of the records revealed a variety of prominent neurotic and psychotic features. The low organization score in this group may reflect intellectual deterioration, regression, intellectual constriction, the influence of neurotic and psychotic processes, or a combination of any of these conditions.

SUMMARY

Unfortunately, comparatively little research has focused on the organization score in the last decade. Norms for Z and g are available for certain age groups, educational and vocational groups and to a lesser extent, for various clinical pictures. Since patient population varies, the norms reported for the clinical groups must of course be viewed as tentative.

Obviously a great many more normative studies are needed for the overall summary scores as well as for their qualitative differentiations across a variety of populations. Furthermore, since the organization score shows some relationship to the number of responses, normative data may have to be computed for different levels of R.

Most of the empirical studies designed to validate interpretive hypotheses for the organization score have dealt only with the summary scores. Some partially confirm some of the hypotheses clinically associated with the score. Others report negative results or results at variance with each other. Even those that are in agreement must of course be repeated and cross-validated.

As we have indicated, to establish the relationship of organization score to level of intellectual functioning, further studies are needed, preferably in reference to different aspects of cognitive functioning rather than to overall M.A. or I.Q.

More extensive work is needed on differential diagnosis to provide a more refined discrimination among groups varying in severity of mental and emotional disturbance. Some attention must be made to the degree of overlap between and among groups, an aspect of research studies which has often been ignored. As we have already indicated, lack of evidence of interscorer reliability is an important area of omission.

Finally, the problem of generalizability of our hypotheses is still with us. Because the organization score reflects how an individual structures and organizes blots into meaningful units, we assume that he can structure and organize his world, solve current life problems, take an integrated approach to life situations, and develop a mature adaptation vis-a-vis the environment, hypotheses we apply, as a result of our clinical experience. These assumptions have yet to be validated.

At the present time, in the absence of more definitive research, the following interpretations are suggested, in the form of hypotheses, which fit in with theory, available empirical findings, and clinical experience.

Hypothesis 1

The organization score reflects the ability to analyze material into component elements, to see relationships between and among them, and to combine and integrate them into a unified whole. The score reflects then, the ability to analyze, to comprehend relationships, to synthesize, to abstract and to conceptualize. It therefore may be used to evaluate the adequacy of certain aspects of an individual's cognitive functioning.

Hypothesis 2

The organization score tells us something about the intellectual capacity of the individual, especially about certain verbal components of intelligence in relation to conceptual activity. While the evidence is contradictory as to the relation of organization to I.Q. or M.A., it appears to suggest a relationship. How extensive it is, is not known at this time, especially since non-intellectual variables appear to be highly influential in its expression. Individuals of high to superior intelligence tend to give high sum organization scores. Those who are mentally defective, retarded, regressed, or deteriorated may be expected to give low organization scores.

Hypothesis 3

In achieving organization, the individual has to exert effort, apply himself, select, weigh, and evaluate his final response in terms of the objective features of the blot areas and in terms of the appropriateness and logicality of his response. The organization score then may be said to reflect intellectual effort, energy, drive, and initiative. In addition, since the individual must persist, break down and resynthesize the stimulus meaningfully—an achievement process—the organization score may likewise suggest achievement potential.

Hypothesis 4

The qualitative differentiations of the g score evaluate the quality of the individual's analytic, synthetic, combinative, and integrative abilities and the efficiency with which he utilizes them. The following hypotheses are offered for the sub-categories of g.

a. **Sum $g+$ wt, Sum org. acts $+$:** Adequate ability to organize, integrate, and control cognitive processes and bring them into appropriate relationships with one another is suggested. These scores may reflect the general ability of the individual to structure his world meaningfully. Individuals of high average to superior intelligence tend to show this kind of organizational score.

b. *g O+*, *g O+ comb*: These scores reveal good native endowment with a high capacity for combinative, abstractive or integrative thinking which, in addition, is highly different. They reflect a freely varied and richly imaginative and creative kind of thinking, and/or thinking dictated by unique past experiences, problems or conflicts, which, however, do not intefere with the clarity or logic of the thought processes. These scores may appear in superior or artistic pictures. They may even appear in pathological context, depending upon the level of intelligence of the individual.

c. *g v+*, *g v−*: Minimal ability to structure a situation, to analyze and synthesize, hence superficial perception and conceptualization. Thinking is vague and unproductive.

d. *g P*: A simple, gross level of perceptual organization may be hypothesized, with proneness to depend upon and stick to the commonplace and the conventional. It suggests a simple structured view of one's world.

e. Sum *g− wt*, Sum org. acts−: These patterns suggest inadequate and inappropriate organization, hence impaired combinative and integrative ability. Reality is misconstrued or twisted, resulting in intellectual misperceptions or distortions. High *g−* scores appear in records of individuals functioning at a low level of intelligence or where considerable emotional disturbance interferes with functioning.

f. *g O−*, *g O− comb*: Thinking is highly different, faulty, irrational, maybe bizarre, dictated by unique past experiences and/or by special problems, preoccupations or conflicts. The *g O− comb!* reflects seriously impaired, illogical, irrational thinking. The pattern reflects excessive fantasizing, irrealistic and autistic thinking. It suggests the presence of disintegrative tendencies or the development of delusional systems.

It should be emphasized that the *g O−* and the *g O− comb* do not always point to pathology. They may reflect ability to relax, artistic creativity, even humor, as Kris (1952) has hypothesized in his discussion of "regression in the service of the ego." Generally in the record where they appear, other patterns point to more mature cognitive functioning. These patterns then help in differential diagnosis, suggesting either cognitive weakness and pathology or temporary relaxation and creative strength.

Hypothesis 5

The distribution of the g patterns within a card may reflect the extent of the stability of the thought processes. Extreme variability in the qualitatively differentiated organization patterns point to marked imbalance and unevenness in the thought processes.

Hypothesis 6

Like other Rorschach patterns, the organization score is especially vulnerable to affective forces. It is increased by expansiveness and liberated energy and decreased by extreme control rigidity, passivity, apprehensiveness. Strong anxiety may increase the g score where it causes the individual to overreact and overstrive; it may decrease the g score, where it inhibits, blocks, or constricts mental functioning.

Hypothesis 7

The g score is influenced by the nature and the success of the defensive strategies utilized by the individual. Repression, blocking, withdrawal, isolation, all tend to lower the g score. Intellectualization may increase the score, reflecting drive, intellectual ambitiousness or exhibitionism, or it may lower the score because of rigidity, thoroughness, and the need to attend to every detail in isolation. Similarly with denial, the score may be increased where, in the attempt to deny thoughts, impulses and feelings, the individual becomes expansive and strives for intellectual attainment or emotional surcease; it may lower the g score, where drive is reduced or where the individual concentrates on details rather than larger more complex but threatening aspects of his environment. Again projection may result in grandiosity, increasing drive and integrative efforts in the intellectual realm, hence the g score increases, or it may result in suspiciousness and withdrawal, constricting the personality and lowering the g score. From the number and the quality of the g score, then, we may learn much about the stability and success of the defensive operations.

Hypothesis 8

The g score has potential value in the differential diagnosis of various kinds of psychiatric disorders. We have ample evidence, of course, that the clinical groupings are far from unitary. Rather than to refer to a specific diagnostic group, our hypotheses for g, as with other Rorschach patterns, should be directed to pathological conditions or features which characterize individuals and which occur in varying degrees. With this in mind, we can say that the g score can furnish certain clues as to the presence of neurotic features, depressed conditions, obsessive compulsive tendencies, elated or manic conditions, and paranoid and schizophrenic disorders. In brain damaged pictures, the g patterns are especially helpful in assessing the extent of the deterioration and impairment. Similarly in old-age groups, the g patterns help in detecting intellectual deterioration, constriction, and the impact of neurotic and psychotic processes.

OVERALL EVALUATION

In general, the organization score is related to intellectual, cognitive, and creative abilities. It is highly useful in assessing the adequacy of cognitive functioning. It helps guage intellectual functioning, drive, initiative, and the efficiency and maturity of the thinking processes. It contributes to diagnostic decisions as to the presence and severity of emotional disturbances and is especially helpful in assessing delusional developments.

Since a strong relationship exists between the simple summation of responses involving organization and the weighted score, both should be computed, using one or the other, depending upon the problem at hand. If the purpose is merely to assess overall level of intelligence, the summary scores are as effective as the weighted scores. The summary scores are not, however, useful clinically, since they obscure the differential patterning which is so helpful in evaluating the nature and the adequacy of reality testing, and the complexity, the appropriateness and the constructiveness of the organizational activity. Furthermore, the differential scores, not the summary scores, contribute to diagnostic decisions as to the presence and severity of pathology.

As yet the interpretation of the organization scores, just as other Rorschach scores, are for the most part a body of hypotheses and clinical observations. Obviously they must be placed on a firmer scientific basis. Research with the organization score, however, because of its multidimensional nature, still presents many methodological difficulties. As has been repeated so often, Rorschach scores take meaning only from the constellation in which they are embedded. The organization score is no exception. Furthermore, organization must be interpreted in terms of its qualitative as well as quantitative aspects and in terms of its interaction with other patterns, a procedure which has not yet shown itself to be amenable to the traditional systematic approach. To make the task harder, the score is influenced by extra test variables—mood, mental set, interpersonal relationships in the test situation, and a host of other variables which have been identified and emphasized in recent literature.

There is, in addition, the problem of integrating Rorschach results with situational, social, and cultural variables. The individual's home environment, the family situation, his interpersonal transactions with others, his social and cultural milieu in general, all shape his intellectual development, his drive, his achievement aspirations, his adaptive potentials and more, all of which affect the quality of his cognitive functioning and hence Rorschach scores including the g.

The problems in establishing acceptably scientific validity of interpretive hypotheses for the organization factor or any of the Rorschach patterns are not unique to the Rorschach. They are inherent in all qualitatively complex clinical investigations with any clinical tool. Because of the difficulties, it is not surprising that validation studies of the organization score have not been vigorously pursued in the last decade. The difficulties, however, should not detract from further research attempts at scientific validation because its clinical utility has been well demonstrated.

If any Rorschach patterns are to be validated, there must be a clear departure from the traditional research paradigm based on psychometric methodology. It would appear more appropriate, and certainly more profitable, to take an idiographic approach and to start with the unit personality itself or a specific personality dimension such as "perceptual disorganization" (rather than discrete scores) and translate it into sets of Rorschach correlates or configurations made up of scores, sequence of scores, summary score patterns, content analysis, and test behavior, all qualitatively and quantitatively evaluated in terms of how they shape up and interact within the individual personality. These configurations in turn should be studied in terms of their interactions with the individual's immediate situation and his social and cultural milieu. Such procedure would cut through the traditional diagnostic groupings and take into consideration the uniqueness and the complexity of the individual personality.

Such an overall research program would lead eventually to the kind of validation of the interpretive hypotheses assigned to Rorschach patterns, including the organization score, which would give it the scientific status and acceptance it deserves.

BIBLIOGRAPHY

Batt, H. V. An investigation of the significance of the Rorschach Z score. Unpublished Ph.D. dissertation. University of Nebraska, 1953.

Beck, S. J. Configurational tendencies in Rorschach responses. *American Journal of Psychology*, 1933, **43**, 433-443.

Beck, S. J. *Rorschach's test. Vol. I. Basic processes* (2nd ed.). New York: Grune & Stratton, 1949.

Beck, S. J. *Rorschach's test. Vol. I. Basic processes*. New York: Grune & Stratton, 1950.

Beck, S. J. *Rorschach's test. Vol. II. A variety of personality pictures.* New York: Grune & Stratton, 1945.

Beck, S. J. *Rorschach's test. Vol. III. Advances in interpretation.* New York: Grune & Stratton, 1952.

Beck, S. J. *The six schizophrenias. Reaction patterns in children and adults.* New York: The American Orthopsychiatric Association, Inc., 1954.

Beck, S. J. *The Rorschach experiment. Ventures in blind diagnosis.* New York: Grune & Stratton, 1960.

Beck, S. J., Beck, A. G., Levitt, E. D., and Molish, H. B. *Rorschach's test. Vol. I. Basic processes* (Revised ed.). New York: Grune & Stratton, 1961.

Beck, S. J., and Molish, H. B. *Rorschach's test. Vol. II. A variety of personality pictures* (Revised ed.). New York: Grune & Stratton, 1967.

Beck, S. J., Rabin, A. I., Thiesen, W. G., Molish, H., and Thetford, W. N. The normal personality as projected in the Rorschach test. *Journal of Psychology*, 1950, **30**, 241-298.

Becker, W. C. A genetic approach to the interpretation and evaluation of the process-reactive distinction in schizophrenia. *Journal of Abnormal and Social Psychology*, 1956, **53**, 229-236.

Ford, M. The application of the Rorschach test to young children. *University of Minnesota, The Institute of Child Welfare Monograph Series*, No. 23. Minneapolis: University of Minnesota Press, 1946.

Freud, S. *The interpretation of dreams.* James Strachey, Trans. New York: Basic Books, 1955.

Friedman, H. Perceptual regression in schizophrenia: An hypothesis suggested by the use of the Rorschach test. *Journal of Genetic Psychology*, 1952, **81**, 63-98.

Friedman, H. Perceptual regression in schizophrenia: An hypothesis suggested by the use of the Rorschach test. *Journal of Projective Techniques*, 1953, **17**, 171-185.

Goldfarb, W. Organizational activity in the Rorschach examination. *American Journal of Orthopsychiatry*, 1945, **15**, 525-528.

Goldfarb, M. R., Stricker, G., and Weiner, I. B. *Rorschach handbook of clinical and research applications.* Englewood Cliffs, New Jersey: Prentice-Hall, 1971.

Guirdham, A. On the value of the Rorschach test. *Journal of Mental Science*, 1935, **81**, 848-869.

Hemmendinger, L. Perceptual organization and development as reflected in the structure of Rorschach test responses. *Journal of Projective Techniques*, 1953, **17**, 162-170.

Hertz, M. R. *Frequency tables for scoring Rorschach responses.* Cleveland: The Press of Western Reserve University, 1936, 1942, 1951, and 1961.

Hertz, M. R. Scoring the Rorschach inkblot test. *Journal of Genetic Psychology*, 1938, **52**, 15-64.

Hertz, M. R. The scoring of the Rorschach inkblot method as developed by the Brush Foundation. *Rorschach Research Exchange*, 1942, **6**, 16-22.

Hertz, M. R. *The summary sheet: The Rorschach psychogram.* Cleveland: The Press of Western Reserve University, 1942.

Hertz, M. R. Evaluation of adjustment in terms of the Rorschach method. Paper read before the Midwestern Psychological Association, Chicago, Illinois, 1951.

Hertz, M. R. Objectifying the subjective. *Rorschachiana*, 1963, VIII, 25-54.

Hertz, M. R. The Rorschach in adolescence. In A. I. Rabin and M. R. Haworth (eds.), *Projective techniques with children.* New York: Grune & Stratton, 1965, 257-270.

Hertz, M. R. *The Rorschach psychogram* (Revised and enlarged). Cleveland: The Press of Western Reserve University, 1969.

Hertz, M. R. A Hertz interpretation: Ellen: A girl, ten years of age. In John E. Exner, Jr. (ed.), *The Rorschach systems.* Appendix, 321-374. New York: Grune & Stratton, 1969.

Hertz, M. R. *Frequency tables for scoring Rorschach responses: Code charts, normal and rate details, F+ and F− responses, and popular and original responses* (5th ed., revised and enlarged). Cleveland: The Press of Case Western Reserve University, 1970.

Hertz, M. R. Projective techniques in crisis. *Journal of Projective Techniques*, 1970, **34**, 449-467.

Hertz, M. R., Grossman, C., and Warshawsky, F. The personality characteristics of a group of institutionalized old people. Paper read at the Midwestern Psychological Association, Chicago, April, 1951.

Hertz, M. R., and Kennedy, S. The *M* factor in estimating intelligence. *Rorschach Research Exchange*, 1940, **4**, 105-106 (abstract).

Hertz, M. R., and Loehrke, L. M. An evaluation of the Rorschach method for the study of brain injury. *Journal of Projective Techniques*, 1955, **19**, 416-430.

Hertz, M. R., and Paolino, A. F. Rorschach indices of perceptual and conceptual disorganization. *Journal of Projective Techniques*, 1960, **24**, 370-388.

Hertz, M. R., and Paolino, A. F. An additional Rorschach index of conceptual disorganization. Paper read before the Ohio Psychological Association, Columbus, Ohio, 1961.

Holtzman, W. H., Thorpe, J. S., Swartz, J. D., and Herron, E. W. *Inkblot perception and personality*. Austin: University of Texas Press, 1961.

Janoff, I. Z. The relation between Rorschach form quality measures and children's behavior. Unpublished Ph.D. dissertation. Yale University Library, 1951.

Jolles, I. The diagnostic implications of Rorschach's test in case studies of mental defectives. *Genetic Psychological Monographs*, 1947, **36**, 89-198.

Klopfer, B., Ainsworth, M. D., Klopfer, W. G., and Holt, R. R. *Developments in the Rorschach technique*. Yonkers: World Book Co., 1954.

Klopfer, B., and Davidson, H. Form-level rating. *Rorschach Research Exchange*, 1944, **4**, 164-177.

Kris, E. *Psychoanalytic explorations in art*. New York: International Universities Press, 1952.

Kropp, R. P. The Rorschach "Z" score. *Journal of Projective Techniques*, 1955, **19**, 443-452.

Leventhal, H. The effects of perceptual training on the *W* and *Z* scores. *Journal of Consulting Psychology*, 1956, **20**, 93-98.

Loehrke, L. M. An evaluation of the Rorschach method for the study of brain injury. Unpublished Ph.D. dissertation. Western Reserve University Library, 1952.

McCandless, B. R. The Rorschach as a predictor of academic success. *Journal of Applied Psychology*, 1949, **33**, 43-50.

Meili Dworetzki, G. The development of perception in the Rorschach. In B. Klopfer (ed.), *Developments in the Rorschach technique Vol. II. Fields of application*, Chapter 5. Yonkers-on-Hudson, New York: World Book Co., 1956.

Molish, H. B. Contributions of projective tests to problems of psychological diagnoses in mental deficiency. *American Journal of Mental Deficiency*, 1958, **63**, 282-293.

Molish, H. B. Contributions of projective tests to psychological diagnoses in organic brain damage. In S. J. Beck and H. B. Molish (eds.), *Reflexes to intelligence*. Glencoe, Illinois: The Free Press, 1959.

Molish, H. B. Psychological structure in four groups of children. In S. J. Beck, *Psychological processes in the schizophrenic adaptation*, Chapter 10. New York: Grune & Stratton, 1965.

Molish, H. B. Critique and problems of research. A survey. In S. J. Beck and H. B. Molish (eds.), *Rorschach's test. Vol. II. A variety of personality pictures*. New York: Grune & Stratton, 1967.

Otis, L. S. What does the Rorschach Z score reflect? *Journal of Consulting Psychology*, 1959, **23**, 373-374.

Phillips, L., Kaden, S., and Waldman, M. Rorschach indices of developmental level. *Journal of Genetic Psychology*, 1959, **94**, 267-285.

Phillips, L., and Smith, J. G. *Rorschach interpretation: Advanced technique*. New York: Grune & Stratton, 1953.

Rapaport, D. *Diagnostic psychological testing*. Vol. II. Chicago: Year Book Publishers, 1946.

Rapaport, D. *Organization and pathology of thought*. New York: Columbia University, 1951.

Reitan, R. R. The relation of Rorschach test ratios to brain injury. *The Journal of General Psychology*, 1955, **53**, 97-107.

Rorschach, H. *Psychodiagnostics. A diagnostic test based on perception*. Bern: Hans Huber, 1942.

Rubin, H., and Lonstein, M. A cross-validation of suggested Rorschach patterns with schizophrenia. *Journal of Consulting Psychology*, 1963, **17**, 371-372.

Sarason, E. K. The discriminatory value of the Rorschach test between two etiologically different mentally defective groups. Unpublished Ph.D. dissertation. Clark University Library, 1950.

Sarason, S. B. *The clinical interaction*. New York: Harper Bros., 1954.

Schmidt, H. O., and Fonda, C. P. Rorschach scores in the manic state. *Journal of Psychology*, 1954, **38**, 427-437.

Siegel, E. L. Perception in paranoid schizophrenia and the Rorschach. *Journal of Projective Techniques*, 1953, **17**, 151-161.

Siegel, E. L. Genetic parallels of perceptual structuralization in paranoid schizophrenia: An analysis by means of the Rorschach technique. *Journal of Projective Techniques*, 1953, **17**, 151-161.

Sinnett, E. R., and Roberts, R. Rorschach approach type and the organization of cognitive material. *Journal of Consulting Psychology*, 1956, **20**, 109-113.

Sisson, B. D., and Taulbee, E. S. Organizational activity on the Rorschach test. *Journal of Consulting Psychology*, 1955, **19**, 29-31.

Sloan, W. Mental deficiency as a symptom of personality disturbance. *American Journal of Mental Deficiency*, 1947, **52**, 31-36.

Taulbee, E. S. The use of the Rorschach test in evaluating the intellectual levels of functioning in schizophrenics. *Journal of Projective Techniques*, 1955, **19**, 163-169.

Taulbee, E. S., and Sisson, B. D. Rorschach pattern analysis in schizophrenia: A cross-validation study. *Journal of Clinical Psychology*, 1954, **10**, 80-82.

Thetford, W. N., Molish, H. B., and Beck, S. J. Developmental aspects of personality structure in normal children. *Journal of Projective Techniques*, 1951, **15**, 58-78.

Thiesen, J. W. A pattern analysis of structural characteristics of the Rorschach test in schizophrenia. *Journal of Consulting Psychology*, 1952, **16**, 365-370.

Thompson, J. The ability of children of different grade levels to generalize on sorting tests. *Journal of Psychology*, 1941, **11**, 119-126.

Thorpe, J. S. Level of perceptual development as reflected in responses to the Holtzman Inkblot Test. Unpublished Ph.D. dissertation. The University of Texas, Austin, Texas, 1960.

Thorpe, J. S., and Swartz, J. D. Level of perceptual development as reflected in response to the Holtzman Inkblot Technique. *Journal of Projective Technique and Personality Assessment*, 1965, **29**, 380-386.

Varvel, W. A. The Rorschach test in psychotic and neurotic depressions. *Bulletin of the Menninger Clinic*, 1941, **5**, 5-12.

Vernon, P. E. The Rorschach inkblot test. Vol. III. *British Journal of Medical Psychology*, 1933, **13**, 271-295.

Werner, H. *Comparative psychology of mental development*. (Revised edition). Chicago: Follett, 1948.

Wilson, G. P., and Blake, R. R. A methodological problem in Beck's organizational concept. *Journal of Consulting Psychology*, 1950, **14**, 20-24.

Wilson, G. P. Intellectual indicators in the Rorschach test. Unpublished Ph.D. dissertation. University of Texas, Austin, Texas, 1952.

Wishner, J. Rorschach intellectual indicators in neurotics. *American Journal of Orthopsychiatry*, 1948, **18**, 265-279.

Zubin, J., Eron, L. D., and Schumer, F. *An experimental approach to projective techniques*. New York: John Wiley & Sons, 1965.

Development proceeds by transformation of structures. Gradually, by a number of smaller or larger leaps and bounds, we achieve different orders, different articulations, different meanings.

KURT KOFFKA

3

*Laurence Hemmendinger
and K. David Schultz*

DEVELOPMENTAL THEORY AND THE RORSCHACH METHOD

In this chapter an attempt is made to assess a particular use of Rorschach's test as a tool for psychological research. The basic approach is through the analysis of the kind and patterning of the test responses.

If research data are to be meaningful, the observations they represent must be guided by questions that are formulated in terms of concepts derived from a systematic theoretical position. This does not necessarily imply the testing of deductions from theory since there are other ways of working within a conceptual framework, e.g., by the ordering of observations selected from diverse sources. The choice and suitability of any particular observational technique (in this case, Rorschach's test) depend in large part on what one wants to observe.

The material which follows is intended to illustrate the research potential of Rorschach's test when used in conjunction with a particular theory. The test as a procedure and the subjects as sources of test responses are the familiar, usual ones; but the analysis of the Rorschach location scores has been carried out consistent with some implications of a particular theoretical framework, namely, Heinz Werner's developmental theory.

DEVELOPMENTAL THEORY

Heinz Werner's developmental approach to behavior states that developmental changes take place in terms of a systematic, orderly sequence, and that a "direction" is implied. The regulatory principle that describes how these changes take place is stated as follows: "When development occurs, it proceeds from a state of relative globality and lack of differentiation to a state of increasing differentiation, articulation and hierarchic integration" (1948, 1953, 1954, 1955).

This orthogenetic principle is not so much a statement allowing predictions about specific developmental events or behavior changes, as it is a manner of viewing, ordering, and interpreting behavior in all its manifold aspects. For example, it is assumed that the orthogenetic principle applies uniformly to all behavior, to the extent that behavior can be viewed as taking place over a period of time. In contrast to this uniformity is the multiplicity of specific developmental changes that may be observed in behavior.

There are three other specific aspects to this developmental conceptualization. These more detailed statements of the orthogenetic principle are that: (a) Changes in development take place according to the principle of abrupt, discontinuous change and developmental shifts—the emergence of new functions, etc.; (b) attained developmental level is characterized by a high degree of variability of functioning—that there is mobility rather than fixity of developmental level of operation; and (c) the achievements of various individuals may have come about by processes genetically quite different—that an analysis of the types of operations underlying a performance rather than the measurement of the accuracy of performance reveals a truer picture, and that the kinds and characteristics of the processes underlying behavior may change.

Werner defines organic development as "increasing differentiation and centralization—or hierarchic integration." The qualitative distinction between "undifferentiated" and "differentiated," "unorganized" and "hierarchically organized and integrated" can be further clarified by using other descriptive terms. Thus, the undifferentiated structure or process is said to be "syncretic," "diffuse," "labile," "indefinite," and "rigid"; when differentiated and organized, the terms "discrete," "articulated," "stable," "definite," and "flexible," are applicable. These terms are paired "opposites," descriptive extremes that have qualitative value for understanding genetic differences (1948).

RORSCHACH APPLICATIONS

This developmental approach is hardly new or revolutionary (Crandell, 1956; Kass, 1956; Reichard, 1956; Stein, 1956). A great many psychological theorists speak of development in terms of a reciprocal sequence of extension, differentiation, and integration of psychological structures and processes (e.g., Freud, Lewin). Recently, a series of attempts have been made to link some of these ideas with regard to development and genetic theory with clinical theory, i.e., to study the characteristic perceptual functioning of different clinical groups, or normal human beings of different ages, and the way perception develops in normal and clinical groups. This research started with the work of Howard Friedman, then at Clark University, who applied the principles of Werner's developmental approach to the structural aspects of Rorschach location scores (Friedman, 1952, 1953).

Friedman applied these qualitative "paired opposites" to Rorschach standard scoring locations. The resulting modified scores are an attempt to get at certain "formal" aspects of the variety of perceptual functioning reflected in a Rorschach response.

Precise definitions of the term "formal" or "structural" are difficult to give, but the meaning here is a simple one: One's concern is with the forming or fashioning of the thing seen. The simple $F+$ or $F-$[1] designation for Rorschach content in a certain location is an attempt to describe adequacy of achievement. The developmental location scores, however, are concerned with the structure, or the arrangement of the parts of the percept, essentially without regard for the content of the structure.

It is true that one cannot deal with structure wholly without

[1] For explanation of scoring symbols, see Appendix, pp. 609 ff. [Editor].

regard for content—indeed, this developmental theory would indicate that one could not do so in a pure sense. Some Rorschach percepts are determined not so much by the structure of the blot as by color or shading, or by the mere something-extended-on-a-ground quality of the blot. "A dog" or "a human," on the other hand, clearly require some orderly arrangement of parts in a fairly well prescribed order. In the latter case, the score deals with the "form" of content, and thus with structure. The second difficulty of dealing with structure in its pure form is that, particularly with mental patients, some percepts are clearly bizarre or erroneous. In this case, one believes that the subject is responding not so much to the qualities of the external stimulus as to some inner experience of his own.

Another important qualification about dealing with pure structure is that at least some of the psychological determinants of structure are imaginal—motor-emotional in nature. Thus, to the extent that non-geometrical, sensory, imaginal, and emotional aspects of form play a role in perception, the attempt to deal only with structure becomes a recognizably artificial one, albeit desirable or necessary.[2]

As a consequence, some of the structural scores defined by Friedman are based upon nonform criteria, some are based upon $F+$ and $F-$ tables, and some are based upon the literal putting together of the forms of the blots; all are attempts to reveal the variety of perceptual functioning previously grouped together under a single unitary location score.

DEVELOPMENTAL LOCATION SCORES

In the following, the criteria for all scores utilized in the Clark University studies are defined, and examples of each score, taken from the test protocols, are given. The usual Detail (D) and rare Detail (Dd) blot areas are those delineated by Beck. The plus and minus form quality is determined primarily from Beck's tables, and in those few cases in which these do not suffice, the tables published by Hertz can be used.

[2]Wertheimer (1957) has described how all perception is organized by a combination of autochthonous (structural) principles, as well as by principles of organization involving idiosyncratic characteristics of the perceiver (past experience, motivation, etc.) and related this specifically to Rorschach percepts.

Wa: An amorphous response in which the shape of the blot plays no determinable role. Such responses are based sole on chromatic or achromatic aspects of the blot, and, in customary scoring procedure, no form element would be included in the score.

 EX: Card I—"Black paint."

   Card II—"Sort of looks like some football team colors—black and red."

Wv: A vague response in which there is diffuse general impression of the blot. Although some form element is present, it is of such an unspecific nature that almost any perceptual form is adequate to encompass the content.

 EX: Card II—"Rock formation."

   Card I—"Could be an island—with water in between and water surrounding it on the outside of the island."

W—: A response in which the content produced requires a definite specific form, which, however, is not provided by the blot. (Goodness of match between blot and content is based upon the plus and minus form tables mentioned before.)

 EX: Card IV—"A starfish."

   Card I—"A frog."

DW: Rorschach's confabulatory response in which "a single detail, more or less clearly perceived, is used as the basis for the interpretation of the whole picture, giving very little consideration to the other parts of the figure."

 EX: Card IV—"A monkey, a chinchilla," solely on the basis of seeing the top central area of the face of a monkey.

   Card IV—"A boat," solely on the basis of seeing the lower projecting central area as "the front."

Wm: A mediocre response in which the gross outline and articulation of an unbroken[3] blot are taken into account so that the specific form implied in the content matches the blot.

 EX: Card V—"A bat."

   Card I—"A mask."

---

[3] A "broken" card is considered as one in which the white background completely surrounds a usual detail (*D*), or the white background isolates the majority of a usual detail from the remainder of the blot, or where a major portion of white background intervenes between the two lateral halves of the total blot. Thus, cards I, IV, V, VI, and IX are considered unbroken, and cards II, III, VII, VIII, and X broken. It should be noted then, that although *Wa*, *Wv*, *W—*, and *DW* can occur on all cards, *Wm* and *W++* can be scored only on unbroken cards, and *W+* only on broken cards. Although normally card VII cannot yield a *Wm* score, it has been found necessary to allow a certain few exceptions. This card brings forth, in a few cases, relatively clear-cut "schematic" *W* responses in which the perceptual functioning is seemingly governed solely by a general contour feature of the blot, as its "U" shape. Such *W* responses, as "harbor," "bridge," "bowl," are scored *Wm*, for it is felt that the gross outline of the contour is clearly involved, rather than any true integration of discrete portions.

W+: A response in which all the discrete portions of a broken blot are combined into a unifying whole, and in which the specific form implied in the content matches the blot.

EX: Card II—"Two fellows at a bar toasting each other."
Card VIII—"A sail boat."

W++: A response in which a unitary blot is perceptually articulated and then reintegrated into a well-differentiated unifying whole, the specific form of which matches the blot.

EX: Card V—"A man dressed up in a grasshopper suit on skates—the finale of a show, and there's two girls resting in his arms."
Card I—"Can imagine it's a fountain with two dogs on each end. . . ."

The criteria for the *W* responses apply to the *D* responses, except, of course, that the blot area referred to is a usual detail. Consequently, with the exception of the *D*+ score which requires a slightly modified definition, only examples will be provided for the *D* scores.

Da:

EX: Card II—Top red area, "Fire."
Card X—"Blue, yellow, brown, and green areas, "That's lighting rooms —lights."

Dv:

EX: Card IX—Large green area, "Looks like a map of some sort."
Card X—Blue area, "That's water . . . a splash of water."

D−:

EX: Card IX—Large top orange area, "Looks like sea lions."
Card VIII—Side pink areas, "That's a bee."

DdD:

EX: Card X—Large pink area, "Cocoons or worms," solely on the basis of the rounded top edge outline.
Card II—One lateral large black area, "Looks like an elephant to me," solely on the basis of an outer edge outline detail as the "head."

Dm:

EX: Card III—Red center area, "Suggests a bow tie."
Card X—Outer yellow area, "This is a little bird."

D+: A response in which two or more discrete blot areas (two or more *D*) are combined into one percept, the specific form of which matches the blot.

EX: Card VIII—The side red figures and top center area, "Two rats climbing up on the tree simultaneously, one on each side."
Card III—All black areas, "Two men beating drums as in a tribal dance. . . ."

$D++$:
>   EX: Card IX—Large green area, "These here look like comedy caricatures —person riding on some sort of animal."
>   Card IX—Orange area designated as a man with hat blowing a bugle.

FaC: A fabulized combination in which two or more acceptably interpreted areas are combined, on the basis of spatial relationship, into one absurd percept.
>   EX: Card VIII—One lateral red area interpreted as a "tiger," the other as a "grapefruit," remainder of blot as a "church," and response becomes, "This is a funny church and the grapefruit is climbing up the church."
>   Card II—Red interpreted as "fire," black as "animal's face," with center white space as "mouth," and response becomes, "It's fire and it's catching on to an animal (onto his chin) 'cause here's his mouth."

CoR: A contaminated response, in which two interpretations to the same area are fused into one.
>   EX: Card V—Entire blot area seen as a "beetle," then seen as a "bear," and response immediately becomes, "A beetle near a bear."
>   Card IV—Entire blot seen as "front of a bug," then as "front of an ox," and response immediately becomes, "Oh, a front of a bug-ox."

This scoring system of Rorschach response location has been created to reflect genetic changes as, for instance, the amount of separation of the blot areas into parts (differentiation), and the organization of these areas together into a "combined" whole (hierarchic integration). Both the developmental theory and onto-genetic evidence allow these scores to be distinguished dichotomously into "genetically low" or "immature," and "genetically high" or "mature" scores. Or, in terms of the theoretical definition of the scores, they may be considered as reflecting levels of operation of the subject.

When these scores are applied to the Rorschach responses of 160 children between the ages of three through ten years, one finds that the basic principle of development appears to be confirmed (Hemmendinger).[4] With increasing age there is a decrease of the undifferentiated, diffuse whole and detail responses, an increase of the highly articulated, well-integrated whole and detail

---

[4] The scoring system was initially developed by Friedman. The research as reported here is in terms of theoretical relationships rather than in its actual historical order.

responses, and an interesting shift from the early whole responses toward small details between the ages of six to eight years, then declining in favor of the integrated whole responses later on.[5]

A detailed look at Hemmendinger's ontogenetic research shows that the data not only reflect the expected sequence of developmental processes but also indicates that development is never quite complete: the adults' behavior retains some of the fused-function global properties that are especially characteristic in young children. Conversely, there are already present in the youngest children traces of what will be their characteristic level or type of operation when they become older. It is not a matter of either/or, but of more or less. Thus, the ontogenetic research provides a developmental scale that can be applied to a wide variety of research problems in which a change of function and/or performance is relevant.[6]

Of particular interest in Hemmendinger's data is the fact that there remain in the perceptual behavior of older children and adults the residuals of the primitive kinds of perceptual functioning so characteristic of the younger children. As had been previously hypothesized by Friedman, the reverse of "growth" or "development" could also be studied by this technique.

---

[5] The comparisons of median per cent, made by the chi-square technique, allow statements about statistically significant differences between age or diagnostic groups; these differences occur in the theoretically indicated directions and places.

[6] In Klopfer's *Developments in the Rorschach technique*, Vol. II, there is an article by Dworetzki describing some of the research into the genetic aspects of Rorschach determinants that have been carried on in Europe. These studies focused on perception (in the same way that Rorschach did) as ways of reflecting the subject's adaptation to reality. Development was conceived of in the same way as described here: "differentiation" and increasing "complexity" as well as growing "flexibility."

Dworetzki first studied perceptual development in the reactions of different children and adult groups to ambiguous figures, e.g., a line drawing of various fruits (*D*) that together have the gestalt of a person on a bicycle (*W*). In her application of the three laws of mental development that are reflected in reactions to the ambiguous figures ["1. General and confused perception of the whole (syncretic perception). 2. Distinct and analytic perception of the parts. 3. Synthetic recomposition of the whole with awareness of the part" (Phillips, 1954, p. 112)], Dworetzki has not so adequately and quantitatively defined the kinds of perception of location areas as has Friedman, but she has related various response determinants, such as movement, shading, and color, to perceptual organization. Dworetzki, furthermore, discusses the influence of color and shading during development, and the development of movement responses themselves. A critical study of this article is fundamental to all future work with the Rorschach and to the developmental approach as an organizing theory.

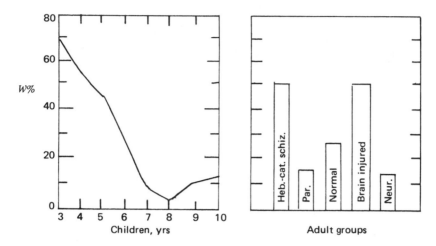

Fig. 3.1. Median Per Cent Whole Responses of All Responses: Child and Adult Groups.

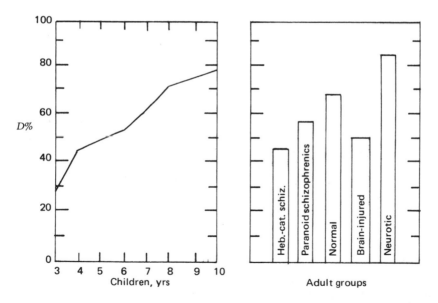

Fig. 3.2. Median Per Cent Usual Detail Responses of All Responses: Child and Adult Groups.

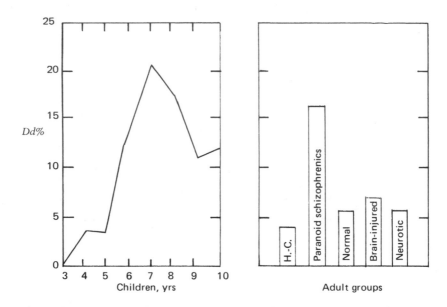

Fig. 3.3. Median Per Cent Rare Detail Responses of All Responses: Child and Adult Groups.

The works of Friedman (1952, 1953), Siegel (1953) Peña (1953), and Frank (1951) deal with perceptual regression. Regression is operationally conceived of as the relative accentuation of genetically low levels of functioning in various clinical groups. The developmental approach would predict that the most seriously impaired clinical groups should show a preponderance of the genetically lowest responses, and that there should be a decrease of these responses and an increase in the genetically high responses with the lesser impaired groups. The relative degree of impairment was predicted from psychoanalytic theory, and would order the clinical groups (in increasing maturity) in the following positions: Hebephrenic-catatonic schizophrenics, paranoid schizophrenics, psychoneurotics, and normal adults.

The other most familiar impaired group of patients are adults who are brain-injured and who have suffered some cerebral damage. Peña (1953) studied such a group of adults and, on theoretical

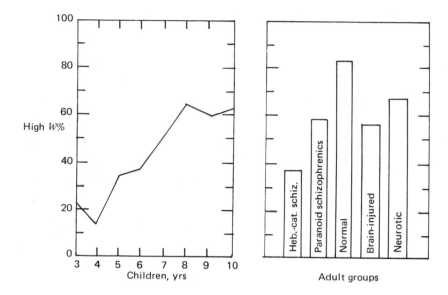

Fig. 3.4. Median Per Cent Developmentally—High Whole Responses of All Whole Responses: Child and Adult Groups.

grounds, hypothesized that they would rate among the other patients on a range between the hebephrenic-catatonic schizophrenics and normal adults.

The over-all evidence is in good agreement with these expecta tions: The hebephrenic-catatonic schizophrenics generally resemble (in their genetic scores) children three to five years of age; paranoids are similar to children six to ten years of age; the psychoneurotics are intermediate between ten year old children and normal adults; and the cerebrally damaged adults are generally like older children, but with some of the perceptual characteristics of the youngest children, and yet possessing some of the stabilizing and economical features of normal adults. These data are shown graphically in Figs. 3.1 through 3.5.

In the researches described so far, ontogenetic concepts have been used either to compare different age groups (the usual comparison) or to study the end products of perception in adult groups. In other

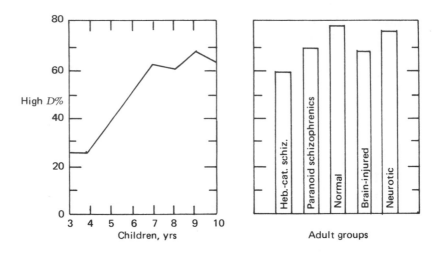

Fig. 3.5. Median Per Cent Developmentally–High Usual Detail Responses of All Usual Detail Responses: Child and Adult Groups.

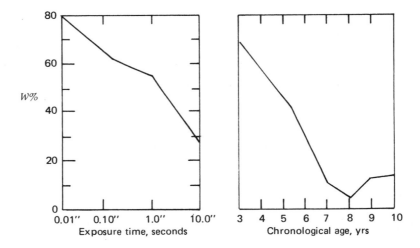

Fig. 3.6. Median Per Cent Whole Responses of All Responses: Normal Adults at Tachistoscopic Exposure, Children at Full Exposure.

words, while the processes of growth and regression have been studied, the intergroup comparisons were made on the basis of the end products of perception and perception itself as a developing process was not studied.

It is also possible to think of perception as a process taking place in time, and to apply the orthogenetic principle to perception as a

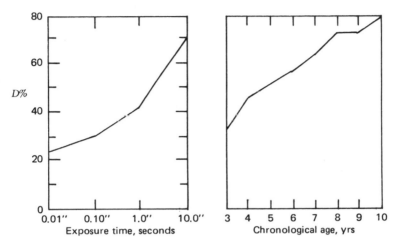

Fig. 3.7. Median Per Cent Usual Detail Responses of All Responses: Normal Adults at Tachistoscopic Exposure, Children at Full Exposure.

developing process rather than as an end product. These are studies of the "microgenesis" of perception. The development of perception is not only predictable from developmental theory but is also demonstrable in tachistoscopic presentation of the Rorschach cards. This was shown in the work of Framo (1952), who studied microgenesis by tachistoscopic exposure of the Rorschach cards to eighty normals. Twenty subjects in each of four groups were presented with the cards exposed for .01 second, for .10 second, for 1 second, and for 10 seconds.

A comparison of the data of Framo's microgenetic study with the data from the ontogenetic study by Hemmendinger shows a striking similarity in the shape of the curves as exposure time increases for normal adults and as chronological age increases for the children. These data are shown graphically in Figs. 3.6 through 3.10. The reader may compare for himself the microgenetic changes and

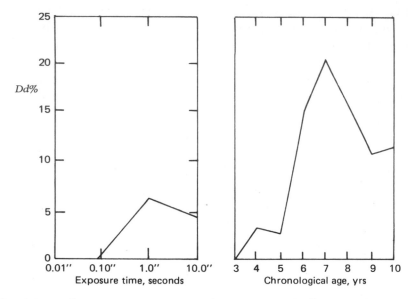

Fig. 3.8. Median Per Cent Rare Detail Responses of All Responses: Normal Adults at Tachistoscopic Exposure, Children at Full Exposure.

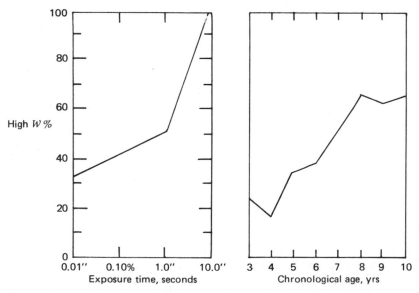

Fig. 3.9. Median Per Cent Developmentally—High Whole Responses of All Whole Responses: Normal Adults at Tachistoscopic Exposure, Children at Full Exposure.

levels with the genetic levels of the two schizophrenic groups, the brain-injured, the neurotic groups, and the genetic characteristics of normal adults, all at standard-time presentation of the Rorschach cards.

The original research reports in detail the comparisons that can be made between these various groups for all of the many genetic location scores, and the reader is referred to them for these data and for the suggestions as to specific clinical use of these comparisons.

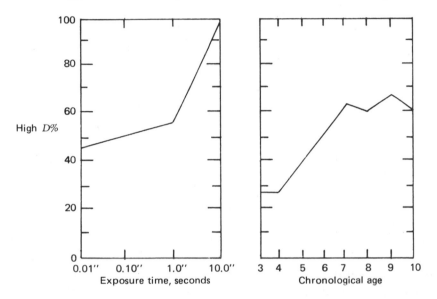

Fig. 3.10. Median Per Cent Developmentally—High Usual Detail Responses of All Usual Detail Responses: Normal Adults at Tachistoscopic Exposure, Children at Full Exposure.

However, the over-all conclusion is that the responses of the clinical groups represent various immature levels of perceptual functioning, and that these levels of functioning are as indicated by the theory (pp. 84 ff.).

The developmental theory further implies that the most immature groups (either children or schizophrenics) would fail to show increased differentiation and hierarchic integration in their perception with time. Part of just such a study has been carried out by Freed (1952), with the same design as Framo, using a group of sixty

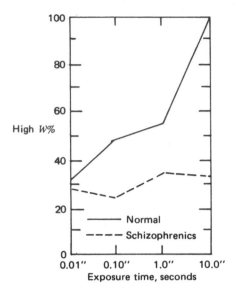

Fig. 3.11. Median Per Cent Developmentally–High Whole Responses of All Whole Responses: Normal and Schizophrenic Adults at Four Exposure Times.

hebephrenic-catatonic schizophrenics as his subjects. At the shortest exposure time, the performance of schizophrenics is not obviously different from that of normals, but as exposure time increases, the schizophrenics lag further behind the normals in the development toward perceptually mature responses. Figures 3.11 and 3.12 show graphically that the schizophrenic groups did not utilize the increase in exposure time for the improvement of perceptual performance.

It would seem that if such a comparison could be carried out for groups of children at various ages, as well as for a greater variety of clinical groups, more light could be shed on how perception takes place in time.

The Rorschach research reported thus far has to do with an attempt to provide supportive evidence for the orthogenetic principle as it applies to growth (ontogenetic or microgenetic studies), and with the application of this principle in describing the levels of perceptual functioning in various adult groups. It is possible to think of these levels separately from "growth;" these genetic levels may be more broadly conceived as reflecting the kind of psychological processes characteristic of different kinds of people. One can, for example, study some of the psychological processes of people who are high social achievers as compared to those who are low social achievers, or various kinds of creative people, or people who are prone toward impulsive or self-destructive behavior, or people who test at different levels of intelligence.

The following brief research reports will illustrate two such uses of these Rorschach scores: Studies in which the Rorschach scores are used to understand certain characteristics of people, and those in which the scores have been used to separate groups (into those of different genetic levels) whose psychological functioning is then studied by other means.

The "level of regression" studies by Friedman, Siegel, Peña, and Frank have shown that psychiatric intactness corresponds to developmental level; one may also conceive of the form of symptom expression as being related to developmental level as indicated by the genetic Rorschach scores. Thus, studies by Misch (1954) have shown

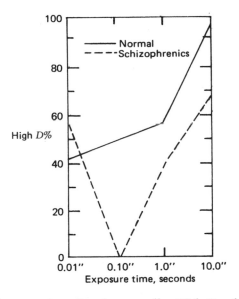

Fig. 3.12. Median Per Cent Developmentally–High Usual Detail Responses of All Usual Detail Responses: Normal and Schizophrenic Adults at Four Exposure Times.

that individuals whose behavior is characterized by immediacy of overt reaction (assault) are developmentally different than individuals whose symptomatology reflects more delayed or mediated behavior. Similar differences have been found by Kruger (1954) for patients who either only threaten suicide or fear perversions from those who make serious suicidal attempts or who demonstrate overt sexual perversions.

In another setting, Fowler (1957) has been able to demonstrate these kinds of developmental differences between subjects of high and low social adequacy and attainment. Becker (1956), in using this approach to studying the process-reactive distinction in schizophrenia, has found a meaningful relationship between the process-reaction dimension and the disturbances of thought processes as reflected at the genetic-level Rorschach scoring system. In addition, Becker found that Whitman's Elgin Prognostic Scale (based on the same factors on which the process-reaction distinction is made) is also related to developmental level as indicated by this Rorschach scoring system. Fine and Zimet (1959), using the same population as used by Brackbill and Fine (1956) in a study of schizphrenia and central nervous system pathology, found differences in developmental level between process and reactive schizophrenics in essential agreement with the work of Becker.

Rosenblatt and Solomon (1954) applied the developmental approach and the genetic Rorschach scoring to the problem of mental deficiency. They were interested in studying some structural aspects of perception, and the differences between the structure of perception in mental defectives and other subjects. They found that it was possible to discriminate among levels of mental deficiency in this way, and that normal children showed more differentiation and integration than defectives of the same mental age. Again, supporting some of the findings of Friedman, schizophrenic and brain-damaged subjects showed vestiges of a former level of functioning higher than that of the mental defectives. There is, furthermore, support for the idea of Friedman that vague whole perception stands for a regressive failure of attempts at integrative functioning on a functional basis, and would enable the clinician to distinguish between "fixation" and "regression."

Except for the studies by Becker (1956) and Rosenblatt and

Solomon (1954), work with this Rorschach scoring system has tended to stick closely to the idea of "genetic and structural aspects of *perception*." It is, of course, possible to think of Rorschach responses, including the location categories, as reflecting other psychological processes, such as thinking. There are two studies not yet reported in the literature (one by Roger Bibace, the other by Charles Hersch) on the apprehension of numerical relationships in adults at different genetic levels and on creativity in artists. There also have been a number of studies from Clark University and Worcester State Hospital on the relationships between genetic level as defined by these Rorschach scores and such other factors as adaptation to stress, social attainment, and various psychological control mechanisms (Hurwitz, 1954; Lofchie, 1955; Phillips and Framo, 1954; Phillips and Smith, 1954; Rochwarg, 1954; Waldman, 1956; Wilson, 1954).

There is, in addition, an attempt by Grace (1956) to relate the developmental continuum of perceptual functioning with social adjustment and the content of the verbalizations. It was found that developmental aspects of content, defined as level of vocabulary usage in terms of frequency of use at various age levels, were related to social adaptation as well as to a variety of genetically conceived scores for the Rorschach.

This brief review of present research with the developmentally defined Rorschach location scores serves to illustrate ways in which the Rorschach method can be used to provide answers to problems in basic psychological science and to specifically clinical-psychological problems.

There are, of course, dozens of immediately obvious comparisons between groups or kinds of people in terms of genetic levels that would be of practical interest to the clinician or psychological scientist who is interested in intergroup comparison data. There are also other uses for this linkage of "theory" and "clinical-observation technique." One is a study of thinking. For example, one would expect that different kinds of "projection" (paranoid projection, infantile projection, and projection in transference phenomena, as well as the projective-test concept of unique and private organizing principles within an individual) would take place by different externalization processes. These externalization processes, like any kinds of organizing processes—e.g., those that create and develop the motivations that further organize thought processes—can be conceived of in developmental terms.

If psychologists were in possession of concepts relating motivating processes and externalizing processes by the developmentally conceived Rorschach factors of "determinants" as well as of "locations," it would be possible to study some of the processes and products of thinking in various age and clinical groups. Some early aspects of this work have been done by Dworetzki (see Wertheimer, 1957); Rapaport has long advocated a distinction between the "fixed tools of thought" (clearly involved in tests like similarities and differences) and "processes of thought," the latter called for especially where already existing concepts are not so relevant (1952). It should be possible to study the conditions of the appearance, and the particular qualities, of processes of thinking by an organized combination of Rorschach inquiry and the subject's further free associations to the apperception of the Rorschach percepts themselves.

It would be anticipated that this inquiry and free association material would reflect some aspect of how thought processes occur and develop. Although there are other, in many ways better, observation techniques than the Rorschach for studying thinking, the congruence of intellectual, motivational, imaginal, etc., factors already recognized in the determination of Rorschach responses indicates that such a research program would be profitable.

No one yet knows enough of what an examination of developmental sequences in the "other-than-form-determined" Rorschach scores would reveal about the creation of the ego's various control functions, although certain implications emerge from the information provided by the genetic location scores and from emphases on $F+$ and $F-$ responses. Many of the present researches in this area are unfortunately based on simple reports of how well signs stand up (Spiegelman, 1956; Stein, 1956); it is suggested that research of the type outlined here can be more than a "sign" approach.

EPILOGUE

by: *Laurence Hemmendinger*
and K. David Schultz

About fifteen years after this chapter was written, an updating exploration was undertaken by the original author and a colleague. The purpose was to learn which research suggestions and predictions from the original chapter were followed up, and what new lines of research specifically using Rorschach's test and Werner's developmental theory have been developed in the intervening years. This exploration not only turned up few studies numerically, but little systematic research to follow up earlier promising findings in regard to both fundamental psychological processes (e.g.: creativity, thinking) and important clinical issues (e.g.: social adjustment and mental deficiency). Indeed, we note that this chapter's bibliography has increased by about twenty references. In some ways the current review is a case study in the history of a research idea.

We will first review those lines of investigation that have been followed, and then offer some thoughts or reasons for what seems like a decline in this line of research. If the tone seems critical, that tone applies to the senior author as well as to his research colleagues from the early 1950's.

It is possible to group the papers to be explored into three categories, as shown in Table 3.1.

TABLE 3.1

Normative Data and Scoring Systems	Psychopathology	Normal Psychological Processes
Ames, 1960	Climes, 1963	Allison and Blatt, 1964
Ames, 1966	Einsdorfer, 1960	Blatt and Allison, 1963
Friedman, 1960	Goldfried, 1962	Dudek, 1972
Phillips et al., 1959	Kaden and Lipton, 1960	Friedman and Orgel, 1964
	Levine, 1959	Hersch, 1962
	Levine, 1960	Kissel, 1965
	Wilenski, 1959	Marsden, 1970

NORMATIVE DATA AND SCORING SYSTEMS

In two monographs written after the first large spread of papers using the developmental scoring systems evolved for the Rorschach, Ames (1960, 1966) has reported valuable scoring norms. One interested in developmental analysis can only speculate how valuable such data might be if it could be—or had been—analyzed using one of the developmental scoring systems (Becker's, 1956; Phillip's et al., 1959) that were evolved subsequent to the original ones (Friedman, 1952, 1953; Hemmendinger, 1953; Siegel, 1953). Such an analysis could shed more light on how perception developed from early childhood through adulthood and old age. The same comment can be made about any other subsequent collection of normative data.

Becker's (1956) additional formulations of a genetic scoring system were briefly described in the original part of this chapter. He combined the location scores of Friedman with confabulatory and contaminated responses, fabulized combinations, perseverations and oligophrenic details into a 6-level system. This procedure has proven especially useful for research purposes by allowing for quantification of developmental scores. Table 3.2 presents the 6 levels (Becker, 1956, p. 232). After assigning a weight to each score in accordance with its level, the weights are summed and averaged. Thus a single developmental level score is arrived at for the whole protocol (DL). While gaining in research practicality, the method sacrifices the patterning and the hierarchical organization and thereby obscures the psychological significance of the developmental level construct.

TABLE 3.2

Becker's Weightings of Developmental Scoring Levels

Levels

1	2	3	4	5	6
Wa	Da	Wv	Dm	D+	W++
W—	DdD	Adx-Hdx	Wm	W+	D++
Dw	D—	Dd+			
ConR	Dv				
FabC	Dd—				
Per					

Phillips, Kaden and Waldman (1959) further expanded Rorschach indices of developmental level to include a total of four aspects of Rorschach performance: adequacy and specificity of form responses (mediocre, minus, vague, and amorphous); determinants used in combination (form dominance versus form subordination); the perception of activity (M, FM, m); and the organization of blot elements (adequate, "integrative" responses, or inadequate organization—fabulized combinations, contaminations, and confabulations). We were able to identify five subsequent publications (Friedman, 1960; Goldfried, 1962; Hersch, 1962; Kaden and Lipton, 1960; and Levine, 1960) that specifically used the modified systems and explored their methodological advantages. One must note in this regard that no system has been compared—or used—often enough to demonstrate any special superiority, and that the overlap among the systems is extensive.

PSYCHOPATHOLOGY

A few studies were undertaken to expand the application of the "age level" or "developmental" scores to other clinical groups, or to partially replicate earlier studies. In general, the reported investigations show that various forms of regression (and lack of progression—at least developmentally lower scores) can be demonstrated for many clinical groups. Regression here means operationally, the appearance of forms of psychological functioning more characteristic of earlier periods of human life.

Climes, Tamous and Kantor (1963) were able to show that patients with psychosomatic illness had more lower age-level scores than patients with purely organic illnesses. They speculated that this is related to differing capacities for coping with stress. Einsdorfer (1960) reported that uncorrected sensory deficits are correlated with greater evidence of lower developmental functioning than is true for people with corrected sensory deficits. The data from Goldfried's (1962) study comparing Rorschach developmental level scores (Becker, 1956) with MMPI ranking according to a set of rules by Meehl and Dahlstrom for "neurotic" and "psychotic" groups suggests that the two measures tap different aspects of functioning—i.e.: the results were negative. Kaden and Lipton (1960), Levine (1959, 1960) and Wilensky (1959) found that level of post-hospital or current ward adjustment of schizophrenics could be predicted from some aspects of the developmental scores.

One may conclude, then, that the developmental scoring systems offer to clinicians added tools in using Rorschach's test to predict some useful things about people—e.g.: form of symptom expression, post-hospital adjustment, and so on. In this context, it is helpful to note that some authors have succeeded in applying these genetic level scoring systems to the Holtzman Inkblot Test.

NORMAL PSYCHOLOGICAL PROCESSES

The survey of Rorschach genetic level research in the area of normal psychological processes shows about as extensive efforts as that in psychopathology—except that it continued for a longer time (see dates of publication). Kissel (1965), Friedman and Orgel (1964) and Allison and Blatt (1964) showed that there is a positive relationship between I.Q. and developmentally high Rorschach scores in children and in adults. Marsden (1970) showed that significant positive correlations held between $W+$ scores and WISC Full Scale, Verbal and Performance I.Q.'s, but only with four sub-test scores (Information, Vocabulary, Picture Completion, and Coding).

Three other researches seem to break new ground. Dudek (1972) explored some relationships between intelligence (WISC), emotional maturity (Cattell's Early School Personality Questionnaire), and concept development (Piaget tests). Blatt and Allison (1963) tried to explore some process aspects of what is meant when one speaks of W responses as an expression of intellectual strivings—abstracting, surveying, and interpreting, and the ability to make syntheses. They used the John Rinoldi Problem-Solving Information Apparatus, which permits sequential analysis of the problem-solving process, and compared scores of Problem-Solving Efficiency with types (quality) of W response. Their findings point again to $W+$ and $W++$ responses as related to intelligent performance.

Hersch (1962) published his dissertation in the cognitive functioning of the creative person, comparing artists, normals, and schizophrenics, using the Phillips et al. (1959) categories. Using Anne Roe's 1946 sample of artists, Hersch demonstrated that artists show evidence of both mature and primitive responses, giving credence to Werner's suggestion that the capacity for creativity presupposes mobility in terms of regression and progression.

SOME THOUGHTS ON THE FATE OF RESEARCH

As far as we have been able to tell only Friedman and Phillips have followed up on this research line, started in 1950. In spite of the fact that it attracted a number of psychologists, and that they explored in various directions, it is clear that clinical practice has benefited more than has the science of psychology.

A number of factors occur to us in an attempt to account for this. One rather obvious factor is the general decrease of interest among clinical psychologists in diagnostic assessment and in psychological testing, as they have turned their attention to psychotherapy, counseling, and kindred therapist-client relationships. This is too familiar to need documentation. What may be less evident is that there has also been a substantial turning away from evaluation/diagnosis as a pre-requisite for selecting appropriate clinical services, and an increased interest in working with normal people—services not thought of as therapy or as treatment. For clinical psychologists, such changes seem correlated with, if not a cause of, a disinterest in tests in any form, and in research on such topics as the concept of regression.

Another factor seems to be the general fate of dissertation research—it is not followed up by clinicians, in part for the reasons suggested above. Another reason has to do with the general requirement for dissertation research—an original study on a new topic, using a new instrument. Such requirements are reasonably applied but tend to discourage researchers, who are not the students of a professor with a major research program or a compelling theoretical position, from engaging in a program of shared research. In fact, much of the research done in the 1950's described in this chapter comes from Werner's students. For the most part, however, dissertation requirements place an emphasis on something unique, new and original in the research. This is as it should be, but it discourages widespread programs of follow-up research using a well-developed instrument, without new minutiae of un-validated scores. This also makes comparison among studies problematic.

Finally there is the growing interest in naturalistic, ethnographic, direct studies of subjects in a naturally-occurring setting. The effort in such research is to tap the processes directly, not in "subjects" but in "persons." Rorschach's test had the early advantage among projective methods of allowing the clinician to tap into processes ordinarily not reportable by the subject. Clinicians, and perhaps researchers, are currently increasingly interested in direct observation of those processes, in their real-life setting, and there is some disdain for indirect methods. The Blatt and Allison (1963) paper shows a rare choice of a research instrument that allows a direct record of process to be made. The suggestion made in the original chapter to use "the subject's further free associations" is in this direction, but has not been followed.

As a case study in the history of a research program, this is not unique. It is all too typical and familiar. There have been some benefits: this combination of test and theory can be fruitful in both clinical-applied and basic science investigations. In the instance of the developmental scores the clinical applications have so far benefited most. It is hoped, however, that our survey of areas of application of this psychologically valuable construct of established scientific trustworthiness[7] will stimulate renewed interest in its further exploration, whether along more traditional lines or in conjunction with current orientations toward the functioning of a person in a variety of situations.

[7] For further evidence on reliability and validity of the developmental scores see Weiner this volume, p. 598 and Goldfried et al., 1971, p. 42-54.

BIBLIOGRAPHY

Allison, J. and Blatt, S. J. The Relation of Rorschach Whole Response to Intelligence. *J. Proj. Techs.*, 1964, **28**, 355-360.

Ames, L. B. Longitudinal survey of child Rorschach responses: older S's aged 10 to 16 years. *Genetic Psych. Monog.*, 1960, **62**, 185-229.

Ames, L. B. Changes in Rorschach response throughout the human life span. *Genetic Psych. Monog.*, 1966, **74**, 89-125.

Becker, W. C. A genetic approach to the interpretation and evaluation of the process-reactive distinction in schizophrenia. *J. abnorm. soc. Psych.*, 1956, **53**, 229-236.

Blatt, S. J. and Allison, J. Methodological Considerations in Rorschach Research: The *W* Response as an Expression of Abstracting and Integrating Strivings. *J. Proj. Techs.*, 1963, **27**, 269-279

Brackbill, G., and Fine, H. J. Schizophrenia and central nervous system pathology. *J. abnorm. soc. Psych.*, 1956, **52**, 310-313.

Climes, S., Tamous, J. C., and Kantor, R. Level of perceptual development and psychosomatic illness. *J. Proj. Techs.*, 1963, **27**, 279-287.

Crandell, V. J. Observations of the use of projective techniques in child development research. *J. proj. Tech.*, 1956, **20**, 251-255.

Dallenbach, K. M. The place of theory in science. *Psych. Rev.*, 1953, **60**, 33-39.

Dudek, S. Z. A longitudinal study of Piaget's developmental stages and the concept of regression. *J. Pers. Assess.*, 1972, **36(5)**, 463-478.

Einsdorfer, C. Developmental Level and Sensory Impairment in the Aged. *J. Proj. Techs.*, 1960, **29**, 129-132.

Fine, H. J., and Zimet, C. N. Process-reactive schizophrenia and genetic levels of perception. *J. abnorm. soc. Psych.*, 1959, **59**, 83-86.

Fowler, N. Psychopathology and social adequacy: a Rorschach developmental study. Unpublished doctor's dissertation, The Pennsylvania State University, 1957.

Framo, J. L. Structural aspects of perceptual development in normal adults: a tachistoscopic study with the Rorschach technique. Unpublished doctor's dissertation, University of Texas, 1952.

Frank, I. K. Perceptual structuralization in certain psychoneurotic disorders: a genetic evaluation by means of the Rorschach test. Unpublished doctor's dissertation, Boston University, 1951.

Freed, E. Perceptual differentiation in schizophrenia: a tachistoscopic study of structural Rorschach elements. Unpublished doctor's dissertation, Syracuse University, 1952.

Friedman, H. Perceptual regression in schizophrenia: an hypothesis suggested by the use of the Rorschach test. *J. gen. Psychol.*, 1952, **81**, 63-98.

Friedman, H. Perceptual regression in schizophrenia: an hypothesis suggested by the use of the Rorschach test. *J. proj. Tech.*, 1953, **17**, 171-185.

Friedman, H. A note on the revised Rorschach developmental scoring system. *J. Clin. Psych.*, 1960, **16**, 52-54.

Friedman, H., and Orgel, S. Rorschach Developmental Scores and Intelligence Level. *J. Proj. Techs.*, 1964, **28**, 425-428.

Fulkerson, S. C. Some implications of the new cognitive theory for projective tests. *J. Consult. Psych.*, 1965, **29(3)**, 191-197.

Goldfried, M. R. Rorschach developmental level and the MMPI as measures of severity in psychological disturbance. *J. Proj. Tech.*, 1962, **26**, 187-192.

Goldfried, M. R., Stricker, G. and Weiner, B. *Rorschach Handbook of Clinical and Research Application.* Prentice-Hall, 1971.

Grace, N. B. A developmental comparison of word usage with structural aspects of perception and social adjustment. Unpublished doctor's dissertation, Duke University, 1956.

Hemmendinger, L. Perceptual organization and development as reflected in the structure of Rorschach test responses. *J. proj. Tech.*, 1953, **17**, 162-170.

Hersch, C. Perceptual structure in creative artists: an analysis by means of the Rorschach test. Doctor's dissertation in progress, Clark University, 1956.

Hersch, C. The cognitive functioning of the creative person: A developmental analysis. *J. Proj. Techs.*, 1962, **26**, 193-200.

Holzberg, J. D. Symposium: implications for projective methods in recent developments in personality theory. *J. proj. Tech.*, 1954, **18**, 418-447.

Hurwitz, I. A developmental study of the relationship between motor activity and perceptual processes as measured by the Rorschach test. Unpublished doctor's dissertation, Clark University, 1954.

Kaden, S. and Lipton, H. Rorschach Developmental Scores and Post-Hospital Adjustment of Married Male Schizophrenics. *J. Proj. Techs.*, 1960, **24**, 144-147.

Kass, W. Projective techniques as research tools in studies of normal personality development. *J. proj. Tech.*, 1956, **20**, 269-272.

Kissel, S. A Brief Note on the Relationship Between Rorschach Developmental Level and Intelligence. *J. proj. Techs.*, 1965, **29**, 45-49.

Kruger, A. Direct and substitute modes of tension-reduction in terms of developmental level; an experimental analysis of the Rorschach test. Unpublished doctor's dissertation, Clark University, 1954.

Kutash, S. B. The impact of projective techniques on basic psychological science. *J. proj. Tech.*, 1954, **18**, 453-469.

Lane, J. E. Social effectiveness and developmental level. *J. Pers.*, 1953, **23**, 274-284.

Levine, D. Rorschach Genetic Level and Mental Disorder. *J. proj. Techs.*, 1959, **23**, 436-439.

Levine, D. Rorschach Genetic Level and Psychotic Symptomatology. *J. Clin. Psych.*, 1960, **16**, 164-167.

Lofchie, S. H. The performance of adults under distraction stress: a developmental approach. *J. Psychol.*, 1955, **39**, 109-116.

Marsden, G. Intelligence and the Rorschach W Response. *J. proj. Techs. and Pers. Assnt.*, 1970, **34**, 470-476.

Meili-Dworetzki, G. The development of perception in the Rorschach. In: Klopfer, B. *Developments in the Rorschach technique.* Vol. II. New York: World Book Co., 1956, 104-176.

Misch, R. C. The relationship of motoric inhibition to developmental level and ideational functioning: an analysis by means of the Rorschach test. Unpublished doctor's dissertation, Clark University, 1954.

Peña, C. D. A genetic evaluation of perceptual structuralization in cerebral pathology: an investigation by means of the Rorschach test. *J. proj. Tech.*, 1953, **17**, 186-199.

Phillips, L. *Developmental theory and social adaptation.* Mimeographed manuscript, Worcester State Hospital, 1954.

Phillips, L., and Framo, J. L. Developmental theory applied to normal and psychopathological perception. *J. Pers.*, 1954, **22**, 464-474.

Phillips, L. Kaden, S., Waldman, M. Rorschach Indices of Development Level. *J. Genet. Psychol.*, 1959, **94**, 267-285.

Phillips, L., and Smith, J. C. *Rorschach interpretation: advanced technique*, New York: Grune and Stratton, 1954.

Rapaport, D. Projective techniques and the theory of thinking. *J. proj. Tech.*, 1952, **16**, 269-275.

Reichard, S. Discussion: Projective techniques as research tools in studies of normal personality development. *J. proj. Tech.*, 1956, **20**, 265-268.

Ricciuti, H. N. Use of the Rorschach test in longitudinal studies of personality development. *J. proj. Tech.*, 1956, **20**, 256-260.

Rochwarg, H. Changes in the structural aspects of perception in the aged: an analysis by means of the Rorschach test. Unpublished doctor's dissertation, Michigan State University, 1954.

Rorschach, H. *Psychodiagnostics* (Eng. translation). Bern: Huber, 1942.

Rosenblatt, B., and Solomon, P. Structural and genetic aspects of Rorschach responses in mental deficiency. *J. proj. Tech.*, 1954, **18**, 496-506.

Schimek, J. G. Cognitive style and defenses: A longitudinal study of intellectualization and field independence. *J. Abn. Psych.*, 1968, **73(6)**, 575-580.

Siegel, E. L. Genetic parallels of perceptual structuralization in paranoid schizophrenia: an analysis by means of the Rorschach technique. *J. proj. Tech.*, 1953, **17**, 151-161.

Spiegelman, M. Rorschach form-level, intellectual functioning and potential. *J. proj. Tech.*, 1956, **20**, 335-343.

Stein, H. Developmental changes in content of movement responses. *J. proj. Tech.*, 1956, **20**, 216-223.

Waldman, M. Personality factors and performances under stress. Unpublished doctor's dissertation, University of Chicago, 1956.

Werner, H. *Child psychology and general psychology.* Mimeographed manuscript, Clark University, 1953.

Werner, H. *Developmental approach to general and clinical psychology.* Mimeographed manuscript, Clark University, 1954.

Werner, H. The concept of development from a comparative and organismic point of view. *The concept of development.* Conference at the University of Minnesota, December 1955. (To be published by the University of Minnesota Press.)

Werner, H. *Comparative psychology of mental development* (rev. ed.). Chicago: Follet, 1948.

Wertheimer, M. Perception and the Rorschach. *J. proj. Tech.*, 1957, **21**, 209-216.

Wilensky, H. Rorschach Developmental Level and Social Participation of Chronic Schizophrenics. *J. proj. Tech.*, 1959, **23**, 87-92.

Wilson, M. T. Regression in perceptual organization: a study of adolescent performance on the Rorschach test. Unpublished doctor's dissertation, Clark University, 1954.

Can we, then, by the citation of some of those instances wherein this thing of whiteness—though for the time either wholly or in great part stripped of all direct associations calculated to impart to it aught fearful, but, nevertheless is found to exert over us the same sorcery, however modified;—can we thus hope to light upon some chance clue to conduct us to the hidden cause we seek?

HERMAN MELVILLE

4

Charles P. Fonda

THE
WHITE-SPACE RESPONSE

Two separate strains of psychological inquiry were incorporated into Rorschach's early assumptions about the white space response. One of these was concerned with perceptual reversal of figure and ground (Rubin, 1915) and the other with schizophrenic negativism (Bleuler, 1912). In this chapter, research stimulated by Rorschach's conjectures will be surveyed. We shall find that substantial progress has occurred in identifying the perceptual processes involved in figure-ground reversal, especially those associated with cognitive differentiation. We shall also consider a few conceptual and method-ological problems, especially those encountered in attempting to distinguish between independence and negativism as the manifesta-tion of an underlying predisposition towards oppositional behavior.

RORSCHACH'S CONCEPT OF THE SPACE RESPONSE

The Primary Space Response

Rorschach (1942, p. 39) described space responses (S)[1] as "those answers in which the white spaces are interpreted rather than the

[1] For explanation of scoring symbols see Appendix, p. 609 ff.

black or colored parts of the figure which surround them." Although he made no reference to the concept of reversal of figure and ground, it is clear that such was the perceptual process he had in mind as mainly responsible for these responses.

His basic assumption was that "space responses always indicate some sort of oppositional trend" (p. 199). Yet he seems not to have been too sure about the "always," for he also said that "if there occurs more than one S in a protocol, abnormality should be suspected" (p. 39). The presumably benign inference to be drawn from the presence of one—or less than one—S in a protocol was not spelled out.

The "oppositional trend" meaning ascribed by Rorschach to S seems to have a considerable degree of plausibility. A person who produces S does indeed seem to be performing in a way contrary to instructions. Instead of interpreting the black or colored parts of the ink blot, as Rorschach quite naturally expected, the subject interprets a white space. "Precisely that is left undone or the contrary is done which one would otherwise expect under the existing conditions." The quotation is from Bleuler's (1912, p. 10) definition of negativism. Inasmuch as Bleuler was one of his most influential teachers, it is not unreasonable to suppose that Rorschach had formulated his concept of the meaning of S in the light of Bleuler's discussion of schizophrenic negativism. He reported, for example, that S responses "are most common in stubborn, eccentric normals and in negativistic, scattered schizophrenics" (Rorschach, 1942, p. 39).

Within his own theoretical model of the dynamic subsystems comprising an organized personality, Rorschach's postulated "tendency towards opposition" was apparently deemed capable of producing a persistent bias in the functioning of the entire system. The salience of this tendency, which may be greater in some individuals than in others, is reflected in the frequency of S in a person's protocol. Rorschach's concept of "opposition" implies a series of bipolar relationships between some central entity (the ego?) and targets selected by it to serve as its adversaries. Although he undoubtedly realized that such bias might pervade the entire personality, he chose to focus mainly on one subsystem—the experience balance—in his efforts to depict the type of targets to be selected.

Thus, when the experience balance is extratensive, i.e., color responses are predominant and the capacity for outer-directed living is relatively well developed, Rorschach expected the most visible targets of opposition to be external to the self. Accordingly, the person's interpersonal stance would be characterized by negative suggestibility, defiance, mistrust, aggressive stubbornness, and tendencies to indulge in polemics and contradictions.

When the experience balance is introversive, i.e., human movement responses are predominant and the capacity for inner-directed living is relatively well developed, the most likely targets of opposition should be within the self. Accordingly, the person's orientation would be characterized by self-criticism, feelings of inadequacy, circumstantiality and self-distrust.

And when the experience balance is ambiequal, i.e., neither color nor human movement responses predominate, the oppositional person's behavior should manifest vacillation, hesitancy, skepticism, indecision and emotional ambivalence.

It is noteworthy that all of the terms employed by Rorschach to describe characteristics associated with S are pejorative. Perhaps this is because most of his subjects were troubled persons under medical supervision. In any event, his concept of the "oppositional trend" has retained much of its apparent cogency during the past half century. For example, after surveying the contemporary applications of ink-blot technology in clinical practice, Exner (1974, p. 238) concluded that "all of the systematizers have emphasized that where S occurs with considerable frequency it may be a form of negativism which can easily impinge upon reality contact and become overtly and/or covertly destructive."

As will be seen later in this chapter, however, the space response has been subjected to a substantial number of research investigations whose findings suggest that the overwhelmingly negative connotation attributed to S by Rorschach may not be amenable to empirical confirmation; instead S often seems to reflect a positive aspect of ego strength.

The Secondary Space Response

What Rorschach recognized as space responses are now called

primary (or main) S in order to distinguish them from secondary (or additional) space responses. The latter designation applies when the white spaces play a more incidental role and no true figure-ground reversal has occurred, the black or colored portions of the blot serving as the principal stimulus. Some authors combine both primary and secondary S into a single undifferentiated category when summing scores within an individual protocol, whereas others include only primary S in the ipsative summary, taking note of secondary S responses separately and counting them as "additionals" for supplementary consideration.

Rorschach's lack of interest in secondary S has apparently been vindicated in subsequent research. Retest reliability coefficients with parallel forms fail to reach significance (Fonda, 1951). Correlations between secondary S and relevant non-Rorschach variables, e.g., perspective reversal (Bandura, 1954 b) and figure-ground reversal Nelson, (1954), do not differ significantly from zero. Moreover, the correlation between primary and secondary S, holding R constant, was found by Bandura to be .08 and non-significant; he concluded that "the practice of using primary and secondary space responses as measures of the same thing seems unwarranted" (p. 117). The combined enumeration of primary and secondary S, therefore, must almost certainly tend to obscure the interpretative significance of any such undifferentiated summation.

The personality correlates of secondary S still await empirical confirmation. Perhaps the best that can be done with them is to consider a variety of more phenomenological interpretations. For example, it has been suggested that an accumulation of secondary S in a record may indicate undue concern with the lack of solidity in the inked figures, an implication being that the subject is acutely sensitive to a lack of stability in his or her own interpersonal relationships and is preoccupied with the resulting sense of insecurity. Interpretations of this kind would seem most plausible when the content of the response is of the "hole," "gap," or "cut-out" variety. When secondary S responses have the appearance of attempts to take into account everything on the ink blot, as in the case of the "lakes," "rivers," or "roads" seen on maps or landscapes, the implication seems clear that obsessive needs for thoroughness and a pedantic attention to detail are in evidence. When the white details are described as "eyes," the examiner is alerted to the probable prominence of paranoid trends in the subject.

The Use of White as Color

In the case of both primary and secondary S, white is occasionally used as a color determinant, although this topic is not discussed in Rorschach's *Psychodiagnostics*. When this occurs, the appropriate symbol (e.g., C', depending upon the system used) is added to the score. White may be employed in a manner analogous to the use of color in formless responses, e.g., "snow" or "ice." Or it may be more adaptively integrated with form, as "a white swan" or "a marble bust." These are all primary S responses, of course, and have figure-ground-reversal significance in addition to the rich implications of the content.

The symbolic significance of whiteness, per se, merits further investigation. Bohm (1972), for example, has described what he calls a "white-shock" reaction, and in this connection it should be noted that writers other than professional psychologists have ventured some intriguing speculations. In a chapter entitled "The Whiteness of the Whale" in *Moby Dick*, for instance, Herman Melville (1942) somewhat obscurely calls attention to an association between whiteness and the ideas of nothingness or death. Conceivably, therefore, sensitivity to whiteness on the ink blots may sometimes reflect susceptibility to eerie and uncanny terrors.

The reader is referred to the discussion of white as a determinant on pages 316 f. in this book.

A CHRONOLOGICAL OVERVIEW

Naturalistic observations relevant to S began to appear in the literature prior to the English translation of the *Psychodiagnostics* in 1942, and these reports continued to proliferate during the decade of the 'forties. Their main concern was to describe typical response tendencies in groups of people identified by one or another categorizing label. Data appeared on S in antisocial psychopaths (Boss, 1931), adolescents (Suares, 1938), juvenile offenders (Zulliger,

1938; Endacott, 1941), alcoholics (Billig and Sullivan, 1942), obsessives (Goldfarb, 1943), conscientious objectors (Rabin, 1945), soldiers (Linn, 1946), variously diagnosed psychiatric patients (Rapaport, Gill and Schafer, 1946), Alorese natives (Oberholzer, 1949), and paretics (Klebanoff, 1949).

Little attention was paid in these reports to the distinction between primary and secondary S or to its relationship with R, but enough provocative speculation was included to whet the reader's interest, and most of the reports tended to encourage a belief that S represents some kind of pathogenic agent in the personality. Toward the end of the decade, Buhler, Buhler and Lefever (1949) reported a comparison between psychiatric patients and non-patients. "Strangely enough," they wrote (p. 46), ". . . normal individuals . . . produce many S, indicating concealed opposition . . ."

During the early 'fifties, experimental work and laboratory studies began in earnest to evaluate the psychometric properties of S and the validity of Rorschach's "oppositional trend" construct. In these studies, the reliability of the S score was established, and the relationships between S and perceptual reversal and between S and R were quantified. Relationships between S and several non-Rorschach variables were demonstrated, but studies concerned with validity of the "oppositional trend" construct yielded equivocal results, and all attempts to confirm Rorschach's hypothesized interaction between the experience balance and S were uniformly unsuccessful. Around the middle of the decade, some clinicians were still treating negativism as a stable personality characteristic reflected in S, but many others were becoming aware of studies that either (a) failed to reject the null hypothesis or (b) demonstrated unexpected relationships between S and socially-desirable variables. New trends in the *Zeitgeist* began to emerge at about the same time, however, and these—coupled with the relative sparsity of S in protocols obtained during routine clinical work—sufficed temporarily to quench interest in further research on the white-space response.

An upsurge of interest in research accompanied the appearance of Holtzman's Inkblot Technique in 1961, but research on S remained in a holding pattern throughout most of the decade of the 'sixties. Clinical concern with the space response survived, however, and proposals for reconsideration of the postulates underlying interpretation of S as an indicator of negativism were reviewed by Nasielski (1965) at the Sixth International Rorschach Congress. These proposals were based upon considerations set forth in an earlier edition of this chapter and, together with alternative suggestions, were discussed extensively at another Rorschach symposium in Paris two years later (Schachter, 1970). Near the end of the decade, a few reports appeared in which S was treated as a dependent variable to be predicted from other data presumed to measure negativism. In these studies, the null hypothesis is rejected, but as will be seen later in this chapter, the theoretical basis for selection of the independent variables is somewhat ambiguous.

The early years of the 'seventies have brought new progress in understanding the processes underlying emission of the S response. From Canada (DeKoninck and Crabbé-Declève, 1971) has come evidence of linkage between S and Witkin's (1965) concept of field independence. And from Boston (M. L. Stein, 1973a) has come a report of successful replication of two previous studies (Bandura, 1952; Finn and Neuringer, 1968), combined with a rationale derived from the writings of White (1959) and Shapiro (1965). Stein's dissertation contains a thoughtful application of some of the concepts elaborated in this chapter, especially those dealing with the strivings for active mastery that accompany a trend towards increased autonomy.

THE RESPONSE PROCESS

The laws of *prägnanz* (Koffka, 1935) provide some clues for determining which portions of a two-dimensional visual display will appear to stand out as figure rather than ground, but the ultimate criterion is strictly empirical. One might with some precision measure the power of an area in the stimulus field to compel perception of figure: the proportion of observers who so view it could be taken as one index of that power. When the power of a given area to induce perception as figure is small, another portion of the constellation must possess correspondingly greater power to generate such perception, since it is known that some portion of every more-or-less heterogeneous field will be experienced as figure.

In one experimental study of this matter, Belden and Baughman (1954) systematically varied the degree of black/white contrast in the configuration of Rorschach card II and found that, no matter how great the alteration, the center white area was perceived as part of the background in from 57% to 93% of the cases studied. When this area is perceived as figure, therefore, it is correct to say that a perceptual reversal has occurred because (a) the area is barren of ink and is alike in color and texture to those portions of the card which are almost invariably experienced as ground, and (b) only a minority of all subjects perceive it as figure. On every occasion when these conditions are present in a Rorschach response, a primary S has occurred.

It is a commonplace observation that when two competing areas in a display possess approximately equal potential for inducing perception as figure, a viewer's experience of the apparent figure will alternate between them. In such instances, the viewer may report that the alternation often seems beyond voluntary control. On the assumption that the rate of alternation is determined, at least in part, by involuntary autochthonous processes, several investigators have explored the extent to which such determinants are related to individual differences in the frequency of white-space responses to ink blots. Their findings, as we shall see, tend to confirm the existence of a weak relationship between these variables.

One of the first investigators to relate S to reversal processes in perception was Bandura (1952) who reported a partial correlation of .32 (holding R constant) between primary S and the rate of perspective alternation in the Necker cube test. This coefficient is significant (for N = 80) at the .01 level. A partial correlation between secondary S and alternation rate, .19, failed to reach significance. That these findings may also apply to figure-ground reversal rates is suggested by Bandura's correlation of .89 between the Necker cube and the Rubin vase/profile tests in a different group of 32 subjects.

High school students served as subjects in Bandura's study; they were instructed to maintain a passive attitude and to try not to force the alternations but let them come naturally. We do not know how an "oppositional" subject would contrive to disobey such instructions, but Bandura found a near-significant correlation ($r = -.25$)

between his subjects' alternation frequencies and ratings on "obedience" by their teachers. By contrast, the positive correlation of .87 between alternation frequencies and ratings on "self-confidence" was significant beyond the .001 level. Perhaps the alternation rate could provide a useful technique for personality assessment: if it slows with depression, as seems likely from these results, it might serve as a convenient indicator of mood swings.

In another well-designed study, Nelson (1954) used a set of 16 cards imprinted with black-and-white figures specifically constructed to provide reliable measurements of individual differences in reversal tendency. He administered the Rorschach to 60 subjects and assigned them to three groups matched on relevant variables (age, sex, I.Q., psychiatric diagnosis, and total R). In Group I, each subject's protocol contained at least one primary S but no secondary S; in Group II, each protocol contained at least one secondary but no primary S; and in Group III, no protocol contained S of any type.

Twenty matched pairs of subjects were drawn from Groups I and III for comparison on the figure-ground reversal measures: in 13 of the pairs, the primary-S member had the higher reversal score; in four of the pairs, the non-S member's score was higher; and in three pairs, there were no differences. The relationship between primary S and reversal of figure and ground in these findings is significant by the sign test at the .025 level. Comparisons between the paired secondary-S vs non-S subjects from Groups II and III failed to reveal a significant difference in reversal tendencies. From these results Nelson concluded that primary S, but not secondary S, probably represents a real propensity for reversal of figure and ground.

Hospitalized psychiatric patients served as subjects in Nelson's study, and he noted a considerable degree of variation in their spontaneous approaches to the task. A few responded only to the black figures; others were able to perceive something in the enclosed areas, either black or white; still others discovered reversals only after having responded to an enclosed white area; but Nelson was most impressed by the small minority who reversed figure and ground easily and shifted attention readily from one aspect of the designs to another. Most of his subjects, however, required a good deal of instruction and guidance and seemed to need more than one trial on each design before finding anything in the white spaces. Once they had been "turned on" to the reversal process and, in effect, had been given permission to look at the white spaces, all subjects eventually managed to find something in them to report.

Scharmann (1959) felt that the gross dichotomy between primary and secondary S might need further refinement. Accordingly, he devised a classification system comprised of eight categories of response to the white spaces. These categories are ranked in order of the degree of perceptual reversal involved, ranging from "genuine" (echte) through "apparent" (scheinbare) to "holes" (Lochdeutungen). Subsequently, Roth (1962) experimentally calibrated for relative reversability eight different published versions of the Rubin vase/profile design and also obtained a reversal threshold for each of the subjects. After scoring these subjects' white-space responses on the Rorschach according to Scharmann's system, Roth tabulated within each category the reversal thresholds of the subjects who had produced them. Biserial correlations computed between the reversal thresholds and the presence or absence of a categorized response parallel in magnitude the order predicted by Scharmann's a priori ranking of the scoring categories, with echte (i.e., primary S) tending to accompany the lowest reversal thresholds. The coefficients are distributed symmetrically around zero, however, and none departs significantly from it. Roth's conclusion is that the data do not confirm the assumption that all responses involving white space are related to individual differences in perceptual-reversal tendencies. These findings are not inconsistent with those of Bandura and Nelson as described above.

From another standpoint, the processes involved in production of S were investigated in a tachistoscopic study by M. I. Stein (1949), who varied exposure times with the standard ink blots through four levels ranging from .01 second to unlimited viewing. He found that S responses tended to emerge only after other response possibilities had been exhausted, and he suggested that "the drive for more responses may lead to a reversal of the figure-ground relationship . . . S responses may highlight a subject's level of aspiration rather than his negativism" (p. 366).

Subsequent studies of the Necker cube and the Rubin design have shown that reversal rates can be voluntarily controlled, and that the degree of control exhibited by field-independent subjects is greater than by field-dependent individuals. Consequently, DeKoninck and Crabbé-Declève (1971) hypothesized that more primary S would be produced by field-independent than by field-dependent subjects; this hypothesis was confirmed in a well-designed study, to be described later, linking S to a personality construct which—compared with reversal rate—may turn out to be more useful to clinicians when confronted by S responses in their clients' protocols.

ACTUARIAL CONSIDERATIONS

A small but impressive body of research on the behavioral correlates of S has accumulated since 1950 and will be surveyed in this chapter. As will be seen, however, this research has been harassed by its share of methodological problems, and some of these will be discussed before turning to the description of specific studies.

Symbiosis Between S and R

Responses elicited by the ink blots are emitted by subjects whose overall output (R) provides a highly reliable measure of individual differences. Within the total array of responses emitted by each individual, a very small number—and sometimes none at all—are identifiable as primary S. Early investigators used a simple binary scoring system to denote the presence or absence of S in a record, but this method was abandoned when it became apparent that implications to be drawn from the presence of a solitary S must be quite different when it occurs in a meager protocol rather than in a more opulent one.

Any significant relationships between S and a non-Rorschach variable are usually paralleled by similar relationships between R and the same variable, and parsimony requires that any apparent relationship with S be shown to be more than a mere artifact of the inclusion of S in R. Actually, of course, the significantly positive correlations between S and R are not entirely due to the inclusion of S as a subset of R. Bandura (1954 b), for example, reported a correlation of .51 between S and the number of other responses in the record (i.e., $R - S$), indicating that approximately 25% of the variance of S in his sample was shared by $R - S$. This degree of sharing represents a so-called "first factor" which has been tentatively identified by the multivariate analysts as "productivity" (e.g., Borgatta and Eschenbach, 1955). First factors are familiar phenomena in psychometric studies, but there is not always a consensus concerning the name or nature of the constructs they represent. Empirical data capable of sorting out various processes involved in the ink-blot productivity factor are still awaited.

Several investigators have attempted to control for R by assigning to each subject a percentage score based upon the division of the number of S in a protocol by its total R. Obtaining an $S\%$ score in this way is convenient and seems quite reasonable, but it involves some rather dubious assumptions because $S\%$ itself is highly correlated with R. Data reported by Bandura (1952), show that the mean $S\%$ of subjects giving less than 30 responses was 2.57; for those with R in the 30-59 interval, the mean $S\%$ was 5.39; and for those with 60 or more R, it was 7.98. Inasmuch as the $S\%$ score is by no means independent of R, serious problems attend its use in studying relationships between S and non-Rorschach variables, as has been shown by Kalter and Marsden (1970). Division of S by R, according to these authors, creates an entirely new variable, the magnitude of whose correlation with non-Rorschach variables bears no consistent relationship to the magnitude of any correlations relevant to controlling for the "productivity" factor included in both S and R.

In attempting to control for productivity when assessing the relationship between S and a non-Rorschach variable, the use of partial correlations or other parametric techniques is defensible when the scores have been transformed to approximately normal distributions. However, it must be borne in mind that the variability of S is not independent of R and tends to shrink systematically as R goes to zero, thus raising the spectre of heteroscedacisty. In such cases, of course, the use of normalized standard-score equivalents to equalize the variance of S within intervals of R remains a possibility.

Another method of control involves the application of nonparametric treatment to the S scores of subjects matched on R. This method, however, may deprive the investigator of an excessive number of subjects or limit generalizability of the findings to those who produce within a specific range of R. It would be preferable, of course, to examine the non-parametric relationships between S and non-Rorschach variables within each of the several subsamples along an extended distribution of scores on R.

An application of these principles to the development of norms for clinical use is exemplified in the work of Slemon, Neiger and Quirk (1965). These authors obtained Rorschach protocols from 200 men and women in Toronto and found the distributions of scores on both S and R to be markedly skewed. Accordingly, they transformed percentile ranks into standard-score equivalents before computing equations for the regression of S (and various other scores) on R. For this computation, S score percentiles within specific intervals of R were identified. Students interested in normative data will find this report useful for identifying S scores at the median and at the 75th, 95th and 99th percentiles within intervals along the distribution of R. For example, when R is between 29 and 44, the median S score is two, and scores of three and five are at the 75th and 95th percentiles, respectively. In the population sampled for this study, S was absent from three-fourths of the protocols having less than 23 R and from half of those with R in the 23-28 range.

Still another way to control for R, of course, is to eliminate its variability altogether. This method was employed by Holtzman, Thorpe, Swartz and Herron (1961) in constructing their Inkblot Technique (HIT). The procedure involves requiring one and only one response to each of 45 cards. Unfortunately, however, S responses under these conditions are quite rare, even though some of the HIT cards were specifically designed to elicit them (Hill, 1972, p. 53). This rarity was highlighted in an item analysis of 15,000-odd responses from some 350 persons to Form A of the HIT: only 51 of these responses were scored S (Holtzman, et al., 1961, p. 255).

Under these circumstances, it is not surprising that the distributions of S scores in all groups tested were found to be too sharply truncated and too severely skewed for parametric analysis. For most groups, the mean S score is less than one and less than its standard deviation. Incidentally, in their Table VI-6, Holtzman et al. (p. 113) show a mean S of 3.8 and standard deviation of 5.8 for a group of 41 schizophrenic patients; according to Holtzman, however, these figures must have been spuriously inflated by "a typographical error that occurred somewhere between the computer printout and the book" (Note 1).

The HIT item analysis revealed that only eight of the cards in Form A and ten in Form B had each elicited S responses from two or more subjects. The authors suggested that these 18 cards be used with subjects instructed to give two responses to each card, thus yielding 36-response records and perhaps increasing the reliability and normalizing the distributions of S. More recently, Holtzman has suggested that "it would be a good idea for someone to construct parallel forms that might contain only ten or twelve blots and for which two or three responses would be given" in order to study S and some of the other very rare variables (Note 1).

The fact that HIT procedures elicit an insufficient quantity of S responses for research was foreshadowed many years ago in a study by Bandura (1952) who instructed his subjects to continue to respond throughout a four-minute exposure of every blot. The mean R of 22.75 for the first two-minute periods was more than twice the mean of 10.54 responses given during the last two minutes; yet the mean percentage of primary S during the first periods was 3% and less than half of the 8% given during the second periods. This finding emphasizes the need for prolonged viewing and multiple responding if adequate samples of S are to be obtained for reliable appraisal; it also suggests that clinicians who are satisfied with relatively brief protocols (e.g., Exner, 1974) are much less likely to encounter S responses in their work.

The Reliability of S

Disregarding the distinction between primary and secondary S and combining them into a single score appeals to many students because it is easier to agree that white space is somehow involved in a response than it is to agree that a true figure-ground reversal has occurred. Moreover, such a combination yields a larger number of responses for assignment to the S category in a single Rorschach protocol, and by analogy to the Spearman-Brown formula, it might be assumed that adding secondary S "items" and thus lengthening the space "subtest" would increase the reliability of the expanded score.

Unfortunately, however, Fonda (1951) found the combined S score to be somewhat less reliable on retest with a parallel series of ink blots ($r = .43$) than the primary S score alone ($r = .53$). Correlations between primary and secondary S, even when scored by the same investigator, are unimpressive. Combination of these two scores has probably introduced enough "noise" into research data to mask the significance of some potential correlations between S and many non-Rorschach variables.

The reliability of primary S increases with the magnitude of R, and external conditions affecting the frequency of both S and R include: (a) the type of administration, i.e., individual or group; (b) the number of inkblots; (c) the duration of exposure of each card; and (d) the number of responses permitted or required. As shown in Table 4.1, the split-half reliability of S, with R held constant, ranges from .17 when only one response is permitted to each of 45 cards, to .60 when unlimited responding is encouraged during

TABLE 4.1

Parametric Reliability Coefficients of Primary S
Independent of R in Four Groups of Subjects

Investigator	Subjects	N	Cards	Exposure	Responses per card	Method*	Reliability coefficient
Bandura (1954)	High school	80	10	4 min.	Ad lib.	S-H	.60
Holtzman et al. (1961)	High school	72	45	Ad lib.	One	S-H	.17
Fonda (1951)	College	150	2 x 10	3 min.	Ad lib.	P.F.	.32
Holtzman et al. (1961)	College	120	2 x 45	Ad lib.	One	P.F.	.22

*S-H: Split-half
P.F.: Parallel forms (14-day interval or less)

four-minute exposures of each of ten cards. With Spearman-Brown correction, the latter coefficient becomes .75, holding R constant, and .80 when the added variance associated with R is included. Under the conditions of his administration, Bandura (1954 b, p. 114) concluded that "the obtained correlations show the space responses to be consistent response tendencies."

THE EMPIRICAL CORRELATES OF S

The Rorschach examination constitutes a standardized interview capable of yielding valuable information concerning content variables; fortunately, it also affords unique opportunities for appraising the more formal, or structural, aspects of personality. In consolidating cues obtained during personality assessment with the aid of ink blots, an examiner incorporates inferences derived from a variety of circumstances, including the relative frequency of emission of S. A number of investigators have undertaken the task of appraising the experimental evidence upon the basis of which such inferences can be sustained. It should be emphasized, however, that the use of psychometric terminology to describe the quantitative aspects of ink-blot responses remains entirely consistent with the view that the Rorschach is not a test but is rather an interviewing technique, or pool of techniques, widely employed by many astute examiners with demonstrable degrees of success.

For didactic purposes, some clinicians have attempted to delineate the processes by means of which they derive inferences from ink-blot responses—including responses to the white spaces—during a diagnostic interview. It is noteworthy that the specific contribution of S to a clinician's overall impression often eludes precise communication, although it is clear that S serves in a variety of ways to help sharpen the focus on a client's attitudes toward self-actualization. In the performance of their duties, clinicians welcome the assistance of behavioral science, and in this section several published inputs from behavioral laboratories will be reviewed.

In a general sense, the discussion is concerned with attempts to appraise the validity of clinical inferences derived from S responses. Several of the studies appear to have been designed to provide evidence concerning predictive or concurrent validity, whereas others seem more deliberately oriented towards some form of construct validation. As will be seen, however, much work remains before an adequate compilation of convergent and discriminant evidence becomes available. The studies to be discussed here are listed, for convenience only, according to the experimental role assigned to S: the studies are identified in Table 4.2 when subjects are selected on the basis of S or when the aim is to complete propositions of the form "if S, then . . ;" studies are identified in Table 4.3 when subjects are selected on some other basis or when S appears as a predicate in the proposition to be tested.

Attempts to identify systematic relationships between S and behavioral tendencies have encountered difficulties in the selection of appropriate criterion variables. The testing of hypotheses concerning S is frequently concerned with variables classified along a bipolar continuum having "negativistic opposition" at one end and "docile acquiescence" at the other. The third, or middle, position, tentatively identified as "autonomy," has only recently begun to undergo rigorous scientific scrutiny.

If one distinguishing characteristic of a testable scientific proposition is its statement in a form capable of disproof, then certainly Rorschach's "oppositional trend" hypothesis would seem to deserve high marks. Evidence that S alone identifies and isolates Caspar Milquetoasts would constitute effective disproof. There is, of course, no such evidence, although a critical examination of the original articles on S, as advocated by Shaffer (1961), occasionally discloses reports which, if replicated and confirmed, might qualify. One such study found high-S subjects to be significantly more cooperative and less resistive than non-S subjects during an experimental stress interview (Ingram, 1954). This study will be reviewed below, but the problematic nature of its findings is demonstrated by Shaffer's (1970, p. 908) impression that they show the high-S subjects to be more "oppositional."

The Null Hypothesis

A customary practice in scientific work is to attempt to reject an hypothesis which states that the variables of interest to the investigator are unrelated. The null hypothesis is, of course, often properly rejected at acceptable levels of confidence, and efforts to do so will be

TABLE 4.2

S as the Independent Variable in Research Studies

Rorschach variables	Author	R control	Statistic	Non-Rorschach variables		
				Non-significant	Significant	
Combined S	Bandura (1952)	Partial r	Parametric transformation	Assertiveness, inadequacy feelings self-distrust	Disobedience, Necker cube reversals	
Combined S	Borgatta & Eschenbach (1955)	Multi-factorial	Parametric		Social intelligence	
Combined S	Eschenbach & Borgatta (1955)	Partial r	Parametric	Antagonism, tension, passive agreement, disagreement		
Primary S	Fonda (1951)	Partial r	Parametric transformation		Question-mark answers	
Primary S	Ingram (1954)	None	Parametric	Assertiveness, persistence, resistance	Cooperation, initiative, rapport	
Combined S	Murray (1954)	S percent Matched groups	Non-parametric	Disagreement, nay-saying, negative suggestibility, opposition		
Primary S	Nelson (1954)	Matched groups	Non-parametric	Extrapunitive, impunitive, intropunitive	Figure-ground reversals	
Combined S	Ray (1955)	S percent Matched groups	Non-parametric		Independence	
Combined S	M. L. Stein (1973b)	S percent	Non-parametric		Disobedience	

TABLE 4.3

S as the Dependent Variable in Research Studies

Non-Rorschach variables	Author	R control	Statistic	Rorschach variables	
				Non-significant	Significant
Viewing time	Bandura (1952)	S percent	Parametric		Primary S
Subjective hostility	Counts & Mensh (1950)	None	Parametric	Combined S	
Field independence	De Koninck & Crabbé-Declève (1971)	Matched groups	Non-parametric		Primary S
Left-handedness	Finn & Neuringer (1968)	S percent Matched groups	Parametric		Combined S
Digits reversed	Fox & Blatt (1969)	Matched groups	Non-parametric		Primary S
Dream deprivation	Lerner (1966)	Matched groups	Non-parametric		Primary S
Objective hostility	Lord (1950)	None	Parametric	Combined S	
Left-handedness	M. L. Stein (1973a)	S percent Matched groups	Parametric		Combined S

discussed here, beginning with several of the less successful attempts.

Non-rejection of the Hypothesis. A glance at Table 4.2 shows that several doctoral dissertations and other studies have attempted without success to reject hypotheses of non-relationship between S and a fairly long list of behavioral correlates. It is often difficult to determine whether failure to reject the null hypothesis is due to invalidity of the postulated alternative, improper choice of criterion variables, or inappropriate research methodology. A few details concerning research design and technology are listed in Tables 4.2 and 4.3.

S and Negativism. The elusive nature of negativism as a personality construct is demonstrated in Murray's (1954) experience with the criterion variables in his study of S. He selected a battery of six tests as measures of negativism but found rather weak evidence of underlying communality among them. Of the 15 intercorrelations, only three are significant, and one of these is in the wrong direction. Some of the tests seem fairly reliable, however, and most of them have satisfactory face validity.

Murray's tests include: (a) the Hull Postural Sway Test, scored for maximum excursion of sway in a direction opposite from that suggested; correlates $-.30$ with the Self-descriptive Inventory. (b) Self-descriptive Inventory, scored for number of items endorsed indicating oppositional behavior, aggressiveness, or negative suggestibility. (c) Naysaying, scored for the number of "No" answers on first administration of an opinion questionnaire; correlates $+.47$ with Testing the Limits. (d) Testing the Limits, scored for the number of suggested Rorschach percepts rejected; correlates $+.24$ with Opinion Disagreement. (e) Opinion Disagreement, scored for the number of shifts on retest away from ostensible responses of the majority on the opinion questionnaire. (f) Compliance, scored for the number of test instructions obeyed.

Scores on each of the criterion variables were subjected to an ANOVA in which the independent sources of variance were considered to be (a) the presence or absence of S, (b) two levels of R, and (c) the three experience types. Scores for primary and secondary S were combined, and S was counted as present when it exceeded 9% of R. In the high-R group, scores ranged from 25 to 51 with a mean at 30; scores in the low group ranged from 16 to 19 with a mean of 17.3. Murray was able to place only two subjects in each of the twelve cells of his 2 x 2 x 3 analysis.

None of the variance in any of the criterion measures was significantly related to S or the experience type or their interaction, although one measure, Naysaying, was significantly associated with R. Murray concluded that "R may be related to negativism, at least as shown by the 'No' answers (the more 'No' answers the fewer R), but S is certainly not" (1957a, p. 45). This embrace of the null hypothesis, however, may be somewhat more ardent than the circumstances warrant: as discussed earlier in this chapter, the use of $S\%$ introduces ambiguity into the scores; combination of primary and secondary S compounds the errors of measurement; and as Murray acknowledged, limiting the size of the sample may have weakened the analysis.

S and Aggression. The several pejorative terms employed by Rorschach to describe characteristics associated with S have been consolidated by some of his followers into a single generic concept: aggression. One investigator who proposed to test the proposition that S reflects aggressive tendencies was Ingram (1954). Her frequently-cited report marks a turning point in our conceptual approach to the interpretation of space responses, even though its findings remain somewhat equivocal. This judgment takes into account the ambiguity of its definition of aggression, together with a few of its methodological mishaps.

In this study, which was concerned with reactions to frustration, Ingram found that "aggressive" characteristics displayed by subjects in an experimental condition could have been predicted more accurately from primary S alone than from entire protocols interpreted by Rorschach experts. Moreover, S was found to be associated with cooperative rapport rather than with resistive behavior, and no consistent relationships were demonstrated between S and hostility.

Only if the null hypothesis had stated that S and participatory interactive behavior are unrelated could Ingram's findings have been accepted as a basis for its rejection. A close reading of the report suggests, instead, that her study was designed originally to test a quite different hypothesis, viz., that S and hostile resistive tendencies are unrelated. The results clearly do not warrant rejection of the latter hypothesis, and perhaps a brief exegesis of Ingram's paper would be in order here.

Methodological strengths and weaknesses are apparent in this study. The disregard of secondary S, for example, is a definite asset; the criterion for admission to one of her eight-member experimental groups was the production of at least two primary S responses during a standard Rorschach administration; in the other eight-member group, none of the subjects produced any S in responding to the ink blots. The two groups were matched on age, sex, ethnicity and I.Q.—but not on R.

Ordinarily, failure to match groups on R would be considered a weakness, but in this case the shortcoming is mitigated to some extent by introduction of the data derived from clinical interpretations of entire protocols. Another weakness is seen in the circumstance that all of the Rorschachs were apparently administered by the investigator who rated the subjects' behavior under frustration. Here again, however, consequences of this error are minimized because the outcomes were contrary to the investigator's own expectations.

In the experimental condition, all subjects were required to participate in two different frustrating situations. During the first session, each subject attempted to solve a difficult puzzle in the presence of an observer; in this situation, the non-S subjects were rated as more "hostile" than the S group. During the second session, each subject was confronted by an authoritarian figure who delivered a direct verbal assault on the subject's self-esteem; in this situation, the non-S subjects were rated as less "hostile" than the S group. The ratings were reliable; the differences between groups were significant; the hostility ratings varied with situations that interacted with S, but the null hypothesis survived with respect to the main effect.

Ingram's conclusion that "the high S group was more aggressive (in a participatory, interactive way)" (p. 27) was based upon unanticipated observations in the second session where the S group was rated higher than the non-S subjects on "initiative," "rapport," and "cooperation," and lower on "resistance."

The outcome pattern in Ingram's study, i.e., failure to reject the null hypothesis coupled with unexpected observations linking S to socially desirable charactertistics, was essentially duplicated shortly thereafter in a study by Eschenbach and Borgatta (1955). In their attempt to reject the null hypothesis, these investigators measured oppositional behavior and its converse, passivity, in terms of four of the categories included in the Interaction Process Analysis (IPA), a method devised by Bales for classifying observations of the behavior initiated by participants in small-group discussion sessions. In this study, each of 125 subjects was observed during four 24-minute encounters with a different pair of strangers on each occasion.

The criterion variables were frequency counts of behaviors recorded in each of the four IPA categories. Two of these categories were considered to be indicators of oppositional behavior; these were (a) shows antagonism, and (b) disagrees. The remaining two, taken as indicators of passivity, were (c) shows tension, and (d) agrees. Untransformed primary and secondary space responses were combined to yield a single S score for each subject. Partial correlations, holding R constant, were computed between S and each of the criterion variables. Positive correlations between S and the first two, and negative correlations between S and the second pair of variables would provide bases for rejection of the null hypothesis.

None of the predicted correlations differed significantly from zero, but several unpredicted relationships did appear; these will be described below in connection with other serendipities.

Hostility and S. The assumption that "emphasis on the use of white space may convey a form of negativism and/or hostility" (Exner, 1974, p. 324) has had a long history even though evidence concerning the relationship between S and hostility remains quite tenuous. Three studies bearing on this issue are available.

One interesting study employed hypnosis to induce hostile feelings toward the examiner (Counts & Mensh, 1950), and protocols were obtained before, during, and after the period of induced hostility. The number of S responses increased progressively throughout this sequence, but so did R, and the investigators found the differences not to be significant. The null hypothesis was not rejected.

In another well-controlled study (Lord, 1950), the Rorschach was administered several times to each subject by different examiners in a counterbalanced order. Each examiner systematically varied the conditions of administration: under one condition, the examiner adopted a deliberately hostile attitude toward the subjects; under another condition, the examinations were conducted in a warm and accepting manner; and under a third condition, the administration was "neutral." More *S* appeared under the hostile condition than during the neutral administration but less than in the warm and accepting situations. The available evidence, therefore, provides no grounds for refuting an assertion that the assumed relationship between *S* and hostility (as a non-Rorschach variable) is entirely chimerical.

Within individual Rorschach protocols, on the other hand, there may be a relationship between hostile content and the presence of *S*, as Weltman and Wolfson (1964) have attempted to demonstrate. These authors inspected 208 records and found that protocols with primary *S*, compared with those without it, were about twice as likely to contain one or more responses having hostile content. The number of individuals who had rotated at least one ink blot was similarly much greater among the subjects with primary *S*, but the report is silent concerning *R*. Inasmuch as *R* is predictable from *S*, the likelihood of responses in several other scoring categories must be similarly predictable from *S*. The importance of controlling for *R*, if the null hypothesis is to be rejected, is thus exemplified in this study.

S and Self-esteem. Up to this point the evidence concerning non-Rorschach variables has consisted mainly of objective information derived from observations of the behavior of subjects under experimental conditions. Next to be considered are studies dealing with evidence concerning the ways that subjects habitually perceive or present themselves. This kind of evidence is collected in three ways: (a) self-descriptive questionnaires; (b) projective techniques; and (c) inferences drawn from continuing interactions with subjects in ongoing real-life situations.

Evidence gathered from self-descriptive questionnaires has failed to indicate that subjects who produce *S* are more likely than non-*S* individuals to describe themselves as uncooperative or disagreeable, or to acknowledge feelings of inferiority (Fonda, 1951); neither do they describe themselves as aggressive, negatively suggestible, or oppositional (Murray, 1954). Nor do subjects grouped according to S-production differ with respect to projective output on the Rosenzweig Picture-Frustration Study (Nelson, 1954).

Perhaps the most definitive information concerning characterological traits in relation to S is still to be found in Bandura's (1952) seminal study of psychological processes associated with Rorschach white-space responses. His criterion variables involved non-laboratory behavior of real importance to his subjects, and he successfully confronted most of the methodological problems that continue to plague investigators in this field of research.

Bandura's criterion variables were rating scales completed on adolescent boys and girls by high school teachers who knew them well. Intercorrelations among these scales show that two relatively independent dimensions were being measured. One dimension was concerned with obedience and will be discussed in the next section. The other dimension was measured by a cluster of three overlapping scales concerned with manifestations of apparent self-esteem; names assigned to these scales are reminiscent of terms used by Rorschach to describe some of the concomitants of S: "self-assertiveness," "self-distrust," and "feelings of inadequacy."

Consensual validity of the rating scales is demonstrated by inter-rater reliability coefficients ranging from .71 to .83. Ratings by five teachers on each of the scales were averaged for each subject, and the scores thus obtained were correlated with scores on S (primary and secondary combined) after both sets of data had been normalized by statistical transformation. Partial correlations (holding $R - S$ constant) between S and each of the "self-esteem" scales were not significantly different from zero, and correlations within the introversive and extratensive groups did not differ significantly from each other.

Bandura's data thus do not support rejection of hypotheses that: (a) S and self-esteem are unrelated; and (b) experience-type and S do not interact.

S and Indecisiveness. One of Rorschach's hypotheses states that S in ambiequal records signifies indecisiveness; some authors (e.g., McCall, 1970) feel that a case can be made for this interpretation without regard to experience type. This position is consistent with one early study in which Fonda (1951) correlated primary S with question-mark answers on two self-descriptive inventories in three groups of subjects classified according to experience type. The coefficients reached significance among the introversives and extratensives but not among the ambiequals, although the three correlations did not differ significantly from each other. The author concluded that "this finding would call into question one of Rorschach's hypotheses with respect to the interaction of opposition tendency and experience type" (p. 376).

Attempts to identify the behavioral correlates of question-mark answers have been generally unproductive except to indicate that they seem to comprise a factorially complex variable having multiple determinants (Rosenberg, 1954). Similar processes may be involved in "cannot-say" answers on the MMPI; speculation concerning these maintains that excessive use of such answers often indicates obsessive indecisiveness, extreme intellectualization, or litigious wariness (Carson, 1969).

Meehl (1969) has suggested that the cannot-say answer may also be a way that self-respecting individuals have of saying "no one has a right to ask me about this particular matter" (p. 275). A remotely analogous interpretation of extreme emphasis on S has been proposed by Schachter (1970), who interpreted excessive emission of S by a young woman as the indication of a need to conceal her true self from others and perhaps from her own awareness as well. (There were 23 primary space responses in her 58-response protocol.)

Rejection of the Null Hypothesis. The studies discussed in previous sections do not warrant rejection of hypotheses that S is unrelated to hostile aggression or negative suggestibility, but the evidence does affirm the existence of reliable individual differences in primary S itself. Further efforts to identify constructs underlying this variable have proceeded both inductively and deductively. Deductive studies that have succeeded in rejecting the null hypotheses will be described here, while reports of inductive research will be considered in a later section.

Psychological Differentiation and S. It is quite clear by now that space responses provide information about individual differences in the availability, selectivity, and strategy of distributing attention. A clinician's perception of the client involves appraisal of that individual's self-regulative mechanisms of adaptive control, including the capacity for ascribing foreground and background characteristics to stimulus situations. Witkin's (1965) review of personality disturbances seen in patients exhibiting various levels of cognitive differentiation preceded an important study by DeKoninck and Crabbé-Declève (1971) which incorporates S into an area of concern to students of field independence, and which expands our understanding of S by facilitating the inclusion of insights derived from that line of inquiry.

The study by DeKoninck and Crabbé-Declève satisfies most of the methodological requirements outlined earlier in this chapter. These authors hypothesized that field-independent subjects would produce more primary S than would field-dependent individuals. From a pool of 52 college students, seven subjects with the highest and seven with the lowest scores on Witkin's rod-and-frame test were administered the Rorschach. Protocols ranged in R from 13 to 70, but the means for the two groups were not significantly different, and the field-independent subjects produced more primary S. Significance of the difference was estimated at the .02 level by a composite rank test.

Studies of psychological differentiation (e.g., Witkin, Dyk, Faterson, Goodenough and Karp, 1962) have identified several personality characteristics associated with various levels of performance on the rod-and-frame test. Longitudinal studies show a gradual increase in level with age while individual differences in comparative standing remain relatively constant. Field-independent subjects are regarded by others as socially more independent and less influenced by authority, tending instead to be guided by values, standards and needs of their own. The ability to keep objects separate from the background and to control voluntarily the incidence of figure-ground reversal is apparently associated with the capacity to function with relative autonomy in the social milieu of everyday life.

S and Independence. Another successful rejection of the null hypothesis was accomplished by Ray (1955), whose study has generated a quantum rise in our understanding of the meaning of the space response. He employed Sherif's autokinetic test to provide a dependent variable in his examination of the relationship between S and the response to prestige suggestion. Significant differences appeared in the autokinetic behavior of Ray's high-S and low-S

subjects: all seven members of his low-S group shifted their reports significantly towards those of a prestige person, whereas among the eight high-S subjects only one compliant individual yielded, six independents maintained their own previously established norms, and one negativistic subject shifted his reports significantly in the opposite direction. This difference between the high- and low-S groups is significant beyond the .01 level of confidence, according to a Mann-Whitney U test. It should be noted, however, that this finding warrants rejection of the hypothesis of non-relationship between S and independence but not of that between S and negativism.

Ray's study highlights the difficulty of obtaining a consensus regarding an operational definition of "oppositional tendencies." His subjects were Air Force fighter-bomber trainees, and the prestige person in his autokinetic situation was identified as a "colonel." Despite objective immobility of the stimulus light, Ray's "colonel" asserted that it moved much more than the trainees had reported; under these circumstances, eight trainees acquiesced, and all but one of these were low-S respondents. Conversely, all but two of the high-S respondents seemed to have a firmer grasp on reality; their scepticism concerning the "social norm," however, was accepted as evidence of "negativism, resistence, stubbornness, contrariness or oppositionality."

Because of the apparent divergence between Ray's findings and those of Murray (1954) concerning response to prestige suggestion (see p. 133, supra), it may be instructive to consider some of the more obvious similarities and differences between the two studies. The similarities are fairly impressive. In both, S was treated as an independent variable, and primary and secondary S were combined into a single score for each subject. Control of R was provided by both investigators: Murray's high-S and low-S groups were both matched at two levels of R, with one mean at 17 and another at 30, whereas Ray's were matched on R at a single mean of 55. Ray's means at 1.14 for the low and 9.63 for the high-S groups probably divided them into more sharply differentiated categories, thus enhancing the likelihood of reliable separation of the groups on the criterion. All of Ray's subjects were extratensive and there were nearly twice as many of these as in Murray's study, although the latter investigator also included equal numbers of introversives and ambiequals as well.

Murray's results are inconclusive: none of his groups exhibited differences associated with $S\%$. Ray's findings were more definitive, despite the fact that he too had used $S\%$ for combined primary and secondary S; this practice, as noted earlier, tends to obscure the role of primary S as an independent variable. Although generalizations from Ray's results may be limited to high-R respondents, it should be noted that identification of autonomous behavior was not included in Murray's design; perhaps the most impressive feature of Ray's findings was the outstanding prevalence of such behavior in his high-S group.

It is tempting and perhaps not unreasonable to imagine that those of Ray's subjects who adhered to their own norms were exhibiting characteristics similar to those of the few subjects in Milgram's (1973) more recent studies of obedience who declined to obey instructions to inflict pain on other people.

S and Disobedience. Moving out of the laboratory and into the more realistic give-and-take of everyday life, two investigators obtained evidence to support rejection of the hypothesis of non relationship between S and the way that subordinates are rated on "obedience" by their authoritarian supervisors. One of these investigators (Bandura, 1952) arranged to have 59 boys and girls rated on obedience by five of their teachers at a Midwestern high school; the other (M. L. Stein, 1973b) obtained obedience ratings on each of 40 corpsmen from immediate supervisors at a U.S. Naval Hospital on Long Island.

In both studies, space responses were combined into a single weighted score for each subject, with primary receiving twice the weight of secondary S. In both studies, the negative correlation between S and obedience was significant beyond the .01 level of confidence. Bandura's partial correlation, holding R constant, was $-.34$; Stein's rank-order coefficient, $-.46$, included covariance associated with R. Signs of these coefficients were interpreted by the investigators as an indication of association between S and "oppositionality." Inspection of their rating scales, therefore, provides an operational description of the meanings assigned to this concept.

The five levels of Bandura's (1952) scale were defined in the following terms:

    I. Docile and compliant; accepts discipline and orders without hesitation.

    II. Willingly accepts orders, without resistance and without hesitation.

    III. Slow in obeying; accepts discipline or orders after brief hesitation and urging.

    IV. Dislikes taking orders; accepts discipline grudgingly; tends to delay and ignore orders.

    V. Refuses to do things unless forced; stubborn and resistive.

Stein employed three scales of a semantic-differential type. Each scale consisted of word pairs separated by numbers from one to seven, as follows:

Acquiescent	1 2 3 4 5 6 7	Contrary
Agreeable	1 2 3 4 5 6 7	Oppositional
Cooperative	1 2 3 4 5 6 7	Stubborn

The raters in Bandura's study were able to reach an adequate consensus on the meaning of "obedience," as shown by a reliability coefficient of .83 in their (normalized) ratings. Reliabilities and intercorrelations among the rating scales in Stein's study are not available.

In authoritarian settings or in relationships based upon dependency needs, overt manifestations of mastery strivings or defenses of autonomy are often perceived and rated by dominant figures as "oppositional" or "negativistic." These terms apply to specific ways of sustaining relationships with other people and, as such, often describe modes of attempting to counteract anxiety associated with personal isolation or social alienation.

Can "oppositionality" be a persisting and socially-desirable personal characteristic? One answer to this question comes from Reik (1974), a longtime associate of Freud, who describes the founder of psychoanalysis as "prepared to go into opposition and to renounce conformity with the 'compact majority.' . . . It was this intellectual freedom from convention and this independence of thought that enabled him to write those eleven volumes that 'shook the world.' It was that readiness to stand alone against an army of antagonists which made it possible to carry his research forward" (p. 32).

Serendipities. As has been repeatedly emphasized, studies designed to test deductions from Rorschach's basic hypothesis ("if S, then some sort of oppositional trend") have encountered problems arising from a lack of precision in defining "oppositional trend." We have seen that hostile, aggressive or negativistic behaviors have not been associated with S in several investigations, whereas other studies have found that the probability of independent or disobedient behavior increases in proportion to the quantity of S. Thus the validity of Rorschach's propositions concerning this variable obviously depends, in part, upon the meaning ascribed to "oppositional trend." Under these circumstances, the application of inductive methods to unanticipated findings is entirely appropriate, and some relevant serendipities will be described here. Eventual replication of these findings could lead to formulation of hypotheses suitable for more rigorous deductive evaluation.

S and "Social Intelligence". Borgatta and Eschenbach (1955) factor analyzed the data on 15 Rorschach and 37 non-Rorschach variables obtained from 125 Air Force enlisted men. Data for this analysis had been collected for the previously described study by these authors (see p. 134 f.). In addition to IPA observations, the non-Rorschach data included scores on the Primary Mental Abilities test (PMA), sociometric responses, biographical items and concurrent behavioral ratings. The authors caution that "what is found in a factor analysis is governed by what was put into it in the first place" (p. 133).

One of the factors emerging from this analysis was identified as "effective (social) intelligence." This factor appreciably loads S—and S alone—among the Rorschach variables; its heaviest non-Rorschach loadings are associated with the PMA Verbal score and with educational level; appreciable loadings are also associated with the PMA Reasoning and Word Fluency scores, an IPA variable (asking questions), and high ratings by superior officers.

In summarizing their findings, these authors felt obliged to warn against comparing their results, which were obtained on a "normal" population, with those obtained by other investigators using "pathological" subjects. It is not unreasonable, of course, to assume that S may be related to adaptive behavior in emotionally mature individuals and to maladaptive behavior in the disturbed.

Dream Deprivation and S. An unanticipated side-effect involving *S* as a dependent variable has been reported by Lerner (1966). In her study of the relationship between dreams and the *M* response, Lerner arranged to interdict dreaming in 20 subjects during an experimental period by administering a combination of amphetamine and pentobarbital. To her surprise, this treatment was accompanied on retest by a substantial increase in primary *S*, significantly (*p* = .005) in excess of the rise of *S* in a placebo-control group. In this comparison, secondary *S* remained unchanged. The author observed that only two of her 20 subjects had "failed to show a post-dream-deprivation rise in at least one of three variables: overall quantity of movement, amount of movement dissolution, or primary space" (p. 85).

Lerner speculated that the increased frequency of *S* in protocols of dream-deprived subjects might reflect striving to master the intense upsurge of kinesthetic fantasies revealed in *M* responses. In support of this interpretation, she noted that nine experimental subjects, compared with four in the control group, had used movement as a primary determinant of *S* on retest. She proposed, therefore, that presence of primary *S* in a record be taken as a reliable sign of capacity for *M*, even when no actual movement response appears.

Lerner's report demonstrates the value of sound methodology in the study of *S*. She used alternate forms of a standard set of ink blots, one before and one after the experimental treatment; these were the 22-card halves of Form A of the HIT, with odd-numbered cards administered in the pre-test. Control for *R* was accomplished by obtaining only two responses to each card; primary and secondary *S* were scored and tabulated separately; satisfactory inter-judge reliability in scoring *S* was reported; and nonparametric tests were employed to evaluate the results.

METAPSYCHOLOGICAL CONSIDERATIONS

The phenotypical character of "negativism" and "oppositional trend" has retarded the alignment of *S* with genotypical concepts in contemporary theories of personality. Bleuler (1912) acknowledged that negativism "does not show itself uniformly but at times is present and at times is absent in accordance with the psychical constellation . . . we are not as yet able to distinguish between the various psychic processes which call forth negativism" (p. 9). Levy's (1955) analysis of oppositional syndromes and oppositional behavior notes that the purpose of such syndromes is to favor the individual's separateness and independence, and he concludes that "what has been called negativism, resistance and oppositional behavior . . . has its origin in a basic protective function . . . We have lost sight of their original positive values . . . of the adaptive features of the mechanism" (p. 222-223). Allport (1937) summed up the situation with his observation that generally negativistic and *contredisant* individuals are encountered too infrequently to justify construction of "negativism" as a measurable dimension of personality. Nevertheless, the search has continued. In their study of response sets, Couch and Keniston (1960) located a group of extreme naysayers for clinical assessment; the typical individuals in this group turned out to be cautious, rational, intellectually controlled and stimulus-rejecting introverts.

The Striving Towards Active Mastery. In an effort to understand the basic personality correlates of S it may be helpful to make use of Freud's (1924, p. 128) concept of the *Bewältigungstrieb*—a "general instinct of mastery." The meaning of this term in ego psychology has been discussed at length by Hendrick (1942, 1943 a, 1943 b), who also credits Angyal (1941) with having formulated the same concept "in an especially constructive way" (1943 b, p. 563).

Hendrick deals with the mastery impulse as one of the so-called ego instincts, others being hunger and self-preservation. According to his formulation, one aim of the mastery instinct is "to control or alter a piece of the environment, an ego-alien situation, by the skillful use of perceptual, intellectual and motor techniques" (1943 a, p. 314). He feels that the mastery-impulse hypothesis provides "an adequate theory of the need to integrate which impels development and use of the executant functions of the ego" (p. 327). In short, *self*-mastery is an indispensable prerequisite in the development of mature and adaptive independence vis-à-vis the environment. It is not to be confused with attempts to dominate and control others, and it should be distinguished from the concept of "aggression." The latter term, according to Hendrick, refers to destructive and possibly disintegrative id impulses, especially to forces motivated by a desire to destroy the rival for a sexual object or the antagonist of a narcissistic need; the aims of the *Bewältigungstrieb* are, by contrast, both useful and constructive. Pointing out that ego pleasures exist which can be differentiated from id gratifications, Hendrick insists that reduction of tensions associated with the drive to attain active mastery is undoubtedly one source of ego pleasure.

In Fenichel's (1945) discussion of the development of active mastery, he takes a position somewhat different from that of Hendrick. Fenichel argues that although the capacity for mastery may depend upon constitutional factors, it is not a separate and specific instinct but depends upon "all of the individual's previous experiences" (p. 117). Active mastery, according to Fenichel, is achieved by the gradual acquisition of ability to bind primitive reaction impulses with countercathexes. In this way, for example, the child's play evolves from mere attempts at discharge to mastery of the external world by means of repeated practice. What happens is that before engaging in a feared activity, the individual passes through an anxious tension of expectation, the overcoming of which is enjoyed. The active repetition, on a limited scale, of what has been experienced passively is one of the principal mechanisms for fighting anxiety. Within the mastery impulse itself there may be a latent tendency to compulsive repetition. "The type of pleasure achieved," says Fenichel, "proves that the person is by no means really convinced of his mastery" (p. 480). The distinction between the impulse to master, on the one hand, and hostility or aggression, on the other, is clarified in Fenichel's observation that mastery can be achieved in the realm of any instinct. Hostile and aggressive impulses must themselves be mastered by the very ego whose autonomy they threaten.

There is something analogous to the latent tendency for compulsive repetition which Fenichel says characterizes the mastery impulse in the fact that each individual's rate of S emission appears to be relatively stable and consistent. It seems that many persons find it necessary to reassure themselves regularly that the capacity to exercise intrapersonal mastery remains intact. Yet the rate of S emission seems not to be highly correlated with transient changes in external events; it follows, therefore, that forces conceived as having power to determine S-emission rate, though perhaps perceived as arising in reaction to environmental conditions, actually emanate from within, from the unconscious regions of the personality, and so might properly be regarded as ego-alien. Inasmuch as conflict over self-determination or self-government may be found at the core of nearly every personality disorder, it is easy to see how Rorschach (1942) could have written so long ago that "study of the space responses defines the neurotic aspects of the record" (p. 200).

The Trend Towards Autonomy. Angyal (1965) considers mastery strivings to be manifestations of a basic endogenous process oriented toward enhancement of the organism's autonomy. The trend toward increased autonomy has no fixed objective but only a general direction. Because the organism lives in a world independent of itself, its autonomy is only partial and must be asserted against heteronomous surroundings. "Every single organismic process," according to Angyal, "is always a resultant of two components, autonomy and heteronomy—self-government and government from the outside" (p. 6). The most direct expression of the tendency toward increased autonomy is "the drive to act, to make things happen for the mere joy of action and for the sake of experiencing oneself as the cause of changes" (p. 9).

Impairments or distortions of this tendency are often seen in clinical practice and appear as either a lack or an excess of autonomous striving. When the lack is generalized, the person behaves like a straw in the wind whose course is completely determined by external happenings; extreme dependency and slavish conformism are familiar examples. Angyal also describes a syndrome of pseudo-autonomy diagnosed as "hysteria with negativistic defenses" (p. 148) which, if occurring in a schizophrenic decompensation, would probably be classified with the catatonic reactions. Manifestations of excessive concern for autonomy include neurotic forms of rebelliousness, intolerance of interference, and repetitive "proving" of oneself by reasserting one's own competence.

The relevance of Angyal's concept of autonomy to the white-space response becomes apparent when it is recognized that figure-ground reversals require an increase of autonomous activity in order to neutralize and counteract heteronomous influences in the stimulus configuration. Appearance of a figure-ground reversal, and hence of the primary S response, becomes an indication that the person has sought reduction of tensions associated with the need for autonomy; the frequency of such occurrences thus reflects the extent to which an individual is concerned with the repetitive need to experience a sense of personal competence and mastery.

The role of competence as an aspect of autonomy has been elaborated in detail by White (1972), and his concepts contribute the rationale for using white-space responses as a criterion variable in M. L. Stein's (1973a) study of the personality correlates of left-handedness. Noting that left-handers are traditionally stereotyped as oppositional, Finn and Neuringer (1968) had already shown that left-handed persons have a higher rate of S-emission than right-handers, and Stein reasoned that left-handed individuals living in a right-handed culture must experience more intense challenges to their sense of competence and autonomy. He found that left-handed individuals, compared with right-handers, not only produce more S but also describe themselves on the Gough Adjective Check List as more "autonomous" and, in addition, are more likely to be rated by their immediate superiors as more "oppositional." (See p. 119, supra.) Drawing upon Shapiro's (1965) discussion of personality styles, Stein interpreted the self-descriptive scores and rate of S-emission as confirmation of his assumption that striving for autonomy is demonstrably more salient an issue for the left-handers in our society.

CLINICAL CONSIDERATIONS

When a clinician's perception of the structure of a client's personality is mediated by the configuration of an entire Rorschach protocol, the contribution of primary S is contingent upon its status relative to R. Preliminary judgments classify the salience of S in the record along a continuum ranging from "deficient" through "optimal" to "excessive," and also provide an estimate of the degree of confidence with which such classification has been made. The soundness of these judgments rests upon adaptation levels acquired by the clinician during previous assessment procedures involving the ink blots, together with whatever normative and statistical data are available in the literature (e.g., Slemon, Neiger and Quirk, 1965).

Total R in Relation to S. It is possible to specify the range of R that is expected to accompany a given number of S. For example, when S is absent, R seldom exceeds 30; but when one or more S is present, R is rarely less than 30. The presence of primary S in a brief record, therefore, is often interpreted as signifying deliberate withholding of R by a stubbornly negativistic client; under these circumstances, the smaller the R, *ceteris paribus*, the greater the pernicious salience of S. Incidentally, somewhat similar reasoning has been applied to interpretations of performance on the WAIS digit-span subtest when more digits are recalled backward than forward. Noting that such behavior is usually taken as a sign of negativism, Fox and Blatt (1969) found that patients who recall fewer digits forward than backward also give more S on the Rorschach than do their matched controls.

Excessive emission of S, when it occurs, can be identified in protocols of any length, but deficiency of S cannot be detected in records having less than 30 responses. The amount of information conveyed by S increases as R is increased beyond 30, and examiners who value such information bear in mind that the production of S is facilitated by prolonged viewing and multiple responding. Given a specific number of R in excess of 30, one can anticipate with some confidence and within a fairly narrow range the precise number of S to be regarded as "optimal."

When S production is at an optimal level, the usual presumption is that, at least with respect to the achievement of active mastery, the ego is functioning adequately. Any noticeable deviation from this level deserves attention. Departures in either direction give reason to believe that the ego is operating defensively in its efforts to ward off anxiety associated with the need for autonomy and active mastery.

Cognitive Differentiation and S. Individual differences in the rate of S emission are remarkably stable and persistent; the rate appears to be unaffected by even major changes in the life situation, and it seems to be singularly resistant to the effects of most types of treatment. Its interpretative significance, therefore, is ordinarily characterological rather than situational or symptomatic, and relationships between its overt behavioral correlates and the underlying dynamics are likely to be equivocal and indirect. Nevertheless, its linkage to the concept of cognitive differentiation provides a useful frame of reference within which to accommodate observations concerning the emission of S and a clinician's overall assessment of the client's potentialities.

A substantial number of generalizations about the personality concomitants of cognitive differentiation have been validated in recent years (Witkin, 1965). Some of these generalizations are relevant to the interpretation of S and may be summarized in the following way.

The level of cognitive differentiation is not to be confused with the degree of personality integration. These two dimensions seem to be relatively orthogonal, although the more complex forms of integration may be seen somewhat more frequently at higher levels of differentiation. When integration is impaired, there is reason to believe that the impairment may be more likely to occur at extremely high or extremely low levels of differentiation. The nature of the impairment tends to vary with the level of differentiation at which it occurs.

Difficulties associated with extreme field dependence and deficient production of S include severe identity problems, inadequately developed controls, and deep-seated dependency needs. Hysterical character disorders and inadequate personalities are typically found at the lower levels of differentiation, as are hallucinated psychotics and catatonic schizophrenics.

At the level of extreme field independence with excessive production of S, individuals who suffer impaired integration are more likely to have maintained a sense of separate—albeit often somewhat peculiar—identity, and to rely mainly upon intellectualization and isolation as defenses. Obsessive-compulsive character disorders and ambulatory schizophrenics with well-developed defensive structures are typically found at the higher levels of differentiation, as are deluded psychotics and paranoid schizophrenics.

S and Psychiatric Nosology. The foregoing generalizations furnish elements of a provisional orientation for the examiner approaching interpretation of S, but emphasis must be given to the observation that no specific psychiatric diagnoses have been unequivocally associated with differential rates of S-emission. Consider, for example, the findings reported by several investigators concerned with the antisocial character disorder.

Scores on both S and the MMPI Psychopathic Deviate (Pd) scale are said to reflect a tendency to disregard society's rules, be they legal, moral, or otherwise. As we have seen, authoritarian supervisors regularly perceive high-S subordinates as less obedient than low-S individuals (see p. 000, supra). And Boss (1931) concluded that, among the antisocial psychopaths in his caseload, "the more white space responses a subject produces, the greater the evidence for deviation with respect to social standards." Unfortunately, Boss did not have a comparison group, and his data do not clearly differentiate psychopaths from other individuals. Moreover, S may also be associated with the ability to evade sanctions that society imposes upon apprehended offenders. In a study by Rosen (1952), S and Pd were significantly related, but his institutionalized psychopaths produced less S than did the other patients in his comparison group. Similarly, Schachtel (1951) discovered that juvenile offenders in a correctional institution produced fewer S than did the youths in a public-school comparison group.

S and the Mechanisms of Defense. The perception of a figure within any two-dimensional display depends upon interaction between objective properties of the stimulus and autochthonous processes within an observer. Perceptual reversal of figure and ground results from spontaneous activity initiated by the observer, and the relative frequency of this activity provides a useful datum for interpretation by the clinician. If this datum is taken as an indication of the intensity of striving for autonomy or active mastery, the clinician will need to relate it to the client's unique personality configuration, with special reference to the preferred defense mechanisms and the person's location on a basic continuum between activity and passivity. If the occurrence of S is viewed in the light of (a) general Rorschach assumptions regarding personality values of M, C, F, etc., and (b) clinically accepted notions about dynamisms that operate in conjunction with the various defense mechanisms, then the following revised adaptation of Rorschach's original interpretative scheme—which took into account mainly the experience balance—may be tentatively proposed.

The first step is to determine from other aspects of the person's protocol, usually from the movement and color responses as described in Chapters 6, 7, and 8, whether the basic orientation is passive or aggressive, and whether impulses from this orientation are being warded off, acted out, or sublimated. Ordinarily, these inferences are not attempted from S alone; once they have been made, however, the rate of S emission enables the clinician to formulate reasonably accurate statements concerning the vigor of attempts to achieve mastery over inner impulses or, conversely, to disguise and conceal them.

When the output of S is deficient and the inner orientation is passive, the dependency needs are either being acted out or are sublimated; acting out leads to extreme submissiveness and slavish conformism, while sublimation often looks like masochism. If the inner orientation is aggressive, the aggression is being warded off by means of repression and inhibition, and the interpersonal facade is likely to be cramped, rigid, indolent, or naive.

When the S rate is optimal and the inner stance is aggressive, the aggressions are either being acted out or sublimated. If the inner stance is passive and the passive needs are being warded off by means of repression and reaction formation, the individual is likely to be seen as domineering, demanding, obnoxious, or irresponsible and may display histrionic rebelliousness or hysterical intolerance of interference.

When the output of S is excessive, the underlying orientation is aggressive, but the aggressive impulses may or may not be acted out. If they are being acted out, the individual is likely to be self-willed, destructive, or disobedient. If they are being warded off, the mechanisms may include reaction formation, isolation, or projection. Which of these mechanisms the client prefers is usually not indicated by S alone but may be inferred from the structure of the entire protocol. If the individual is using reaction formations against ego-alien aggression, most of the time the person will seem to be sweetly reasonable, compliant, and scrupulously trustworthy. If isolation and intellectualization are the preferred defenses, the individual will probably appear to be obstinate, pedantic, vacillating, and compulsive. Finally, if projection turns out to be the principal defense, the individual is likely to be suspicious, truculent, grandiose, or deluded.

SUMMARY

In this chapter, a core meaning of the primary S response has been developed by coordinating the perceptual process of figure-ground reversal to the Freudian concept of a drive to achieve active mastery. Some contemporary theory builders have identified the striving for mastery with a more basic trend towards increased autonomy. Alignment of the meaning of S with these concepts enriches the usefulness of Rorschach interpretations by facilitating the incorporation of implications and generalizations from a systematic theory of personality.

Rorschach's original description of S as an indicator of "some sort of oppositional trend" attributed unequivocally pejorative implications to this response in patterning out the structure of an individual personality, but subsequent experience with the ink blots has shown that S is usually a manifestation of more positive values. Indeed, the maintenance of autonomous mastery is regarded as one of the principal components of ego strength.

Ideal personality integration is thought to be achieved when each component of ego strength, including the trend towards autonomous mastery, is functioning at an optimal, rather than a maximal, level, and it is recognized that the constructive potentials reflected in S may be effectively negated by the particular configuration of impulses and defenses in which it occurs.

The secondary S response, which uses the white space but does not entail complete reversal of figure and ground, was briefly discussed. A consensus holds that it may have unfavorable connotations, but in light of its unreliable and arcane character, systematic interpretation is not recommended.

The primary S response, on the other hand, appears to have been one of Rorschach's most provocative discoveries, and although its true meaning remains to be more fully explored, it gives promise of becoming an indispensible adjunct in the art of dynamic personality assessment.

REFERENCE NOTE

1. Holtzman, W. H. Personal communication, November, 1974.

BIBLIOGRAPHY

Allport, G. W. *Personality: a psychological interpretation.* New York: Holt, 1937
Angyal, A. *Foundations for a science of personality.* New York: Commonwealth Fund, 1941.
Angyal, A. *Neurosis and treatment: a holistic theory.* New York: Wiley, 1965.
Bandura, A. A study of some of the psychological processes associated with the Rorschach white space response. Unpublished doctoral dissertation, University of Iowa, 1952.
Bandura, A. The Rorschach white space response and "oppositional" behavior. *Journal of Consulting Psychology,* 1954, **18**, 17-21. (a)
Bandura, A. The Rorschach white space response and perceptual reversal. *Journal of Experimental Psychology,* 1954, **48**, 113-118. (b)
Beck, S. J., and Molish, H. B. *Rorschach's test. Vol. 2. A variety of personality pictures* (Rev. ed.). New York: Grune & Stratton, 1967.
Belden, A. W., and Baughman, E. E. The effects of figure-ground contrast upon perception as evaluated by a modified Rorschach technique. *Journal of Consulting Psychology,* 1954, **18**, 29-34.
Billig, O., and Sullivan, D. J. Prognostic data in chronic alcoholism. *Rorschach Research Exchange,* 1942, **6**, 117-125.
Bleuler, E. The theory of schizophrenic negativism. *Nervous and Mental Disease Monographs,* 1912, No. 11.
Bohm, E. *Lehrbuch der Rorschach-Psychodiagnostik.* (4th ed.) Bern: Huber, 1972.
Borgatta, E. F., and Eschenbach, A. E. Factor analysis of Rorschach variables and behavioral observation. *Psychological Reports,* 1955, **1**, 129-136.
Boss, M. Psychologisch-charakterologische Untersuchungen bei antisozialen Psychopathen mit Hilfe des Rorschachschen Formdeutversuches. *Zeitschrift für die gesamte Neurologie und Psychiatrie,* 1931, **133**, 544-575.
Buhler, C., Buhler, K., and Lefever, D. W. *Development of the basic Rorschach score with manual of directions* (Rev.). Los Angeles: Rorschach Standardization Studies, No. 1, 1949.
Carson, R. C. The validity scales. In J. N. Butcher (ed.) *MMPI: Research developments and clinical application.* New York: McGraw Hill, 1969.
Couch, A., and Keniston, K. Yeasayers and naysayers: Agreeing response set as a personality variable. *Journal of Abnormal and Social Psychology,* 1960, **60**, 151-174.
Counts, R. M., and Mensh, I. H. Personality characteristics in hypnotically-induced hostility. *Journal of Clinical Psychology,* 1950, **6**, 325-330.
DeKoninck, J-M., and Crabbé-Declève, G. Field dependence and Rorschach white-space figure-ground reversal responses. *Perceptual and Motor Skills,* 1971, **33**, 1191-1194.
Endacott, J. L. The results of 100 male juvenile delinquents on the Rorschach ink-blot test. *Journal of Criminal Psychopathology,* 1941, **3**, 41-50.
Eschenbach, A. E. The relationship of basic Rorschach scoring categories to observed three-man-group interaction behavior. (Doctoral dissertation, University of Florida, 1955). University Microfilms No. 12,769.
Eschenbach, A. E., and Borgatta, E. F. Testing behavior hypotheses with the Rorschach: an exploration in validation. *Journal of Consulting Psychology,* 1955, **19**, 267-273.
Exner, J. E., Jr. *The Rorschach: a comprehensive system.* New York: Wiley, 1974.
Fenichel, O. *The psychoanalytic theory of neurosis.* New York: Norton, 1945.
Finn, J. A., and Neuringer, C. Left-handedness: a study of its relation to opposition. *Journal of Projective Techniques and Personality Assessment,* 1968, **32**, 49-52.

Fonda, C. P. The nature and meaning of the Rorschach white space response. *Journal of Abnormal and Social Psychology*, 1951, **46**, 367-377.

Fox, E., and Blatt, S. J. An attempt to test assumptions about some indications of negativism on psychological tests. *Journal of Consulting and Clinical Psychology*, 1969, **33**, 365-366.

Freud, S. The predisposition to obsessional neurosis. In *Collected papers* (Vol. 2). London: Hogarth, 1924.

Goldfarb, W. A definition and validation of obsessional trends in the Rorschach examination of adolescents. *Rorschach Research Exchange*, 1943, **7**, 81-108.

Hendrick, I. Instinct and the ego during infancy. *Psychoanalytic Quarterly*, 1942, **11**, 33-58.

Hendrick, I. Work and the pleasure principle. *Psychoanalytic Quarterly*, 1943, **12**, 311-329. (a)

Hendrick, I. The discussion of the "instinct to master." *Psychoanalytic Quarterly*, 1943, **12**, 561-565. (b)

Hill, E. F. *The Holtzman Inkblot Technique: a handbook for clinical application*. San Francisco: Jossey-Bass, 1972.

Holtzman, W. H., Thorpe, J. S., Swartz, J. D., and Herron, E. W. *Inkblot perception and personality*. Austin: University of Texas, 1961.

Ingram, W. Prediction of aggression from the Rorschach. *Journal of Consulting Psychology*, 1954, **18**, 23-28.

Kalter, N., and Marsden, G. Response productivity in Rorschach research: a caution on method. *Journal of Projective Techniques and Personality Assessment*, 1970, **34** (3), 10-15.

Klebanoff, S. G. The Rorschach test in an analysis of personality changes in general paresis. *Journal of Personality*, 1949, **17**, 261-272.

Koffka, K. *Principles of gestalt psychology*. New York: Harcourt, Brace, 1935.

Lerner, B. Rorschach movement and dreams: a validation study using drug-induced dream deprivation. *Journal of Abnormal Psychology*, 1966, **71**, 75-86.

Levy, D. M. Oppositional syndromes and oppositional behavior. In *Psychopathology of childhood*. (P. H. Hoch and J. Zubin, eds.) New York: Grune & Stratton, 1955.

Linn, L. The Rorschach test in the evaluation of military personnel. *Rorschach Research Exchange*, 1946, **10**, 20-27.

Lord, E. Experimentally induced variations in Rorschach performance. *Psychological Monographs*, 1950, **64** (10, Whole No. 316).

McCall, R. J. Review of the Rorschach. In O. K. Buros (ed.), *Personality tests and reviews*. Highland Park, New Jersey: Gryphon Press, 1970.

Meehl, P. E. Comments on the invasion of privacy issue. In J. N. Butcher (ed.), *MMPI: research developments and clinical application*. New York: McGraw Hill, 1969.

Melville, H. The whiteness of the whale. Chap. 42 in *Moby Dick or the white whale*. New York: Dodd, Mead, 1942. (Originally published, 1851.)

Milgram, S. *Obedience to authority*. New York: Harper & Row, 1973.

Murray, D. C. An investigation of the Rorschach white space response in an extratensive experience balance as a measure of outwardly directed opposition. (Doctoral dissertation, Northwestern University, 1954). University Microfilms No. 9,260.

Murray, D. C. An investigation of the Rorschach white space response in an extratensive experience balance as a measure of outwardly directed opposition. *Journal of Projective Techniques*, 1957, **21**, 40-46. (a)

Murray, D. C. White space on the Rorschach: interpretation and validity. *Journal of Projective Techniques*, 1957, **21**, 47-53. (b)

Nasielski, S. Remise en question de l'interprétation des résponses localisées dans les espaces blancs (Dbl.) au test de Rorschach. In *Sixiéme Congrés International du Rorschach et des Méthodes Projectives* (Vol. 2). Paris, 1965.

Nelson, W. D. An evaluation of the white space response on the Rorschach as figure-ground reversal and intellectual opposition. (Doctoral dissertation, Michigan State College, 1954). University Microfilms No. 11,147.

Oberholzer, E. Rorschach's experiment and the Alorese. In C. DuBois (ed.), *The people of Alor*. Minneapolis: University of Minnesota Press, 1944.

Rabin, A. I. Rorschach test findings on a group of conscientious objectors. *American Journal of Orthopsychiatry*, 1945, **15**, 514-519.

Rapaport, D., Gill, M., and Schafer, R. *Diagnostic psychological testing: the theory, statistical evaluation, and diagnostic application of a battery of tests* (Vol. 2). Chicago: Year Book Publishers, 1946.

Ray, J. B. The meaning of Rorschach white space responses. (Doctoral dissertation, University of Oklahoma, 1955). University Microfilms No. 14,018.

Ray, J. B. The meaning of Rorschach white space responses. *Journal of Projective Techniques*, 1963, **27**, 315-323.

Reik, T. *The search within*. New York: Aronson, 1974.

Rorschach, H. *Psychodiagnostics, a diagnostic test based on perception*. (Trans. P. Lemkau & B. Kronenburg.) Bern: Huber, 1942.

Rosen, E. MMPI and Rorschach correlates of the Rorschach white space response. *Journal of Clinical Psychology*, 1952, **8**, 283-288.

Rosenberg, N. An investigation of the use of the question-mark response in objective personality tests. (Doctoral dissertation, Syracuse University, 1954). University Microfilms No. 10, 415.

Roth, E. Zwischenraumdeutungen im Rorschachversuch und ihr Zusammenhang mit Wahrnehmungsgesetzlichkeiten. *Schweizerische Zeitschrift für Psychologie und ihre Anwendungen*, 1962, **21**, 339-348.

Rubin, E. *Synsoplevede Figurer*. Copenhagen: Gyldendal, 1915.

Schachtel, E. G. Notes on the Rorschach tests of 500 juvenile delinquents and a control group of 500 non-delinquent adolescents. *Journal of Projective Techniques*, 1951, **15**, 144-172.

Schachter, M. Contribution a l'etude des interprétations des espaces blancs (détails intermaculaires, Dbl.) dans le test de Rorschach et de leur signification. *Annales Medicopsychologiques*, 1970, **1**, 229-351.

Scharmann, T. Actualgenetisches zum Rorschachtest. *Zeitschrift für experimentelle und angewandte Psychologie*, 1959, **6**, 519-533.

Shaffer, L. F. The blot's escutcheon. *Contemporary Psychology*, 1961, **6**, 420-422.

Shaffer, L. F. Review of the Rorschach. In O. K. Buros (ed.), *Personality tests and reviews*. Highland Park, New Jersey: Gryphon Press, 1970.

Shapiro, D. *Neurotic styles*. New York: Basic Books, 1965.

Slemon, A. G., Neiger, S., and Quirk, D. A. Adjusting for the total number of responses in calculating the Rorschach apperception type. *Journal of Projective Techniques and Personality Assessment*, 1965, **29**, 516-521.

Stein, M. I. Personality factors involved in the temporal development of Rorschach responses. *Journal of Projective Techniques*, 1949, **13**, 355-414.

Stein, M. L. Personality correlates of left-handedness. (Doctoral dissertation, Boston University, 1973). University Microfilms No. 73-23,518. (a)

Stein, M. L. An empirical validation of the relation between Rorschach white-space and oppositionality. *Perceptual and Motor Skills*, 1973, **37**, 375-381. (b)

Suares, N. Personality development in adolescence. *Rorschach Research Exchange*, 1938, **3**, 2-11.

Weltman, R., and Wolfson, W. Rorschach S: oppositional tendencies or mastery strivings. *Perceptual and Motor Skills*, 1964, **18**, 821-824.

White, R. W. Motivation reconsidered: the concept of competence. *Psychological Review*, 1959, **61**, 297-333.

Witkin, H. A. Psychological differentiation and forms of pathology. *Journal of Abnormal Psychology*, 1965, **70**, 317-336.

Witkin, H. A., Dyk, R. B., Faterson, H. F., Goodenough, D. R., and Karp, S. A. *Psychological differentiation*. New York: Wiley, 1962.

Zulliger, H. *Jugendliche Diebe im Rorschach Formdeutversuch. Eine seelenkundliche und erzieherische Studie*. Bern: Haupt, 1938.

CATEGORIES OF ANALYSIS: DETERMINANTS

5 | Sheldon J. Korchin
and Dale G. Larson

FORM PERCEPTION
AND EGO FUNCTIONING

I

Perceiving, whether highly structured objects or inkblots, always represents a joint interaction of the organism and the stimulus. "The percept . . . develops as an organized response to a matrix of stimulation in which the structure of the environment and the structure-giving tendencies of the perceiver converge in the determination of a unitary response" (Murphy, 1947). The more structured the stimulus, the more likely will field organizational properties decide the final perception; the less the external structure, the greater will be the contribution of the individual perceiver. However, the personality is active in every perceptual act, whether the outcome is a personalized distortion or the attainment of a veridical concept of reality. The interpretation of form responses in the Rorschach depends on the assumption that in neither case does perception consist simply of the passive reception of "what is there." In Stern's (1937) classic dictum, there is "Keine Gestalt ohne Gestalter." Humans organize selectively, and the percept bears the imprint of individual styles of cognition.

In this chapter the adequacy of Rorschach form perception, interpreted as an index of the integrity of ego functioning, will be examined. In a strict sense, the final Rorschach response involves

159

more than a narrowly defined perceptual act; rather it is the resultant of a coordinated series of cognitive activities in a total process of forming, testing, critically evaluating, and communicating perceptual hypotheses. The term "form perception" is used in the present context as a shorthand designation for this total process. "Form level," operationally $F+\%$,[1] describes the accuracy with which the form qualities of the blot are used. Although often described as "ambiguous stimuli" or, in Rorschach's original phrase, "indeterminate forms," the inkblots do have contours and are in varying degree organized. The responses given by a subject may be more or less congruent with the form of the blot. This dimension of Rorschach performance—the degree to which the subject is attentive to, or departs from, the "reality" represented in the blots—can therefore be taken as a measure of the subject's ability to deal with, and his respect for, reality in general. In this general sense, it becomes a measure of ego strength, or at least the central component of reality testing. Accurate form perception is a necessary, if not sufficient, characteristic of a strong and mature ego.

From the beginning, the scoring and interpretation of the number and quality of form responses have been of central importance in all approaches to the Rorschach. Rorschach workers have, however differed in their conception and treatment of form. Controversy, over the past 50 years, has "muddied the form level waters" (Weiner, 1966) and innovations in form level scoring have usually failed to achieve widespread use. Recently, however, there is new interest and fresh streams of investigation are revealing the value of systematic study of what Rorschach referred to as "sharpness" or "clarity of form visualization." Rorschach simply determined the "percentage of clearly visualized forms" by dichotomizing good and poor form responses on a combination of statistical and empathic criteria. Since Rorschach, two main trends have emerged in the evaluation of form quality. In the Rorschach-Beck-Hertz tradition, statistical criteria of frequency of occurrence have been used to assess form quality. Analysis is limited to form-determined responses, and responses are scored in plus or minus terms, with no finer distinctions. By contrast, Klopfer, Piotrowski, Rapaport and Schafer, and Mayman rely more on the qualitative judgments of the examiner. At the same time, they have, with the exception of Piotrowski,

---

[1] For explanation of scoring symbols, see Appendix, p. 609 ff. [Editor].

introduced finer, qualitative distinctions in order to evaluate aspects of perceptual appropriateness other than "accurary" as such.

We will examine these various approaches to form level scoring and interpretation, as part of an effort to conceptualize the relation between form perception and ego functioning. Some of the differences in form perception among clinical and personality groups will also be examined, and an attempt will be made to distinguish the mechanisms responsible for good or poor form responses. Finally, we will consider the question of what constitutes optimal form perception.

II

According to Rorschach (1921), a high proportion of $F+$ responses depends on: (1) the ability to concentrate; (2) the availability of clear memory images (engrams); (3) the ability to bring such memory images into consciousness; and (4) the ability to select from among these the most fitting for the stimulus. It assumes control of the perceptual and associational processes and a capacity for critical interpretation. For Rorschach these abilities were the *sine qua non* of intelligence. More generally, he related form to "rationality" and "disciplined thinking;" it is an application of "la fonction du réel."

The production of $F+$ responses is dependent on the ability to organize, integrate and control perceptual and associational processes and to bring these into appropriate relation with one another. It depends on the capacity to block the intrusion of unconscious and emotional factors. Achieving adequate form perception, as Rapaport, Schafer and Gill (1946) emphasized, results from the individual's capacity to delay the discharge of impulse, thus allowing for the critical development of the reality-appropriate response. Time is required for the integration of $F+$ responses, as Stein (1949) showed in his studies of Rorschach performance under tachistoscopic conditions. Compared to the more immediate and passive color response (see Chapter 1 in this volume), the form response requires greater organizational effort. Thus Beck (1948) states, "F plus, then, is the critical work of the intellect." It depends on the effective functioning of the highest levels of cerebral organization.

Over the years $F+$ has come to be viewed, more broadly, as a general index of ego strength. Commenting on the then current interpretations of form level, Kimball (1948) noted that "Beck's interpretation of $F+$ and $F-$ response as indicative of strength of Ego looks promising, but needs further clarification and research before it can be accepted as valid." Both research support and conceptual clarification were forthcoming, and today form quality is most consistently viewed as a measure of the reality testing aspect of ego strength (Klopfer, et al., 1954; Weiner, 1966; Piotrowski, 1957; Beck, 1966, 1968; Mayman, 1970). Perhaps the clearest expression of this trend is found in Mayman's system. Each of his form-level scoring categories is interpreted as reflecting a particular mode or style of testing reality.

Beck extends good reality testing to the social domain: "Adequate reality testing is indicated in accurate form perception $(F+)$. Insofar as the patient sees the form which healthy persons see, he perceives as they do. Extended into the function of judgment, the testee's judgment is like that of healthy persons. A further inference is that his values are consistent with those of people about him, of his society. The degree to which one respects the values of his society is also the measure of one's respect for himself. It is ego. $F+$, Rorschach's *gute Formen*, is thus a measure of the person's 'good form' not only in the test's technique. It is good form socially" (Beck, 1966, p. 95).

III

The concept of reality testing, on closer consideration, turns out to be more complex and multidimensional than might seem true at first glance. Important, for example, is the distinction between the appropriateness of judgment in the external world (outer reality testing) and accurate knowledge of one's inner experiences (inner reality testing). The complexity in the concept is illustrated by Bellak, Hurvich, and Gediman's statement that:

> . . . in evaluating reality testing in an individual with constricted, compulsive personality features, the ability to distinguish internal from external may be quite good, and accuracy of perception may be quite high, while inner reality testing is poor, the latter because this individual tends not to be aware of inner psychological events and reactions (1973, p. 271).

Thus, Bellak, Hurvich and Gediman distinguish three components of reality testing: (1) the ability to distinguish between ideas and perceptions; (2) the accuracy of perception; and (3) the adequacy of inner reality testing. In a similar vein, Meyer and Caruth (1964) suggest that outer and inner reality testing might be differentially reflected in form and content aspects of the Rorschach test. Thus, a disturbance in outer reality testing of the sort which might lead to misperceptions of the environment would be revealed in $F-$ responses. On the other hand, disturbances of inner reality testing which might be evidenced by an inability to judge the appropriateness of a fantasy could be reflected in the Rorschach by the attribution of inappropriate or bizarre qualities to the percept. As examples, Meyer and Caruth offer two responses to Card V: (1) A bat, eating people. Vultures; and (2) A cat. The first response (suggesting failure of inner reality testing) is an unrealistic interpretation of a correctly perceived object; the second (suggesting deficient outer reality testing) is a realistic concept arbitrarily assigned to a misperceived reality. As noted earlier, these distinctions remind us that a co-ordinated series of cognitive acts, rather than a simply defined perceptual act, is involved in the formation of Rorschach responses. It was Schafer (1954) who introduced the concept of "spread" within a single response, noting the ways in which a given response might reflect reality adaptiveness in some ways and ego disruption in others.

In an important theoretical contribution to the understanding of Rorschach form perception, Schachtel (1966) notes the ways in which the qualities of form responses reflect the nature of an individual's relatedness to reality. The abstractive, identifying, and object-ifying functions of form perception cannot be fulfilled unless perception is accurate and a firm "perceptual hold" of reality is maintained. Individual form responses can be located on a continuum of "type of relatedness" as well as one of "accuracy" ($F+$ to $F-$). The kinds of inferences permitted by such qualitative distinctions among accurate form responses are illustrated in Schachtel's discussion of Rapaport's (1946) "special $F+$" and ordinary $F+$ response categories:

> The special $F+$, thus, tend to be based on an attitude of flexible openness toward and interest in the inkblot, freedom of association, decisiveness of perceptual grasp and organization. Hence, they do not point to inhibition, repression, and impersonal objectivity and do not constitute an impoverished

type of perception. They tend to correlate positively with a dilated experience type, and form perception of a convincingness equal to the special $F+$ is also likely to occur in responses where form is combined with shading, color, and particularly kinesthetic factors. The ordinary $F+$, on the other hand, tend to represent the attitudes and traits traditionally ascribed to all form responses, and they may go together with a coartated as well as a dilated experience type. (Schachtel, 1966, p. 116).

While Rorschach himself did not distinguish qualitatively, for example, between the fairly accurate form response and one of superior quality, he was interested in the sort of psychological dimensions Schachtel is discussing; he was concerned to understand the differences between the poetic and prosaic in psychological functioning. Indeed, Schachtel is here approaching the significance of qualitative distinctions among types of form responses with some of the integrative zeal Rorschach applied to the test as a whole.

IV

Scoring form level: What is accuracy?[2]

The problem of scoring starts from a truly different question: "What is accuracy?" Inherent in the definition of good form—that the percept offered fit the "realities" of the blot—is the problem of knowing what that reality is and how to judge that the given response fits. Basically two types of criteria have been used—one statistical and the other empathic—each derived from a somewhat different answer to the question.

Frequency of occurrence. One way of deciding what is accurate is in terms of the responses actually given by a sizable sample of normal individuals. On probabalistic grounds alone, it would seem reasonable that pathological thinking would usually lead to diversity of response, whereas reality-directed thinking would more usually result in greater

---

[2] The purpose of this section is to examine some of the methodological issues involved in scoring, rather than to consider in any detail the several proposed scoring systems. For critical reviews of alternate approaches to the scoring of form, see Kimball (1950a), Weiner (1966), Exner (1969) and Mayman (1970).

commonness of response. A large group of healthy individuals, from the same culture, sharing basic experiences, should more often give similar than diverse responses to the same stimulus. On this basis, frequency of response can be taken to define reality. Thus, Beck et al. state:

> Our starting assumption is that since there is no accuracy, or reality at all within these originally chance inkblots, therefore the forms which these normal people perceive in them are the absolute accuracy or reality that obtains in the blots. (1950, p. 263)

In establishing standards for plus and minus, Beck takes as a basic criterion that $F+$ should differentiate healthy from unhealthy psychological functioning.

> Under differentiation I have in mind selections of persons of good intellectual control who see their world accurately, separating these from those who see less of the world in this manner, and from those who twist much of it. The groups in our society who see their world in clear outlines, are presumably they who make up the rank and file, and those who run our society—that is, the average and superior. The next premise is that the forms they see in the Rorschach test are the reality that obtains in these figures. They are F plus. Contrarily, the forms that a feeble-minded or a schizophrenic group see, and that are not seen by the healthy, are not real. (Beck, 1944, p. 155)

In a later statement Beck tempers this distinction by pointing out that a normal sample does not have "carte blanche to interpret the presented blot figures arbitrarily and to call anything which they see an F plus" (1950, p. 263). Thus, the criterion for including a new response found in the Spiegel Company sample of 157 normals into the existing list of $F+$ was that it can be seen by at least three individuals.

Using this criterion and extensive samples of subjects, Beck has carefully evolved norms for plus and minus responses. His translation of Beizmann's *Handbook for scorings of Rorschach responses* (1970), which is a compilation of more than 10,000 responses, represents a significant contribution to the standardization of $F+$ and $F-$ responses. Similarly, Hertz (1951) has derived norms from the responses given by an adolescent population and has recently (1970) published a revision of her tables. In his original work Rorschach (1921) used the form-determined responses of 100 normal subjects as the basis for deciding plus and minus, though apparently coupling a judgmental with this statistical criterion.

The judgment of the examiner. A second criterion for the accuracy of response depends on the empathic judgment of the examiner. In its simplest form this consists of the decision: "Does it seem to fit? Can I see the response which the subject gives as making sense in terms of the blot?" Implied in this criterion is the assumption that what is accurate is what another—albeit skilled and experienced—individual can appreciate as an adequate solution to the problem. Whereas an occurrence criterion assumes that what is actually given by healthy individuals defines accuracy, this criterion assumes that what can be appreciated by healthy individuals is accurate. Although these approaches imply two logically different solutions to what is ultimately a metaphysical question, we do not really know to what degree estimates based on them do differ in practice. Some experiments (Kimball, 1950b; Walker, 1953), in which judges evaluated the "goodness of fit" of numbers of responses taken from published lists of plus and minus based on occurrence are relevant and will be considered shortly.

Klopfer and Kelley (1942), Piotrowski (1957), and Rapaport, Schafer and Gill (1946) have depended principally on the judgment of the examiner.

Whatever the criterion used, there is likely to be a problem in the evaluation of the essentially new response. Take, for example, the very creative response which, although unusual and original, is not (in some absolute sense) minus. Although it differs from the commonly agreed-upon solutions, it need not violate the "realities" of the blot. Yet, in a literal interpretation of an occurrence criterion it cannot be $F+$ if it has never or rarely been reported before, nor, however, is it $F-$.[3] Although it is more likely that the sensitive examiner will appreciate the response, still his ego has limits for accepting the unknown. Copernicus was "accurate" though his contemporaries neither independently held his view of the universe nor certainly did they recognize the correctness of his position when evaluating it.

Although not dependent on published lists of plus' and minus', it

---

[3] All Rorschach workers have been sensitive to this problem. Beck, for example, counsels that when dealing with an original response, the judgment of the examiner is called into play to decide whether the new response is more like known $F+$ or whether it is more similar to known $F-$.

is unlikely that any examiner evaluates each response *de novo*. As in any judgmental act, there is always a frame of reference, perhaps in part derived from the examiner's own observations of occurrence (i.e., "clinical experience"), or perhaps consisting of implicit definitions of the limits of accuracy. The establishment of norms based on frequency of occurrence has the advantage of providing explicit standards, but the examiner's judgment is by no means obviated. This is always true in evaluating the wholly new response, and often true in deciding whether the given and listed response is in fact the same. Although a wholly qualitative system may put more strain on the examiner's judgment, and allow greater play to his projections, the obvious dangers in trusting his empathy exist in some degree whatever the method used, the more so if the examiner is inexperienced or under emotional strain. Thus, in one study, Kimball (1950b) found that 100 *W* responses were given significantly higher ratings for accuracy by inexperienced than by experienced judges. There was considerable disagreement among judges; many responses were rated at virtually every point of her six-point scale. Moreover, the examiner's judgments are made within the same interpersonal context as the subject's responses. Consequently, estimates of accuracy are subject to halo effects and may reflect the action of countertransferent tendencies. Withal, the critical judgment of the examiner is indispensable in any scoring system, and these dangers merely point up the necessity for training and discipline.

Some empirical studies of form level suggest a method for reducing the subjectivity of examiner judgments which, at the same time, may provide new criteria for form-level norms, dependent neither on frequency of occurrence nor on individual examiner judgment. A number of responses are shown to a number of judges, each of whom evaluates the accuracy with which they match the blot. Whether a response is called plus or minus depends on the extent of agreement among the judges rather than its frequency in the records of normal subjects. Thus, in a study by Walker (1953), 100 normal adults naive to the Rorschach method judged 299 *W* responses (191 plus and 108 minus) from Beck's norms simply in terms of whether the response did or did not seem to fit the blot. Although the plus' and minus' arrived at through group judgment were significantly related to Beck's plus' and minus', it was found that the $F+\%$ arrived at by this method significantly differentiated normals from paranoid schizophrenics, whereas Beck's $F+\%$ did not. In another study, Kimball (1950b) had 103 judges, varying in experience with the test, rate on a six-point scale of accuracy 100 responses from Beck's and Hertz' lists. If a response was rated 4 or better by 50% of the subjects, it was considered plus; if 2 or below by 50% of the subjects, it was considered minus. She found that the populars were generally rated highly, although they were not always considered to be the most accurate. In a number of cases, the plus and minus standards arrived at by this method did not agree with the Beck or Hertz standards. This type of approach has the obvious advantage of supplying quantitative norms of examiner judgments, thus minimizing the uncertainties inherent in single-examiner evaluation, while preserving the theoretical rationale of a judgmental criterion.

Which responses should be scored for accuracy? Originally, Rorschach scored only pure form-determined (F) responses for accuracy. As time has gone by, the Rorschach-Beck $F+$ ratio has been extended or supplanted by approaches which do not limit the judgment of plus-ness or minus-ness to pure F responses. Klopfer (1939) warned that the evaluation of form level should not be restricted to pure F responses but should also be made where F is combined with other determinants. Indeed, he considered, as we shall see shortly, the appropriate use of determinants to be a constructive specification which contributes to the form level of the response. Hertz (1951, 1970) in her $R+\%$ and Rapaport, Schafer and Gill (1946) in their "extended $F+\%$" evaluate all responses which use form either as their sole or principal determinant. More recently, Lerner (1968) has proposed a substitute for the "extended $F+\%$." Her $B+$ ratio includes *all* blends of form, irrespective of primacy, and excludes pure form. She argues that the logic of the extended $F+\%$ (even as the original $F+\%$) reflects the value-laden assumption that FC is superior to CF and that accuracy of perception does not even apply in instances where there is manifest affect. The $B+$ ratio, on the other hand, does not discount the adaptive aspects of emotionally intense percepts and can thus more fairly assess "those who might not share the traditional Anglo-Saxon preference for an FC response style" (p. 535).

Speaking out against an overly sharp and arbitrary separation of the realms of affect and intellect, Schachtel (1966) states:

> . . . It is a very widespread pejorative view of affects as being disorganizing and/or primitive forms of behavior which has led to a too-narrow view of intellect and reason as opposed to affect, and of affect as something rather questionable and at best to be tolerated, provided it is properly controlled. Rorschach himself wrote, rightly, that his whole test, not just the giving of form responses, requires adaptation to external stimuli; this he considered an action of the 'fonction du réel.' Thus, the omission of the color, shading, and movement responses from the problem of reality-testing and its expression in Rorschach's test would lead to grave errors. Actually, competent clinicians know this. But it is important to be aware of the described restrictive undercurrent in the clinical concept of 'reality' and its expression in the Rorschach literature (pp. 62-63).

Have we built into our measure of reality testing the blind spots in our own? Does it reflect an overemphasis on intellectual control? The search for a less restricted and more sensitively tuned measure of reality testing than the traditional $F+\%$ has led to developments in the form level literature anticipated by Schafer (1954) when he wrote:

> Some $F+$ responses represent greater integrative and imaginative achievements than others. Card IV as a "skin" is $F+$; as a "worm's eye view of a man sitting on a stump" it is $M+$. No distinction is drawn in the form level scoring between the superior accuracy and integration of the latter and the simplicity and obviousness of the former. Recognizing the existence of the absurd $F-$ at one extreme and the superior $F+$ at the other, we must attend to the qualitative as well as the quantitative aspects of success and failure in achieving accurate form. The $F+\%$ and the extended $F+\%$ are merely general orientation points for this aspect of our investigation and do not tell the whole story about reality testing (p. 179).

What factors other than the closeness of fit between the percept and the blot contours might be used in developing a more subtle form level scoring, to take account of examples such as those offered by Schafer? Klopfer has suggested the importance of appropriateness in the use of determinants. Thus, in discussing cloud responses, Klopfer et al. (1954) note:

> (W to Card VII). Clouds are characteristically indefinite in shape, and although they are by reason of shading effects particularly appropriate to this card, the excellence of the fit applies to determinants rather than outline. It is the characteristic indefiniteness of shape of the concept that prevents this response from being classified as "accurate" (p. 209).

For Schachtel, the use of determinants in addition to form, if they do not detract from the perceptual appropriateness of the response, is a form of enrichment which suggests a stronger relation to reality. Accuracy of perception is a fundamental requisite for a firm "perceptual hold," yet a highly accurate fit does not insure the capacity to respond fully to one's world.[4] "Superior accuracy" does not simply mean more accuracy. Perceptual accuracy is one component of reality testing, and, in several uses of the term, only one aspect of form level. Klopfer's form-level rating scheme (1944, 1954) is the most ambitious attempt to rate factors other than accuracy *per se*. Unfortunately, its cumbersomeness does not endear it to working clinicians.

How well the response matches the contour of the blot cannot readily be appraised if the response lacks sufficient clarity. Indeterminate, vague and amorphous responses have been treated differently in the major Rorschach systems. Beck (1944) scores them as $F+$ or $F-$, though he does not include these scorings in his form level summary score. Piotrowski (1957) and Beizmann (1966) use an $F\pm$, while Klopfer and Kelley (1942) simply score F. Sarason (1954) considers such responses as lacking "complexity" rather than accuracy and also includes organization elements in this complexity dimension. Weiner (1966) notes the lack of perceptual articulation in these responses and relates this to an inadequate sense of reality. In his view, sense of reality and reality testing are two separable components of one's relation to reality. Beck's scoring of these responses as plus or minus would suggest that they are either good fitting or poor fitting responses when, in actuality, they occur in many changeable forms and could be assigned to any of the ink blots. Because of his criterion for accuracy, Beck's accurate responses need not fit the blots very well. However, his $F+$ amorphous responses, though not literally accurate, may be quite appropriate in the sense in which Klopfer et al. (1954) used the term. In their system basal ratings of 0.0 and 0.5 are given to "indefinite" and "semi-definite" responses respectively. The form level of these responses could, in their approach, be raised by the appropriate use of determinants.

[4] The psychological significance of these points is illustrated by some findings Maria Rickers-Ovsiankina (1954) has reported.

Current Approaches to Form Level Scoring

It has long been recognized that restricting judgment of perceptual accuracy to form-determined responses alone would preclude the "whole story about reality testing" from being told. The form level scoring systems which we will now describe represent significant chapters in this story. In differing ways they assess the dimensions of form level marked by grossly inaccurate percepts at one extreme and those of superior accuracy at the other.

Klopfer's break with tradition. Following Rorschach's lead, Beck simply dichotomized F responses into those with good and poor form. Klopfer and Kelley (1942) divided form responses into the unusually good ($F+$), unusually poor ($F-$), and a large average category (F) which constituted about 90% of all form responses. Later, Klopfer (1944, 1954) proposed an approach to form level rating in which the examiner makes quantitative rating of each response depending on his estimate of the accuracy with which the percept fits the blot outlines, the type and degree of specification of the response, and the degree of organization. This last criterion overlaps conceptually with Beck's Z score. A fifteen-point scale results, extending from -2 through zero to $+5$, with .5 intervals. Each response is rated in two steps. First, a basal rating is assigned to the percept based on the examiner's judgment of the definiteness and accuracy of the percept. Then a credit of .5 is added for each constructive specification or for a successful organization, and a .5 credit is subtracted for specifications or organizations which weaken the match between the concept and the blot. Various conditions are specified for the addition and subtraction of credits.

Rapaport, Friedman, and Mayman. Rapaport and his colleagues (1946) distinguished four levels of quality: $F+$, $F\pm$, $F\mp$, and $F-$. In addition he distinguished four qualitative categories: "special $F+$" for the sharply defined and very convincing form response; "special $F-$" for the definite but arbitrary form responses; Fv for the vague response, and Fo for the mediocre but acceptable form response.

Drawing upon the work of Dworetzki (1939) and Beck, and making only slight changes in Rapaport's system, Friedman (1953) interpreted his scoring categories within the theoretical framework of Werner's (1940) organismic psychology (also see Hemmendinger's chapter in this volume). Individual percepts are assigned to categories reflecting Werner's developmental stages.

Friedman's translation of form level scoring into developmental terms is an ingenious application of the Rorschach and has been used with considerable success in a number of investigations. Those scores which are considered higher developmentally are $W++$, $D++$, $W+$, $D+$, Wm, and Dm; Wv, Dv, Wa, Da, $W-$, $D-$, DW, DdD, $FabC$, and $ConR$ represent developmentally lower scores. Scoring criteria and applications of the Friedman method are discussed by Goldfried, Stricker, and Weiner (1971) and by Hemmendinger, Chapter 3 in this volume. All developmentally high responses suppose a specific form which matches the blot outline well. Friedman suggests using Beck's or Hertz' tables where accuracy decisions are required; vague and amorphous responses are not scored plus or minus. In Friedman's system the examples of Schafer cited above would be scored: "worm's eye view of a man sitting on a stump" = $W++$; "skin" = Wm (mediocre whole). Considerable interpretive significance is attached to each of these scoring categories. The $W++$ response reflects developmentally higher functioning, for it involves both differentiation and reintegration of the constituent parts. By contrast, the Wm, although relatively high developmentally, shows little organization. The two responses have been found to differentially discriminate clinical groups. The value of studying the qualitative aspects of W responses was demonstrated in a study of Rorschach correlates of intellectual functioning. Allison and Blatt (1964) found that it was the higher forms of W responses ($W++$, $W+$, and Wm) rather than the lower forms ($W-$, Wa, and Wv) which best predicted measured intelligence.

Friedman's scoring system focuses on the structural aspects of responses; degree of accuracy, perceptual articulation, and organization are used to order responses on a developmental continuum. His inclusion of the Fabulized Combination ($FabC$), Contamination Response ($ConR$), and Confabulated (DdD, DW) responses, which reflect deficits in reasoning and are not traditional form level scoring categories, adds discriminative power to his system but limits the comparisons which can be made between his system and traditional approaches. Mayman's (1970) form level scoring system is more truly an outgrowth and extension of the Rorschach tradition, both in theoretical orientation and the scoring categories used.

Mayman interprets his form level categories as reflecting qualitatively distinct modes of reality testing. They represent a range of reality appropriateness which has reality-adherence at one extreme and reality-abrogation at the other. In the patterning of form level scores an individual's style of adhering to and testing reality can be seen. Unlike Friedman's system, which is primarily suited for nomothetic applications, Mayman's system, as his clinical examples illustrate, is useful in the idiographic study of individual protocols. This more differentiated approach to form level scoring has been adopted by a number of clinicians and its research value has been demonstrated in a number of studies (Kahn, 1967; Lohrenz and Gardner, 1967; Pryor, 1968; Smith and Coyle, 1969). Mayman's form level scores have been successfully related to a number of independent measures of adaptive capacity and ego strength. In what has been a major research application, they have been used as a primary component of Holt's measures of "defense effectiveness" and "adaptive regression" (Mayman, 1970; also see Holt's chapter in this volume). Mayman's categories are: $F+$, sharp convincing forms easily seen by the examiner; $Fw+$, reasonably plausible but not terribly convincing forms; $Fw-$, forms that bear only a slight resemblance to the blot area, not very plausible, or based on only one point of resemblance; Fv, vague form responses differing from the Fw response only in degree of formlessness; Fs, spoiled form response, to be used when the subject gives what is basically a familiar and good response (Fo or $F+$) but then introduces specifications which have the effect of markedly lowering the acceptability of the response; and $F-$, wholly arbitrary percepts. Lohrenz and Gardner (1967) have shown that the system is easily taught and that good interscorer reliability is readily achieved.

Mayman makes it clear that he is measuring outer reality testing.

> To avoid construct diffusion, it is important to remember that reality testing assessed by this scoring system refers only to the form quality of a percept, not to the fantasy or inner object-world in which that percept may have become embedded. A person may elaborate an $F+$ response into a psychotic confabulation without spoiling the $F+$ properties of the percept. . . . the dereism of confabulatory *fantasies* should not be confused with arbitrary

misperceptions of reality. The *F*– response is not a crazy thought, or image, or fantasy; it is an arbitrary percept in which the person claims to see something which simply is not there (1970, p. 20).

Like Schachtel (1966), Mayman (1970, p. 14) believes that the "form quality of the Rorschach responses indicates in microcosm the attitude with which a person maintains his hold on his object world."

V

Let us now consider in closer detail the various psychological mechanisms which may account for *F*– responses. An optimum form level, viewed as an index of ego strength, assumes the intactness of the integrative functions of the ego (to focus attention, discriminate, consciously scan and select from memory), the availability of experience (memory or associational context), and the subject's desire to be accurate (in general, his set and motivation in the task). Deficiency in any of these factors singly or in combination may result in *F*–, but the quality differs with the particular factors involved. This is recognized in such distinctions as Beck's between personal and impersonal *F*–.

The Effect of Need

A personal *F*– may occur when the pressure of internal needs is great and the reality organization of the subject is overwhelmed. The response, given with minimal respect for the contours of the stimulus represents in one or another fashion the subject's need expression. However, the existence of strong drive as such is not sufficient to produce *F*–; there must be simultaneous weakness in the subject's ability to control the emergence of the drive and its effect on conscious perception. Thus, in studies of semi-starvation there is no decrease in form level (Kjenaas and Brozek, 1952).

The Effect of Defense

Not only the drive, but the defense against its expression may lead to perceptual distortion. Though it is precisely the defensively constricted individual who achieves very high $F+$ levels, in other instances defensive action may lead to the hasty production of harmless but poor responses. If the blot stimulates threatening fantasy, the reported response may represent a denial of such a percept or involve the avoidance of the suggestive area. Clearly, the nature of the defense may influence the adequacy of the percept as well as its content.

The Lack of Integrative Ability

However, the subject may simply be unable to meet the demands of the task and to integrate a response from the available stimulus material. This implies not a pressure of uncontrollable impulse, but rather a deficit in the control itself. The subject lacks *Gestaltungskraft*, and hence may give $F-$ responses which are, however, "impersonal." The brain-injured patient required to make something of the meaningless stimuli may do no more than give the obvious responses. Staying within the limits of his ability, there is minimal distortion but little richness or variety. However, venturing beyond these limits or because of the anxiety generated by his inability to cope with the tests, his performance deteriorates and $F-$ responses appear. An interesting illustration of such a process was seen in a patient examined by the senior author. This man, a physician with a long-standing barbiturate addiction, gave a well-elaborated airplane as a whole response to Card I. Most of the succeeding cards he again described as airplanes; in each case, however, giving considerable technical information about the particular model, style, and construction. While impressing the examiner with his knowledge, most of these responses were little related to the forms of the blot. This patient used a particular fund of knowledge to cover his inability to integrate responses in terms of the stimulus qualities unique to each blot. Perseveration of response leading to lowered form level has been described often in the brain-damaged and senile. However, perseverative response can also appear under the pressure of inner need, although in such cases the $F-$ produced will be more clearly personal. Thus, the neurotic patient with obsessive sexual thoughts may give genitalia in response to every conceivable, and many inconceivable, portions of the blots. Klopfer and Kelley (1942) have distinguished the two forms of perseveration by the terms "mechanical" and "fixed idea." Other types of pathological thinking leading to lowered form level are seen in confabulation, contamination, positional responses or the like. Though all are $F-$, the distinctions among them are of diagnostic value.

Paucity of Associational Material

Still another source of poor form perception lies in the paucity of associational material out of which to construct responses. This may well be the more important determinant of the feeble-minded individual's low $F+$ than either a lack of integrative capacity, or, certainly, the overwhelming pressure of need. Since the final response depends on the subject's perception of the blot area and then drawing from his experience a likely percept to fit its perceived contours, it is clear that any reduction in the fund of material from which a response can be drawn, whether due to cultural isolation or limited intelligence, will reduce the possibilities of $F+$ responses.

Task Set, Interpretation and Motivation

Form level also reflects the motivation of the subject in the task. An individual may be capable of, but unconcerned with, good form. It has often been assumed that the motivation of the subject in this as in any test procedure is "to do as well as you can." Thus, by presenting him with a piece of "reality" one can see how well he is able to deal with the demands of that reality. But the subject may be unconcerned with our reality and rather prefer to do it his own way. One extreme is typified by the schizophrenic, another by the compulsive who, in Rorschach's phrase, "takes the test very seriously."

Test behavior depends, both generally and specifically with regard to $F+\%$, on the subject's interpretation of the test situation —the purpose of being tested, the rationale of the procedure, the behavior required of him—and on his relation with the examiner. It has too often been assumed that the test performance is strictly the resultant of the interaction of the test stimuli and the subject's personality, while neglecting to note that this behavior occurs within a social setting and is conditioned by the preexisting orientations of the subject. Schachtel (1941), Sarason (1954), and Schafer (1954) have described in considerable detail the dynamics of the patient-test and patient-examiner relationships. That such factors may have considerable influence on the final protocol is also attested to by a variety of empirical studies in which the attitude of the subject, relation to examiner, and other such test-situational factors have been experimentally manipulated (Gibby, 1951; Hutt, Gibby, Milton and Pottharst, 1950; Lord, 1950; Zubin, Eron and Schumer, 1965).

Rorschach early recognized that $F+\%$, along with sequence and approach, is one of the factors which can most easily be varied voluntarily and, by extension, through the action of more subtle attitudinal and situational factors. Set for accuracy, a subject with adequate intellectual resources can reach a perfect hundred. And as Schachtel (1941) notes, many subjects enter the examination with the expectation that their intellectual abilities are under test, that there are "right" responses, that "the essential requirement of the task is doing systematic accurate work rather than letting their imagination play" (p. 438). Their relation to the examiner may be defined in authoritarian or competitive terms. In other cases, a lowering of form level may reflect a regression of the subject in terms of his set toward the task and examiner, just as the excessively high $F+\%$ shows the others' need to appear exact and meticulous to the examiner. A common experience is the basically well integrated subject tested prior to, or early in, psychoanalysis who, projecting the role of analysand into the Rorschach situation, applies the "first rule" willy-nilly and gives loose and personal responses. How free the "free association" part of the examination is, often reflects the subject's role definition, and his willingness to relax his criticalness as his ability to apply it. Thus, Rychlak and Boland (1969) found that subjects could be appropriately self-critical when asked to rate how closely their original percepts fit the blot contours. Further, using such ratings allowed a more refined form level score which better related to various personality measures.

Certainly, it is important to distinguish such behavior from a more enduring inability to give accurate responses. For this, it becomes important to understand the meaning to the particular subject, possibly through direct inquiry or through the observation of other cues in the situation. The subject who interprets the situation com-petitively—"I'll show him!"—may be driven by a quantity ambition and consequently produce large numbers of responses, some of them poor. Similarly, another, awed by the omniscient doctor and feeling that his fate hangs on the outcome, may limit himself to safe and accurate responses. Recognizing the importance of task-motivational factors also indicates the value of varying them in the interest of discovering the range of potential response. By manipulating the demands of the task—as in "testing the limits"—the production of plus responses (or, conversely, the relaxation of critical attention) can be encouraged. If none are forthcoming, then one can speak more readily of incapacity.

These considerations point up the rather obvious fact that the final production cannot be taken as a literal representation of the subject's capacity for reality-contact, but that it may well be deter-mined by test-situational, motivational and attitudinal factors, some of which, in turn, reflect enduring and habitual personality trends, others more transitory ones.

VI

Differences Among Personality and Clinical Groups in Form Level

Beck gives the mean $F+\%$ for normal subjects as 84 and the critical minimum for psychological health as 60. With these values for reference some of the differences among personality groups may be briefly characterized. It has generally been found that the $F+\%$ rises from early childhood (Klopfer and Davidson, 1944; Rabin and Beck, 1950; Thetford, Molish and Beck, 1951; Vorhaus and Kay, 1943), though a lowering is found in the adolescent years which may well reflect temporary ego weakening of this emotionally stressful period (Beck, Rabin, Thiesen, Molish and Thetford, 1950; Thetford, Molish and Beck, 1951). During the adult years the level is stable, falling again in advanced age (Caldwell, 1954; Davidson and Kruglov, 1952; Thetford, Molish and Beck, 1951; Vorhaus and Kay, 1943). $F+\%$ is high in adults with superior intelligence, and decreases at lower levels, being lowest in the feeble-minded. The brain-injured patient may have an adequate form level, perhaps in a constricted and coarctated record, but it will tend to be lower under emotionally stressful conditions or in more confused patients. In schizophrenia the level is generally low, decreasing with the extent of confusion, excitement and intellectual deterioration (Weiner, 1966). The greater the involvement and disorganization of the thinking processes, as in Beck's S-1 schizophrenic reaction pattern (1954), the lower the form level. Studies have shown that with clinical improvement there is a general rise in $F+\%$ (Kisker, 1942; Piotrowski, 1939; Goldman, 1960). In agitated and manic states the $F+\%$ is quite low. Similarly, the very anxious individual, generally less able to integrate perceptual and associational processes, also tends to a somewhat lower level. Interestingly, however, the depressed patient can have an exceedingly high form level, as does the rigid and pedantic normal. This finding will be commented on later, for it makes the important point that form level is not a simple and direct function of mental health and psychological maturity, but rather is curvilinearly related.

$F+\%$ and Behavior Under Stress

Overt behavior is always the result of a number of interrelated personality processes operating in terms of the various demands and constraints of particular situations. Consequently, as Ainsworth (Klopfer, Ainsworth, Klopfer and Holt, 1954) points out in her review of Rorschach validation research, one is inclined to look askance at "single variable" studies attempting to predict behavior in complex situations. Yet, where it is possible to derive pointed hypotheses relating test variables to measurable behavior, and one can reasonably manipulate the experimental situation, such research can contribute greatly to the understanding of the test variables.

The hypothesis that subjects with good form perception should function better in experimentally-induced stress situations has been tested in a number of experiments. Baker and Harris (1949) measured the intelligibility and variations of intensity of speech during non-stress and stress conditions. While all subjects showed a significant decline in both intelligibility and variability under stress, both form level and color-form integration (*FC:CF*) were positively correlated with the increased variability of intensity. Williams (1947) found that the maintenance of digit-symbol test performance under stress was correlated with both $F+\%$ ($r = .71$) and color-form integration ($r = .35$). The multiple R using both Rorschach variables was .82. However, these findings could not be replicated in subsequent experiments (Carlson and Lazarus, 1953; Eriksen, Lazarus and Strange, 1952). Although not reporting $F+\%$, Hertzman and his co-workers (1944, 1949) found that the ability to tolerate anoxic conditions in high altitude pressure chambers is related to a number of Rorschach indices of psychological health. The records of subjects with low anoxia tolerance were more often marked by low M, color and shading shock, refusal or inability to respond, no *FC*, and negative color balance ($CF + C > FC$). Using a multiple-choice group Rorschach, Smith and George (1951) studied the proportion of form-determined responses ($F\%$) as an index of control, using the decrement in performance of digit symbol and information tests given before and after severe criticism as a measure of stress response. There was a significant nonlinear relationship between $F\%$ and stress measure. Control in this situation increased with $F\%$ to the 50% level; above this point control broke down. Taken together, these experimental studies suggest that subjects with more accurate form perception are better able to perform under stress. They supplement clinical and personality studies, and in general give support to the interpretation of form perception as an index of ego control.

Optimal Form Perception and Psychological Health

The healthy ego is not only able to maintain critical control but also is able to relax it as well. Psychoanalytic ego psychologists have pointed out that creative behavior often depends on regression, which is, however, under control and "in the service of the ego" (Hartmann, 1950, 1951; Kris, 1950; Rapaport, 1950, 1951). In play, in art, and in spontaneous social intercourse, the psychologically healthy individual does not have to maintain a vigilant reality-testing, but voluntarily releases control in the interest of spontaneous affective expression or fantasy. Indeed, it has been argued that artistic production may depend largely upon this ability for controlled regression. Stated another way, Lawrence Kubie has suggested that creative thinking may depend upon the free utilization of preconscious processes and involve the relative constraint of both the logic and reality-orientation of conscious thought as well as the distortion of the unconscious.

The fact that form level is not linearly related to psychological health was recognized by Rorschach, who pointed out that optimum and maximum are not synonymous.

> . . . we find the best forms in the pedants and depressed subjects, especially in psychotic depressions. These subjects take the test very seriously. They search laboriously for good forms, bringing to bear all their attention and faculties of self-criticism so that they achieve an F plus percentage of almost 100, though the answers are extraordinarily stereotyped, showing a poor range of variation (1921, p. 57).

More recent writers have invariably pointed to the fact that the highest level of F+ is found in the constrictively-defended individual who is neurotically unable to relax control. "The critical-controlling processes may have become rigid and intolerably accurate, making for meagerness of productivity and for rigidity in thinking and behavior" (Rapaport, Schafer and Gill, 1946, p. 194). Such behavior is usually paralleled by a generally high proportion of form-determined responses indicating the decreased spontaneity and the inhibition of fantasy and affective processes. In Schachtel's (1945) interpretation, both the pedantic and depressed patient share a lack of relatedness to the world in general, which, within the Rorschach situation, does not permit any spontaneous interest in the ink blots. Each views the task as something imposed from outside by a strange and threatening authority which one is relatively powerless to deal with. The pedant has to a degree repressed the feeling of strangeness and helplessness, and the compulsive defenses are in the forefront. By contrast, the depressive is overwhelmed by his inadequacy and guilt and by the attendant affect. But both "have to check constantly whether they are really on the right track, the depressive considering this unlikely, the pedantic making sure he has followed the right protocol" (1945, p. 439).

Schachtel (1966) does note, however, that Rorschach's own data contradict his assertion that pedantic and depressed subjects had the highest form level scores; in fact, his sample of artists had the highest

$F+\%$, which was then followed by the depressed and pedantic people in his sample. However, the high $F+\%$ of the artists, though not those of the other two groups, tended to go with dilated experience types and many W responses. Did Rorschach's artists give a high number of "special $F+$" responses? Would their responses receive higher scores in the Klopfer system or be $W++$ if scored by Friedman?

Thus, the psychologically healthy individual, viewed in terms of form perception, emerges as one whose perception is neither diffuse nor distorted nor rigid, but it is accurate. The central integrative functions upon which such behavior depends emerge in psychological maturation and are damaged in psychopathology. They are part of the ego organization, which includes also the self-concept and internalized value systems. Before concluding, we should like to consider the relationship between accurate form perception and such values, and more specifically to distinguish between reality-oriented behavior, on the one hand, and social conformity, on the other, in the well-functioning personality.

In the concept of the "ego" two highly related but conceptually separate types of psychological phenomena can be distinguished. First, there are the organized values, attitudes, conscious needs, goals and ideals which define the psychological self. These are the center of the personality organization from which the individual gains identity and continuity. This is "ego" in terms of its content, and can be distinguished from ego in a more structural sense. For the present discussion, clarity might be served by using a term such as "self." Second, the term "ego" defines the capacity to organize and synthesize experience, perceive, remember, plan, and, in general, exercise control over behavior. The term "ego strength" has come into use to describe variations in the adequacy of such functioning. Thus far, the ego functioning seen in $F+$ has been discussed principally in terms of this latter meaning.

Ego and self are clearly parallel and related concepts. In psychological development, the individual must be capable of distinguishing self and not-self before a self-system can emerge. The ability to relate past memories, present events, and future consequences in causal sequences paces the emergence of the self as a temporally continuous structure. The delay of gratification which makes possible the development of ego functions allows the self, as subject to be gratified, to have internalized goals which can be represented in fantasy. Similarly, in the developed organism, self and ego processes remain tightly related. The individual who has incorporated unrealistic goals may of necessity have to resort to irrational mechanisms to live without anxiety. Thus, the existence of strong ego functioning assumes an organized self-system. In social behavior, critical judgment implies a set of values in terms of which such judgment is made. Although many of these are derived from the cultural environment, they are integrated within the psychologically individual self.

Accurate form perception implies an awareness of, and in general a respect for, the social values which define the rules of organized social life. The ego-strong individual has learned the conditions allowing expression and those requiring inhibition of impulses, and he has the control necessary for directing their expression or inhibition. Similarly, he can flexibly accept various roles in a complex and changing social situation. He is neither, on the one hand, compulsively constrained to a single pattern of behavior, nor, on the other, does he lose the identity of the self in chameleon-like adaptation.

But knowledge of social definitions does not imply conformity to them. Perceiving accurately does not mean valuing things as everyone else does. The existence of an integrated self involves holding values which to greater or lesser degree must be in conflict with social demands. Prior to the formation of the ego, there is conflict between the blind expression of instinct and the requirements of social reality, but the reality testing which arises in the mediation of these conflicting demands also provides a basis for a new conflict between the values of the self and social demand. Indeed, psychological maturity requires the ability to accept social disapproval and isolation in the pursuit of long-term goals, and not to have one's self-esteem dependent upon the approval which goes with conformity.

Thus, deviance does not imply social weakness. True, the individual with profound unresolved emotional conflicts will have poor reality contact and be characterized by aberrant behavior. The existence of certain deviant values may be presumptive evidence of a deficit in psychological growth, while holding others may put such strain on the ego's resources as to require distortion for their maintenance. But the fact of deviance is neither proof for nor against ego strength. It is precisely the weak ego who is unable to assert independent values and who "escapes from freedom" through conformity. And, conformity, as so often happens, depends on continued self-deceit, compromise, and the renunciation of one's own perceptions for its justification and continuance.

In sum, the healthy individual is capable of detachment and objectivity in perceiving and organizing both internal and external events. He knows social standards, and may in the main abide them, but he is not compulsively constrained by them. He has interiorized value systems which are the unique expressions of his development and give direction to his behavior. He is not compelled to judge his actions by existing social standards, nor does he feel it necessary to flout them. There is sufficient flexibility to adjust to changing demands, but this behavior is not so fluid as to conform to the immediate requirements of the social world or to the pressures of inner needs.

BIBLIOGRAPHY

Allison, J. and Blatt, S. J. The relationship of Rorschach whole responses to intelligence. *Journal of Projective Techniques and Personality Assessment*, 1964, **28**, 255-260.

Baker, L. M. and Harris, J. S. The validation of the Rorschach test results against laboratory behavior. *Journal of Clinical Psychology*, 1949, **5**, 161-164.

Beck, S. J. *Rorschach's test, Volume I.* New York: Grune & Stratton, 1944 (3rd ed., Revised with A. G. Beck, E. E. Levitt and H. B. Molish, 1961).

Beck, S. J. Rorschach F plus and the ego in treatment. *American Journal of Orthopsychiatry*, 1948, **18**, 395-401.

Beck, S. J. *Rorschach's test, Volume III, Advances in interpretation.* New York: Grune & Stratton, 1952.

Beck, S. J. *The six schizophrenias.* New York: The American Orthopsychiatric Association, 1954.

Beck, S. J. Emotions and understanding. *International Psychiatry Clinics*, 1966, **3**, 93-114.

Beck, S. J. Reality, Rorschach, and perceptual theory. In Rabin, A. (ed.) *Projective techniques in personality assessment: A modern introduction.* New York: Springer, 1968, p. 115-135.

Beck, S. J. and Molish, H. B. *Rorschach's test, Volume II, A variety of personality pictures* (2nd ed. rev.) New York: Grune & Stratton, 1967.

Beck, S. J., Rabin, A.I., Thiesen, W. G., Molish, H., and Thetford, W. N. The normal personality as projected in the Rorschach test. *Journal of Psychology*, 1950, **30**, 241-298.

Beizmann, C. *Livret de cotation des formes dans le Rorschach.* Paris: Centre de Psychologie Appliquée, 1966. *Handbook for scorings of Rorschach responses.* English translation by S. J. Beck, New York: Grune & Stratton, 1970.

Bellak, L., Hurvich, M. and Gediman, H. K. *Ego functions in schizophrenics, neurotics, and normals: A systematic study of conceptual, diagnostic, and therapeutic aspects.* New York: Wiley, 1973.

Caldwell, M. The use of the Rorschach in personality research with the aged. *Journal of Gerontology*, 1954, **9**, 316-323.

Carlson, V. R. and Lazarus, R. S. A repetition of Meyer Williams' study of intellectual control under stress and associated Rorschach factors. *Journal of Consulting Psychology*, 1953, **17**, 247-253.

Davidson, H. and Kruglov, L. Personality characteristics of the institutionalized aged. *Journal of Consulting Psychology*, 1952, **16**, 5-12.

Dworetzki, G. Le test de Rorschach et l'evolution de la perception. *Archives de Psychology*, 1939, **27**, 233-396.

Eriksen, C. W., Lazarus, R. S. and Strange, J. R. Stress and its personality correlates. *Journal of Personality*, 1952, **20**, 277-286.

Exner, J. E. Jr. *The Rorschach systems*. New York: Grune & Stratton, 1969.

Friedman, H. Perceptual regression in schizophrenia: An hypothesis suggested by use of the Rorschach test. *Journal of Projective Techniques*, 1953, **17**, 171-185.

Gibby, R. G. The stability of certain Rorschach variables under conditions of experimentally induced sets: 1. The intellectual variables. *Journal of Projective Techniques*, 1951, **15**, 3-25.

Goldfried, M. R., Stricker, G. & Weiner, I. B. *Rorschach handbook of clinical and research applications*. Englewood Cliffs, N.J.: Prentice Hall, 1971.

Goldman, R. Changes in Rorschach performance and clinical improvement in schizophrenia. *Journal of Consulting Psychology*, 1960, **24**, 403-407.

Hartmann, H. Comments on the psychoanalytic theory of ego. In *The psychoanalytic study of the child, Volume V*. New York: International Universities Press, 1950, 74-96.

Hartmann, H. Ego psychology and the problem of adaptation. In D. Rapaport (ed.) *Organization and pathology of thought*. New York: Columbia University Press, 1951, 362-396.

Hertz, M. R. *Frequency tables for scoring responses to the Rorschach inkblot test*. Cleveland: Western Reserve University Press, 1951.

Hertz, M. R. *Frequency tables for scoring Rorschach responses*. Cleveland, Ohio: Case Western Reserve University Press, 1970.

Hertzman, M., Orlansky, J. and Seitz, C. P. Personality organization and anoxia tolerance. *Psychosomatic Medicine*, 1944, **6**, 317-331.

Hertzman, M., Smith, G. M., and Clark, K. B. The relation between changes in the angioscotoma and certain Rorschach signs under prolonged mild anoxia. *Journal of General Psychology*, 1949, **41**, 263-271.

Hutt, M. L., Gibby, R. C., Milton, E. O. and Pottharst, K. The effect of varied experimental "sets" upon Rorschach performance. *Journal of Projective Techniques*, 1950, **14**, 181-187.

Kahn, M. W. Correlates of Rorschach reality adherence in the assessment of murderers who plead insanity. *Journal of Projective Techniques*, 1967, **31**, 44-47.

Kimball, A. J. *Evaluation of form-level in the Rorschach*. Doctoral Dissertation, University of California, Berkeley, 1948.

Kimball, A. J. History of form-level appraisal in the Rorschach. *Journal of Projective Techniques*, 1950, **14**, 134-152. (a)

Kimball, A. J. Evaluation of form-level in the Rorschach. *Journal of Projective Techniques*, 1950, **14**, 219-244. (b)

Kisker, G. W. A projective approach to personality patterns during insulin shock and metrazol convulsive therapy. *Journal of Abnormal and Social Psychology*, 1942, **37**, 120-124.

Kjenaas, N. K. and Brozek, J. Personality in semi-starvation. *Psychosomatic Medicine*, 1952, **14**, 115-128.

Klopfer, B. Theory and technique of Rorschach interpretation. *Rorschach Research Exchange*, 1939, **3**, 152-194.

Klopfer, B., Ainsworth, M. D., Klopfer, W. G. and Holt, R. R. *Developments in the Rorschach technique, Volume I. Technique and theory.* Yonkers-on-Hudson: World Book Co., 1954.

Klopfer, B. and Davidson, H. Form level rating: a preliminary proposal for appraising mode and level of thinking as expressed in Rorschach records. *Rorschach Research Exchange,* 1944, **8**, 164-177.

Klopfer, B. and Kelley, D. M. *The Rorschach technique.* Yonkers-on-Hudson, New York: World Book Co., 1942.

Kris, E. On preconscious mental processes. *Psychoanalytic Quarterly,* 1950, **19**, 540-560.

Lerner, B. A new method of summarizing perceptual accuracy on the Rorschach. *Journal of Projective Techniques and Personality Assessment,* 1968, **32**, 533-536.

Lohrenz, L. L. and Gardner, R. W. The Mayman form-level scoring method: Scorer reliability and correlates of form level. *Journal of Projective Techniques and Personality Assessment,* 1967, **31**, 39-43.

Lord, E. Experimentally induced variations in Rorschach performance. *Psychological Monographs,* 1950, **64**, No. 316.

Mayman, M. Reality contact, defense effectiveness, and psychopathology in Rorschach form-level scores. In Klopfer, B., Meyer, M. M., Brawer, F. B. and Klopfer, W. G. (eds.) *Developments in the Rorschach technique. Vol. III. Aspects of personality structure.* New York: Harcourt Brace Jovanovich, Inc. 1970, 11-46.

Meyer, M. M. and Caruth, E. Rorschach indices of ego processes. *Journal of Projective Techniques and Personality Assessment.* 1965, **29**, 200-218.

Meyer, M. M. and Caruth, E. Inner and outer reality testing on the Rorschach. *Reiss-Davis Clinic Bulletin,* 1964, **1**, 100-106.

Murphy, G. *Personality: a biosocial approach to origins and structures.* New York: Harper, 1947.

Piotrowski, Z. A. *Perceptanalysis.* New York: Macmillan, 1957.

Piotrowski, Z. A. Rorschach manifestations of improvement in insulin treated schizophrenics. *Psychosomatic Medicine,* 1939, **1**, 508-526.

Pryor, D. B. Correlates of the Mayman form level scoring system. *Journal of Projective Techniques and Personality Assessment,* 1968, **32**, 462-465.

Rabin, A. I. and Beck, S. J. Genetic aspects of some Rorschach factors. *American Journal of Orthopsychiatry,* 1950, **20**, 595-599.

Rapaport, D. On the psychoanalytic theory of thinking. *International Journal of Psychoanalysis,* 1950, **31**, 161-170.

Rapaport, D. *Organization and pathology of thought.* New York: Columbia University Press, 1951.

Rapaport, D., Schafer, R., and Gill, M. *Diagnostic psychological testing, Vol. II.* Chicago: Year Book Publishers, 1946. (Revised and edited by Robert R. Holt, International Universities Press, 1968.)

Rickers-Ovsiankina, M. A. Longitudinal approach to schizophrenia through the Rorschach method. *Journal of clinical and experimental Psychopathology,* 1954, **15**, 107-118.

Rorschach, H. *Psychodiagnostik.* Bern: Bircher, 1921 (English translation by Paul Lemkau, Verlag Hans Huber, 1942).

Rychlak, J. F. and Boland, G. C. Empirical cross-validation of Herman Rorschach's theory of perception. *Journal of Projective Techniques and Personality Assessment,* 1969, **33**, 11-19.

Sarason, S. B. *The clinical interaction.* New York: Harper, 1954.

Schachtel, E. G. The dynamic perception and the symbolism of form. *Psychiatry,* 1941, **4**, 79-96.

Schachtel, E. G. Subjective definitions of the Rorschach test situation and their effect on test performance. *Psychiatry,* 1945, **8**, 419-448.

Schachtel, E. G. *Experiential foundations of the Rorschach test.* New York: Basic Books, 1966.

Schafer, R. *Psychoanalytic interpretation in Rorschach testing.* New York: Grune & Stratton, 1954.

Smith, S. and George, C. E. Rorschach factors related to experimental stress. *Journal of Consulting Psychology*, 1951, **15**, 190-195.

Smith, W. H. and Coyle, F. A. Jr. MMPI and Rorschach form level scores in a student population. *The Journal of Psychology*, 1969, **73**, 3-7.

Stein, M. I. Personality factors involved in the temporal development of Rorschach responses. *Journal of Projective Techniques*, 1949, **13**, 355-414.

Stern, W. *General psychology.* New York: Macmillan, 1937.

Thetford, W. N., Molish, H. B. and Beck, S. J. Developmental aspects of personality structure in normal children. *Journal of Projective Techniques*, 1951, **15**, 58-78.

Vorhaus, P. and Kay, L. Rorschach reactions in early childhood; Part II. Intellectual aspects of personality development. *Rorschach Research Exchange*, 1943, **7**, 71-78.

Walker, R. G. An approach to standardization of Rorschach form-level. *Journal of Projective Techniques*, 1953, **17**, 426-436.

Weiner, I. B. *Psychodiagnosis in schizophrenia.* New York: Wiley and Sons, 1966.

Werner, H. *Comparative psychology of mental development.* New York: Harper, 1940.

Williams, M. An experimental study of intellectual control under stress and associated Rorschach factors. *Journal of Consulting Psychology*, 1947, **11**, 21-29.

Zubin, J., Eron, L. D. and Schumer, F. *An experimental approach to projective techniques.* New York: Wiley, 1965.

Imagination imitates and competes with reality.

6

THE MOVEMENT RESPONSES

Zygmunt A. Piotrowski

MEANING OF HUMAN MOVEMENT RESPONSES

Movement is the cause of all life and vibration is the fundamental process of all existence, organic and inorganic. Human movement responses elicited by the Rorschach plates (symbolized by the capital letter M)[1] provide, more than any other single test component, specific and significant information about the individual's role in interhuman relationships that matter to him. Another special feature of the M is that it allows conclusions pertaining to character changes which have occurred in the past, including childhood. Other test components being similar, two persons with M of contrasting natures are indeed strikingly different; e.g., producing exclusively self-assertive, unhampered overt movements, such as "dancing" or "a giant jumping over a tree stump," reveals a self-confident basic attitude toward others and one's own future, while responding to the same plates with "two persons bending under the weight of whatever they're carrying" or "a man lying on a log, sleeping" discloses a dependent and passive attitude, being easily defeated by difficulties and waiting for others to guide and to make the important decisions for one. The assertive-M subject overcomes gravity and inertia, while the compliant one gives in to gravity and expects to be led.

[1] For explanation of scoring symbols see Appendix, p. 609 ff. [Editor].

My definition of the meaning of human movement responses was first formulated in 1937 as a result of theoretical considerations but has been retained because of ample empirical evidence: "The M represent the conception of life, according to which the individual makes his adjustment to reality. . . . The M stand for the most individual and integrated strivings which dominate his life . . . [they reveal] the attitude that he takes toward his own future, toward other people, toward his own work, toward what worries and pleases him" (Piotrowski, 1937). This concept was greatly elaborated over the years and reformulated in *Perceptanalysis* (1957): "My concept of the M makes it comparable to a steering mechanism which directs the individual to play certain definite roles in those interhuman relationships that are vital to him; the M determine external conduct directly or indirectly but always materially and, therefore, are accessible to direct observation in the external motor behavior. . . . It is not necessary for one to be fully aware of his life role in order to have one and to be directly influenced by it. . . . The M indicate prototypal roles in life, i.e., definite tendencies, deeply embedded in the subject and not easily modified, to assume repeatedly the same attitude or attitudes in dealing with others when matters felt to be important and personal are involved. There is dislike and unwillingness to act in a manner not foreseen in the prototype or incompatible with it. . . . The prototypal M roles reveal whether the individual tends to be a leader or a follower, whether he likes to demonstrate his strength or to seek the protection of a psychologically stronger person, whether interhuman relationships are experienced as enervating or stimulating, whether the individual is exhibitionistic or self-effacing, aggressive or cooperative, active or passive, etc. The prototypal role can be desirable or not, can be acceptable or unacceptable, can be an aid in the struggles of life or a severe handicap. It is not necessarily a model pattern likely to make the individual successful in life. It may involve an action pattern which causes failures, frustration and unhappiness. . . . The M indicate traits stabilizing the relation between the individual and his environment" (Piotrowski, 1974). By stability is meant constancy and regularity of subjective attitudes and overt social interaction.

Rorschach had a different conception of the M. He stated that the M disclosed the individual's attitude toward his own inner psychic processes, toward "tendencies in the subconscious," and thus had no direct relation to overt psychosocial relations. Beck re-stated Rorschach's position explicitly: "The M response, as Rorschach understands it, really reproduces movements or activities that the subject is carrying on within his mental life. Since these mental activities are those in which we should like to engage in the outer world but cannot, or dare not, they are our fantasy life" (1944, p. 92). Rorschach defined differences between types of M also in terms of the individual's attitude toward his inner fantasy life: The self-assertive M indicates that the "subject actively struggles against his introversive tendencies," while the compliant individual "surrenders himself to his imagination" (1942). On another page of his *Psychodiagnostics* we find this unequivocal statement: "The factors which are essentially 'inner' or self-determined, and are expressed primarily in the experience of motion in the test, are in some way opposed to physical activity, to actual execution of motion. I would like to add an example so that this conclusion is not left simply hanging in air. Dreams are 'inner' or self-determined productions, and kinesthesias play an important role in them. On awakening, necessary movements, physical motion begins at once. This movement sets the dreams aside. There is, however, a way to recall dreams: lie perfectly motionless on awakening in order not to cover up the kinesthesias of the dream by present physical move-ment" (Rorschach, 1942). From the conjectured analogy between the M and dream imagery, Rorschach concluded that the action tendencies and attitudes disclosed by the M are "opposed to physical activity, to actual execution of motion." This conclusion may be questioned because of contradictory empirical evidence and also because of the investigators' failure to discriminate between potential and actual "execution of motion" or, to be exact, of an indicated action tendency. Forgetting dreams is not tantamount to casting off the action tendencies revealed by dream events. It is a truism since the inception of organized society that humans harbor desires which influence their actions in various ways, whether they are aware of their desires or not. Forgetting dreams simply means becoming unaware of them but it does not mean freeing oneself from the desires which created the dream events: these desires retain the potential for overt manifestation. Thus, Rorschach's phrase "opposed to actual execution of motion" can refer only to the time of dreaming and cannot imply lasting inhibition of overt action. Indeed, when one lies in bed dreaming, one cannot do anything else purposefully and deliberately without interrupting the dream. By the same token, when one produces M responses looking at the Rorschach plates, one cannot simultaneously perform the activities or assume the attitudes and poses indicated by the M. These responses are potential, not actual, actions. One might say they are initial stages of actions at a very low level of intensity. Carefully controlled and precise electromyographic investigations probably would demonstrate a parallelism between the patterns of electric currents during the spontaneous production of various types of M and during overt manifestations of actions indicated by the same M.

EVIDENCE IN SUPPORT OF MEANING OF M

The first (and so far) only relevant experimental study of the M was made by Mirin (1955). Behavior toward others in personally important situations is the essential meaning of M. Every direct investigation of psychosocial behavior in situations of importance to the individual collects the most relevant information for a validation of the meaning of M. This was done by Mirin. He did not rely on the subject's words, on what they might have said they would or might do, but on direct observations of what they actually did in a situation relevant for the validation of the M. Mirin created such a situation; participating in it personally, he challenged the patients (one at a time) and made them respond openly to his challenge. An immediate recall experiment of a new kind was designed. Two, not one, subjects were tested at the same time and they had to agree on the response; neither was credited with success unless their common single response was "correct." When they failed to reach an agreement or when one of them could not answer, neither received credit even when one of the pair answered correctly. Rorschach test records of the 30 patients had been obtained before Mirin met the patients, who believed Mirin was one of them. For the experiment only those patients were selected who produced either exclusively assertive M or exclusively compliant M. Mirin's purpose, unknown to his teammates, was to influence them and to make them accept as "correct" his response to particular test items; he would sometimes insist on an answer he knew was false and sometimes on the answer he knew was correct but which his mate missed. The results were positive and significant. Compliant-M patients yielded and aceeded to Mirin's answer, withdrawing their own which they had already voiced. By contrast, assertive-M patients did not give in and held on to their own response, sometimes becoming argumentative. This experiment confirmed the thesis that the type of M discloses the actual role which an individual assumes in a psychosocial situation when he feels emotionally involved.

Many people produce not one but several different types of M, assertive, compliant, at times also blocked, with their numerous variants. In fact, when the number of M in a test record rises above five, the M are of at least two of the three main types: assertive, blocked, and compliant (Piotrowski, 1974). This poses a problem because each M influences handling of interhuman relations in its own specific way. The M, as it were, do not compromise, compete or block one another but influence the subject's psychomotor system separately, in turns. The individual's psychological constitution, his health, strength, courage, prudence and experience as well as external social conditions and regard for the future determine which of the diverse roles, revealed by the different types of M, will be enacted in particular encounters with others. One has to learn through experience how to carry out in action one's multiple potential roles and which role to choose for what kind of social interaction. This process of learning is only partly conscious. Possession of traits, indicated by multiple types of M, is not an unqualified blessing. However, it is an asset because it is associated with imagination, intellectual liveliness and spontaneous interest in understanding human psychology and social relations. All those who are greatly and consistently curious about motives, feelings and enduring aims of others produce more M than others of similar intellectual level and education. According to his friend, Roemer (1938), Rorschach himself produced more than thirty M; so large a number of M had to contain many which differed from one another in subtle nuances, while other M probably were easily differentiated because of striking differences in type, assertive versus compliant, overt movement versus immobile pose. There is a prevailing impression among clinicians that psychologists and psychiatrists with many *M* have a better understanding and grasp of projective personality tests and make better psychotherapists than those with average numbers of *M*.

Hammer and Jacks (1955) made a survey of relative frequencies of assertive and compliant *M* in test records of rapists, who had obviously imposed their will by force on their victims, and of men who, using seductive appeals and petty bribery, had induced children to expose their genitals. Significant differences were found between these two groups of offenders. Assertive *M* were associated with the rapists' violently aggressive behavior, and compliant *M* were associated with the restrained and passive seductiveness of pedophiles. The choice of a prepuberty child for a pregenital sexual experience also marks the pedophiles as ineffectual, diffident and dependent.

Parker (1968) constructed a careful and detailed technique for the validation of the meaning of *M*. It utilizes the subject's associations to his *M* and a standard questionnaire. Independent of the subjects' own evaluation of their *M*, qualified clinical psychologists rated each of the subjects' *M* separately on a scale. Two aspects of the *M* were rated: first, the affect the subject was likely to experience if he expressed, in overt social interaction, the movement or pose indicated by his *M*; and, secondly, what effect would the subject's overt action have upon the mood of the other person with whom the subject would be interacting. The mood could be pleasant, unpleasant or neutral emotionally (on a five-point scale). Three groups of subjects were compared. Every person included in these groups produced at least one *M*; non-*M* individuals were eliminated. The first group consisted of 30 male students in an introductory psychology course. The other two comprised schizophrenics, 30 male and 30 female. Each patient had an I.Q. of over 100 and at least 8 years of school; patients with organic cerebral disorders, alcoholism, psychopathic personality and intellectual confusion were eliminated. Analysis of findings confirmed the statement that the *M* reveal action tendencies which actually influence the subject's handling of others in personally important matters. Moreover, they confirmed the assertion that subjects project attitudes they consider unfavorable into *M* figures of opposite sex. When *M* are appraised in different ways, a single common factor of comfort-discomfort accounts for the relationships among the rating scales. There was some supporting evidence that different information was elicited from M-actions than from subjects' additional associations to these M-actions. This highlights the difference in validity between the primary visual associations to the blots and the additional verbal elaborations of the M-contents; these verbal associations are not visual in the sense that nothing graphic corresponds to them on the blot. The primary visual response is much more valid than the secondary verbal comments. Primary association is defined as every element in a test response which corresponds to something visual in the stimulus blot, in other words, only the direct interpretations of something physically seen in the blot (Piotrowski, 1974). The Parker method and results demonstrated that several meaningful types of M can be discriminated. This differentiation makes it possible to identify correctly the subjects' preferred roles in life which they act out with a comfortable feeling and the roles they disown consciously which make them uncomfortable when they relate to others in accordance with these roles.

A man "saw" in plate III "two women, dancing around a fire; they seem to be nude, I guess." The primary associations were the two women projected into the side gray details; the fire which included the bottom center gray, interpreted as pieces of wood or stove, and the central red viewed as flames; the bodies of the dancers were seen unclothed. The subject felt that he was looking at a genuine dancing scene. When asked to add anything he wished to his original response, he replied: "I'd feel pretty ridiculous, dancing around a fire, nude." Feeling ridiculous was the secondary association. He did not say that the dancers felt ridiculous; on the contrary, they seemed to him engrossed with their dance. Moreover, no graphic blot detail was pointed out by the subject as indicating awkwardness or embarrassment. Other examples of secondary association are: "I have reservations about being a clown;" "I've always wanted to travel, and I wouldn't mind meeting someone like this."

Group testing is less reliable and less productive than testing one individual at a time. Nevertheless, the M are such powerful predictors of behavior in situations which involve the individual that even group testing yields helpful information. During World War II the author was administering the Rorschach to groups of 40 men. Lack of time prevented individual testing. The men were Army prisoners at the Ft. Jackson Rehabilitation Center; about 80% of them had been court-martialed for repeated absence without official leave. The purpose of the Rorschach and other tests was to obtain data for a prompt evaluation of personality which would form the basis for a recommendation for parole or denial of parole (Piotrowski, 1965). There was a follow-up on every paroled man, covering the first six months after restoration to active duty in the Army. On the basis of the follow-up reports the men were divided into a good and poor group. When the report came that a man had been court-martialed again, for whatever reason, he was placed in the poor group. All other followed-up men were placed in the good group. The reports were used to check the accuracy of the preparole predictions of future behavior on active duty. The types of M produced during the group testing at the Rehabilitation Center was among the few criteria to which the author attached much significance. The types of M had been divided into favorable and unfavorable, on the basis of a preliminary study on a small number of cases. One type of M was classified as favorable: M in which two (rarely more) figures were seen as cooperating freely, without difficulty, restraint or mutual dislike or quarrel; cooperation was used in the sense of doing something together without fighting over it or feeling restrained by inner attitudes or external obstacles. Nothing else was required for inclusion among the favorable M. The M could be assertive and self-confident or it could be compliant and dependent; this distinction was irrelevant. The unfavorable M comprised two classes of M: (a) M in which appeared only one figure, and (b) M with two or more figures in which the movement or pose was described as at least partly inhibited or restrained by external forces, when doubt of completing the action successfully was expressed, or when there was inconsistency in the activities described in the M. Anything thwarting a movement, or any interference of one figure with the activity of the other, disqualified an M for inclusion in the favorable class of M. Examples of favorable M are: "Two men working on some engine"; "two bears standing at a bar"; "men or women sort of bowing" (in courteous and friendly salutation); "two old hens [meaning women] gossiping"; "squatting with knees touching together"; "waiters serving"; "sitting at a table and toasting each other"; "dancing" (a pair); "two men tearing a crab apart." The essential point is the cooperation of the men even though it is destructive to a cooked crab; the men are sharing it and do so harmoniously. Had the men fought each other over the crab the M would have been classified as unfavorable. Examples of unfavorable M are: "Two men try to move this heavy bag" but cannot; "ugly persons trying to kiss through a partition"; "two Martians trying to pull this apart but I don't know if they can do it"; "two people dancing or pulling a tire off a wheel" (subject could not decide which); "washing clothes or trying to pick up a basket"; "sitting on the ground or maybe bowing"; "tug of war" undecided; "kneeling down but raising hands up"; "men trying to get the same thing which only one of them can have." The second class of unfavorable M consisted of one figure M, e.g., "a giant climbing down a pole"; "a ballet dancer, dressed as a butterfly, standing on her toes"; "a man, bending forward, is climbing up a mountain." Good parole conduct was predicted only for men with exclusively favorable M. Poor parole conduct was predicted for men who produced at least one unfavorable M, regardless of how many favorable M he also may have produced. No predictions on the basis of the Rorschach test were made when the record contained no M at all. All these men were seen after the group testing in order to ascertain whether the lack of M was due to psychodynamically irrelevant reasons, such as poor writing, misunderstanding of directions. When an M was elicited during this inquiry, it was coded and used in prognosis. Sixty-eight per cent of the men with a follow-up (115 out of 168) produced at least one M. Among the 115 M cases, 69 gave no unfavorable M; of these, 57 (or 83%) conducted themselves well on parole and in active military service. Each of the remaining 46 had at least one unfavorable M in his test record; 32 (or 70%) of them had been convicted and sentenced by a general court-martial during the six months following restoration to active duty. Altogether, in the total group of 115 men, parole behavior had been correctly predicted in 77% or in 89 cases.

It may be a surprise that the difference between assertive and compliant M was irrelevant in predicting the adjustment of privates to Army life during a war. However, the surprise should vanish if one considers the psychosocial conditions of a private in the Army. His main duty is to carry out orders; he is told what to do and is expected to do it well. No personal initiative is expected of him; in fact, it might get him into difficulties. The close and crowded living quarters require that routines be respected to prevent disorder and arguments. Therefore the compliant M man can easily adjust to such conditions. Since everybody must obey the same orders and there are many of them, his compliance becomes an asset rather than a liability. Moreover, personal and disruptive competitiveness is strongly discouraged and all essential bodily needs are provided by the Army. Under these conditions compliant men can adjust as well as assertive ones if not better. To be an individualist and have the inclination to be independent in making decisions about intended changes in one's living conditions, as is indicated in M in which only one figure appears, makes adjustment to military life (especially when one is a private) difficult. Good self-control is necessary to follow all the rules.

If the M reveal the psychological roles which influence and direct actions and attitudes in situations in which individuals are involved, then M should change when an individual's handling of significant social relations changes. Indeed, this is the case. Schizophrenics are the best subjects to demonstrate the parallelism between M changes and actual psychosocial relationships. These patients undergo marked personality changes within a short time much more frequently and conspicuously than the rest of us—except, of course, victims of sudden and grave cerebral disorders. The following sample M are taken from test records of schizophrenics who had been tested before insulin coma treatment and after treatment. The clinical psychiatric evaluation of their post-treatment condition was made, in each case, after post-treatment hospital observations of at least two months duration. All of the patients were admitted to a psychiatric hospital for the first time; their ages varied from 18 to 24 years with the one exception of a man who was 28. M obtained before treatment will be indicated by the capital letter B, those after treatment by the capital letter P.

The following five patients improved: they became more active, more interested in relating to others, much less tense and anxious, and their thinking improved in lucidity and realism. (a) male, B

— "Men holding a pot, they're letting it down." P — "Men, seems they're lifting it up from the fire." (b) male, B — "Swimming mermaids," [pl. X]. P — Repeated the pl. X response and added "Two girls dancing the cancan" [pl. VII, reversed]. (c) female, B — "This distinguishes some kind of dog. I don't know. A French poodle dog. That's what threw me off the track [points to bottom center detail]. Seems they're resting their front paws on this" [pl. III]. P — "Two women washing clothes. Each is doing her own laundry" [pl. III]. (d) female, B — "Angels with wings—just standing" [pl. I]. "Two figures bending over or holding something, some kind of interpretive dance pose" [pl. III]. P — "Two angels, side by side, their hands are raised." "Two boys, their hands are over their heads. Jubilant postures. Halleluia!." (e) male, B — "Two people eating at a table. Actually they look like ducks" [pl. III]. "This looks like a devil, he's looking down on something, looking through something like binoculars" [pl. IV]. P — "Looks like two people kissing or something" [pl. II]. "Two women talking over the back fence" [pl. VII]. Some of the improved patients gave no movement response before treatment but produced one or two after treatment.

The following five patients failed to improve intellectually, emotionally and socially after insulin treatment: (f) male, B — "Two men or women lifting an object." "Two people, facing away. They're bent forward and stretch their arm out" [pl. V, reversed]. P — "Two people holding valises" "Two people lying" [pl. V, right side up]. (g) male, B — "Two disfigured men, their arms raised to strike each other." "Gossiping women." P — "Distorted men facing each other with upraised hands." "Two women laughing." (h) female, B — "Two people scratching their backs" [pl. III, reversed, bottom reds]. "Two little girls trying to kiss each other." P — "Two freaks, two circus freaks in tuxedos, clowns." "Two old-fashioned ladies, saying goodbye to each other and waving hands." (i) male, B — "Guerilla warfare. Submachines. Shooting." "Ballet. Girls dancing on their toes." P — "Witches arguing." "Ballet dancers. Dynamic. They're hitched together for a moment, back to back." (k) female, B — "Two women bending and holding a bundle. They're out of balance, falling backward." "Man sitting on a tree stump." P — "Two women standing in a queer position and holding something." "Man sitting on a stump."

Rorschach test evaluations of personality changes are not limited to an analysis of the *M*. However, since the *M* pertain to the most significant personality traits, and, as a rule change least and last, they contribute very pertinent information. The *M* indicate the individual's deep-seated mode of behaving in social interactions felt to be personal and important. They do not change easily because they are results of emotionally charged struggles to solve repeated conflicts with others and with oneself. Originating in early childhood, the conflicts are resolved by the development of a new and enduring manner of handling significant social relations. The new role grows under the influence of two desires: security and alleviation of anxiety (Piotrowski, 1974). This process begins within the first five or eight years; consequently it is largely unconscious. Individuals are commonly unaware of its causes as well as of its result. The appearance of *M* when they were absent on a previous examination, or their disappearance on subsequent examinations, also is important. Careful inspection of the pre- and post-treatment *M*, quoted above, disclosed that the *M* changes of the improved group in the post-treatment period disclosed increased inner freedom, greater self confidence, more activity and intensified countergravity tendencies. The reverse is true of *M* changes in the unimproved group after treatment. These *M* changes reflected adequately personality changes which had been observed while the patient remained in the hospital and after release from the hospital.

The *M* play a great role in schizophrenia research because they indicate traits which help the patients to resist the damaging effects of the psychosis. Schizophrenics without any *M* suffer, as a group, a more conspicuous and more rapid personality impairment than those who have at least several *M*. Generally, short term prognostic signs are easier to construct and are more highly valid than long term prognostic indices. Prediction of the course of schizophrenia seems to be an exception to the usual rule. The marked fluctuations in behavior and achievement that frequently occur after the onset of the manifest psychosis largely account for the difficulty of short term prognoses. In the first three to five years after onset of schizophrenia, the patient's inner condition and overt behavior reflect not only the direct crippling effects of the psychosis, but also his secondary, neurotic-like attempts at self-cure which may be even more maladaptive than the direct influence of the psychotic process upon the central nervous system; while most, if not all, of the secondary effects vanish or are greatly reduced usually within five years, the primary or direct effects tend to last even when they are mild. In all illnesses, including psychoses, the mild cases far out-number the serious ones. After twenty-five years and many trials, Piotrowski succeeded in constructing a long-term-prognostic-test-index, the LTPTI, for schizophrenia (Piotrowski and Efron, 1966).

In its final version, the LTPTI consists of 12 signs. Four validation studies were done altogether. Two of them were done "blind." This means that those who scored the test records for the presence or absence of each sign did not know which of the patients improved and which did not; the classification of the schizophrenics into improved and unimproved (by three criteria) was made independently of the scoring of the Rorschach test records by psychiatrists and research psychologists who had not seen the Rorschach records (Piotrowski, 1966). One of the groups for which the LTPTI predictions were made "blind" was the Medfield Foundation, consisting of 18 male and female patients, tested many years earlier and followed for years by the Foundation. The LTPTI classification agreed with the Foundation classification in 83 per cent of the cases. The second "blind" group consisted of 68 male patients of the Lyons Veterans Administration Hospital, the great majority of whom was chronic and elderly; 75 per cent of these patients were classified by the LTPTI in agreement with the results of their lengthy and manysided "Psychiatric Evaluation Project." A third validation group consisted of 70 male and female patients, originally studied at the New York Psychiatric Institute and followed for at least three years (with an average follow-up period of 6.6 years); the agreement between the LTPTI classification and follow-up clinical evaluation was 90 per cent. The fourth validation group consisted of 103 additional New York Psychiatric Institute male and female schizophrenics; the two independent classifications agreed in 82 per cent of the cases. Improvement after a long follow-up period of at least three years was predicted for every schizophrenic who obtained an LTPTI score of less than two points; lack of improvement, i.e., remaining the same or getting worse, was predicted for every schizophrenic patient who received an LTPTI score of at least two points. The LTPTI predictions rely almost exclusively on personality impairment, especially intellectual or perceptual, and not on emotional shocks or personality assets. There is a marked difference in relevant test reactions related to short-term and to long-term prognosis in schizophrenia; for example, the number of M is irrelevant to short-term prognosis but very important in long-term prognosis (Piotrowski, 1969). Producing more than four M was achieved by patients who eventually improved or remained essentially the same; five or more M were not found in records of those who had become worse with time. It is also typical of organic cerebral cases and of epileptics to lose the capacity for creating human movement responses.

A detailed illustration of how to apply and interpret the LTPTI is offered in the analysis of Delia's test record (Piotrowski, 1969a). Delia communicated her feelings and thoughts so well and her behavior in convential situations and in the clinic was so proper that she was given a favorable prognosis and a non-psychotic diagnosis. Yet, within less than two years after testing, she regressed conspicuously in her emotional, intellectual, social and occupational life.

Indispensable to the construction of the LTPTI was the long follow-up. The second significant contributory factor was the large number of the follow-up patients: 259 schizophrenics who differed in age, sex, decade of testing and treatment; social, ethnic and economic background. The predictive power was quite satisfactory in all four validation groups. These conditions of a long-term research made it possible to discover a principle of irreversible schizophrenic regression, namely: The degree of irreversible schizophrenic regression can be measured in terms of percentage of time during which the patient is delusional (Piotrowski, 1969). This percentage grows as regression deepens; it begins with seconds per day to a full time delusional state in cases that regress the most.

There is no substitute for follow-up in personality research. No valid predictions can be made unless one knows which personality traits are transient and which endure, and only careful and patient follow-up fact finding can provide this necessary knowledge. This observation pertains to clinical criteria as well as to test results, to psychotics and neurotics, to men who violently attack and injure others and to resigned, depressed individuals. The gradual increase of time during which the patient indulges in delusional thinking would not have become apparent without seeing many schizophrenics for a long time and over several decades; about sixty of them were seen several times and some were visited in state hospitals for more than ten years.

Long-term studies of patients who will die in a suicide are, of course, particularly time-consuming and difficult to organize. A psychologist rarely examines a patient who will later commit suicide. Even when he does, he is usually not appraised of their death. During my forty years of working with the Rorschach technique, I examined only eight patients more than once before their suicidal death. The number is small, but the trend of personality changes, from the earliest Rorschach test to the last, not only is definite, but very similar in all eight cases; the degree of the change in personality differs from patient to patient but not the direction of the change. The nature of the change makes good psychological sense. Nevertheless, many more patients should be tested and studied over long periods to learn how reliable the congruence of findings is in those eight cases.

In this group of eight patients, a professional man's two psychological examinations were separated by the longest interval of more than five years. This extensively educated and versatile professional man with great professional and social responsibilities was examined five and one-half years earlier and again three weeks before his suicidal death. The changes in his M, the whole Rorschach record, the Thematic Apperception Test and free drawings were conspicuous and consistent on all tests. He had become hypochondriacal, regularly consulted many physicians, including psychiatrists, and was known to have attempted suicide before. Apparently every one who knew him, including relatives, felt that during the last month of his life he was more serene, displayed more interest and was much less anxious than he used to be. Anxiety had been the outstanding symptom. It was a general belief that he would not commit suicide or even attempt it. The Rorschach also indicated greatly reduced anxiety in the period of five and one-half years to three weeks before his self-destruction. He was indeed calm when last seen. This external calm and absence of signs of internal tension and intellectual disturbance was taken as proof of the patient's reconciliation with life. Another explanation of the calm can be advanced and seems to be relevant and valid, namely, that the patient had made a determined decision to die. He was ready to die without fear and regret; consequently he lost the fear and anxiety about life. With anxiety vanished neurotic ambivalence which had seriously distressed him for more than thirty years (Piotrowski, 1968). During the last psychological examination, the three projective techniques agreed in their conclusion that the patient was severely constricted, resigned, passive and emotionally withdrawn. He related to others easily on a superficial level, covering his emotional disinterest in them by pleasant small talk. A new tendency appeared: the tendency to alleviate anxiety states by increasing overt motor behavior despite a conspicuous reduction of anxiety. Dark or black color responses were produced for the first time three weeks before his self-inflicted death; such responses are closely associated with depressive moods which are "partly welcome and partly unwelcome" to use Rorschach's phrase (Piotrowski, 1974).

During the first examination, the patient's Rorschach record contained the following M: "I see two comic animals, perhaps playing with each other. Perhaps bears with the faces here" [pl. II, gray areas]. "Here are two characters, playing with each other. They seem to be people, female I should say. There is a suspicion of breasts. Something in their hands which I cannot make out. With the hips extended in the rear. The breasts extended in front, in a rather peculiar position" [pl. III]. "Two childish goblins or gnomes, making faces at one another, perched rather precariously, balancing on points of rock or something underneath. Curious little tail and foreshortened body, I mean, out of scale" [pl. VII]. "Two laughing grotesque animals that might come from the imagination of Lewis Carrol. Alice in Wonderland creatures. Branching proboscis, curious laughing eyes and mouth. Big belly" [pl. IX].—Over five years later the following two M were obtained: "More interesting. Black figures. Look like gesticulating human creatures, engaged in some sort of manual activity; possibly dancing. The foot of the creatures appears to be a hoof, in shape of hoof. Here they are doing something with their hands; the arms are lowered" [pl. III]. "Here you have two gnomes or playful comic creatures with a tassel or cap on their heads, facing each other. Just head and shoulders, not the whole body" [pl. VII].

A reduction of the number of M had occurred, from four to two, revealing a reduction in inner fantasy life. The two M which had been omitted in the second examination contained animals performing movements typical of humans, but not of animals. The bears in pl. II and the Alice-in-Wonderland creatures in pl. IX stand erect on their hind legs the way humans normally stand. For this reason the responses were classified as M. Human movement responses in which animals perform are rare; they appear to reveal that their creators level a silent accusation of hypocrisy at the world. One can describe them as disillusioned idealists who have not yet recovered from the painful shock they had when they discovered that the world is not as honest and fair as they had been made to believe in their childhood. The patient was a very ethical and socially minded person who had experienced many disappointments which hurt him. In the last month of his life, he got over his shock, lost his illusions about the world and faced psychosocial realities with few, if any, illusions. However, he took his life. The M that were repeated underwent some changes. Motions of hands were prominent in the figures of pl. III on both occasions the females with their "rather peculiar position" of an exhibitionistic nature were displaced by two male black figures with hoofs (devils?), "possibly dancing." The M are dynamic self-portraits. There is no doubt that suicide was against the principles of this avowed religious man; shortly before he took his life, the "devil" in him danced. Gnomes were seen in pl. VII both times but with a distinct difference. During the first testing, they were "childish" and behaved childishly, "making faces at each other" and "balancing on points of rock." With a "curious little tail and foreshortened body" they were disproportionate. At second testing, the gnomes were playful and comical, but only their heads and shoulders were seen. With this reduction of the figures, the impression of disproportion was eliminated; the figures ceased to be "out of scale." Now they faced each other silent and composed; no mention was made of "curious little tails" and they did not need to maintain a precarious balance. Thus the second examination changes of the M indicate a marked restraint of movement, desistance from clowning, a sober and darker mood with outward calm. With conspicuously developed resignation and reduced ambitious striving, the patient became capable of a more realistic and sober look at the world. He found the world overwhelming (Piotrowski, 1968).

So far all group studies of suicide with the Rorschach test were made on survivors of suicidal attempts. Few people die in their first suicidal attempt; frequently, several are made before the fatal self-destruction. After thirty years Piotrowski was able to collect Rorschach records of 35 men and women who had died by their own hand. These effected suicides had made, on the average, two suicidal attempts before the last, fatal one. Therefore this group was matched with 25 patients who had survived two suicidal attempts that were serious enough to cause their hospitalization and were alive at a follow-up of at least six years. The test records of the 60 patients were then scrutinized for signs which discriminated between the effectors and the attempters. Rorschach reactions which were reported to differentiate between suicidal attempters and depressed patients without a history of suicidal tendencies, let alone attempts, were culled from literature; moreover a comparison of average frequencies of the conventionally coded responses also contributed a number of signs. The result was a suicide scale consisting of 14 signs, 12 of which were associated with probable suicidal death and two with probable survival of suicidal attempts (Piotrowski, 1970). What interests us here are the M that discriminated. Sign 9 was scored when there was at least one mention of death, regardless of whether it was in a form or a movement response, human or animal. Examples of "death" M: "hanging" by a rope, "jumping into a fiery furnace," "falling off a (high) mountain ledge"; 43% of effectors and 28% of attempters were credited with sign 9. "Dancing" M were placed in a category of their own; this sign 10 was found in 34% of effectors and 20% of attempters. The next sign, 11, was credited when the patient produced at least one human or animal movement expressing a pleasant and joyful activity. This was the second most discriminating sign of the scale; 37% of effectors and only 4% of attempters had this sign. Examples of joyful M are: "New Year's revelers," "ducks gazing at each other fondly," "pleasant dogs, they're rubbing their noses together"; "two men mixing a punch bowl." "Dancing" was classified exclusively as sign 10. At first sight it is surprising to find more dancing and joy in the test records of the effectors. On second thought, however, the finding is not or should not be unexpected. After all, it is easier to live in a chronic, stable depression than alternate between depressions and periods of self-confidence and gratifying interpersonal relationships. The statistical data on suicide are only an additional demonstration of the sensitivity and power of the Rorschach test to reflect personality traits of great importance to people. These traits involve the whole personality and reveal how the individual evaluates life: whether it is worth living or not (Piotrowski, 1970).

The M pertain to the least changing and most significant personality traits, both from the individual's subjective view and from the standpoint of the personality analyst, because they disclose lasting and important motives of behavior in social interactions. The "personality" accessible to projective tests, in particular to the Rorschach, is the role the individual plays in interhuman relationships when his vital personal matters are involved; the term "role" connotes not only overt behavior, conscious and unconscious, but also internal, subjective attitudes, feelings, self-evaluations, ego ideals, promptings, impulses and counterdrives, inhibitions, fears and anxieties, and their numerous varieties, conscious and unconscious (Piotrowski, 1974). More than any other component of the test, the M reflect the core of personality with its beliefs, emotions and psychomotor activities. Even small qualitative differences among the M have their distinct and enduring meaning. Every movement has a feeling all its own.

ASSOCIATION OF M WITH SPECIAL TRAITS

The foregoing accumulation of evidence regarding the positive correlation between M and overt behavior (whenever physically or socially possible, that is, in the absence of powerful external inhibitors) is of necessity incomplete. Ward's review of "the meaning of the movement response and of its changes during therapy" carefully covers a good deal of literature and concludes "that the movement response does tap a unitary concept and does provide a direct reflection of overt observable behavior" (1966, p. 427). No condition provides a better opportunity to learn what an individual's habitual handling of significant interpersonal relations is than his prolonged and intensive psychotherapy. Evidence brought forward in the preceding part of this chapter demonstrated still another point, namely, that the difference in types of M seems at least as important,

if not more, than the absolute number of M. There are three fundamental types: assertive, compliant and blocked (Piotrowski, 1974).
So rare are the blocked M that the differentiation is practically
limited to assertive and compliant M. In a study of 13 cases who
underwent a long, psychoanalytically oriented therapy (three sessions a week), the number of M was about doubled in the first six
to twelve months of treatment, but the types of M were changing
slowly and gradually (Piotrowski and Schreiber, 1952). These qualitative changes of M paralleled clinically observable personality changes,
the patients' self-descriptions and occasionally obtained estimates
of relatives. The changes of M of the improved patients were marked
primarily by two features: (a) by an increasing free expansiveness
and decrease of restraint in the movements performed by the M
figures; and (b) by the gradual change of the physical characteristics
of the M figures in the direction of increasing similarity to the
patient, in terms of age, sex and other personal traits. There were
of course individual differences in degree of change. Not every patient
changed in the same way, but the trend of the changes, when any
occurred, was in the direction of greater and freer expansiveness
and activity, diminished aggressiveness and disagreement between
two figures of the same M and reduced physical difference between
the patient and his M figures. Simultaneously some of the undesirable
M, not all, disappeared in later examinations; they included the
hostile and aggressive M, the passive and blocked ones. Incidentally,
negative color responses[2] which indicate avoidance of emotional
involvements dropped, and positive color responses which indicate
desires to get affectionately involved with others increased more
easily and strikingly than desirable changes in the quality of M.
Subsequent analyses of Rorschach records of improved and unimproved patients by psychotherapy confirmed the conclusions of
the Piotrowski and Schreiber study; it is desirable to obtain multiple
test records, at the beginning and after termination of treatment,
and also during treatment if treatment lasts a long time. Since the
number of M varies more frequently and more widely than the type
or quality of M, and since the change of the type is gradual and
reflects important personality changes, then the type of M is more

---

[2] For explanation of these terms see Piotrowski 1974, p. 225 f.

significant than the absolute number of M for personality analysis. Some schizophrenics who had not been receiving psychotherapy and had not experienced a traumatic shock sometimes suddenly produce different types of M; this is a sign that the patient's personality is undergoing a considerable endogenic change.

Attempts were made to demonstrate experimentally that the production of M increases when the Rorschach test is given following a period or during a period of deliberate inhibition of physical activity by comparison with the number produced under normal examination conditions. Cooper and Caston (1970) in their systematic review of the matter, point out the conceptual complexity of the problem and the technical, experimental inadequacies in dealing with the problem. Many different concepts are meaningfully involved and no technique used was able to provide relevant and reliable empirical referents of the concepts. Thus none of the experiments could settle the issue of whether there is or is not any stable and valid relationship between physical restraint of the subject and a change in the number of M produced by him. First of all, the results of the different experiments were contradictory, and second, the quantitative absolute differences in the number of M between the experimental situation and normal testing were small if at all present. It is true that Rorschach related the M to imagination or fantasy, but the M reflect much more than just imagination. The general observation that it is easier to fantasize when one is physically inert usually implies daydreaming. Fantasies are many; they vary and get complicated. The M, on the other hand, are few, as a rule, and vary little unless sudden and marked personality changes occur. The actions and attitudes indicated by the M are not assumed all the time or in all life situations but only in those in which the subject feels involved. How important to a student is a school experiment, for most of the subjects were college or university students. If the subject is indifferently participating and does not view the situation as seriously involving his personal scale of values, then the experiment does not investigate the meaning of M. If he does cooperate and wants to do what is expected of him, then he follows instructions and lets the experimenter control the situation, curbing whatever personalized and idiosyncratic reactions he might make. The experimental situations are not serious enough as challenges to test the serious psychosocial implications of the M as defined in the first part of this chapter. It is like trying to reach the moon in a toy paper plane. Those experiments were vague conceptually and defective in technical design. The strongest argument against the possibility of coming up with valuable results is that the type of M is of much greater relevance in studies of that sort than the mere number of M. Differences between implications of assertive and compliant M were overlooked in those experiments. A person with assertive M behaves differently from another who produces compliant M even if the absolute number of M is the same for both. The compliant subject readily assumes physically inactive postures, but not the assertive subject. It is quite probable that overlooking the meaning of the differences between the two categories of M is responsible for the contradictory findings, and the small size of the increase in M which there was an increase. The changes reported in the number of M in the normal testing condition and in the preceding experimental condition are within one standard deviation of changes between two normal examinations, particularly when the test was not administered individually but to groups. An increase in M is not always desirable. In the psychology of personality, as in all biological sciences, it is a truism that the maximum is not the optimum. Maintaining homeostasis is the condition of health. Speaking of physical activity, many Rorschach test components other than the M are more relevant to an estimate of an individual's liveliness. These components include the degree and regularity of the speed with which the blots are interpreted, color responses, shaded gray and dark color responses, ratio of color to shaded gray responses, number and differentiation of whole responses, etc. This fact adds to the unlikelihood of finding any reliable and high correlation between decrease of physical activity and rise in the number of M.

Booth (1945) used a strictly perceptanalytic principle to classify M: axial and lateral. The axial M which he calls primary are visually constructed around the middle vertical axis of the blots. Instead of seeing in this middle vertical line a border at which the two symmetrical halves meet, he views it as a dynamic center which unites both halves forming one integrated unit. Axial M reveal a greater capacity for individualism and creativeness. Axial M are less frequent than the lateral M, which in itself also indicates that the axial M are more difficult to produce, and thus require a greater effort of imagination and higher intellectual capacity which makes creators of axial M more deviant from the average. Examples are: "a giant walking" [pl. IV] and "a ballet dancer dressed as a butterfly" [pl. I]. Lateral M contain two figures, separated by the middle which is nearly always a white area. Examples are: "two men toasting each other" [pl. II] and "two women turned their heads to say something to each other" [pl. VII]. The lateral or secondary M indicate capacity to work within traditional frameworks of social organizations, a preference for activities controlled by conventions and not intended to make significant changes in the individual's social milieu. Having studied 120 patients with organ dysfunctions, Booth found that his "locomotor" group, consisting of 30 arthritic and 30 Parkinsonian cases, produced a significantly larger relative number of axial M, while his 60 arterial hypertension group produced the larger percentage of lateral M. This is a new and fruitful contribution to the psychology of movement responses.

Another group with organ dysfunction are the myopes who were examined by Marilyn Rosanes (1967). She compared the near-sighted, normal-sighted and far-sighted with one another, having 20 subjects in each of the three groups. The myopes produced mainly compliant and blocked M, while the hyperopes responded mainly with assertive M. The lower self-confidence, greater fear and greater caution of the myopes was indicated also by the difference between the sum of shaded gray responses and the sum of weighted color responses. Light shading responses measure automatic control over undesirable impulses, while color responses measure energy or emotional interest in others, both positive and negative. The average differences between shading and color measures were: in the myopes 2.20, in the emmetropes (normal-sighted) −1.55, and in the hyperopes −4.48. Excess of control over impulse was found only in the myopes. The hyperopes, on the other hand, showed the greatest excess of impulse over automatic, self-regulating control. They were confident enough and oriented in the environment well enough to take risks which sometimes result from impulsive and free behavior. The author concluded that near-sighted individuals exhibit significantly more covert anxiety with a decrease of psychomotor activity than do the normal and far-sighted. During the

Rorschach examination corrective lenses were worn by the forty subjects who needed them.

Multiple personalities are rare and published Rorschach records of them are quite infrequent. It seems that, among other features, records of these patients contain at least several M and that the types of the M differ a good deal from one another. All generalities must be cautiously made because of lack of a sufficient number of cases. It is probable at any rate that each different M or sets of M constitute the core of one of the multiple personalities. The two personalities which seem to be always present resemble Dr. Jekyll and Mr. Hyde, the good and the bad, the constructive and the destructive person; when there are more than two dissociated personalities, they are variants of the first two. Wagner and Heise published Rorschach records of three cases of multiple personalities with a theoretical explanation by Wagner (1974). Gertrude, fourteen years old at the time of testing, had three other personalities beside her main one. She consistently denied knowledge of the other three personalities. "Gertrude was sweet, shy, softspoken, and enjoyed solitude. She was described as cooperative and calm but was said to have a flat affect. . . . A second personality, Joan, was in every way opposite to Gertrude. Joan was violent, excitable, vile, and insolent. She threatened everyone, inmates and staff alike." The differences between the Rorschach records of the two personalities are conspicuous. What strikes one at first glance is the very even pace of interpretation of Gertrude (all her initial reaction times were below 8 seconds), and her cooperation indicated by the full explanation of her percepts, phrased in complete sentences. Joan's seven initial reaction times were also below 8 seconds, but the remaining three, to plates IV, V, and VI, were 25", 11" and 16" respectively, revealing: marked anxiety states, ambivalence about handling her depressive states, and lasting mood disturbances. The tendency to long periods of mood disturbance is concluded from her reacting with strikingly increased reaction times to three consecutive plates all of which present a gradation of dark and light grays without chromatic colors. After plate VI, Joan's interpretation changed by comparison with the preceding part of the record. In the first part, her unimaginative interpretations were mixed with descriptive remarks; then followed responses like these: fires, smoke, mouth of a dragon, insects clawing at each other, and last but not least a ribbon. Since our emphasis is on the *M*, let us consider Joan's sole *M*: "A flying man, he's going to fly away. He looks like a devil. His horns are sticking up here and he's wearing a cape. Horns and cape" [pl. V]. Devils have bad intentions. We do not know whether Joan's devil was getting ready just to fly away to find another place to stay or whether he was about to go on a fiendish mission. The sticking out horns imply aggression. The main aspect of any *M* is its visual-motor aspect: the devil was still on the ground; he was "going to fly away," still waiting for his flight. Seeing a man standing and prepared to fly is a response no more plausible (to plate V) than to see him actually in flight with his cape spread like the wings of a bird or plane. Unknowingly Joan was faced with a choice between two equally plausible images. Her unconscious selected a pose rather than an overt motion. The realization of the planned flight, that is, the removal of herself from her present conditions of living, was frustrated by unconscious forces. Joan was then kept bound to live in conditions which made her feel very anxious and threatened; she could not sever the painful emotional ties with others and get away. The "three insects, all clawing at each other" [pl. I] as well as the devil with his sticking up horns and his inherent capacity for evil testify to Joan's potential aggressiveness. However, the postponement of the flight reveals compulsive inhibition of aggression.

The distinct shifts in quality of content and manner of responding, at plates IV and VII, indicate a paranoid attitude. Gertrude gave *M* responses to five plates. Her *M* in plates I and IV are sadomasochistic. They contain a powerful, threatening and active pursuer whose intended victims are passive, seemingly unaware of the danger and taking no protective measures. Since the *M* are dynamic self-portraits, both the pursuer and the victims represent Gertrude. Comparison is the basis of all judgments including emotional attitudes; we cannot understand anything without having some notion and feelings about its opposite. Therefore every sadist must have some taste for masochism, and vice versa. Gertrude's pl. III *M* was: "Two men, oh, yah, no, it's two women. They've got some food there and it's cold and they're trying to warm themselves by the fire. They just killed someone and there's blood all over. I guess they're going to eat the person they killed." This response, too, is sadomasochistic with an additional element of cold-blooded unconcern for the fate of the victim which contrasts sharply with concern for personal warmth and comfort; the figures try to warm themselves before consuming their victim. The "blood all over" does not disturb them; the initial reaction time was only two seconds. The remaining two M were: "Two angels dancing" [pl. VII] and a number of witches gathering around the large white center "to see what the crystal ball has to say" [pl. IX]. Angels and witches are fictional characters; they are free of violent aggressive intentions in Gertrude's record. She made two remarks: "Am I giving you creepy ones?" when she spoke of the men or women about to eat a person they killed, and "I like to have something good in there beside evil things" after she projected the dancing angels. She had at least some awareness of her potentialities as Dr. Jekyll or Mr. Hyde. In four of the M, the acting figures did not attain their goal; they were "trying." This sign of compulsive delay of overt action or reaching the goal is much more pronounced in Gertrude's than in Joan's record. Gertrude's only M without any indication of restraint or postponement of overt activity were the good dancing angels. Therefore this M had the highest chance by far (among all of Gertrude's M) to be directly and frankly manifested in overt social interactions. Unimpeded dancing is one of the healthiest and a frequent M. It is a deep-seated, enduring drive to let people know what one can do, to attract their favorable attention and thus to secure for oneself their respect and support, making possible pleasant and constructive interhuman relationships. Ginny was a third personality; she was more easily controlled than Joan but resembled Joan more than the other three personalities. Ginny "saw" in plate V "a man with wings." Asked what it made her think of, she replied: "I'm gonna fly away. They aren't gonna keep me locked up." It is therefore quite probable that Joan's "devil" (in the same plate V) was getting ready to escape rather than do mischief. The fourth personality, Isadora, was described by the staff as fairly similar to Gertrude. These two shared several M with each other but not with the other two personalities. It seems that multiple personalities offer the best opportunity to check and develop in detail the statement that the M reveal lasting and persistent action tendencies which influence effectively the individual's role in interhuman relations that matter to him. The individual is his own control; a multiple personality is a person with several sub-personalities which can dissociate themselves from the major personality and function differently and independently of the other ones.

Margaretta Bowers, psychiatrist and hypnotist, and Sylvia Brecher (1955), clinical psychologist, reported the case of a forty-two year old man in whom multiple personalities emerged during the course of hypnotic investigation. The three dissociated autonomously functioning personalities were always the same age, 38, 16 and 4 years respectively. In his conscious state the patient was not aware of his three sub-personalities, each of which reported distinct dreams and Rorschach responses. Limiting ourselves to the *M*, the conscious, major personality age 42, gave the following *M*: "Two nuns saying their prayers together and sticking their tongues out at each other, and they are praying over a casket, kneeling with their hands up [pl. II] ; "These look like waiters and they're thinking about roosters and are holding the water pitchers in their hands" [pl. III] ; "Two boys lying on their backs with their arms folded, daydreaming. Lying back on something soft" [pl. V] ; "Two Spanish dancers, they're dancing and holding their feet together" [pl. VII]. The patient came voluntarily to the psychiatric hospital to seek help for his depression, inability to tolerate the tensions of his marriage, and to overcome a fear of committing suicide. He kept himself rigid all the time; expressed feelings of inadequacy and self-deprecia-tion. When regressed to age 38 under hypnosis, he produced: "It looks like two men facing each other. Heads look as if out to each other. They look as if they're lowering something, the way the arms are stretched. Like lowering a boat into the water" [pl. III] ; "Looks like two women. The arms are holding the cape, and the feet are hidden by the long train of the cape" [pl. X, reds]. His father died when the patient was 38. The father's ideals were "to play the game" and "to be a good loser." The plate III *M* suggests lowering of the coffin into the grave; and the plate X *M* could symbolize withdrawal since the women are all wrapped up, the lateral outward extension of the red areas being one of each woman's arms holding the cape in place. The 38 year old personality was suspicious, cold, calculating and tended to be domineering. When regressed to age 17, the patient produced only one *M*: "These look like two men dancing. They're

standing in a funny position. The legs are like men's legs" [pl. III].
In this state of a 17 year old adolescent, the patient was relatively
self-assured and defended energetically his views in matters in which
he was interested and involved emotionally. He was polite but
definite. His knowledge of the strategies and tactics of both armies
in the Civil War was enormous and detailed. Having a southern
background, he defended the aims and moves of the Confederacy
ardently. He insisted idealistically on frankness and truthfulness.
Too passive and depressed to fight for himself, he took up the
defense of what he felt was a big and just cause. Finally, regressed
to age 4, he produced no M, but gave two animal movement responses
which in prepuberty children's records have a meaning similar to that
of the M in the records of adults. These responses were: "Doggies,
kissing" [pl. II]; and "Elephant. Hiding in the trees? Hiding from
me! He's looking at me" [pl. IX]. Animal movements are also
dynamic self-portraits. However, they manifest themselves in overt
behavior when the subject is in a state of narrowed consciousness.
The patient's mother was aggressive and melancholy; she engaged
in solitary drinking and used to wander around the house nude to
keep cool. When regressed to age 4 under hypnosis, the patient was
mother's "little Harry" and "saw" mother, "two mommies" to be
exact, in plate VII. However, this percept elicited no kinesthetic
associations. Little Harry was cheerful, active, mischievous, imitative
and aggressive; he was the most outgoing of the four personalities.
The 38 year old personality was the only one clearly schizophrenic.
All of them had depressive trends, even little Harry. He was affection-
ate as his "kissing doggies," but though feeling like an elephant,
he hides in trees from little boys and watches them. To have to avoid
and escape potentially pleasant relationships is depressing. This case
demonstrates that autonomically functioning multiple personalities
produce clearly different Rorschach records, and that these differences parallel observed overt psychosocial behavior. Furthermore,
the types of M of the separate personalities are reflected in the roles
these personalities play in social interactions. The Rorschach serves
then as a reliable and objective test of the authenticity of the personalities, dissociated from the major, conscious personality, and of the
authenticity of age regressions.

The M can perform still another function in multiple personality research, namely that of predicting personalities which have not yet emerged and of which there is yet no evidence clinically. "Piotrowski predicted that there would be another personality. He based this on the variety of *M* and *FM* [animal movements] responses in the patient's conscious Rorschach which were not fully accounted for in the Rorschachs of Butch and Henry [two of the patient's dissociated personalities] . . . the two together did not equal Dick [the major, conscious personality]. There was something missing . . . [Later] we realized that this personality was trying to emerge . . . his name was Little Harry" (Bowers and Brecher, 1955). The prediction of the eventual appearance of yet another personality was made with the aid of the premise that multiple personalities are not a result of a basic personality change but of splitting into several units functionally independent of one another. It can be assumed that the patient's conscious personality was too brittle to withstand the tensions caused by the clashes of strong and incompatible action tendencies or basic motives; dissociation then is the solution. The basic motives operant in important social interactions are thus divided into compatible functional units which the patient can tolerate one at a time. M. Bowers' perceptiveness and remarkable hypnotic skill summoned up the patient's diverse personality trends and their complex psychology.

Some of the most violent, brutal and murderous assaults are committed in mental states resembling the dissociation characteristics of multiple personality. Such acts seem motivated by self-defense; what is horrible and morbid about it is that the reduction of anxiety, the catharsis and the marked alleviation of extreme hostility is achieved at the expense of physical injuries and human lives of the victims by whom the violent aggressors feel directly threatened. Their victims are, as a rule, close to them. In great contrast to these uncontrolled murderous spasms is the calculated behavior of the political assassins. Characteristic of the assassin, who acts independently, on his own initiative, and not as a loyal member of a secret group of conspirators carrying out the group's decision, is the long and careful planning of killing a politically important person, personally unknown to the offender, with whom the offender has not had even indirect contacts, but whom he has selected to be the object of his wrath, envy, hatred and sadistic preoccupation. Such offenders suffer from exaggerated but frustrated ambitions, have no lasting affection for anyone, are proud but feel demeaned by the success of others. They are extremely revengeful, secretive and lead a lonely existence. A persistent desire is to attract the attention of the world to themselves by committing a spectacular murder of someone in the limelight. Being at heart suicidal, they are ready to sacrifice their lives in order to perform the sensational deed. Hunting their chosen prey is a continuous preoccupation. The anticipation of killing excites them and gives meaning to their existence. They are realistic enough to foresee that their criminal act will also be the end of their freedom and perhaps even of their life, but they are ready to take the risk. This makes them very dangerous. Their chief goal, which psychopathologically boosts their worth in their own eyes, is the sadistic thought that one day they will deprive the very successful political leader, admired by crowds or at least known by all, of the power he exercises, of his enjoyments and even his life. Arthur H. Bremer (1973) is a member of this class of lonely men who dreamt of achieving notoriety by killing a well-known and influential political figure. He kept a diary which is most revealing. His motive was not an ill conceived self-defense and pathological manner of reducing inner tension. He had not been impulsive; on the contrary, he demonstrated self-control to appear harmless and thus to be able to perpetrate his act undisturbed by security guards. The M of such individuals are permeated with physical violence, bloody scenes, and an obsession with aggression.

The control and eventual treatment of the individual impulsive assailant will remain insoluble until we develop an objective measure of dangerousness of satisfactory validity. In the absence of such criterion, no rational planning or consistent action are possible. Megargee (1970), in his inclusive and discriminating review of predictability of violence by means of psychological tests, emphasizes that "taking small samples of behavior to estimate other behavior . . . inevitably involves errors and inaccuracy." Relevant to this principle is the 1952 Piotrowski and Abrahamsen study about which Megargee remarks that "it does demonstrate how the integration of several different variables, in this case formal Rorschach scores, Rorschach content, and the influence of alcohol, might be associated with overt aggressive behavior while simpler relationships cannot be found." About half of the violent acts against persons, including rape, are committed under the influence of alcohol. Relatively few are offenders who assault others in both states: that of sobriety and that of intoxication. Another point to keep in mind is that different types of animal movements and of human movements alternate in exercising influence upon overt social behavior (Piotrowski, 1974). Considering the difference between the psychological functions connoted by the two categories of movement responses, it appeared probable that: (a) If any animal movement response of a physical aggressor was more assertive, expansive or active than any of his human movement responses, then he perpetrated the act of physical aggression in a state of narrowed consciousness (brought about most frequently by alcohol or other drugs but occasionally in panic or by a delusional state); (b) if, however, any of the human movement responses was more assertive, expansive or active than any of the animal movement responses, then the physical aggression occurred in a state of lucid consciousness or sobriety. This statement was checked against the known mental condition of offenders at the time when they were violent, forcing their victims to submit to rape. The mental state of 100 men at the time of crime was unknown to the scorers of the Rorschach records and the classifiers of their movement responses to assure objectivity of scoring and of collecting facts about the offense. Each man had to produce at least one human movement and one animal movement to be included in the study (Piotrowski, 1974). The above statement was confirmed in 84 of 100 convicted and sentenced rapists. It applies also to predictions of expansive non-criminal behavior.

Predictions of violent and dangerous behavior, based on direct observations and records of past behavior have failed. Research findings and tests have so far also been discouraging. Tests have so far failed to reflect sufficiently and validly the complexity of human nature, the diversity and incompatibilities of goals, the impulses and their controls, the degree and nature of concern for oneself and its difference from concern, if any, for others, the quality of judgment and its influence upon overt behavior; to know what "right" behavior is and to act "right" are very different processes, particularly in offenders. What test can answer validly some of the basic questions one asks oneself when trying to predict behavior, e.g., in connection with an application for parole? To begin with (a) what is the man's capacity to deceive and to hide his true feelings and intentions? (b) how did his past violence affect his personality if at all? (c) what triggers his impulsive and cruel assaults? (d) how is his course of action influenced by unexpected obstacles? etc.

There is indeed one test that can tackle such questions with reliability and persuasive validity. It was given a try as a "blind" measure of dangerousness and produced quite satisfying results. It is PAR (the Piotrowski Automated Rorschach), a computerized system for the interpretation of responses to the Rorschach plates, based on the perceptanalytic, revised Rorschach method (1973). It emphasizes, as a source of information about personality, the visual images freely associated to ambiguous visual stimuli, the inkblots. Movement responses play a key role in the prediction of violent aggressive behavior.

Hay Associates received from a law enforcement authority Rorschach records of 40 men, all of whom threatened physical injury or death. The task was to separate the men likely to carry out their threats from those who limit themselves to verbal threats and minor physical aggression without murderous or vicious intent. A five-point scale was used for rating the men's Rorschach records: imminently danger-ous, dangerous, likely to become dangerous; not likely to become dangerous, innocuous. Frank B. Martin and this writer classified the PAR printouts in the five categories "blind;" that is, they did not know the history of the men, their past records, and they did not codify the test records for computer processing. They knew the subjects were male, their ages and that the men had voiced threats and committed violent acts which (within the group) varied from greatest intensity to the mildest. Placing all men rated as dangerous in one category and all non-dangerous men into another, the percentage of men put in the same category independently by both FBM and ZAP was 85%. The raters disagreed on only three men in each category. Thus the reliability of rating was high and PAR must have an obvious relation to dangerousness to make pos-sible such a high agreement between two independently rating judges. Degree of validity was measured by comparing ratings based solely on the PAR printouts with ratings based on records of past behavior, criminally offensive and psychopathological (mental hospitals) histories. The two raters, working independently, had to decide whether, considering each man's past behavior, he was likely to be dangerous or not dangerous to others in the future. They agreed in 62% of cases. The average ratings of the two PAR analysts and the average ratings of the two biographical raters agreed in 77% of cases. Differences in the training and experience of the raters had an influence on the degree of agreement. The more experienced PAR rater and the more experienced biographical rater agreed in 80%; the less experienced raters agreed with each other in 62% of cases. Considering the complexity of the data and the lack of any relevant and valid predictive criteria of dangerousness, the results are encouraging. PAR meets Megargee's requirement that complex (and, of course, consistent and reliable) test methods be used in investigations of dangerousness: "the integration of several [PAR has over 300] different variables . . . might be associated with overt aggressive behavior while simpler relationships cannot be found" (1970).

There was a difference in the relative frequency of many rules and rule sets between the dangerous and the non-dangerous men. Moreover, 22 of the PAR rules occurred in the printouts of only one of the groups, 12 in the dangerous and 10 in the non-dangerous group. The most striking difference between the two sets of rules is one in the capacity for effectual carrying out of intentions. Aggression is a function of controls as well as impulses.

TYPES OF *M* IN VARIOUS GROUPS

People can have the same kind of social relations or perform the same occupational tasks for several different reasons. Therefore one cannot always expect to find in the test records the type of *M* which is associated with the individual's social interaction. It is easier to give a highly valid personality evaluation using Rorschach test data than to conclude with high accuracy the Rorschach record a person would produce. One reason for it is the greater sensitivity of the Rorschach by comparison with observation under the usual social conditions and without a prolonged and intimate psychological probing. Another reason is that similar human behavior may have dissimilar motives and causes. Wagner set out to check whether actors and strippers have a larger number of exhibitionistic M than normals, neurotics and schizophrenics (Wagner, 1965; Wagner and Hoover, 1971). He did find that the former group had significantly more exhibitionistic M than the latter group. Exhibitionistic M were defined as human movement responses which involved activities performed for the benefit of an audience, such as skating, dancing, playing an instrument, or specially adorned figures to attract the viewer, such as costume wearing performers, people dressed for a ball, wearing tight toreador pants, decked out in their Sunday best. Piotrowski compared in an unpublished study neurotics with conversion symptoms to neurotics with hysteria but no conversion. Schizophrenics and cerebral cases were excluded. The ages and intellectual levels were the same, on the average. The conversion cases produced about one-half of the M produced by the non-conversion group, the averages being 2.4 and 4.2 respectively. Significant differences in types of M were found, and the greatest was in the relative frequency of Mp or movement projection. Of the 30 conversion cases, two-thirds had at least one Mp, while of the 30 non-conversion cases only one-tenth. Mp is a rare response and not a genuine movement: the subject does not visualize any movement or blocked movement but mentions it only as a secondary, verbal association to a form response. In this Mp, "stones, you could pick them up and throw," the patient "saw" only a pile of stones in plate VII; there was no figure or part of one (e.g., a hand) to throw the stones. Any element in a response to which nothing graphic corresponds in the stimulus blot is of secondary dynamic importance. We assume hypothetically that an Mp reveals an unrealized tendency to act in accordance with the movement indicated in the response but inhibited and repressed from overt manifestation if not always from consciousness. It is one important sign of the conversion neurotic's inability to come to grips with interpersonal relationships. Another sign is the greater frequency of ambivalent M in the conversion group (42% versus 28%). An ambivalent M is an alternative, e.g., "two men fighting or perhaps lifting something together." The majority of ambivalent M of the conversion group contained an aggressive movement; there was only one such ambivalent M in the non-conversion group.

Rorschach had an intense interest in the M. This is demonstrated by the amount of thought and space he devoted to the *M* in his *Psychodiagnostics* and by his own responses to his own test. According to Roemer, he and Rorschach spent a good deal of time discussing the scoring and meaning of *M*. Rorschach said that scoring *M* was the most difficult part of coding (1938). One of Rorschach's observations was that people differing strikingly in the number of *M* have a difficult time understanding each other in matters involving human relations because of the great difference in feeling about others, in acting socially and in their scales of values. Piotrowski and Dudek (1956) reported that disagreeing marital partners contemplating divorce continued living together when the numbers of their *M* were about equal; when the difference exceeded two points, a significant percentage of couples parted. All 50 couples tested were in psychotherapy because of marital difficulties. Bricklin and Gottlieb (1961) confirmed this finding but did not limit themselves in their investigation. They analyzed types of *M* and other test components and constructed a Marital Compatibility Prognostic scale. This therapeutically helpful scale is another instance of improving the test's sensitivity to complex and important human problems by using patterns of test elements instead of only one or several. Bricklin and Gottlieb suggest that when husband and wife each earn a poor score on their Marital Compatibility scale, communication between them should be discouraged and each should be urged to enter individual psychotherapy. Talking things over does not always help; sometimes it separates.

Differences in number and types of *M* are significant not only when people are in difficulties but also when they are successful. Rorschach records of 110 top executives examined by Hay Associates were scrutinized for components associated with continued success and promotions in top business positions and for components associated with failure to retain a top position in a large corporation once it had been attained. Each man was followed for at least four years. On the basis of their past records and follow-up information, the men were divided into a group of 52 successes, 16 intermediate successes and 42 failures. By far the most significant test component associated with success or lack of it was the type of *M*. On the Perceptanalytic Executive Scale for the selection of top managers, the *M* occupy the first place because of the relatively high correlation between type of M and managerial success. This is not surprising in competitive and hard working men. The more active and intense the life a man leads, the easier it is to validate the conclusions drawn from his M. The differences between the successful and failing groups were significant (with P below .01) on every one of the 15 positive signs and 11 of the negative signs; the remaining six of the 32 signs differentiated with P above .01 but below .10 with the exception of one sign (P below .20). Piotrowski and Rock (1963) described the signs and analyzed ten sample records, summarizing also the occupational achievement of each of the ten men. Freedom from obsessions and compulsions was the outstanding trait which differentiated the continually successful top executives from the other two sub-groups. This inner freedom was reflected also in the animal and human movement responses. Large mammals easily overcame obstacles or the force of gravity. Typical were M in which two human figures were engaged in a common counter-gravity activity, cooperating harmoniously and acting confidently, unhampered in any way.

ANIMAL AND INANIMATE MOVEMENTS

There is no space for an extensive presentation of animal and inanimate movements. There is some difference of opinion on how to score these responses and whether to use these movement categories at all. It seems that the main reason for this is that Rorschach did not include them in his book *Psychodiagnostics*. The same is true of dark and light shading responses which Rorschach introduced into his system after the publication of his book. The reader is referred to *Perceptanalysis* in which he will find a lengthy discussion of the animal and inanimate movements as well as of human movements.

However, one brief remark is in order about the animal movements because it is an addition and correction of previous presentations. The types of animal movements change more than had been thought previously. Very intelligent, mostly obsessive patients in long and intensive psychoanalytically oriented therapy changed, among other components, also the types of their FM. Each patient was given the Rorschach at least three times, at the beginning, in the middle and after termination of treatment. We noted in the middle period an increase of compliant, passive or sadomasochistic animal movements. This increase or first appearance of these undesirable responses coincided with a phase of treatment during which acute conflicts with parents, hitherto repressed, were emerging from the unconscious; this new awareness caused much anxiety and strong emotional reactions (Piotrowski and Schreiber, 1952).

In the perceptanalytic Rorschach system, the category of inanimate movements is reserved for overt or blocked movements of physical, inanimate objects only (Piotrowski, 1974). Unless so limited in denotation, the meaning ascribed to them does not apply. They reveal action tendencies shaping social interactions which the subject experiences as desirable but feels that they are unrealizable for him. Actions and attitudes indicated by human and animal movements are not felt to be unrealizable by the subjects who produce these movement categories. Therefore, one might assume that the content of the inanimate movements should be different from that of human and animal movement responses. This is the case of the great majority of adults who are rather well integrated psychologically. It is not the case of a considerable percentage of prepuberty children and of some adults with poorly integrated personalities. Such individuals actuate at some times or in special psychosocial conditions only parts of their personalities, parts which have a functional autonomy to a noticeable degree. Such individuals have a low awareness of their inconsistencies in relating to others on the fantasy and actual inter-action levels.

Imagination expressed in movement responses—and especially in human movements—imitates reality which has a powerful influence. Experience with reality is an essential factor in shaping imagination and anticipation of the future. Imagination also competes with perception of reality because it often leads to attempts to modify perceived reality so as to suit the individual's expectation. More imagination and more creative power are revealed by the movement responses than by any other component of the Rorschach test.

BIBLIOGRAPHY

Beck, S. J. *Rorschach's Test: Basic Processes*. New York: Grune & Stratton, 1944.

Booth, C. G. Organ function and form perception. *Psychosom. Med.*, 1945, **8**, 367-385.

Bowers, M. K., and Brecher, S. The emergence of multiple personalities in the course of hypnotic investigation. *J. clin. & exp. hypnosis*, 1955, **3**, 188-199.

Bremer, A. H. *An Assassin's Diary*. New York: Harper's Mag. Press, 1973.

Bricklin, B., and Gottlieb, S. G. The prediction of some aspects of marital compatibility by means of the Rorschach test. *Psychiat. Quart. Suppl.*, 1961, **35**, 281-303.

Cooper, L., and Caston, J. Physical activity and increases in *M* responses. *J. proj. Techn.*, 1970, **34**, 295-301.

Hammer, E. F., and Jacks, I. A study of Rorschach flexor and extensor human movement responses. *J. clin. Psychol.*, 1955, **11**, 63-67.

Megargee, E. I. The prediction of violence with psychological tests. In: C. D. Spielberger (ed.) *Current Topics in Clinical and Community Psychology*. New York: Academic Press, 1970, 97-156.

Mirin, B. The Rorschach human movement response and role taking behavior. *J. nerv. ment. Dis.*, 1955, **122**, 270-275.

Parker, R. S., and Piotrowski, Z. A. The significance of actors of Rorschach human movement responses. *J. proj. Techn.*, 1968, **32**, 33-44.

Piotrowski, Z. A. The *M*, *FM* and *m* responses as indicators of changes in personality. *Rorschach Research Exch.*, 1937, **1**, 148-157.

Piotrowski, Z. A. *Perceptanalysis: A Fundamentally Reworked, Expanded and Systematized Rorschach Method*. Philadelphia, Pa.: Ex Libris (2217 Spruce St., 19103). 3rd print., 1974. (Orig. publ., 1957).

Piotrowski, Z. A. The Rorschach inkblot method (as a diagnostic test). In: B. B. Wolman (ed.). *Handbook of Clinical Psychology*. Baltimore: Williams & Wilkins, 1965, 522-561.

Piotrowski, Z. A. Psychological test prediction of suicide. In: H. L. P. Resnik (ed.). *Suicidal Behaviors*. Boston: Little, Brown & Co., 1968, 198-208.

Piotrowski, Z. A. Long-term prognosis in schizophrenia based on Rorschach findings: The LTPTI. In: D. V. Siva Sankar (ed.). *Schizophrenia: Current Concepts and Research*: PJD Publications, 1969, 84-103.

Piotrowski, Z. A. Delia: A relatively well-functioning young woman and her bizarre Rorschach record. In: J. E. Exner, Jr. (ed.). *The Rorschach Systems*. New York: Grune & Stratton, 1969, 297-314.

Piotrowski, Z. A. Test differentiation between effected and attempted suicides. In: K. Wolff (ed.). *Patterns of Self-destruction*. Springfield, Ill.: C. C. Thomas, 1970, 67-81.

Piotrowski, Z. A. *PAR: the Piotrowski Automated Rorschach*. 3rd rev. ed., 1973. (In operation: Hay Associates, Philadelphia).

Piotrowski, Z. A., and Abrahamsen, D. Sexual crime, alcohol and the Rorschach test. *Psychiat. Quart. Suppl.*, 1952, **26**, 248-260.

Piotrowski, Z. A., and Dudek, S. Z. Research on human movement response in the Rorschach examinations of marital partners. In: V. W. Eisenstein (ed.). *Neurotic Interaction in Marriage*. New York: Basic Books, 1956, 192-207.

Piotrowski, Z. A., and Efron, H. Y. Evaluation of outcome of schizophrenia: The long-term-prognostic-test-index. In: P. Hoch & J. Zubin (eds.). *Psychopathology of Schizophrenia*. New York: Grune & Stratton, 1966, 312-334.

Piotrowski, Z. A., and Rock, M. R. *The Perceptanalytic Executive Scale: A Tool for the Selection of Top Managers*. New York: Grune & Stratton, 1963.

Piotrowski, Z. A., and Schreiber, M. Rorschach perceptanalytic measurement of personality changes during and after intensive psychoanalytically oriented psychotherapy. In: G. Bychowski and J. L. Despert (eds.). *Specialized Techniques in Psychotherapy*. New York: Basic Books, 1952, 337-361.

Roemer, G. A. Vom Rorschachtest zum Symboltest. *Zbl. Psychotherapie*, 1938, **10**, no. 6.

Rorschach, H. *Psychodiagnostics: A Diagnostic Test Based on Perception.* New York: Grune & Stratton, 1942. (Orig. publ. Bern: H. Huber, 1921). '

Rosanes, M. B. Psychological correlates to myopia compared to hyperopia and emmetropia. *J. proj. Techn.*, 1967, **31**, 31-35.

Wagner, E. E. Exhibitionistic human movement responses of strippers: An attempt to validate the Rorschach *M. J. proj. Techn.*, 1965, **29**, 522-524.

Wagner, E. E., and Heise, M. R. A comparison of Rorschach records of three multiple personalities. *J. proj. Techn.*, 1974, **38**, 308-331.

Wagner, E. E., and Hoover, T. O. Exhibitionistic *M* in drama majors: A validation. *Perceptual & Motor Skills*, 1971, **32**, 125-126.

Ward, A. J. The meaning of the movement response and of its changes during therapy: A review. *J. proj. Techn.*, 1966, **30**, 418-428.

It is our contention that every experience not only refers to the fundamental spheres of "self" and "world," but also to the sphere of the body. Human existence consists in living at once in these three spheres, which form an inseperable unit.

PAUL SCHILDER

7

Martin Mayman

A

MULTI-DIMENSIONAL VIEW OF THE

RORSCHACH MOVEMENT RESPONSE:

Perception, Fantasy, Kinesthesia, Self-Representation, and Object-Relationships[1]

Forms, colors and chiaroscuro of the Rorschach ink blots provide the raw material out of which the perceptual-associative process fashions Rorschach responses. Most Rorschach inferences are based upon the manner in which the subject uses this source of stimulation —how he experiences and responds selectively to these properties of the blots, and the extent and nature of their influence upon his thought processes.

It has become customary to include with these determinants, a fourth, movement, to account for the fact that some figures seen in the blots seem to be in motion. However, it is by no means obvious what the corresponding raw datum is for the movement response, and, if such a blot-stimulus for *M* responses[2] can be identified, how often it is the only, or even the main, determinant of the movement im-

---

[1] The first half of this paper was presented at a Rorschach seminar at the Menninger Foundation in 1956. The full paper was read at the Colorado University Medical School in 1962. The discussion of self/other relationships appears more fully, and in relation to some research data, in a paper presented at a 1966 APA symposium, published in the Journal of Personality Assessment (Mayman, 1967).

[2] For explanation of scoring symbols see Appendix, p. 609 ff. [Editor].

pression. This question, if systematically pursued, opens up several lines of inquiry, and shows why movement responses are easily the richest, most revealing, consistently most interesting responses which occur on the Rorschach test.

Rorschach theorists have identified at least five "determinants" of the movement response: (1) The inkblot-properties which help evoke movement percepts; (2) The contribution of fantasy to movement perception; (3) Kinesthesia, and its relation to the self-expressive character of movement responses; (4) Object-representation in the content of the human movement response; and (5) Empathy and identification as reflected in the movement response.

It is this complexity which explains why the only important divergence among Rorschach theorists occurs in their treatment of movement responses. Each has emphasized one or two of these five determinants of the movement response to the exclusion of other aspects. No one has yet advocated scoring for, and interpreting separately, all five dimensions of the movement response process. Only in this way, however, will we ultimately resolve what are only apparent, not real, conflicts regarding proper scoring and interpretation of the M response.

1. The Perceptual (Objective) Determinant of the Movement Response.

It was Rapaport's (1945) discussion of the M response which first called attention to the purely perceptual determinant of movement responses. Rorschach had explained the M response by postulating a kinesthetic "engram" stirred associatively by a blot-outline. According to Rorschach (1921), this movement engram, or memory trace, is qualitatively different from the memory traces of static objects, and merges with a human percept making it seem as if the person seen in the blot is animated by that kinesthesia. The action seems real but is only the projection of a reawakened memory trace of a kinesthesia.

The adequacy of the engram concept, and of association theory in general, to explain such perceptual experiences was called sharply into question by the Gestalt psychologists. Rapaport, following the Gestaltists, wanted to make a complete break with the nineteenth century association theory which Rorschach had been using in his explanation of the *M* response. Rapaport sought to account for the movement response on some different basis more in line with Gestalt theory. He argued that the only genuine movement responses were those in which the subject sees and associates to an actual, demonstrable, perceptual imbalance in the ink blot. A simple stick figure such as   ⟨   or   ⟨   is an unstable gestalt whose imbalance normally is felt directly by the observer. The first figure seems to be falling forward, the other, toppling backward. Rapaport argued that kinesthetic engrams need not be invoked to explain these percepts. He suggested that the person, unconsciously piqued by the imbalanced gestalt, sees that gestalt in flux. Without being aware of it, he introduces perceptual *praegnanz*; he sets matters right, so to speak, by attributing to that image a direction of change toward an imminently better-balanced, more stable configuration. The figures above will be seen for example, as "something bending over," or "straightening up," or "pulling against something which keeps him braced in that position." All of these impressions either add a stabilizing force or imply a direction of change toward a more stable position.

Such sensitivity to "visual rhythms," to use one of Rorschach's terms, is no mean achievement. If nothing else, it requires that one be able to transcend an atomistic survey of a blot area and pay attention, rather, to its dynamic composition. If one takes hold of an area in piecemeal fashion, one does not see the more complex configurations in which such imbalanced gestalten usually occur. The subject will not be prompted to see the more dynamic form and will make do instead with simpler, more static interpretations. This is one reason why people who are intellectually limited give few *M*'s. They are more prone in general to see relatively simple forms. They view details too discretely to become aware of such subtle perceptual properties as intrinsic balance, imbalance, or dynamic composition. It is to this disturbance of the perceptual-organizing process that we can attribute Werner's (1940) finding that organically brain-damaged patients are deficient in the capacity to perceive *M*'s, and Rorschach's (1921) finding that patients who are mentally deficient are most prone to give oligophrenic responses which in almost all instances

prove to be fragments of what could have been developed into good
M responses had the patients been capable of grasping the more complex gestalt.

Rapaport's most telling argument in support of this hypothesis
was his finding that M responses, scored according to his hypothesis, co-vary with the intensity, vigor and sweep of ideational activity.
Rapaport, Gill and Schafer (1945) cite a wealth of supportive data
for the hypothesis that M's indicate ideational potential, the number
of M's correlating not only with I.Q., but with such specifically over-
ideational forms of psychopathology as obsessional states, paranoid
conditions, phobic conditions and over-ideational borderline states
(called "pre-schizophrenic" by them in 1945).

Some important and valuable corollaries of Rapaport's hypothesis which are uniquely explained by his rationale should be noted
before we set it aside. The sensitivity to dynamic composition and
the sense of flowing inter-relatedness of certain blot areas can go
awry in a number of ways. We may observe an over-readiness to leap
across natural gulfs, to ignore natural blot-boundaries, to indulge in
a sweepingly overriding sense of perceptual cohesion, to an extent
which breaks with good reality testing and culminates in an $M-$ response. On such occasions, the subject is so overly impressed with
the intrinsic movement impression in a blot area that this single
perceived quality serves as virtually the sole basis for an interpretation
which does not fit the area at all, for example, seeing Card VII
upside down as "a fat pudgy man with his arms spread." Here, the
arms and legs are the basis for the percept, which coalesces into a
single impression despite the arbitrariness of the ensuing organization.
The person is carried away so completely by the impression of dynamic imbalance that he abandons himself to this single perceptual
property and suspends reality testing as he puts his associative
processes to work rationalizing this impression, much like the paranoid patient who feels and rationalizes with intense conviction his
arbitrarily perceived connections.

Another miscarriage of the sense of dynamic composition may
involve the "perception" of relationships where none exist: either
a feeling that one Rorschach card is the same as, or a continuation
of, another blot in some way, or else the feeling that the separate
areas in a blot are disarranged but would form a new and better

configuration if one area were transposed, tilted, or fitted to another in a different way. In both these instances, a present configuration flows into the shape of one which the person can only feel but does not yet see. Such overriding awareness of relatedness indicates both the ideational vigor and the interpretive arbitrariness which such paranoid patients are so capable of and use so extensively in their thinking.

Such impressions represent a misguided and overworked sensitivity to the dynamic composition of the blot forms. Just as one learns in the course of development to modulate the labile, intense, impressionable response to color, so too, the physiognomic sense of movement and change which is so much a part of the life of early childhood, is converted into a more stable, less animated, more predictable world, as the ego takes over the task of carrying on its work-a-day relationship with stable objects of its experience. $M-$ responses and "relationship" responses are regressive revivals of physiognomic response tendencies which have usually been long since overcome by the growing ego.

We also occasionally find evidences of an attempt to bind this tendency on the Rorschach test. The need to see things as balanced, and therefore as stable, static, and under control, interferes with the ability to tolerate imbalance long enough to see an M response. This occurs most often in cases with conspicuous compulsive defenses, where M's drop away as the patient becomes more and more concerned with sterile preoccupations. But it is important to stress that in these cases, too, this does not represent a purely perceptual failure to delay long enough to see and use the perceptual imbalances which underlie good movement responses. The subject is also reacting to the "imbalance" within himself which the perceptual imbalance reminds him of. The quick restitution of an outer balance serves to blot out the reminder of his own inner imbalance and his own disturbing potential for inner flux.

These are all corollary hypotheses which accompany and lend support to Rapaport's explanation of the M response process. However, even if we grant Rapaport's contention that perceptual imbalance is an important component of many M responses, it is neither a necessary nor a sufficient factor to account for the full range of characteristics which set Movement responses apart from all other responses on the Rorschach test. Even Rapaport went beyond this rationale for M responses when he limited the movement score only to human or humanoid figures seen in motion. There are surely many animal movements or even inanimate movement impressions which are just as soundly based upon perceptual imbalance as are the human movements. If human movement responses differ from animal movement responses, then this must be on the basis of other considerations than perceptual imbalance. Moreover, Rapaport does not account for the occurrence of movement responses where no perceptual imbalance exists but where he agrees with other Rorschach workers that an M score is in order. The postulation of perceptual imbalance as a component of the movement response does not rule out the existence of other determinants of these responses which may be as important, or more important, than the purely perceptual determinant which Rapaport made so much of.

Several times in the above remarks I have verged on a discussion of kinesthesia in the M response. Before turning to this aspect of Movement perception, it would be advisable to consider first the most ubiquitous component of M responses, their immersion in the ongoing fantasy life of the subject.

2. The Fantasy Component of the Movement Response.

The M response differs from most other responses in its vividness, its aliveness. It seems to draw more heavily upon fantasy than does the usual non-M response. In fact, the M response often seems to be a fragment of arrested fantasy. This is easily confirmed in almost any Rorschach test situation if, following an M response, the examiner invites the subject to continue his response, so to speak. If asked something like, "Hands together, as if what?", the subject will almost always immediately add something in a way which strongly suggests that the "new" material had been part of an integral fantasy of which only a part had been verbalized in the response proper. It makes good sense to him to be asked to continue developing his response. Apparently, he puts only a fraction of the total response into words. The rest may be there ready-made and available, but either preconscious, or else conscious but withheld, until it is elicited by the examiner.

Fantasy animates the movement response. One does not usually see just "two people bending over." The people are ordinarily more animated and more real than that—they are "bowling," or "bowing to each other," or "lifting a table." This kind of animation on the Rorschach Test is probably not too distant a derivative of the animism of childhood, and it is certainly not limited to *human* movement percepts on the test. When someone sees on Card X, for example, "creatures sweeping upward toward some ultimate objective," the response is clearly in movement, in this instance a form of primitively animistic movement. Animism may be successfully held in check and converted into a good movement response, but it may also appear in much more archaic forms on the test, sometimes even in representations much like the infant's panic, the adult nightmare, or the psychotic delusion. Thus, "A piece of meat, blotchy as if maggots are crawling all over it."

Those Rorschach theorists, like Klopfer (1942), who score movement on the basis of "aliveness," have, in doing so, extended the movement score to cover a wide range of non-human M responses in which fantasy spills over in the response process and gains plastic representation in the ink blot forms. As such, they are appropriately taken to indicate "richness of inner life." But if the movement score is to be so equated with fantasy potential, then not even Klopfer goes far enough in his innovations for the scoring of Movement responses. There are some responses which do not involve either movement *or* aliveness, but which have animistic vividness that would justify their being included in a score which seeks to measure "rich inner life." These are the responses which may, following Rapaport's suggestion, be scored "fabulized" responses. Usually a fabulized response entails some living creature in an action of some sort, but not always. The fantasy may be expressed in a response much like a stage setting in which living creatures might at any moment make their appearance but haven't yet arrived. For example, the tiny spire projections on the "nose" of the popularly seen faces on Card VII have been called. "A town off in the distance with a church steeple visible and a few other spires. A little hamlet snuggled into the valley of some rolling hills." This response has an immediate realism which is the special earmark of the richly fabulized response. Every good M incorporates some of this quality; to be able to give a good M one must have available a stream of fantasy that one can dip into to help vivify the response. But, as in the above example, static fabulized responses can occur, and may draw as richly from fantasy as do movement responses. They are as legitimate an index of rich inner life as is the total M score, or the combined M, FM and m score. The wealth of a person's fantasy life is best measured by the number and intensity of the "fabs," not the number of M's and FM's. When a record is vividly animated by fantasy which envelops each response, whether these be animate movements, inanimate movements, or the fabulizing of an unpeopled but living scene, we may infer rich fantasy life and a capacity to slip back and forth easily between the immediate objective reality and the subjective mirroring in fantasy of that reality. A five-point Fabulizing Scale has been developed which shows some promise of more precisely measuring the degree of fantasy potential indicated by movement (and other) Rorschach responses than do other more conventional Rorschach scores (Mayman, 1960, Voth and Mayman, 1963).

As with some other Rorschach determinants—color particularly —we find that the mature ego has learned to subdue the highly subjective, highly personalized, occasionally animistic modes of expression characteristic of childhood. More and more, these qualities are consigned to the realm of daydream, fiction and poetry, while the person comes to share with others a more impersonal, less colorful but more communicable set of experiences. But this abandonment of fantasy may be carried to extremes. A person who carefully avoids fabulizing, or who shows no inclination in this direction, may have cut himself off too completely from his inner life. Such people often seem shallow and stimulus-bound. In Rapaport's phrase they often show relatively little autonomy from reality (Rapaport, 1958). Usually, they also seem frightened of what might emerge if they were to open themselves to more subjective experiences. Such people act as if they have insufficient inner resources to do otherwise; they tie themselves to reality because they have no alternative (not unlike the mental defective or organically brain-damaged person who clings compulsively to a monotonous routine).

Rorschachs obtained from people in states of motor inhibition or restricted freedom of movement, have been shown to be richer in Rorschach movement perception (Singer et al., 1952; Meltzoff et al., 1953), suggesting that inhibited motor discharge touches off a reverberating circuit of kinesthesias. But these studies report only on the number of M responses, not the total Fab score. More recent studies on stimulus deprivation (Goldberger and Holt, 1961; Mayman and Voth, 1969) suggest that it may rather be imagination in general, not kinesthesias in particular, which acquires renewed cathexis as the input of exteroceptive stimuli diminishes, just as it is visual imagery, not kinesthesia, which emerges with greatest vividness when one drops off to sleep.

Certainly it seems reasonable to say at this point that Rorschach records rich in both fabulized and movement responses are likely to be elicited from introversive, obsessive and schizoid individuals (Voth and Mayman, 1963). Of course, fantasy may also be richly represented in Rorschach records obtained from some grossly infantile-hysterical character disorders, rather than being submerged with the general repression of inner life which so commonly occurs in most hysterical neuroses. It is also important to remember that a certain optimal range of fantasy expression occurs in Rorschachs of bright, imaginative, and creative normal subjects as well.

As with any expression of fantasy in test productions, an analysis of their content can be most instructive. The imagery which finds its way into all Rorschach test responses, M's in particular, may have rich personal significance, but a comprehensive discussion of this component of the M response belongs better in a discussion of content interpretation (Schafer, 1954; Mayman, 1967).

3. Kinesthesia, and the Self-Expressive Character of the M Response.

The fact that any Rorschach response may be fabulized tells us something we already know from other sources: that every experience, particularly fantasy, is invested with self-feeling and is to some extent self-expressive. However, many Rorschach theorists have felt that the movement response, more than any other Rorschach response, is particularly relevant to questions of self-experience and self-expression (Schachtel, 1950). This is probably because of the dependence of the movement response on ingrained kinesthetic memories, and their relation to a person's characteristic stance vis-a-vis the people and things in his world.

Children's thought is at first largely sensori-tonic. Articulate thought emerges from a sea of sensori-affective and kinesthetic experiences. The child thinks with his body.* When the baby is in pain or need he yells or thrashes about, or reaches imperfectly for what he wants. When an adult guesses the child's wish and meets it, the success of the child's random acts helps crystallize the magical anticipation that wishing will make it so, especially if accompanied by the proper magical gesture; thought, wish and act are one (Ferenczi, 1913). Werner (1940) reports a wealth of data illustrating how the child early in life defines his relationship to his world in such "syncretic" terms.

If we assume that a person not only experiences these kinaesthesias, but retains some memory of them, it follows that each newly learned action adds to a rapidly growing repertoire of kinesthetic memories. What, after all, does the word "I" mean? If we take the grammatical structure literally, the "I" is the subject of some transaction with the objects of one's world; the I is always linked with some verb, usually an active one. Grammar and syntax only express a psychological truth it takes a child months and years to learn, namely, that one's being-in-the-world, to borrow an existentialist phrase, is defined by the transitive and intransitive verbs of his language; that one becomes an autonomous self as one becomes the initiator of activity which can change his world; that one establishes himself in his world by acting upon it. One can almost trace the emergence of a sense of personal identity and autonomy in the transitions from an "I am" (or more likely, a "me" ego-state) to the "I have" or "mine" ego-state, to the "I can"—"I will"—"I do" ego-states. The changing predicate reflects the changing scope of the evolving self. Not only does the ego's boundary expand but the emerging self shifts progressively from the passive to the active voice as it becomes rooted in increasingly self-responsible, self-initiated action systems. The child who can say "I" with emphasis has learned what it means to be master of his own musculature, and to have his musculature be instrumental in his mastering of his world. Perhaps the first clear expression of the decision-making "I" comes with the development

---

*This is true not only of the child. Studies on the motor theory of thought (Latif, 1934) show that to a great extent muscle innervations are an inseparable accompaniment to thought. Even psychoanalysts hold that thought is really "a form of experimental action" (Freud, 1911).

of the "no" reaction. This form of self-assertive experience is closely linked with the "I have" forms of experience, that is, with the taking and keeping actions which are among the first expressions of autonomy by the child, and add importantly to his growing repertoire of ego-experiences. Both the "no" response and the "I keep" or "I take" response are transitional stages in the shift from the passive "I am" to the active "I can do."

The child who has repeatedly undergone certain traumatic experiences may come to build a particular recoil experience into his ego-system. A child who is emotionally cowed may become kinesthetically cowed as well. Those people who are set to cringe at almost any form of criticism may actually go through life cringing inwardly, that is, kinesthetically, when events stir up the unconscious memory of a host of parental injunctions like, "Go away!" "Don't touch!" "Be quiet!" "Don't run!" "Come here!" When we speak of the super-ego or of parental introjects, we speak of those ways in which the child has been programmed to react as he does. He becomes primed to recoil as if he were still confronting the internalized voice of a reproachful or mocking or crushing or engulfing parent. There is reason to believe that each such readiness to recoil is kinesthetically real, not just a figure of speech.

There may be a kinesthetic basis for many metaphors which express feelings with particular vividness. When one says he feels like "sinking through the floor" or "crawling into a hole" or "rolling up into a ball," such metaphors should perhaps be taken literally. The person may be expressing a kinesthetic, quasi-conscious memory of just such an early experience. These phrases may refer to ingrained, kinesthetically rooted stances taken by the ego in response to early traumata, and may express embedded reaction-tendencies of the self, built into the person's character structure and retained largely in kinesthetic form.

To return to the thought which led to these reflections, those self-feelings that are bound up in kinesthesias are different in quality from the self-feeling involved in the pleasure of making contact with familiar and warmly personal objects. Both enhance one's self-experience, but there is an essential difference between the self-feeling that derives from one's valued objects and the self-feeling that is rooted in one's kinesthetic action-potentials.

We may assume that those kinesthesias which find their way into a person's movement responses are drawn from a repertoire of kinesthetic memories which express some of his core experiences of selfhood. This is true of all movement responses, not just human movements. Purposeful, goal-directed, socially appropriate, total body activity is not the ego's only form of kinesthetic experience. We have all had the experience of crawling on all fours; we know what it would feel like to "explode"; we know the buoyancy of feeling "like a feather in the breeze." In fact, most, if not all, tension-states expressed in animal movement and in inanimate movement responses are by no means alien experiences. Crawling, falling, drifting, chewing, crushing, pouncing, tearing apart, are not unfamiliar tension-state experiences. Some are infantile. Some are very archaic feeling states, linked with impulses which normally would be wholly repressed, but they are not beyond the pale of human experience. They may come to expression in less ego-syntonic form than those mature kinesthesias which find their way into good human movement responses. The "m" tensions are likely, in fact, to be least ego-syntonic of all movement experiences. The "m" is a metaphoric expression of forces which seem impersonal, not subject to personal control. These forces intrude on the self; they come at one from outside; they happen willy-nilly. Subjectively they have the same attributes as those ego-alien forces which are relegated to the "id." In fact, "m" responses generally indicate some failure of repression which permits unsuccessfully repressed impulses to spill over into subjective awareness in essentially ego-alien form. Such tension-state experiences, and their associated fantasies, may indicate the existence, in the form of somewhat alien, archaic ego-states, of intra-psychic tensions which have remained unassimilated, that is, unsublimated, in the person's functional ego-system. Animal and inanimate movement responses are often metaphoric representations of such infantile or archaic ego-states in various degrees of insubordination to the prevailing ego-synthesis. As Klopfer (1942) puts it, "The little *m*'s indicate hostile and uncontrollable forces working *on* him rather than as sources of energy at his disposal." This is rarely the case with those kinesthesias which find expression in *human* movement responses.

One must be careful, however, in translating a Rorschach image into a statement about the subject's inner experience of impulses. One must, for example, decide whether the person is the subject or object of the represented action, i.e., whether he is an active or passive participant in the movement metaphor, relying on such clues as the tone of voice, the gestures, and the further elaborations which come in response to an "As if . . . ?" question. The person might say, for example, "As if a little animal were just about to cross the road when a car came along and crushed it," or he might say with a bit more relish, "As if a steamroller had run over some animal and flattened it out." In the first, the experience is presented from the point of view of the little animal; in the other, from that of the massive object doing the crushing. We must ask in each instance what the quality is of the ego's participation in a response: is it active or passive? attacking or masochistic? Of course, at a very regressed level of experience, the clear distinction between subject and object fades away, and the act may be experienced in the form of, "crushing is taking place" or "anger is about to explode," and one may quickly vacillate between being the subject and being the object of these destructive intents, as often happens in borderline psychotic people or those with very infantile personality structures.

4. The Interpersonal (Relationship) Implications of the *M* Response

There is more to a movement response than kinesthesia; there is also the figure carrying out the action. In telling us about this observed other, the subject reveals much about himself.

Hertzman and Pearce (1947) carried out a somewhat informal but important study. They administered Rorschachs to a number of subjects who subsequently went into therapy. After six months' treatment, the personal images which appeared in each patient's pre-treatment Rorschach record were reviewed by the therapist to see which of the images had distinct personal relevance in the light of the material which had emerged in psychotherapy. They found that 75% of all human figures appearing in the Rorschach protocol had identifiable, though presumably largely unconscious, personal meaning for the subject. What implications can be drawn from the fact that such personal images are available at all, let alone that they are "discovered" in the ink blots so frequently, and with a warmth, openness and even a kind of intimacy which does not usually characterize other Rorschach responses?

A number of studies are brought to mind by these questions. Pious (1950) reports on an interesting observation he made in the psychoanalysis of an obsessive-compulsive man who suffered an acute schizophrenic break shortly after he started treatment. Pious noticed that the patient's condition would disintegrate during any period of separation from the analyst unless the patient was able to retain a mental image of his analyst during the separation. If the image of his analyst were to dissolve, the patient went into a panic and his condition disintegrated until he could once again reconstitute his image of the analyst. It was clear in the material that the image was not just a percept or just a conceptualization of the analyst; it carried some of the *essence* of the analyst. The image, when available to the patient, was part of an enduring presence to which he could turn for comfort.

This patient's panic was not very different from the panic which infants experience in the absence of their mothers if they are too young to be able to retain in fantasy a stable image of the mother which reassures them that the mother hasn't vanished. I once had an interesting experience which first brought this realization home to me. I was baby-sitting for a friend, the mother of an eighteen-month-old child, while she was out shopping. The little boy was asleep, but awoke before she returned and made whimpering noises. I went into his room, and he stopped whimpering long enough to look at me, see who I was, whereupon he began crying in earnest. Soon he was screaming with mounting agitation. He hadn't yet begun to talk, nor had there been any evidence of fantasy play as yet, but he did understand speech. I began talking to him to try to distract him and noticed that when I mentioned "Mommy" the crying subsided a bit. So I began telling him a story about Mommy. It was a very, very dull story: Mommy had put on her coat, then Mommy took her hat, then Mommy went out to the car, "And now your Mommy is driving in the street, and Mommy is thinking about Johnny and how she is going to give Johnny a kiss when she comes home. When Mommy comes back she is going to drive into the driveway . . . etc." As long as I talked about *her* he listened and did not cry. As soon as I stopped, the crying resumed. It was for me a dramatic confirmation of the role that imagery and language play in the evolving life of a child. So long as Johnny could keep an image of his mother in mind—something which he could not yet accomplish on his own—he felt reassured. It was just a few weeks later, coincident with the appearance of fantasy play and shortly afterward of speech, that this capacity seemed to mature sufficiently for him to become more able to tolerate her absence for short periods of time. Even this one incident would suggest that the sense of well-being, one's sense of secure belonging, is contingent upon the availability and the quality of such personal images which people one's fantasy life (particularly the unconscious fantasy life). Where, as in Pious's patient, one fails to preserve one's significant others by some mental representation, one may lose his existence even in the unconscious fantasy system, and one is then left to his own bewildered, panic-stricken state of aloneness.

The existence within the self of a storehouse of unconscious imagoes of early self/other relationships provides the substrate for all subsequent relationships. One's repertoire of object-representations, and the feelings and relationship predispositions tied up in these images, may reveal much about a person's introjects. His fund of personal images reflects the socialization process to which an ego-system has been exposed. It also tells us something of the imprint which socialization has made on him, and what he, even as an archaic unformed self, made of those interactions and events which he lived through from his first glimmerings of sensori-affective awareness.

A person brings to the Rorschach response process a large part of his repertoire of internalized images of self and others, images which "people" his inner life. The most compelling images, of course, are most often those which remain largely unconscious, but the more readily available images can hardly be unrelated in some fathomable way to the unconscious images.

The task of the Rorschach examiner is not simply to take stock of the personal images which appear on the Rorschach, but to identify the part these images play in the person's ego-system: To what extent can the image be taken as a protagonist of what one feels himself to be? To what extent does the image express what he admires and would like to be? To what extent is it an imago of a feared other? Much work needs to be done yet on the criteria for determining the particular relevance for the individual of the personal images he projects in his Rorschach responses.

5.   Empathy and Identification in the *M* Response.

Any Rorschach image, whether in movement or not, and whether of a human being or not, may have important personal meaning, but it is from the human *M*'s that we can most directly learn something of a person's capacity to establish empathic contact with another human being.

That human movement responses are linked with a capacity for forming empathetic interpersonal relationships has been suggested by the findings of a number of studies.* One should be careful, however, to evaluate empathetic potential not by the *number* of *M*'s in a record, but by their quality. For one thing, the number of *M*'s may be a measure only of the extent of fantasied involvement with others. The occurence of a wealth of *M* responses may not signify a corresponding capacity for forming mature relationships with others. On the contrary, the patient may be quite inhibited in his actual relationships, and carry on much of his social intercourse on the private stage of fantasy where he is protected from the potentially painful vicissitudes of real interpersonal relationships. *M*'s should be associated with other indications of responsiveness and warmth, before they may be taken as an unambiguous expression of the capacity for mutuality and rapport.

Equally important is the need to distinguish between empathy and identification in determining the quality of the self-other relationship between the subject and the fantasied other in his *M*

*Kelly and Fiske (1951) in their predictive study on good and poor clinical psychology trainees found that *M%* has more predictive value than most of the variables studied. King (1958) showed that the number of *M* responses in a record is positively associated with the degree to which a patient defines his problem in self/other terms and is concerned introspectively with the quality of his interpersonal relationships. Holt and Luborsky (1958) found that the eight psychiatric residents who were independently rated highest in "empathy" produced significantly more *M* responses than the lowest eight. Frankle (1953) showed that the adequacy of social work students in forming interpersonal relationships was positively correlated with the number of *M* responses they gave. And in Roe's study on creative scientists gave more *M* responses than did artists, physical scientists or biological scientists. Schachtel (1950) has written of this at some length.

response. Empathy is a higher level psychological attainment than identification. Empathy involves a successful two-way relationship. In empathy, an experience is shared; in simple identification, the self-other distinction is blurred or lost. In identification, the ego becomes the other, or by projection, the other becomes an externalized facsimile of the self or some part of the self. Identification dissolves self-other differences in order to reduce to an absolute minimum the separateness of self from other; empathy does not. Identifications are not amenable to conscious self-reflection; empathy is carried out consciously or preconsciously, and under ego control. Empathy and identification differ in the degree of ego-intactness maintained in interaction with one's real or internalized objects. In empathy the ego preserves its integrity. There is a sharing, but without fusion. There is a feeling with, but not a total immersion *in*, the experience of the other person. Identificatory relationships, on the other hand, are those in which one could easily engulf others, or is prone to use others as a screen for his own self-actualization. He may be shrewd or adroit in his interpersonal relationships, but this interpersonal adeptness is not yet empathy. He may be sensitive to how people respond to him and may guide his actions according to these cues, all the while separated from others by an emotional gulf which prevents the intimacy or mutuality one would find in a mature empathetic interaction. He may be unable to keep from losing himself in others, a form of ego-diffusion antithetical to the more mature capacity to appreciate and feel with others without becoming engulfed by them.

The intensely narcissistic person may sometimes *seem* to empathize deeply and respond intensely to another. He may suddenly feel sorry for another person who feels lost, abandoned, and needs to be nurtured. This compassion may strike us as mature until we come to realize that it is a form of identification, a reversal of roles which allows one the vicarious experience of being nurtured, and is a piece of "empathy" limited to this particular experience. For example, we find that narcissistic women may be very good mothers to their children only so long as the child remains relatively helpless and in need of their nurturant care. When the child starts becoming an individual in his own right, with feelings which sometimes run in very different directions from the mother's, these women begin to fail as mothers. The capacity to relate to another person on the basis of *identification* exists, but not the ability to tolerate and sustain a relationship in which there are differences between the self and the other, differences which can be appreciated and shared on the basis of *empathy* in a way that doesn't dissolve the uniqueness of one or the other.

Such distinctions between an empathic relationship and an identificatory relationship hold for the *M* response as well. Whether a person is prone to relate himself to his fantasied others on the basis of empathy or on the basis of identification should become apparent through an analysis of the kinds of *M* response he gives. One characteristic of some narcissistic *M*'s would be the spilling over of the kinesthesia into action. The person acts out his response. Momentarily, he becomes the person he is describing. He infuses himself into the imagined person with whom he is in momentary relationship as he develops his response. The self becomes too directly engaged in the fantasy. There is a loss of distance between self and other, a temporary partial fusion of self and other.

One can distinguish empathic *M*'s from identificatory *M*'s in other respects as well. Other distinguishing characteristics of the two kinds of *M*'s suggest themselves:

Responses based on empathic forms of interpersonal relatedness	*Responses based upon more extensive forms of dissolution of ego-boundaries*
1. A wide range of images of others; a wide range of characterizations.	1. The response is reported with extreme vividness and conviction.
2. Movement perceptions take into account the many real nuances of the perception. The subject sees and describes the "others" with objectivity.	2. The perceived action is largely fabulized rather than inherent in the percept itself. In contradistinction to the reality-orientation of the empaththetic *M*, in these, the affect-content or action which the subject "sees" is not ordinarily associated with that response, and may even be projected onto the blot in quite arbitrary fashion.
3. The quality of the percept: the Subject feels a warmth, interest, pleasure, amusement in the doings of these figures, but in a way which makes it clear he is talking about someone else.	3. The response is reported with intense absorption in the behavior of the perceived figures; he infuses himself into the figure he is describing, vicariously sharing in the other's experiences.

The ability to empathize without over-identifying is the ear-mark of the good psychotherapist. He must be able to appreciate what his patients feel without having those feelings become his own. When he gets caught up in the feelings of the other he becomes less effective as a therapist. It is probably impossible to keep from slipping on occasion from empathy into identification, but sufficient ego strength (i.e., a firm sense of one's own identity) forestalls this degree of identification from occurring too often.

We have been considering inferences about a person's capacity for empathic contact, which can be drawn from M's a subject finds in the Rorschach blots. There are also conclusions to be drawn from his *inability* to find any M's, or his doing so only very selectively. Generally, responses which imply a richness in the capacity for empathic, mutual sharing of experiences are not singled out for special comment, but their absence *is* remarked upon. A person who fails to see the common M responses is assumed to shy away from interpersonal involvement. One reason he does this may be a confusion in his sense of personal cohesiveness such as we find most commonly in schizophrenics, where closeness carries for them the threat that they will be engulfed and will completely lose their identity. Or interpersonal distance may be maintained for fear of expressing certain forbidden impulses or of acting out some ego-alien identity-fragment. In these instances, repression may extend to the point of elimination, or the greatly inhibited expression, of those self-expressive impulses which would appear in M response fantasies.

Empathy is an essentially friendly act, and we can draw useful inferences not only from its presence or absence in the human contacts a subject portrays, but also from its exclusiveness. What kinds of people does the subject find it easiest to be friendly with in the Rorschach blots? Does a man seem inclined, for example, to surround himself exclusively with women, and if so, why? Is he disposed, rather, to seek out (or find himself beset by) very phallic men? Or passive men? By large, frightening animals, or inoffensive weak ones? Such inherent preferences, which give form and emotional tone to a person's object world, often tell us much about his characterologically based interpersonal posture toward his world (Mayman, 1957).

A person may shy away from human involvement to an extent which may leave him feeling estranged from others, expressed on the Rorschach in a dehumanizing of figures which are usually seen by others as human beings. When people are experienced as "strange," "alien," "frightening," etc., one may infer a drastic change in a person's internal milieu; the self has become alienated from its human situation and people are no longer sensed as friendly, safe, supportive, engaging or comfortable, but rather as impersonal, even inhuman, objects who are threatening or unreachable or ungiving. This from of withdrawal from interpersonal mutuality in a subject's M responses may imply not only a warping of relationships, but a severe pathology in his sense of self (Krohn and Mayman, 1974). Such responses on the Rorschach are usually prototypes of a corresponding coldness and/or estrangement in the way people are experienced in reality, and are associated with a stunting of the person's own sense of his own humanness.

CONCLUSION

When a person is asked to spend an hour immersing himself in a field of impressions where amorphousness prevails and where strange or even alien forms may appear, he will set in motion a reparative process the aim of which is to replace formlessness with reminders of the palpably real world. He primes himself to recall, recapture, reconstitute his world as he knows it, with people, animals and things which fit most naturally into the ingrained expectancies around which he has learned to structure his phenomenal world. The kind of world that he recreates for himself will call forth core dispositions which enliven (or deaden) his sense of self and which shape the world he finds himself in. This complex set of processes comes uniquely into play when one "sees" living, moving people or things in the Rorschach blots. Traditional ways of scoring movement have been too closely tied to one or another Rorschach system to take full advantage of the wealth of information a person's movement responses affords us about this multiplicity of determinents which enter into his way of relating himself to his world.

BIBLIOGRAPHY

Ferenczi, S. (1913). Stages in the development of the sense of reality. In S. Ferenczi, *Contributions to Psychoanalysis*, London: Hogarth Press, 1952.

Ferenczi, S. (1919). Thinking and muscle innervation. In *Theory and Technique of Psychoanalysis*, London; Hogarth Press, 1960.

Frankle, A. H. (1953). *Rorschach Human Movement and Human Content Responses as Indices of the Adequacy of Interpersonal Relationships*. Doctoral Dissertation: The University of Chicago, 1953.

Freud, S. (1911). Formulations regarding two principles of mental functioning. *Standard Edition*, v. 14.

Goldberger, L. and Holt, R. R. (1961). Experimental interference with reality contact: Individual differences. In P. Solomin, P. E. Kulzansky, P. H. Leiderman, D. J. H. Mendelson, R. Trumball, and D. Wexler, eds. *Sensory Deprivation*. Cambridge; Mass.: Harvard University Press, 1961.

Hertzman, M. and Pearce, J. (1947). The personal meaning of the human figure in the Rorschach. *Psychiatry*, **10**, 413-422.

Holt, R. R. and Luborsky, L. (1958). *Personality Patterns of Psychiatrists*, New York: Basic Books.

Kelly, E. L. and Fiske, D. W. (1951). *The Prediction of Performance in Clinical Psychology*, Ann Arbor: The University of Michigan Press.

King, G. F. (1958). A theoretical and experimental consideration of the human movement response. *Psychological Monographs*, 1958, #72.

Klopfer, B. and Kelley, D. M. (1942). *The Rorschach Technique*. Yonkers, New York: World Book Company.

Krohn, A. and Mayman, M. (1974). Object representations in dreams and projective tests. *Bulletin of the Menninger Clinic*, **38**, 445-466.

Latif, I. (1934). The physiological basis of linguistic development and of meaning, *Psychological Review*, **41**, 55-85, 153-176, 246-64.

Mayman, M. (1960). Measuring fantasy on the Rorschach Test. Unpublished, 27 pp.

Mayman, M. (1967). Object-representations and object-relationships in Rorschach responses. *Journal of Personality Assessment and Projective Techniques*, **31**, 17-24.

Mayman, M. and Voth, II. M. Reality closeness, fantasy and autokinesis: a dimension of cognitive style. *Journal of Abnormal Psychology*, **74**, 635-641.

Meltzoff, J., Singer, J. L. and Korchin, S. J. (1953). Motor inhibition and Rorschach movement: a test of the sensory-tonic theory. *Journal of Personality*, **21**, 400-410.

Pious, W. L. (1950). Obsessive compulsive symptoms in an incipient schizophrenic. *Psychoanalytic Quarterly*, **19**, 327-351.

Rapaport, D. (1958). The theory of ego autonomy: a generalization. *Bulletin of the Menninger Clinic*, **22**, 13-35.

Rapaport, D., Gill, M. and Schafer, R. (1945). *Diagnostic Psychological Testing, v. 2*. Chicago: Year Book Publishers. Second edition by R. R. Holt, International Universities Press, 1968.

Roe, A. (1953). A psychological study of eminent psychologists and anthropologists, and a comparison with biological and physical scientists. *Psychological Monographs*, 1953, #67.

Rorschach, H. (1921). *Psychodiagnostiks*. New York: Grune and Stratton, 1949.

Schachtel, E. G. (1950). Projection and its relation to character attitudes and creativity in the kinesthetic responses. *Psychiatry*, **13**, 69-100.

Schafer, R. (1954). *Psychoanalytic Interpretation in Rorschach Testing*. New York: Grune and Stratton.

Singer, J. L., Meltzoff, J. and Goldman, G. D. (1952). Rorschach movement responses following motor inhibition and hyperactivity. *Journal of Consulting Psychology*, **16**, 359-365.

Voth, H. M. and Mayman, M. (1963). A dimension of personality organization. *Archives of General Psychiatry*, **8**, 366-380.

Werner, H. (1940). *Comparative Psychology of Mental Development*. New York: International Universities Press.

Werner, H. (1945). Motion and motion perception: a study in vicarious functioning. *Journal of Psychology*, **19**, 317-327.

Vowels: black A, white E, red I, green U,
blue O,
Someday I shall name the birth from
which you rise. . . .*

J. N. ARTHUR RIMBAUD

8 | *David Shapiro*

A

PERCEPTUAL UNDERSTANDING
OF COLOR RESPONSE

INTRODUCTION

The practical Rorschach problem of the interpretive meaning
of color response has not been a subject of much debate among
clinical Rorschach workers. It is safe to say that there are not many
working with this test clinically who would disagree, in essentials,
with Rorschach's own original formulation:

> The C and CF answers express the more ego-centric affective respon-
> siveness, while the more adaptive affective responsiveness is expressed in
> the number of FC's (Rorschach, 1949, p. 33).†

However, notwithstanding its general acceptance and its wide
areas of clinical applicability, it must be noted that in certain spe-
cifics this formulation has not always proved to be an accurate one.
For example, ordinary clinical experience suggests at least two
types of cases—severe narcissistic or psychopathic character disorders and chronic schizophrenics—in whose Rorschachs pure color
or color-dominated responses may appear conspicuously without
evidence of corresponding affect-experience in the ordinary sense.
Nor has the general acceptance of Rorschach's interpretive prin-

---

*Translated by Muriel Rukeyser.
†For explanation of scoring symbols, see Appendix, pp. 609 ff. [Editor].

ciple linking color with affect been matched by an equally wide acceptance of any of the proposed explanations of this linkage.

Some Rorschach workers, convinced of the linkage but not able to explain it, have in effect tried to skip over the problem of rationale simply by assuming some sort of given, intrinsic affective value to color. Others have assumed the existence of culturally established, highly charged and affective associations to colors. But as has often been pointed out, this explanation does not explain; at best it only postpones the explanation.

An understanding of the meaning of color response can come only through an understanding of the perceptual processes involved in it. Specifically, the issues are these: Does color perception, and therefore color response, involve special perceptual processes which are essentially different, for example, from those involved in form perception? If so, different in what respects? And, can the nature of those differences clarify the interpretive meaning of color re-sponse, especially in those cases where the affect-color linkage seems not to hold up?

The aim here will be to answer these questions, which have, I believe, an intrinsic interest quite aside from their practical implications for test interpretation. In line with this aim, we will put aside for the time being questions of the interpretive meaning of color response, and first concentrate only on the nature of color experience and the color response process as such.

It is important to begin with a reminder to the reader of the three basic contributions, in addition to Rorschach's own discussion, to the understanding of color response. These are: Schachtel's (1966), Rickers-Ovsiankina's (1943), and Rapaport's et al. (1968). Each of these contributions takes as its starting point the assumed relationship between color response and affect, but each also contains certain views, or certain principles, of color perception or color response as such. It is not possible to summarize the three contributions here, but I would like simply to indicate these views or principles of color perception, since the following discussion will lean on them, particularly on Rapaport's, quite heavily.

Schachtel refers to the subjective experience of seeing color. He points out that this experience is of something perceived without effort of will, or of one's attention being captured, in contrast to the experience of form perception. He suggests the example of walking into a room in which there is a colored area on the wall—the color "strikes" one. The perception of color, therefore, requires little activity on the part of the perceiver and may be described as primarily a *passive* process.

Rickers-Ovsiankina speaks more explicitly of the nature of the perceptual processes themselves. A color perception, she states, is a relatively *direct* sense datum as compared with the complex, more energy-consuming processes, e.g., of gestalt organization, involved in form perception. Color perception may also be described, therefore, as a more *immediate* process than form perception. Rickers-Ovsiankina presents important evidence for this point, some of which will be referred to later (see also pp. 11 ff. of this book).

Rapaport's emphasis is somewhat different. He considers, first of all, that color response is merely an indicator of affective response, not necessarily affectively toned in itself any more than the dial of a gasoline gage needs to contain fluid. Although he does not discuss explicitly the nature of color experience as such, he speaks to the problem of the integration of the "impact" of color with articulated form. The Freudian concept of capacity to delay tension discharge is central to Rapaport's discussion, and he indicates that, in general, the more successfully form-integrated color responses reflect a capacity for such delay sufficient to allow for the optimal integration of color impression and form. The color-dominated responses, in contrast, generally represent an insufficient integration of the perceptual impact of color with form; and the pure *C* responses reflect a "short-circuiting," an absence of the delay capacity which is a precondition for further perceptual and associative elaboration. One may assume therefore that, from this point of view, color experience as such *requires less complex psychological organization* (i.e., discharge-delaying organization) than the perceptual articulation of form.

I have previously (Shapiro, 1956) attempted to define a mode of perception which may be associated with color experience in general, and I have proposed in that connection the concept of *perceptual passivity*.[1] This concept, I believe, is essentially con-

---

[1] Suggested by a concept of activity-passivity developed by Rapaport (1953) in connection with drive-restraining psychological organizations, i.e., "activity" describing a condition of active organization, control, and modulation of drives, and "passivity" describing a condition of helplessness in the face of those drives.

sistent with the views of color perception contained in the three contributions described, with one qualification regarding Schachtel's position which is discussed below.

Perceptual passivity refers to the perceiver's relationship to the visual stimuli. It means a condition of relative absence, immobilization, or temporary relaxation of active perceptual organizing capacities, and, accordingly, a condition in which the perceptual experience is to a large extent dominated by, and subject to, the most immediately manifest and sensorially most vivid aspects of the visual surroundings, such as color. Such perception would tend to be, *though would not necessarily be*, associated with conditions of impaired or less highly developed psychological organization. And perception of this sort, in contrast to perception which organizes more actively such as in complex perceptual form articulation, would ordinarily be accompanied by a subjective feeling of passivity of the sort Schachtel describes, an experience of being held, distracted, or struck by the stimulus. But, this subjective feeling of passivity is not a reliable indicator of the objective condition of passivity in the sense described; the *feeling* of passivity, in such a connection, may be avoided, as will be demonstrated later. With this qualification, therefore, the assumption that color experience tends to be associated with a passive mode of perception is consistent with the three views described above.

One corollary, namely, a developmental one, may be added to this conception of color perception. We know, from Werner's work (1948) in particular, that perception undergoes a development, in mode or style, from infancy to adulthood. Werner indicates that the very young child is "stimulus-bound," i.e., he is passively subjected to sensory stimulation. In contrast, he describes, normal adult perception is relatively more free from the influence of adventitious aspects of sensory stimulation, and is characterized by increased articulation and increased dominance of form as the basis of reaction to stimuli. This picture of perceptual development suggests that color experience tends to be a more prominent aspect of visual life in childhood than in maturity.

These formulations regarding color perception will be considered in the following sections as working hypotheses, to be examined in the light of certain experimental, clinical, and Rorschach literature. I believe these hypotheses to be essentially sound, but the place of color experience in perception is by no means settled by them. The data to be considered have, therefore, not been selected with a view merely to substantiate these initial formulations or to render them more convincing, but rather to clarify and extend them. In the final section, the interpretive or clinical significance of color response, and with it the question of the color-affect relationship, will be reconsidered and the formulations will be recast.

DATA ON COLOR PERCEPTION

The data that will be taken up in this section are not for the most part Rorschach data but pertain more to color perception in various other situations. The studies considered fall roughly into three groups: (1) Developmental data including experimental studies of children's sorting behavior that seem to throw light on certain aspects of children's perception, and some data from developmental Rorschach studies; (2) studies of special pathological states—schizophrenic and brain-damage conditions—in which certain changes in perception appear and seem associated with thought disorder; and (3) the material collected by Senden (1932), describing the early visual experiences of previously blind people with surgically repaired vision.

Color Perception in Children

The relative prominence of color in the visual experience of very young children is obvious even to the casual observer. Their response to brightly colored objects, as compared with uncolored or less saturated ones, is unmistakable.[2] It is quite clear also, in general observation, that this response is not only a matter of sensory pleasure, but is more far-reaching. Objects tend, to a much greater extent among children than adults, to be *identified* primarily or exclusively in terms of color. For example: a 2½-year-old child sees a brilliantly colored maple tree in autumn, at a range

[2]Children's preference for bright colors, in contrast to adults' preference for pastels, is documented in a study by Honkavaara (1958).

quite close enough for her to identify even the shape of the leaves; she can readily identify them when they are green but, in this case, exclaims that it is an apple tree. A good deal of experimental work appears to confirm this heightened significance of color for children.

A number of studies have been carried out on object-sorting behavior in children which are of interest here for one reason in particular: the experimental task, which is usually to sort simple geometrically formed objects either on the basis of form or color, has an appreciable perceptual component.

Revesz (1925) and Thompson (1941) have reported such studies, and additional studies of this sort are described by Werner (1948). The results indicate a clear tendency in the groups of young children to sort initially on the basis of color rather than on the basis of form—at least as "form" is defined by such materials as triangles, circles, squares, etc. Several similar studies have been made on a relatively large scale with subject populations covering a fairly wide and continuous age range, an advantage over those which compare younger children with only one or two older age groups. Descoudres, in an experiment described by Werner, and Lindberg (1938), using his ring test,[3] have been able to demonstrate a more or less *continously* increased preference for form and decreased preference for color as a sorting basis through the age ranges of 3 to 18, and 7 to 14 respectively.

Since these experimental tasks put no special logical advantage on either the color or the form sorting, it seems justifiable to assume that the results reflect, at least in part, a developmental change of a perceptual sort, i.e., a change in the relative perceptual importance of form and color factors within the task. Insofar as the direction of this change is clearly toward a decrease in the significance of color with age and maturation, the results support our general assumptions. However, it is not clear from the data alone exactly what this developmental shift in the significance of color consists of. The difficulty of interpreting the results is, in fact, compounded by a special problem, namely, the likelihood that the task itself

---

[3] Lindberg's results are especially clear-cut, possibly because his procedures involve printed material and thus escape the problem, which is often insufficiently considered, of whether a child's form-choice has more to do with the perceived form configuration or with concrete object qualities of the cut-out forms. I imagine that this problem is one of the reasons why studies of this kind do not *always* show the sort of development described, although the preponderance of such studies do.

is subjectively something different for the younger children from what it is for the older ones or for adults. It is likely, for example, that for the youngest children tested the task is one of immediate identification of 'the most manifest similarity among the objects presented. For the older subjects, the task is probably something closer to finding the logically most essential aspect of the objects or representations, even though the nature of the test does not prejudice the logical choice one way or the other.

Three ways of understanding the development suggest themselves: (1) The difference in *attitude* toward the task and in *understanding* of its nature, and the undoubted inclination of the younger children to proceed in a more immediate and less detached fashion are primarily responsible for the shift from color emphasis to form emphasis; (2) the shift represents a *perceptual develpment* in which color experience actually comes to occupy a modified and on the whole less significant position in visual life; and (3) there may be, along with maturation, an actual *diminution of color sensitivity*, as the psychophysicist would measure it. These three possibilities by no means exclude each other, and it is not out of the question that all three are correct. It is, in other words, possible that the more immediate response and less detached attitude of the younger children are associated with a mode of perception in which such sensory qualities as color have heightened significance and are actually subjectively more vivid. These issues will come up again later in connection with other data.

It is of interest to compare the results of the sorting studies of children with developmental Rorschach data. Systematic Rorschach studies as well as clinical reports on children's Rorschachs seem quite consistent and unvarying regarding the appearance of color response in children. Klopfer and Margulies (1941), Ford (1946), Ames (1952), and Halpern (1953) have all described that among the color responses in Rorschach records of very young children pure *C* responses tend to predominate; in somewhat older children *CF* responses occupy a more important role and the pure *C* responses drop out rapidly; and at a still later age, *FC* responses play an increasing part. It is not necessary to consider here the specific age ranges which seem to be correlated with these phases.

There is, however, one aspect of the Rorschach data on children which seems, at first, to contradict the general picture of a more or less continuous development from a predominance of pure *C* to increasingly form-dominated color response. Most Rorschach workers have noted the fact that, among the very youngest children tested—2 to 2½ years of age, for example—color responses tend to be few or even to be absent altogether. This matter, noteworthy in itself, also involves certain more general issues that warrant discussion.

The explanation of the apparent discontinuity in the development of color response can be found in the nature of the demands which the Rorschach itself imposes. The Rorschach test does not require of a subject simply any perceptual reaction. It requires rather a response that meets certain standards of conceptualization if it is to be counted as a *response* at all. The Rorschach instructions, regardless of their minor variations, clearly indicate that mere verbal expression of a sensory impression of color is inadequate. What is called for is the integration of that impression with form aspects of the card, if possible, or at the least an integration of the color impression with an appropriate, more or less realistically representational content. As far as the Rorschach is concerned, most pure *C* responses are already at the bottom of the conceptual scale; mere color naming is generally considered off the response scale altogether (some Rorschach workers considering such responses to be in the pure *C* category, others not counting them among responses at all). However, it is clear that color responsiveness in children, if one foregoes the technical response standards of the Rorschach test, extends far below this conceptual level. For example, Werner (1948) indicates that, on the basis of studies of bodily reactions, very young infants seem to be able to discriminate the primary colors.

The absence, therefore, of what may be technically accepted as color responses in the Rorschachs of very young children by no means indicates an actual absence of responsiveness to the color stimulus. The situation can be summed up as follows: As one goes *down* the chronological scale, Rorschach responses altogether become progressively more diffuse, global, and concrete and, correspondingly, the predominant mode of color response shifts from *FC* to *CF* to pure *C*; before this, color may well occupy a prominent part in the over-all impression but this is the point at which the

Rorschach response scale, so to speak, stops. The significance of this issue in evaluating the Rorschach data on children with respect to color response is easily illustrated. Both Ames and Ford, for example, consider color-naming responses as beneath the conceptual level required for Rorschach responses, and they do not include color naming in their over-all tabulations or in their tabulations of pure color responses. Ford, however, reports that 48% of her three-year olds gave color-naming responses, and Ames also reports a high incidence of color naming in the early age range. These tabulation procedures, as far as ordinary Rorschach work is concerned, are not in question, but the apparent absence of color responsiveness in very young children looks very different in this light.[4]

Dworetzky (1939, 1956) makes essentially this same point in connection with her extensive developmental study, and offers some empirical confirmation of it. With her Rorschach subjects (1939) from approximately 4 years old through puberty she found, in line with the other work described, a gradual diminution of pure color and color-dominated responses in favor of form-dominated responses. Among her three- to four-year-old subjects, however, color tended to drop out altogether as a basis for scorable responses, very much as has been described. She was able to note, however, that various aspects of the test behavior and other aspects of the test performance of these children (e.g., number of subjects who gave their first response to a red area) indicated the attraction and stimulation value of the color for them, notwithstanding that they were not, at this age, able to use the color to produce scorable responses.

With this amendment, the Rorschach data on children are quite consistent with the sorting results described but, in at least one

[4] It may be mentioned that essentially the same issue appears in Stein's (1949) tachistoscopic experiment with the Rorschach. With normal adults as subjects, he administered the Rorschach tachistoscopically, the exposures ranging down to .01 second. In general, the bright color determinants steadily *decreased* as exposure time was *increased*. Pure color responses dropped especially rapidly with increased exposure time. In apparent contradiction to this development, at the very shortest exposure time, Stein found a drop in color responses. He indicates, however, that the card was considered rejected and no responses were counted if the subject responded in such a way as the following: "It looked like it was colored but it didn't mean anything to me" (p. 363). It seems clear, in this illustration, that color was in fact an effective stimulus, but that there was insufficient time for sufficient mobilization of the organizing and associative processes necessary to arrive at a percept which would be technically acceptable as a Rorschach response.

sense, they offer more. The sorting data are, aside from behavioral observations, limited to a single dimension: the number who sort one way as compared with the number who sort another way. The quantitative Rorschach data, however, contain additional dimensions, namely, those defined by the Rorschach scores, and it is accordingly possible to see clearly an answer to one question which could not be answered on the basis of the sorting studies alone. Although the Rorschach data do not indicate that color responsiveness *per se* diminishes with development, they do indicate unmistakably that the relative significance of color as the central and overriding aspect of the percept diminishes. What can only appear in the sorting data as a progressive diminution in number of color choices, appears in the Rorschach data to be a modification of the position of color in the final percept, namely, from an immediate color experience which tends to dominate a final percept to one in which the color is progressively integrated, in essentially a secondary position, with form articulation. Dworetzky (1939) relates this change in the nature of color response to a more general perceptual development from a "receptive and global" stage to a more "active and analytic" one.

Perceptual Tendencies Associated with Impairment of Thought Processes

Studies of schizophrenic and brain-damaged patients with color-form sorting tests (or the more complex Vigotsky test) offer valuable data on perceptual tendencies in these groups also, especially so since certain of these studies include relatively detailed clinical or behavioral description.

Weigl's study (1941) on patients with cerebral lesions and Hanfmann and Kasanin's (1942) on schizophrenic patients show a consistent result in regard to color versus form preference. These patients, in contrast to normal adults, have a decided tendency to make sortings *first* or *exclusively* on the basis of color.

In addition to the quantitative results, however, these investigators observed certain qualities of behavior or attitude which tended to be associated, respectively, with color and form sorting. Repeatedly, these authors describe the apparently passive, gripped, or stimulus-bound quality of the patient's perception of the material in connection particularly with its color qualities.

Weigl, for example, says, in describing his impression of the (typical) color choice of one of the brain-damaged patients: this response "*was forced upon* [him] by the sensorially manifest aspects of the situation" (1941, p. 2) [my emphasis].

This is in contrast to the apparent attitude of detachment and reflective choice which is usual in the normal subjects and is typically associated with form choice.

Weigl explored further the differences in attitude associated with the form and color choice respectively by inquiring into the immediate responses of the normal subjects when they first looked at the given material and before they had time for reflection. It turned out that, "without exception . . . their first impression was that of 'color variety' in which the colors of similar qualities seemed to join together" (1941, p. 10). Here again, the subjective experience of something happening, visually, beyond deliberate control in connection with the immediate color response is noteworthy ("seemed to join together").

In Hanfmann and Kasanin's study of thinking in schizophrenia (1942), with the Vigotsky test, observations of this sort are described in greater detail. Specifically, these authors note a relationship, although a significantly limited one, between the visual qualities of the materials to which their subjects seemed to respond and the level of thinking, primitive or concrete, "intermediate," or abstract and truly conceptual, which they demonstrated in the test. They state:

> Color, and to a lesser degree general size (height and area), seem to have a more immediate perceptual, at times even physiognomic appeal, and consequently prevail on the primitive level. Shape (prevails as a basis for sorting) on the intermediate level . . . on the level of true classifications there seems to be no definite preference for any one quality of the blocks . . . (1942, pp. 39-40).

On the most primitive, concrete level the sorting is not made with a detached, "objective" attitude or with any concept or principle in mind; it is made rather on the basis of the most (visually) impressive groupings which immediately "thrust themselves" upon the subjects. On this level, characteristic of the schizophrenic patients, the sortings tend to be made in terms of color. At a higher level, the "intermediate" level, there is a somewhat greater tendency toward a detached attitude and a conceptual principle, and here the shape of the objects seems to outrank color in its perceptual significance and becomes the basis of sorting. At the highest conceptual level, characteristic of the more intelligent normal-control cases, the attitude is a detached and objective one, and the subject is no longer *directed by* the immediate sensory or perceptual impressions but can, as it were, *make use of* these impressions, shift freely from one to another, and consider them without bias for the purpose of solving the logical task.[5]

The pertinence of these studies of thought disorder is twofold: First of all, they confirm our expectation of an increase in the significance of color under circumstances of disorganization or primitivization of thought. Secondly, they give evidence of the behavioral and subjective attitude of passivity in relation to the visual stimulus which is associated with this increased color significance. The second fact gives special meaning to the first. It indicates that the significance of color in these conditions is not merely increased but also different in quality. These differences in the quality and significance of color experience appear then to reflect differences of a more general sort in the mode of perception, and, at the same time, in thought organization. Although the normal subjects,[6] as a whole, are undoubtedly

[5] The substantial identity of these conclusions with those of Goldstein and Scheerer (1944), and others in studies of abstract and concrete behavior, is evident. Goldstein and Scheerer do not report, and are essentially not interested in, the relative frequencies of color and form choices. Their interest is rather in description of the qualities of the abstract and concrete attitudes (e.g., dependence upon a unique aspect of an individual object; "matching" as opposed to "sorting;" capacity to learn with aids; shifting; etc.), either of which may eventuate in color or form choice where those are alternatives. It is undoubtedly true that there is no perfect relationship between the operating mode of perception or attitude and the final sorting choice (form or color). This fact was mentioned in connection with the sorting studies of children, and another aspect of the same fact is indicated in the Hanfmann-Kasanin results described above. Nevertheless, the general tendency for color choice to be associated with the more concrete attitudes seems clear. This is implicit in the Goldstein-Scheerer monograph also, particularly in their repeated emphasis on passive "surrender" to the most sensorially vivid aspects of the stimulus as one critical feature of the concrete attitude.

[6] Of course, when we speak here of "normal" adult perception, we refer to the general group tendency. Hanfmann (1941), with the Vigotsky test, was able to distinguish several groups along the same dimension among normal subjects. She found that her subjects could be divided according to their approach to the task as follows: (1) those whose approach was characterized by "active thinking"—"subjects of this type show a strong preference for shape as a basis for groupings," and (2) those she characterizes as intuitive, "in whose approach the perceptual . . . factors seem to predominate." These subjects, she reports, favor color and over-all size of blocks in groupings. Of course, perceptual factors operate in the response of both groups, but in different ways. The division must be between those whose perception and response tend to be more passively dominated by the gross sensory aspects of the stimulus, and the more "active" subjects whose perception is not dominated by these aspects and whose approach is in terms of what would ordinarily be logically more relevant features, primarily shape.

perfectly capable of considering the color, or of weighing in a detached way its possible significance, it does not have for them the compelling, griping quality[7] that it has for the pathological subjects.[8]

The question that was raised before, concerning whether the heightened perceptual significance of color or its compelling quality is associated also with heightened subjective vividness and a lowered color threshold, as a psychophysicist would measure it, is still not answered. Some light, though it is not conclusive, is thrown on this interesting question by the work of Senden (1932) discussed in the following.

Visual Pathology: Senden's Survey

The last data to be taken up concern perceptual experiences associated with a certain type of visual pathology. These are the remarkable data on the early visual experiences of the newly seeing (after operation) formerly blind, collected by Senden (1932).

The most significant features of these data, from the standpoint of our interest, may be summarized as follows: In the earliest visual experiences of these previously blind people, there is a remarkable deficiency in form vision. Not only is there an initial incapacity to recognize forms (on the basis of anticipated transfer from previous, nonvisual familiarity), which would not be so surprising to us, but there is an extraordinary difficulty in this initial phase in *learning* to identify forms or in learning to "see" forms of any degree of complexity. For example, even after a period of some weeks of visual experience, a typical patient had extreme difficulty in distinguishing a triangular cardboard cutout from a circular one, and the distinction could finally be made only by laboriously tracing the edge, visually, taking note of corners, etc.

In contrast to this marked incapacity for perceptual form-articulation, color recognition was very rapid in this initial stage, almost

---

[7] See also, in this connection, the concept of the "insistence" value of color in the gestalt literature, e.g., Katz (1935).

[8] Clinical observations of brain-damaged patients, e.g., Schilder (1953), also provide very interesting descriptions of the increased significance of color and the modifications in its appearance under these circumstances. It is an open, but interesting, question whether the greatly increased vividness and the compelling quality of colors in the case of a person under the influence of Mescaline or similar drugs, e.g., Huxley (1956), can be related to the same general process.

immediate for most of the patients reported. It is, however, not only the fact of the ease and rapidity of color vision and color recognition, in contrast to form vision, that is of interest. Senden's material also makes it clear that one reason for this rapid acquisition of color recognition was the very fact that vivid color sensation occupied an unusually dominant position in the earliest visual experiences of these people.

The case descriptions included by Senden leave no doubt about the general quality of these early visual experiences and the subjective feelings that accompany them. The sensation is of helplessness and passivity in the face of a confusion of attention-demanding stimuli: "A plethora of impressions . . . from which he obtained relief only by closing his eyes" (1932, p. 60), "too many things . . . he becomes confused . . . only the colors interest him" (p. 64), are typical descriptions.

Senden summarizes them as follows: "There is now the experience of a tremendous wealth of visual impressions which overwhelmed him who only recently gained sight" (1932, p. 57).

This "plethora of impressions," it must be remembered, does not consist of articulated form impressions but rather of the most gross and diffuse sensations of light and color, movement, figure, and background. The sensations are often of unusual vividness and brilliance, frequently actually painful, and Senden speaks, in this connection, of a "sensory oversensitivity," at this stage of vision.

There can be little doubt that the exceedingly compelling and vivid qualities of these visual sensations are of a piece with their diffuseness, and are essentially antagonistic to perceptual form articulations of any degree of complexity. The accomplishment of form articulation and reliable object recognition, out of this state of vision, becomes a task of such magnitude that it frequently precipitates a personal crisis which is overcome only after laborious training procedures.[9]

This process of increasing capacity for form recognition and perceptual form articulation is not, according to Senden's data, a gradual

[9] It should be mentioned that the more recent results obtained by Wilson and Riesen (1966) with chimpanzees reared in darkness fully confirm the incapacity for perceptual form articulations without a prior development of experience. Riesen speaks of "form blindness" in the early vision of these champanzees. Brightly colored, shiny, or moving objects provided much more effective visual stimuli.

and continuous one. The development appears to consist of distinguishable phases. The critical phase, which appears to coincide with the time of the personal "crisis," seems to be one in which the rudiments of form perception are being laboriously acquired. It is during this period that the patient slowly emerges from the experience of being passively subjected to sensory stimuli of great vividness, at the same time compelling and distracting, into a stage in which the *basic equipment* for more active perceptual articulation is available. Senden says:

> When the blind-born operated person has acquired a certain fund of form-conceptions and is able to increase this fund independently in approaching new visual objects with a searching mind and by using previously acquired concepts, then learning how to see is no longer a problem . . . they [doctors or educators] can leave the rest to the patient . . . (1932, p. 93).

One other noteworthy feature of this perceptual development deserves to be mentioned. During this same critical period, in the course of the patients' efforts toward an adequate visual orientation, it is observed that *object identifications* often tend to be made, at first, on the basis of color. There appears, in other words, to be a development which very likely consists of several overlapping phases, from identification of objects at first on the basis of their most conspicuous and gross visual aspects to later perceptual identification primarily in terms of more abstract form qualities. It is the earlier phase of identification by color that is of special interest here. It reveals a process by which color sensation, initially only passively experienced and antagonistic to clear form articulation, comes to serve an active function, to be *used* actively, and the beginnings of an integration of color and form are suggested. This issue will be taken up below.

Summary and Reformulations

In certain respects the data of all these studies confirm the initial assumptions; in other respects they seem to raise new questions.

Color does appear to have increased significance for children, in conditions of pathologically impaired mental organization, and in conditions of primitive and undeveloped visual capacity as well, as compared with normal adults. It has greater significance, in other words, in all those cases in which optimal perceptual organizing capacity has not yet been achieved or has been impaired. This fact, together with the subjective experience of its compelling quality, in contrast to the more detached and subjectively deliberate or, in the case of the newly seeing person, effortful feelings associated with form articulations, seems consistent with the assumption that color experience involves more passive and immediate processes, and becomes more prominent under conditions that make for a passive perceptual mode. But the data suggest more than this general principle.

Senden's material suggests that the two types of visual experience, the passive and immediate experience of what is sensorially most vivid, on the one hand, and the more active and detached articulation of form, on the other, may originally be antagonistic to each other. It is primarily his description of the critical phase, in which the effort is made to achieve form vision and to overcome the distraction of what is simply vivid in the visual field, which suggests such an antagonism. At the least, it is clear that the overcoming of a passive and hypersensitive relationship to visual stimuli and the acquisition of basic elements of form perception, and with them a more active and autonomous way of seeing, *are two aspects of the same process.* The details of this transition are not clear. But it does seem clear that a stage is reached in which the acquisition, in effect, of basic tools of form perception at the same time allows for easier resistance to the otherwise compelling and distracting sensory qualities of the visual field. These latter no longer dominate perception, and rapid and less effortful visual learning experience becomes possible. This marks the end of the critical phase of learning to "see" in the patients.[10] If color is, in the earliest visual experiences, an extremely compelling and dominating aspect of the visual field, what happens to it as perception becomes progressively dominated by active and complex form articulations? It is obvious that color neither disappears nor retains fully its original gripping and too vivid quality. *Its place in perception is modified and, in one way or another or to varying degrees, it becomes integrated with the now predominantly formal perception, and secondary to it.*

---

[10] The process is very suggestive of what has been described by Harlow (1949) as "learning to learn," and, in fact, Riesen (1966) has considered this type of hypothesis in explaining his data with chimpanzees.

It has been noted by painters and others, e.g. Schilder (1953), that looking at a landscape upside down causes the colors to become more vivid. This process accomplishes the partial disruption of familiar, recognizable forms. Probably much the same thing is accomplished with the use of a reduction screen. The existence of color constancy, as well as the loss of color constancy (Katz, 1935) with the use of reduction screens or other devices such as a tachistoscope which obscure or eliminate form outlines, offer additional evidence of the significant changes that come about in color experience as color sensation is integrated with form and with meaningful or familiar objects. It cannot be assumed that this integration *necessarily* involves a diminution in the vividness of the color experience, but I believe that this is the predominate tendency.

To speak of an "integration" of color sensation with form suggests, however, something more than merely a modification of the subjective experience of color. Form vision is an adaptive function of first importance, and this fact raises the following question: Does color sensation, when integrated with predominantly formal perception, have a functional or adaptive position in vision, and if so, what is it? Ordinary visual experience suggests three such functions that color sensation may perform within form-dominated perception, although all three are undoubtedly functions of secondary adaptive importance in vision: (1) Color sensation enriches a visual experience by investing it with an ordinarily pleasing sensual quality which is not present otherwise; (2) simply by adding another dimension to visual experience, color sensation makes finer articulations possible and lends greater individuality to a given form articulation; and (3) color sensation may be an *aid* to form articulations, and under optimal conditions can undoubtedly make form recognitions easier, faster, and more accurate; in this sense, color performs an economical function. In these ways, at least, color sensation comes, *in the later stages of perceptual development*, to enhance form articulation and to fulfill adaptive functions. It should be added that the ultimate value of color sensation in fulfilling these functions seems to derive from *just those qualities of sensorial immediacy and directness which originally appear to be antagonistic to form vision*.

At the same time as we may speak of color sensation as predominantly integrated with form in normal adult perception, it cannot be forgotten that all individuals are capable of and ordinarily exercise a *range* of perceptual modes. We see differently from time to time, and we are capable of a variety of shifts in mode of vision. These shifts in way of seeing seem to be partly determined by the nature of the stimulus as, for example, when bright lights or, for that matter, vivid colors compel attention or distract us. Partly, however, the nature and the range of such shifts is undoubtedly a matter of individual differences. A painter, for example, may have an unusually great capacity for certain sorts of perceptual shifts; Katz (1935) has suggested that painters may have a capacity to perceive color in its "reduced" quality, i.e., as it would be seen ordinarily through a reduction screen. It can be assumed that the variety of ways of seeing, in a given individual, is itself organized in a way which is superordinate to each single perceptual mode. Beyond that, however, it seems justifiable to assume that the extent to which perception remains passively gripped by the sensorially more vivid aspects of the stimulus or "stimulus-bound" (as in the early phase of Senden's cases), to that extent the development of a wide range of ways of seeing or of the capacity for deliberate shift from one way to another must be limited.

Along with the fact of the range of color experience in perception, it must be remembered that, although we have talked schematically of the development of color experience from an originally more dominant position in a stage of perceptual passivity to a position secondary to and integrated with form in later, form-dominated perception, actually this transition must include a number of developmental phases and must be a gradual and extended process. Senden's cases suggest some of the intermediate phases, e.g., that phase in the newly seeing patients in which object identification is attempted primarily on the basis of color. The developmental sorting studies cited make clear the gradual nature, in normal development, of the modification of color significance. The sorting studies of pathological cases give evidence of the regressive changes that can occur, in this respect, in individuals whose visual capacities can certainly not be compared with Senden's cases of "form blindness." One can only conclude that the variations and transitional states in the development of active, form-dominated perception are many, and that the ways in which color may be integrated with form perception are equally numerous. Some of these will be discussed in the following section in connection with specific varieties of Rorschach color responses.

Before turning to these, which will also provide opportunity for more specific development of our general thesis, we can sum up as follows:

Color perception as such is a more immediate and passive experi-ence than form perception, requiring less in the way of perceptual tools or organizing capacity. It is associated with a passive perceptual mode in that it becomes more dominant, more compelling in quality, and perhaps even antagonistic to form articulation in conditions in which active perceptual organizing capacity is impaired or is only rudimentary; at the same time, under optimal conditions, color becomes integrated with form perception, is itself modified in subjective experience, and acquires new functions of economy and enrichment.

RORSCHACH COLOR RESPONSES AND THEIR INTERPRETIVE SIGNIFICANCE

A color response involves, from our point of view, the operation of a perceptual mode of the sort or within the range described above; i.e., a perceptual mode which retains, at some level, a significant aspect of passivity. In psychological conditions of impairment of controlling, integrative, and expressive functions, we expect an im-pairment of active perceptual organizing functions also; the more immediate perceptual route offered by the color stimulus may then be especially opportune. Conditions of excessive affect pressure con-stitute one *special case* within this general class. There are many others. At the same time, under conditions where perceptual organiz-ing and integrative functions operate well, passive and immediate sensory experience will still play a significant role, but it will be of a different sort and the sensory experience will be of a different quality. In general, the degree and quality of color response, including the subjective quality of the color itself insofar as this can be deter-mined, will reflect the characteristic forms and qualities of immediate and passively experienced tension discharge. It will either be well-integrated, expressive, and adaptive, in which case it will tend to lose its distinctiveness, both subjectively and objectively in the over-all integrated operation; or it will be primitive, unmodulated, and per-haps eruptive, in which case its distinctively passive character will be conspicuous both objectively and, ordinarily, subjectively.

The varieties of color response on the Rorschach are very numerous, only grossly covered by our scoring schemes, and it is doubtful that all of these varieties can be accurately placed on any single continuum. Nevertheless, a very rough sort of continuum does exist, namely, from the completely formless pure *C* response to the highly articulated and well-integrated *FC+* response. The discussion here, and the brief excerpts from Rorschach protocols that accompany it, will be divided into three loose categories: pure *C* responses, *CF* responses, and *FC* responses. It should be kept in mind, however, that our aim is not a manual of interpretation but rather illustrations of our approach.

Pure *C*

It has been indicated in the discussion of the previous section that even the most primitive pure *C* response which is scorable as such does not reflect the most immediate and primitive perceptual response to color, but is already, or it could not be a scorable response, integrated to some extent with appropriate content. The only exception to this would be color-naming responses which are clearly on the borderline of scorability. Nevertheless, the pure *C* responses as a whole, and particularly those varieties that are met with in cases of chronic schizophrenia, do seem to approach the immediacy and directness of an altogether diffuse and unformed color experience. As mentioned before, these responses have been described by Rapaport (1953) as "short circuiting" the ordinarily more highly developed channels of perception and association. That is to say, the processes of active perceptual organization which operate in normal adults are in these cases by-passed to a considerable degree. This describes the condition of perceptual passivity, and, in Rorschach testing, such responses are in fact sometimes accompanied by indications of a relative helplessness and of a subjective feeling of passivity in relation to the stimulus, which are very close to those described previously in connection with the sorting studies of pathological cases and with the early experiences of the newly operated blind.

Pure color responses, such as those found in the records of chronic schizophrenics, and color-naming responses, which are an even more "pure" type of color response, provide difficulties for an understanding of color responses which ties their meaning exclusively to affects. Cases in which these primitive varieties of color response tend to predominate are, of course, just those whose affects are often described as shallow, "blunted," and the like.

At the same time, it is true that one sometimes meets with these responses in cases where the pathology may include exceedingly impulsive, perhaps psychotic, actions or exceedingly wild, unmodulated, unpredictable, and by ordinary standards inappropriate affect expressions. Sometimes both of these conditions may exist together in the same person, blandness being sporadically interrupted by impulsive outbursts. Since we know that pure C response can be a dominant Rorschach feature associated with any of these—blunted affect, impulsive actions, or unmodulated outbursts—it is clear that its essential significance relates to a factor which underlies all of them. This factor is just that condition of "short circuiting" or immobilization of integrative, modulating, and impulse- and tension-discharge-delaying functions, a short-circuiting which, as we have described, reflects itself also in a relative primitivization of the perceptual process. Perception tends, in such conditions, to become more diffuse and global (see Chapter 3 of this volume) and, with immobilization of the active form-organizing capacities that give it its autonomy, perception becomes also more bound to the sensorially most impressive aspects of the stimulus.

In organic cases of color naming and in connection with the pure C responses of blunted and deteriorated chronic schizophrenics, one gets no feeling of *affect* discharge or affect pressure. On the contrary, the impression is often of a concrete report of a sensory experience without any but the most direct, immediate, and primitive content and quite without the affective connotations which more highly organized color responses frequently have. Nor is there, in general, any indication of sensual-esthetic satisfaction in the color perception. Such satisfactions appear, and richer and more highly refined content and affect associations as well, only when some greater sense of autonomy and deliberateness is present in the perceptual act, i.e., only when active perceptual organization as a whole is more advanced.

The issue may be illustrated with several color responses, one a pure C and one scored F/C arb., from the Rorschach of a 42-year-old male chronic schizophrenic. This patient had barely managed an ambulatory adjustment for many years and, when seen at a psychiatric sanitarium, he was undergoing some further decompensation which made hospitalization necessary. His Rorschach contained 47 responses, somewhat more than one would have expected from the extent of his general dilapidation, but probably reflecting those retained adaptive capacities that had permitted him to function at a marginal level outside of hospitals for so long. Contamination, gross confabulations, perseverative responses, confused and peculiar verbalizations, and gross fluidity of thinking were all conspicuous in his test. His $F+\%$ was low. Among the determinants, he had one M, the popular on card III, four FC of which two involved an arbitrary use of color, one CF, and five pure C responses.

The following response, it will be noted, is quite innocuous and ordinary in content, but it is unusual in the extent to which it reveals the processes involved:

> To card VIII—"These two red things here [the animal figures] look like rats . . . [pause] . . . only they're red . . . red rats . . . I never heard of that . . . only the shape looks like rats."

In this response, the form, certainly one of the most clear-cut and obvious in the Rorschach, was accurately perceived. But it is clear at the same time that this perception is not at the level at which we are accustomed to thinking of form perception. The concreteness of the response is obvious. An adequate form perception implies the capacity to abstract perceptually the outline or shape without regard for or distraction by the other sensory stimuli which may happen to surround or be enveloped by that shape. Here, this capacity was clearly not present. Once impressed by the gross, concrete sensory stimulus, the patient was not able to restrain his response to the color, to say nothing of making use of it, for example, in an adequate FC response.

A subjective feeling of helplessness and passivity which one might expect would accompany this process is, in fact, conveyed not only in his verbalization in connection with the original response but also in the inquiry.

When the examiner later returned to this response and asked, "Red rats?" he answered, "Very peculiar . . . but I mean I saw them that way . . . you don't see red rats . . . but they're shaped like rats."

The patient was still bound to the color and unable simply to over-look it, even though he was well aware of the inadequacy of his pro-duction. A feeling of helplessness of this quality and extent seems substantially the same thing as what has been called "impotence" in the Rorschach behavior of organically brain-damaged patients. The similarity of the whole response, also, to some of the behavior that has been described, in connection with both the concrete sorting behavior of the pathological group and the perceptual reactions of Senden's cases, is noteworthy.

This response quoted was followed immediately by another one, and it seems possible to see in this sequence the further breakdown of an already extremely inadequate detachment, and the patient's even greater passivity in the face of the color stimulus. This second response was a pure C. He continued, ". . . and the redness [now all of the red area on card VIII] reminds me of tincture of merthiolate . . . like I have on my hand here."

His reference of the ink-blot color to the red tincture of merthiolate on his hand, which he held up in front of him at that moment, reveals again the loss of an attitude of active, detached perceptual organizing of the ink blot. Instead, he is held by the color even to the extent that the immediately striking color relationships over-ride the ordinary separation, altogether unquestioned in the attitude of most subjects, between the card and the remainder of the visual field around it.

It will be noted that there is no suggestion here of affect dis-charge in connection with the color response; as mentioned, bland-ness and impoverishment of affect were clinically conspicuous in the patient. The color, after all, is itself only a *sensory* stimulus and response to it can only be productive of, or reflect, affective response when the psychological organization being stimulated is capable of such a response. But, as has been described, a passive perceptual mode and the high responsiveness to the color that tends to be associated with it is far from being limited to such conditions. In the case of this patient, the impairment of perceptual organizing and integrating capacities was so great as to make the color stimulus attention demanding and passively experienced to the extent of not only precluding adequate integration with perceived form elements but also of overriding logical considerations and even detachment from the Rorschach card itself. Such a degree of impairment of perceptual organization and perceptual control must reflect a general impairment of psychological organization and control functions including an impairment of what are, after all, the relatively highly organized and differentiated discharge channels that would be necessary for true affect experience. Color response of this sort, therefore, cannot be said to reflect affectivity, but rather a condition of such disorganization or impairment of control functions as to preclude affective response in any ordinary sense of that term.

It happened that six months later this patient had recompensated to a considerable degree, and it is interesting to compare his handling of the same stimulus on card VIII at that time. His response was: "This looks like a rat—the same on the other side . . . [long pause] . . . I was going to say it looks like ink—I said it before . . . I can't see anything else." He handed the card back abruptly.

In the inquiry he was asked, "Ink?" He answered: "Because I think I said all the red looked like ink the last time . . . it doesn't look like ink this time . . . it feels funny . . . it feels like a lot of things disappeared the way I looked at things before."

In an unusually explicit way, and just because the process here is such an effortful and tenuous one, these verbalizations describe certain aspects of the patient's now reconstituted functioning. It is clear that his reference to the difference between this and the previous experience does not primarily have to do with the content of the response; it is altogether ordinary and unremarkable. His remarks seem rather to derive from a vague subjective feeling of increased control, perhaps including increased repressive capacity, but, more important in this instance, including a control that manifests itself in the capacity to detach himself from the over-all concrete sensory impression and to restrain immediate response to the color stimulus in particular. He is able now, although obviously barely able, to achieve a true form response. In the normal subject, of course, this process functions so smoothly and so quickly as not to be noticeable.

It may be mentioned that the color determinants in this second Rorschach consisted of two *FC*, two *CF*, and only one pure *C*, and that, along with this indication of better organization, at the time of the second testing, this man was a good deal more emotionally responsive in general clinical observation.

What about those cases of severe regression, e.g., chronic schizophrenics, where no color response appears at all? How is it that color, if it is the more immediately manifest stimulus, can be completely absent in these cases where impairment of perceptual organizing capacity along with impairment of thought and affect organization is otherwise obvious? The problem may at first appear all the more peculiar in view of the fact that it is always among the same clinical groups—chronic schizophrenics, severe schizoid character disorders, and perhaps some of the more severe narcissistic character disorders —that one finds cases in which color responses are altogether absent and other quite similar cases in which pure C responses are a dominant feature. It is not unusual, in fact, to find in retesting these patients that a Rorschach with one or two pure C responses will be replaced by one with no color at all, or vice versa.

It is just this close relationship between pure C responses, on the one hand, and complete absence of color response, on the other, that contains the central point. It will be remembered that a similar issue arose in connection with the apparent disappearance of color responsiveness in very young children, and, also, at very short exposure times in tachistoscopic presentation of the cards. In each of these cases the essential point is the same. It is this: the pure C response tendency and the complete absence of color response do not stand, as it were, at opposite ends of a scale of perceptual organization, but rather side by side.[11]

This fact may be made more clear if one considers that the two perceptual tendencies have an essential feature in common, namely, *that something* is conspicuously absent in both of them. What is absent is exactly the capacity to achieve an adequate degree of integration of the sensory experience of color with appropriate content and with form articulation, the capacity to use the color actively in any degree, and it is this capacity which essentially distinguishes an adequate color response from *both* the pure C response and the total absence of color response.[12] I do not mean to imply by this that the conditions which give rise to pure C responses, on the one hand, and

[11] This observation is confirmed by the following studies: Rickers-Ovsiankina, M. A. Prognostic Rorschach indices in schizophrenia, *Rev. diagn. psychol. and personal. explor.*, 1955, 3, 246-254; and Rickers-Ovsiankina, M. A., Knapp, R. H. and McIntyre, D. W. Factors affecting the psychodiagnostic significance of color perception, *J. proj. tech.*, 1963, 27, 461-466. [Editor].

[12] There are many analogies to this situation, both in psychological phenomena and elsewhere: flood and drought, inhibition and vulgarity, stinginess and waste—all these look

to a total absence of color response, on the other, are identical, but only to clarify their relationship to each other and the relationship of both to more advanced and more adequately organized color responses.

There appear to be at least two sorts of conditions which may be responsible for a total absence of color response. First of all, in cases of chronic schizophrenia, or possibly some cases of organic brain damage, there may be an incapacity to articulate and to give expression to the color experience as a distinct perceptual dimension at all, at least at a level of a scorable response. Color naming would, again, be just on the borderline of scorability, and is likely to appear in such cases. In other types of cases, particularly schizoid or paranoid but not necessarily psychotic characters, one often suspects on the basis of clinical observation an underlying defensiveness or guardedness in the absence of color response. The guarded detachment which is so characteristic of these people seems to preclude the degree of abandonment which might be implied in responding to the color stimulus at all. Here, too, however, one may easily overestimate the gap between a total absence of color response and a helpless, immediate response to color, as in a pure *C*, if one forgets that a complete avoidance of color reflects, first of all, an *incapacity* for adequate form- and content-integrated use of it. Such a defensive avoidance of the color stimulus, therefore, is likely to be separated by only a very thin line from a passive, helpless response to it. In fact, one sometimes gets some clinical confirmation of this when, in the course of a Rorschach test, one has been impressed by such a total avoidance up until the last card or two when a pure *C* response finally occurs. It would not be correct, in any event, to assume that a defensive, total avoidance of color reflects simply an avoidance of expression of affects, because the incapacity for an adequately organized response to the stimulus, which is indicated by the necessity for such an avoidance, is precisely what suggests that more or less adequately organized discharge channels, such as are assumed for ordinary affective experience, are not in existence. The likelihood is, therefore, that such an avoidance will again correspond to a degree of

---

superficially like polar opposites, but on closer look they are often associated and always for the same reason, namely, an absence of development, or an impairment, of modulating and controlling organizations or discharge structures.

blandness, possibly sporadic impulsive actions, and possibly even sporadic outburst of diffuse affect, but not simply to inhibition or lack of expression of otherwise well-developed and continuous affect experience.

The *CF* Response

The *CF* response is a much more common sort of color-dominated response than the pure *C*, and its quality and interpretive significance in many ways are much more varied. We will have to limit ourselves here to discussing a few types of *CF* responses.

It is among records in which color response is predominantly of the *CF* type, much more than among those dominated either by pure *C* or *FC*, that one finds the cases where color truly seems to reflect a lability and unusual vividness of affects. Even among cases with a dominant *CF* tendency, however, it is necessary to distinguish at least two important groups: one, characterized in fact by vivid and usually unstable emotional reactions, and a second group characterized much more by impulsive action, frequently with only little or shallow affect accompanying the action, and sometimes even with a psychopathic coolness or blandness. Roughly speaking, these two groups are, diagnostically, the hysterical category, in the first case, and the category of narcissistic or impulsive character disorders, in the second.

The *CF* responses, of course, stand between the more immediate and passive pure *C* responses and the more highly articulated *FC* responses. It will be remembered from the previous discussion that the development from the most passive and concrete sort of perception, in which color tends to be a dominant feature, to a more active perception, in which color is primarily integrated with and secondary to form, must include many overlapping intermediate phases. Senden's material only hints at such phases, and this is not surprising in view of the fact that visual development in his cases was compressed into an extraordinarily short period. Still, he describes, for example, a phase in which the newly seeing person attempts object identifications primarily on the basis of color, yet with some attention also to at least the more gross or visually more evident form characteristics. There is no intention here to suggest any exact parallel between such a phase of perceptual development and a specific sort of Rorschach response; such a parallel would be misleading. But it is important to note that such intermediate phases do exist, that there are various levels and degrees of integration of passive and active perceptual modes, and that these, in turn, must reflect various levels of more general psychological organization.

Of the two types of subjects to be considered first for whom the *CF* response is frequently a dominant Rorschach feature—impulsive, action-oriented, highly narcissistic people, on the one hand, and hysterical, extremely and unstably emotional people, on the other —no one can doubt that in both cases there is an impairment of capacity for delay of tension discharge or an impairment of impulse- or affect-organizing, modulating, and expressive functions. Yet it is clear that this impairment is not on the same level as that evident in the case of chronic schizophrenia described before. In these non-psychotic cases, no matter how great the pressure to discharge may be, or how abrupt or extravagant the discharge itself may be, the form or channel which that discharge takes is still in its essentials reasonably adapted to reality, i.e., it is a nonpsychotic form of dis-charge. Even though, therefore, abrupt, impulsive action or affect discharge reflects an impairment of control functions, this manner of discharge still generally presupposes a level of psychological organization which is distinctly more advanced and more intact than that of the schizophrenic case discussed before.

These people of the two types mentioned will typically find the immediate and visually obvious perceptual route offered by the color a congenial or provocative one. The subjective sense of im-mediacy and of being passively "struck" by a vivid color stimulus is, in fact, often very clear in the behavior and verbalization of these subjects. The fact remains, however, that as quick and passive as the response appears to be, as attention demanding as the color may be in these cases, the perceptual response does not reach the level of passivity, either in objective response product or in subjective sense of helplessness of the schizophrenic pure *C* response. The immediate and passive aspect of the perception is to some extent integrated with form-organizing and articulating capacities. A certain level of intact organization, *within which* an impairment of discharge control appears, is reflected therefore in the perceptual mode represented by a dominant *CF* tendency.

Of course, the *CF* tendency, itself, may be more or less prominent in a wide range of subjects. *CF* responses may reflect not only the sorts of impairment of controls that eventuate in pathologically abrupt and diffuse discharges through action or affects but also may reflect, at other times, the capacity for the wide range of affect discharges, immediate enough but quite nonpathological, which we call spontaneity. Or they may reflect a capacity for various degrees and types of more sensuous abandonment to the stimulus.

There are presumably differences in the perceptual quality of these sorts of *CF* responses, and there are marked differences in the subjective experience that accompanies them. Sometimes the quality of the subjective experience will be suggested by the behavior and tone of voice of the subject and sometimes by the "tone" of the content of the response itself. For example, the response "paint dripping" to the upper red areas of card III or the response "lipstick smear" to the upper red areas of card II suggest a different subjective experience from that suggested by the response "bursting fireworks" to the whole of card X. However, both of these responses will fall within the *CF* scoring category.

The first illustration is from the Rorschach of a young man diagnosed a narcissistic character disorder. An outstanding feature of his history and his life was impulsive action, frequently with a psychopathic flavor; business decisions, the buying of a car, even marriage or divorce were carried out speedily, with a minimum of reflection, and, as far as one could tell, with quite limited amounts of affect. In many ways, in fact, his affects could be described as shallow or bland, although not to the degree of a schizoid or schizophrenic person. His Rorschach was a long one, 77 responses, although many of the responses were pretentious and empty. His color responses included three *CF*, one *C/F*, and two pure *C* together with eight *FC* and *F/C*. In many ways the *CF* responses may be considered most characteristic of the man; both the *FC* responses, on the one hand, and the pure *C* responses, on the other, tended toward a *CF* quality. Many of his responses, including the color responses, were delivered in an exhibitionistic way, with special pleasure when he felt they might be considered remarkable or unusual, and his manner was one of dictating what he felt confident would be an interesting record.

To card II, for example, after an initial *W* response of "clowns," he went on, "... then, blood ... blood stains," a pause followed by another response that did not become clear until the inquiry, "... toilet ... this isn't particularly pretty," this last with particular emphasis as though to call attention to how disturbing the idea was.

A few responses later, he returned to the colored areas with the following: "It seems to be like red underwear there;" a few responses further on, he said: "Upside down it looks like an explosion ... like a volcano exploding;" finally, his last remark on handling the card, again with special emphasis, "I don't like that red."

The "toilet" response turned out to be associated loosely with the previous "blood" response and included all of the black, center white, and lower red areas of the card; when asked about this in the inquiry, he said: "Ah, I was afraid you'd get to that. It seems to be a blast of blood. That's been a big problem of mine ... it seemed to be associated with blood coming out of my rectum. ..."

Thus, there were three color-dominated responses to the card, exclusive of the surrounding comments and elaborations: "blood," the vaguely formed "red underwear," and the equally vaguely formed "volcano."

I have tried to convey with these excerpts the exceedingly impulsive and diffuse quality of this patient's whole Rorschach. The immediacy and relative absence of restraint with which gross, only weakly articulated, and vivid sensory impressions appear as conscious percepts and, in that sense, as finished products are obvious. It is noteworthy, however, that notwithstanding this immediate and impulsive quality, there was no indication of affect fluctuations in connection with the color responses or, for that matter, during the entire test. In contrast to the typical reaction of hysterical neurotics, this patient seemed quite at ease with the immediate, impulsive style of his color responses.

In certain ways, in the primitive quality of the pure C responses and the diffuseness of many others as well, this record seems close to a schizophrenic one. Yet it is still different in several respects, speaking with regard to the issue of color alone. As primitive as the color responses often are, they remain predominantly on a level on which there is some degree of integration with form, and they include, in fact, a number of form-dominated color responses. Just as the patient's general behavior was characterized by extremely impulsive discharge through action—which was, however, never essentially disorganized action—had some direction, and was not unmindful of at least proximal realistic demands, so his perceptual mode was passive, impulsive, and dominated by immediate response to the most sensorially vivid stimulus, yet never without a certain degree of active perceptual organization, and never passive to a degree in which the sensorially vivid overrode or immobilized the capacity for form organization altogether.

There is another feature related to this. In this man's behavior, there was no indication whatever that he experienced a *subjective feeling* of passivity or helplessness. There was no evidence that he felt "struck" by the color stimulus, in spite of the fact that to the observer he *appeared* immediately attracted and gripped by it. On the contrary, there was every evidence of a subjective feeling of deliberateness and autonomy even as he gave the most (perceptually) impulsive responses. This situation closely paralleled certain aspects of the clinical observations. The patient's quick, impulsive behavior could not help but strike anyone as reflecting an *incapacity* to delay, to hold back, and to consider long-range consequences or possible alternatives; yet the patient himself in no way *felt* at the mercy of his impulses, but rather felt that every action was deliberate and willful, or at least allowed by him. Is the observer right, or is the patient? The answer seems to be that in certain respects both are right. The impairment of restraining and organizing functions, perceptual and otherwise, is certainly present and manifests itself in the ways described, but, again, this impairment is not so extensive that certain basic integrative functions are altogether overwhelmed or immobilized. The existence of some such level of intact organization must be, at least, one prerequisite for this man's capacity to maintain a subjective feeling of autonomy. This type of discrepancy between the subjective feeling of autonomy and the objective evidence of passivity will present itself again in a more gross form in connection with the productions of hypomanic patients, to be discussed later.

Probably the most frequently encountered records in which *CF* responses have an important place are those of hysterics. These records demonstrate more than any others a relationship between vivid, color-dominated responses and equally vivid and labile affects.

As we said before, the labile and volatile affects of hysterical people reflect also an impairment or inadequacy of controlling and integrative functions; the immediate, provocative quality of the color stimulus for them, the perceptual "short-circuit" that occurs, is often especially apparent. It is so apparent because it is frequently accompanied by small-scale, but actual, affect discharges. However, just as an impairment of control which manifests itself primarily on a level of abrupt *affect* discharge, without discharge in action and without conspicuous impairment of thinking processes, implies an essentially more intact organization than would be indicated otherwise, so, typically, the impulsive color-dominated response of the hysteric, notwithstanding its immediacy, does not violate form aspects of the stimulus (as in the first, schizophrenic case), nor does it reach a level of diffuseness in which form aspects are ignored.

The following excerpts are from the protocol of a 39-year-old hysterical woman. Her adjustment had been characterized for many years by typically hysterical features: a general repressiveness and lack of reflectiveness, a good deal of romantic fantasy, and, above all, a conspicuously labile emotional life. It was, in fact, an increasing difficulty in emotional control, manifested in outbursts of tears or anger, that had caused her to seek psychiatric help.

Her Rorschach, except perhaps for one feature, was much as one might expect. There was only one M response, but an abundance of color responses including three FC, one F/C, two CF and three C/F. The total number of responses was 49; this unusual feature in an hysterical record is probably attributable to a rather ambitious, tenacious, compulsive aspect of her makeup.

Her first color response, which was her first response to card II was as follows: "Oh, my heavens! [flushes . . . a brief burst of nervous laughter] . . . Oh! . . . well, I could say it would look just like some pictures in a gynecological magazine or book of some kind."

In the inquiry, it became clear that this response was a rather vague W, determined largely by the immediate color impression which suggested menstruation, though it was integrated to some extent with form by way of the sexual-anatomical content. Other color responses which appeared later in the Rorschach had much the same perceptual quality as this one, though without the sexual content.

Her first response to card IX is an example: "That looks like a burst of something . . . just looks like a great big burst of color more than anything else;" and the first response to card X was: "Goodness! It looks like something . . . under a microscope . . . in color."

Both of these responses are *W*, and both were accompanied by the same sort of tension and affect discharge which was apparent in connection with the earlier response. In these responses also, however, she managed to achieve some degree of integration of color with form, though a quite weak one.

The exclamations, flushing, and nervous hesitations that accompanied these responses leave little doubt of a subjective experience of being struck by something or being taken by surprise. When one sees such reactions, in a Rorschach of this sort, it is tempting to assume that the color somehow contains an intrinsic affective value. The tone of the response content, e.g., "bursting," may also be construed to suggest this. Yet even in this case such an assumption is not necessary. It is necessary only to assume that the *perceptual* response to the color stimulus will, in its level and degree of immediacy, bear the stamp of whatever level of impairment or relaxation of control functions may exist. The qualities of that level will be reflected in the special visual qualities and formal aspects of the perception, ordinarily in its content as well, and in the special quality of the subjective experience that is associated with the perceptual process.

These special qualities of a response are often not revealed in scores. For example, both the color responses of this hysterical patient and those of the previous case are predominantly of a *CF* sort. But it would be as incorrect to miss the difference in level of color-form integration, the difference in degree of perceptual diffuseness and immediate sensory domination, the difference in content-tone, and the difference in subjective experience between this patient's responses and the previous patient's as to miss the difference between romantic fantasy and impulsive marriages.

One of the most interesting examples of the significance of color response appears in the records of hypomanic cases. At the same time, color response in these cases involves certain special problems.

The expansive, poorly controlled affect of hypomanic people is sometimes described as "forced" emotionality; similarly, the large number of color-dominated responses which usually accumulate in the Rorschach records of these people are sometimes described as "forced" or "artificial" color responses. What is the meaning of this description, and what process is described by it?

The fact that the color responses of hypomanic patients often appear forced seems to derive from two aspects of those responses: (1) They often consist largely of C/F responses, i.e., color-dominated responses in which the color and form are inadequately or only very effortfully and tenuously integrated; and (2) the fact that many of these responses are given in the manner of, or accompanied by, the driven expansiveness and high mood which are characteristic of hypomania; frequently the content of the responses themselves suggests that high mood (Schafer, 1954). In connection with the first of these facts, the inadequate integration of color and form, there is a certain ambiguity. In a response in which color and form are inadequately integrated, the question remains open as to whether the color is "artificially" added to what was originally a form perception or, on the contrary, the form is inadequately integrated with what began as a vivid color experience. As to the second factor mentioned, the expansive way in which such responses tend to be produced and in which the color in particular tends to be described, it must certainly be said that this accurately reflects one level of the hypomanic person's subjective experience; he does obviously *feel* that he is producing deliberately, actively, and creatively, and he may very well feel so about his color use. But as we have already seen in the case of the narcissistic character disorder, the subjective feeling of activity and creativeness, and of autonomy in perception, by no means necessarily precludes that the state is objectively a relatively helpless one.

There is an alternative to understanding these color responses as "artificial:" The abundant color reaction of these people reflects essentially a state of relative passivity in the face of this stimulus, a too immediate response to it, and an incapacity to integrate it adequately with form; but, in contrast to other conditions in which this passivity or helplessness is experienced *subjectively* as such, in hypomanics it is covered by denial. It is somewhat like a person who finds himself riding a wild horse and, though actually quite out of control, proclaims himself a great rider because he is able to go so fast.

In the color response, then, what is "artificial" and forced is not essentially the vividness of the color but the inadequate integration of it with form and content, and the denial of helplessness implied often in the content tone. One qualification has to be made: In the analogy, the fiction of good horsemanship can only be maintained if the rider is able to avoid falling off altogether, and so it is with the color response; to the extent that the capacity for active form integration fails altogether and *CF* or *C/F* responses give way to pure *C* responses, one may expect that what was only high mood will give way to chaotic action and to a subjective sense of disorganization.

Both paranoid and hypomanic features, clearly of borderline psychotic degree, were outstanding in the clinical picture of the patient whose Rorschach will be described. Along with the usual expansive mood, there were many quite megalomanic ideas, particularly in connection with her interest in world affairs. There were 76 responses in the Rorschach, of which three were *M* responses and 22 were color responses. Among the color responses were two pure *C*, two *C/F*, seven *CF*, six *F/C*, and five *FC*.

The first color response was the first response to card II, given almost immediately upon looking at the card: "A top of a woman's dressing table with spilt nail polish and mascara all over the place."

The domination of this response by the gross sensory impression is conspicuous. The emphasis on spilling or spilling over is also noteworthy because it appears repeatedly in connection with other color responses in the remainder of the test.

For example, to the same card: "This part looks somewhat like a map of Russia—that would be very interesting—down here where the red is sort of spilling over into Red China and here into the eastern satellite states."

Or, to card VIII: "An aerial view of the Mississippi . . . flood stage . . . spreading over its banks." This whole response was determined primarily by the blue-green color in the center of the card, but included the other colors as indicating "a more turbulent area."

Other color-dominated responses, to illustrate further the vivid and gross quality, included the three red areas of card III seen as "red lights" and, again, the whole of card VIII seen as "the flame of a Bunsen burner."

The exceedingly poor control, including both impulse and affect control, is reflected not only in the immediacy of the perceptual response to the color impression and by its essential diffusiveness but also in content, as in the theme of "spilling over" or "overflowing" banks. She was, however, sufficiently intact to maintain not only a consistently high mood but also a superficial manner of detached intellectual interest throughout most of the test. This degree of actual intactness, i.e., the kernel of truth that was probably indispensable to her otherwise empty sense of autonomy, was reflected in the degree of form articulation she generally did manage to achieve in her color responses as well as in the quantity of her productions. Just such a capacity for enough active, integrative effort to go through at least the motions of productiveness and, as it were, to challenge the underlying sense of incapacity seems essential to a sustained hypomanic mood. It is difficult to observe such things, but it may be that with those responses which are least articulated formwise and, at the same time, with those in which the color experience is most immediate, vivid, and compelling (e.g., "red lights"), the sense of detachment and control did break down temporarily.[13]

It seems more difficult to account for those expansively toned color responses sometimes given by hypomanic patients to areas of color on the ink blots which are, in themselves, quite pale.

An example of this type of response is the following to the upper center area of card IX, from a mildly hypomanic patient: ". . . and here all the colors of the card [which she had previously responded to separately] blend in a rainbow. . . ."

It is this type of response which, as far as I can see, constitutes the strongest argument for an assumption of "artificial" or forced response to color. However, even here, this thesis seems doubtful.

The patient whose response is quoted above had, almost immediately upon seeing the card, named and described each of the colors in the different parts of the blot. This process revealed her initial reaction to the colors; it represented, as such color description ordinarily does, an altogether inadequate attempt to use them actively. Following that, there was a gross, and again inadequate,

---

[13] Such an apparent vividness of color experience is also encountered on occasion in the Rorschachs of borderline or schizophrenic paranoid patients in more acutely disturbed states. One such response from a patient, and his only color response, was to card III: "Like the headlights of a car [center red] coming toward you on the beach at night." The vividness of this response harks back to the early phase of Senden's patients.

attempt at integration of all the color with form; she described the whole blot as a "varicolored doublet." Notwithstanding their inadequacy, the integrative efforts in connection with the color were, therefore, clear enough. Again, up to the last response—the "rainbow"—the effortful and forced quality seemed to reside, as in the previously described case, in the inadequate form integration rather than in the color reaction itself. This was the background of the "rainbow" response at which the patient arrived finally. It may very well be that this last color response contained not simply a reaction to the pale area indicated, but was actually a further integrative effort to deal with *all* of the other, previously named, colors in the blot (". . . and here all the colors . . . blend"). In effect, then, this final color response, in which the color experience itself seemed forced and artificial, is seen as another effort to deal actively with the initially passive color experience. I believe that careful analysis will usually show this type of process in connection with such responses.

Responses of this sort seem to underscore that the defensive efforts in hypomanic conditions include not only denials of a sense of helplessness to deal with compelling sensory stimuli but also an aspect of active exercise of the remaining intact integrative functions, as though to challenge those underlying feelings. It is probably this active exercise that lends some substance to the content of the denials. It is in this sense only that an artificial-use-of-color hypothesis seems to have validity.

FC Response

On the whole, the processes that go into making an *FC* response seem more difficult to understand and more complex than those involved in the color-dominated responses. Perhaps this is so because the higher integrative capacities that go into the making of this type of response are less well understood. It also seems true that the interpretive meaning of *FC* responses varies more widely than that of more primitive color responses. In general, after all, people differ more widely from each other in the more complex mental functions than they do in the developmentally more primitive ones. It will be necessary to discuss the *FC* response in somewhat more general terms than has been the case with the other categories, since specific illustrations cannot, in this case, sufficiently convey the main aspects of the argument. First, I will sum up the understanding so far.

As a result of the absence of capacities for active perceptual organization, more primitive perception involves a more passive relationship between the perceiver and the stimulus, in which color, because of its sensory quality and its ease of apprehension, becomes an especially compelling, vivid, and distracting aspect of the visual field. Because of these same qualities, color originally is probably antagonistic to form perception; the perceiver is distracted from form elements by what is sensorially more vivid. In certain types of adults, such an antagonism between color and form perception still operates to some degree, and, as we can see through the Rorschach, the more immediate response to the vivid sensory stimulus seems to abort or override the development of highly organized form articulations; or, the achievement of highly articulated form perception is possible only at the relative sacrifice of responsiveness to the more immediate and sensorially more vivid stimulus. However, optimally, as form perception develops, an integration between it and the originally antagonistic or distracting color sensation is achieved. The problem is, what does this integration actually consist of?

As described before, one significant intermediate stage in the integration of color and form in perception is achieved in the movement from being only gripped or distracted, passively, by the sensory experience to active *use* of that sensory experience for object identification. But the adaptive value of object identification predominately or exclusively on the basis of color is extremely limited, and vision ultimately, if it is to have significant adaptive value at all, must be predominately form vision. The development must be progressively away from what merely happens to be sensorially most impressive in the visual field and toward what is logically most essential.[14] Color must be displaced from a position of dominance, and it is displaced along with the development of capacities for active perceptual organization and the increasing freedom, concomitant with this development, from altogether passive response to what is sensorially vivid. However, color may still retain functions of value; by its very quality of sensory immediacy and ease of apprehension, color ex-

---

[14] With the development of perceptual constancies, the perceiver achieves an adaptively valuable degree of independence even from transient and accidental variations in form or configuration.

perience normally plays a significant role even in perception that is very largely dominated by form.

Let us continue at this point in Rorschach language. If we regard a good *FC* response, i.e., a response whose character is predominately defined by the form or configuration of an area of the blot but in which the color of that area also plays a significant and appropriate part, is it correct to say that such a perception has been achieved in a rapid but essentially additive fashion, by a process through which the component of color supplements the form perception through additional organizational effort? This question, most likely, must be answered in the negative, for two reasons. First of all, there is the fact that in the process of integration with form the perceptual experience of color undergoes some change. In a broad way, this is indicated by the body of the material discussed here, but specifically, it can be confirmed by such simple devices as a reduction screen. Therefore, the process is certainly an integrative and not an additive one. In addition, if we ask whether an object or representation is more easily or more rapidly identified when it is with or without appropriate color, we see at once that under such circumstances, far from being a burden to the perceptual process or requiring more effort than already required by the organization of the form perception, appropriate color is an aid, can make accurate apprehension of the object or representation a speedier and easier affair, and functions more like a *useful* short-cut. It is, of course, partly for just such reasons of perceptual economy that color is useful in communication generally. That very immediacy which is inherent in color sensation, and which is originally antagonistic to highly organized form perceptions, can serve perceptual articulation in an economical way, assuming still that it does not override or short-circuit form elements altogether.

We know that there is more to the story. Apparently at the same stroke in which apprehension of color can provide a perceptual economy, it can enliven a form and lend an additional richness or sensory pleasure. Exactly what the sensory pleasure consists of, how it is related to the over-all perceptual organization, and in what possible ways it may be connected with the economical function of color, if at all, are questions which we cannot answer. But that is no reason to ignore the fact.

It is assumed, then, that within predominantly form-oriented perception, color retains from its original compelling quality both an economical and an enriching function. An optimal integration of this sort between form and color seems to be reflected in the *FC* type of response. The enrichment of virtually any form response when it is integrated successfully with color is self-evident. To call the large human figures on card II, for example, "Halloween witches," making use in that image of the red and black costume is to see something more distinct, more vivid, and more individual than to describe these same figures without the dimension of color. The same thing can be said for the ordinary "green caterpillars" or "green tomato worms" on card X, as opposed to describing these same figures as simply "snakes" on the basis of their form alone. The economical function of color in the Rorschach situation itself may be questioned, because, after all, in that situation there is no objective need for economy of recognition. Even so, the availability of a more economical mode of perception will have advantages; the subject who can allow color as well as form to suggest imagery is able not only to produce richer responses but also to produce them more easily. The capacity, for example, to allow the red and black colors on card II to suggest, together with the form, an appropriate content should, if the process works smoothly, be a less effortful one than a delineation which must rely on form exclusively to suggest an appropriate content.

The condition that is reflected in successful perceptual integration of form and color and, at least ideally, in the *FC* type of response, is one in which the immediate sensory experience of color is neither so compelling and distracting as to preclude adequate form articulation (and content elaboration) nor has it to be avoided altogether, but can be *used*. This condition implies a more autonomous perceptual attention (in contrast to a condition in which attention is bound to the vivid sensory qualities of the visual field) and a wider range of perceptual sensitivity than would otherwise be the case. It implies, therefore, rather a capacity for a more flexible and therefore more adaptive sort of perception.

Insofar as they can be determined, the subjective feelings typically associated with the color impression on the Rorschach when it is well integrated with form are not feelings of *helpless* passivity or of disruption of sense of (perceptual) autonomy; for example, such phenomena as have been described by the term "color shock" do not appear in connection with these responses. It is, in fact, only consistent with the integrated character of this perceptual process and the economical or enriching use of the immediate color impression that the visual quality of the color *as such* should be less attention demanding and that the subjective experience in connection with the color *as such* should tend to be less distinct, except insofar as it endows the whole perception with a special vividness or ease of apprehension.

FC responses have been considered, in line with Rorschach's original assumptions and the color-affect linkage, to reflect a more adaptive, reality-tuned emotional responsiveness. However, I believe that, here too, the characteristics of the perceptual mode represented by this score suggest a somewhat broader significance. This perceptual mode suggests a psychological organization in which passive and immediate experience or discharge may appear on a level not antagonistic to, or disruptive of, control functions or adaptive necessities, and which is not associated with a subjective experience of helplessness or loss of autonomy but on a level and of a quality integrated with and valuable to adaptive direction and interest in the ways indicated.

FC responses, therefore, may reflect not only an adaptive responsivenessness in the narrow, socially oriented sense but also a range of sensitivity, a mobility of attention, and a susceptibility to pertinent impression all of which are equally significant in connection with such functions as judgment, planning, and, in general, style of thought. They may reflect, also, capacities for more durable, subjectively self-consistent, and also more individually stamped sorts of feelings, involvements, and interests.

Of course, it has again been expedient to speak in ideal, almost typological terms. It will be clear enough to anyone who is familiar with the Rorschach that a great deal that has been said here about the *FC* response can apply equally well to many responses that may be scored *CF*, and it is equally true that many responses which, technically, require an *FC* score do not convey at all the sense and meaning that has been described. Several of these latter sorts of responses, *FC* responses which, as it were, fall short of their goal will be considered further.

Most such inadequate *FC* responses are of a specific type; the integration of form and color is simply unsuccessful, not in the sense that it flatly violates reality but that it produces no essential unity in which one feels, of both the color and the form, that each contributes something to the other and perceptually modifies the other. These responses are usually scored *F/C*. For example, the upper red areas on card II may be seen, the card turned sideways, as representations of animals colored red for decorative purposes as in a stage backdrop; or the popular animals on card VIII may be seen as polar bears with a pink color because they are in a sunset. In such responses the form and the color seem to approach an additive combination; the form is not significantly influenced, or further delineated, or specified by the presence of the color, and the appearance of the color is probably subjectively no different than it would be if detached from this particular form, or seen through a reduction screen—it is uninfluenced by the form which marks its boundaries.

Sometimes it is said that these responses also contain a "forced" use of color. But here again, what is forced is not the response to color *per se*, but the integrative effort. Certainly there seems in such responses to be an integrative effort, but the resulting integration fails, at least partially, in that the color does not fulfill to any appreciable extent its essential functions, i.e., it does not particularly enrich or enliven the form, nor does it seem to have aided or to have been suggestive in the articulation of that form. What is the failure of the integrative process here? It can be made clear by a comparison with more successful form-color integration.

The condition for a successful *FC* response is a susceptibility to the immediate color impression in which that impression offers itself as a possibility to a mobile attention, but not gripping that attention and not, as it were, intruding itself until it becomes an aspect of the final, integrated percept. In the process of the *F/C* response, as much as one can reconstruct it, this does not quite happen. Visual attention seems in this case not to be so mobile and autonomous; although, many times, the subjective attitude toward the color seems to be one of detachment, actually the color seems to offer itself quite insistently. (Both the subjective detachment and the underlying insistence and attention-demanding quality of the color for these subjects are often conveyed in the explanations of their response, in inquiry, which may run as follows: "Well, the color *was there*, so I *had* to explain it some way.") In contrast to the process of a pure *C* or color-dominated response, this insistence of color seems not to be of a sort which aborts (or "short-circuits") form articulation but, nevertheless, occurs to the extent that the color, in contrast here to the successful *FC* process, does establish its final quality independently of the final, complete percept, and perhaps thereby limits, or at least does not extend, the range of acceptable content possibilities.

One sometimes gets the impression with *F/C* responses that a primitive and exceedingly immediate color response has barely been avoided. This expresses, in another way, the fact that the color aspect of these responses often seems so unmodulated perceptually and so little more than a direct and concrete report of a sensory impression (and, in fact, simple color descriptions do frequently appear in these same records, though given in a detached way and not intended as official responses). Yet, insofar as a logical coordination is achieved between the color and form, and a quality of detachment is maintained, a "short-circuit" is avoided. It will, in fact, be found in many cases where *F/C* responses figure prominently that there is a general avoidance of and an apparent incapacity for a freer or more frankly immediate response to the color, a playful use of it, or a sensory enjoyment of it, and *CF* responses will tend to be absent in these cases. Thus, the *F/C* response seems, on the one hand, in some way to be associated with a relatively unmodulated, sensorially direct, and insistent perception of color, yet, on the other hand, at least in one context in which it frequently appears, it seems associated with an avoidance of free response to color. What is the meaning of this apparently paradoxical circumstance?

It seems possible in certain cases that capacities for active perceptual form articulation have been achieved, not together with a more or less gradual modification of the perceptual position and function of more immediate sensory experience but only by way of an excessive detachment of attention from such sensory experience in favor of form elements. It is not clear how such a detachment of attention might be achieved and maintained, though possibly the persistent and unvarying fixing of attention on form elements of the visual field (such as we see in many obsessive-compulsive Rorschachs) is itself a critical factor in maintaining it. This sort of detachment is quite different from the more flexible and mobile attention described before. It does achieve facility in form articulation, but at a cost of more immediate sensory experience; it does achieve a degree of active, autonomous visual attention, but the range of that attention is limited; and it often has a quality of strain and of being only a short step from losing its autonomy to compelling sensory stimuli (as, in fact, in some rigid, compulsive Rorschachs, the detached accumulation of pure form responses is abruptly interrupted by a pure C response). The F/C response seems to involve such a detachment, but a detachment of a partial or less complete and wavering sort. It appears to involve a compromise in which a color experience, which is initially insistent and attention compelling and which, as we have said, establishes its final quality in the perception independently, is yet regarded with a degree of detachment until the form articulation is also independently established, and only then is it fully and officially admitted. It is some process such as this, I believe, that gives the F/C response its peculiar quality of an effortful combination of elements which are not really integrated perceptually.

F/C responses of this sort are found frequently in overcontrolled, compulsive people. They seem to reflect a kind of responsiveness, adaptivity, or spontaneity that may be described as "forced" in the same sense that the response itself may be called "forced;" i.e., one senses in this kind of responsiveness some quality of discrepancy or incomplete integration between a not quite sufficiently modulated impulse or tension discharge and the intent or direction with which it is coordinated and which it is supposed to serve.

This type of F/C response is by no means the only one; the process which has been described may have a number of variants, and so, accordingly, may the specific perceptual quality of the response and its specific interpretive meaning. It must be added, also, that there are various shades of responses that fall somewhere between the type of F/C response described and a successful FC. A less rigid, and perhaps more smoothly functioning, detachment, which is still essentially of this sort may allow for better integration of the color with form, and may even eventuate in a response scorable as FC. Such conditions are among those taken up below.

There are, of course, many different perceptual qualities even among *FC* responses in which form and color are, according to our criteria, perfectly well integrated. Two sorts of cases will be considered now in which such *FC* response seems to have a significance somewhat different from, and which in some ways falls short of, the general *FC* quality described. These are, first, cases in which one or two *FC* responses comprise the *only* color responses, and, secondly, cases of an apparent overabundance of *FC* responses.

There are several types of Rorschachs in which a few *FC* responses will comprise the only color response. First of all, there are the Rorschachs of extremely inhibited people, which are likely to be quite constricted in general. Secondly, there are the records of compulsive people, which are dominated by a large number of meticulous, pure-form responses. The general problem of these cases may be put as follows: Can *FC* responses, in such contexts, be said to reflect the wider range of perceptual sensitivity or the susceptability to immediate sensory experience and the readiness to use it, which were previously described as characteristic of the *FC* tendency? Or, to put the issue another way, is it possible that a perceptual organization in which a frank, immediate responsiveness (of a color-dominated-response type) is so decisively avoided may still allow for such flexible use of color as the *FC* score has been said to imply? The answer appears to be "yes," but with certain qualifications.

It seems that in these cases of rigid and inhibited psychological organization a *limited* sort of attention may be allowed to the colors in the Rorschach. It is true that the functioning of a psychological control organization such as this seems to dictate a relatively consistent detachment from, or avoidance of, color in favor of exercise of more active, more controlled form-organizing perceptual capacities. Within this general orientation, however, the rigidity or constriction may be more or may be less severe, and the restriction of attention to form elements may be more or less marked. In connection with the *F/C* response we have seen one way in which such rigidity may *waver*, and one way in which detachment may be *partially* relaxed. When the general control organization is functioning more smoothly, some greater mobility of perceptual attention may be achieved, but perhaps only to an extent and under conditions which do not challenge the essential dominance of the more actively controlled form-organizing perceptual mode.

What are such conditions? For example, attention may be allowed to the more muted colors (e.g., the "brown-grey mice" in card X), whereas it is not allowed to the more vivid ones; or, attention may be allowed to colors in connection with form percepts which are very obvious and easily articulated, whereas it is not allowed otherwise. In the cases under discussion, where one or two *FC* responses comprise the total color response, richer responses involving the more vivid colors or larger colored areas (e.g., "Halloween witches in black and red costumes" on card II) are not likely to be present. In other words, the sort of mobility of perceptual attention which is associated with the *FC* response is not an all-or-none affair; it may operate within various limits and with various sorts and degrees of restriction. The perceptual quality of the resulting response will vary accordingly, and so will its interpretive significance. Thus, even one or two *FC* responses within such otherwise rigid or constricted records will generally reflect some of the flexible, responsive, or sensitive traits generally associated with the *FC* tendency, but in muted ways or within limited areas which are not inconsistent with the quality of the general control organization.

The second type of case considered in order to illustrate the various perceptual qualities which are possible within the *FC* category is that type in which there is an unusual abundance, in a sense even an excess, of *FC* responses. These *FC* responses, in contrast to the rigid or inhibited Rorschachs discussed above, may appear together with many *CF* and even pure *C* responses. It might be asked, with some justification, how *FC* responses could be too abundant, in view of their generally adaptive significance. The answer is, of course, in the fact that such a context suggests that the individual *FC* response must have a somewhat different quality and significance from what is usual.

One such record, for example, obtained from a male overt homosexual, included seven *FC*, two *F/C*, and four *CF* out of a total of 27 responses. Only five of these 27 responses were pure-form responses; wherever color was present and available, some sort of color-form response was preferred to a pure-form response.

Actually, his emphasis on color went further, in a certain way, than even this tabulation can demonstrate. In his verbalization generally, and particularly in the inquiry, wherever a response was by objective criteria a product of both color and form aspects, he invariably underscored the color aspect.

For example, his remark, "It had to be something—the color just suggested it," was a typical answer to inquiry, even in connection with obviously well-articulated perceptions. Or, his description of card IX, "An arrangement of tropical plants—arranged more just for the combination of colors than for the beauty of the flowers themselves," or even on card I, "The first thing I thought of was kind of the outline of a bat—maybe the color more than anything else."

We have indicated that the *FC* response reflects, ideally, a type of sensitivity to the color stimulus and a capacity to use it which result in an enrichment of the final perception and an economy in the perceptual process. This sort of readiness to make use of the more immediate color experience, together with form elements, has been described as indicating a more flexible kind of perception and a more freely ranging visual attention. But it is clear in the case described that we cannot speak simply of a *readiness* to use color in this way; instead, for this patient, there appears to be a marked *reliance* on some use of the immediate color experience, together with form elements, to achieve a reasonably well-delineated response. Pure *F* responses, in other words, tend to be supplanted by *FC* responses. What does this mean, and, specifically, what is the interpretive meaning of *FC* in these circumstances?

It will be helpful, at this point, to consider certain features of the clinical picture that this patient presented. He was a capable enough person who arranged and organized his life in a way that for the most part would indicate to an observer some stability and direction. The patient himself, however, did not particularly feel such a direction or, at least, did not feel that it originated from him and was controlled by him. Whatever he did was felt by him either to be vaguely impulsive, or dictated by external necessity, or submissive to another person's wishes, and, in fact, his activities tended to be so arranged as to leave such issues unclear. He experienced little or no sense of active choice, decision, or autonomous action. Clear-cut and self-aware planning, especially of a long-range sort, was largely absent, although as mentioned, the objective course of his life was by no means chaotic.

Throughout the Rorschach, along with his tendency to underscore the color determination of his responses, this patient repeatedly emphasized their intuitive, impressionistic nature (e.g., in such comments as, "It was the first thing I thought of . . . ," "It just looked that way at a quick glance . . . ," "The color just suggested it . . ."). The verbal emphasis on the impressionistic nature of actually well-articulated responses is consistent with the perceptual tendency described; i.e., it is consistent with what appears to be a *reliance on the suggestive value* of the more immediate and sensorially more impressive aspect of the stimulus for the initiation even of what may finally become a well-articulated percept. This sort of reliance seems generally to be involved when the *FC* mode dominates and tends to supplant pure-form articulations.

This tendency does not imply a severe impairment or "short-circuit" of form-articulation capacities. It does indicate, however, that complex form-articulation capacities either have not been maximally developed or tend to be avoided in favor of more impressionistic shortcuts to the achievement of articulated percepts. This perceptual mode, therefore, may be considered one that fulfills the adaptive requirement of perceptual articulation with the least amount of active and controlled perceptual organizing. The color experience here will not be an altogether compelling and attention-demanding one but, in its suggestive and percept-initiating value, will probably draw greater attention and assume greater visual importance than might ordinarily be the case in an *FC* response.

This type of dominant *FC* tendency will not necessarily be associated with impulsive behavior or affective lability. Nor will it, on the other hand, be associated with the sort of adaptive flexibility previously described in connection with the *FC* response. It will rather tend to be associated with that kind of life style which, though sufficiently well-organized and adaptive, is somewhat lacking in, or shrinks from, controls and the degree of detachment from transient external pressures that make for clear and autonomous direction, for the capacity to make long-range plans, for sustained though not necessarily rigid convictions, etc., and which, because of that insufficiency, relies heavily although quite selectively on the manifest external pressures of the moment and the passively experienced internal response to them. Such people prefer to feel "it happened to me" rather than "I did it." Where this dominant *FC* made is surrounded by color-dominated response, the character will usually have a somewhat more impulsive quality; where color-dominated responses are fewer, it will generally be more submissive in tone.

It is clear, then, that within the *FC* category, as in the other major scoring categories, there exists a range of perceptual qualities with a corresponding range of interpretive meanings. One additional point may be noted at this time. It is apparent that at the FC end of the color-response scale as at the other, pure C end, the value of the color-affect hypothesis tends to diminish and the supposed linkage becomes foggy. Although the various sorts of subjective experiences and forms of tension discharge other than affects which have been described in connection with various types of color response are not unrelated to affect experience in its ordinary meaning, it is in the CF range that the linkage between color and affect has its principal validity.

SUMMARY

We have selected a sample from the ordinary range of Rorschach color responses for the purpose of examining a variety of perceptual modes in which color plays some part and to illustrate an interpretation of color response in terms of the perceptual processes involved in it.

This perceptual understanding of color response rests primarily on three factors, which, of course, are separated and abstracted here only for purposes of exposition: (1) The more strictly sensory and perceptually immediate quality (i.e., requiring a minimum of perceptual organizing or deliberate direction of visual attention) that is intrinsic to color as a visual stimulus; (2) the special, more passive or immediate *aspect* which may be seen in one form or another or on one level or another in all Rorschach color responses; and (3) the nature of the individual perceptual organization and integrative capacities which will determine the quality and significance of this aspect of visual experience, from an altogether attention-compelling and distracting experience, antagonistic to form articulation, to a sensitive and smoothly operating use of color to facilitate and enrich an articulated percept. The quality of color response will therefore reflect aspects of the perceptual and general psychological organization, which pertain to the more passive and immediate varieties of subjective experience and tension discharge, and will indicate, also, something of their specific quality.[15] From this point of view, the affect-color linkage must be regarded as a special case of a more general phenomenon.

[15] For a more general study of relationships between cognitive modes and general psychological organization, see Shapiro (1965).

BIBLIOGRAPHY

Ames, L. B., Learned, J., Metraux, R. W., and Walker, R.N. *Child Rorschach responses.* New York: Paul Hoeber, 1952.

Dworetzky, G. Le test de Rorschache et L'evolution de la perception, *Arch. Psychol.*, 27, 1939.

Dworetzky, G. The development of perception in the Rorschach. In: Klopfer, B. et al. *Developments in the Rorschach technique. Vol. II.* Yonkers: World Book Co., 1956, 104-176.

Ford, M. *The application of the Rorschach test to young children.* Minneapolis: University of Minnesota Press, 1946.

Friedman, H. Perceptual regression in schizophrenia: An hypothesis suggested by the use of the Rorschach test. *J. genet. Psychol.*, 1952, 81, 63-99.

Goldstein, K., and Scheerer, M. Abstract and concrete behavior: an experimental study with special tests. *Psychol. Monogr.*, 1944, 53, 239.

Halpern, F. *A clinical approach to children's Rorschachs.* New York: Grune & Stratton, 1953.

Hanfmann, E. Study of personal patterns in an intellectual performance. *Character and Personality*, 1941, 9, 315-325.

Hanfmann, E., and Kasanin, J. Conceptual thinking in schizophrenia. *Nerv. ment. Dis. Mongr.*, 1942, No. 67.

Harlow, H. F. The formation of learning sets. *Psychol. Rev.*, 1949, 56, 51-65.

Honkavaara, S. The "dynamic-affective" phase in the development of concepts. *J. Psychol.*, 1958, 45, 11-23.

Huxley, A. *Heaven and hell.* New York: Harper, 1956.

Katz, D. *The world of color.* London: Routledge and Kegan Paul, 1935.

Klopfer, B., and Margulies, H. A. Rorschach reactions in early childhood. *Rorschach Res. Exch.*, 1941, 5, 1-23.

Lindberg, B. J. *Experimental studies of colour and non-colour attitude in school children and adults.* Copenhagen: Leven & Munksgaard • Ejnar Munksgaard, 1938.

Rapaport, D. Some metapsychological considerations concerning activity and passivity. Paper read at the Austen Riggs Center, 1953.

Rapaport, D., Gill, M. M., and Schafer, R. *Diagnostic psychological testing* (1945) Revised edition by R. R. Holt. New York: International University Press, 1968.

Revesz, G. An experimental study in abstraction in monkeys. *J. comp. Psychol.*, 1925, 5, 293-343.

Rickers-Ovsiankina, M. A. Some theoretical considerations regarding the Rorschach method. *Rorschach Res. Exch.*, 1943, 7, 41-53.

Rorschach, H. *Psychodiagnostics.* Bern: Hans Huber, 1942.

Schachtel, E. *Experiential Foundations of Rorschach's Test.* New York: Basic Books, 1966.

Schafer, R. *Psychoanalytic interpretation in Rorschach testing.* New York: Grune & Stratton, 1954.

Schilder, P. *Medical psychology.* New York: International Universities Press, 1953.

Senden, M. *Raum and Gestaltauffassung bei operierten Blindgeborenen.* Leipzig: Barth, 1932. (Translation of notes on original by Laboratory of Psychology, Cornell University, 1950.)

Shapiro, D. Color-response and perceptual passivity. *J. proj. Tech.*, 1956, 20, No. 1, 52-69.

Shapiro, D. *Neurotic styles,* New York: Basic Books, 1965.

Stein, M. I. Personality factors involved in the temporal development of Rorschach responses. *J. proj. Tech.*, 1949, 8, 355-414.

Thompson, J. The ability of children of different grade levels to generalize on sorting tests. *J. Psychol.*, 1941, 11, 119-126.

Weigl, E. On the psychology of so-called processes of abstraction (transl.). *J. abnorm. and soc. Psychol.*, 1941, **36**, 3-33.

Werner, H. *Comparative psychology of mental development.* Chicago: Follett Publishing Company, 1948.

Wilson, P. D. and Riesen, A. H. Visual development in rhesus monkeys neonatally deprived of patterned light. *J. Compar. and Physiol. Psychol.*, 1966, **61**, 87-95.

In the quiet of night when awaking
Loneliness treads near my place
How to go on living and laughing?
Darkness stares into my face.

Is there still a scent from candles
And a mother's softness near?
How the smoke envelops me in blackness
And only melancholy's here. *

ALBIN ZOLLINGER

9 | *Ewald Bohm*

THE

BINDER CHIAROSCURO SYSTEM

AND ITS THEORETICAL BASIS [1]

It may be a matter of chance that Binder's fundamental essay (1933), although it appeared as early as forty years ago, even today remains little known in the United States. The work is seldom mentioned, and even then not always correctly. Nevertheless, European workers consider Binder's writings among the most important publications in the field.

It is no easy task to work one's way through this treatise and to master its complicated trains of thought. The effort is worth while, however, since the Binder system offers a number of advantages. Only after the analysis of a considerable number of test protocols did Binder arrive at his classification criteria. Following Rorschach, he treats the chiaroscuro reactions, analogous with form, color, and movement responses, in the light of the experiences determining them, whereas in scoring systems based on the distinction among surface, depth, and texture, the treatment appears to be more

---

*Translated by Morton Felix.

[1] This chapter is a translated, modified and updated version of the author's publication *Das Binder'sche Helldunkelsystem*, Rorschachiana, **V**, 1959, pp. 3-21.

closely related to the content of the responses than to the underlying experiences. The widely used systems of Klopfer (1954) and
Beck (1944) utilize three-dimensionality as a criterion for classification of chiaroscuro responses. Binder, too, realized that in many of
these interpretations three-dimensionality plays a role, but he did
not consider this factor an essential or invariable aspect of the
shading. Their summative nature rather than three-dimensionality
is considered by Binder to be the distinguishing feature of chiaroscuro
responses. It is consequently advisable to keep apart these two things
—the mode of experiencing the shading and the criterion of three-
dimensionality. I record the three-dimensional responses as "perspective," and take their occurrence into account as an independent
phenomenon.

Binder's system has the further advantage that it is based on a carefully considered and very usable theory of feeling. Theory and practice are synthesized in a way which we do not meet even in Rorschach's
own writings. It therefore seems appropriate to begin the presentation
of his system with an exposition of this theoretical basis.

BINDER'S THEORY

Peripheral and Central Phenomena

In his theory, Binder essentially follows the Munich branch of the
objectivistic, phenomenological school. He distinguishes between
peripheral and *central* psychic phenomena.[2] In order to account for
the great adaptability in coordinating functions between the incoming
sensory and outgoing motor "sides" of the organism's periphery,
Binder postulates a mediating agent which he calls the "sophropsyche," a term borrowed from Braun (1928). The sophropsyche is
a set of cognitive-conative systems, culminating in an "integrative
organ" (Binder, 1933), the ego. Since the ego represents primarily
the phylogenetically late developed "higher" mental activities, it is
to be thought of as peripheral in nature. In contrast to these ego-
syntonic processes, the ego-alien deep-seated urges and emotions
constitute the core of the person or the id, and are to be considered
central in terms of Binder's basic dichotomy. This differentiation
does not coincide with that between "conscious" and "unconscious."

---

[2] This distinction into peripheral and central phenomena should not be interpreted as
paralleling the differentiation of neurological processes into peripheral and central [Editor].

Peripheral as well as central processes may be conscious, part-conscious, or unconscious, according to the extent to which inner awareness is focused on them. Through constant interaction, the ego and the id combine into the superordinate unity of the individual.[3]

Characteristics of Feeling

According to Binder, all feelings are characterized by the following four criteria:

1. Feelings always show "a peculiar warmth;" they are pleasant or unpleasant; they have a quality of like or dislike; in other words, they are never indifferent.

2. Feelings show "a peculiar subjectivity." One may distinguish "a subjective and an objective component of feeling," but, in contrast to the objective one, the subjective component can never be absent.

3. Feelings *per se* are not "directed," but a direction may be superimposed upon them from the outside.

4. "Feelings are not acts, but merely states which the individual experiences passively" (1933, p. 4).

The latter feature distinguishes them from strivings, which involve psychomotor activity. However, introspectively, feelings and strivings may be experienced as closely linked.

Categories of Feeling

In accordance with the above division of psychic phenomena into peripheral and central, Binder arrives at the following classification of feelings:

I. Peripheral, reactive, discrete feelings.
    (a) Sensory   (b) Dispositional
II. Central feeling-tones (moods).
    1. Central, reactive, total-feelings (*Gesamtgefühle*).
    (a) Sensory   (b) Dispositional
    2. Endogenous vitality-feelings (*Lebensgefühle*).

[3] The ego concept presented here as a "sophropsychic integrative organ" interpolated between the centripetal and centrifugal "sides" of the human organism and possessing regulative functions, essentially corresponds to Freud's conception of the ego. Freud's ego is "the organized part of the id" (1936, p. 24), and has "controlling, mediating, and integrating functions" (pp. 15-16). In *The Question of Lay Analysis*, Freud writes: "We recognize in man a psychical organization which is interpolated between his sensory stimuli

The *peripheral discrete feelings* are aroused by sensations, perceptions, and ideas, and are closely connected with them. Usually they constitute rather specific reactions of consciousness and possess a relative independence within the momentary state of the person. Different discrete feelings may exist side by side at the same time. The *sensory* discrete feelings are connected with a palpable sensory element of a perception and their objective feeling component is pronounced. The *dispositional* discrete feelings are based on an "act intending a single object of perception, of ideation or of thought." They are directed and intentional (joy at, dislike of, love of, fear of). Here the subjective part is more evident (Binder, 1933, pp. 5-7).

The *central total-feelings* are also of a reactive nature, and are aroused by peripheral experience. Where an entire sensory area is experienced as total impression, a *sensory* total-feeling arises. A diffuse multiplicity is experienced, which through some common basic feature is merged into a whole. When a circumstance of broad implications combines a wide area of objects and events into a total situation, a *dispositional* total-feeling arises. Such sensory and dispositional total experiences may give rise to a "feeling resonance" in the deeper layers of the personality, which will then diffuse into a broad total-feeling. Total-feelings, as a rule, reverberate for a long time and their directional character is so faint that intentionality can no longer be ascribed to them. The subjective feeling component is preponderant. Two different total-feelings cannot exist at the same time in consciousness. The total-feelings are identical with Kuelpe's "generalized feelings" (*Gemeingefühle*) (1922).

The *vitality-* or *life-feelings*, finally, are the "deepest central emotional background of everything experienced." They are not reactive, but endogenous. They are purely subjective and they are not directed. They are "tied to the totality of the ... indistinct organic sensations and fused with these into a uniform experience"

---

and perception of his bodily needs on the one hand, and his motor activity on the other; and which mediates between them with a certain purpose. We call this organization his 'I' (ego)" (1927, p. 33).

Binder's conception of the id as the emotive and conative core of the personality, now conscious, now semiconscious, and now unconscious, differs however in one respect from Freud's id conception. The Freudian id is indeed also "the oldest of mental provinces" (1949, p. 14), the original core of the personality, but it is always unconscious: "Everything which goes on in the id is unconscious and remains so" (1927, p. 38).

(Binder, 1933, p. 6). The endogenous vitality-feelings blend to a great extent with the reactive total-feelings. Thus these central feeling tones together form the *moods*, in which an endogenous and a reactive side are to be distinguished. At times, however, as a consequence of the general spreading tendency of feelings, very intensive and prolonged peripheral feelings may expand into the center of the personality, and then assume the character of a mood. These moods will then acquire an object-oriented, concrete direction. Thus there are no sharp lines of demarcation among the various categories of feeling.

Psychiatric Implications

According to these views of Binder's an *endogenous mood distur-bance* constitutes "an organically determined fluctuation of the vitality-feelings," which also influences the mode of reaction of the total-feelings. This leads to a constantly heightened readiness for like reactive total-feelings. Occassionally, however, as, e.g., in light depressions, euphorically toned discrete feelings may appear. The *reactive mood disturbance* is the occurrence of a central total-feeling produced by a complex experience or by the expanding of very strong and lasting discrete feelings. Here, too, the readiness is increased for responding in a like feeling tone to almost every stimulation from outside. As a rule, the vitality-feelings remain unaffected in reactive depressions, although there are cases in which the total-feelings are of such depth that they may engulf even the vital feelings. The *autochthonous mood lability* consists of abnormally frequent changes of the vital feelings, the phases of which, however, last for at least a few hours. The *common reactive mood lability* appears to be a constitutionally based anomaly of central total-feelings, which respond readily even to mild stimulation, but fade rapidly. This kind of mood fluctuation may be very transitory. When total-feelings of only a single quality occur, Binder speaks of *one-sided reactive mood lability* (1933, p. 8). In psychopaths this type of lability seems to be rooted in temperament, while in neurotics, it is more likely to be functional in nature.

Like Ribot (1903) and Szymanski (1926), Binder distinguishes four basic mood qualities, the euphoric and three dysphoric ones, namely, the sad, the anxious, and the irritable. In addition, these qualities may appear in mixed forms (1933, p. 8).

Emotion and Perception

The problem under consideration in this section makes it desirable to say a few words about Binder's ideas regarding the relationship between perception and emotional experiences. He develops these ideas from the supposition that there are two principal attitudes under which it is possible to grasp a number of simultaneously occurring visual stimuli:

1. One may apprehend every sensory pattern as separate and interpret it objectwise. Such an attitude will be accompanied by a number of sensory and dispositional discrete feelings. Since the perceived "complex" is experienced as an aggregate of independent items, as something summative, mosaiclike, only incomplete fusion of these discrete feelings can occur. In the resulting so called "mixed feelings," the separate affective components can easily be discerned by directing one's attention toward them.

2. One may also take in the perceptual totality at a glance, without attending separately to its different sensory components. They are simply experienced as a diffuse multiplicity. Since the perceptual impression is a holistic one, awareness of its common undertone within the multiplicity is what primarily characterizes this experience and leads to sensory total-feelings or mood reactions. Any dispositional total-feelings arising at the same time will be fused with them.

These two extreme attitudes may combine. In such cases, single, especially striking, sensory items will be perceived separately and with object character, so that they are experienced as "figure" on the "ground" of diffuse total impressions into which the remaining perceptual material blends.

To a certain extent, both modes of experience may be brought about intentionally. The objective nature of the presented stimuli, however, greatly influences the mode of experience. If the visual stimuli consist mostly of sharply offset, disparate elements, the experience is usually correspondingly mosaiclike, and there is no "true total impression." On the other hand, visual stimulus material containing indistinctly separated details that blur into each other and are similar to each other is likely to produce a total impression, especially where these details are "tuned to" a common keynote. Such visual impressions thus bring about reactive moods (central total-feelings). We know these differences from art. The genre picture or still life of Dutch realists appeals to our discrete feelings. It has been justly said about such a picture as the well-known "Iron Mill" by Adolph von Menzel (1875) with its multitude of well-defined details that here the eye could find no focal resting point. The landscapes of the Romanticists and the Impressionists, on the other hand, characteristically tend to arouse moods in the observer. In the same way we may distinguish between these two kinds of effect in music and in literature.

In nature, *chromatic colors* mostly appear to us in such a clearly differentiated way that this independence of distinct color blots from each other is experienced as a multitude of single objects. Accordingly, the emotional reaction is one of discrete feelings. The above-mentioned "mosaiclike impression of a whole" has been created. In the same way, placing a variety of equally bright color patches side by side in a painting fails to produce any moods.

On the other hand, the *chiaroscuro scale* of white-grey black is typically experienced in quite a different way. In nature it occurs mainly in the grey of dawn, in twilight, in a moonlit landscape, fog, darkness, or the "floating light of distant atmosphere," where the chiaroscuro values blur indistinctly into each other, and thus "automatically" result in a total impression. The mood tends to be euphoric when brightness prevails, and dysphoric when darkness dominates. The creation of diffuse total impressions is particularly facilitated by chiaroscuro stimuli, because they are more homogeneous than the greatly varied chromatic hues, and thus one of the two conditions for the appearance of total impressions (indistinct delineation and similarity among the given elements) is always fulfilled in the case of chiaroscuro material. The perception of a colored landscape usually calls forth a combination of the two approaches. The play of lights and shadows produces the "background" of the experience, the total-feeling, the mood, whereas single, especially conspicuous, chromatic colors provide the "figure" which arouses certain discrete feelings as leitmotif.

The essence of these reflections by Binder culminates in a state-ment that is basic for his Rorschach theory: "Chiaroscuro values primarily affect the total-feelings, produce mood-reactions; the hues of the chromatic colors mainly affect discrete feelings" (1933, p. 11).

This proposition, however, does not apply without certain excep-tions. The assumption that color perception, by virtue of its "object character," arouses discrete feelings, refers only to the *surface colors* (in the meaning of Katz, 1930), which in the Rorschach test cor-respond mainly to the *FC responses.*[4] The *film colors*, on the other hand, do not show this strong affinity to discrete feelings, but seem to stand in a closer relationship to moods. In the Rorschach, this concerns especially the pure *C* and possibly also certain *CF* responses, as is well demonstrated by protocols of patients with agitated mood disturbance. Binder, who does not mention the work of Katz, was nevertheless fully aware of this psychologically important distinction between colors. He speaks (p. 12) of the justification for the expres-sion "color mood," where a color is so predominant that it strikes the keynote which evokes a total color impression, and, hence, a mood reaction. This applies particularly to "large, relatively uniform color areas." This wording, with the examples he gives—"forest-green, ocean-blue, sunset-glow"—suggests that Binder had in mind more or less the same phenomena as those referred to by Katz as "film colors." Far more complicated conditions probably exist in such cases as the glaring color contrasts of an annual fair, which as a rule do not evoke any moods (unless one squints to bring about artificially a total impression). Besides the over-all brightness, it is the general impact of noise and motion that is here mainly responsible for the mood effect.

In practice, a second exception from Binder's conceptual frame-work is of even greater importance. Occasionally chiaroscuro material may be experienced in a mental set toward detail, and in such cases will then lead to peripheral discrete feelings in the same way as do the chromatic colors. "This, however, is only possible," Binder says, "where in the totality of presented stimuli the shadings are suffi-ciently clearly demarcated, and are of sufficiently differing bright-ness, so that the individual shading actually is able to produce the effect of a separate form" (p. 12). We shall later see that this ex-

---

[4] For explanation of scoring symbols, see Appendix, pp. 609 ff. [Editor].

ception has suggested the main principle of classification in Binder's chiaroscuro system.

Emotion and Overt Behavior

Of relevance to Binder's theory of feelings are his ideas on the psychology of overt behavior. They center around the controlling functions of the "sophropsyche" discussed earlier in this chapter (p. 304 f.). All organizational mental activity is seen as representing a synthesis between sophropsychic cognitive patterning, on the one hand, and emotional-motivational forces, on the other. This synthesis results in a global formation "which is at once reason, feeling and striving" (p. 14). The role of the sophropsychic steering in this process is that of a regulating agent of infinite plasticity. It is directed against peripheral as well as central emotions and strivings, not in the sense of denial but of control (p. 14). Such steering does not prevent the arousal of emotions and motivations *per se*, it only checks selectively the overt expression of those that cannot be effectively integrated into rationally formed structures. "Normal steering is thus 'a striving for organization' in perception, thought and action" (p. 15).

Empathy

To complete the review of Binder's theoretical system, we shall touch upon his treatment of the controversial concept of *empathy*. Binder agrees with Scheler (1923) and Klages (1923) that the direct apprehension of another person's expression "does not result from empathy." Empathy is rather the projecting of one's own emotions and strivings, and of accompanying kinesthetic experience, into an external object. The sensory discrete feeling is most easily "objectivized" in this manner; "it is localized completely in the object" (p. 15). Volkelt (1927) calls this "subjective, unaccentuated empathy," as, e.g., in "the cheerful yellow of the flower." On the other hand, there is no projection of dispositional discrete feelings; the enjoyment of the flower remains my own, and cannot be perceived as a property of the flower. With sensory and dispositional total-feelings, on the other hand, empathy is a frequent phenomenon. When the observer is in a sad mood, the landscape seems to be full of sadness; it acquires an "emotional character." But the mood is also felt as one's own ("subjectively accentuated empathy," according to Volkelt).

BINDER'S SCORING SYSTEM

Binder's Rorschach material consisted of the records of 51 normals, 101 psychopaths, 58 neurotics, and 61 psychotics, altogether 271 cases. The patients were diagnosed by means of detailed case studies at the psychiatric university clinic in Basel.

Analyzing the protocols, he soon realized that it would not be possible to assign any single interpretation to all chiaroscuro responses. On the basis of careful, nonsuggestive inquiries into the experiences of his subjects, he arrived at a differentiation of the chiaroscuro responses into two large main categories, with quite different interpretative significance: (1) The faceted responses emphasizing a number of individual discrete shadings, which today are usually called *shading responses*; and (2) the *chiaroscuro responses proper*, which are based entirely on a diffuse total impression of chiaroscuro. In conformity with Rorschach's original scoring, Binder denotes the former group (C) responses, and scores them $F(C)+$, since their form by definition can only be good. This implies a narrowing of the category to which Rorschach originally gave the score. As Binder says, he now uses the symbol "in a much more precisely defined manner" (p. 27). The other group, Binder identifies as chiaroscuro or Ch responses proper.

Classification of Chiaroscuro Responses

Shading or (C) responses. Score: $F(C)$. The frequency of these responses is inversely proportional to that of the other group, the Ch responses, and inversely proportional to the frequency of M. They have a high negative correlation with W and a high positive correlation with D and Dd (pp. 33, 38, 57). The $F(C)$ is a rather rare category of response, and since the score is so often wrongly used, we shall quote Binder's definition verbatim:

> ... Within the selected blot area, the subject, from among all the conspicuous shadings, *picks out each individual one*, primarily emphasizing the

delimiting forms of the individual shadings, and only secondarily their chiaroscuro values (pp. 26-27).

Binder emphasizes the rarity of the $F(C)$ responses elsewhere with these words:

> In each $F(C)$ response, *several* single shadings must be used, and each of them must be interpreted separately. These individual shadings must be objectively different in brightness and clearly delineated from each other (p. 31).

The shading response is thus a matter of summative multiplicity. In most cases, these responses are very minutely elaborated. As an example, Binder quotes the following response to the upper projection of card VI:

> A fountain in the shape of a slender Triton of black marble [deep black]. It is clearly seen how the water emerges above his head and flows down across the marble. Behind it [the half-moon shaped detail] a Roman bowl made of light, strangely clouded marble. All over the bowl peculiar gargoyles are placed [the featherlike parts]. They are already half crumbled and in places overgrown with dark moss (p. 27). The score is D $F(C)$+ *Arch. O+.*

An example in which the space details are combined with $F(C)$ and even seen in perspective is the following response to card II:

> A parkway in glaring sunlight [white space], both sides lined with dark, overhanging trees [the black]. The street narrows down in the distance to a little path [light grey middle stripes of the point] lying in shade because both sides of it are lined with a fence, perhaps made of rocks. The lane leads up to a pagodalike pavilion [pointed detail] (p. 27). The score is *WS* $F(C)$ + *Na.*

The $F(C)$ response, which occurs only rarely in the records of psychopaths and neurotics, always indicates a low threshold for sensory discrete feelings and for rather specific nuances of affective adaptability, while sophropsychic control is adequate and central feeling tones are rarely involved. Two groups of $F(C)$ responses may be distinguished. A preponderance of darker shadings suggests "peripheral feelings of depressive-anxious bend" in insecurely functioning persons (pp. 36, 38). The *FC* occurring in these protocols are mostly a cool blue or green. In the other group, the light, single shadings are especially emphasized, intimate landscapes with idyllic nuances are affectionately described, finely chiseled, attractive or quaint heads are seen, or soft furs almost sensually enjoyed. This type of $F(C)$ interpretation reveals the arousal of gently pleasurable emotional tones in compliant, plastically adapting individuals. These subjects also produce considerable numbers of FC responses, usually warm reds and yellows. It may be said that in a subject of extratensive experience type the $F(C)$ are an indicator of sensitivity, whereas in the record of a subject of introversive experience type they rather suggest oversensitivity. In combination with the white-space interpretations [S $F(C)+$], the $F(C)$ responses have the meaning of wish fulfillment, as Rorschach realized.

Elsewhere (Bohm, 1972, p. 166) I have called the $F(C)$ responses "the auxiliary troops of the color," since in deducing the total affectivity from a protocol the $F(C)$ must always be considered in conjunction with the color responses. The $F(C)$, like the chromatic FC, reflect the subject's emotional adaptability; however, the former indicate an especially finely nuanced capacity for empathy. There are three major kinds of color-shading configurations:

(a) $F(C)$ may occur in a protocol (at times with FCh or even ChF) without color responses. These are nearly always cases of "substitute contact," in which the subject tries to offset his lack of direct emotional adaptation and empathy by a more intellectualized, indirect, hesitant form of contact.

(b) In the case of a preponderance of $F(C)$ over FC, the sensitivity of the subject approaches oversensitivity, particularly in the case of an introversive experience type.

(c) Finally, $F(C)$ may occur together with a predominance of labile color responses, i.e., together with CF and C, and no or very few FC. This combination has proved to be typical of the specific form of oversensitivity found in schizoid persons who, behind a withdrawn facade, conceal an oversensitive core, so that their reactions are at times quite puzzling to the observer. As Kretschmer has expressed it so beautifully, they are "like bare Roman houses, villas, that have closed their shutters against the glaring sun, while in their subdued inner light feasts are being celebrated" (1944, p. 159).

Chiaroscuro responses proper or *Ch* responses. Lacking a common designation for the two major groups, Binder uses the term "chiaroscuro responses" for both $F(C)$ and Ch responses, although he applies the chiaroscuro symbol Ch only to the group of genuine chiaroscuro responses. They are either W responses or refer to large details of the blot. The frequency of Ch responses is inversely proportional to frequencies of $F(C)$ and of color responses. Ch responses have a high positive correlation with W, a clearly negative correlation with D, and a high negative correlation with Dd. In these responses, "no single shadings are selected;" rather the interpretations are based on a diffuse total impression of the chiaroscuro values. "The delimiting forms of the individual shadings receive no attention" (p. 28). The outline form, however, may play a more or less significant role. On the basis of the latter criterion, Binder divides the Ch responses, in analogy with the color responses, into three subgroups, as follows:

(a) *The FCh+ or FCh− responses* (depending on the quality of the form perception) are responses in which the outline form is emphasized primarily and clearly, "while the diffuse chiaroscuro impression is given less weight than the delimiting form" (p. 29), e.g., "Scarecrow draped with dark material" (card IV) or "The silhouette of the ruins of a castle on rocks (upper half of card VI in $>$ position). "Animal skin" (especially for cards IV and VI) should be scored *FCh* only where the chiaroscuro factor is emphasized (pp. 66, 67).

(b) *The ChF responses* are interpretations in which the chiaroscuro impression is so much in the foreground "that the form delineations of the area are only faintly and unclearly perceived, if not entirely disregarded" (p. 30), e.g., "Stormy clouds" (card VII), "X-ray pictures of an animal" (card IV), "Dark-wooded mountain slope, a sort of mountain ridge" (card V).

(c) In the *pure Ch responses*, finally, the form factor of the blots is entirely ignored in the interpretation, "so that the subject reports nothing but a diffuse chiaroscuro impression" (p. 30), e.g., "Stormy mood" (card IV), "Like a nightmare" (card IV), "The play of the waves" (card I, right side).

The Ch responses are more frequent in neurotics than in normals, and still more frequent in psychopaths. In contrast to the $F(C)$, which reflect peripheral discrete feelings, the Ch interpretations are always connected with central feeling tones, mostly of a dysphoric nature. In the case of the FCh, sophropsychic control of these moods may be assumed, since such responses usually accompany a high $F+\%$, an orderly succession, and a normal apperception type. Control of moods is inadequate with the *ChF*, and entirely absent in the pure *Ch*. In the case of the *FCh*−, a striving for self-control is still present, but because of inadequately differentiated judgment, it is no longer effective.

Borderline Cases

To complete the discussion of Binder's classificational system, some bordeline cases should be mentioned in order to differentiate them from the chiaroscuro responses. Binder emphasizes about all these borderline cases that they are *not* "genuine chiaroscuro responses" (p. 23).

1. Interpretations of the *white areas* occur in two variations. Such a response either is a *secondary* reference to the white color (e.g., "Lampshade of white china" to the space detail in card II), and is scored simply *F*; or is a *primary* reference to the white color (e.g., "Snowman" to the space detail in card IX), and, as a genuine color response, is scored *FC*. That these primary references to white are genuine color responses is indicated by their occasional appearance in conjunction with chromatic color responses (as figure-ground fusion, one might say). An example is the response to the central red in card VIII combined with the white space above: "Elegant red kimono with especially nice white collar." These "genuine" white color responses seem to have a whole series of possible interpretations. As Binder himself mentions, they may be the expression of an euphoric mood. Rorschach found reference to the white as well as to the grey and black colors in epileptics, and sometimes also in disorganized schizophrenics. I myself have observed the use of black, grey, and white color as a not uncommon component of the ixothyme[5] syndrome. More recently Zulliger reported (1954, pp. 58, 269) that he had found white-color responses mostly in records of oversensitive and easily hurt subjects who endeavor to hide their sensitivity. Furthermore, it should be remembered that, when the white color serves as a determinant, space responses are involved, and hence their interpretative significance must also be considered. In any case, they are never assigned a chiaroscuro score.

[5] The ixothyme constitution, according to Stroemgren, is a normal type, with character features analogous to those found in exaggerated and pathological form in epilepsy (1936).

2. Similarly, responses to which only the outline of a darker or lighter inner detail has contributed, and in which the light-dark gradation has not played a role, do not belong in the chiaroscuro category. Such interpretations are frequently given to the black or the light figures inside the so-called boot on card IV, where the black is often seen as a human figure or a geographical map (e.g., Jutland), the light part as a dog or lion. These are either pure form or movement responses. The same detail may, of course, be perceived in quite different ways, as in the following example by Binder: one subject interprets the two dark stripes in the middle line of card IV in position V as "Man, of whom only his long legs and his hips are plainly seen, while the upper part of his body [in the middle column] is indistinct." This is a pure form response $(Dd\ F+\ H\ O+)$. Another subject, however, interprets the same detail as "A sinister figure —only the legs and the abdomen are clear; on top it looks as if it were shrouded in a dark cloud. A mummified Egyptian—a giant from olden times" (p. 23). Here, besides the form, the chiaroscuro values have clearly played a part, and the score is ChF. This important distinction is often overlooked, and responses which are not determined by shading are scored as if they were, thus causing misinterpretations.

3. Again, the use of shading secondarily as an elaboration does not constitute a genuine chiaroscuro response. If, e.g., the subject says on card III: "Two men who take their hats off to each other," and then after a pause goes on: "One might also say, if one wishes, that they are English schoolboys because they are dressed in dark clothes" (p. 24), then this is a common popular response, and must be scored $W\ M+H\ P$. At most, we may, with Zulliger, indicate the tendency as $FCh \rightarrow$. The full score, then, would be $W\ FCh \rightarrow M+H\ P$.

4. Finally, a whole group of responses must be distinguished from the genuine chiaroscuro responses, because the subjects do not react emotionally but purely intellectually to the chiaroscuro impression. Binder calls these responses "intellectual chiaroscuro responses" (p. 25). They usually are given by subjects who want to put on airs "to create an impression of specialized knowledge and education." There are three kinds of such responses.

a. The chiaroscuro namings are a special kind of description and should be dealt with as such, i.e., they are not given any score, but instead "chiaroscuro description" is noted. Here an effort to make an impression has induced the subject "in spite of lack of ideas nevertheless to say something." Binder illustrates this kind of response with the following example: "A person familiar with the technique of charcoal drawing is reminded of it by the shadings because everything is so blurred together" (p. 25).

b. Another variety of intellectual chiaroscuro response is somewhat more concrete, and may be scored as real interpretation. It does not matter much whether they are scored F— or ChF responses, as long as they are marked "intellectual chiaroscuro response" and are kept apart from the genuine chiaroscuro scores. Binder describes them as "scientific reminiscences," and gives this example: "When in a chemistry experiment two fluids are mixed together, then such clouds are created in one of the substances" (p. 25).

c. A third, rather rare subgroup of the same phenomenon includes the responses which might be called *descriptions of the chiaroscuro symbolism*. They are closely related to schizoid symbolic interpretations. They are scored in the same way as are the "scientific" reminiscences. An example is the following reaction to card VII: "That [lower third] would be the dark grey life—and here [midline] it then goes through the narrow gate of death up to heaven [white space] which appears quite white" (p. 26).

DARK SHOCK

An outgrowth of Binder's chiaroscuro scoring system are his reflections on the dark shock, the aspect of his work that is most familiar to American readers. He observed this phenomenon first in "persistent neurotic depressions." It consists of failure to respond to the dark cards, especially to card IV or, more frequently, inhibition of interpretations on these cards, reflected in Dd or Do responses, poor form, trite stereotypes, disturbance of succession, or unusual perceptions (Binder, 1933, p. 279).

Since Binder drew attention to the existence of dark shock, it has been found on all achromatic Rorschach cards, and today we know that dark shock may appear as a component of such psychopathologic Rorschach syndromes as phobias, psychasthenias, etc. It is always an indicator of pervasive anxiety. As such it is less frequent than the color shock which is characteristic of peripheral and more isolated emotional imbalances. Dark shock may occur alone or together with color shock, in the latter case with or without interference phenomena on cards IV or VII (Bohm, 1972, p. 127 ff.). Furthermore, the possibility of shock compensation and the simultaneous presence or absence of depression symptoms all have to be taken into consideration for an adequate evaluation of the dark shock on an individual Rorschach protocol.[6]

In a recent experiment (Bohm, 1973) I have been able to demonstrate that the dark shock constitutes a physiologically measurable "diminutive anxiety attack," i.e. manifest anxiety. While a group of 62 subjects, equally divided among men and women, responded to the Rorschach cards, changes in their skin temperature were recorded by means of a spot galvanometer. The subjects consisted of clinically diagnosed normals, various forms of neuroses, and psychopathies. The measurements revealed beyond the .05 level of statistical significance that as a rule (1) dark shock is associated with decrease in skin temperature; (2) color shock is not associated with decrease in skin temperature; (3) epileptoid subjects have no decrease in skin temperature even with dark shock. These findings, especially when related to certain aspects of the interference phenomenon (Bohm, 1973, p. 10), hold promise of providing helpful clues toward a differential diagnosis between neurosis and psychopathy.

Mohr (1947) has given us some interesting speculations regarding the psychogenesis of dark shock. Symbolically, black is frequently perceived as the "opposite of the impression of life inherent in light." It is lifeless, empty, dead. Since in a variety of cultures death is viewed as atonement for man's sins before God, the black color has become symbolic of the divine and of guilt. As pictured in the Prometheus legend, victory over nature has left man with a fear of the forces of nature, which, it may be postulated, is now transferred to the black, the dark of night.

Hence Mohr has deduced the following symbolic significance of the black color: Its *positive* meanings are the stable, the unalterable, the solemn (*viz.*, its use in formal clothes), the symbol of authority, the majesty of death, the divine. The *negative* meanings are guilt,

---

[6] For more details on the symptomatic value of dark shock, see Bohm, 1972, p. 124-129, 245 f, 271 ff., and Bohm, 1967, p. 77 and p. 107.

rebellion, anxiety and judgment. Since the father is the first authority in the life of the small child, it appears understandable in the light of the above relationships, that those of Mohr's subjects who were in conflict with their father felt an "unpleasant, somber, anxious mood" on cards I, IV, and VI, whereas persons not bothered by such conflicts react to these cards "with moods of security and calmness." Negative reactions to the dark cards were also observed in girls who had experienced conflict with a man. Here, of course, man may mean the father figure, but the black may also directly symbolize "evil," the negative masculine, as it is found in the symbolism of some Western cultures.

However valuable these observations may be for the understanding of individual Rorschach protocols, the reader should be warned against mechanically considering the card IV "*the* father card," just as card VII cannot be called "*the* mother card." Not every disturbance on card IV in the form of dark shock must necessarily rest upon a father conflict or on a sexual conflict with a man. Such a conclusion may only be drawn where it is made probable by the total picture of the particular Rorschach protocol. Psychological insight and clinical experience are of particular importance here.

SOPHROPSYCHIC CONTROL

To demonstrate concretely how Binder applies his scoring system to a psychological analysis of Rorschach protocols, we shall present in some detail his deductions with respect to sophropsychic control (see p. 304 and pp. 311 ff.).

Today it has become customary in superficial Rorschach practice simply to "read off" the degree of reality adaptation of an individual from the $F+\%$, as well as from the relation of the FC and FCh to the other color and chiaroscuro scores. This, however, does not provide an adequate picture of the subject's reality adaptation; rather a more complex pattern of test factors has to be taken into consideration.

Thus, Binder infers sophropsychic inhibitory tendencies from the particular manner in which his hypersensitive, asthenic subjects handle their chiaroscuro responses. For example, in sensitive psychopaths, a Ch response is frequently followed by an $F(C)$ response of labored objectivity. Binder gives the following example: First the subject responds to card VI in position > with, "A wreck in a sea of ice. Everything snowed under and covered with ice, quite abandoned. And below, the melancholy reflection. Arctic loneliness." The score is $D\ FCh+\ Na\ O+$. Then the card is placed in $\wedge$ position, and the subject interprets the upper projection: "That is a newt in an embryonic stage seen under the microscope in transmitted light. The inside of the embryo, alimentary canal, ganglia, etc., are already firmly formed and hence appear dark. Then round it a semi-transparent mantle. In front, a little darker, the embryonic eyes. On both sides the extremities, flippers, etc., partially formed toward the periphery —the darker fibers of the tissue are clearly seen." The score is $D\ F(C)+\ A\ O+$ (Binder, 1933, p. 235).

The first response reflects a relatively intensive mood reaction to the general diffuseness of the chiaroscuro. An emotion of such intensity may be expected to reverberate for some time, and so the second response is again prompted by the light-dark effect of the blot. What is significant, however, is that this time the interpretation does not fall into the Ch category, quite contrary: by means of pedantic elaborations on minute gradations in shading, the patient constructs an over-rational association. Any peripheral discrete feelings that had been touched off in this context, and that would have to be disphoric in tone because of perserveration of the earlier total-feeling, are blocked. The response is one of marked dry objectivity. It appears plausible to see in this strained scientific affectation an effort to compensate for the initial display of mood disturbance. Such $F(C)$ reactions of stressed matter of factness, devoid of any accompanying feeling, do not occur in the records of normal subjects. They are the result of compensatory mechanisms directed at the upsurge of an emotional attack. The quoted Rorschach responses thus might be viewed as a miniature reproduction of the inner struggle characteristic of the sensitive psychopath.

Sophropsychic inhibition may also affect directly the content of the shading responses, e.g., in the way the interpreted object is projected into great spatial distance. Thus an inner rejection of feeling expresses itself in spatial symbolism, as in the following reaction to card VI:

> A cold winter landscape, but seen from far away. In the middle line a brook frozen over in spots, on each side a dark earth slope. Then above there is still some dirty snow; one can see the snow streaks running between

the dark stones. Farther out some isolated grey snow patches are still seen on the slightly rolling ground. But it is all seen from very far away, as if you were flying in an airplane far above it. The score is $D F(C)+NaO+$ (p. 236).

The implication here is that the subject wants to place himself "at a distance" from his feelings.

Occasionally the rejection of initially experienced moods through sophropsychic inhibition also affects the Ch responses. The inhibition may be expressed through either spatial or temporal distance, as in the well-known phrase, "bird's eye view," or as in the following for card VI, main part, in V position: "As if one were standing on a mountain looking down at a distant prairie fire on the plains. Nothing but fire and smoke." Score: $D Ch Na O-$ (p. 253). At times the rejection of feeling is even given conscious representation, as in the following response to card IV:

> Something depressing. Maybe a desolate landscape with a chaos of strange rocks. And there [dark stripes in the middle above] a very small slender figure seen from the back. It turns away from the landscape. Yes, I have experienced something like that myself. Score: $W ChF Na O-$ (p. 253).

Other interpretations stand out by their forced, dry objectivity, as in the following response to card IV:

> The map of an island with a rugged coast. A certain island in the Malay Archipelago has such a shape, but I cannot think of its name. In the interior the shadings, that is how one indicates the contours on such a map. But I don't know—this is indeed somehow a quite unfamiliar island. Score: $W FCh+ Map$ (p. 254).

Similarly, on card VI: "A newspaper-holder with torn newspapers" ($W FCh+ Obj O+$) (p. 254). And finally, the blocking of feeling can be inferred from the sudden appearance of a white space or an artificial form interpretation after several Ch responses (p. 255).

The overcompensation of the mood effect may show itself when, immediately after several mood-colored "genuine" Ch responses, a Ch response of monumental architecture, devoid of mood, appears. A subject first gives the following interpretation to the side figure of card I in > position: "Like a cemetary. There [bat's wing] a cypress, old and bent, and beside it overturned gravestones. Gives a sinister impression," $D FCh+ Na O+$. And then the somber mood is overcompensated in the following response (card I in V position): "The

outline of a triumphal arc or something like that. Crude rocks.",
WS FCh+ Arch O+ (p. 256). The overcompensation can also be
recognized in the use of religious symbols, as in the following reaction to card IV: .

> Torn clouds, quite dark—that is the first impression I got from that pic-
> ture. But if one tries hard, one might see there above the clouds the Madonna
> floating with open arms, W ChF Scene O— (p. 256).

In all forms of sophropsychic inhibition, a capacity for control may
thus be assumed, which is of special importance regarding indications
and prognosis for psychotherapy.

CONCLUSIONS

By way of conclusion I should like to submit that through his ingenious interpretations of chiaroscuro reactions to the Rorschach blots,
Binder has thrown new light upon the important and complex role
played by moods in the total structure of the personality. With his
patterns of emotional reactions on the one hand, and indicators of
rational controls, on the other, he has so enriched Rorschach theory,
that it is nowadays hard to imagine the Rorschach field without
Binder's share in it. Hence it seems justifiable to term the European
variations upon the original method of Rorschach, the Rorschach-
Binder method.

BIBLIOGRAPHY

Beck, S. J. Rorschach's test. Vol. I. Basic processes. New York: Grune & Stratton, 1944.
Binder, H. Die Helldunkeldeutungen im psychodiagnostischen Experiment von Rorschach.
  Schweiz. Arch. Neurol. Psychiat., 1933, 30, 1-67 and 233-286.
Bohm, E. Lehrbuch der Rorschach Psychodiagnostik (4th ed.). Bern: Hans Huber, 1972.
Bohm, E. Experimentelle Untersuchungen ueber die Schockphaenomene des Rorschach-
  Tests. Schweiz. Z. f. Psychol. u. ihre Anw., 1973, 32, 150-162.
Bohm, E. Psychodiagnostisches Vademecum, 2nd ed. Bern: Hans Huber, 1967.
Braun, E. Psychogene Reaktionen. In: Bumke, O. (ed.). Handbuch der Geisteskrankheiten.
  Vol. 5. Berlin: Julius Springer, 1928.
Freud, S. An outline of psychoanalysis. Strachey, J. (Tr.) New York: Norton, 1949.
Freud, S. The problem of anxiety. Bunker, H. A. (Tr.) New York: Norton, 1936.
Freud, S. The question of lay analysis. Proctor-Gregg, N. (Tr.) New York: Norton, 1927.
Katz, D. Der Aufbau der Farbwelt. Leipzig: J. A. Barth, 1930.

Klages, L. *Ausdrucksbewegung und Gestaltungskraft*. Leipzig: J. A. Barth, 1923.

Klopfer, B., Ainsworth, M. D., Klopfer, W. B., and Holt, R. R. *Developments in the Rorschach technique. Vol. I.* Yonkers: World Book Co., 1954.

Kretschmer, E. *Körperbau und Charakter*. Berlin: Julius Springer, 1944.

Külpe, O. *Vorlesungen über Psychologie*. Leipzig: S. Hirzel, 1922.

Mohr, P. Die schwarze und dunkle Farbe der Rorschach-Tafeln. *Rorschachiana*, 1947, 2, 24-36.

Mohr, P. Die schwarze und sehr dunkle Tönung der Rorschachschen Tafeln und ihre Bedeutung für den Versuch. *Schweiz. Arch. Neurol. Psychiat.*, 1944, 53, 122-133.

Ribot, T. *Psychologie der Gefühle*. Altenburg: O. Bonde, 1903.

Scheler, M. *Wesen und Formen der Sympathie*. Bonn: F. Cohen, 1923.

Stroemgren, E. Om den ixothyme Psyke. *Hospitalstidende*, 1936, 79, 637-648.

Szymanski, J. S. *Gefühl und Erkennen. Abhandlungen aus der Neurologie, Psychiatrie, und ihren Grenzgebieten, Heft 33.* Berlin: S. Karger, 1926.

Volkelt, J. *System der Aesthetik*. Munich: C. H. Beck, 1925-1927.

Zulliger, H. *Der Tafeln-Z-Test*. Bern: Hans Huber, 1962.

Were it not for the motion and the colourplay of the soul, man would suffocate and rot away in his great passion, idleness.

CARL G. JUNG

10

Jerome L. Singer
and Serena-Lynn Brown

THE EXPERIENCE TYPE:

SOME BEHAVIORAL CORRELATES

AND THEORETICAL IMPLICATIONS

The concept of the experience type emerges from *Psychodiagnostics* as one of Herman Rorschach's most important contributions. Indeed, the rather warm and human quality of Rorschach's pages dealing with the ratio of human movement and color responses suggests that the author felt a close personal identification and an intuitive excitement about this material which are readily communicated to the reader. That people with differing life experience should see different things in ambiguous ink blots was almost a truism in Rorschach's day, but that a *specific* type of response determinant —human movement or color—should effectively measure a long-standing and important personality characteristic remains to this day a puzzling observation that calls for theoretical comprehension. Rorschach also concluded from his observations that, while relative emphases on human movement (introversive tendencies) or color (extratensive tendencies) represented human variations along two separate dimensions, some underlying relationship existed which merited juxtaposition of the two types of responses in order to estimate the experience type. For Rorschach the M:sum C relationship[1] apparently reflected a deeply ingrained life style most

---

[1] For explanation of scoring symbols, see Appendix, pp. 609 ff. [Editor].

likely constitutional in origin, although modifiable to some extent by mood swings, aging, extreme situational disturbance, or psychotherapy. The ratio for a given individual derived from his ink-blot protocol indicated a pattern that could be observed in day-to-day behavior, but which went beyond this readily observable level and suggested potentialities as well. As a concept the experience type had implications for unifying a vast number of personality characteristics ranging from the modes of expressing intellectual abilities to artistic talent, approach to interpersonal relationships, vocational potential, suitability of marriage partners, therapeutic accessibility, stress reaction, psychopathological symptomatology, and type of social or cultural interests.

Despite these potentialities, the concept of experience type in actual practice, as Beck (1946) has noted, has proved difficult to use and is often relatively neglected in diagnostic reporting. This chapter represents an attempt to explore the data now available from an increasing body of experimental research, with the hope of exposing some of the known facts that bear on Rorschach's concept and some of the problems which arise concerning its theoretical worth. The focus of the chapter will be as much as possible upon the M:sum C relationship, and subtle nuances such as content of either human movement or color responses will not be considered here. Two general questions will be raised and will serve as the organizational framework for the chapter:

1. Are Rorschach's original observations concerning the experience type confirmed by other investigators using more formal and improved research methods?

2. Are data or formulations available which suggest the possibility of relating Rorschach's experience type to more general theories of perception and personality?

BEHAVIORAL CORRELATES OF THE EXPERIENCE TYPE

Since Rorschach emphasized the "empirical" nature of his results and explicitly stated that his conclusions were grounded in his observations rather than deduced from a theory, these observations must bear up under the detailed scrutiny of others if they are to be accepted. The heightened awareness of the existence of selective perception and recall which derives from the work of Freud and Rorschach makes it all the more imperative to check on the reported observations of these original and independently-minded investigators.

Although analysis of an individual Rorschach protocol calls for consideration of the interrelations of several response categories and their qualitative features, the argument that experimental variation of specific aspects of the Rorschach method violates the meaning of the technique overlooks the crucial question of how the interpretative scheme originated. In order for Rorschach to derive his conclusions about the meaning of the different determinants he must have had at one time to consider them in relative isolation and to correlate gross behavior with extreme scores on the various test dimensions. Since Rorschach did not hesitate to suggest overt behavioral characteristics associated with high M, high sum C, and M:sum C, it may be well to begin with his specific statements and consider some approaches to verify them.

Other chapters have dealt in detail with the specific significance of the human movement and the color responses. It may suffice here to state that for Rorschach, human movement (kinesthetic) responses to the ink blots gave an indication of gross tendencies for fantasy and imaginal activity which were linked to overt inhibition or delay of motor response. Color reactions represented affective tendencies which also bore a relationship to overt mobility. By juxtaposing human movement responses and the weighted sum of color responses, one is afforded an indication of gross reaction tendencies that bear on relative capacities to resort to introversive or extratensive patterns in many areas of human functioning. The following table suggest some of the characteristics of persons who show predominantly either M or sum C in their experience types. As the experience type ratio becomes more nearly equal for both components, one may expect a richness of capacity for both inner- and outer-directed living:

Kinesthesis Predominant:	*Color Predominant:*
More individualized intelligence	Stereotyped intelligence
Greater creative ability	More reproductive ability
More "inner" life	More "outward" life
Stable affective reactions	Labile affective reactions
More intensive than extensive rapport	More extensive than intensive rapport
Measured, stable motility	Restless, labile motility
Awkwardness, clumsiness	Skill and adroitness.

(Rorschach, H., 1942, p. 78)

It is obvious from this table that Rorschach felt he had observed direct behavioral manifestations of the experience type patterns. It remains the task of the experimenter to formulate the terms in Rorschach's table operationally so as to permit specific verification. For some reason, despite Rorschach's obvious interest in such experiments, little has been attempted in the past. Only recently has a body of data emerged which permits some evaluation of the validity of Rorschach's formulation of the experience type.

A critical issue which is outside the scope of this chapter, but which must be mentioned because it is frequently overlooked, is that of the essential validity and reliability of Rorschach's scoring system itself (see Chapters 16 and 17). To the extent that human movement scores are not clearly distinguishable from animal or inanimate movement (FM and m), or color from shading or texture, we cannot anticipate clear-cut results from attempts at experimental validation. Certainly there is considerable question concerning the relative effect of color on the ink blots (Ainsworth, 1954; Siipola, 1950). It appears possible that the outstanding feature in color responses is the relative diffuseness of the reaction (Ainsworth, 1954; Fortier, 1953; Siipola, 1952; Wittenborn, 1950b) and this may conceivably apply to shading or black-white as well as to color. Hays and Boardman (1975) have recently shown, however, that the chromatic Rorschach cards are generally found to be more positive and active but less potent, as determined by use of the Semantic Differential technique of Osgood, Suci and Tannenbaum (1957), than their achromatic counterparts, although some differences in connotation, suggesting chromatic ambiguousness, were also discovered. It is also possible that the experience type may be sacrificing information, since achromatic responses, either diffuse ones such as "Black clouds" or articulate ones such as "Face of a black poodle," are not considered in the $M:C$ computation. It is conceivable as well that the experience type may fluctuate according to mood in a manner not compatible with the simple constant ratio pattern that Rorschach proposed. Thus present test-retest reliability measurements would not be an adequate method for use in determining constancy in Rorschach data (Erginel, 1972). Another criticism of the Rorschach concerns the effect of experimenter expectation on the frequency of certain responses, notably M and sum C. Recent evidence shows, however, that experimenters led to expect either *M* or *C*-dominated experience balances had no significant effect on the responses of the people they were testing (Strauss, 1968; Strauss and Marwit, 1970).

Constitutional Factors and Physiological Correlates

What are some of the areas of human functioning in which we can expect manifestations of correlates of *M* and sum *C*? Obviously the constitutional make-up of the individual comes to mind, since Rorschach did feel the experience type was, within limits, an inborn response predisposition. This must mean that one may expect almost from birth gross differences in children along the dimensions of activity inhibition, delaying capacity, and, gradually, of the tendency to use fantasy. European psychologists have sought to link physique to introversive-extratensive personality characteristics: The work of Schmidt (1936) and the research of the students of Kretschmer which have been reported on and followed up by Eysenck (1953) suggest at least the possibility that gross introversive or extratensive characteristics are associated with body type, on the one hand, and perceptual preferences for form or color responses, on the other. Wenger (1938, 1942a, 1942b) has found evidence of gross motor differences in children that might be taken as forerunners of subsequent introversive-extratensive tendencies. There is insufficient data on these points as they apply specifically to the Rorschach, for the obvious reason that, by the time it is possible to obtain suitable protocols from children, so much learning and variation in identification patterns have occurred as to prevent any clarification of the constitutional elements.

Developmental studies of Rorschach response patterns and of perception and concept formation indicate a general tendency for more primitive color responses to emerge prior to more controlled color and human movement, thus coinciding with children's progress from diffuse motor reactivity to increased control, as well as from egocentric speech with minimal delay of fantasy to socialized speech and greater internalization of fantasy. These studies do not, however, come to grips with the *origin* of individual differences in the experience type, and, hence, offer no support to any constitutional theory.

Some indirect but suggestive evidence for the viewpoint that identification possibilities in the family setting may account for variation in experience type comes from the work of Goldfarb (1945, 1949), who reported that children raised from very early life under impersonal institutional conditions show primitive and markedly extratensive Rorschach characteristics in addition to difficulties in delaying capacity and conceptualization. Recent evidence supports the hypothesis that early family relationships may determine later Rorschach responses. Bene (1975) has shown that boys with close and positive relationships with their mothers exhibit higher M productivity than those with ambivalent or negative relationships. No correlation between M response and relationships with fathers was shown. Bene interprets these findings as evidence that M response capacity is determined in boys at an early age when the relationship with the mother is of primary importance.

There have been relatively few attempts to relate the Rorschach experience type or M and sum C to various physiological measures. One intriguing study along this line has been reported by Rabinovitch et al. (1955), who found EEG distinctions between extremes in the experience types and tentative evidence that high introversive subjects showed more "harmonizing activity" from various cortical areas. Since little is known of the correlates of the EEG measures, however, speculation as to the meaning of these findings is limited. Certainly we cannot conclude from this evidence that the experience type is constitutionally based, but merely that there appear to be concomitant cerebral activities which accord with Rorschach reaction tendencies. The same caution applies to a study by Brower (1947) which provides some evidence of relationships of FC and general responsiveness to color cards (R VIII, IX, X/total R), to pulse pressure, and to diastolic blood pressure. A study more clearly translated into Rorschach concepts is that of anoxia tolerance reported by Hertzman et al. (1944). These investigators found that the threshold for breakdown under anoxic conditions as measured by physiological and psychological instruments was lower for extratensives than introversives, suggesting greater response to environmental alterations by the high sum C group. It should be noted, however, that the group most susceptible was made up of the constricted subjects who gave few M or C responses. Generally it appears that persons who block or show impoverished use of various Rorschach determinants prove least stress-tolerant or flexible, and that production even of relatively uncontrolled color responses is indicative of more adaptive capacity in various situations (Levine, Glass and Meltzoff, 1956; Stein and Meer, 1954). Another study of interest along these lines is one by Broekmann (1970), who used psychophysiological methods to attempt to validate the Rorschach color-emotion form-control hypothesis. This investigator recorded from subjects giving both color and form responses, and found some differences in the rate of vasomotor change, skin resistance, and heart rate between subjects, suggesting the possible existence of two groups of individuals, "emotional" and "controlled," who react differently, both physiologically and verbally, to the Rorschach through their usage of color and movement responses. Steel and Kahn (1969), on the other hand, found no correlation between muscle tension and M response, although their data do indicate that there may be a relationship both between kinesthetic activation and a high M content, and heightened change in muscle potential during aggressive content responses. The implicated trends in both of these experiments are quite interesting, and suggest the need for further studies on these topics.

A suggestive model for research in this area is to be found in the work of Block (1957), who reported that subjects who showed considerable psychogalvanic responsiveness in a lie-detector situation also revealed perceptual and behavioral characteristics similar to those which might be expected of Rorschach extratensives. Block did not base his classification into "over" and "undercontrollers" on Rorschach data, and it is suggested that a repetition of his study, using Palmer's (1956) useful method for classifying experience types, might throw further light on the correlation of the experience balance with the lie-detector measure.

For the present it must be concluded that very little of a systematic nature is known concerning the physiological or constitutional correlates of the M:sum C ratio. Hunter's (1937) findings of Negro-white differences in the experience type have been questioned by Palmer (1955) as being possibly an artifact of her mode of inquiry. Palmer (1955) himself found no racial differences in his experience-balance measure. Even if Hunter's results were accurate, they might well reflect subcultural group differences rather than differences in racial temperament. Studies by Felzer (1955) and Palmer (1955) have failed to yield evidence of clear-cut sex differences in the experience type, although both obtained some very tentative suggestions of greater adaptive affect on the part of the women. Studies of sex differences vis-à-vis the M response indicate that this area may offer a clearer between-sex differentiation. Kleinman and Higgins (1966) showed a significantly higher M production among women than among men. Raychaudhuri (1971) has also reported that females, "feminine" males, and subjects classified as "creative" all showed high M productivity, while no significant difference in M response was shown either for "masculine" females or between "creative" subjects of both sexes. He explains these findings in terms of both sociocultural factors and sex-role demand. However, Aronow (1972) questions the validity of Raychaudhuri's conclusions on the grounds that intelligence and education were not sufficiently controlled for in his study. Certainly these factors could have a bearing on the outcome of experiments utilizing a creative-non-creative dichotomy. An extensive series of questionnaire studies of daydreaming (Singer, 1974a, 1974b, 1975) have indicated evidence of a "positive-vivid" daydreaming style that is associated more with psychological femininity and creativity in keeping with Raychaudhuri's results. Dawo (1952) has reported a shift from introversive to extratensive experience types in female medical students tested in the intermenstruum and again at the onset of menstruation, but this conclusion is rendered somewhat questionable by the fact that the second testing was with the Behn-Eschenburg ink blots which have been shown to yield more FC responses and less M than the original series (Eichler, 1951; Singer, 1952a). Confirmation of Dawo's finding would not necessarily provide evidence of a physiological component in the M:sum C ratio, since the emotional response of these women to the psychological meaning of the period might well be involved.

Other work attempting to quantify physiological variables and the Rorschach M response has been directed to pairs of identical and fraternal twins, but evidence in this area is highly contradictory as well. While Troup (1938) showed little concordance in M and sum C scores of both identical and fraternal twins, Hamilton, Blewett and Sydiaha (1971) found a very high correlation, approaching test-retest reliability, between the identical twins, thus suggesting a possible genetic involvement in disposition towards certain responses. They have proposed that their disagreement with Troup's data may be due to the different methods of statistical analysis employed, or to the fact that Troup controlled for intelligence by using twins with I.Q.'s only within a certain range, while they did not, and thus she may have done away with an important source of variance in the Rorschach response. The necessity for further experimentation in this area is clear.

Perceptual Correlates

A knotty problem in understanding the experience-type concept derives from Rorschach's contention that M and sum C represent reaction tendencies and also modes of perceptual experience which presumably influence subsequent reaction tendencies. Thus the fantasy world of the M type leads to special kinds of selection in what is perceived, whereas the C type's emotional response or motor interchange with his environment similarly leads to a selection in perceptual experience. Palmer (1955, 1956) has pointed to some of the problems inherent in Rorschach's concept, and has suggested a solution in terms of functional dimensions similar to those which will be discussed below. In actuality, research data in the sphere of perceptual correlates of the experience type are largely limited to studies of behavioral correlates of the M and C components rather than to investigation of the mode of "experiencing."

Since one component of the M response is motion, it has seemed logical to compare Rorschach M tendencies with tendencies to perceive illusory motion, specifically the ϕ and other autokinetic phenomena. In view of the complex nature of the ϕ phenomenon and its extensive theoretical ramifications, several attempts have been made to relate M responses to low thresholds for stroboscopic or similar illusory motions. Werner (1945) observed that endogenous mentally defective children showed lower threshold for ϕ and other forms of illusory motion than did the matched exogenous mental defectives. Since these two groups differed significantly in Rorschach movement responses (endogenous subjects showing more M and a more introversive protocol as well as generally more controlled or, at least, phlegmatic motor behavior), it is likely that M and ϕ bore some relationship, although no data specifically on this point were presented. Werner perhaps more than any other investigator has proceeded to draw extensive theoretical conclusions concerning perception and developmental theory from this inverse relationship of motion perception and overt motor activity. Klein and Schlesinger (1951) also obtained some evidence that high-M subjects showed greater tendency to perceive ϕ than did low-M subjects, although their results are somewhat inconclusive when total Rorschach responses are considered.

Singer and Basowitz, in an unpublished study, also observed a relationship between a scoring of the M:sum C ratio and threshold for ϕ, the more introversive subjects showing lower thresholds for perception of illusory movement. Schumer (1949) has reported a trend for subjects with numerous M to show less variability in perception of ϕ, although ϕ threshold itself did not prove to discriminate between high- and low-M subjects. Two studies employing perception of autokinetic motion as correlates of M have also obtained suggestive, if not conclusive, results. Murawski (1954) found that immobilized subjects with expectations of recovering motion showed a positive correlation between Rorschach M and a tendency to perceive the autokinetic phenomenon. Schumer (1949) used the autokinetic situation as a measure of influence and suggestibility in the manner of the social psychological studies that have derived from Sherif's work. In this case, a negative correlation between M and extent of autokinetic perception emerged. The crucial difference between the apparently contradictory findings of Schumer and Murawski appears to lie in the fact that Schumer's procedure by its experimental instruction employed the autokinetic phenomenon in a social situation involving conformity or suggestibility. Hence Schumer's results are consistent with Rorschach's view that high-M subjects, being presumably more independently-minded and less responsive to external stimuli, should prove less suggestible. Leiman (1951) employed two perceptual measures for comparing high- and low-M subjects. One involved perception of motion in kinesthetic figures which were presented tachistoscopically. The high-M group showed a trend toward reporting motion in the figures sooner than did the low-M subjects. Results obtained with the Street gestalt figures (silhouettes of figures which have been cut up and which subjects are required to integrate perceptually in order to ascertain their content) were even more conclusive. High-M subjects proved significantly more effective at integrating the cut-up silhouettes into meaningful wholes. Leiman has interpreted his basic data as supporting a view that "closure accuracy" is one of the basic components in formation of M responses. Matarazzo et al. (1952) instructed their subjects (students and patients with anxiety neuroses) to report sensations other than merely flickering in response to an intermittent flickering light. They then scored these reported sensations by means of Rorschach determinants and found significant positive relationships for both movement and color between the flicker reactions and Rorschach responses. For the patients alone the color relationship failed to hold, but the association of flicker movement and Rorschach movement persisted.

Perceptual data seem in general, therefore, to indicate that tendencies to structure Rorschach ink blots with movement correspond roughly with more general sensitivities to perceive illusory movement. The M type of person has not been shown, however, to be more responsive to general motion around him. The noteworthy point is that in the situations described the movement is not actually taking place in the stimulus constellations but is contributed by the subjects as a result of an integration of certain favorable environmental conditions. This is a crucial consideration, theoretically, since the implication of Rorschach's view of M and of the extensions of these views by Werner (1945) is that certain persons by inhibiting direct reaction tendencies tend to develop sensitivities or predilections for *imposing* motion, either on ambiguous stimuli or on stimuli in what may be called "the mind's eye." Schumer's data point up the fact that when perception of motion is utilized as part of an environmental situation in which suggestibility plays a role, the relationship of M and motion perception is altered. So it would seem that, as there is less support from the stimulus itself for perception of motion, the introversive person becomes the more likely to *impose* motion on it; conversely, with more stimulus support, the more likely is the extroversive person to *perceive* motion in it. Indirect evidence for this supposition may be adduced from studies which suggest that introversive subjects (as judged by questionnaire measures rather than Rorschach protocols) show lower size constancy in perceptual experiments (selecting an object of the same size as a distant standard), where it is known that inability to isolate the stimulus from the environmental objects which surround it enhances size constancy (Singer, 1952b; Weber, 1939).

Further research into perceptual correlates of Rorschach's experience type is clearly necessary if we wish, on the one hand, to gain a greater understanding of what goes into the making of a particular response and, on the other, to advance beyond Rorschach empiricism to a theory that encompasses perception, imagination, and action.

Motor Activity and Environmental Responsiveness

One of the most fruitful outcomes of Rorschach's concept of extratensiveness has been the possibility of linking the motor habits and expressive behavior of the individual to habits of thought and perception. Through the medium of the color responses, and even more the experience type as a whole, the way has been opened for exploring such linkages and ultimately relating them in a theory of ego function or personality, generally. Indeed, although the linkages of the Rorschach ratio to other perceptual responses are relatively tenuous at the moment, data bearing on the relationship of the experience type to action tendencies and environmental responsiveness are more clear-cut. This may be, in part, because the perceptual situations utilized have themselves involved fairly subtle processes of dubious reliability, and, in part, because Rorschach's own conclusions about his response categories were no doubt derived to a great extent from observation of gross motor tendencies.

Most current theories of personality and ego development emphasize as a basic developmental dimension the gradual control, differentiation, and socialization of motility (Freud, 1923; Lewin, 1935; Luria, 1932; Piaget, 1932; Rapaport, 1951; Werner, 1948). In Rorschach terms this implies a certain general pattern of response tendencies for various age groups. One should expect with increasing age in children an increase in M and a change in the nature and weighting of color responses from pure C and CF towards FC. This is roughly what has been found in normative studies (Ainsworth,

1954; Ford, 1946; Klopfer and Margulies, 1941; Thetford, Molish and Beck, 1951). The M response begins to appear most typically in the records of children of school age, at a time when there is a sharp increase in the demands on the child for inhibition of motor behavior and socialization of speech and gratification patterns. The increasing introversive trend of the experience type and the greater control of the color responses correspond with Piaget's descriptions of changes in the verbal behavior of children as well. Where once the child moved directly towards the source of gratification or spoke out his thoughts whether heeded or not, he must now check the impulse, raise his hand to request permission, or remain quiet during a lesson. In varying degrees, then, internalization of response is rewarded and, as reading is learned, the tools for internalization are vastly improved. Since effective and creative living involves a flexible shifting between control, internalization, delay, and direct action or spontaneous affect, one would ideally expect an optimal rather than maximal development of introversive tendencies. Levi and Kraemer (1952) and Thetford (1952) provide some data on variations in introversiveness and motor control, or precocity, which have pathological implications.

Witkin, Dyk, Faterson, Goodenough and Karp (1962) stress the development of a field approach as an essential personality characteristic the child employs as a filter in order to determine the structuring of incoming stimuli from the environment. They show strong evidence for an "analytical" field approach, correlated with a tendency to imbue Rorschach inkblots with structure and an ability to overcome embedding contexts in both intellectual and perceptual situations, and a "global" field approach, correlated with an inability to organize or structure amorphousness such as that contained in the Rorschach cards and an inability to escape the influence of embedding contexts. They have discussed an apparent correlation between assertive M responses and subjects showing high field-independence, and have also found a correlation between field approach, impulse control, and responses utilizing color on the Rorschach, indicating that subjects with a global field approach exhibit less ability to control their impulses than subjects with an analytical field approach.

More direct studies of responsiveness, impulsivity, and control seem also to accord with Rorschach's views. The work of Siipola and Taylor (1952) on responses to ink blots under free and pressure conditions affords evidence that fast responders give fewer M responses and that persons who give unstructured responses such as C and CF respond more rapidly. Similarly, as pressure for response is increased, there is greater tendency for C and CF responses to emerge. The authors conclude that the M tendency in contrast to the C tendency characterizes the person who excels in "the ability to delay." These findings were also confirmed by Bieri and Blacker (1956a). The latter investigators reported that extratensive subjects showed faster reaction times in producing all types of Rorschach determinants than did ambiequals and introversives, in that order.

Since the trait of impulsivity is obviously related to inability to delay, one would expect some relationship between measures of impulsive behavior and the M:sum C ratio. Holtzman (1950) failed to find such a relationship in a study of normal persons rated by their neighbors, while Gardner (1951) did obtain positive results in a study of normal adults rated by clinical psychologists who knew them well. Thiessen et al. (1953), studying equated groups of children differing in ratings of impulsivity, found ample support for the relationship of sum C and, particularly CF and C, to impulsivity and also to maladjustment, but the M:sum C ratio itself did not prove discriminating in the form in which it was employed. Misch (1954), in a careful effort to obtain data on extreme impulsivity, selected two groups of individuals who differed in assaultiveness; one consisted of chronically assaultive criminals, the other of psychiatric patients who had a history of assaultive threats but who had never carried these verbal threats into action. The "motoric" group was characterized by more primitive Rorschach records, including more CF and C and less M than the "verbal" group. Finney (1950), comparing assaultive psychiatric patients with others who had never been assaultive during their hospitalization, found significantly more CF and sum C in the records of the former group but no differences emerged in M. In general, grossly comparable results were obtained in a study by Singer et al. (1956), in which color and shading responses and ward ratings of aggressiveness and diffuse energy had sizable loadings on a common factor, whereas M and a rating for ward cooperativeness were linked on still another factor.

Other evidence bearing on inhibition of motor response or environmental reactivity comes from a variety of studies. Mann (1953) employed a clever criterion of environmental responsiveness or lack of imaginative inner resources. He obtained series of free associations from subjects, and totaled those associations to the immediate situation or the examination room, to obtain his measure. A negative correlation between M and environmental responsiveness, and a sizable positive correlation between sum C and this criterion emerged. This result seems clearly an indication of a relationship between introversiveness and the ability to free oneself from passive response to the environment. Ideational fluidity, a basic component of imagination, must also be involved, to be sure. Levine, Glass, and Meltzoff (1956) sought to obtain evidence of inhibition of a habitual motor response by studying the Rorschach records of subjects who, in taking the Wechsler Bellevue Digit Symbol subtest, erred by writing the letter "N" instead of its mirror image, which is the corect symbol. A significantly greater percentage of these subjects than of controls gave fewer than two M responses on the Rorschach. Results obtained when color responses were considered, however, indicated that, for this sample, the more color, the less likelihood of a reversal. The authors found that coartated subjects were most likely to err and introversive patients with dilated experience types least likely to do so.

Herman (1956) employed a clever measure of motor control in comparing equated groups of introversive and extratensive Rorschach groups. The subjects were asked to define out loud a list of words such as, "point," "knot," "twist," "squeeze," and "rub." Extratensives used significantly more gestures and body movements in the course of their oral definitions. Two studies employing a simple waiting-room observation procedure devised by Rickers-Ovsiankina (1937) have found that schizophrenic adults grouped on the basis of Rorschach M and sum C differed correspondingly in the amount of spontaneous movement and speech during a 15-minute wait. Although M and particularly active M proved most discriminating, both Singer and Spohn (1954), and Singer and Herman (1954) found clear evidence of an influence of the experience type in the fact that rated amount of activity in the waiting period increased progressively through the four subgroups of high M: low sum C, high M: high sum C, low M: low sum C, low M: high sum C, or, in other words, as the group ratios changed from marked introversion to marked extratension.

Separate mention should be made here of a series of studies which have employed a motor inhibition task modified from Downey's Will-Temperament Scale. This technique calls for the subject to write a brief phrase as slowly as possible without stopping motion of the pencil. Performance on this task consistently proved to correlate with M (Meltzoff, Singer and Korchin, 1953; Singer and Herman, 1954; Singer and Spohn, 1954; Singer et al., 1956), but also yielded differences between subjects with introversive and extratensive experience types (Herman, 1956; Singer and Spohn, 1954). Meltzoff and Levine (Levine and Meltzoff, 1956; Meltzoff and Levine, 1954) have demonstrated that Rorschach M responses, motor inhibition, and cognitive inhibition (ability to inhibit a habituated association and rapidly substitute a new one) are related, thus affording support to the entire theory of the linkage of motion perception, action, and thought. However, in testing the generalizability of the theory that motor inhibition stimulates fantasy, Prola (1970) found that in fact when motility is restricted prior to administration of the Thematic Apperception Test, no change in movement fantasy, non-movement fantasy, or total fantasy was shown. He thus suggests that the heightened Rorschach M production after motor inhibition reported on in the literature may be a specific attribute of the M response itself. Conversely, however, it may be argued that the lack of significant change found by Prola may be specific to the TAT, or may be an artifact of some as-yet unknown aspect of its form or administration. Only further research in this area will settle this question.

Research with children does afford some additional evidence of relationships between movement responses and motor behavior or impulsivity. Studies reported in Singer (1973a) suggest that young children who indicate imaginative predisposition as measured by M responses do tend to play more pretend or fantasy games and to be less overtly aggressive or impulsively active than children with little fantasy predisposition. A recent report by Goldberg (1974) also indicates that boys seen in an urban clinic who show more signs of fantasy on Rorschach measures (M) as well as TAT measures of imagination (the Transcendence Index) are signficantly less likely to show overt aggressive and violent behavior. Despite these encouraging findings, we cannot but notice some lacunae in the structure thus far built up in support of Rorschach's view of the experience type. These gaps appear particularly in the area of expression of affect. Although it is true that much of the data on motor and impulse control are indirectly relevant to affectivity, the fact remains that there are few studies which deal with the relationship between M:sum C and ease or inhibition in revealing feelings of anger, love, sympathy, or sadness. Indeed, while free expression of feelings and spontaneity both in imaginativeness and in affect are facets of psychotherapy, concerning which individual Rorschach examiners have much to say in their reports, little effort has been made to carry out systematic studies along this line.

Two studies by Wagner and Hoover (1971, 1972) which approach this problem most closely report that drama majors, cheerleaders, and drum majorettes give significantly more exhibitionistic M responses than a matched control group. Teltscher (1964) has also reported that extremely active college athletes gave far fewer Rorschach M responses than a sedentary, literary-minded, but otherwise intellectually comparable, college sample. However, while these may be interesting findings, they only begin to address this problem. Recent studies by Singer and various collaborators with very young children do suggest that children who show more M responses not only play more imaginatively but are rated by observers as showing more positive affect and liveliness (Singer, 1973a, 1975). The studies on aggressive behavior cited above are relevant, but there has been no attempt to evaluate potentialities for warmth, for giving love, or for effective assertiveness rather than destructive aggression. One technical difficulty among others here is the fact that the FC response, presumably indicative of adaptive rapport, is one of the least reliable of major Rorschach determinants both in retest and scoring (Blechner, 1954; Eichler, 1951; Felzer, 1955). But perhaps there has been too much preoccupation with "pathology" to the detriment of a fuller understanding of the richness of personality. Perhaps, too, the populations available to researchers for extensive or intensive study have been clinic or hospital patients, thus leading to an overemphasis on behavior that is socially distressing.

Whatever the reasons, it seems essential that some attempts be made to carry through research on affective expression as a correlate of the experience type if one of the most vital assumptions of Rorschach analysis is to be verified and if the Rorschach factors are to be brought into conceptual relationship with more general personality theories. Some valuable first steps towards effecting this increase of our understanding have come in studies by Piotrowski and Schreiber, described in detail in Chapter 6, and in an ingenious experiment by Meltzoff and Litwin. Piotrowski and Schreiber (1951) found valuable evidence of increases in dilation of the experience type in the course of psychoanalytic psychotherapy as contrasted with supportive psychotherapy. Changes in both M and sum C seemed to mirror personality changes in the individual patients. Ward (1966) has written a comprehensive review of change in Rorschach M during therapy as a manifestation of change in both behavior and fantasy. From his evidence it appears that M may be predominantly a reflection of the overt social behavior of the patient, and must be interpreted individually.

Meltzoff and Litwin (1956) studied conscious inhibition of affect by exposing normals to a Spike Jones "Laughing Record," which they had already demonstrated evoked an almost universal laughter response in a sample of their population. They found that when subjects were instructed to listen to the record without laughing, the high-M group proved more successful than the low-M individuals. They also observed an interesting progression and some individual differences in the modes of control employed. Some subjects at first employed motor control to avoid laughing, e.g., tightening lips, and later resorted to cognitive or fantasy methods, e.g., thinking of sad events. Some of the subjects emphasized motor methods, others fantasy, thus opening an avenue for exploration of such problems as symptom choice. Should further studies support these observations, a way may be opened for elaborating on Rorschach's original observations on mode of schizophrenic reaction, sense involved in hallucinations, obsessive or compulsive symptomatology, etc., as a function of experience type.

Even these two stimulating reports point up some of the problems raised in introducing this area, however. It should be noted that in both studies the M determinant proved most significant. The influence of the color factors therefore remains more shrouded in doubt. In addition, the very form of the Meltzoff and Litwin experiment calls for an emphasis on control of affect. In this experiment, success or compliance with experimental instructions hinged on control.

But what of the problem of *excessive* control of affect through ideation—the intellectual defenses? Little has been done in that connection. And what of the many times in life when a spontaneous, warm laugh or smile carries with it more than a thousand words or images in building constructive human contacts? Clinically, Rorschach examiners have often been aware that the rich use of FC and good CF responses betokens the sympathetic and loving person who can also assert himself clearly when crossed. Rioch (1949), for example, in her studies of Rorschach records before and after psychoanalytic therapy, found evidence of increased FC responses and richer use of color in patients felt to have relaxed emotionally. One change in color responses reported by Piotrowski and Schreiber in the course of psychoanalytic treatment was a greater resort to warm colors, while Rickers-Ovsiankina (1955) found that chronic schizophrenics who improved were chiefly distinguished from a static group by the former's avoidance of the red and pink portions of the blots. When the improving subjects do respond to these portions, however, their reactions are significantly less frequently of the form-dominant type than is the case in the static group. Some unpublished data collected by Singer on schizophrenic patients with dilated and constricted experience types also indicate that the patients with many movement and color responses were generally rated the most attractive and interesting personalities in the wards. Although the dilated personalities often showed persisting severe symptomatology, they were capable of establishing relationships and of evoking affection of a sort from other patients and the staff of the hospital.

The capacity for spontaneous intellectual or emotional release or playfulness, what Kris (1950) terms "regression in the service of the ego" is almost certainly what was meant by Rorschach in his discussion of the adaptive features of the FC and the good CF responses. Exploration of this facet of the experience type through formal experiment remains to be done, however (Holt, 1954 and Chapter 11, this volume). It seems very likely to be related to talent and expression in what has been termed the "performing arts," and may have been expressed in Rorschach's reference to "reproductive ability and skill and adroitness" as characteristics of the color-predominant experience type.

Inner Life: Thinking, Fantasy, and Imagination

The correlates of the experience type in the area of the inner experience and in the capacities for fantasy, "individualized intelligence," and "creative ability," as Rorschach described them, have proved most fascinating to subsequent Rorschach workers. This is the domain of the M response *per se*, although Rorschach makes clear that both M and C—fantasy capacity and affective expression —can exist side by side, and do so in really well-rounded, gifted human beings. It may therefore be assumed that sum C is not inversely related to fantasy, but merely *unrelated* in itself to this area of functioning. Here Rorschach was perhaps unwittingly going beyond any systematic knowledge he could have been able to acquire, by positing a relationship between M, sum C, and their behavioral correlates that could only be expressed by rather complex mathematical functions and tested by statistical treatments far beyond his ken. Simple attempts to correlate Rorschach introversion with questionnaires concerning social and thinking introversion have yielded negative results, but this may in part reflect limitations of the questionnaires involved (Royal, 1950; Singer and Herman, 1954; Thiessen, Favorite and Coff, 1953). If attention is paid to specific characteristics of behavior presumably exemplifying inner life, considerable support exists for Rorschach's linkage of the introversive experience balance, and particularly M alone, with fantasy. In the area of cognitive attitudes and problem solving, for example, Rosenthal (1954) has reported clear-cut differences in the approach to solution of the Katona match stick problem of otherwise equated groups of introversive and extratensive normals. The introversives thought longer about the task and thus had longer reaction times, while the high sum C subjects manipulated the problem sticks far more frequently. Thus, the contrasting experience types appear to reflect different modes of approaching the problem situation. The word *different* is important for one cannot say "superior" or "inferior" in this connection inasmuch as Rosenthal's groups were *equally proficient* in solving the problem. This finding suggests that, as Barron (1955) has pointed out, we may be dealing with differing life styles which cannot be ranked as favorable or unfavorable except in relation to a highly specific cultural or intellectual demand. A similar result was obtained in a study by Singer and Opler (1956). A group of Irish-American schizophrenics, who were more introversive on the Rorschach than a corresponding Italian sample of patients, failed to obtain superior Porteus Maze Test Quotients despite the fact that they were considerably more restrained and apparently planful in their mode of performance. Kurz and Capone (1967) have taken another approach to the problem of correlating M response with changes in cognitive functioning on a concrete to abstract continuum. They studied M productivity and its relation to cognitive development and ability to both take a variety of roles and to understand one's behavior in the context of those roles. This is an interesting way of conceptualizing the difficulty, but the results they obtained were inconclusive, apparently because they required only two responses per card with no inquiry, and thus may have contributed to a paucity of M responses in their subjects.

Barron (1955) investigated correlates of M alone by developing a new series of all black ink blots standardized in a fashion so as to yield a threshold score for tendency to see human movement. A group of Air Force officers who showed low thresholds for perceptions of humans in motion were described in the following terms by psychologists who had observed them in a variety of interview, social, and stress situations: "1. Highly cathects intellectual activity; values cognitive pursuits. 2. Gets along in the world as it is; is socially appropriate in his behavior. 3. Is introspective; concerned with his self as object; frequently self-aware. 4. Has high degree of intellectual ability." Officers with a high threshold for M responses, on the other hand, were described in the following terms: "1. Has narrow range of interests. 2. Allows personal bias, spite, or dogmatism to enter into his judgment of issues. 3. Prefers action to contemplation. 4. Is rigid; inflexible in thought and action." Despite this impression created by their behavior, these M-disposed officers did not actually prove more intelligent or imaginative on a series of formal tests than the officers with high thresholds for M response. Thus Barron concludes that M may tap "thoughtfulness" as an intellectual *disposition* rather than as an ability. However, since the officers with high thresholds for perceiving M were generally described in clinically less "flattering" terminology, e.g., "rigid, inflexible, allows bias, spite, or dogmatism to enter into judgment of issues," there still is the possibility that an extreme lack of M tendency may indicate a liability for effective functioning. King (1960) has also shown that persons with more frequent M responses showed greater interpersonal awareness and sensitivity.

A study by Barrell (1953) with a design rather similar to Barron's also led to results linking Rorschach M tendency with assessment ratings of "broad interests, imaginative and independent minded." Significant positive correlations between M (with the effect of total responses partialed out) and a combined score for the Miller Analogies Test and the Primary Mental Abilities word fluency subtest emerged for Barrell's sample of Veterans Administration trainees, suggesting that some association between M and achievement measures of abstraction and ideational productivity does exist. One feature of Barrell's study was his finding that a distinction between $M+$ and $M-$ could be made since much of the correlation with intellectual variables occurred for the $M+$ response. As is plain from the summary of studies thus far, there has been little consideration in research for the form level of the M response as such, although certainly important differences in clinical interpretation often hinge on the form level of M. There seems to be a serious neglect in the literature of studies dealing with the qualitative characteristics of the experience type, as a matter of fact. Such studies could include, from a structural standpoint, the form level of the movement and color components and, from a dynamic standpoint, the actual content of these percepts. Parker and Piotrowski (1968) have made an initial attempt to perform a content analysis of actors and actions involved in the M responses of college students and hospitalized schizophrenics, but their data showed little significance except in a correlation between M content and development and therapeutic transference. Further research on these points is highly desirable.

Dana (1968) has reviewed a large number of research findings on the Rorschach M and has presented six constructs to define the human movement response; delay, time sense, intelligence, creativity, fantasy, and interpersonal relations. Motor inhibition has been equated with tolerance for delay, and has been employed in fifteen minute waiting paradigms (Singer and Herman, 1954; Singer and Spohn, 1954), motoric "freezing" designs (Singer, Meltzoff and Goldman, 1952), and in writing inhibition procedures (Levine, Spivack, Fuschillo and Tavernier, 1959; Meltzoff and Levine, 1954; Meltzoff, Singer and Korchin, 1953; Singer and Herman, 1954; Singer and Spohn, 1954; Singer, Wilensky and McCraven, 1956), all providing strong correlations between ability to delay and M productivity. Time sense has been measured by correlating accuracy of time judgment with M production (Kurz, Cohen and Starzynski, 1965; Levine and Spivack, 1959; Levine, Spivack, Fuschillo and Tavernier, 1959; Singer, Wilensky and McCraven, 1956; Spivack, Levine and Sprigle, 1959), and by the use of other time-dependent measurements. The correlation of intelligence with M response shown is significant and has been replicated several times (Levine, Glass and Meltzoff, 1957; Levine, Spivack, Fuschillo and Tavernier, 1959; Spivack, Levine and Sprigle, 1959).

The main basis for listing creativity as a determinant of M is Rorschach's definition of the experience balance as primarily reflecting the creativity of the individual. Although difficult to define experimentally, some research has concentrated on determining an M:creativity relationship, although the results of these experiments are presently highly contradictory (Griffin, 1958; Hersch, 1962; Richter and Winter, 1966). The evidence linking the M response alone with various measures of imaginativeness or fantasy capacity is by this time quite convincing. One obvious avenue to test this linkage has been by correlating Rorschach M with various measures of fantasy disposition drawn from the Thematic Apperception Test or similar story-telling techniques. Thus, one may attempt an over-all rating of story originality or develop a more quantitative scheme such as scoring transcendent items, e.g., the number of characters, incidents, or emotions not actually depicted in the stimulus card but introduced into the story by the subject. Both types of analysis have yielded consistently positive correlations with M and M:sum C (Hays, Gellerman and Sloan, 1951; Herman, 1956; Lane, 1948; Murawski, 1954; Pickering, 1950; Schumer, 1949; Shatin, 1953; Singer and Herman, 1954; Singer, Wilensky and McCraven, 1956; Vernier, Claire and Kendig, 1951).

Important data dealing with the relationship of M to fantasy processes and daydreaming was presented by Page (1957) and Singer and Schonbar (1961), who showed that frequency of reported daydreaming was correlated with M productivity and various factors concerning attentional and curiosity processes (Singer and Antrobus, 1963). Some work has also been done indirectly in this area by attempting to correlate sleep deprivation (Loveland and Singer, 1959; Palmer, 1963) and dream deprivation (Lerner, 1966) with changes in M production. The interpersonal relations construct has been defined by both an individual capacity for conceptualization of relationships with others, particularly with parents (Singer and Sugarman, 1955), and by an external measure of the accuracy with which the individual is perceived (Mueller and Abeles, 1964), and has also shown a reasonable correlation with M response. Dana feels that if M is regarded as an indicator of a mature ability to reach out and deal with one's environment, these six constructs can be easily understood as a clinical test for M capacity. He sees the individual who exhibits high M productivity as possessing the abilities to delay before acting and to focus attention appropriately, an ordered time continuum, an intellectual approach to reasoning and problem-solving, a useful command of fantasy and memory, constructive utilization of anxiety, and both viable ego controls and a solid sense of self-identity and self-worth, as well as worthwhile and warm interpersonal relationships. Dana and Cocking (1968) have attempted to empirically test the contribution of each of these constructs to total M response by use of the Brunswik Lens Model (Brunswik, 1956), but as yet they have not found a valid means of utilizing these cues in the inferential and predictive processes involved with clinical judgment. However, this approach offers hope to those who would eventually like to see Rorschach interpretations based on a foundation of empirical fact. A really critical study finally linking Rorschach M to perceptual responses, daydreaming, TAT measures, and measures of delay and inhibition still remains to be done, although Singer, Wilensky and McCraven (1956) took several steps in that direction in a factor analytic study with schizophrenic patients.

Although data bearing on M and fantasy disposition alone clearly relate one to the other, the results for a correlation between M:sum C and fantasy are somewhat equivocal. In several studies (Hays, Gellerman and Sloan, 1951; Herman, 1956; Pickering, 1950), introversive experience types yielded clearer correlations with fantasy than extratensive scores. At the same time, in other studies (Shatin, 1953; Singer and Herman, 1954, Singer et al., 1956), sum C showed either no correlation with fantasy measures or a positive one. The various components of sum C as well as the many qualitative complexities attendant on color reactions (Shapiro, 1956, and Chapter 8, this volume) seem to confuse the picture in study after study, since no investigator has been able to effect a thorough comparison of all types of scoring and weighting of color or of the movement and color relationships. There seems little doubt, however, that introversive or high-M subjects with introversively or ambiequally dilated experience types show greater fantasy disposition in story-telling activities than do low-M subjects, and are also more likely to show greater originality in associations (Schumer, 1949), greater cognitive complexity in perception of persons (Bieri and Blacker, 1956b), and more planfulness and time perspective (Singer et al., 1956). A study by Gibby et al. (1955) which compared hallucinated with deluded psychotics found, contrary to Rorschach's original reports, significantly more M in the former group and more FC and total C in the latter group. The extremely low frequency of M limits generalization since both groups are decidedly extratensive in their experience types.

A highly significant feature of fantasy disposition is, presumably, the willingness to introspect and to face up consciously to problems and difficulties, or at least to attempt a solution by ideational means rather than by somatization, direct motor activity, or repression. To this extent a dilated or moderately introversive experience type should prove an asset in beginning psychotherapy. Recently Temerlin (1956) selected two groups of patients in psychoanalysis who were apparently equated in all respects except that one group showed "flexible, productive behavior" in the first 20 sessions of psychotherapy, associating freely, taking responsibility for work at their treatment, etc., while the second group was "rigid, unproductive, blocked often, and was unwilling or unable to express the content of awareness, passively describing experiences in an affectless manner." Although specific Rorschach data were unfortunately not available, Temerlin found that the "productive" group showed considerably more variability in the perception of motion in an autokinetic situation, i.e., they could see movement more frequently. Temerlin attributes this motion perception to a "tolerance for experiencing self." Barron's (1955) *M*-disposed officers were more frequently described by assessors as "more self-involved," whereas Shatin (1953) found that Rorschach *M* was also associated with willingness to give open expression to unpleasant feelings in stories on the Thematic Apperception Test. Further evidence on this point is forthcoming from a study by Singer et al. (1956), who found in a group of schizophrenics that *M* was positively correlated with willingness to admit distress after a failure experience. Finally, Palmer (1956), in an elaborate comparison of Rorschach experience types and Minnesota Multiphasic Personality Inventory responses, found that inventory items dealing with self-dissatisfaction and self-awareness were more characteristic of introversive subjects, whereas items involving self-satisfaction or lack of awareness characterized extratensives.

It seems clear that introversiveness is very likely linked with self-knowledge, or at least conscious tolerance of distress or difficulty, perhaps because the person who has the capacity or disposition for fantasy has at his disposal a means for experiencing the difficulty without necessarily having "to take arms against a sea of troubles and, by opposing, end them." Clinical experience suggests that the extreme of this capacity is perhaps as maladaptive as its absence or as total extratensiveness; excessive rumination and resort to the ideational leads to inaction and gradually increases anxiety instead of coping with it. A clinical study of the origin of intellectuality presents some stimulating treatment of this possibility (Kupper, 1950).

Imaginative, sociodramatic or make-believe play represents one important expression in childhood of divergent thinking or creativity. A series of studies using various forms of Rorschach or Holtzmann blots to measure imaginative predispositions do seem to find modest relationships between the *M* response and the likelihood that children will engage in make-believe during free play (Singer, 1974a; Singer and Singer, 1974). Considering the degree to which situational factors modify play patterns in early childhood, the consistency of these results is intriguing.

It appears that to some extent the tendency to deal on a fantasy level with conflicts or frustrated wishes serves as a temporary "experimental action," an alternate response pattern in a controlled and potentially productive manner. Unless this mode of response is reinforced, however, either by eventually leading to satisfaction of the original wishes or, perhaps, by yielding other socially accept-able rewards (prestige, approval of friends and family, creative achievement), the marked resort to constructive fantasy seems to wither away. This appears to be the case in certain precocious but disturbed children (Levi and Kraemer, 1952) and in schizophrenic children (Thetford, 1952). It can be observed clinically in many schizophrenic adults who show considerable fantasy and obsessive rumination early in the course of their illness (with corresponding high M or dilated experience types), and who then, as they find no relief, settle into a chronic torpor or passive hospital adjustment with much sleeping and a decline in fantasy. The same trend appears demonstrable in nonpsychotics who have been blocked in their motor activity by illness. Murawski (1954) found considerably more Rorschach movement responses in a group of subjects who were immobilized by physical illness but who retained hope of recovery of motion than in a similarly immobilized group who had no ex-pectation of recovery. Wittkower (1949), describing tuberculous adults, reported that enforced bed rest leads to heightened fantasy at the outset but this declines in time. Diabetic children were shown by Mitsunaga (1970) to appear as introversive types on the experi-ence balance, with a large production of active movement and positive striving responses. Richards and Lederman (1956), using Levy's momentum blocks, found that children physically handi-capped from birth, or soon after, showed significantly *less* vigorous activity in their movement percepts than children who became handicapped after a considerable period of normal motility. Nickerson (1969) investigated the question of whether or not paraplegics who had constructively adjusted to their condition would exhibit intro-verted and intellectualized living styles, a great deal of fantasy life, and high M response. Although her data did not demonstrate these relationships, they did offer support for Singer's theoretical structure of M as a product and measure of the inhibition potential of the ego (Singer, 1955). Nickerson's data also gives support to Rorschach's basic premise that M productivity correlates with individual kines-thetic imagery, as she found that M is negatively related to having flaccid, as opposed to spastic, paralysis.

One final aspect of the introversive experience type is in the area of artistic achievement or creativity. Here is a complex problem that merits separate consideration. To some extent clinical experience and a variety of researches suggest that creativity or originality is greatest in persons with dilated experience types, as Rorschach found. It is this dilation-coarctation dimension rather than introversion-extratensiveness which appears to be crucial. Dudek (1968a) has looked at the relationship between M productivity and ease of creative expression, and has found a highly significant correlation between the two. She sees M as an active function, representing the potential for creative experience or ideational productivity, with no guarantee that this will result in creative productivity of any kind. To test this hypothesis, she compared the Rorschach M of successful and unsuccessful artists, and found that, contrary to her postulated expectation, there were no significant differences in the M responses of "good" and "bad" artists, although M did reflect the creativity or ideational richness of the individual. Primary process thinking in the Rorschach protocol was shown to be correlated with the productive use of that creativity, however (Dudek, 1968b). Dudek has also suggested that Rorschach M may in fact not be an adequate index for all types of creativity, as, for instance, that found in scientific thought (Dudek, 1967). To the extent that story-telling on the Thematic Apperception Test may be considered a measure of creative productivity or originality in associations, there is some evidence cited above that bears on this point. But what of evidence based on a life pattern of achievement? To what extent does the introversive ratio reflect a creative interest in people or a more general creativity expressed, say, in achievement in manipulating nonhuman symbols as well? Shakespeare, Dostoievsky, or Hugo were men whose minds must have teemed with vivid imagery of human interaction, and yet they themselves were often vigorously active. If some celestial Rorschacher examined these men and found few or no M and no indication of a dilated M:sum C ratio, the whole significance of the experience type would be called into question. Would that be the case, however, if Beethoven's Rorschach yielded no M or even few C responses? Certainly Beethoven's must have been a rich and vibrant inner life, but it was at the very least so full of sound as to leave much less room for human imagery than might be expected in a novelist's fantasy. Roe (1952) found that physicists show more m than psychologists, who tended to be most productive of M and of sum C as compared with other scientists.

Her study, however, yielded evidence which suggests that a knowledge of ideal Rorschach patterns played some role in their reactions. Too little is known as yet to provide a definitive answer on this point.

Clinical experience has suggested some support for Rorschach's view that both M and sum C must be fully developed for optimal human functioning. It is possible in our society or in Western civilization generally that an individual with many M and low sum C could function effectively as a creative artist or as a specialist in some profession or skilled vocation. It seems less likely that this could be the case for someone with no M and a great many CF or pure C responses. But neither extreme would necessarily represent an individual living to his fullest potential as a person. The grossly introversive person might prove to be essentially detached and distant in his interpersonal relations, and even if he were to form a close human relationship, it might be still marked by an element of deliberation that would limit its development. The grossly extratensive person might be capable of passion and great warmth but little stability and little sense of direction, which could only lead to painful human relationships. Schachtel (1943, 1950), for example, has demonstrated in brilliant fashion the various complex facets of human interaction and creativity which may be gleaned from both human movement and color responses. The type of experimental research cited in this chapter scarcely touches on many of the issues raised by Schachtel or other astute observers of human nature who have used the Rorschach blots as their adjunctive tools. Yet, however trivial in themselves may seem tasks like slow writing or verb definition, they are theoretically consistent with the more general and subtle interpersonal behaviors with which clinicians deal, and they serve, in addition, to point out research models which by successive approximation may gradually test clinical hypotheses and elaborate on our scientific comprehension of the Rorschach.

SOME THEORETICAL CONSIDERATIONS

A theoretical formulation suggested or supported by the empirical data summarized in this chapter must remain sketchy at best, because so little of the research on Rorschach concepts has been addressed to theoretical problems. The relationship of Rorschach's experience type to Jung's introversion-extraversion *attitudinal* continuum has been reexamined by Klopfer (1954) and Bash (1955). (See also McCully, Chapter 15, this volume.) It seems clear that Rorschach's *M*:sum *C* ratio is similar in many ways to the final formulation by Jung. In *Analytical Psychology*, introversion-extraversion represent extremes of a general personality orientation which interact with two other general dimensions—the *functions* of thinking-feeling and sensation-intuition—in the definition of any given response pattern characteristic of an individual. Both Rorschach's and Jung's conceptions of intro-extraversion unquestionably represent powerful and comprehensive schemata for evaluating the manner in which individuals experience their world. They provide the psychologist with a useful reference frame for interpreting and organizing the complexities of overt behavior as well. Jung, however, unlike Rorschach, stressed the principle of *complementarity*, which indicated that, if an introversive orientation is not overtly apparent, it is unconsciously present. Jung's conceptions have a certain power in reflecting a comprehensive picture of personality *structure* in contrast with *dynamics*. Failing precise operational definitions of the *function* dimensions, it is difficult to relate the theory of *Analytical Psychology* to the data thus far summarized.

Bash (1955), in an ingenious manner, has sought, however, to test the theory of *complementarity* in the experience type. Subjects to whom Rorschachs had been previously administered were exposed to 200 consecutive presentations of card IX, and were instructed to offer a response for each exposure. Sequences of 50 responses were scored for *M*:sum *C*. It was found that introversives on their original records gradually reversed their experience types to a decidedly extratensive ratio, whereas initial extratensives gradually became markedly introversive. Ambiequals showed no change. This remarkable result in a very simple experiment bears repetition, particularly with the view of clarifying the basis for the reversal. It might be argued, for example, that the introversive subjects, having given so many *M* responses, had nowhere else to go, if they wished to vary their reaction, but to color. However, keeping stimulus characteristics (Zubin, 1956) of the blot in mind, a simpler explanation than Bash's may be possible. While the Jungian constructs remain at a rather high level of abstraction, it might indeed be worth while to sample a variety of human performances which lend themselves to inclusion within the definition of the various Jungian functions, and then, if possible, to obtain some method for tapping conscious and unconscious manifestations of these functions and for evaluating the introvert and extrovert mode of utilizing each function. This suggests a rather grand factor analytic design, and, in some respects, is not too different from the program being carried out by Eysenck (1948, 1953).

The Jungian concepts, although certainly suggestive for comprehending the experience type at the level of a general typology, appear to be extremely limited in one respect, however. They do not afford, except possibly for the case of symbolic content analysis (Mindess, 1955), a suitable basis for answering the crucial questions concerning *the linkage of specific determinants of ink-blot response to specific behavioral tendencies.* As a matter of fact, no theory has succeeded in this connection, and there is still a considerable gap between studies analyzing the stimulus properties of the blot (Arnheim, 1951; Eckhardt, 1955; Zubin, 1956) and those studies which attempt to relate a certain form of perceptual behavior to personality variables (Rickers-Ovsiankina, 1943; Schachtel, 1943; Schachtel, 1950; Shapiro, 1956, and Chapter 8, this volume; Werner, 1945). The effectiveness of a theory in dealing with Rorschach data depends on whether it provides a rigorous basis for understanding the linkage of motor activity, affectivity, and fantasy to motion perception, and whether it affords some conception of the etiology of these functions, their developmental aspects, and the nature of individual differences. In addition, the theory must offer some explanation for the association of human movement perceived in ink blots with fantasy and motor inhibition, and for the association of color with motor responsiveness and affective expression. It must also account for the movement:color ratio as representing a complex dimension of human variation. Although no single theory seems capable at present of meeting these criteria, there has been a confluence of thought from psychoanalytic ego psychology, developmental psychology, and cognitive psychology, which appears to be opening the way for the development of a formulation incorporating the Rorschach experience-type data (Holt, 1954; Schachtel, 1943; Shapiro, 1956, and Chapter 8, this volume; Singer, 1955; Werner and Wapner, 1952).

Perhaps the greatest progress in this respect has come in connection specifically with the human movement response. At the perceptual level, Werner (1945) and Werner and Wapner (1952) have made important strides through the medium of their concept of the vicarious functioning of sensory and motor processes, which are linked by body tonicity. Their theory provides an important clue to the linkage of motion perception with inhibition of overt movement, which is essential in comprehending the origin of the M response. At the level of perception and motor activity, this theory has been specific enough to be tested and supported in several studies. Meltzoff, Singer and their co-workers (Meltzoff, Singer and Korchin, 1953; Singer, Meltzoff and Goldman, 1952), for example, have found that Rorschach movement responses increased immediately after periods of motor inhibition. Werner's theory as yet does not fully specify the implications of this sensory-tonic vicariousness for fantasy and more general personality dimensions, however, nor does it provide sufficient basis for understanding why *human movement* rather than *animal* or any other type of movement on the Rorschach should be most closely related to motor inhibition. Some intriguing possibilities relating Werner's theory to recent findings on the effects of sleep and Rapid Eye Movement, EEG Stage 1 deprivation may be cited. Palmer (1963), Lerner (1966), and Feldstein (1972) all found some evidence for modifications in M responses as a result of systematic interference with normal sleep cycles. While these results are not definitive, they do encourage more careful explorations of the continuity between night dream fantasy and waking imagination.

Psychoanalytic ego psychology, as first expounded in Chapter 7 of Freud's *Interpretation of Dreams* (1953), and subsequently developed in its application to thought by Rapaport (1951), suggests some possibilities for specifying the origin of movement and color responses and their general significance. The central concept in Freud's theory of the shift from primitive, diffuse, wishful, primary-process thought and perception to a secondary process characterized by organization, reality groundedness, planfulness, and abstraction is that of *delay*. Thought develops in effect when the child is compelled to deter immediate gratification, either because it is impossible of attainment or because a more valued gratification is desired. In the course of the delay, the motor impulses already oriented towards action in the direction of the gratified object must be checked. Thought, which Freud termed "experimental action" (Freud, 1946), intervenes to sustain the child by discharging smaller quantities of energy, presumably through fantasy of the reward or planning directed towards obtaining it. Here Werner's theory seems to supply a specific bridge to explain how checked motor reactions find a vicarious expression in illusory motion perception or imaginal movements. One need no longer accept notions of energy to see the advantages of alternative response potentialities in the individual.

Learning to defer gratification, with an attendant resort to an imaginal or conceptual level of behavior, is a tremendous step in maturation. By freeing the organism from the spatial and temporal limitations of immediate perception and motor response, it makes possible mastery of the future and of countless new environments, while, as Freud has so acutely noted, some sustaining satisfaction is possible, since the image or name of the reward is present in the course of the fantasy or planning activity. In this process must lie the origin of an awareness of self and of a self-concept, since the delay of gratification and the fantasy clearly differentiates the organism from the immediate environmental situation. This differentiation, once effected, partially alters the perceptual field of the child and makes possible more self-directed responses. These responses unquestionably form the basis for a symbolism and an organization of behavior, which becomes part of the Freudian "ego" or Mead's (1934) and Sullivan's (1953) "self-system."

Because learning opportunities, family and cultural demands, and constitutional dispositions differ, children undoubtedly vary tremendously in their rate and extent of development of motor inhibition, fantasy tendencies, and sense of self. The Rorschach experience type and specifically the M response may well represent a unique if crude method of estimating these individual differences in motor inhibition, fantasy, and self-differentiation.

The specific element of human content in the M response must still be explained, however. Here the psychoanalytic theory of identification, as delineated in an intensive survey by Lair (1949), provides some clues. The delay between arousal of a need and its fulfillment may be sustained by fantasy about the parent who will bring relief. To the extent that a certain consistency in delay with assurance of the eventual coming of the parent is part of the life pattern of the child, the parental image in fantasy becomes a temporary source of satisfaction and, perhaps later, in itself an instrumentality by means of which the child, through imitation of this image, learns to master other frustrating situations. In family constellations which are characterized by considerable emphasis on deferment of gratification, but with the ultimate promise from parental figures of reward, fantasy of humans must undoubtedly be enriched. A dependency on fantasy about humans seems to be fostered in this way, particularly if parental figures are relatively loving and rewarding. Lair (1949) has attempted some formulation of the role of a benign parent in the learning of language and symbolic thought. Two studies (Shatin, 1953; Singer and Sugarman, 1955) have offered some evidence that neurotic and schizophrenic subjects who show relatively numerous Rorschach M responses describe parental figures in TAT stories as more nurturant or less rejecting than do patients with few M. The work of Bene (1975) and the extensive studies of daydreaming (Singer, 1974a, 1975) also offer support for this view.

Constitutional or cultural factors aside, therefore, a given family constellation may make for the development within a child of a pattern of behavior characterized by relative ease of delayed gratification, identification with parental goals and behavior fantasy, a heightened awareness of self-other or self-environment distinctions, and increased planfulness, introspectiveness, and concern with human relationships. The pathological extreme of this pattern may be occasioned by a parent-child relationship that so emphasizes control of motor response and dependence on the adult, or the adult's image, for gratification that it renders the child impotent for direct action or expression of affect. Fantasy, introspection, and self-responses are the only things the child can count on without the parent, and he grows to feel that all direct action or motor activity will reveal him as inept or inexperienced. An outcome of such a childhood pattern may be an individual with a lopsided introversive experience type, whose color responses are few or absent, and who is clinically characterized by extensive obsessional preoccupations, withdrawal, gross conscious concern about inferiority and insecurity, and considerable inhibition in acting upon sexual or aggressive desires.

Individuals in this group may function effectively in certain spheres of intellectual activity and may prove extremely creative in their thought about human relationships or in poetic and dramatic imagery, but they continue to be blocked in intimate human contacts of a direct sort (Kupper, 1950). This clinical formulation suggests a concrete exemplification of the general theory of delay and fantasy development. It remains to be seen, however, whether systematic research will support such characterizations. Suggestive possibilities are present in some data obtained by Opler and Singer (Opler and Singer, 1956; Singer and Opler, 1956), who compared schizophrenic subjects coming from cultural backgrounds which differed in their relative emphases on impulse control and maternal influence. Irish patients, whose parental constellations and cultural milieu favored delay, showed themselves to be more given to fantasy (Rorschach M, TAT imaginativeness) and delay (time estimation, voluntary slowness of writing, ward cooperativeness and absence of assaultive behavior) than a corresponding sample of Italian patients. In symptomatology and case histories, the Irish emphasized excessive impulse control and obsessional or religious delusional preoccupations, compared with the Italian patients, whose histories revealed more open antisocial or acting-out behavior, more sexual activity of all sorts, and more hypochondriacal bodily rather than inter-personal preoccupations in their delusions.

Let us now consider the sum C term of the experience type formula, its origin, its perceptual basis, and behavioral implications. The whole question of the relationship of color and affect is beyond the scope of this chapter; the problems involved have been covered by Fortier (1953), Rickers-Ovsiankina (1943), Schachtel (1943), and Shapiro (1956 and Chapter 8 of this volume). The common core of theory linking the various points of view concerning the relationship of color to affect and impulsivity appears to emphasize the relatively immediate impact of color, which evokes what Schachtel has called a "passive" reaction, Rickers-Ovsiankina, a response "involving less complex processes of organization and articulation," Shapiro, following Rapaport's theory of affect, a process involving "less delay," and Hays and Boardman (1975), a response more positive and active, using the Semantic Differential technique of Osgood et al. (1957), than that given to identical achromatic representations, but in general less potent than the responses elicited by those same achromatic cards. Certainly the developmental theory of Werner (1948) concerning hierarchic levels of integration in perception and motility from diffuse and syncretic response to more complex, differentiated, and articulated reactions has provided both a viewpoint and data which afford a basis for comprehending why pure C or CF responses may be associated with impulsivity, egocentricity, and immaturity in general. Several questions remain unanswered by this formulation, however. Recent studies have questioned the specific issue of whether it is the color *per se* or rather the diffuse, poorly articulated, nature of the response which is associated with diffuse or hasty motility or affect (Siipola and Taylor, 1952; Wittenborn, 1950a; Wittenborn, 1950b). Even Shapiro, who has carried the concept of delayed discharge in relation to color a step further by delineating three steps of passivity in response to color, has not indicated whether shading or black and white reaction differ in this respect from chromatic reactions. Does a diffuse C'F response carry a different behavioral import than a CF? The theoretical basis for a distinction between these response tendencies does not seem apparent as yet, at least with a specificity that can explain the *perceptual* basis for the distinction.[2]

The second problem raised in the linkage of color to affect by means of a "delayed discharge" theory is how to distinguish between M and C. If M represents the outcome of a long period of development in the personality of the capacity to free the individual from the pressure of immediate drives, and if FC in effect represents a similar example of this development, we are faced with the necessity of explaining why we differentiate between the two responses and between records with high sum C and those with no M. Indeed,

[2] David Shapiro replies: If I understand the general question properly, I would have to say that I do not think it can be answered in this form. The point is that the color stimulus seems to permit more immediate and subjective, less detached, objective and articulated reactions than other visual stimuli. This is why, I together with others have argued, color-response becomes in various forms an indicator of certain less detached, more immediate and subjective reaction modes and tendencies in the personality, to put the matter loosely. So the disjunction in Singer's question, Is it the "color per se or rather the diffuse, poorly articulated nature of the response?" does not seem to me a justifiable one. If it turned out that the perceptual processes involved in achromatic "color" responses or shading responses were of the same relatively immediate sort of color responses, then, of course, the significance of these responses would be the same. But I am not at all sure that that is the case. [Inserted by the editor.]

Wittenborn (1950a, 1950b) has, on an empirical basis, questioned the association of FC with CF and C, and has claimed that his data support only a distinction between presence or lack of perceptual control. No simple solution seems forthcoming at present. Although Rorschach made it clear that movement and color measured different functional dimensions, he also took an important step by indicating the close association between affectivity and motility. The question as to how color and human-movement responses to ink blots come about and how they come to be linked to different personality dimensions persists as long as we cannot demonstrate a distinction between the behavioral correlates of the two types of responses.

A study by Singer, Wilensky, and McCraven (1956) may point up the difficulty of an attempt to derive a comprehensive theoretical basis for the M:sum C ratio. A large battery of tests including the Rorschach and various behavioral situations were administered to a group of 100 schizophrenic patients. The tests and behavior samples were chosen because it was felt that most of them would have relevance to a dimension linking fantasy capacity with inhibited motility, planning, lack of impulsivity, or delaying capacity in general. Factor analysis of the matrix of intercorrelations yielded four factors. Factor A's heaviest loadings were for Rorschach M, Barron's Human Movement Threshold, Porteus Maze Test Quotient, Downey's Motor Inhibition Test, and rated cooperativeness with ward routine. This factor clearly links Rorschach M with a capacity for delay in the motor sphere. Factor B showed highest loadings on measures of productivity and aspiration. Factor C had highest loadings from FC, C', CF, R, and FM, as well as aggressiveness, uncooperative ward behavior and diffuse energy level in ward behavior. Factor D resembled factor A since its high loadings were from M and Barron's M-threshold, but here the other tests with appreciable loadings did not involve control of motor activity, but seemed to reflect imaginativeness, introspectiveness and lack of external interests.

Consideration of these results suggests tentative support for Rorschach's view of the experience type with its two dimensions. Factor A may clearly be termed a "delay" factor, and it resembles a similar result obtained in a factor analysis by Foster (1955), using different behavior samples with the Rorschach ink blots. Factor C seems definitely to represent a pressure for outward living which might be termed "emotional surgency," and which again parallels a finding by Foster. Indeed, a second-order factor analysis reveals an inverse linkage between factors A and C, which seems in accord with Rorschach's uniting M and C in a common ratio while insisting that they still represented different functional dimensions. At the same time, the very high loading of C' on factor C, although supporting Piotrowski's (1950) empirical interpretation of C' as associated with acting-out tendencies, complicates the picture somewhat in so far as it may be appropriate to make a distinction between chromatic color and black-grey reactions. The emergence of two separate M factors, one linking M with motor inhibition, the other with introversion and imagination, is also puzzling. It may perhaps reflect a pattern peculiar to pathology, since the sample was made up of severely disturbed patients. Nevertheless, it remains possible that the linkage of fantasy, control of hostility, and motion perception is far more complex than any description thus far attempted would suggest. Unfortunately, in this study and in most described in the literature, it was not possible or not planned to consider in detail the various nuances of M or sum C, and to incorporate a specific M:sum C measure in the matrix.

A Tentative Theoretical Formulation of the Experience Type

In attempting a brief formulation which will incorporate Rorschach's experience type within a more general framework, the authors hope chiefly to provide a good target for experimental sniping. The basic tenet of this chapter has been that experimental and theoretical exploration in the Rorschach method is not only possible but genuinely interesting, and fruitful not only for the practical purpose of validating a clinical tool but also for generating hypotheses about the nature of human personality.

To begin with, it is postulated that two dimensions of variation in human behavior exist at birth which have relevance for the concept of the experience type. These dimensions may well be considered aspects of a basic temperament relatively built into the constitution and modifiable only within limits by subsequent learning. One dimension might be termed "capacity for internal experience," and it may be reflected in speed of assimilation of visual percepts, general tendency for rapid formation of associations, general intelligence, and capacity for development of imagery. Subsequently, it may be related to ease of language development. The other dimension might be termed "activity" or "motility" and includes rapidity of autonomic arousal, a constitutional factor suggested by Wenger's work (1938, 1942a, 1942b), rapidity of movement, and a low threshold for affective response. In crude terms, it may be that every child differs in the amount of energy available for expression along these dimensions, or in the differentiation and sensitivity of the organ systems or neural patterns relevant to these dimensions. It seems likely that differences in gross quantity of energy exist so that some children show marked development along both dimensions whereas others show little in one or both. It seems reasonable to suppose that just as some persons are put together in such a way as to enhance full and long employment of their physiques, others are born already possessing the potential capacities for richer use of imaginal and affective resources in interpersonal relationships.

To some extent, these dimensions together may well represent what Maslow (1949) has termed "the expressive component of behavior." The inner-living dimension would certainly represent a scale along which the autonomous ego functions, described by Hartmann (1950), would vary for each person. The rewards and frustrations of life are then brought to bear upon each child, and accident and parental attitude undoubtedly affect this behavior along each dimension. Parental emphasis on delay or routine may afford opportunity for fantasy development in some children and may reward such development, thus increasing its emergence as a conflict-free area in which the child finds considerable satisfaction and even practical use. In children initially lacking this possibility, but pressed for delay, other mechanisms may develop, e.g., somatization. Close parental ties may also enhance this development. In the sphere of affect or motility, parental demands for rapid response and for affective interchange may prove too much for the phlegmatic child, enhancing conflict and, as the emotional response sought is not forthcoming, leading to rejection by parents. The hyperactive sensitive child whose parents cannot tolerate timidity or aggression may be forced to suppress his affective potential by whatever means available. Affectivity would thus become part of the conflictual sphere of the ego, subject to a variety of defense mechanisms, one of which might be, in a child with fantasy potential, intellectualization or withdrawal into daydreaming. Cultural values will come into play here from the peer group and the school situation, thus enhancing further development along one or both of these dimensions. In a family setting in which open emotionality is acceptable and in which warmth enhances the value of adaptive affectivity, one might expect moderate control of motility and expression of feeling but little denial or repression.

Some outcomes of various family constellations may be sketched briefly. Given an individual already possessing constitutional potential for introversive living, with the concurrence of a close relationship with parents in a family where the mother is often nurturant and fosters identification with order or with ideal values ("Be a good boy for mother"), a highly developed inner life characterized by respect for mental process, deferment of gratification, fluidity of imagery, planning ability, and concern with human problems and human interaction may develop. An individual of this sort may well choose an occupation in keeping with this pattern (as Roe's [1952] data suggest), but if circumstances lead to other work, humanistic interests may persist. Such a person might still prove to be cold, reserved, and distant in his direct interchange with others, and might win respect but perhaps not love. Sexual activity could perhaps be mechanical or characterized by extreme inhibition, while at the same time the introversive development might enable the individual to write sensual poetry or to emphathize deeply with the experience of lovers. If, however, in such a person, the family constellation had perhaps more balance with a pattern permitting affective expression and encouraging motility, both potentialities might be developed and lead to the richness correlated with the dilated experience type.

Since at least in our society the influence of the mother temporally precedes that of the father, one might speculate on a chronological sequence of identification patterns necessary for optimal development of both M and C dimensions. Bene's findings concerning the correlation between higher M production and a close mother-male child relationship lends strength to this speculation (Bene, 1975). An early experience with a reasonably nurturant mother who emphasizes control and delay may aid in fantasy development and ego formation through identification and imitation. For fullest development of the affective and action capacities, it would appear that, at least for a male child, some identification with the father subsequently reinforced by peer-group association is necessary. The father who moves about, works at chores, shows interest in sports, swears and expresses open hostility on occasion as well as affection, and can tolerate these tendencies in the child, offers a model for development of affective and motor spontaneity. As a matter of fact, the term "spontaneity" may perhaps involve separation of activity in the ideational and affective dimension—a markedly introversive individual may be capable of clever ideas and original thoughts or wit which can be put on paper, without having, however, much capacity for emotional responsiveness or motor freedom. Someone lacking such inner potential, but developed in the motor-affect area, may prove to be warm, sympathetic, and easily moved, and may be capable of great freedom of movement or bawdy but winning humor. Of course, translating these generalizations to the M:sum C ratio of a Rorschach protocol, it should be kept in mind that quality and content of the component responses in each ratio term would obviously require consideration in this connection.

Combining Rorschach data bearing on these two dimensions into a common ratio can now be seen as a method for tapping potentialities and capacities for spontaneity in two great spheres of human variation—the ideational and the affective. Other dimensions undoubtedly exist and are of equal importance for clinical purposes, e.g., anxiety level, masculinity versus femininity, reality orientation, etc. The M:sum C ratio, if it can be perfected, and really rational rather than arbitrary weightings could be made available, may tell us much of the gross patterns of fantasy, affectivity, and motility, and of the spontaneity potential in the ideation and affect of the individual. A rich development in one sphere may afford evidence of potentiality for effective and satisfactory living even when there is minimal or disturbed development in the other sphere. Important differences between people which are often attributed to specific dynamic conflicts or distortions may in part be a reflection of gross temperamental differences represented by strikingly different experience types. Rorschach's suggestion that the M:sum C ratio be applied to ascertaining the suitability of marriage partners is worth some empirical consideration in this connection. As Barron (1955) has suggested, the *M* type may represent not so much a distinctively *effective* mode of adjustment as a *style of life*. It is interesting in this connection that the psychologists who assessed the high-*M* individuals in Barron's study and who felt them to be more intelligent, may well, if Roe's (1952) data are valid, have been *M* types themselves. The experience type, by reflecting the balance between development in two crucial areas of human behavior, appears to go beyond expressiveness, however, to provide important clues to two major spheres of human life, two great dimensions of human variation along which we may observe the fulfillment of man's potentialities for thought and feeling.

BIBLIOGRAPHY

Ainsworth, M. D. Problems of validation. In: Klopfer, B., Ainsworth, M. D., Klopfer, W., and Holt, R. *Developments in the Rorschach technique* Yonkers: World Book Co., 1954, Chapter 14.

Arnheim, R. Perceptual and aesthetic aspects of the movement response. *J. Pers.*, 1951, ·19, 265-281.

Aronow, E. Comment on Raychaudhuri's 'Relation of creativity and sex to Rorschach *M* responses'. *J. Personality Assess.*, 1972, **36(4)**, 303-306.

Barrell, R. P. Subcategories of Rorschach human movement responses: A classification system and some experimental results. *J. consult. Psychol.*, 1953, **17**, 254-260.

Barron, F. Threshold for the perception of human movement in inkblots. *J. consult. Psychol.*, 1955, **19**, 33-38.

Bash, K. W. Einstellungstypus and Erlebnistypus: C. G. Jung and Herman Rorschach. *J. proj. Tech.*, 1955, **19**, 236-242.

Beck, S. J. *Rorschach's test.* New York: Grune & Stratton, 1946.

Bene, E. An effect on Rorschach *M* responses of a boy's relationship with his mother. *J. Personality Assess.*, 1975, **39(2)**, 114-115.

Bieri, J., and Blacker, E. External and internal stimulus factors in Rorschach performance. ·*J. consult. Psychol.*, 1956a, **20**, 1-7.

Bieri, J., and Blacker, E. The generality of cognitive complexity of people and inkblots. *J. abnorm. soc. Psychol.*, 1956b, **53**, 112-117.

Blechner, J. E. Constancy of Rorschach movement responses under educational conditioning. *California J. Ed. Res.*, 1953, **4**, 173-176.

Blechner, J. E. Constancy of Rorschach color responses under educational conditioning. *J. exp. Ed.*, 1954, **22**, 293-295.

Block, J. A study of affective responsiveness in a lie-detection situation. *J. abnorm. soc. Psychol.*, 1957, **55**, 11-15.

Broekmann, N. C. A psychophysiological investigation of the Rorschach colour and form determinants. *J. Proj. Tech. & Personality Assess.*, 1970, **34(2)**, 98-103.

Brower, D. The relation between certain Rorschach factors and cardiovascular activity before and after visual-motor conflict. *J. gen. Psychol.*, 1947, **37**, 93-95.

Brunswik, E. *Perception and the representative design of psychological experiments.* Stanford: University of California Press, 1956.

Dana, R. H. Six constructs to define Rorschach *M. J. Proj. Tech & Personality Assess.*, 1968, **32(2)**, 138-145.

Dana, R. H. and Cocking, R. Cue parameters, cue probabilities, and clinical judgment. *J. clin. Psychol.*, 1968, **24(4)**, 475-480.

Dawo, A. Nachweis psychischer Veränderungen gesunder Frauen während der Menstruation mittels des Rorschach Versuches. *Rorschachiana*, 1952, **1**, 238-249.

Dudek, S. Z. Creativity and the Rorschach human movement response: An analysis of the relationship between quantity and quality of *M* and creative expression in artist and non-artist groups. *Diss. Abstr.*, 1967, **27(11-B)**, 4120-4121.

Dudek, S. Z. *M* an active energy system correlating Rorschach *M* with ease of creative expression. *J. Proj. Tech. & Personality Assess.*, 1968a, **32(5)**, 453-461.

Dudek, S. Z. Regression and creativity: A comparison of the Rorschach records of successful vs. unsuccessful painters and writers. *J. nerv. ment. Dis.*, 1968b, **147(6)**, 535-546.

Eckhardt, W. An experimental and theoretical analysis of movement and vista responses. *J. proj. Tech.*, 1955, **19**, 301-305.

Eichler, R. A comparison of the Rorschach and Behn ink-blot tests. *J. consult. Psychol.*, 1951, **15**, 186-189.

Erginel, A. On the test-retest reliability of the Rorschach. *J. Personality Assess.*, 1972, **36(3)**, 203-212.

Eysenck, H. J. *Dimensions of personality.* London: Routledge and Kegan Paul, 1948.

Eysenck, H. J. *The structure of human personality.* New York: John Wiley, 1953.

Feldstein, S. REM deprivation: the effects on inkblot perception and fantasy processes. Unpublished doctoral dissertation, City University of New York, 1972.

Felzer, S. B. A statistical study of sex differences on the Rorschach. *J. proj. Tech.*, 1955, **19**, 382-386.

Finney, B. C. Rorschach test correlates of assaultive behavior. *J. proj. Tech.*, 1950, **14**, 15-30.

Ford, M. *The application of the Rorschach test to young children.* Minneapolis: University of Minnesota Press, 1946.

Fortier, R. H. The response to color and ego functions. *Psychol. Bull.*, 1953, **50**, 41-63.

Foster, A. The factorial structure of the Rorschach test. *Tex. Rep. Biol. Med.*, 1955, **13**, 34-61.

Freud, S. *The ego and the id.* London: Hogarth, 1923.

Freud, S. Formulations regarding the two principles in mental functioning. In: *Collected Papers. Vol. IV.* London: Hogarth, 1946, 13-21.

Freud, S. The interpretation of dreams. In: *Standard edition of the complete psychological works. Vol. V.* London: Hogarth, 1953, 339-628.

Gardner, R. W. Impulsivity as indicated by Rorschach test factors. *J. consult. Psychol.*, 1951, **15**, 464-468.

Gibby, R. G., Stotsky, B. A., Harrington, R. L., and Thomas, R. W. Rorschach determinant shift among hallucinatory and delusional patients. *J. consult. Psychol.*, 1955, **19**, 44-46.

Goldberg, L. Aggression in boys in an urban clinic population. Unpublished doctoral dissertation, City University of New York, 1974.

Goldfarb, W. Psychological privation in infancy and subsequent adjustment. *Amer. J. Orthopsychiat.*, 1945, **15**, 249-254.

Goldfarb, W. Rorschach test differences between family reared, institution reared, and schizophrenic children. *Amer. J. Orthopsychiat.*, 1949, **19**, 624-633.

Goldman, A. E. Studies in vicariousness: degree of motor activity and the autokinetic phenomenon. *Amer. J. Psychol.*, 1953, **66**, 613-617.

Griffin, D. P. Movement responses and creativity. *J. consult. Psychol.*, 1958, **22**, 134-136.

Hamilton, J., Blewett, D., and Sydiaha, D. Ink-blot responses of identical and fraternal twins. *J. genet. Psychol.*, 1971, **119(1)**, 37-41.

Hartmann, H. Comments on the psychoanalytic theory of the ego. In: *The psychoanalytic study of the child. Vol. V.* New York: International Universities Press, 1950, 74-96.

Hays, J. R. and Boardman, W. K. An analysis of the function of color in the Rorschach. *J. Personality Assess.*, 1975, **39(1)**, 19-24.

Hays, W., Gellerman, S., and Sloan, W. A study of the verb-adjective quotient and the Rorschach experience-balance. *J. clin. Psychol.*, 1951, **7**, 224-227.

Herman, J. A study of some behavioral and test correlates of the Rorschach experience type. Unpublished doctoral dissertation, New York University, 1956.

Hersch, C. The cognitive functioning of the creative person: a developmental analysis. *J. proj. Tech.*, 1962, **26**, 193-200.

Hertzman, M., Orlansky, J., and Seitz, C. Personality organization and anoxia tolerance. *Psychosom. Med.*, 1944, **6**, 317-331.

Holt, R. R. Implications of some contemporary personality theories for Rorschach rationale. In: Klopfer, B., Ainsworth, M., Klopfer, W., and Holt, R. *Developments in the Rorschach technique. Vol. I.* Yonkers: World Book Co., 1954, Chapter 15.

Holtzman, W. H. Validation studies of the Rorschach test: Impulsiveness in the normal superior adult. *J. clin. Psychol.*, 1950, **6**, 348-351.

Hunter, M. Responses of comparable white and Negro adults to the Rorschach test. *J. Psychol.*, 1937, **3**, 173-182.

King, G. F. An interpersonal conception of Rorschach human movement and delusional content. *J. proj. Tech.*, 1960, **24**, 161-163.

Klein, G. S., and Schlesinger, H. J. Perceptual attitudes toward instability: Prediction of apparent movement responses from Rorschach responses. *J. Pers.*, 1951, **19**, 289-302.

Kleinman, R. A., and Higgins, J. Sex of respondent and Rorschach M production. *J. proj. Tech. & Personality Assess.*, 1966, **30(5)**, 439-440.

Klopfer, B. Rorschach hypotheses and ego psychology. In: Klopfer, B., Ainsworth, M., Klopfer, W., and Holt, R. *Developments in the Rorschach technique. Vol. I.* Yonkers: World Book Co., 1954, Chapter 16.

Klopfer, B., and Margulies, H. Rorschach reactions in early childhood. *Rorschach Res. Exch.*, 1941, **5**, 1-23.

Kris, E. On preconscious mental processes. *Psychoanal. Quart.*, 1950, **19**, 540-560.

Kupper, H. L. Psychodynamics of the "intellectual." *Int. J. Psychoanal.*, 1950, **31**, 85-94.

Kurz, R. B. and Capone, T. A. Cognitive level, role-taking ability and the Rorschach human movement response. *Percept. Mot. Skills*, 1967, **24(2)**, 657-658.

Kurz, R. B., Cohen, R., and Starzynski, S. Rorschach correlates of time estimation. *J. consult. Psychol.*, 1965, **29**, 379-382.

Lair, W. S. The psychoanalytic theory of identification. Unpublished doctoral dissertation, Harvard University, 1949.

Lane, B. M. A validation test of the Rorschach movement responses. *Amer. J. Orthopsychiat.*, 1948, **18**, 292-296.

Leiman, C. J. An investigation of the perception of movement on the Rorschach inkblots. Unpublished doctoral dissertation, University of Kentucky, 1951.

Lerner, B. Rorschach movement and dreams: A validation study using drug-induced deprivation. *J. abnorm. Psychol.*, 1966, **71**, 75-86.

Levi, J., and Kraemer, D. Significance of a preponderance of human movement responses in children below age ten. *J. proj. Tech.*, 1952, **16**, 361-365.

Levine, M., Glass, H., and Meltzoff, J. The inhibition process, Rorschach M, color responses, and intelligence. Paper read at Eastern Psychological Association meetings, Atlantic City, 1956.

Levine, M., Glass, H., and Meltzoff, J. The inhibition process, Rorschach human movement responses, and intelligence. *J. consult. Psychol.*, 1957, **21**, 41-45.

Levine, M., and Meltzoff, J. Cognitive inhibition and Rorschach human movement responses. *J. consult. Psychol.*, 1956, **20**, 119-122.

Levine, M. and Spivack, G. Incentive, time conception and self-control in a group of emotionally disturbed boys. *J. clin. Psychol.*, 1959, **15**, 110-113.

Levine, M., Spivack, G., Fuschillo, J. and Tavernier, A. Intelligence and measures of inhibition and time sense. *J. clin. Psychol.*, 1959, **15**, 224-226.

Lewin, K. *A dynamic theory of personality*. New York: McGraw-Hill, 1935.

Loveland, N. T. and Singer, M. T. Projective test assessment of the effects of sleep deprivation. *J. proj. Tech.*, 1959, **23**, 323-334.

Luria, A. P. *The Nature of human conflicts*. New York: Liveright, 1932.

Mann, L. The relation of Rorschach indices of extratension and introversion to a measure of responsiveness to the immediate environment. Unpublished doctoral dissertation, University of North Carolina, 1953.

Maslow, A. The expressive component of behavior. *Psychol Rev.*, 1949, **56**, 261-271.

Matarazzo, R. G., Watson, R. I., and Ulett, G. A. Relationship of Rorschach scoring categories to modes of perception induced by intermittent photic stimulation—a methodological study of perception. *J. clin. Psychol.*, 1952, **8**, 368-374.

Mead, G. H. *Mind, self, and society*. Chicago: University of Chicago Press, 1934.

Meltzoff, J., and Levine, M. The relationship between motor and cognitive inhibition. *J. consult. Psychol.*, 1954, **18**, 355-358.

Meltzoff, J., and Litwin, D. Affective control and Rorschach human movement responses. *J. consult. Psychol.*, 1956, **20**, 463-465.

Meltzoff, J., Singer, J. L., and Korchin, S. J. Motor inhibition and Rorschach movement responses: A test of the sensory-tonic theory. *J. Pers.*, 1953, **21**, 400-410.

Mindess, H. Analytical psychology and the Rorschach test. *J. proj. Tech.*, 1955, **19**, 243-253.

Misch, R. C. The relationship of motoric inhibition to developmental level and ideational functioning: an analysis by means of the Rorschach test. Unpublished doctoral dissertation, Clark University, 1954.

Mitsunaga, A. A study of diabetic children by Rorschach test. *Jap. J. Clin. Psychol.*, 1967, **6(2)**, 87-96.

Mueller, W. J. and Abeles, N. The components of empathy and their relationship to the projection of human responses. *J. Proj. Tech. & Personality Asses.*, 1964, **28**, 322-330.

Murawski, B. The perceptual and imaginal effects of immobilization: a clinical study. Unpublished doctoral dissertation, Harvard University, 1954.

Nickerson, E. T. Some correlates of *M. J. Proj. Tech. & Personality Assess.*, 1969, **33(3)**, 203-212.

Opler, M. K., and Singer, J. L. Ethnic behavior and psychopathology: Italian and Irish. *Int. J. soc. Psychiat.*, 1956, **2**, 11-23.

Osgood, C. E., Suci, G. J., and Tannenbaum, P. H. *The measurement of meaning*. Urbana: University of Illinois Press, 1957.

Page, H. A. Studies in fantasy—daydreaming frequency and Rorschach scoring categories. *J. consult. Psychol.*, 1957, **21**, 111-114.

Palmer, J. O. Rorschach's experience-balance: The concept, general population characteristics, and intellectual correlates. *J. proj. Tech.*, 1955, **19**, 138-145.

Palmer, J. O. Attitudinal correlates of Rorschach's experience-balance. *J. proj. Tech.*, 1956, **20**, 208-211.

Palmer, J. O. Alterations in Rorschach's experience balance under conditions of food and sleep deprivation: A construct validation study. *J. proj. Tech.*, 1963, **27**, 208-213.

Parker, R. S. and Piotrowski, Z. A. The significance of varieties of actors of Rorschach human movement responses. *J. Proj. Tech. & Personality Assess.*, 1968, **32(1)**, 33-44.

Piaget, J. *The language and thought of the child*. New York: Harcourt, Brace, 1932.

Pickering, W. D. A comparison of predominant verbal levels on the Thematic Apperception Test with the Rorschach experience-balance. Unpublished doctoral dissertation, University of Pittsburgh, 1950.

Piotrowski, Z. A. A Rorschach compendium, revised and enlarged. *Psychiat. Quart.*, 1950, **24**, 543-596.

Piotrowski, Z. A., and Schreiber, M. Rorschach perceptanalytic measurement of personality changes during and after intensive psychoanalytically oriented psychotherapy. In: *Specialized techniques in psychotherapy.* New York: Basic Books, 1951.

Prola, M. A re-evaluation of the motor inhibition: fantasy hypothesis. *J. Proj. Tech. & Personality Assess.*, 1970, **34(6)**, 477-483.

Rabinovitch, M. S., Kennard, M. A., and Fister, W. P. Personality correlates of electroencephalographic findings. *Can. J. Psychol.*, 1955, **9**, 29-41.

Rapaport, D. *Organization and pathology of thought.* New York: Columbia University Press, 1951.

Rapaport, D. On the psychoanalytic theory of affects. *Inter J. Psychoanal.*, 1953, **34**, 177-198.

Rapaport, D., Gill, M., and Schafer, R. *Diagnostic psychological testing. Vol. II.* Chicago: Year Book Publishers, 1946.

Raychaudhuri, M. Relation of creativity and sex to Rorschach *M* responses. *J. Personality Assess.*, 1971, **35(1)**, 27-31.

Richards, T. W., and Lederman, R. A study of action in the fantasy of physically handicapped children. *J. clin. Psychol.*, 1956, **12**, 188-190.

Richter, R. H. and Winter, W. D. Holtzman ink-blot correlates of creative potential. *J. Proj. Tech. & Personality Assess.*, 1966, **30**, 62-67.

Rickers-Ovsiankina, M. Studies of the personality structure of schizophrenic individuals. I. *J. gen. Psychol.*, 1937, **16**, 153-178.

Rickers-Ovsiankina, M. Some theoretical considerations regarding the Rorschach method. *Rorschach Res. Exch.*, 1943, **7**, 41-53.

Rickers-Ovsiankina, M. Prognostic Rorschach indices in schizophrenia. In: *Review of diagnostic psychology and personality exploration.* Bern: Hans Huber, 1955, **3**, 246-254.

Rioch, M. J. The use of the Rorschach test in the assessment of change in patients under psychotherapy. *Psychiatry*, 1949, **12**, 427-434.

Roe, A. Analysis of group Rorschachs of psychologists and anthropologists. *J. proj. Tech.*, 1952, **16**, 212-224.

Rorschach, H. *Psychodiagnostics.* Bern: Hans Huber, 1942.

Rosenthal, M. Some behavioral correlates of the Rorschach experience-balance. Unpublished doctoral dissertation, Boston University, 1954.

Royal, R. E. An experimental investigation of the relationship between questionnaire and Rorschach measures of introversion. Unpublished doctoral dissertation, University of Pittsburgh, 1950.

Schachtel, E. G. On color and affect. Contributions to the understanding of Rorschach's test. II. *Psychiatry*, 1943, **6**, 393-409.

Schachtel, E. G. Projection and its relation to character attitudes and creativity in the kinesthetic response. Contributions to the understanding of Rorschach's test. IV. *Psychiatry*, 1950, **13**, 69-100.

Schumer, F. Some behavioral correlates of Rorschach human movement responses. Unpublished doctoral dissertation, Yale University, 1949.

Schmidt, B. Reflektorische Reaktionen auf Form und Farbe. *Z. Psychol.*, 1936, **137**.

Shapiro, D. Color response and perceptual passivity. *J. proj. Tech.*, 1956, **20**, 52-69.

Shatin, L. Rorschach adjustment and the Thematic Apperception Test. *J. proj. Tech.*, 1953, **17**, 92-101.

Siipola, E. The influence of color on reactions to inkblots. *J. Pers.*, 1950, **18**, 358-382.

Siipola, E., and Taylor, V. Reactions to inkblots under free and pressure conditions. *J. Pers.*, 1952, **21**, 22-47.

Singer, J. L. The Behn-Rorschach inkblots: A preliminary comparison with the original Rorschach series. *J. proj. Tech.*, 1952a, **16**, 238-245.

Singer, J. L. Perceptual and environmental determinants of perception in a size constancy experiment. *J. exp. Psychol.*, 1952b, **43**, 420-427.

Singer, J. L. Delayed gratification and ego-development: implications for clinical and experimental research. *J. consult. Psychol.*, 1955, **19**, 259-266.

Singer, J. L. (ed.) *The child's world of make-believe: Experimental studies of imaginative play.* New York: Academic Press, 1973a.

Singer, J. L. Daydreaming and the stream of thought. *Am. Scient.*, 1974b, **2(4)**, 417-425.

Singer, J. L. *The inner world of daydreaming.* New York: Harper and Row, 1975.

Singer, J. L. and Antrobus, J. S. A factor-analytic study of day dreaming and conceptually-related cognitive and personality variables. *Percept. Mot. Skills*, 1963, **17**, 187-209.

Singer, J. L., and Herman, J. Motor and fantasy correlates of Rorschach human movement responses. *J. consult. Psychol.*, 1954, **18**, 325-331.

Singer, J. L., Meltzoff, J., and Goldman, G. D. Rorschach movement responses following motor inhibition and hyperactivity. *J. consult. Psychol.*, 1952, **16**, 359-364.

Singer, J. L., and Opler, M. K. Contrasting patterns of fantasy and motility in Irish and Italian schizophrenics. *J. abnorm. soc. Psychol.*, 1956, **53**, 42-47.

Singer, J. L. and Schonbar, R. A. Correlates of daydreaming: a dimension of self awareness. *J. consult. Psychol.*, 1961, **25**, 1-6.

Singer, J. L. and Singer, D. G. Enhancing imaginative play in pre-school children: Television and live adult effects. Paper presented in symposium on Play at American Psychological Association, New Orleans, 1974. In Press, *J. of Communication,* 1976.

Singer, J. L., and Spohn, H. Some behavioral correlates of Rorschach's experience-type. *J. consult. Psychol.*, 1954, **18**, 1-9.

Singer, J. L., and Sugarman, D. Some Thematic Apperception Test correlates of Rorschach human movement responses. *J. consult. Psychol.*, 1955, **19**, 117-119.

Singer, J. L., Wilensky, H., and McCraven, V. Delaying capacity, fantasy, and planning ability: A factorial study of some basic ego functions. *J. consult. Psychol.*, 1956, **20**, 375-383.

Spivack, G., Levine, M. and Sprigle, H. Intelligence test performance and the delay function of the ego. *J. consult. Psychol.*, 1959, **23**, 428-431.

Steele, N. M. and Kahn, M. W. Kinesthesis and the Rorschach *M* response. *J. Proj. Tech. & Personality Assess.*, 1969, **33(1)**, 5-10.

Stein, M. I., and Meer, B. Perceptual organization in a study of creativity. *J. Psychol.*, 1954, **37**, 39-43.

Strauss, M. E. Examiner expectancy: effects on Rorschach experience balance. *J. consult. clin. Psychol.*, 1968, **32(2)**, 125-129.

Strauss, M. E. and Marwit, S. J. Expectancy effects in Rorschach testing. *J. consult. clin. Psychol.*, 1970, **34(3)**, 448.

Sullivan, H. S. *An interpersonal theory of psychiatry.* New York: Norton, 1953.

Teltscher, H. O. A study of the relationship between the perception of movement on the Rorschach and motoric expression. Unpublished doctoral dissertation, Yeshiva University, 1964.

Temerlin, M. K. One determinant of the capacity to free-associate in psychotherapy. *J. abnorm. soc. Psychol.*, 1956, **53**, 16-18.

Thetford, W. N. Fantasy perceptions in the personality development of normal and deviant children. *Amer. J. Orthopsychiat.*, 1952, **22**, 542-550.

Thetford, W. N., Molish, H. B., and Beck, S. J. Developmental aspects of personality structure in normal children. *J. proj. Tech.*, 1951, **15**, 58-78.

Thiessen, J. W., Favorite, L., and Coff, P. An investigation of the relationship between clinically-observed emotional behavior in children and Rorschach test indicators of emotional response. Paper read at the Eastern Psychological Association meetings, Boston, 1953.

Thornton, G. R., and Guilford, J. P. The reliability and meaning of Erlebnistypus scores in the Rorschach test. *J. abnorm. soc. Psychol.*, 1936, **31**, 324-330.

Troup, E. A comparative study by means of the Rorschach method of personality development in twenty pairs of identical twins. *Genet. Psychol. Monogr.*, 1938, **20**, 461-556.

Vernier, C., and Kendig, I. V. Analysis of the relationship between various measures of creative productivity in two projective tests. *Amer. Psychologist*, 1951, **8**, 349 (abstract).

Vernon, P. E. The significance of the Rorschach test. *Brit. J. Med. Psychol.*, 1935, **15**, 199-217.

Wagner, E. E. and Hoover, T. O. Exhibitionistic *M* in drama majors: A validation. *Percept. Mot. Skills*, 1971, **32(1)**, 125-126.

Wagner, E. E. and Hoover, T. O. Behavioral implications of Rorschach's human movement response: Further validation based on exhibitionistic *M*s. *Percept. Mot. Skills*, 1972, **35(1)**, 27-30.

Ward, A. J. The meaning of the movement response and of its changes during therapy: A review. *J. Proj. Tech. & Personality Assess.*, 1966, **30(5)**, 418-428.

Weber, C. O. The relation of personality trends to degree of visual constancy correction for size and form. *J. appl. Psychol.*, 1939, **23**, 703-708.

Wenger, M. A. Some relationships between muscular processes and personality and their factorial analysis. *Child Develop.*, 1938, **9**, 261-276.

Wenger, M. A. The stability of measurements of autonomic balance. *Psychosom. Med.*, 1942a, **6**, 94-95.

Wenger, M. A. A study of physiological factors: The autonomic nervous system and the skeletal musculature. *Human Biol.*, 1942b, **14**, 69-84.

Werner, H. Motion and motion perception: a study on vicarious functioning. *J. Psychol.*, 1945, **19**, 317-327.

Werner, H. *The comparative psychology of mental development.* Chicago: Follett, 1948.

Werner, H., and Wapner, S. Toward a general theory of perception. *Psychol. Rev.*, 1952, **59**, 324-333.

Wittenborn, J. R. A factor analysis of Rorschach scoring categories. *J. consult. Psychol.*, 1950a, **14**, 261-267.

Wittenborn, J. R. Level of mental health as a factor in the implications of Rorschach scores. *J. consult. Psychol.*, 1950b, **14**, 469-472.

Witkin, H. A., Dyk, R. B., Faterson, H. F., Goodenough, D. R., and Karp, S. A. *Psychological differentiation: Studies of development.* New York: John Wiley and Sons, Inc. 1962.

Wittkower, E. *A psychiatrist looks at tuberculosis.* London: National Association for Prevention of Tuberculosis, 1949.

Zubin, J. The non-projective aspects of the Rorschach experiment: I. Introduction. *J. soc. Psychol.*, 1956, **44**, 179-192.

CATEGORIES OF ANALYSIS: CONTENT

*We come now to a theme of the utmost importance,
the distinction Freud established between what he
called "primary processes" and "secondary processes." It was perhaps his most fundamental
contribution to psychology.*

ERNEST JONES

11

Robert R. Holt [1]

A

METHOD FOR ASSESSING PRIMARY

PROCESS MANIFESTATIONS AND THEIR

CONTROL IN RORSCHACH RESPONSES

When Rorschach gave us his test—his blots, his way of administering the experiment, as he called it, and interpreting the results—he
also left us a system of scoring the responses. Essentially, this was a
way of abstracting from a complex performance four or five important dimensions—dimensions which hundreds of Rorschachers since
have found most useful. Hermann Rorschach was perfectly open in
pointing out the intuitive and heuristic nature of these scoring
categories. One of the first points he made in his monograph was that
the theoretical basis of the test was almost nonexistent.

Since Rorschach's death, other hands have worked to expand and
perfect the scoring, but mostly this has meant increasing its differentiation and making explicit the criteria for assigning particular
scores. Attempts to work out a theoretical rationale of the test, or to
construct new scoring systems on a theoretical basis, have been few
indeed. Although the majority of workers have followed Rorschach

[1] Preparation of this chapter has been supported by a United States Public Health Service
Research Career Award, Grant No. 5-K06-MH-12455, from the National Institute of Mental
Health.

The first part of this chapter has been reprinted with some revisions from an article that
appeared in the *Journal of Projective Techniques* (Holt, 1956). I wish to express my indebt-

in working within the framework of some kind of psychoanalytic theory in their thinking about personality, only rarely has this led to attempts to set up new ways of scoring the test.

THEORETICAL BACKGROUND

This chapter reports an attempt to develop one such supplementary method. It is used on classic psychoanalytic theory, and is limited specifically to the problem of finding operational definitions for the concepts of primary and secondary process. Though I am a great deal more skeptical about the value of Freud's theories than I was when I did the major developmental work on the scoring system reported here, I still strongly believe that much of what he wrote about the primary process was based upon clinical observation and profound insights that will have lasting value, whatever the fate of his metapsychological elaborations may be.

Psychoanalysis popularly has the reputation of being a voluntaristic, antirational theory, one that portrays thought as the plaything and creature of man's impulses. Actually, of course, Freud did *not* deny that logical, rational, realistic, and efficient mental processes exist, or even that they make up a great part of conscious mental life, a part which his therapy aimed to enlarge. He grouped them under the conceptual heading *secondary process*. The term *secondary* was a warning, however, that another type of thinking preceded genetically and had priority for our understanding of unconscious processes. In his studies of neurotic patients, he found that their dreams and symptoms were not the random coughs and sputters of a faulty engine, but intelligible and highly meaningful products of a peculiar kind of mental operation. This he called the *primary process*. He found evidence of its working in slips of the tongue and other

edness to Dr. Roy Schafer, whose book (Schafer, 1958) has been stimulating and helpful in the development of the point of view expounded here, and who has contributed useful criticisms of the manual that embodies the scoring system.

The version of this chapter that appeared in the first edition of *Rorschach Psychology* was written with the active coauthorship of Dr. Joan Havel (now Grant), who had worked intensively with me for several months during the development of the major formal aspects scores. When I wrote to her about taking part in this revision, she declined on grounds that her work in recent years has taken her into other areas and that she lacked familiarity with the scoring manual in its current form. I have followed her suggestion that she no longer be listed as coauthor, but want to express my thanks for her creative and thoughtful participation in early stages of the work reported here.

errors, in jokes, in the thinking of primitive people, of children, of persons under extreme stress and strong affect, and in the creative processes of artists.

Most definitions of the primary process fall into the waiting semantic trap that encourages us to believe, when we postulate a process, that (a) it exists in pretty much the same form in different people, (b) it is the functioning of some structure, and (c) this hypothetical structure is a causally efficacious entity: it does things, e.g., thinks for us. The thinking I am interested in is done by people—not by egos, not by primary or secondary processes, not by cognitive or neurological structures. But people do tend to think in somewhat similar ways. Some of the time, they disregard considerations of time, ignore logical contradictions or clashes between what they assert and verifiable aspects of reality; they shift fluidly—madly and maddeningly—from topic to topic, transferring attributes or implications from one thing to another that doesn't deserve it. In this style of thinking, which is what we call primary process, they think in an inappropriately concrete and pictorial way, combining and associating ideas or images in seemingly arbitrary ways or on more trivial bases —like assonance—than one would expect. When thinking has these characteristics, it is often though not always wishful, overweeningly preoccupied with relatively infantile, crude, unsocialized, bodily (in a word, instinctual[2]) passions. These, then, are the main defining characteristics of primary process thinking: when a person thinks in all these ways, we call it "the" primary process.

One needs only to imagine such a state of affairs to realize that it is an ideal conception rather than the description of an empirical possibility. Just as the rational man of the enlightenment is an ideal type never to be encountered, neither is his opposite, the id incarnate. In much of what Freud wrote about these concepts, it is fairly clear that he did not think of them dichotomously, but as defining the extremes of a logical continuum. Any actual thought process, even that of a baby or a deteriorated schizophrenic, has to be located somewhere in between the two poles. Rapaport (1951), Hartmann (1950) and Kris (1952) are quite explicit about this way of viewing primary and secondary process.

[2] I shall use the common term "instinctual" to refer to motives having these characteristics, without implying that I believe Freud's concept of instinct or *Trieb* is actually a useful one; see Holt, 1975b.

Out of the many points that might be made in discussing these concepts, I want to emphasize three.

1. The more primary the thinking, the more wishful it is. That is a shorthand way of referring to several attributes, hinted at above. It seems safe to assume that all thinking is motivated, and a wish is a motive. But that would not be a useful way of trying to define primary process, since it would be far too overinclusive. "Wishful thinking" usually implies what a person does when he lets his desires play too great a role in his assessment of reality. The limits of "too great" remain to be spelled out, of course. We cannot escape from the necessity of using judgment in defining and recognizing the qualities of thinking we call primary. It takes judgment to arrange motives on a scale from the most instinctual—"primitive" and unsocialized—to the most refined and socially acceptable, a necessary operation if we are to use this distinction (the heart of what Hartmann called "neutralization" but which he unfortunately assigned as a qualitative characteristic of an unmeasurable, ineffable psychic energy) in scaling thinking between the extremes of primary and secondary. It is a matter of the kind of wishes, then, *and* how illogical or unrealistic thinking becomes as the person inappropriately speaks or acts as if he is closer to attaining his desires than he actually is.

2. Primary thinking can be recognized, therefore, not only from the thinker's preoccupation with crude wishes but also by certain peculiar *formal* characteristics. These include autistic logic instead of straight thinking, loose and nonsensical types of associative links, and distortion of reality in numerous ways. But the most notable formal deviations of primary thinking were described by Freud as the "mechanisms of the dream work." *Condensation* is a process resulting in the fusion of two or more ideas or images. *Displacement* is a shift of emphasis or interest from one mental content to another (usually a less important content in terms of relevance to conflict or instinctual aims). *Symbolization* is the replacement of one idea or image by another, a concrete visual presentation which may have various formal features in common with what is being symbolized but which disguises the latter's dynamic significance. A person may use any of these devices defensively, since they produce changes that usually conceal the original meanings of the material on which

they exert their effects. Thus, in the formation of dreams, the dream thoughts undergo transformations in ways that make these threatening materials acceptable to the dreamer's superego standards.

The operations of condensation, displacement and symbol-formation are by no means confined to the production of dreams and neurotic symptoms. They are conspicuously present in the language of schizophrenics; indeed, schizophrenia has been described (perhaps too glibly) as a state in which conscious mental life is dominated by the primary process instead of the secondary. Any interference with normal cognition and motivational control may result in the emergence of primary thinking—in reverie states, under the influence of drugs, in slips of the tongue, in febrile deliria, and so forth.

3. The final point I want to underscore about the primary process has to do with humor and other enjoyable sides of life. It is one of humanity's great gifts to be *able* to abandon reality voluntarily for a little while; to shake free from dead literalism, to recombine the old familiar elements into new, imaginative, amusing, or beautiful patterns. Among modern psychoanalysts, Ernst Kris has been particularly interested in artistic creativity and humor. He is well known for his contention that the ego of a mature and healthy person can at times relax, abandon secondary-process standards in a controlled and reversible way, and *use* the freedom and fluidity of the primary process productively; this he calls *regression in the service of the ego* (1952). A person who is not asleep and dreaming may therefore fragment and recombine ideas and images in ways that flout the demands of reality on either of two bases: because he cannot *help* it, due to a temporary or permanent impairment, or because he *wants* to, for fun or for creative purposes, and is able to because he is not too threatened by his unconscious wishes. Thus, the third point is that we find primary thinking in conscious subjects either out of strength or out of weakness. In the former case, it is more likely to appear in a playful or esthetic frame of reference, accompanied by pleasant affect. If, on the other hand, primary thinking breaks through the usual defenses uninvited and unwanted, the subject may feel anxious or threatened and is likely to act defensively.

Most of what Freud had to say in his attempts to account for the properties of dream thinking and his other theorizing about the primary process was couched in terms of psychic energy, which he generally assumed to be responsible for everything that happens in a person's mental and behavioral life. Attempts to clarify his propositions concerning psychic energies, forces, and structures, which Freud called metapsychology, have failed because of their internal inconsistencies, logical fallacies, and failure to square with established facts (Holt, 1975b). As a result, his relatively operational, clinical propositions about primary and secondary process thinking lack the backing of a general theoretical model that enjoys widespread acceptance. Fortunately, they are able to stand on their own merits until such a theory arrives.

Why should the Rorschach test performance lend itself to analysis in terms of primary and secondary processes? If one accepts the idea that thought processes may be arranged in a continuous series from the most primary to the most secondary, we can apply these concepts to *any* sample of mental activity, though we know that anything obviously primary in character is exceptional when we are dealing with people who are not psychiatric patients. Taking the Rorschach, however, is a situation with a number of more or less unique features that favor the emergence of primary modes of cognition. First of all, the subject is called on to produce a series of visual images. Freud thought imagery to be a preferred mode of operation for the primary process; without the requirement (such as the TAT imposes) to produce a connected narrative, there is less demand for organizing and synthesizing and less necessity for secondary-process thinking. Moreover, the ink blots offer complex stimulus configurations, richly enough varied to evoke and support almost any kind of image that may be latent in the viewer's mind, yet without actually and unmistakably representing anything in reality. By releasing the subject from the more stringent of ordinary requirements for logical thought organization, and by sanctioning, as it were, the emergence of any kind of ideational content, the test thus offers a means of assessing both the nature and extent of wishfulness in thinking, and its formal structure as well—the first two points made above about the primary process. We know, however, that subjects react to this test in different ways, and permit themselves different degrees of freedom in their responses. The test thus also offers a means of assessing the third aspect of primary cognition referred to above: the characteristic response of the person to the emergence of primary material into consciousness, or his characteristic defenses against its emergence.

I have found, however, that test records administered in the usual way often leave me in the dark about the person's reaction to the primary-process material emerging in his responses. Only part of the time do the subject's behavior (as noted by the tester) and his verbalizations indicate his inner feelings about what he sees and says. I therefore took up a suggestion of a colleague, Dr. Fred Pine, and added an additional question to the inquiry on each response: "How did you feel about it?" Sometimes it is necessary to expand on this simple question by explaining that the tester is interested in the subject's reactions to each thing that he saw in the blots, whether seeing it was pleasant, unpleasant, or a matter of indifference. Such a direct questioning approach is accepted well by patients and research subjects alike, and it not only yields the information needed for rating the effectiveness of the subject's controls (*DE*, see below) but also often provides data of considerable clinical value. Of course, the answers given cannot always be taken at face value; clinical judgment cannot be eschewed when dealing with the primary process.

The objection might be raised: How can you speak of primary *process* when you have only a *product* to deal with? The point is well taken; but the process is an intervening variable that is not directly observable—we can infer it only from its products. A scoring system thus could either attempt to work with inferences to the hypothetical process (something that is difficult at best and impossible without extensive free associations), or one can stick to the product itself and concentrate on its properties of still retaining the hallmarks of the processes that produced it. I have followed the latter course, hoping by minimizing inference to attain greater reliability and usefulness.

I take it for granted, therefore, that aspects of the primary process are at work during the generation of many responses that are not scorable by the present system. Is this a loss? On the contrary, it is a gain, for theoretically we all use the primary process continually in our unconscious fantasies, and to penetrate to that level would thus not produce individual differences. It is, however, both theoretically and practically valuable to identify the extent to which *communicated products of thought* are allowed to retain the stigmata of their unconscious origins despite the mediating defenses and controls from which they emerge.

THE SCORING SYSTEM

I will not go here into the history and development of the scoring method to be described. They have been reported elsewhere (Holt, 1956; in preparation). The system consists of three groups of scoring categories, corresponding to the three aspects of primary thinking just discussed, and several rating scales which are applied to each response. The first group (Content Variables) has to do with evidences of wishfulness in the content of the test responses; the second (Formal Variables), with deviations in response structure; and the third (Control and Defense Variables) with the subject's reaction to the emergence of material in either of the first two categories. The rating scales deal mainly with over-all aspects of the response, and include attempts to summarize and integrate the other scores.

Before presenting the scoring system in detail, I should like to make several points about the method as a whole. First, the system is intended as a research tool, not as a clinical instrument, and is better suited for use with groups of subjects rather than for individual analysis. The scoring is too cumbersome and time-consuming for routine clinical use. Nevertheless, it has been applied with illuminating results to some individual case analyses (see, for example, Silverman, 1965) and many clinicians report that having learned the scoring system permanently affects their clinical use of the Rorschach for the better.

Second, the system is not intended to supplant existing scoring, but to supplement it. Rorschach responses are so rich and multi-dimensional that many noncompeting systems may usefully be applied to them, depending on one's interests and purposes.

Third, the system was constructed mainly on the basis of records taken from adults—some in treatment and some not, but mostly well-educated and of a relatively high socio-economic level. Moreover, these subjects took the test with the awareness that they were being judged for a serious purpose—diagnosis, acceptance into professional training, or research. I have no solid data on the limits of the system's applicability, either to subjects of different backgrounds or to subjects who take the test in a different setting. It has been applied to Rorschachs from nursery-school children on up to those from the aged, from persons suffering from all kinds of pathology, and from people in a variety of cultures, speaking a good many different languages. It is very hard to say how far it retains its validity in such extensions. My impression is that the more a subject differs from the above-described reference group on whose Rorschachs it was based, the more problematic the interpretation of findings becomes. Some categories were added and some other, minor changes were made as a result of the attempts to score children's records (in particular, those of Safin, 1974), but a number of real difficulties in such application remain.

Fourth, there are no categories specifically designed to measure secondary-process thinking. In effect, we are concentrating on the lower portion of the primary-secondary continuum, leaving most of the secondary part of it undifferentiated. Partly the decision was one of interest, partly it is attributable to the relative unsuitability of the Rorschach as a test of the secondary process. For a differentiated account of secondary-process functioning, we must look to multi-dimensional tests of abilities and adaptiveness, intelligence tests like those of David Wechsler and J. P. Guilford, and to the work of Jean Piaget. Though secondary-process operations are involved in the control and defense categories we score, the emphasis is not on getting "measures" of the secondary process but on estimating the efficiency of these operations in coping with the primary-process aspects of responses. Thereby we are enabled to distinguish with some success between maladaptive and adaptive regression (regression in the service of the ego).

I have said nothing so far about the relation of the ideational and structural characteristics of primary thinking, nor is this a question I am prepared to answer at this time. It may be the encouragement given by the test to abandon modes of thinking grounded in physical reality that facilitates the emergence of wish-centered ideation, but it may also be that the urgency of the wishes itself leads to structural distortion of responses. The fact that responses with (apparently) neutral content do sometimes contain formal deviations suggests, however, that the latter are caused by a weakening of perceptual-organizing functions, induced by the structure of the test. In some instances, it is true, deviations in each category occur together, but this is by no means always the case. The fact of such differences poses some interesting questions about the nature of primary thinking and its relation to personality structure, questions I hope may be approached through the application of the present scoring method.

CONTENT VARIABLES

I have made the assumption that *all* thought and perception are organized to some extent by wishes as well as by the given requiredness of external reality and the logical structure of ideas. What is at issue, thus, is not whether a thought process involves wishes or not, but the *extent* and the manner in which motives are involved in cognition.

The problem of scoring Rorschach content for primary process becomes then a question of establishing criteria by which the degree of wishfulness may be identified. One asks first whether any relevance to the kinds of motives considered instinctual by Freudian analysts can be seen in a given response. Since taking the test is not a situation in which there can be any realistic striving for direct gratification of a basic motive, I assume that any libidinal or aggressive imagery that occurs is not part of normally goal-oriented behavior but rather evidence that the response is inappropriately wishful.[3]

Content variables are divided into two major groups, depending on whether the content of the implied wishes is libidinal or aggressive. Once one abandons Freud's dual instinct theory, as I have done since the system was first devised, there is no necessity to stick to just these divisions; and surely a good case can be made for including manifestations of passive and dependent wishes without oral coloring, but I have not done so. My impression is that they are not particularly frequent in Rorschach responses anyway, so ignoring them makes little practical difference.

---

[3]Note that the special test-taking situation gives the Rorschach an advantage over a sample of cognitive functioning in a real-life situation. In the latter, wish-relevant imagery does not necessarily indicate primary process, but is, in fact, necessary for the realistic gratification of needs—the basic function of the secondary process. In the test situation, the subject is, of course, motivated (as, for example, by the desire to please the examiner, to show off, to get out of the hospital, etc.), but in terms of the Freudian theory of motivation, these needs are rather remote derivatives of the two basic instincts, which are not *directly* gratified thereby.

Both of these subdivisions have two main sections, noted as "Level 1" and "Level 2." These represent two levels of closeness to the primary-process pole, as defined by several criteria. One of these has to do with a "primitive-civilized" dimension: the more the type of motivational expression described or implied is socialized and discussion of it is appropriate to communication between strangers in a professional situation, the more the thinking concerned is felt to be secondary; we then score Level 2 (if anything). Conversely, the more direct, intense, or blatant the wish, the closer the response is to the primary process; the score given is Level 1. In a sense, we have here a control distinction built into the content scoring.

A second criterion has to do with the degree to which the response focuses on the body, and the erogenous zone or organ most directly involved. In general, percepts of isolated, libidinally-relevant organs are scored Level 1, while mention of the organ among other parts of a body (or of a face) usually earns no more than a Level 2 score.

In addition, Level 1 includes a good many pathological fantasies, which differ from simple, direct references to the form of gratification in question in that their "blatancy" is probably a function of defensive exaggeration.

The set of content scores, as it stands, represents a compromise between what I thought, on theoretical grounds, should be included and what I found, on the basis of several groups of records, had to be included. It is one of several ways of classification that were considered and tried out on a group of cases. I make no claim for its completeness, and consider it still open to revision.

It will be seen that in the first portion—libidinal responses— emphasis seems to have been put on bodily channels of expression rather than on psychological derivatives: thus, "mouth" rather than "helplessness." This is not because we consider the first more primary, but because the ink blots lend themselves more readily to images of concrete objects than to descriptions of feeling states, and because the latter raise many theoretical problems. I have not entirely neglected such wishes, but it will be noted that I have not included all types of content that might be used by the clinician in drawing inferences about motivation. I have tried, as much as possible, to stay close to the most obvious kinds of scorable content and to reduce the numbers of inferences necessary for the scorer.

TABLE 11.1

Summary of Primary- and Secondary-Process Variables

Content Variables

L. *Libidinal*
    L 1. Level 1—*L* 2. Level 2
       O. Oral receptive
       O-Ag. Oral aggressive
       A. Anal
       S. Sexual (phallic-genital)
       E-V. Exhibitionistic-voyeuristic
       H. Homosexual (sexual ambiguity)
       M. Miscellaneous libidinal
Ag. *Aggressive*
    Ag 1. Level 1—*Ag* 2. Level 2
       A. Attack (sadistic aggression)
       V. Victim of aggression (masochistic)
       R. Results of aggression

Formal Variables
(Formal Aspects of Content)

C. *Condensation*
    C-ctm 1. Contamination (fusion of two separate percepts)
    C-ctgn 1. Contagion
    C-int 1. Interpenetration
    C-co 1 or 2. Composition
    C-a-c 2. Arbitrary combinations of separate percepts
    C-arb
       1. Arbitrary combination of color and form
       2. Rationalized inappropriate color
D. *Displacement*
    D-chain 1. Chain association
    D-dist 2. Distant association
    D-clang
       1. Clang association
       2. Puns and malapropisms
    D-fig 2. Figures of speech
    D-time 2. Displacement in time
Sym. *Explicit Symbolism*
    Sym-C Color or shading symbolism
       1. idiosyncratic
       2. conventional
    Sym-S 1. Spatial symbolism
    Sym-I Image symbolism
       1. idiosyncratic
       2. conventional

TABLE 11.1 (Continued)

Ctr. Contradiction
　　　Ctr-A 1. Affective contradiction
　　　Ctr-L 1. Logical contradiction
　　　Ctr-R 1 or 2. Serious or less serious contradiction of reality
V. Verbalization Scores
　　　V-I 1. Verbal incoherence
　　　V-C 1. Verbal condensations
　　　V-Q 1. Queer verbalizations
　　　V-P 2. Peculiar verbalizations
　　　V-S 2. Verbal slips
Miscellaneous Distortion of Thought and Perception
　　　Au Lg 1. Autistic logic
　　　M L 1. Memory loosening
　　　Intr 1. Intrusion of irrelevancy
　　　Un Rel 1. Unrealistic relationships
　　　Trans 1. Fluid transformation of percept
　　　S-R 1. Self-reference
　　　Au El 1 or 2. Autistic elaboration
　　　Impr 2. Impressionistic response
　　　Do 2. Fragmentation
　　　F-msc 1 or 2. Miscellaneous formal deviations

Control and Defense Variables

R. Remoteness
　　　R-min. Minimal remoteness
　　　R-eth. Remoteness—ethnic
　　　R-an. Remoteness—animal (ego syntonic)
　　　R-(an). Remoteness—animal (ego-alien)
　　　R-pl. Remoteness—plant
　　　R-ia. Remoteness—inanimate
　　　R-dep+. Remoteness—depiction
　　　R-geo+. Remoteness—geographic
　　　R-time(+). Remoteness in time
　　　R-fic s(+). Remoteness, fictional—specific
　　　R-fic n(+). Remoteness, fictional—non-specific
　　　R-rel(+). Remoteness—religious
　　　R-fan(+). Remoteness—fantasy
　　　R-fig(+). Remoteness—figurative
　　　R-cond. Remoteness—conditional
Cx. Context
　　　Cx-C(+). Cultural context
　　　Cx-E(+). Esthetic context
　　　Cx-I(+). Intellectual context
　　　Cx-H(+). Humorous context

TABLE 11.1 (Continued)

Postponing Strategies
    Del. Delay
    Blkg. Blocking
Miscellaneous (Mostly Pathological) Defenses
    Refl(+). Reflection
    Eu. Euphemism
    Vulg. Vulgarity of verbalization
    Mod+. Adaptive modification of response
    Ratn(+). Rationalization
    Neg(+). Negation
    Minz. Minimization
    Cphb−. Counterphobic defense
    Self-D−. Self-deprecation
    Rep−. Repudiation or disavowal of a response
    Va−. Vagueness of percept or communication
    Prj−. Projection
    Obs−. Obsessional defense
    Iso−. Isolation
    Eva−. Evasiveness and avoidance
    Imp−. Impotence
    S. Sequence; sequence changes—alternation of scorable and unscorable, Level-1 and Level-2 responses: *S-C* 1-0, *S-C* 1-2, *S-C* 2-0, *S-C* 2-0.
O. Overtness
    O-beh. Overtness—behavioral
    O-vbl. Overtness—verbal
    O-exp. Overtness—experiential
    O-pot. Overtness—potential
General Ratings of Total Response
    FL. Form Level of Response
    DD. Demand for Defense
    DE. Effectiveness of Defense

A word about the symbols used to designate the catgories: Just as it is convenient to say FC^4 instead of writing out form-color, so, too, the scoring categories introduced here need a set of convenient symbols for use in scoring. Abbreviated designations appear in the heading along with each category name. The numbers 1 and 2 refer to Levels 1 and 2; the letters are abbreviations of key words in the category name. Thus, *L 1 O* means Libidinal content, Level 1, Oral; *Ag 2 R* means Aggressive content, Level 2, Results of hostile or destructive action. In the Formal categories, *C* (except in *Sym-C* 1, color symbolism) stands for Condensation (*V-C* 1 = Verbal Condensation, Level 1; *C-co* 1 = Condensation, composite image, Level 1). The abbreviations for Control and Defense categories are (I hope) self-explanatory, except for the Sequence variables: *S C* 2-0 means Sequence, Change of percept from Level 2 to unscorable (no primary process). All of the scores have been summarized for ready reference in Table 10.1.

Libidinal Content[5]

Level 1 (crude, direct, "primitive" content)

L 1 O. Oral receptive: Mouth, breasts—score when seen in isolation; sucking; famine; vomit.

L 1 O-Ag. Oral aggressive: Teeth, jaws—score when seen in isolation; cannibalism; castrative or sadistic biting; parasites.

L 1 A. Anal: Buttocks—score when seen in isolation or with other Level 1 content; feces or other excretory reference; hemorrhoids.

L 1 S. Sexual: Genitalia; indirect references to sexual organs are scored except for those of plants ("phallic symbol"); ejaculation; sexual acts; any reference to illegal or illicit intercourse.

L 1 E-V. Exhibitionistic-voyeuristic: Nudity; pornography; explicit voyeurism or exhibiting genitals.

L 1 H. Homosexual; Sexual ambiguity: Overt homosexual acts; less blatant homsexual acts ("two men kissing"); ambiguity of sex of genitalia; hermaphrodites.

---

[4] For explanation of standard scoring symbols, see Appendix, pp. 609 ff. [Editor].

[5] This is a condensed version of the actual *Scoring Manual*. I want to thank Ms. Carlan Robinson for her help in preparing this condensed version. For reasons of space, most examples of scored responses and some explanatory material have been omitted. The same is true for the presentation of the formal, control, and defense portions of the scoring system.

L 1 M. Miscellaneous: Menstruation; birth process; contraceptives; urine.

Level 2 (indirect, controlled, "socialized" wishful content)

L 2 O. Oral receptive: Breasts; mouth—score when seen as part of person or animal and emphasized; stomach; kissing; any reference to use of alcohol or drugs ("drunks"; "joint of grass"); pigs; smoking; eating or drinking, active attempts to get food; cooking; food or drink; containers, utensils for food or drink; hunger; persons with oral identity or social role.

L 2 O-Ag. Oral aggressive: Poison; biting; teeth, jaws, beak —when seen as part of organism and emphasized; animals feared because of their biting; verbal aggression; spitting.

L 2 A. Anal: Buttocks or corresponding region—when seen as part of person or animal; intestines; toilet; tail of animal—when seen in isolation or emphasized; disgust; dirt; suppository.

L 2 S. Sexual: Breasts; kissing; socialized or aim-inhibited references to implicitly genital sexuality; virginity; symbols of romance; technical names for sexual organs of flowers; abstract reference to genitality; woman's legs (given by a man).

L 2 E-V. Exhibitionistic-voyeuristic: Underwear, partial nudity; peering, leering; looking emphasized; eyes in isolation or emphasized; unusual views; stage performing or performers; masks; concealment; blind person.

Do not score: References to eyes as vehicle of hostility or disapproval (score *Ag 2 A*).

L 2 H. Sexual ambiguity; homosexual: Transvestism; latent or sublimated homosexual acts; uncertainty about sex; contradictory sexual descriptions.

L 2 M. Miscellaneous: Internal sexual anatomy; embryo; fetus; pregnancy; urinary anatomy; narcissism.

Aggressive Content

My co-workers and I began the scoring of aggressive content somewhat uneasily accepting the usual psychoanalytic instinct theory even though we never were happy with the notion of a death instinct. Today the drive conception itself seems highly inappropriate to the phenomena of rage, hostility, cruelty, and aggressiveness, particularly the assumption (backed up by few if any data) that there is an upwelling, inner, aggressive impulse that must in some way be "discharged." I think it quite possible that seeing a dangerous wild beast in a Rorschach blot can indicate that the respondent harbors unexpressed anger, but it seems equally plausible that such a response indicates persisting fear or anxiety, such as may occur as the residue of a traumatic fright. Until research demonstrates some way of differentiating two (or more) classes of responses corresponding to different motivations, we shall have to continue to classify them all under "aggressive content," with the preceding caveat.

Besides the basic Level 1–Level 2 distinction, aggressive content is subdivided into three types: *attacks*, *victims*, and *results* of aggression. They may be viewed as three points on the active–passive dimension, *attack* being sadistic in orientation, *victim* being masochistic, and *results* even more so logically, though perhaps not psychologically. If two persons or animals are seen in some kind of struggle with no clear indication that one is seen as aggressor and the other as recipient, score under *attack*; but in a response like the following, where both roles are depicted, score both *Ag 2 A* and *Ag 2 V*: "A bully hitting a terrified child."

Level 1 (murderous or palpably sadomasochistic aggression)

Ag 1 A. Attack (Sadistic Aggression): Vivid sadistic fantasies; primitive annihilation of persons or animals; murder, even if not sadistically elaborated; torture.

Ag 1 V. Victim of Aggression (Masochistic): Castration or explicitly sexual masochism; extreme victimization; nightmarish helplessness; suicide.

Ag 1 R. Results of Aggression: Aftermath of sadistic, lethal action; decayed or putrified flesh; mutilated persons or animals; mutilated object or plant when the response implies the effects of really ferocious action.

Level 2 (hostility or aggression of a socially tolerated kind—usually non-lethal)

Ag 2 A. Attack: Explosions, manifestations of violent symbolic anal expulsion; fire; fighting, physical conflict; hostile acts that are not reciprocated or where the victim is not specified; volcano; frightening creatures of childhood fairy tale and fantasy; skeletons in a threatening context; persons or animals about to attack; frightening or potentially dangerous people or animals ("a lion"); threatening or potentially dangerous parts of animals or people ("claws"); personifications of the punishing superego in religion and mythology ("the devil"); abstract dangers or concepts of violence ("the inferno;" "war signal"); weapons, other threatening or frightening objects; anger, hostile affects and facial expressions; crime and criminals.

Ag 2 V. Victim of Aggression (of the kind scored Level 2): People or animals in pain, suffering, illness; frightened or threatened persons or animals; figures or objects in states of precarious balance; defensive objects or activities.

Ag 2 R. Results of Aggression: Injured persons or animals; deformed persons or animals, monsters in the medical sense; persons or animals with parts missing; blood; death, dead persons or animals with no ill will involved; decayed or rotten plants or objects; aftermath of fires, explosions (including "destruction"); dead or injured plants or parts of plants; broken objects.

FORMAL VARIABLES

Primary-process thinking was first defined in terms of certain formal characteristics. In considering how these might appear in responses to the Rorschach, Joan Havel (who was my main collaborator in this part of the work) and I thought first of the formal characteristics of dreams—condensation, displacement, and symbolization. But there is obviously a considerable difference between Rorschach thinking and dream thinking. The Rorschach, being anchored in consciousness, provides only a very crude equivalent of the dream process. We thus had to derive the scoring categories from the unique situation presented by the test. The formal categories refer both to the perceptual organization of a given response and to the thought process that underlies giving it. They are an attempt to measure deviations from the logical, orderly thinking grounded in experience with the real world that characterizes the secondary process. Let me emphasize again that these categories should not be taken evaluatively. Although some of them we have learned to recognize as clearly pathological (for example, the contamination response), this was not the basis for their inclusion here. The abbreviations indicate the classification of each category as Level 1 or Level 2. These formal variables represent formal aspects of content rather than the formal, perceptual-structural scores of location and determinants with which they should not be confused. Note, however, that they include a couple of the latter.

C. Condensation

C-ctm 1. *Contamination* (fusion of two separate percepts): Overlapping images of separate objects, persons, etc., are fused into a single percept; fusion of two mutually exclusive views of the same thing (often, both external and internal views of a body).

C-ctgn 1. *Contagion:* Loss of boundary between self and percept ("the man looks sad. I feel like crying when I see that—please take it away").

C-int 1. *Interpenetration:* Partial fusion of two separate percepts, which may be seen in the same area, the S unable to decide between them; response may reflect a weak but conceivable compromise between incompatible percepts; preference for one percept is expressed but S is unable to relinquish the other; interpenetration of ideas without image-fusion.

C-co 1. *Composition* (Level 1): Impossible fusions, hybrid organism; improbable fusions ("a two-headed lobster"); percept of a face with parts organized in an unrealistic way.

C-co 2. *Composition* (Level 2): Composite images that actually exist in mythology, art, folklore; realistic fusions of separate organisms ("Siamese twins").

C-a-c 2. *Arbitrary combinations of separate percepts:* Two separate but contiguous percepts are placed in some kind of meaning relationship that violates reality. Responses that might be acceptable if kept separate are reported as being in impossible, or implausible but possible, combinations. The first includes those that violate the laws of physical reality; the second violates reality in a less absolute sense, since it is to be scored for combinations that could conceivably occur, though they are *unlikely* to.

There are three principal types of *impossible combinations*: (1) discrepancy in size; (2) putting together things that do not occur together in reality; (3) mixing natural and supernatural frames of reference. Also scored here are arbitrary linkages, in which the underlying assumption seems to be: Two areas of the blot are touching, therefore they cannot be separated and the description of what they represent must take this relationship into account ("women, sort of stuck together"—card VII—attached at lower center; "some sort of flying animal—held back by this mass here, because it seems attached" —card VI—animal is top detail, mass is rest of card).

C-arb 1. *Arbitrary combination of color and form:* Score whether given without criticism or recognition of incongruity ("red bears"), or given with spontaneous criticism or negation ("a sheep —I don't know why it should be green, but it is"). If color named is not particularly inappropriate to the concept, but the shade of that color in the blot is unrealistic ("red fox" for popular animal on card VIII), score *weak*.

C-arb 2. *Rationalized inappropriate color:* S mentions a color that is unnatural for the percept described, even though rationalized more or less convincingly ("a man with pink paint all over his head" —card IX, bottom *D*).

D. Displacement

D-chain 1. *Chain Association:* Fluid associative thinking, going from one idea to another without the overall guidance of an organizing set or anticipation.

D-dist 2. *Distant Association:* Nonsense, or inappropriate elaboration; S strays off the point according to some loose principle other than clang association.

D-clang 1. *Clang Association:* Assonance is used to get from one idea to another.

D-clang 2. *Puns and Malapropisms:* Substitution of one word by another of similar sound, or by a homonym, often with humorous intent (in which case score *Cx-H*).

D-fig 2. *Figures of Speech:* Metaphor, hyperbole, or inappropriate simile, but score only if idiosyncratic or unusual enough to attract notice.

D-time 2. *Displacement in Time:* Inappropriate or impossible introduction of an attribute, activity, etc. from a different era of time than the one implied by the rest of the response ("two knights, taking off their helmets for a cigarette").

Sym. Explicit Symbolism

Sym-C 1. *Color or Shading Symbolism, Idiosyncratic:* The term "symbol" must be used, or a close synonym ("the red denotes strength towards evil"); also, physiognomic or synaesthetic responses ("a concert—the colorfulness and weirdness"—card X, *W*).

Sym-C 2. *Color or Shading Symbolism, Conventional:* Stereotyped conventional meanings of color ("green with envy").

Sym-S 1. *Spatial Symbolism:* Use of spatial relations between blot areas to stand for an abstract idea or attribute that is not directly pictured.

Sym-I 1. *Image Symbolism, Idiosyncratic:* Use of an idiosyncratic concrete image to stand for an abstract idea ("the spots outside represent thoughts in his head").

Sym-I 2. *Image Symbolism, Conventional:* The symbolic equivalence is cited by S, not made up by him ("explosion—could represent anger").

Ctr. Contradiction

Ctr-A 1. *Affective Contradiction:* S indicates that he experiences contradictory affects simultaneously; affective fluidity; inappropriate affect ("Fu Manchu—that's pretty, he's disemboweled himself").

Ctr-L 1. *Logical Contradiction:* Mutually incompatible qualities, activities, or attributes are assigned to a single percept; S both asserts and denies something about blot or response, contradicting himself.

Ctr-R 1. *Contradiction of Reality* (serious): Deliberate molding of the blot's reality ("I make the picture into what I want it to be —it looks sunny but I want it to be cloudy, so I see it that way").

Ctr-R 2. *Contradiction of Reality* (less serious): People or animals are seen with impossible, unlikely, or inappropriate attributes or activities ("headless man conducting an orchestra;" "mice with a pensive look"); S distorts the reality of the blot by describing achromatic color as chromatic ("blue water . . . subtle green of the moss" —card VI).

V. Verbalization Scores

V-I 1. *Verbal Incoherence:* The course of thought is extremely autistic, resulting in a use of words that fails to communicate and becomes incoherent ("a bundle of love, how do you like that for an answer, wrapped up in endearing young charms—dementia praecox").

V-C 1. *Verbal Condensations:* Portmanteau words or phrases in which the condensed elements are discernible; neologisms in which condensation is not evident ("chest-monks"; "a batterfly").

V-Q 1. *Queer Verbalizations:* Psychotic distortions of usage, failure to maintain appropriate set ("a twat—I don't get the same sensation as if it were real"; "a crab, I was hoping for an octopus").

V-P 2. *Peculiar Verbalizations:* Linguistic usage that is autistic enough to sound odd although the meaning may be quickly understood ("part of a lady's vagina"; "a fine dog—noblest of all dogs").

V-S 2. *Verbal Slips:* Slips of the tongue (whether noticed and self-corrected or not).

Miscellaneous Distortion of Thought and Perception

Au Lg 1. *Autistic Logic:* Responses cast in a fallacious syllogistic form ("everything's so small it must be the insectual kind of thing;" "snakes." [How much of the card represents the snakes?] I don't know, because when they coil around they're endless"); autistic aspect of the reasoning may result from a blending of both concrete and abstract meanings of words; reasoning on a positional basis (*Po* responses); wild generalization or a jumping to conclusions about the identity of a larger unity on the sole basis of a minor part (*DW* responses).

M L 1. *Memory Loosening:* A factual error made by someone who can be presumed to know the correct information ("the opening of the vagina into the stomach").

Intr 1. *Intrusion of Irrelevancy:* An irrelevant idea suddenly inserted into the record ("a vampire bat. What the hell is my I.Q.?"); S replies tangentially and unresponsively ("[What made it look like fur?] Here are four wonderful faces").

Un Rel 1. *Unrealistic Relationships:* S sees an unrealistic relationship between blots ("the butterfly of the previous picture again"); S sees an unrealistic relationship between elements of one card, other than the kind scored in *C-a-c* 2.

Trans 1. *Fluid Transformation of Percept:* S describes an experience in which one thing turns into another under his very eyes, so to speak.

S-R 1. *Self-Reference* (of a magically unrealistic kind): Indications that S feels the test or the thing seen has reference to him personally ("an arrow being shot at me").

Au El 1. *Autistic Elaboration* (Level 1): The presence of thematic, often dream-like fantasying; impossible types of fantastic material ("Aztec figure—stone-like, an idol figure . . . hips, legs, some sort of symbol—sexual, I guess I'd say vagina . . . here a dinosaur figure—now they're fighting over this woman, because of the sexual symbols—horrible—frightened—and she can't talk, her mouth is closed").

Au El 2. *Autistic Elaboration* (Level 2): Inappropriately thematic elaboration that does not become bizarrely unrealistic ("two bunnies, looking at each other. They've noticed each other and turned their heads to look each other up and down, as if to say, 'Well, who are *you*?' And soon they'll scamper on about their business, wondering where the other came from").

Impr 2. *Impressionistic Response:* The response is given as "a feeling," or "an impression"; abstract movement responses.

Do 2. *Fragmentation:* Only a part is reported where most Ss see a whole percept (Rorschach's "oligophrenic detail").

F-msc 1 or 2. *Miscellaneous Formal Deviations* (Level 1 and Level 2): Perseveration (Level 1), the third appearance and subsequent ones of essentially the same content *and* poor form level; taking the blot as reality (Level 1); physiognomic response (Level 1) to a property of the blot other than color ("it looks like a protocol, or an announcement, because it has a flourish to its structure").

CONTROL AND DEFENSE VARIABLES

The following categories are scored only in conjunction with responses that have received scores on either content or formal variables. The use of these categories seems to represent an attempt on the part of the subject to contain the material, implying some awareness (not necessarily conscious) that the response needs to be justified or defended against (see *DD*, below). Some of these ways are obviously more satisfactory than others: thus, the control implied by a "successful introspection" or an "esthetic context" score seems more adequate than that involved in "repudiation" or "projection"; plus or minus signs are added accordingly.

R. Remoteness

This group of categories resulted from an effort to apply to the Rorschach essentially the same concept that Tomkins introduced for the TAT (1947, pp. 78-82). When an unacceptable impulse is expressed in a response, it may be made more acceptable if S puts distance between himself and the response by making the latter remote in time, place, person, or level of reality. An R-score is given to every response for which a primary-process content score has been recorded. In addition, any R-score from R-geo on *may* be scored for formally deviant responses when the remoteness has any relevance to the formal quality scored.

R-min. Minimal Remoteness: The response involves *persons* (or parts of persons) *here* and *now*, implicitly or explicitly *existing* in reality. Assume that time, place, etc., are close unless it is stated or clearly implied otherwise. In addition, "food," "feces," "blood" and other human bodily products are all scored *R-min* unless it is clear from context that they are animal.

One or more of the following (*R-eth* through *R-cond*) may be scored for any one response.

R-eth. Remoteness—Ethnic: A person in the response is different from S in ethnic group.

R-an. Remoteness—Animal (ego syntonic): Actors (main figures in responses) are non-human mammals; interaction between human and mammals when the impulse is attributed to the animal.

R-(an). Remoteness—Animal (ego-alien): Actors are sub-mammalian; include also bats and birds (see Linton, 1954).

R-pl. Remoteness—Plant: Main figure is a plant of any type, including bacteria ("burnt tree stump").

R-ia. Remoteness—Inanimate: Neither persons nor animals involved; inanimate objects or abstractions; inanimate actions ("explosion"; "bell").

R-dep+. Remoteness—Depiction: Actor is seen as *depicted* in a painting, drawing, sculpture, etc. (Note: This and some other categories have plus signs because of empirical findings that they are associated with various adaptive attributes of personality.)

R-geo+. Remoteness—Geographic: Explicit geographical remoteness; persons, objects, etc., explicitly put at a distance ("African cannibals"; "spacemen fighting on Jupiter").

Each of the following six categories is scored with a plus sign when appropriately used; without, when inappropriately used.

R-time. Remoteness in Time (past or future): ("torturing of the Inquisition"—*R-time+*).

R-fic s. Remoteness, Fictional—Specific: Reference to a specific fictional character, animal, or object ("Mephistopheles", "the Inferno"—both *R-fic s+*).

R-fic n. Remoteness, Fictional—Non-specific: Reference to non-specific characters or objects from fiction ("ghost"; "Wotan's magic fire"—both *R-fic n+*).

R-rel. Remoteness, Religious: Religious character or context, from current world religions; ancient Greek deities are *R-fic*.

R fan. Remoteness, Fantasy: Characters or context are from dream or explicit fantasy ("frightening figures out of a nightmare").

R-fig. Remoteness, Figurative: Use of figures of speech ("Kentucky—it has that carrot-like shape"—*L 2 O, R-fig+*).

R-cond. Remoteness, Conditional: When primary process is in a conditional part of a statement, or when the whole statement is unusually tentative and "iffy" ("he'll get well again, unless he dies of starvation"; "it might look like a vagina if I stretched my imagination").

Cx. Context

This kind of score refers to the setting in which the response is presented and by which the S presumably attempts to "explain away" or make more acceptable the primary-process aspect of his response. Four kinds of context are distinguished below. They are scored as being either successful (+) or not in dealing with the content or formal element involved in the response. A given context is considered successful when the explanation or justification it provides for the response is sufficient to cover its deviant elements and to make the total response acceptable as a communication. It is considered unsuccessful when it only partly explains these elements or when it is essentially irrelevant to their presence in the response, or when it entails forcing or straining after control.

Cx-C. Cultural Context: Reference to a ritual, custom, mythology, occupational role or other social reality ("witches dancing around a fire, at Halloween"; "they [figures on card III] have beak-like mouths, the way that African tribe does"—both +).

Cx-E. Esthetic Context: Reference to one of the arts ("series of paints squeezed on the card, like a pallette"—*Cx E*, without +, because the reference is not convincing).

Cx-I. Intellectual Context: Reference to scientific, technological, or professional fact or knowledge. Terminology should have at least a slight technical or intellectual flavor ("a dissection of the spinal cord"; "prostate and *vas deferens*").

Cx-H. Humorous Context: Humorous and fanciful elaboration of material (*Cx-H+*: "Two people, with both male and female organs —guess you could say they're ambisextrous;" *Cx-H*: "Blackboard that hasn't been cleaned properly—some kid running out of paint, smudging everything up [laughs]").

Postponing Strategies

Del. Delay: The first emergence of the particular aspect of primary process being scored is in the inquiry, with no prior hint in the original response. Score also if the whole response is given only as an additional during inquiry, or if there is a considerable interval of time between the first enunciation of the response and the appearance of the scored primary process.

Blkg. Blocking: Responses that occur only after two minutes or more of vain effort, usually accompanied by protests and complaints, and those that occur only on readministration when S had initially rejected the card.

Miscellaneous (Mostly Pathological) Defenses

Refl. Reflection: Attitude of self-observation or criticism, expressed in two main ways: introspection ("I've had two impressions which are quite contradictory, but the second seems to be dominant, so I'll mention it first"); and criticism of response ("*it isn't sensible* to think the penis is on top of the woman, but it looks like it"). Both exist in successful forms, like the examples just given (+) and unsuccessful variants (no sign added).

Eu. Euphemism: The substitution of a "genteel" or roundabout word for a direct one ("a man's private parts").

Vulg. Vulgarity of Verbalization: Crude, shocking slang where neutral terms are standard and technical ones are often used.

Mod+. Adaptive Modification of Response: S begins by giving a response with scorable primary process, and then edits or modulates it so that in the end the primary process has moved from Level 1 to Level 2, or from either of these levels to unscorable ("men with breasts—no, projecting lapels").

Ratn. Rationalization: S begins a response with an instinctual content or formal bizarreness but then adds details that he hopes make it more acceptable or plausible, although the level of the scorable material is not changed thereby ("a woman dressed in only a corset, being pulled in opposite directions by two men. It's a satirical dance—she's fat and dowdy but is pretending to be in danger of assault from these dashing, cloaked figures"). A + may be added if the effort succeeds.

Neg. Negation: Conscious appearance of an idea with a simultaneous denial of its existence or applicability. Usually, the second aspect is presented in negative form: "Two animals, but not hateful." Or S may attribute "good" qualities to something threatening that slipped by his defenses, trying to decontaminate or purify it ("a lion —a nice, gentle one"). Sometimes the negation of an impulse is built right into the response in such an integral way that it must be considered a successful defense, in which case score *Neg+* ("mask"; "virgin").

Minz. Minimization: Under this heading fall attempts to control (chiefly content) deviations by two main devices: seeing them in tiny areas (as small as the "arrowhead" *Dd* on card II or smaller), and in the concept itself, introducing modifications or qualifications that have the effect of making the threat a literally small one ("a *baby's* arm and fist"; "a lion *cub*").

Cphb–. Counterphobic Defense: Mastering anxiety by images of attacking or doing daring things in the situations where one is most afraid; belittling phobic images or poking fun at them.

Self-D–. Self-Deprecation: S criticizes himself in an inappropriate way, in conjunction with a response containing primary process ("I must be crazy to see things like that").

Rep–. Repudiation or Disavowal of a Response: Attempts to retract an entire response or to deny that it was ever given ("penis —no, no, don't write that down, it really looks like a snake instead"; "two cloaked figures, holding knives"; in inquiry, S cannot find knives, and finally says: "I couldn't have said knives, there aren't any there").

Va–. Vagueness of Percept or Communication: S complains along with or after giving a response that he does not really see it or sees it indistinctly; language used in a vague, fragmented, fluid, or otherwise defective way as an apparent defense against primary process material.

Prj–. Projection: Projection of responsibility for the response; extreme rejection of response, test, or experimenter ("if it's supposed to be a sex organ I fail to see it"—also *Neg;* "that's completely non-dimensional, idiotic, stupid!").

Obs–. Obsessional Defense: Any of the classical obsessive-compulsive defenses if clearly relevant to the primary-process aspect, or more prominent in the response in question than in non-scored responses; it must be a relatively decompensated, maladaptive form of an obsessional defense: doubting, vacillation, obsessional "worrying" of a percept, or indecision about it. Score if there is the equivalent of at least two waverings between possibilities ("should I try for more responses or should I stop here? I can give you more, but maybe you're getting tired"; "two men—perhaps waiters bringing a tray, but that isn't a very good tray—they could be 18th-century dandies bowing to each other, or even cowboys, with those high-heeled boots, but then that wouldn't account for this business" —breast area; card III).

Iso–. Isolation: Decompensated or maladaptive manifestations of isolation; affective deadness or frozenness; ideas or percepts ordinarily experienced as related are seen as separated.

Eva–. Evasiveness and Avoidance: Slippery attempts to evade examiner's questions; refusal to commit oneself; manifestations of the escape form of avoidance ("couple of heads [?] heads of nothing, heads of skeletons—heads of anything").

Imp —. *Impotence:* Inability to explain a response when asked by examiner.

S. Sequence: Ability to use primary process from time to time, interspersing it with more neutral secondary process material. Alternation of scorable and unscorable responses; alternation of Level-1 and Level-2 responses. For example, when a Level-1 or Level-2 response is followed by a neutral one, the former is scored, respectively, either *S C* 1-0 or *S C* 2-0; when a Level-1 response is followed by a Level-2 response, the former is scored *S C* 1-2.

O. Overtness

In part an elaboration of a distinction formerly made between *potential* and *active* types of aggression, these categories also incorporate the distinctions introduced by Tomkins (1947, p. 30f.) under the heading of "*level* . . . the plane of psychological function involved."

O-beh. Overtness—Behavioral: Motivations expressed in terms of behavioral action ("animals fighting"; "people kissing").

O-vbl. Overtness—Verbal: Verbal statements of intention, desire, or emotion attributed to figures ("two gossips quarreling"; ". . . this one says, 'let's make out' ").

O-exp. Overtness—Experiential: Motivations expressed as wish, longing, feeling, sensation, thoughts, or emotion ("hungry animal"; "angry face"; ". . . he worships her from afar").

O-pot. Overtness—Potential: The motive is expressed only as a potentiality ("animals, poised to leap at each other's throats").

GENERAL RATINGS OF TOTAL RESPONSE[6]

Form Level Scoring

The first column on the scoring sheet after the identification of response by card and number is for the form level symbol, which must be given to each response. We follow the system developed by

---

[6] In addition to the ones given here, the full manual includes a section on Creativity ratings, and rules for scoring Combinations and Integrations. They are omitted here, as they are optional, not bearing directly on the assessment of primary process thinking.

Mayman out of proposals by Rapaport et al. (1968). (See also Lohrenz and Gardner, 1967.) This scoring is a necessary first step for making the *DE* rating (see below).

The column at the left presents numerical equivalents, which may be used to derive an overall quantitative summary score for Form level.

Rating	*FL*	
7	*F+*	Sharp, convincing forms, easily seen by examiner.
6	*Fo*	Popular and near-popular forms; fixed list in manual.
5	*Fw+*	Reasonably plausible, but not terribly convincing forms; takes a little stretching to see.
4	*Fw−*	Forms that bear only a slight resemblance to the blot area; not very plausible, or based on only one point of resemblance.
2	*Fs*	Spoiled form responses, to be used when the subject gives what is basically a familiar and good response (which would have been scored *Fo* or *F+*) but introduces some specification that has the effect of markedly lowering the acceptability of the response as a whole as a percept.
1	*F−*	Arbitrary forms, very little or no resemblance.
5	*Fv+*	Vague forms that fit the blot quite well, and non-definitive form combined with appropriate use of color or shading.
4	*Fv*	Vague forms with no other determinant, or forced use thereof (as in *C/F* or *CFarb*).
3	*Fa*	Amorphous responses, in which form plays *no* role (and could not, by the nature of the concept). Usually pure *C*, *C'* or *Ch*.

DD. Defense Demand of Response

Under this heading, the shock value of the response is to be rated: the degree to which the very nature of the underlying idea, or (in the case of the formal variables) the way it emerges, demands that some defensive and controlling measures be undertaken in order to make the response a socially acceptable communication. (Note that we do *not* try to score differently for each S; criteria are *general*.) Scores at the upper extreme are usually given to blatant, Level-1 sexual or aggressive *content*, but formal aspects also make varying demands that the "craziness" of the conception be concealed or explained away. In part, this rating represents an elaboration of the Level 1—Level 2 distinction.

1. *No apparent need for defense:* Here fall responses that con-

tain aspects of the primary process only implicitly, or references to matters that would hardly be noticed if referred to at a polite tea party; e.g., food; *Do*.

2. *Slight need for defense:* The content and structure of the responses rated at this level are only slightly unusual in conversation, and arouse only slight degrees of tension. Also, any response containing both Level-2 content and Level-2 formal scores must be rated at least 2; e.g., "animals fighting"; verbal slips.

3. *Moderate need for defense:* The content and formal deviations scored here are at a level that might cause moderate tension or social embarrassment if they occurred in conversation. Also, any response combining Level-1 content and Level-2 formal, or Level-2 content and Level-1 formal must be rated at least 3; e.g., "buttocks"; impossible combinations.

4. *Considerable need for defense:* The level here is set by the example of sexual organs. It is possible for most people to refer to such things in a doctor-patient setting, but it is not permissible in ordinary formal conversations. Also, any response combining any kind of Level-1 content and Level-1 formal material must be rated at least 4; e.g., genitals; *DW*.

5. *Great need for defense:* Shocking ideas which could under no circumstances be introduced into a social conversation without extensive controls and defenses. Such responses are almost pathognomic of psychosis, since they imply both a serious breach of judgment in order to be mentioned, and the availability to awareness of ideas that are usually kept unconscious; e.g., "two men eating a dead body"; autistic logic.

6. *Greatest need for defense:* Sometimes it happens that a response contains content that would be rated 5 and also formal deviations that are at the 5 level. The result is about as much primary process and need for defense as can be packed into a single response; responses rated 6 occur exclusively in psychotic records. (For an example, see under −3a, *DE*.)

DE. Effectiveness of Defense

Each response that contains any scorable content or formal element is to be rated on the effectiveness of controlling and defensive measures in reducing or preventing anxiety, and making a successful, adaptive response to the examiner's demand to interpret the blots.

DE is rated on a 6-point scale, ranging from +2 to −3, by half-point steps. Positive values indicate good control and adaptive regression, negative ratings indicate more pathological defensive efforts and maladaptive regression. Distinguish carefully the *success-fulness* of control or defense, and the response's creativeness, which is separately rated (see note 6). A completely successful response *may* be at the bottom of the creativeness scale, or at the top.

Note that two types of ratings are given, distinguished by the letter *a* following the *undefended* type. An *undefended response* is defined as one that lacks any control and defense category except *R-min*, the sequence or overtness categories (or any combination of these). It is assumed that if someone is quite mature and unthreatened by the primary process, he may feel no need to defend a response containing a good deal of it; therefore, the lack of any scorable defenses is not considered a detriment if the response is in other respects successful.

Procedure for scoring: Consider first of all the form level of the response, and assign a tentative approximate *DE* as follows:

If *FL* is	tentative *DE* is
F+	+2
Fo	+1.5
Fw+	+1
Fv+	+1
Fv	0
Fw−	0
Fa	−.5
Fs	−1
F−	−1

Second, consider the accompanying *affect*: expressive behavior and verbal indications of threat, enjoyment, etc., from the protocol and affect inquiry. Adjust the rating up or down by .5 or 1 full point, taking into consideration the appropriateness, genuineness, and intensity of the affect. Thus, appropriate pleasure and enjoyment may raise either a +1.5 or a +1 to +2; appropriate but minimal indications of pleasure (e.g., inferred from *Cx-H+* in the absence of affect inquiry, or from the mere statement, "I like it") may raise a

−1 to −.5, +1 to +1.5, etc. Expressions of anxiety, distress, repug-
nance, guilt, shame, disgust, or embarrassment may lower the *DE* by
−.5, −1, or even −1.5 if intense and uncontrolled. If there is no
internal evidence ˚of affect and no affect inquiry, or if the latter
yields a feeling of indifference, neutrality, etc., do not change the
DE. Inappropriate expressions of enjoyment may lower the rating;
but be careful not to lower it once under affect and again because
a defense with a minus sign is present, when the latter is *Cphb*−
scored for precisely the same inappropriate expression of enjoyment.

   Third, consider the Control and Defense scores, raising by as
much as one point for those with + signs, and lowering by as much
as a point for those with − signs appended. No absolute rule can be
laid down, but in general if the numbers of positive and negative
controls balance one another, do not change the rating; a single +
control or a couple without signs will usually warrant raising the
DE by +.5 (and similarly for minus controls). Control and Defense
categories that do not carry signs are generally considered to operate
more in the adaptive than the maladaptive direction, but they must
not be given much weight.

   Fourth, make a final adjustment of the rating, changing no
more than one point up or down, relying on your clinical judgment.
You may consider various unscored aspects of defense: indications
of defensiveness, evasion, or disruption that were not scored because
they did not refer directly to scorable primary process, various
interpersonal maneuvers in S's relation with examiner, the failure of
expected determinants to appear, the presence (or absence) of
Combinations and Integrations (see footnote 6), and slight changes
in verbalization or form level when the primary process aspect of the
response is introduced. Use all of your clinical sense!

   +2. *Completely successful control and defense, in a successful response:* Good form level (*F+* or *Fo*); no disturbance; if any affect, it is positive; "good" control and defense categories; response is a
perfectly acceptable communication, with no deviations of language.

   "Here I can also see the outlines of a man—gangster-type
individual with hat brim over his eyes. [Inq.] Looks like a gangster
in one of the English stories they show over TV." Card VI, *D F(C)+H*;
Ag 2 A; *R-fic n+, R-geo+, Cx-E+, O-pot. (DD:* 2)

   +2a. *Highly successful response, undefended:* Above description applies, except that no control and defense category is scored other than *R-min*, sequence or overtness.

"A woman's sexual organs—here are the lips, the opening, even this little hole back here could be the anus. [Inq.] The color and shape. (?) Oh, I enjoyed seeing it." Card II, *Drs FC+* Sex; *L 1 S (L 1 A)*; *R-min*, *O-pot*. (*DD*: 4)

+1.5. *Successful control and defense:* This rating is given mainly to *Fo* responses that lack any special reasons for being raised to the top level; but it may also be occasionally given when an otherwise +2 candidate has a slight defect, or as a result of raising responses with poorer form level.

+1.5a. *Successful response, undefended.*

+1. *Mostly successful control and defense:* This rating is generally given to responses with good form level that are lacking in some respect (affect or controls), to otherwise unremarkable *Fw+* and *Fv+* responses, or to those with poorer form level that have been raised because of special evidences of effectiveness.

+1a. *Mostly successful response, undefended.*

+.5. *Fairly successful control and defense.*

+.5a. *Fairly successful response, uncontrolled.*

0. *Only moderately successful control and defense:* This level does not contribute to S's total score in the direction of either adaptive or maladaptive regression. If, on the whole, you feel that the primary process in a response is under good enough control to be a positive asset, raise the score to +.5 or more; if you feel that it is poorly enough defended against so that its emergence is a liability for S, which he would have been better off without, lower it to at least −.5. Usually, if the affect is appropriately positive *and* form level is *Fw+*, *Fv+* or better, *DE* is no worse than 0, no matter how bad the control scores are.

0a. *Only moderately successful response, undefended.*

−.5. *Slightly unsuccessful control and defense.*

−.5a. *Slightly unsuccessful response, undefended.*

−1. *Relatively unsuccessful control and defense:* Responses with this degree of ineffective defense occur in neurotic records and are not uncommon in Rorschachs given by normal persons. The degree of disorganization implied is not great, but the response must be clearly on the side of maladaptive regression.

−1a. *Relatively unsuccessful control and defense, undefended.*

−1.5*a. Mostly unsuccessful control and defense, uncontrolled.*

−2. *Unsuccessful attempts at control and defense:* "Makes me think of a mouse with entrails hanging out, I don't know why. (?) Real horrible looking−ugly." Card IV, *W F− A; Ag 2 R; R-an (Imp− tend). (DD:* 4)

A poor response, poorly defended−only the remoteness of its being an animal and the change to a neutral but still poor response (an *F−* following) for defense. The remark in affect inquiry shows how ineffective these controls were.

−2*a. Unsuccessful response, undefended:* In addition to the *R-min*, Sequence and Overtness controls that do not preclude our considering a response as undefended, *Imp−* should also be added. It rarely is encountered at higher levels, but wherever it is found, it is an expression of a *failure* of defense rather than a type of defensive effort.

"This opening here−I can't tell you why, unless it's the reddish tinge−I get a vaginal impression. (?) Mucous. (?) I couldn't say." Card III, *Dr FC− Sex; L 1 S; Impr 2; R-min, Imp− wk, O-pot. (DD:* 4)

Starting level is −1; there was no affect inquiry and no clear indication of disturbance. The weak *Imp−* alone would warrant lowering only a half point, but the additional half point is subtracted for the clinical impression of uneasiness and ineffectiveness.

−2.5. *Very unsuccessful control and defense.*

−2.5*a. Very unsuccessful response, undefended.*

−3. *Disorganized responses with only pathological attempts at defense:* Almost pathognomic of psychosis.

−3*a. Pathological disorganized responses, undefended:* "It looks like an insect, on two parts of it, and looks like somebody's chest. (?) That doesn't look like an insect; it looks like part of a body (*W*) 'cause it looks like part of a man's chest. And it looks like he has some kind of a disease, with two insects inside . . . (What's happening inside?) He's in the hospital." Card VIII, *W Fs At−A; Ag 1 R, Ag 1 V; C-ctm 1, Intr 1, Ctr L 1; R-min, Rep− tend. (DD:* 6)

Clearly a psychotically disorganized response, with only a feeble attempt at repudiation of the "insect" idea, which immediately breaks down as the contamination emerges unmistakably. This is a rare example of the maximum of *DD*, because either the Content or Formal scores alone would have been rated 5.

Once all of these categories and rating scales have been applied to each Rorschach response, they are tallied on special psychogram sheets prepared for the purpose. Most of the time, of course, the great majority of the 167 listings (all possible Content, Formal, Control and Defense, Form Level, Creativity, *DD* and *DE* rating points or categories) will be blank. Then these basic frequencies are combined to form a variety of indices, the number and nature of which will vary somewhat according to one's interests and purposes. Research has not yet given a definitive word on which ways of combining the bits into indices are most widely useful. Most frequently used, however, are percent total primary process (the proportion of *R* containing any manifestation of primary process), percent Content (proportion of *R* containing any libidinal or aggressive material), percent Formal (proportion of *R* scored for any Formal indication of primary process), and percent Level 1 and Level 2, respectively (proportions containing any Level 1 scores, or any Level 2 scores; sometimes Content and Formal are subdivided into Levels 1 and 2, similarly); mean *DD*, mean *DE*, weighted mean Form Level, and the Adaptive Regression Score (ARS). The last is the product of *DD* and *DE*, response by response, summed and divided by the number of primary process responses (which is also the divisor for mean *DD* and *DE*).

A word about the applicability of the present system to the Holtzman Ink Blot Test: in principle, there is obviously no reason why the primary process scoring system should not be used with Holtzman's test, with its demonstrated advantages for certain kinds of research. Indeed, several investigators have made successful use of this particular combination (Podkomenyi, 1965; Gray, 1969; Irizarry, 1971; Myers, 1972). There is one troublesome drawback, however: there exists no form-level manual for the application of Mayman's FL system to the Holtzman blots. Since there are so many blots, each of which contains many areas to which responses are frequently given, it would be an enormous labor to produce such a manual, larger by several times than the 44 pages of the mimeographed FL manual currently distributed along with my primary process scoring guide. Even in its absence, if two scorers are thoroughly trained and experienced in the application of Mayman's system to Rorschach blots, and work together scoring a variegated sample of HIT's on the same categories, they can develop a satisfactory enough level of reliability for most research purposes.

RELIABILITY AND VALIDITY

In brief outline, this is the system we have worked out for scoring Rorschach records for the primary process and how it is handled. Obviously, such a detailed system is cumbersome until it is thoroughly learned, but even then, scoring is not a quick affair. It is necessary to scrutinize each remark of the subject quite carefully and weigh it against many kinds of standards. What evidence is there that such a system can be reliably scored, and that the scores are valid, i.e., lead to verified predictions about the behavior that is theoretically to be expected?

Reliability

Our efforts to check scorer agreement show that many individual categories are difficult to score reliably, but when these are combined in certain over-all indices, agreement is excellent.

The following figures on interrater reliability come from a series of researches all of which used the ninth draft of the manual (quite similar to the tenth and latest). McMahon (1964) tested his agreement with another scorer with considerable experience in the method on 20 cases randomly selected from his samples of 40 schizophrenics and 40 medical patients in VA hospitals. Here are his product-moment correlations:

Percent total primary process	.94
Percent content	.94
Percent formal	.85
Percent Level 1	.89
Percent Level 2	.93
Mean DE	.56

In a study using Mean DD, Mean DE, and Mean $DD \times DE$, Bachrach (1968) reports that interrater reliability coefficients "for all relevant variables were greater than .89." His subjects were psychotherapists in training, both psychologists and psychiatrists. Bachrach was trained during a week's visit to New York University, and he then trained the other scorer.

The same indices were used by Allison (1967) in a study of 20 divinity students, all of whose Rorschachs were scored by two psychologists independently (neither of whom had been trained at the Research Center for Mental Health). The reliabilities obtained were: Mean DD = .99, Mean DE = .81, Mean DD x DE = .67.

In a 1968 study, Benfari and Calogeras, neither of whom had had any previous training in primary process scoring, obtained the following reliabilities with 40 college students: "Inter-rater agreement for Content was .90, .85 for Formal aspects, .95 for Defense demand and .90 for Defense effectiveness."

Another study used a sample of only 11 adult volunteers (Oberlander, 1967). Rorschachs were scored for form level, "the extent of primary process intrusion," DE, and mean DD x DE. Interrater reliabilities, "calculated with the use of Ebel's formula . . . ranged from .88 to .95."

Rabkin (1967) randomly selected 25 protocols from a group of 100 Rorschachs given at various times to patients in the Menninger Foundation Psychotherapy Research Project, and had them scored by another experienced scorer also trained by me. Just before the scoring for Rabkin's study was undertaken, we worked out the present rules for scoring DE, a change over the ninth edition as used by others. The results were satisfactory enough to encourage the belief that the problem of DE's fluctuating reliability might have been solved, though only time will tell. Here are Rabkin's reliability coefficients:

Percent total primary process	.92
Percent content	.94
Percent formal	.90
Mean form level (weighted)	.92
Mean DD	.86
Mean DE	.90

Validity

The problem of validating any psychological test has been discussed many times, and contains many tricky and complicated issues, some of which I have discussed elsewhere (Holt, 1968, 1970a, 1971, 1975a). The most troublesome and obvious roadblock to straightforward concurrent validation of any attempt to measure the primary process and ways in which it is handled is the lack of any generally accepted criterion measure. In point of fact, there does not exist any other way of gauging these subtle aspects of human functioning with better face validity than the system presented here.

Nevertheless, some data exist to help answer the practical question: What do these scores mean, and what are they good for? In 1966, I published a collation of available evidence on the correlates of the various Content scores, indicating a substantial amount of construct validation for the proposition that they measure libidinal and aggressive motives. In 1970 (b), I published another survey of research on attempts to predict artistic creativity by means of Rorschach indices of adaptive regression, testing Kris's (1952) hypothesis that "regression in the service of the ego" is prerequisite for achievement in the arts. In brief, the results were mixed, varying from incredibly high correlations (.90; Pine and Holt, 1960) to negligible ones not significantly different from zero, depending on the nature of samples, the ways of computing an ARS, and the criterion of creativity. Negative findings from well-executed studies came entirely from samples of females, a fact that has been replicated several times since.[7] I concluded:

> The weight of the evidence seems to me impressively positive, in light of the many limitations of the pieces of research that have been done. True, the Rorschach primary process scores that have shown statistically significant relationships to measures of creativity have varied from study to study, but then so have the populations sampled and the kinds of creative functions considered as criteria. With so much error variance on both sides of the equation, it is remarkable that so many positive findings have come through.... (Holt, 1970b, p. 305f.)

The adaptive Regression Score is the nearest thing to an overall summary of the entire scoring system, and since it purports to be a measure of the degree to which primary process thinking is well controlled and available for adaptive use as against being poorly controlled and expressing thought disorder, it has been of special interest in a good deal of research. The following brief review will concentrate, therefore, on evidences of this score's predictive utility. First, however, I shall present a few findings with its predecessor,

[7] Various attempts to explain this remarkable finding may be found in Pine and Holt, 1960; Holt, 1970b; and Rosen, 1971.

the first attempt to devise an index of regression in the service of the ego, which was worked out by Goldberger (1961). He first rank-ordered a group of subjects on Percent Total Primary Process and on Percent Level 1, added ranks for each S and re-ranked them, which yielded a measure of *amount* of primary process with, in effect, double weighting for the more primitive manifestations. Then he ranked the following *control* score for each S: the number of responses with high *DD* ratings and good *DE* ratings was divided by the number of responses with poor *DE* ratings regardless of *DD* (responses with good *DE* but low *DD* were not considered). Finally he re-ranked Ss taking into account both the amount and the control scores, putting at the top those who were high on both the weighted proportion of primary process in their Rorschachs *and* on the effectiveness with which it was controlled; in the middle fell the Ss who expressed least primary process; and at the bottom of the rank order came those who had large amounts but ranked lowest on control.

Goldberger's first findings were with 14 male college students who spent 8 hours in a state of perceptual isolation ("sensory deprivation"), lying on a bed in a sound-deadened room with halved pingpong balls fixed over their eyes. He and I independently and reliably rated their tape-recorded spontaneous verbalizations for a number of aspects of thinking, and other trained raters scored the Rorschachs that had been given to them earlier. Two findings were significant at the .05 level: Goldberger's ARS was correlated with controlled primary-process thought during isolation (rho = .54) and with the amount of time Ss spent sleeping (rho = .65)—a sensible way to while away the otherwise boring day. Because the sample was so small, the following predicted rank correlations are significant at only the .10 level: Unpleasant affect −.50, pleasant affect .47, self-stimulation .46, unimpaired secondary-process thought .45, and adaptive syndrome of reactions to isolation .50. (The last is a cluster of the following intercorrelated variables: pleasant affect, controlled primary process thought, unimpaired secondary-process thought, imagery, verbal output, immobility—remaining motionless as instructed, and self-stimulation—ability to find ways of getting some input without violating the rules of the experiment.) The basic finding, that a good adjustment to isolation is predicted by Rorschach ARS, has been replicated in four additional studies, using slightly different ARS formulas and isolation measures (Wright and Abbey, 1965; Wright and Zubek, 1969; Myers and Kushner, 1970; Myers, 1972). Indeed, it has a claim to the status of the best-established finding in the entire literature relating personality and adaptation to perceptual isolation.

Using Goldberger's method, Bergan (1965) found adaptive vs. maladaptive regression strongly related to the vividness of imagery in 14 college men's dreams (p < .01), and positively related (p < .05) to the self-rated intensity of 14 female undergraduates' waking auditory imagery and to the accuracy with which they could judge musical pitch. Derman (1967) found that Goldberger's index significantly distinguished subgroups of 32 male college students who —on the basis of MMPI scores—were classified as either "ambulatory schizophrenics" or normals. Maupin (1965) divided 28 male undergraduates into 3 groups according to the strength of their response to two weeks of daily training in Zen meditation. This criterion was significantly (p < .001) predicted by a modification of Goldberger's method of measuring adaptive regression.

In most of the research, however, Goldberger's method has been supplanted by the simpler ARS score (mean DD x DE). The latter uses much of the same information, but does not require ranking and therefore can be used more flexibly, with larger samples, and with less loss of power; its drawback is that it does not give more extreme scores to Rorschachs containing large amounts of primary process, especially of the Level 1 variety.

One group of researches suggest that the ARS measures an openness to affective and imaginal types of experience when such openness is adaptive. Allison (1967) found this index to be significantly (p < .05) related to reports of intense religious conversion experiences by 20 male theological students. Bachrach (1968) found a correlation of +.79 (p < .01) between ARS and independent ratings of empathic behavior in recorded samples of psychotherapeutic sessions with 22 therapists in training. Using several measures of the cognitive control principle, tolerance for unrealistic experiences (Klein, Gardner and Schlesinger, 1962), Feirstein (1967) found that their composite was correlated .49 (p < .05) with ARS in 20 male graduate students. Weiss (1971) found ARS to be significantly related (p < .05) to a combined measure of sensitivity to emotional and nonverbal communication; her Ss were 50 college students, 30 males, 20 females.

Another group of researches have in various ways supported the interpretation that adaptive regression characterizes good psychological adjustment, as Schafer (1958) indicated it should. Oberlander (1967) found an rho of .74 (p = .01) between adaptive regression and the flexibility of autonomic nervous system functioning, as measured by the reactivity of the pupil in a sample of "11 young adult volunteers." Gombosi (1972) reports a positive relationship (p < .05) between the ARS and a clinical rating of the level of identity formation, made from interviews with 30 male college students. With a similar male sample of 20, Rosen (1971) found the ARS correlated as follows with   factorial scales from an inventory she constructed to measure aspects of Erikson's "basic trust:" Acceptance, .49; Trust in Others, .46; total Trust, .48 (for each, p < .05). In a sample of 20 female college students, however, the ARS was not reliably related to any of her questionnaire scales; instead, it was *negatively* related to trust as rated from the TAT (−.38; p < .10). In his studies of maturity in Haverford college men, Heath (1965) found that *mean DD* x *DE* discriminated in the predicted direction between the 12 best-organized and the 12 least organized upperclassmen (p < .05), and a few years later differentiated the 10 most and 10 least organized upperclassmen (p < .05), in both cases as rated by faculty and fellow classmates. In the larger of these two samples this measure of adaptive regression was highly and significantly correlated with a number of test measures of adjustment (e.g., MMPI general maladjustment −.43, p < .05; incongruence of self-image −.66, p < .01) but few of these correlations held up in other samples studied in this country and abroad (Heath, 1968). There is no good theoretical reason, however, to expect even a perfectly valid measure of adaptive regression to be highly and consistently correlated with gross measures of adjustment, maturity, or good organization. Clearly, the world contains many a contented and effective citizen who has no conscious access to primary-process modes of thought, and no need for any.

A research project on a cognitively complex form of problem solving came up with a surprising correlate of the ARS. Blatt, Allison, and Feirstein (1969) used the John-Remoldi PSI apparatus (John,

1957), with 50 male graduate students at Yale as Ss. The machine confronts S with 9 lights in circular array, each controlled by one or more button-switches; there is also a center light, not directly controlled by any button. It goes on, however, to indicate success when S discovers how to turn on the other lights in the correct sequence. The machine records each button-push, affording measures of problem-solving efficiency. The principal measure of efficiency, number of unnecessary pushes, correlated $-.40$ ($p < .01$) with the ARS: the more adaptive regression, the more efficient the problem-solver. Before trying to concoct any ingenious theory about how primary process can help with this kind of logical efficiency, we should realize that the finding is illusory; mean Defense Effectiveness was an even better predictor of efficiency ($r - -.16$) and when it is partialled out, the relation between ARS and unnecessary button-pushes drops to .13. DE, being a measure of maintained efficacy of responding despite the presence of potentially disruptive primary process material, is a more plausible predictor of ability to keep one's head and not retrace one's steps under the pressure of being timed at a complex problem.

By virtue of its derivation, mean DE is necessarily correlated with ARS, sometimes as highly as .95 (Fishman, 1973); in the study just cited, the correlation was .69. Let us look back at some of the other findings in the above summary and check the null hypothesis that DE is the whole story.

In the Rosen study (1971), each of the correlations with ARS is matched by an equivalent or higher correlation with mean DE, so that trustful males and mistrustful females seem better characterized as effective in coping with their own primary process (regardless of its amount or intensity) rather than as capable of adaptive regression. But in the researches by Allison (1967), Bachrach (1968), and Feirstein (1967), the several criteria were considerably less strongly related to mean DE. Similarly, Blatt and Feirstein (MS) found, in a later study, that the variability of heart-rate while 26 male graduate students were solving a pair of complex problems was highly correlated with ARS ($r = .59$, $p < .01$) but considerably less so with mean Defense Effectiveness ($r = .44$, $p < .05$). The contrast is even more striking when the Rorschach indices are restricted to Content scores: then ARS is correlated .64, mean DE only .45, with variability of cardiac rate. Here, apparently, the ARS predicts a person's open-ness to emotional experience without being disrupted by it, during complex cognitive performance.

It seems safe to conclude, therefore, that though it is in some ways not yet a wholly satisfactory measure (being more highly correlated with one of its components, Defense Effectiveness, than one might like), the Adaptive Regression Score is a promising measure with an encouraging degree of construct validity. More scattered, but cumulatively promising, evidence of similar kinds is slowly accumu-lating concerning many of the other scores yielded by the primary process system—enough evidence of usefulness to encourage me to publish the manual in full, with norms and a complete summary of research using it (Holt, in preparation).

BIBLIOGRAPHY

Allison, J. Adaptive regression and intense religious experiences. *Journal of Nervous and Mental Disease*, 1967, **145**, 452-463.

Bachrach, H. Adaptive regression, empathy and psychotherapy. *Psychotherapy: Theory, Research and Practice*, 1968, **5**, 203-209.

Benfari, R. C., and Calogeras, R. C. Levels of cognition and conscience typologies. *Journal of Projective Techniques and Personality Assessment*, 1968, **32**, 466-474.

Bergan, J. R. Pitch perception, imagery and regression in the service of the ego. *Journal of Research in Music Education*, 1965, **13**, 15-32.

Blatt, S. J., Allison, J., and Feirstein, A. The capacity to cope with cognitive complexity. *Journal of Personality*, 1969, **37**, 269-288.

Blatt, S. J., and Feirstein, A. Cardiac arousal: Affect discharge or signal function. MS sub-mitted for publication.

Derman, B. I. Adaptive vs. pathological regression in relation to psychological adjustment. Unpublished doctoral dissertation, University of Georgia, 1967.

Feirstein, A. Personality correlates of tolerance for unrealistic experiences. *Journal of Con-sulting Psychology*, 1967, **31**, 387-395.

Fishman, D. B. Holt's Rorschach measure of adaptive regression, mathematical artifact, and prediction of psychotherapy outcome. *Journal of Personality Assessment*, 1973, **37(4)**, 328-333.

Goldberger, L. Reactions to perceptual isolation and Rorschach manifestations of the pri-mary process. *Journal of Projective Techniques*, 1961, **25**, 287-302.

Gombosi, P. G. Regression in the service of the ego as a function of identity status. Un-published doctoral dissertation, Boston University, 1972.

Gray, J. J. The effect of productivity on primary process and creativity. *Journal of Pro-jective Techniques and Personality Assessment*, 1969, **33**, 213-218.

Hartmann, H. (1950). Comments on the psychoanalytic theory of the ego. In: H. Hartmann, *Essays on ego psychology*. New York: International Universities Press, 1964.

Heath, D. H. *Explorations of maturity*. New York: Appleton-Century-Crofts, 1965.

Heath, D. H. *Growing up in college: Liberal education and maturity.* San Francisco: Jossey-Bass, 1968.

Holt, R. R. Gauging primary and secondary processes in Rorschach responses. *Journal of Projective Techniques,* 1956, **20**, 14-25.

Holt, R. R. Measuring libidinal and aggressive motives and their controls by means of the Rorschach test. In: D. Levine (ed.), *Nebraska Symposium on Motivation, 1966.* Lincoln: University of Nebraska Press, 1966. Reprinted in P. M. Lerner (ed.), *Handbook of Rorschach scales.* New York: International Universities Press, 1975.

Holt, R. R. Editor's introduction. In: D. Rapaport, M. M. Gill, and R. Schafer, *Diagnostic psychological testing.* New York: International Universities Press, 1968.

Holt, R. R. Yet another look at clinical and statistical prediction: Or, is clinical psychology worthwhile? *American Psychologist,* 1970, **25**, 337-349. (a)

Holt, R. R. Artistic creativity and Rorschach measures of adaptive regression. In: B. Klopfer, M. M. Meyer, and F. B. Brawer (eds.), *Developments in the Rorschach technique, Vol. III: Aspects of personality structure.* New York: Harcourt, Brace, Jovanovich, 1970. (b)

Holt, R. R. *Assessing personality.* New York: Harcourt, Brace, Jovanovich, 1971.

Holt, R. R. Clinical and statistical measurement and prediction: How *not* to survey its literature. *JSAS Catalog of Selected Documents in Psychology,* 1975, **5**, 178, MS No. 837. (a)

Holt, R. R. Drive or wish? A reconsideration of the psychoanalytic theory of motivation. *Psychological Issues,* 1975, **9**, (4, Whole No. 36), 158-197.

Holt, R. R. *Measuring primary process.* Book in preparation.

Irizarry, R. Anxiety, repression, and varieties of antisocial behavior in psychopaths. *Journal of Personality Assessment,* 1971, **35**, 56-61.

John, E. R. Contributions to the study of the problem-solving process. *Psychological Monographs,* 1957, **71**, No. 18 (Whole No. 447).

Klein, G. S., Gardner, R. W., and Schlesinger, H. J. Tolerance for unrealistic experiences: A study of the generality of a cognitive control. *British Journal of Psychology,* 1962, **53**, 41-55.

Kris, E. *Psychoanalytic explorations in art.* New York: International Universities Press, 1952.

Linton, H. B. Rorschach correlates of response to suggestion. *Journal of Abnormal and Social Psychology,* 1954, **49**, 75-83.

Lohrenz, L. J., and Gardner, R. W. The Mayman form-level scoring method: Scorer reliability and correlates of form level. *Journal of Projective Techniques and Personality Assessment,* 1967, **31**(4), 39-43.

Maupin, E. W. Individual differences in response to a Zen meditation exercise. *Journal of Consulting Psychology,* 1965, **29**, 139-145.

McMahon, J. The relationship between "over-inclusive" and primary process thought in a normal and a schizophrenic population. Unpublished doctoral dissertation, New York University, 1964.

Myers, T. I., and Kushner, E. N. *Sensory deprivation tolerance as a function of primary process defense demand and defense effectiveness.* Unpublished MS, Naval Medical Research Institute, Bethesda, Md., 1970.

Myers, T. I. *Psychobiological factors associated with monotony tolerance.* Silver Spring, Md.: American Institutes for Research, 1972.

Oberlander, M. I. Pupillary reaction correlates of adaptive regression. Unpublished doctoral dissertation, University of Chicago, 1967.

Pine, F., and Holt, R. R. Creativity and primary process: A study of adaptive regression. *Journal of Abnormal and Social Psychology,* 1960, **61**, 370-379.

Podkomenyi, A. The effects of sensory deprivation on primary process thinking. Unpublished doctoral dissertation, Adelphi University, 1965.

Rabkin, J. Psychoanalytic assessment of change in organization of thought after psychotherapy. Unpublished doctoral dissertation, New York University, 1967.

Rapaport, D. (ed.). *Organization and pathology of thought*. New York: Columbia University Press, 1951.

Rapaport, D., Gill, M. M., and Schafer, R. (1945-46). *Diagnostic psychological testing*. Revised edition by R. R. Holt. New York: International Universities Press, 1968.

Rosen, M. Trust, orality and openness to sensory experience: A study of some personality correlates of creativity. Unpublished doctoral dissertation, New York University, 1971.

Safrin, R. Primary process thought in the Rorschachs of girls at the oedipal, latency, and adolescent stages of development. Unpublished doctoral dissertation, New York University, 1974.

Schafer, R. Regression in the service of the ego: The relevance of a psychoanalytic concept for personality assessment. In: G. Lindzey (ed.), *Assessment of human motives*. New York: Rinehart, 1958.

Silverman, L. H. Regression in the service of the ego: A case study. *Journal of Projective Techniques and Personality Assessment*, 1965, **29**, 232-244.

Tomkins, S. S. *The Thematic Apperception Test*. New York: Grune & Stratton, 1947.

Weiss, R. A study of some personality correlates of sensitivity to affective meaning. Unpublished doctoral dissertation, New York University, 1971.

Wright, N. A., and Abbey, D. Perceptual deprivation tolerance and adequacy of defenses. *Perceptual and Motor Skills*, 1965, **20**, 35-38.

Wright, N. A., and Zubek, J. P. Relationship between perceptual deprivation and adequacy of defenses as measured by the Rorschach. *Journal of Abnormal Psychology*, 1969, **74**, 615-617.

Nothing is inside, nothing is outside:
What is within is also without. *

JOHANN WOLFGANG GOETHE

12 | *Florence R. Miale*

SYMBOLIC IMAGERY
IN RORSCHACH MATERIAL

Hermann Rorschach's (1942) initial presentation of his method, published first in 1921, emphasized almost entirely the formal characteristics of the responses. Shortly after the publication of *Psychodiagnostics*, Rorschach wrote, with Emil Oberholzer, the posthumously published paper *The Application of the Interpretation of Form to Psychoanalysis* (1942), in which he recognized the extent to which the utilization of content enhanced the value of the formal characteristics and explored ways in which scoring and content could be used together in psychological interpretations. But Rorschach died in 1922 and as his monograph became famous, in the late nineteen thirties and forties, psychologists were captivated by the promise that scoring, adding up of scores, arranging them in ratios, graphing them, developing norms for them, would provide an objective, scientific personality test, uncontaminated by the talent or training or experience of the clinician. Psychodiagnosis would no longer be an art—it was being advanced to the status of a Science.

The trouble was that the scores weren't scores at all. In mental testing, scores are based on frequency distributions, on the assumption that many traits and abilities are distributed in the population according to the normal curve. For example, intelligence tests have

*Translated by F. R. Miale.
The original: "Nichts ist drinnen, nichts ist draussen: Denn was innen, das ist aussen."

been constructed on the reasonable (and to an extent verifiable) assumption that certain aspects of intellectual functioning are distributed normally in the population, that there are about as many idiots as geniuses, about as many people above average as below in the ability to do certain important kinds of reasoning, and in retaining certain useful items of information. But there is no evidence at all that "scores" of M or W or C[1] are normally distributed. The term "score" has been unfortunate. The "scores" are shorthand signs which note aspects of the blots to which a subject responds. The "scores" are important. But to treat them as the basic Rorschach material and to play statistical games with them, is about as inappropriate as interpreting X-ray photographs by use of a ruler instead of the use of a skilled roentgenologist.

For psychodiagnostic purposes, content cannot be divorced from the context of the total Rorschach record: scorable features, unscorable qualitative aspects, quantitative aspects, even reaction and response time. For the purpose of putting into focus my approach to the use of symbolic material, the emphasis of this chapter will be on content. But I shall return to the important question of the interrelations of content and scoring. (See p. 609 ff.)

Two theses elaborated elsewhere (Miale, 1959) underlie the discussion in this chapter. One is that self-expression in projective material is not different in kind from that which occurs in life situations, that the tendency to project oneself onto that which is ambiguous in the environment is a tendency which applies in very similar ways to life behavior and to behavior in response to projective stimulus material. This thesis, long regarded as providing the rationale for the use of projective material, has been called the "projective hypothesis" (L. K. Frank, 1939). Every reaction of a subject is a reflection, or projection, of his private world (Rapaport, 1942). I should like to state it as follows: Personality tends to be an organized and consistent whole; to the extent that a person handles a situation in his own way, despite pressure from convention or pride or social expectations or immediate environmental influences, he will do it in a way which is thoroughly consistent with his whole personality.

And the difficult and subtle job the psychologist is called upon to

---

[1] For explanation of scoring symbols, see Appendix, p. 609 ff. [Editor].

do is to identify the ways in which the individual is *being himself*, to focus on the *unwittingly manifested* aspects of the response or expression, while the person who is being observed is concentrating on quite other, and usually quite different aspects of the stimulus situation and of his reaction to it. Handwriting analysis provides perhaps the clearest analogy here. A person, while writing, is generally concerned first with content, then perhaps with aspects of handwriting like legibility and attractiveness. He is not occupied with (and could modify very little if he were) features like writing stroke, pressure, relative size of different parts of letters, or the type of curve he uses in connecting vertical strokes of his pen—to mention a few of the many features of handwriting which the graphologist utilizes. Similarly, if not as clearly, the Rorschach interpreter utilizes features of the material which are not subject to conscious selection or control by the subject, who indeed may suppress sexual associations, or show off his sophisticated knowledge of art, but cannot do much that is essential about the images that, as it were, jump out at him from the inkblots.

The second underlying thesis is that projective material need not involve "breakthrough" of unconscious contents for it to be diagnostically valuable, that because of an essential unity between conscious and unconscious, the conscious material obtained by projective methods may be interpreted in terms of the whole personality, with its unconscious as well as its conscious aspects. McCully (1971) says, ". . . identifiable features in the stimulus materials may set going processes which cut across the whole spectrum of psychic potentiality. This includes conscious processes, ego reactions, attitudes, judgments, material associated with an individual's development and construction of his defense shield, and data from commonly shared or collective substance, the repository of man's psychological experiences" (p. 31).

As Mindess (1955) points out, "In the Rorschach literature generally, a visible confusion surrounds the problem of content analysis" (p. 248). This chapter will be concerned with several aspects of the problem of content analysis in the Rorschach: (1) the reference of Rorschach symbols; (2) their metaphoric character; (3) the relation of content analysis to use of scoring categories.

1. *The reference of Rorschach symbols.* Mindess (1955) has surveyed the various uses of Rorschach content made by different workers in this field. For example, Brown (1953), cited by Mindess, draws from Rorschach content conclusions referring variously to:

> *inner states* (e.g., A dress, a suit of clothing, or a tailor's dummy seen in Card I "signifies a sense of inner emptiness, great distance from people, with inability to empathize with them, cathexis withdrawal . . .")
>
> *early memories* (e.g., Faces seen in Card I, depending on the expression, signify "the most enduring impression of the earliest facial expressions and moods experienced in contact with the parental figures.")
>
> *organic conditions* (e.g., A womb seen by women in the white space of Card II "hints at either sterility or a possible hysterectomy.")
>
> (Italics by Mindess)

For Walter Klopfer (1954), cited by Mindess, the referents of the content, while they do not range over so wide a field, still are confusingly varied.

> Nature responses sometimes seem to reveal *attitudes* on the part of the subject *about certain elemental forces in himself.*
>
> Describing the figure as being pulled about or otherwise engaging in actions over which it has no apparent voluntary control may lead us to think of schizoid or obsessive *tendencies within* the perceiving subject.
>
> The specific idea of clowns, if repeated, may be associated with an *attempt to regard others or oneself* as foolish or ineffectual.
>
> The animal may be seen as hovering or otherwise in a threatening position which may be *how the subject views the world.*
>
> (Italics by Mindess)

Some writers interpret some Rorschach symbols in terms of people and events in the subject's life history. Thus Brown (1953) interprets the response to Card II, "Two animals fighting over a bone," as: "This projects sibling rivalry for parental favors" (p. 261). Phillips and Smith (1953) state that the response *cow* "suggests a relationship with a kind, mild, passive and easily led mother figure" (p. 121), and the response *eagle* "suggests powerful, dominating, omnipotent, patriarchal father figure, with whom subject compares himself unfavorably" (p. 281).

Ainsworth (1954) in an illustrative case study, suggests that the interpreter consider the question, "What can be inferred about her attitudes towards and her relationships with other people from the human figures she sees in the blots? What sex are the figures? What age? What characteristics have they?" (pp. 653-654) Then, interpreting the record with a knowledge of the history, Ainsworth identifies various human figures as the subject's mother, father and grandfather. For example, she says, "Card IX seems to give a picture of home life, with the mother (witch) and the grandfather (old man with the red nose) both talking at once, neither willing to listen or agree with the other and both trying to get in the last word" (p. 681). She states also, "The father is an idealized fantasy figure; the real father is known very slightly. Perhaps this is why in Card IV she sees the clothing but not the man" (p. 681).

The dilemma of the psychologist concerned with the problem of the reference of Rorschach content is illustrated in only slightly exaggerated form by the problem of a student writing a sequence analysis of a record. In connection with a particularly striking image, the "sinister black angel" (discussed below on pages 430 f.) she wrote:

> It is not possible to determine who this figure represents. Is it his mother, or his wife, or his sweetheart? Perhaps later responses will provide the answer.

The problem takes on a different aspect, however, if we refer to the projective hypothesis, which implies the similarity between projection as it operates in everyday life and projection as it is revealed in projective methods. The self-reference of projection in life situations is evident. It would seem to follow from the projective hypothesis itself, or at least to be a reasonable extension of this hypothesis, that projective material may likewise be considered self-referent.

The hypothesis of self-reference has been applied by Jung (1953) to dreams and other symbolic material not derived from projective methods. He speaks (p. 83) of two levels of dream interpretation, the "objective" and the "subjective." These may be of equal validity, one in terms of the dreamer's experience of and response to life situations and to the people and relations involved in them, the other in terms of the way in which the dream contents symbolize aspects the dreamer's own personality. According to Jung's concept of projection, these two levels are very closely related in life, since the dreamer's images of the objects and the people in his environment have a large element of projection in them. The way one views a person in waking life as well as in dreams, is to a considerable extent a function of the aspect of oneself that the other person symbolizes. While Jung concedes that interpretation on the "objective" level can often be of value clinically, his emphasis is on the "subjective" or self-referent interpretation. He says, "The dream is the theatre where the dreamer is at once scene, actor, prompter, stage manager, author, audience, and critic" (1928, p. 162).

In the same way, I am suggesting that Rorschach symbols may be viewed as self-referent, as faithfully representing inner states of the subject, aspects of his personality. The following ideas will be presented in support of this assumption: (a) it is broad enough to include many of the other meanings proposed; (b) it avoids certain difficulties of other kinds of interpretation; (c) most important, sample Rorschach interpretations based on the self-referent hypothesis will be presented along with excerpts from case history material and psychotherapists' reports which point to the validity of these "blind" interpretations; and (d) the intrinsic relationship between content and formal scoring features of a Rorschach record will (finally) be demonstrated.

a. The self-referent hypothesis is broad enough to include many of the other meanings ascribed to Rorschach symbols. As mentioned above, the question is frequently asked: Does this figure represent the subject's father? Is that one his mother? Is this one representative of his view of women? If we assume that the Rorschach symbol represents primarily an aspect of the subject's own personality, we may add that his image of his actual father or mother or lover is determined to a considerable degree by aspects of his own personality. Such aspects of his personality have often had their origins in relations with parents and siblings, and are likely to be projected in a person's view of figures in the environment. A man's standards of conduct, for example, may grow quite directly from the demands which his father imposed upon him, and also determine his reactions to external authority. A woman's conception of her feminine role is likely to be closely related to the sort of woman her mother was, and this conception will, in turn, color her view of women about her.

Therefore, if we interpret the Rorschach image as revealing aspects of the subject's own personality, we will also be able to make inferences about his images of important figures in his environment and his relations with them, as well as inferences about the genesis of these qualities. Other aspects of his attitudes toward himself and others, of how he views the world, even his organic conditions (cf. above p. 424), may likewise be inferred from a self-referent interpretation of Rorschach material. This point will be illustrated with specific examples in the interpretations to follow.

b. The self-referent hypothesis avoids certain difficulties of other interpretations. It was pointed out above that some writers interpret Rorschach symbols in terms of generalizations about life history. While such interpretations are not necessarily incorrect, they tell us very little about the particular individual we are studying. To explain a given subject's problem in terms of sibling rivalry (cf. above p. 424), castration anxiety, or Oedipus complex, is to clarify very little of its particular character if, as is widely held, these are universal experiences. Again, while inferences can sometimes be made from Rorschach material as to significant past experiences of a person or as to his overt behavior, simpler methods of obtaining such information exist. As a matter of fact, the Rorschach, like projective methods generally, is not a particularly good instrument for obtaining such information, since it can assess only the subject, not the situations in which he behaves. As Schafer (1954) says, ". . . Since at present there seems to be no evidence in Rorschach test records to support or refute genetic reconstructions concerning specific, important, early experiences and relationships, and since current representations of the remote past are historically unreliable even though revealing of current pathology, interpretation can and should pertain only to the present personality structure and dynamics of the patient or to changes in these in the relatively recent past" (p. 145).

Thus, the most relevant use of the Rorschach method is not to find out what experiences a person has had, but rather to learn what his experiences mean to him, and what he has become through them. It is the meaning of an experience in the present, not the fact of its occurrence in the past, which is significant for an understanding of the person.

c. Sample Rorschach interpretations based on the self-referent hypothesis. The method to be followed here will be to select single Rorschach responses for interpretation, rather than whole records.

This method permits the selection of striking images, ones whose significance can be understood without intensive training in projective methods. It will, furthermore, be possible under these conditions to consider content in relative isolation, with little concern for scoring, sequence and the like. It should be emphasized that for *clinical* purposes isolation of content from other aspects of the material is not appropriate. A later section of this chapter will discuss the intimate interrelations among these various aspects of the responses. I made each interpretation without knowledge of the subject except for that obtained by examining the projective materials and, in some cases, also administering them. After each interpretation, pertinent data from case history or psychotherapist's report or both will be presented briefly as evidence for the relevance of the interpretation.

A hypothetical example will contrast the self-referent hypothesis with other approaches to projective material; later, actual cases will be presented. A subject may see in the blots a series of images of contest, competition and mutual hostility. The figures in the side details of Card I may be trying to wrest the center from each other, those in II arguing, in III competing, in VII fighting, etc. One might infer from this that there are strong aggressive impulses in the subject. As Walter Klopfer (1954) says, "When such aggression is taking place, (as with people fighting or attacking one another), it may be indicative of the presence within the subject, at some level, of severe feelings of hostility against the world" (p. 381). Or one might focus on the implication that he views people as hostile. Again, one might conclude that his environment, early or current or both, contained much conflict and aggression, that his parents, for example, were ill-matched, or actually quarrelled a good deal. Any or all of these inferences may be valid in an individual case. If the self-referent character of Rorschach symbols is borne in mind, however, the problem of interpretation is not one of arbitrarily choosing one of these possibilities over the others. It is rather a matter of recognizing the essential quality within the subject's personality which must be present if any of the above-mentioned conditions is of such central importance as to pervade his responses: Any person who responds to the inkblots in this fashion is one who is involved in intense internal conflict; one in whom aspects of himself are at war with one another.

For one person this conflict may be symbolized in his mind by (and have its origins in) his ill-matched or quarrelsome parents; for another it may be externalized in attitudes of hostility toward others; for a third it may be expressed in projection onto others who are then viewed as hostile toward him. Any or all of these expressions of the conflict may be present in the person. It is possible, too, that in a particular case, the conflict may be represented in none of these ways, but simply experienced directly as inner struggle, as opposition within the self. For example, Janet, age 21, produced the following responses:

> Two old ladies tugging at one another. Woman in the middle rather horror ridden, with her hands up in the air and the other two, to me, just seem sort of stodgy—one pulling on one side and one pulling on the other (Card I).

> Two odd men playing around for some reason—I mean it does not look like they are really fighting (Card II).

> Butlers or something, anyway some stiff looking people. I have the impression they are pushing against each other (Card III).

> Like two gnomes perched on top of a couple of chunks of ice. They look sort of mad at each other—I mean like they are daring each other to do something; they have taken issue over something. They don't look like they are out to kill—sort of gritting their teeth. Almost look like they are arguing their point, each one pointing in the opposite direction trying to prove some point or other (Card VII).

> The top of this looks to me like two people fighting, and the two people in green underneath are trying to separate them and pull them apart (Card IX).

> At the top they sort of look like beetles talking to each other in a rather angry fashion (Card X).

Janet, who was depressed and had obsessive-compulsive symptoms, did not show hostile attitudes toward others, nor did she feel that others were hostile towards her. There was very little expression of aggression between her parents (who were Quakers). However, her therapist said, "Janet consistently and obsessively hated herself more than anyone I have ever known." The self-hatred came to a climax in a subsequent suicide attempt.

A 30-year old man described Card I as a "sinister black angel" which he designated as female. If we consider this response as primarily a reflection of the man's own personality, we may proceed as follows. He is here concerned with those aspects of his personality which he least associates with his conscious, masculine self and, in the culture in which he lives, are generally considered feminine. These include such aspects as feeling as against logic, aesthetic as against matter-of-fact approach, indirection as against directness, and so forth—only a deeper study of all the material would make clear which aspects of so-called feminine psychological qualities were most outstanding in this man's conception. The problematic nature of these aspects of his personality is suggested by the paradoxical concept of the sinister angel. This response further reveals a man who views the world and himself—and more especially those aspects of himself which can be called feminine—in terms of dichotomies, in terms of black and white, sinister and angelic, good and bad. The black angel seems to represent irrational forces within him, which he equates unconsciously with "woman." (Perhaps she provokes the welling up of such forces.) And telescoped with this is the guilt that he experiences about his irrational urges, and the accompanying depression. The use of the black color as a determinant suggests depressive mood.

This is the kind of man who, as a projection of his moralistic (black-white) attitude toward his own "feminine" qualities, views all women as either saints or prostitutes. Such an attitude frequently develops in men who are very much attached to dominating mothers. The psychiatrist's report confirmed the statement about his mother and about his attitude toward women. There was a long history of pre-marital and extra-marital relations, and he complained that he "couldn't keep his mind off women." He also expressed the wish that he "could get sexual satisfaction without complications," and the idea that if this were possible, his "whole life would be transformed." At the same time, he was always searching for the "ideal relationship that would lead to the ideal marriage." (His marriage had ended when his wife left him, he reported, "simply because she was upset by my depressions.")

The significance of the analysis of this Rorschach response did not lie primarily in the interpreter's ability to discover the subject's attitude toward women, or the nature of his relation with his mother —either of which might be determined more easily than by means of the Rorschach. What made the Rorschach material useful in understanding him and in planning treatment was the meaning of the response as a reflection of a dynamic component of his own personality. It contributed to the understanding of his distrust of his artistic abilities and interests, a distrust which was combined with a longing for artistic expression. It illuminated, too, the dichotomous, all-or-nothing, attitude toward the expression of feeling in relations with others, and toward his own accomplishments, which are described in the following paragraphs from the psychiatrist's report:

> There was great ambivalence in his relation to others as well as to himself. On the one hand, he felt that he could easily be abused by employers and friends. On the other, he accused himself of having done a great deal to hurt other people, especially his wife. As he expressed it, "I have to be very casual and cold, or I get too warm. I want very much to like someone and to be liked, but I can't spread it out in the right proportions."

> He was subject to spells of depression which he tried to relieve by drinking. When he drank, he felt more at ease with people, but when the effect wore off, he became depressed again, often to the point of crying. Then he accused himself of being sentimental and rejected this as a feminine quality.

Two further illustrations of the application of the self-referent hypothesis to Rorschach material will be taken from the record of Maud, a woman of 33. She gave the following response to Card III:

> Looks like a couple of butlers, or men in full dress suits, bowing to each other. [Two other responses were given, then she returned to the men.] The men look very supercilious. [She put down the card, as though finished, then picked it up again, something she did frequently during the Rorschach.] They seem to be pulling something. [She continued in the Inquiry]: They are bowing and scraping. [She proceeded to point to details of clothing]: Breeches, coat, shoes, stiff white collars. The black and light tones look like black and white.

What is to be inferred from the content and language of this response? That her father was a stiff, formal person, with little personal warmth? On the hypothesis that a woman's ideas about men tend to stem from her father's characteristics, this is a reasonable inference from her particular way of viewing these male figures. This inference was validated by the case history, but it should be added that it was a fact learned easily from the subject—a Rorschach was certainly not necessary to obtain this information. Is our conclusion to be that her attitude toward men alternates between servile respect and snobbish superiority, in the way the character of the Rorschach image varies? This, too, is a reasonable conclusion, and one which the case material confirms; but it is merely a statement of easily ascertainable attitudes. Of far greater importance to the psychologist are the dynamic bases for such attitudes (which include the dynamic *effect* of her relation with her father). If the unconscious determinants as well as the conscious attitudes and defenses are to be understood, the image must be viewed as a reflection of the subject's own personality; the characters are inner figures.

How can "butlers or men in full dress suits" be inner figures in the psyche of a woman? In the "sinister black angel" response we saw how the female figure could represent the "feminine" aspect of a man's personality. Correspondingly, this response sheds light on the "masculine" side of this woman's personality. The sharp shift between superciliousness and obsequiousness in the attitudes of the figures, as well as the fact that they are also seen as pulling in opposite directions, indicates that there is intense conflict in this woman about qualities associated with masculinity.

The role of men, in the culture in which Maud grew up, is exemplified in the traditional position of the father in the family. Masculinity represents authority. The man is expected to be dominating, directing, assertive. Apparently when Maud experiences a life situation as calling for her to play a role of this sort, as demanding decision and authoritative behavior, she becomes involved in conflict between her passive and aggressive impulses. Called on to play a role which represents authority, her opposition to authority is evoked, and she is plunged into self-opposition.

This inner war is manifested also in the obsessive indecision which is revealed both in the fluid, shifting concepts and in her uncertainty about giving up the card, in her lack of ability to set up limits and function within them. This fluidity, in turn, seems to reflect the fluidity of the boundaries of her ego, that is, the lack of clarity about her individual identity.

The history revealed that her most severe problem, the one that impelled her to seek therapy, was her inability to hold any job, regardless of the adequacy of her ability and training for the actual work. The difficulty was twofold: on the one hand, she alienated her associates and her superiors (but especially the latter) by her arrogance and aggressiveness; on the other hand, she became acutely anxious about her ability to handle the work, and was unable to organize her work and to make decisions. In her relations with men, she played a role of exaggerated passivity and dependence as a way of achieving dominance. She had no insight into this. Her view was that she was expressing love and devotion—she did not see how demanding she was.

Also revealed in the response is her emphasis on facade and social role, manifested not only in the stress on details of clothing, but also in the contrasts between superiority-inferiority, superciliousness —bowing and scraping. From the exaggerated emphasis on facade, too, one would infer great deficiency in her sense of personal identity, a lack of clear individual values, a fear of exposing her emptiness to others, and difficulty in distinguishing between form and substance. This seems to reflect also a tendency to evaluate people in terms of the effectiveness of their social fronts.

Instead of saying simply, as many subjects do, "Men in evening clothes," she needs to bring in the dimension of social position —butlers or men in full dress suits—while at the same time she implies a helplessness in determining at which end of this important scale these people are because their surface adornments are the same. The correctness of the clothing—the facade—is evidently so important to her that she makes a point of saying in effect, "I know these are shades of grey, not black and white, but for the sake of maintaining an effective facade (to make the evening clothes proper), I am ignoring such distinctions." Thus her value judgments are oversimplified, and she treats issues as though they consisted only of blacks and whites, even when she knows that the real situation is more complex. The concern with the achromatic color also reveals the depressive mood which accompanies her preoccupation with the problem expressed in the response.

Her uncertainty about her personal identity was manifested in a number of ways. One was in her highly unrealistic professional aspirations: she wanted to be a movie star or a great writer. A more immediate and more dramatic expression of both her identity problem and her tendency to live in terms of black-white extremes was her way of dressing. Much of the time she was extremely well-groomed, with the sort of hair style that required elaborate daily setting, and she wore striking dresses in the latest fashion. At other times, however, when she was depressed, there was a startling change. She would neglect her appearance to the point of leaving her hair uncombed and her clothing soiled and unmended.

One further illustration, from the same record: in response to Card VII, she said:

> Upside down, looks like a very fat woman with her guts shot out—everything removed but her head and part of her dress. (In the inquiry, she elaborated): Hair (top large details), two legs (lower details), two arms (side extensions). All scooped out. I don't think I even have the right to see anything like that. It's too imaginative. It doesn't really look like anything.

My report on the Rorschach, written with no knowledge of the subject's history, said that the content of this response "makes the observer wonder whether a precipitating factor in her present symptoms might not have been an induced abortion experienced under extremely traumatic psychological circumstances." This speculation was confirmed by the history which was later obtained. But such an observation does not really constitute interpretation of projective material, since, first, many women have experienced induced abortions, and under traumatic circumstances, without giving such a response in subsequent Rorschachs; and second, the fact of the experience, while it might help to explain the choice of this content for a Rorschach response, explains not at all the particular form which the response takes: the use of a Whole with white space, the extremely poor form level, the bizarre quality, the combination of violence and passivity in the concept, the choice of details to be emphasized (head and part of her dress), or the final negation of the concept. Only when the focus is shifted, and the image is seen as a metaphoric portrayal, from one angle, of this personality, do all these things take on meaning.

To indicate the interpretive approach, without an exhaustive analysis of the response: The most striking aspect of this image of a woman is the inner emptiness. The person is only a head and a costume, only intellect and social exterior. The image carries the quality of violence ("guts shot out," "all scooped out,") and helplessness (the passive victim, not the perpetrator of the violence, is portrayed). Here, as in the response to Card III, the passive-aggressive conflict is strongly implied; now we see its effect on her efforts to play a feminine role. When her feminine qualities, the passive, receptive, "feeling" aspects of her personality are called into play, she becomes overwhelmed by feelings of the inadequacy and insufficiency of her femininity as well as by a violently aggressive defensiveness against revealing her weakness. So she is helpless, ineffectual and inappropriate in her role as a woman.

Her inner emptiness was revealed in her life in her extreme dependence on externals. Her daydreams of public acclaim, which she thought were real plans for the future, her exaggerated emphasis on her appearance, her need for her friends to reiterate explicitly their regard for her, were all indications of her reliance on externals. Her inadequacy in the feminine role was revealed in her relations with men, discussed above, in which she was extremely aggressive and "masculine" under the guise of helpless femininity. Her difficulties about her femininity were expressed in her relations with women, too. Although she could not permit men any degree of dominance over her, she chose as women friends those on whom she could become exaggeratedly dependent, who would make every decision for her.

So far we have utilized responses involving human figures to illustrate the approach to the Rorschach symbol as self-referent. But what of the animals, the plants, the islands, the explosions, the articles of clothing, the items of food, which are so frequent in Rorschach records? These are commonly used to throw light on interests and conscious preoccupations of the subject, on his mental breadth or stereotypy [see Rorschach (1942) and Beck (1946)]. However, important information may be obtained by treating these responses, too, as reflections of deeper aspects of the personality.

Jung's (1953) interpretation of dream symbols as "subjective" embodies this approach. He says that interpretation on this level "detaches the underlying complexes of memory from their external causes, regards them as tendencies or components of the subject . . . All the contents of the dream are treated as symbols for subjective contents" (p. 83). He illustrates this approach in connection with the following dream of a patient: She is about to cross a wide river. There is no bridge, but she finds a ford where she can cross. She is on the point of doing so, when a large crab that has lain hidden in the water seizes her by the foot and will not let her go (p. 80).

Jung comments, "The dreamer is the whole dream; she is the river, the ford, and the crab, or rather these details express conditions and tendencies in the unconscious of the subject" (p. 83). With the aid of the dreamer's associations, but essentially on the basis of the intrinsic qualities of the images, he interprets the river the dreamer must cross as an inner obstacle to her development, and the crab which comes up from the bottom of the river to attack her as an aggressive instinctual aspect of her personality which threatens her from the depths of the unconscious.

A similar approach to Rorschach symbols has been proposed by Mindess (1955):

> The general level of meaning can be investigated in two ways: either on the basis of *physical appearance* (i.e., determining the symbol's referent by asking what it looks like, what it resembles), or on the basis of *intrinsic quality* (i.e., determining the symbol's meaning by asking what is its function, what—on a higher level of abstraction—is its essential nature). The former approach is utilized when one interprets trees, table legs, totem poles, etc., as phallic symbols because they are elongated. The latter approach is employed when one interprets fighting animals, vicious monsters, etc., as symbols of hostile impulses because their psychological quality is essentially one of hostility (p. 251).

The criterion of physical resemblance undoubtedly has significance. When a Rorschach record abounds in table legs and totem poles, or when every projecting detail in the blots captures the subject's attention, the inference that there is a problem about male sexuality is inescapable to the interpreter. The limitation of this approach, however, lies in its generality. To say that a person is preoccupied with sex, or has a problem about it, or to say (if the table legs and totem poles are seen as sawed-off), that a castration complex is present, is to say very little that is distinctive about the individual. As Schafer (1954) says in reference to interpretation of "food" or "mouth" responses simply as indicative of "orality", " . . . unless we describe the manifest form of appearance of the trends in question, their relative intensity, how they are controlled, etc., these archaic, instinctual concepts tell us little about the patient. In all of us, presumably, there are noteworthy amounts of orality, anality and other instinctual trends" (p. 149).

Mindess has made a real contribution in suggesting that Rorschach symbols be interpreted in terms of their intrinsic quality. I think it is necessary to go further, beyond what he calls the "psychological quality" of the response, to consider the specific meaning of the referent of the concept. Just as the human figure responses are regarded as reflecting some aspect of the personality of the subject, so the self-referent hypothesis must be applied to responses with other contents. The particular aspects of the person to which these responses refer can be determined by an examination of the corresponding concepts. Mindess himself implies that it is necessary to go further. After discussing the meaning of a car as a dream symbol in terms of its intrinsic quality, Mindess says, "The attributes of the specific car which appear in the dream may then reveal significant characteristics of the patient's emotional relations to his surroundings" (1955, p. 251). He does not develop this idea in relation to the Rorschach method, however.

Animals are creatures guided by instinct and impulse. Thus an image employing animals may be interpreted to refer to this realm of psychic existence. And different instinctive qualities are connected with different animals—lions and rabbits will not be used to represent identical qualities. The crab, armored, aggressive, primitive dweller in the depths, is an image different in important respects from the snail, which, while also armored, uses defenses of passive withdrawal. To illustrate:

A woman sought psychiatric treatment because of depression. She was a successful business woman, soft and sweet on the surface, forceful and aggressive in her work. She was married to a mild, passive man. For many years she had felt great satisfaction in her dominant role. Now, at forty, life was no longer satisfying. She felt inadequate as a woman, rather as though she were acting a part rather than living a life. The incongruous combination of "masculine" striving and "feminine" surface, as well as her sense of futility about her achievement is strikingly represented in her response to the whole of Card IX: "The head of a bull with a pink chiffon fichu around his neck—he looks as if he's blowing bubbles."

A forty-nine year old man was seen a number of times by a psychiatrist who made a diagnosis of paranoid schizophrenia and recommended commitment to a mental hospital despite the fact that he was sufficiently oriented to get along outside a hospital and had an income sufficient to support him. Hospitalization was recommended because of the extraordinary intensity of the patient's hostility. It seemed extremely likely that there would be an eruption of violence, toward others or toward himself. External manifestation of the deterioration of his personality, and of the growing intensity of his hostilities, had been very marked in the two years previous to examination, after he had lost his license to practice medicine because of a conviction on a charge of criminal abortion. In the Rorschach, he saw in Card IV, "With his head down, a wild bull— a ferocious animal." In Card V, he saw, "An animal whose front and hind parts have different usages—the hind part with scoops with which the animal could scoop out the flesh of his enemies, the front part innocuous." The latter image suggested that his sadism must have found considerable outlet in his profession ("scoop out flesh") and even greater danger was indicated now that he was no longer practicing.

The self-referent character of Object responses in the Rorschach may be illustrated in connection with clothing responses. Articles of clothing serve both as protection and as social front and adornment. A Rorschach record which is pervaded by references to clothing in its protective aspects—heavy cloaks, bundled-up figures, enveloping wraps, etc.—will suggest a personality in which there is much emphasis on need to avoid exposure, on reluctance at self-revelation, with implications of the guilt or inadequacy or weakness which requires the protective covering. Where emphasis on clothing stresses its exhibitive aspects (costumes, formal dress, etc.), interpretive stress will be on the importance of facade and social role, and perhaps, depending on specific qualities of the clothing content, e.g. elaborate stage costumes, on exhibitionistic or self-dramatizing defenses against the weakness in personal identity.

The significance of clothing responses in the record of Maud has already been mentioned. Her full Rorschach record shows a marked emphasis on clothing. The great effort to compensate for the inner emptiness and to find some safety and protection for her weak

individuality by playing a part, is expressed in the variety of gar-
ments and costumes in the record. There is even a costume without
a person, in Card VI—as though the individual has disappeared
entirely, through identification with a social role. The appearance
in Card VII of the response of the "woman with her guts shot
out," already discussed (p. 434) is thus further illuminated. The
special intensity of the quality of emptiness is clearer against the
background of the efforts to cover it. In the same way, by identifying the intrinsic qualities of any image, whether human, animal or
inanimate, the interpreter can understand the language of Rorschach
content. For the referents of such images possess qualities which
are also psychic qualities.

2. *The metaphoric character of Rorschach symbols.* The previous
sentence suggests a characteristic of Rorschach images that has not
been made explicit—their metaphoric character. Interpretation of
the image in terms of intrinsic quality implies that the symbol of
dream or projective material is a direct representation of the inner
situation of the person, not the product of a process of disguise and
distortion (Freud, 1938). Here, too, Jung's (1954) approach to the
dream illuminates projective material. He speaks of:

> ... the false belief that the dream is a mere facade concealing the true mean-
> ing. But the so-called facade of most houses is by no means a fake or a
> deceptive distortion; on the contrary, it follows the plan of the building and
> often betrays the interior arrangement. The "manifest" dream-picture is the
> dream itself and contains the whole meaning of the dream. When I find sugar
> in the urine, it is sugar and not just a facade for albumen. What Freud calls
> the "dream facade" is the dream's obscurity, and this is really only a pro-
> jection of our own lack of understanding. We say that the dream has a false
> front only because we fail to see into it. We would do better to say that we
> are dealing with something like a text that is unintelligible not because it
> has a facade—a text has no facade—but simply because we cannot read it.
> We do not have to get behind such a text, but must first learn to read it
> (p. 149).

Elsewhere Jung (1920) states, "... the symbol in the dream is
approximately equivalent to a parable; it does not conceal, but it
teaches" (p 309). Similarly, Calvin Hall (1952) emphasizes the
representative, metaphorical, character of dream symbolism:

> The function of dreaming as we have said many times is to reveal what is
> in the person's mind, not to conceal it. Dreams may appear enigmatic be-

cause they contain symbols, but these symbols are nothing more than pictorial metaphors, and like the verbal metaphors of waking life, their intention is to clarify rather than to obscure thought. What is the difference between a person awake exclaiming, "He's a majestic individual," and a person asleep conjuring up an image of a king? There is no difference except in the medium of expression. The verbal metaphor expressed by the adjective "majestic" and the dream image of a king represent the same conception (p. 215).

The metaphoric character of the symbol in dream and in Rorschach image may be clarified by looking into the nature of metaphors themselves. Such an investigation was made by Asch (1955) in a study of the use of metaphor in the description of persons. He points out that there are a great many words which are used to describe both physical and psychological properties:

> There is hardly a term in English which, while describing some physical aspect of things or events, does not also describe some psychological aspect of persons. People too are deep and shallow, narrow and wide, hard and soft, bright and dull. Our language draws upon nearly the entire range of visual, auditory, tactual, kinesthetic, thermal and olfactory experiences for a description of psychological properties. We also call to our aid a great range of events observable in nature to convey the facts of psychological experience. We liken our consciousness to a stream; ideas can be at its surface or buried in its recesses (pp. 29-30).

Asch goes on to demonstrate that the psychological referents tend to be the same in a variety of languages, a fact which points to an intrinsic, rather than an arbitrary, basis for the psychological application of the terms. When a temper is described as fiery, or a manner as icy, or an attitude as mulish, the description is understood by the listener because certain universally perceived qualities of fire or ice or mules, certain generally shared meanings of these concepts, are also descriptive of psychological properties of human beings, properties which have something intrinsically in common with those of the physical objects of forces.

What is true for the symbols of everyday language, seems to be true also for the symbols of projective material. The connecting link between the process of forming and that of interpreting a symbol can be seen as lying in the intrinsic nature of the relation between the symbol and its referent. We are here concerned not with the *process of forming symbols*, but with their interpretation.

To describe a particular orientation to the interpretation of symbolic content, is not to imply that the interpreter follows, in reverse, the path which the user of the symbol in Rorschach response or dream followed in its formation. To say that the psychologist can understand an aspect of the symbol by treating it as though it were a metaphor for some aspect of the personality, is not to suggest that the one who formed the image necessarily arrived at it by steps like those which are followed when a speaker or writer invents a metaphor or an allegory in order to make a point.

Mindess (1955) was quoted above (page 436) as saying that the understanding of a symbol in terms of its intrinsic quality involves a "higher level of abstraction." While it is not clear that he means the symbol is abstract only, the point is important enough to merit discussion. Like the metaphor or allegory, in which an abstract point is embodied in concrete form, the symbol cannot be adequately described as involving a process of abstraction alone. In projective material, the abstraction underlying the symbol is contained in and enriched by the specific character of the concrete image, every detail of which is important.

In this connection, the artistic symbol provides an illuminating analogy to the projective one. Arnheim (1953) writes:

> In the work of art the generalities are not hidden when we contemplate the particulars; nor do we need to abandon the realm of concreteness in order to grasp abstractions. On the contrary, the most abstract affirmations of the artist are the ones received by the eyes of the beholder most directly. Such concepts as large and small, high and low, active and passive, near and far, enclosing and enclosed are immediately perceived as sensory properties whereas the more specific content of subject matter demands recourse to knowledge, learning, memory. The triangle which symbolizes the hierarchic conception inherent in much Rennaissance art is directly seen by the eye: but it takes more than vision to recognize a woman, let alone, a Madonna.
>
> ... in the work of art particulars and universals are simultaneously and immediately present. A given event acquires visual form by a compositional pattern which defines it as an example of a most general kind of event. Raphael's triangular composition not only makes the Madonna and her child visible, but also interprets the scene as a situation symmetrically structured around a dominating climax. The indivisible oneness of the general and the specific permits and indeed requires the spectator to see the various levels of meaning in constant interaction. These levels remedy each other's

deficiencies by exchanging their virtues. The trite emptiness of the general is animated by the liveliness of the specific, and the trite irrelevance of the particular is elevated by the inherent generality of its form.

Thus the work of art symbolizes all the levels of reality that lie between the phenomenon and the idea. It counteracts the impoverishment of vision which results when any one of these levels is viewed in isolation of the others and encourages the synthesis of conception which is the mark of wisdom (pp. 96-97).

The analogy between metaphor and Rorschach response which is now so strongly suggested should have implications for Rorschach interpretation. Consequently a study was undertaken to test whether a valid interpretation of the content of a Rorschach response could be made by untrained people instructed to approach the response as a metaphor. It was expected that, if our assumptions about the metaphoric character of Rorschach symbols were correct, such interpretation would be possible. Two responses were chosen, each of which seemed to symbolize a very general aspect of the personality of the subject who had given it.

The latter point needs to be emphasized. Many responses would not be suitable for such a test since their contents tend to symbolize the personality of the subject as it is expressed in reaction to a particular kind of stimulus situation, which is represented by the attributes of the blot used and by the determinants involved. Further, content symbols vary in subtlety and in complexity. For these reasons, no broad generalizations are indicated, even if it should turn out that people without training can interpret carefully selected responses as metaphors.

The two responses were presented for interpretation to two groups of high school seniors. To one group they were presented as Rorschach responses, with the age and sex of the subjects given. The other group was offered the responses in the context of a lesson on metaphors. The students were asked to describe a person (of the age and sex of the actual subject) about whom such a metaphor might be used. No mention was made of Rorschach to this group. The first of the two responses was to the whole of Card IV: "An enlarged photograph of a microscopic insect." The subject was a man of thirty diagnosed psychopathic personality, with a history of imprisonment for armed robbery. The social and psychiatric histories, as well as the projective material as a whole, gave a picture of his personality as one of extreme weakness with compensatory ego inflation, a picture epitomized by the response selected. As Miale and Selzer (1976) report, the second response, "A chameleon, climbing," to the side pink details of Card VIII, had been given, with slight variations as to the movement of the chameleons, by five of sixteen leading defendants at the Nuremberg War Crimes trial: Schacht, Frank, Fritzsche, Von Neurath, Kaltenbrunner. These details are seen as animals by nearly all subjects, most often as rodents or bears. "Chameleons" is an extremely rare response, in Germany as well as in America. The chameleon, who changes his color to fit his surroundings, symbolizes the opportunism of these prominent Nazis, while the idea of climbing reflects their ambition.[2]

The subjects were students in two twelfth grade English classes.[3] There were 36 (29 boys and 7 girls) in Class M, the one presented with the responses as metaphors, and 39 (25 boys and 14 girls) in Class R, which was given the task of interpreting Rorschach responses. Median I.Q. in both groups was 130. In Class R, after a brief discussion of the Rorschach method, the students were asked to write an interpretation of each response, read aloud and written on the blackboard. They were asked to describe "the kind of person you think would have responded in this manner to these blots."

Group M was given a lesson in figures of speech, with emphasis on the metaphor. (Example: "What kind of man is a lion, a rat, a carbon copy on grey paper?") The students were asked to write answers to the question: "What kind of man is suggested by each of the following metaphors?" They were asked to avoid using metaphoric language in interpreting the metaphors. Time was the same as in the other group: about 15 minutes for both images.

In order to establish a reliable basis for comparing the characterizations by the two groups of students, the author made a preliminary list of the categories into which the characterizations fell, and two judges, uninformed of the purpose of the study, working independently, classified the material. The agreement between the two judges in classification of the responses was such that the hypothesis of chance agreement could be rejected at less than the .01 level.

---

[2] For a detailed analysis of the Rorschach records of the sixteen Nuremberg defendents see Miale and Selzer, 1976.

[3] For more details, see Miale, 1959.

The students' characterizations for each of the two responses were summarized separately under several headings. Only those entries on which the two judges were in agreement were included. There was agreement on 81% of the entries for the "insect" response, and on 89% for the "chameleon."

Characterizations of the "insect" response fall into three main categories. The differences between the two groups of students with respect to the three categories is demonstrated by a chi-square of 9.91 at less than .001 level of significance. The first deals with central personality characteristics. Twenty-two of the 43 characterizations in the metaphor group fall in this category as compared with only one in the Rorschach group. In contrast, the second category involves superficial or extremely general characterizations. Only five of the 43 descriptions in the metaphor group fall under this heading, whereas 52 of the 53 descriptions in the Rorschach group are classified in this category. A third category, relating to physical appearance, was used by 16 subjects, all of them in the metaphor group. The nature of the instructions would seem to be responsible for this result. The Rorschach group was asked to interpret psychological test material and therefore could not be expected to focus on physical appearance. The metaphor group, on the other hand, was told that the metaphors described persons, and there was no stress on psychological as against physical aspects of the persons described. Many subjects in the metaphor group who described physical appearance also mentioned psychological characteristics.

Characterizations of the "chameleon" response fall into two categories. Again there is one category which represents central personality qualities, and another which refers to highly general or superficial aspects of the person. Thirty-two of the 39 descriptions by the metaphor subjects fall into the first category, and only seven into the second. On the other hand, 38 of the 44 characterizations by the Rorschach subjects fall into the second category, while only six involve central personality features. Most of the members of the Rorschach group apparently approached the responses in terms of the conscious meaning for the subject. They searched for a rational explanation on a conscious level for the choice of content and then tended to make judgments about the appropriateness of this choice.

One typical description from the Rorschach group, referring to the "insect" response, reads:

> The man apparently has some knowledge of biology or insects. It is possible he was connected with some branch of science, judging from the language he used. The man may have an excellent memory, because of the fact that his description was accurate. It tends to indicate an intelligent mind. There is also the possibility that the person could be a teacher.

Another student in the Rorschach group wrote:

> The man doesn't know much about science or insects; has high school education. Probably a normal person.

Typical reactions to the "chameleon" response by members of the Rorschach group are the following:

> He might have a good knowledge of nature. He seems to be imaginative. He probably doesn't have a good sense of values nor a mathematically inclined mind. His answer gave me the impression that the person was weak-minded.

> He didn't know much about chameleons. Since they look like animals and that's about what he said they are, he was a mature, sensible man relating exactly what he saw. He was a successful, happy, well-adjusted man.

As these examples suggest, there was wide disagreement among members of the Rorschach group. The subject who gave the "insect" response was characterized as educated or intelligent, and as uneducated or unintelligent, by approximately the same number of students in this group (9:10). Similarly, while 15 students spoke of an interest in or knowledge of science, five centered their descriptions on lack of interest in or knowledge of science.

The Rorschach group generally failed to make valid judgments. A few of the interpretations were, however, quite accurate. The subject who gave the "insect" response *was*, as three or four students indicated, a person who attempted to impress others on the basis of a smattering of scientific knowledge. However, to very few students in this group did it occur that the response was symbolic, that it represented something basic in personality, or that it was self-referent.

On the other hand, the task assigned to the Metaphor group, that of interpreting metaphors, not psychological material, led the members of this group to view the material as self-referent and as representing more basic personality attributes. It led also to more valid judgments, and far fewer contradictory ones. The inferiority and weakness of the "insect" subject and the ambitious opportunism of the "chameleon" subject were referred to by a large proportion of the students in this group. Following are some typical descriptions by members of the Metaphor group, for the "insect" response:

> This is a description of a man who tries to do everything in a big way so as to make himself known, but really he is very small and petty underneath. In other words, he is trying to make up for his bad traits by putting on good airs.

> This man seems to be a man bloated with his own glory when actually there is no glory to be bloated with.

> He is oversized in figure, and in thought of himself. He thinks much more of himself and his stature in life than is true. His importance in the world is much less than he believes it to be.

The following are typical reactions by members of this group to the "chameleon" response:

> This man, at 50, is still rising in the world. His present success is due to his adaptability, for he has few inherent values (the chameleon's changes are superficial) to prevent him from molding himself to best agree with those in power. What ideas he really does have are disguised and changed if necessary to promote his advancement.

> "A chameleon, climbing" suggests a middle-aged man fighting for position in either the social, political or economic world. The political idea is easiest to explain, for the chameleon suggests a changing of colors or a change of party and platform to achieve office or position.

To summarize the results of the investigation: psychologically untrained individuals tended to give much more meaningful personality descriptions when they interpreted carefully selected Rorschach responses as metaphors than when they tried to interpret them as projective material. The subjects who interpreted the material as Rorschach responses (without, of course, knowing anything about the Rorschach method) referred to more superficial aspects of personality, showed greater disagreement among themselves, and, in most cases, failed to make valid judgments. In contrast, a large proportion of the Metaphor group, who based their judgments on the intrinsic qualities of the images, made significant and valid statements, and the agreement among members of this group was greater. These findings seem to offer support for the view that Rorschach symbols may be understood metaphorically, in terms of their intrinsic quality.

3. *The relation of content analysis to use of scoring categories in the Rorschach.* In the summary of his posthumously published paper, a case analysis, prepared in collaboration with Oberholzer, Rorschach (1942) first interprets "the formal psychogram," and then discusses "the comparison of the formal psychogram and the content" (p. 215). Since the original publication of this paper, in 1924, Rorschach workers have been concerned with the question: Having scored and tabulated the responses (i.e., constructed the "formal psychogram"), and having analyzed the symbolic images of the content, on the basis of what principles does one relate the two sets of material? The implication is that the "formal," scorable, characteristics of the Rorschach record, and the content, are different in kind, separate features which must be integrated in order to arrive at a picture of the total personality. In a leading textbook on the Rorschach method, for example, Klopfer and Ainsworth (1954) state:

> Rorschach interpretation is carried out in two major steps, quantitative analysis and sequence analysis, followed by a final step of integrating the findings from these two separate steps in the interpretative process (p. 249).

Again, these authors state:

> The final step in the interpretative process is to bring together those hypotheses that seem applicable to the individual on the grounds of the quantitative analysis of his record with those that have emerged through the sequence and content analysis, retaining those that are confirmed by both analyses and those that are compatible with the total picture, while discarding or modifying others as seems advisable in the light of the integrated picture of the personality that has been built up (p. 250).

Even aside from the methodological dangers inherent in the circularity of the approach advocated, such separate treatment of the two kinds of data does not seem to lead to maximum utilization of the potentialities of the Rorschach material. For example, a high proportion of *Fc* (definite form with use of shading as texture) is generally considered to represent much "sensitivity" in a personality. Discussion of the interrelations between such a characteristic as "sensitivity" and other features of a person, without qualifying the term at the outset, must of necessity be so vague as to have no utility. The "sensitivity" indicated by high Fc may represent: subtle awareness of nuances in others' feelings, accompanied by appropriate, adaptive response to them; a tendency to be easily hurt; raw, irritated exposure to sensory stimuli; crude, undifferentiated sensuality, etc. Which one of these is represented, or what variation of one, or what combination of two or more, or what alternation among them corresponding to the nature of the life situation which evokes the reaction, all depend on features of the Fc responses other than their quantity. These features include the objective qualities of the blots to which the responses refer, the form level of the responses, qualitative features and content.

The point of view which I have found most useful in understanding Rorschach responses is that the formal characteristics and contents are not different in kind. Rather, the same symbolic characteristics which determine the meaning of the content of a response, also determine the meaning of the scorable aspects of the Rorschach stimuli. The same relation of metaphorical equivalence between aspects of the subject's personality and characteristics of the image or the referent of the image is basic in both cases. Thus, just as an island represents isolation; clothing, the need for protection against exposure; or a snarling tiger, an aggressive animal-like impulse; so the "formal" characteristic of color represents emotional challenge. Color shares with emotion intensity, liveliness, warmth, excitement, as language attests. Emotions, we say, give color to our life. The manner in which color is handled in the Rorschach is symbolic of the subject's way of dealing with emotional challenge. Color combined with form (FC) indicates quite a different mode of handling such challenge than does pure color (C). Form is by definition contained; it is determined by its contour which contains it. Correspondingly, an FC response is more contained, disciplined, and thus more adaptive, than the diffuse, uncontained, sometimes explosive emotional response indicated by C. Likewise, texture represents nuances, subtle distinctions in the Rorschach blots. Thus, sensitivity to nuances of shading in this material corresponds to sensitivity to subtle environmental influences. As these examples suggest, then, the nature of the scorable features and of the content is essentially the same, and the two may be dealt with in the same way.

I suggest further that the shift in emphasis from scoring category to quality of response to content represents a transition from the general to the particular. When we interpret a Rorschach record only from the quantitative material, we are doing the most general kind of personality description. As we move to include more and more of what are usually called the qualitative features of the formal material (types of animals, kinds of texture, kinds of movement, intensity of color, etc.), we come closer to a specific description of the particular personality. When we go beyond these, to a consideration of the specific meaning of the content, what we are doing is considering the particular individual's expression of the more general characteristic described by the category in which the response is placed.

We may illustrate this kind of coordinated procedure in relation to content by analyzing a reaction to Card IV. The outstanding feature of this card is its strong shading, which tends to evoke reactions reflecting a subject's response to nuances in experience, particularly to subtleties in relationship. Lewis, age 30, says:

> A strange little animal—looks like he'd be seafaring, and he probably has a hard shell too. [Then spontaneously in the inquiry]: He would have a hard shell because he has no agility, no mobility, nothing to defend himself with. He has a human expression, puppy-like. I don't think, though, that we would become very good friends—his strangeness would leave me cool. Also, he is probably a dirty animal, the kind you find in muddy backwaters. He has a rough skin—there is some bone structure, but it shades off to show his soft underside. Eventually, in the process of evolution, he would die off. Anything that looks like that, I would suggest he keep his armor. (Score: $W\ Fc\ A$)

My analysis of the response illustrates the interpretive procedure in moving from the general to the specific aspects of the subject's concept:

Formal Features:

W Score	Mental approach is that of generalization.
Fc Score	Sensitivity is aroused, subject responds with effort at adaptation.

Form Level	Vague concept, unprecise form, reflect the inadequacy of the adaptive effort.

Qualities:

Hardness, roughness	Becomes defensive in an effort to erect a barrier against too close involvement. Inference is that this is because he fears loss of detachment.
Hard-soft contrast	Feelings of ambivalence; conflict between tendency to surrender to and to resist involvement.

Content:

Animal	Instinctual aspects of the personality are activated.
Sea animal	Concept of submerged, primitive animal suggests that "animal" aspects of the personality operate in an immature, undeveloped way with little awareness.
Hard shell because he has no agility, no mobility, nothing to defend himself with	His defensive armor is the result of an effort to compensate for the vulnerability. Unable to adapt in a flexible, differentiated way, he is inordinately threatened by environmental stimuli and erects an exaggeratedly strong barrier of defensiveness and resistance to influence.
He has a human expression, puppy-like.	In his very effort to deny his instinctual, animal qualities, he loses the capacity to distinguish clearly between the more evolved, developed "human" qualities and the more primitive animal ones.
	This sentence contains the one positive reaction to the animal he sees. The image here is an appealing one; it suggests that there might be some hope for gratification of instinctual needs. But the appealing "puppy-like" expression is too inappropriate on a hard-shelled sea animal. The promise of pleasurable gratification is not strong enough to overcome his sense of alienation from his impulses.
Probably a dirty animal, the kind you find in muddy backwaters	His impulse life operates in a realm far from his conscious values (in muddy backwaters). Unable to accept his instinctual needs as part of himself, he experiences them as strange,

Strange little animal	dirty, and guilt arousing, and they are denied an opportunity to find a legitimate outlet integrated with the rest of his personality.
Rough skin—bone structure shades off to show his soft underside	Despite, and in a way because of, the great defensive effort, the essential weakness and vulnerability remain. He is not confident that he can maintain his detachment in the face of a real challenge to his artificial show of strength.
Eventually, in process of evolution, he would die off	The adaptation is ineffective, not appropriate to the demands of reality. The direction of development is regressive.
Anything that looks like that I would suggest he keep his armor	The weakness goes deep. Only the hard facade offers any possibility for survival.

In this response, then, it is possible to see how a situation which arouses this man's sensitivity finds him extremely weak and essentially defenseless, so that he meets such situations with an effort to cover his weakness and feelings of ambivalence with a defensive, hard facade. We also see how ineffectual the result is of this effort. In this context one can see the way in which the subject's contempt for the "animal" qualities of his own nature has kept these qualities at an immature, unevolved level, operating in a childish way that is poorly integrated with his conscious, rational functions.

At the time that this Rorschach response was obtained, the psychiatrist whom Lewis had recently consulted had the impression that Lewis possessed a strange and contradictory combination of neurotic and psychopathic traits. In his work, which was in the field of advertising, and in his personal life, there was much ambivalence, anxiety, and indecision hidden behind a brash and over-confident facade. He said he considered himself the best man of his age in his field, but said, too, that he obtained no satisfaction from his work, felt useless, as though he were wasting his life. He expended much effort thinking up ambitious business schemes, seven or eight at a time, and said he felt he could do anything he set out to do. But after a short time he would drop his schemes and take to planning new ambitious projects.

The psychiatrist said, "Lewis refuses to admit that there is any such thing as emotion . . . he has a rigid, inflexible countenance, finds it difficult to say 'Thank You' or 'Please'. . . . The big problem in therapy is to reduce the rigidity, the defensiveness against emotional involvement. . . . He feels he can accomplish anything that can be accomplished, and at the same time has very strong feelings of inferiority. He has no acceptance of his limitations."

Lewis did not remain in treatment for long. At intervals, at the urging of others, he would consult psychiatrists but would terminate treatment whenever it became uncomfortable, whenever he was pressed to face his weaknesses. The anxiety and uncertainty about himself became much less apparent, and his manner colder and more aggressive. In a second Rorschach obtained five years after the one from which I have quoted, he called Card IV "a primeval animal, gray, with rattlesnake coloring and the texture of shell." Here there is no longer any sign of apology or of conflicting feelings. The sense of his own weakness and vulnerability, which was present in the concern that the animal keep his armor to protect his soft underside, has been replaced by a crystallization of the rigid defensive attitude.

Viewed in the light of the foregoing material, the problem of how to relate scoring categories and content in the Rorschach changes its character. It is a matter of integrating separate features only if we artificially separate the features to begin with. Rather I have suggested that the specific content of a response represents the subject's particular individual expression of that personality feature which is represented generally by the scoring category into which the response falls.

By way of conclusion it may be appropriate to refer to Weiner's remarks about symbolic interpretation elsewhere in this volume (p. 602 f.). His warning against confusing "reasonable certainties" about the subject which are based on representative behavior, with conjectures about content based on a questionable series of inferences, is well taken. As I have attempted to show in the body of this paper, however, interpretation in terms of self-reference and intrinsic quality may offer another perspective which can help lessen the gap in the inferential sequence. If the self-referent character of Rorschach symbols is borne in mind, the procedure is not one of arbitrarily choosing one interpretation over another one. It is rather a matter of recognizing how the essential nature of the personality is reflected equally in the content, the quality, and the scoring category of a subject's response. Supported by evidence from biographical data,

I have illustrated this coordinated procedure with a number of Rorschach samples.

This is not to suggest that interpretation in terms of intrinsic quality is necessarily more valid in a particular case than representational interpretation. In fact, in some instances the latter may be of greater clinical relevance. Rather, I am attempting to emphasize the importance of recognizing the value of symbolic interpretation in projective methods. A symbol, unlike a mere sign, as Jung has so frequently emphasized, is by definition ambiguous and may have many levels of meaning. By considering the symbolic meaning of Rorschach content, as of dreams, the material is thus interpreted at more than one level.

BIBLIOGRAPHY

Ainsworth, M. D. Illustrative case study. In B. Klopfer, Mary D. Ainsworth, W. G. Klopfer, and R. R. Holt, *Developments in the Rorschach Technique*. Vol. 1, Yonkers-on-Hudson, New York: World Book Co., 1954, Pp. 601-687.

Arnheim, R. Artistic symbols—Freudian and otherwise. *Journal of Aesthetics and Art Criticism*, 1953, **12**, 93-97.

Asch, S. E. On the use of metaphor in the description of persons. In H. Werner (Ed.), *On expressive language*. Worcester, Mass.: Clark University Press, 1955.

Beck, S. J. *Rorschach's Test*. Vol. II. *A variety of personality pictures*. New York: Grune & Stratton, 1946.

Brown, F. An exploratory study of dynamic factors in the content of the Rorschach protocol. *Journal of Projective Techniques*. 1953, **17**, 251-280.

Frank, L. K. Projective methods for the study of personality, *J. Psychol.*, 1939, **8**, 389-413.

Freud, S. The interpretation of dreams. In *The basic writings of Sigmund Freud*. New York: Modern Library, 1938.

Hall, C. S. *The meaning of dreams*. New York: Harper, 1952.

Jung, C. G. *Ueber die Energetik der Seele und andere psychologische Abhandlungen*. Zurich: Rascher, 1928.

Jung, C. G. *Two essays on analytical psychology*. New York: Pantheon, 1953

Jung, C. G. *The practice of psychotherapy*. New York: Pantheon, 1954.

Klopfer, B., Ainsworth, M. D., Klopfer, W. G., and Holt, R. R. *Developments in the Rorschach Technique*, Vol. I, Yonkers-on-Hudson, New York: World Book Company, 1954.

Klopfer, W. G. Interpretative hypotheses derived from the analysis of content. In B. Klopfer, M. D. Ainsworth, W. G. Klopfer, and R. R. Holt, *Developments in the Rorschach Technique*, Vol. I, Yonkers-on-Hudson, New York: World Book Company, 1954, Pp. 376-402.

McCully, R. S. *Rorschach theory and symbolism: a Jungian approach to clinical material*. Baltimore: The Williams and Wilkins Company, 1971.

Miale, F. R. *An approach to projective material*. Doctoral dissertation, Graduate Faculty of Political and Social Science, New School for Social Research, 1959.

Miale, F. R. and Selzer, M. *The Nuremberg Mind: The psychology of the Nazi leaders*. New York: Quadrangle The New York Times Book Company, 1976.

Mindess, H. Analytical psychology and the Rorschach test. *Journal of Projective Techniques.* 1955, **19**, 243-252.

Phillips, L. and Smith, J. G. *Rorschach interpretation: advanced technique.* New York: Grune & Stratton, 1953.

Rapaport, D. Principles underlying projective techniques. *Character and Personality*, 1942, **10**, 213-219.

Rorschach, H. *Psychodiagnostics.* Berne, Hans Huber (1921) 1942.

Schafer, R. *Psychoanalytic interpretation in Rorschach testing.* New York: Grune and Stratton, 1954.

> *"Everything that can be thought at all can be thought clearly. Everything that can be said can be said clearly."*
>
> LUDWIG WITTGENSTEIN

13 | *Margaret Thaler Singer*

THE
RORSCHACH AS A TRANSACTION

In this chapter an approach will be described for using the Rorschach as a method for exploring aspects of interpersonal verbal communication. The Rorschach will be viewed as a bit of reality being looked at by two or more persons in a conversational transaction. A special focus upon a number of deviances which can occur in such conversations over a shared task will be outlined.

Describing the process of communication, or the exchange of meanings between individuals, has been a concern of scholars since the time of ancient Greece. The history of philosophy and linguistics revolves around issues of how meaning is attained and transmitted or shared. In recent times linguists and others have begun to study the pragmatics of language (the relation between signs and the user of signs). General systems theory and its many subdivisions, including communication, games, and information theories, suggests that both the speaker and the hearer be considered within the conceptualized system (von Bertalanffy, 1950, 1962; Bateson, 1972; Watzlawick et al., 1967). Or as Richards (Ogden and Richards, 1956) put it: "Communication takes place when one mind so reacts upon its environment that another mind is influenced, and in that other mind an experience occurs which is like the experience in the first mind, and is caused in part by that experience."

For many years, Dr. Lyman Wynne and I have been using the Rorschach and other projective devices to assess how an individual shares attention with others and tries to communicate meaning to them. (See Singer and Wynne, Wynne and Singer references.) We have been particularly interested in studying the sharing of attention and meaning within families. The rationale for this being that families can be viewed as systems, and that the styles of communication within families are part of the family system. It has been in this framework of studying families that our particular use of the Rorschach has emerged. Here we shall concentrate on the Rorschach, although we have applied the same principles to devising scoring manuals for use with the Thematic Apperception Test (Singer and Wynne, 1966; Jones, 1974), the Object Sorting Test (Wild, Singer, Rosman, Ricci and Lidz, 1965), and Proverb Interpretation (Singer, Wynne, Levi and Sojit, 1968).

Here I shall illustrate how the Rorschach and other standardly administered assessment devices can be used, not in the traditional way with primary emphasis upon the revelation of an individual's intrapsychic experiences, but with an emphasis upon identifying, formalizing and interpreting the *impact* of his or her verbal communication upon others.

IMPACT VERSUS PSYCHODIAGNOSIS

Verbal behavior samples gathered and analyzed with the intention of studying the impact of a person's conversational style can be utilized in personality research and in the formulation of clinical decisions and individual treatment plans. To do so, a shift must be made from using the Rorschach or other behavior primarily to infer intrapsychic phenomena and instead, using it to conceptualize the probable impacts or effects of the person upon others who must deal with him or her in intimate, ongoing relationships (Singer, 1974).

To this end we have used psychological assessment techniques in ways which appear close to traditional approaches yet diverge from them in important respects (Singer and Wynne, 1965a, 1965b, 1966a; Singer, 1967; Singer, 1973, 1974; Wynne and Singer, 1966; Wynne, Singer, Bartko and Toohey, 1968, 1975). At first glance to a casual listener or reader, we may seem to be taking only a slight change in perspective for our interpretations, but in actuality we are proposing a rather major reorientation regarding the analysis of Rorschach and other verbal behavior.

We feel the Rorschach task is an analog of those many occurrences in daily life in which two individuals attempt to establish a consensually shared view of reality. During a viewing and discussing of reality, one person offers a focus of attention, labels what he "sees" and offers his interpretation to the other. In turn this person then responds to the offered focus of attention in some way. The Rorschach offers a relatively standardized starting point for sampling to what extent attentional foci and meanings are mutually shared during such a verbal transaction. We feel that for both personality research and the making of clinical decisions and therapy plans, this method of studying the stylistic features of an individual's communication provides highly revealing psychological insights of a nature quite different from the usual psychodiagnostic yield of assessment devices. Making inferences about a person's possible impact upon others when he attempts to share attention and meaning with them appears to be a highly fruitful approach for exploring the interpersonal dimensions of personality in contrast to the intrapsychic phenomena emphasized in standard Rorschach assessments. The validity of predictions based on this approach attests to its usefulness. (See Singer and Wynne, Wynne and Singer references.)

In our research, we have used a subject's verbal Rorschach behavior to differentially predict what kinds of thought sequences, mental images and attentional foci he will evoke in a listener. In gaining an understanding of how this person functions interpersonally, our descriptions of a subject's conversational and attentional style sensitizes the clinician to formal communication problems which may have important effects on his client's interpersonal transactions.

FAMILY COMMUNICATION STYLES

In our work with families containing either index schizophrenic, neurotic or normal offspring, we assume that both innate and experiential factors are co-determinants of behavior (Singer and Wynne, 1965a, 1965b; Wynne, Singer, Bartko and Toohey, 1968, 1975). Because of a long standing interest in trying to study the so-called thought disorders seen in young adult schizophrenics, we chose to focus upon one major aspect of the experiential factors, namely, the sharing of attention and meaning during family verbal interactions. We were especially interested in what links might exist between the thought disorders of the schizophrenic young adults and the communication styles of their parents. A good deal of research which attempted to establish some concordance between the psychiatric diagnosis of parents and their offspring has been rather inconclusive. Thus in a series of studies, we have analyzed the recorded and transcribed verbal transactions of parents (1) as they individually talked with a tester over projective and other psychological test material (Singer and Wynne, 1963, 1964, 1965a, 1965b, 1966a, 1966b, 1967); (2) as the parents talked together as a couple with a research interviewer (Morris and Wynne, 1965); (3) as the parents transacted together and with their children in test situations, without staff present (Loveland, Wynne and Singer, 1963; Singer and Glasser, 1975); and (4) as parents, offspring and staff met in family therapy sessions (Morris and Wynne, 1965; Palombo, Merrifield, Weigert, Morris and Wynne, 1967). In this research the focus has been upon the formal, stylistic features which characterize communication; especially on how parents focus their own attention and how they go about sharing meaning. We have been primarily interested in studying *how* parents communicate and relate to other persons, and for the present have relegated to a secondary position the study of the *content* of their transactions (Wynne and Singer, 1963a, 1963b; Singer, 1964; Wynne, Singer, Bartko and Toohey, 1975).

On both theoretical and empirical grounds we feel that the particular forms or styles in which attention is established is an enduring feature of family transactions and makes formative contributions to the ego structure of the growing child. We find that in families containing a young adult schizophrenic offspring both parents tend to have frequent difficulties in establishing a focus of attention and sharing meaning (Singer, 1967). Communication in these families is especially disturbed at the attentional level (i.e., where are we looking?), whereas in the families of borderline, neurotic, and normal individuals, communication disorders are more prominent *later on, after* an attentional focus has been shared by two or more persons.

THE RORSCHACH AS A STANDARDIZED STIMULUS

In the transaction with a person administering the individual Rorschach, a subject is asked to say aloud what he thinks each blot looks like. His words can be regarded as the outward, visible products of his attentional processes. First, he has to join the focus offered by the tester who has proposed the task; then attend to the images and ideas that come to awareness in his own mind and to select appropriate ones to express aloud to the tester. Thus this person's spoken words reflect the orderliness, or lack of it, of his attentional processes as he is using them at that moment in a verbal transaction with another person. It is assumed that those attentional and communicational features detectable in the Rorschach task are structural, that is, quasi-stable (Rapaport, 1957) stylistic attributes. It is further assumed that these samples of attention and language in this particular task are representative of how a person deploys his attention and uses language in similar labeling and descriptive exchanges with other persons. In our scoring manual various communication deviances are cited which we feel reduce the visualizableness of verbal communication and disrupt a listener's attention; that is for a number of reasons a listener cannot piece together the words offered to him by a speaker to form a coherent, consistent picture or frame of reference in his or her head based upon the remarks of the speaker (Singer, 1967, 1975).

RORSCHACH ADMINISTRATION

Because of our interest in the details of communication, we work with verbatim typescripts of tape-recorded Rorschach interchanges. Certain methodologic precautions are necessary in this research.

It is essential that communication patterns be sampled in a comparable way from one subject to the next. Therefore, what the examiner says and does must be standardized as much as possible, including guidelines for his or her behavior when the subject asks questions or diverts from the task.

Thus, communication samples must be verbatim, preferrably tape recorded, and include comments of both subject and examiner.

Otherwise, important, indeed essential, aspects of the communication may be omitted or selectively recorded and independent checks on comparability of the data will not be possible.

Also, the interviewer or tester should not be informed of the psychiatric diagnosis or symptom picture of the subject, or the family from which he or she comes, because such information could covertly bias the tester's attitudes and behavior (Wynne, Singer, Bartko and Toohey, 1968, 1975).

Conversely, investigators who diagnose the subject should do so without knowledge of the tests or any clinical or research reports based upon them.

Interjudge reliability must be established and maintained at an adequately high level. This is a methodologic criterion which is, unfortunately, too often neglected in psychiatric research.

Ideally four separate staff members or groups of staff should be available in research of this kind—for administration of the procedure to the subject, for accurate transcription of the material, for independent clinical diagnosis and evaluation, and for blind scoring or rating of the Rorschach behavior. We have provided manuals and guidelines for each of the groups involved in our research (Wynne, Singer, Bartko and Toohey, 1968, 1975).

COMMUNICATION DEVIANCE MANUAL

The variety of communication deviances that can be fruitfully identified in a Rorschach protocol may be gleaned from a glance at a listing of our scoring manual items (Figure 13.1). An early version of this manual appeared in 1966 (Singer and Wynne, 1966); a subsequent revision was completed in 1973 (Singer, 1974). It is this latter version of the manual which will be described and considered here. We have separate manuals for scoring Individual, Spouse and Family Rorschachs.

The communication deviance scoring manual contains 41 items, grouped into five clusters. Raters assign as many of the features as are detected in any response: The items are individually discrete and at the same time they are not mutually exclusive. The manual describes and illustrates types of communication anomalies or

FIGURE 13.1

Rorschach Scoring Codes

C. *Commitment Problems*

1. Abandoned abruptly ceased remarks
2. Unstable percepts
3. Responses in negative form
4. Subjunctive "if" responses
5. "Question" responses
6. Derogatory, disparaging remarks
7. Nihilistic remarks
8. Failures to verify own responses
9. Forgetting responses
10. Partial disqualifications

R. *Referent Problems*

1. Unintelligible remarks
2. Gross indefiniteness and tentativeness
3. Inconsistent and ambiguous references
4. References to "they" and the intent of others
5. Abstract, global terms
6. Cryptic remarks

L. *Language Anomalies*

1. Ordinary words or phrases used oddly or out of context
2. Odd sentence constructions
3. Peculiar or quaint, private terms or phrases
4. Euphemisms
5. Slips of the tongue
6. Mispronounced words
7. Foreign terms used for no particular reason
8. Clanged association, rhymed phrases and wordplay
9. Reiteration

D. *Disruptions*

1. Interruptions of examiner's speeches
2. Extraneous questions and remarks
3. Nonverbal, disruptive behavior
4. Humor
5. Swearing
6. Hopping around among responses
7. Concrete-set responses

FIGURE 13.1 (Continued)

CA. Contradictory, Arbitrary Sequences

    1. Contradictory information
    2. Incompatible alternatives and incompatible aspects of images
    3. Retractions and denials
    4. Odd, tangential, unappropriate responses to preceding speaker
    5. Negativistic, temporary card rejection followed by a response
    6. Illogical combinations of percepts and categories
    7. Non sequitur reasoning
    8. Assigning meaning illogically on basis of non-essential attributes of cards
    9. Contaminations

deviances which have the effect of puzzling, diverting or confusing a listener instead of permitting him or her to follow and comprehend a line of thought. These communication or transactional deviances are maneuvers, wordings, reasoning, or phrasings which have a disturbing impact upon a listener. Examples from first viewing Card I responses of the father and mother of a chronic schizophrenic young woman will best illustrate what we score. The family is upper middle class, the father with college and the mother with high school education. Traditional Rorschach scoring would heed only the mother's content of bat, face and bell. However, a tape-recorded transcript of her transactional communication conveys the potentially bewildering impact her remarks create in a listener's mind. The numbers and phrases inserted in parentheses are those shown in Figure 13.1 and follow the passage to which they apply. Following the standard instructions, the mother replied:

    1. (2 seconds) Oh, bat. *(W)*[1]
       Is it good to ahm say the first thing that comes in your mind? (*D2, extraneous question; mother is changing task set a bit, introducing notion about "first thing" which was not implied in the instructions.*) (Tester replied: That's ok, but also tell me other things the blot suggests.)

       Well, that's sort of ah, (*C1, abandoned idea*) I don't know why, (*C8, failure to verify own idea*) but that's what it looks like to me.

---

[1] For explanations of standard Rorschach scoring symbols, see Appendix, pp. 609, ff. (Editor).

2. I see pe-oh what looks like a face (upper lateral detail) on one of them. (*R3, ambiguous or indefinite reference point*) Right here. Right over there. Yeah. With the head. (*R3, ambiguous reference point*) Could be a black angel I guess, if (*C4, "if" conditional remarks*) it were white, (*CA1, contradictory remark*) but it's black, so I can't say angel. (*CA7, reasoning problems*) And it only has one wing, so that wouldn't be very good. (*C10, disqualification without actually taking back the response*) There's the ha- looks like a hand there (outer "wing" detail).

3. This looks like a bell. (low center) Ah, I don't know, about all I can see there. I'm not very imaginative.

One can readily see that while this mother would attain adequate traditional Rorschach scores, her communication deviances are such as to really bewilder a listener. The following are her husband's individual Rorschach responses to the first viewing on Card I. The tester had given the standard instructions and the father opened with:

> You know, I thought I'd seen you somewhere before, but I could not remember where. Maybe that just . . . (*C1, abandoned idea*)

1. Aah, that's a bat. (*W*) (25 second pause) Sir? (Odd, but not classifiable. Tester encouraged him to keep card a bit longer and see what else came to mind.)

    Father replied: Oh! You mean you use the same one? (*R3, ambiguous remark*) Oh, I'm finished. I said it was a bat. Oh, you can see more than one thing. (*CA5, quitting, then continuing; D2, distracting questioning*)

2. Well, a uh, a dissected frog (whole). Don't care which way I look at it, which angle, or upside down, or . . . (Tester: That's ok, you may look at it from any angle.)

3. A lady's fur jacket. (*W*) That's about all I say (*L1, odd usage*) outa that one . . . If it doesn't make any difference what you say if you do this the way you see it, then how does that prove anything? (*R1, unintelligible remark*) (The puzzled tester replied: Oh, I think so.)

These parents well-illustrate the vast difference between what a traditional psychometric approach to scoring might reveal and what scoring their Rorschach behavior as a sample of the impact of their communicative transactions might indicate.

We will not present the inquiry portion of these parent's interaction over the blots, for suffice it to say they continued in their idiosyncratic style. However, this brings us to the point that the two viewings of the Rorschach cards should be regarded as separate tasks tapping two somewhat different skills. One task calls for *what* and one for *why* behaviors. The first viewing calls for the person to label *what* he sees; the inquiry or second viewing taps his skills at explaining to another person *why* he said what he did. The first viewing is a labeling procedure; the second a reasoning procedure. Thus, we separately analyze the data obtained on the first and second viewing of the cards and make separate inferences about the labeling and reasoning behaviors elicited on these two occasions.

A BRIEF OVERVIEW OF THE
COMMUNICATION DEVIANCE MANUAL

As Figure 13.1 reveals, the 41 types of deviances are classed into five groups: commitment problems, referent problems, disruptions, language anamolies, and contradictions. Space does not permit the presentation of the actual manual with its many examples of what to score and what not to score as deviances.* Rather, only one or two examples of each are given. Raters assign the applicable code to the passages where such deviances occur. Multiple scores may be assigned any passage as the categories are not mutually exclusive, but merely ways to code various forms of transactional deviances. Each of the types of deviances will be briefly described and illustrated with one or two examples. Potential users of this approach for the Individual as well as for the Spouse and Family Rorschach are urged to consult the extended manuals prior to proceeding with use of this type of analysis of Rorschach communication (Singer, 1973; Singer and Faunce, 1975).

Commitment Problems

When a listener is confronted with any one of the ten varieties of commitment problems described in this section, he is apt to wonder: *Does he* (the speaker) *really mean what he is saying?* The way in which the idea is phrased by the speaker leaves doubt in a listener's

---

*Mimeographed copies of the manual along with special typing, unitizing and scoring procedures are available through correspondence with the author for use with Individual, Spouse and Family Rorschach procedures.

mind about the status of the idea—has he abandoned it, disqualified it, down-graded it, or intended it to be taken seriously. The speaker in various ways seems less than fully committed to the idea. The following items class ways in which a speaker causes a listener to wonder if he should really pay attention and heed what the speaker is saying:

C1. *Abandoned, abruptly ceased, uncorrected remarks:* A speaker says aloud a bit of an idea, only to abandon it.

"And I don't know what the artist ah—or what this ah—but it seems in every one of them there is something that is significant to me."

C2. *Unstable percepts:* A speaker can indicate that what he is viewing is so changing that one is not sure just what to pay attention to.

"Here is a bat, but now when I look here, his head has moved down here. First of all, I said this was an ear, but I think that must be a part of his head."

C3. *Responses in negative form:* A speaker cites what he does not see, and is thus not committed to the notions expressed.

"It doesn't look like a sheep."

C4. *Subjunctive, "if" responses:* A speaker qualifies his ideas with conditions that are not present and a listener does not know how to regard the remarks.

"It could be scary, if you were a nervous type."

C5. *Question responses:* Instead of making a statement about what he sees, the speaker puts his idea in question form.

"Is that a girl?"

C6. *Derogatory, disparaging, critical remarks:* Ideas are given but down-graded.

"That might represent two people, look mighty goofy to me."

C7. *Nihilistic remarks:* These disqualify the context of meaningfulness.

"I think it might be part of a flower at the top, but they're just blobs. I don't see how you can read alot of things into them."

C8. *Inability or failure to verify own responses:* A certain disclaiming of responsibility for one's own ideas can occur and puzzle a listener.

"Well, this suggests to me, I don't know why, a sort of underwater light."

C9.   *Forgetting responses:* The speaker forgets what he said; his commitment seems ephemeral.

"What did I see here?"

C10.   *Partial disqualification:* The speaker disqualifies aspects, but does not totally retract an idea; he leaves meaning half-standing.

"Like a couple of characters doing a dance, dressed alike. More like dogs than people. They don't look like any particular kind of dog, and they don't look exactly like monkeys. They're just sort of figures that are created by this ink."

Referent Problems

Six subclasses of referent problems are described in this section. When referent problems occur the listener hears things worded in ways that cause him to ponder: *What is he talking about?* From what the speaker says, a listener can not be sure he is sharing the proper referent point. What is being alluded to is ambiguous or inconsistent, in any of a variety of ways. Those described in this section are:

R1.   *Unintelligible remarks:* Certain passages are not followable and leave a listener totally adrift about the intended meaning.

"To do with birth again I feel. They're sort of uh, about to give birth itself I think to one another."

R2.   *Gross indefiniteness and lack of specificity:* Remarks scored here are so indefinite, unspecified and vague that a speaker could be talking about almost anything.

"Might be some insect, or something like that, insect kind of thing, laying down, tore up here, just looks like something blotted down, could be almost anything."

R3.   *Inconsistent and ambiguous references:* Within related statements the speaker shifts tense, gender, number and referents leaving a listener unsure about what is intended.

"Here's a ballroom *dress*. You see the top and then *she's* got one tier and then there's a third tier."

"That's the same shape as *the other one* we had a while ago, only *it's* in color."

"See this bear up here? There's his feet and there's *your* tail."

R4.   *References to the intent of others:* The speaker indicates that the meaning he is assigning derives from the acts or intentions of other persons.

"*The fellow* who prepared the map used the red colors to represent something, but I don't know what."

R5.   *Abstract, global terms and technical phrases:* The speaker uses technical jargon, esoteric references, and global, abstract terms. The listener cannot share the referent point with him because the labeling process has not been sufficiently specific or visualizable.

"There are a *pair of beings.*"

"That reminds me of a *helgramite.*"

R6.   *Cryptic remarks:* The speaker responds with a brief, telegraphic word or remark. The listener has to try to guess the intended implication

"Semper Fidelis."

"The dance of the inferno."

"Pantomine."

"Friendship."

Language Anomalies

This section contains the criteria for classifying oddities in word choice, word order and word usage. When a speaker uses words peculiarly and places them in odd order, plays with their sounds, and even invents words, he reduces the likelihood that a listener will be able to follow his remarks. Again if we ask what is the experience of the listener when he hears a language anomaly, we can see the impact. He asks himself mentally, "Do I know what he is talking about." The listener knows roughly what the speaker is talking about, but has to stop to process or puzzle over the words and feels he has not kept up with the flow of the transaction.

Meaning is not reduced by most common grammatical errors and common slang expressions such as "he ain't," "he don't," and "that's got no wings." These are not the kinds of usages which impair meaning. Rather it is the appearance of idiosyncratic and peculiar words and phrases which puzzle and distract a listener. Here are scored those instances in which a speaker's wording causes a listener to wonder: *Did I really hear that? Did I get that right?* Nine sub-categories of language anomalies are scored:

L1.   *Ordinary words or phrases used oddly, incorrectly or out of context:* Ordinary and correctly pronounced words or phrases are used in odd, incorrect or unexpected ways.

"These are *symptoms* of vertebrae."

"I *pronounce* this the same as I say before."

"This one has *some readings* of human shapes."

L2.   *Odd sentence construction:* Word order seems peculiar. Words seem dropped into sequence in a loose, incorrect way.

"Little mouths *with ducks.*"

"Mannekin, you know, *they put on dresses.*"

"I see ribs and *of the esophagus.*"

L3.   *Peculiar, quaint, or private terms and phrases:* The speaker makes up, and modifies words and common sayings, creates neologisms and idiosyncratic labeling.

"It's *raggeldy pointed* on the left."

"That is a bodygeist." (sic)

L4.   *Euphemisms:* The speaker uses euphemisms and roundabout ways of labeling.

"That's the fore and aft department." (for front and back of the torso).

L5.   *Slips of the tongue:* A seeming slip of the tongue makes it necessary for the listener to make inferences about the meaning the speaker probably intended to select.

"That looks like a mother and her little father there."

L6.   *Mispronounced words:* Mispronounced words are distracting occurrences.

"That's an *ogray*" (ogre).

"That is a *carticaytchure*" (caricature).

L7.   *Foreign terms used for no particular reason:* The use of foreign terms for no reason by a native American speaker is distracting.

"What is that creature that flies at night? Die Fledermaus?"

"Here is that blitzkriegen machine, a tank you'd call it."

L8.   *Clang associations, rhymed phrases, and word play:* In this testing situation, when a subject rhymes words, plays with their sounds, or puns, he is diverting his and his listener's attention away from the message and onto the sheer mechanical sounds of words involved.

"Lamb's skin, ram's skin."

"This is a very well illu*strated straight* line."

"Imag*ination* is the worst *nation*."

"Looks like a *bat*. I'll *bat* you never heard that before."

L9.   *Reiteration*: The same words or phrases are repeated three or more times in close proximity.

"This has two *cows*, the figure of two *cows*, in the middle, two buffalo or two *cows*, two *cows* I guess, yeah, *cows*."

Disruptions

Here are scored seven types of occurrences which have a distracting, disrupting effect upon a listener. The listener as he hears these types of remarks says in effect to himself: *I can't keep up, I am losing track*. The speaker in one way or another diverts himself and the listener away from the shared task they set about to do.

D1.   *Interruptions of the examiner's speech*: In the Rorschach procedure the examiner speaks primarily to give the instructions at various times. Interrupting him thus distracts both the subject and the examiner.

The tester began the instructions and a father interrupted with, "Oh, boy, parchesi."

D2.   *Extraneous questions and remarks*: Here the speaker disrupts the task by getting off onto side issues.

"Could a person be affected by a vaccination?"

"You got me buffaloed, doc."

D3.   *"Nonverbal" disruptive behavior*: The subject engages in acts which in themselves are disruptions of the task.

The subject gets up and walks around; starts to draw on test cards; silently reads the back of the card; hunts for his glasses, tissues, or cigarettes; hums, whistles, or mumbles; slips his shoes on and off; rearranges the furniture.

D4.   *Humor*: While humor can be a great social facilitator, within the testing situation it tends to be distracting on the whole and is scored as a disruption.

(Parent ends viewing card by saying:) "I pass." (laughs) (This is humor based upon alluding to the test cards as if this is a "card game.")

"It looks like a bat, right off the bat."

D5.　*Swearing*: This upsets the general tone of the transaction and distracts from the central task. Score here profanities, blasphemies and curses, but not terms such as darn, heck, gosh and drat it.

D6.　*Hopping around among responses*: Jumping back and forth among ideas without properly announcing and carrying a listener along can be a diverting and puzzling event.

In the follwoing example (one person's replies to Card I) responses 1 and 3 are both involved in the "hopping":

Card 1: "Mm, I don't think I need my glasses for that."

1.　"Well, my first thought is that it's more like a bat than anything I've—can think of.

2.　And then, ah, to me there's a similarity to the pelvic bone region of a person.

Are we supposed just to keep naming things, or as many as we see in it? (yes, mmhmm) Or - and that's it? (Anything that occurs to you that you can make out in it.)

3.　There's a little bit of a similarity to a butterfly, but not too—not too much.

4.　I have seen a flying uhm squirrel, however, I'm gonna have to admit it doesn't have a tail here. Think the same might be . . .

1.　It would be more like a bat I guess than it would be a . . .

3.　Did - I did I say a butterfly, didn't I?"

D7.　*Concrete-set responses*: The Rorschach instructions set up an *interpretive* set toward the blots. If the speaker falls into a concrete-set in which he feels he must try to *recognize* the cards, he diverts himself and his listener from the task they set out upon, namely, his saying what the blots suggest to him.

"I don't know what those cannibals would be doing with bowling balls and a necktie."

"Doctor, I'm afraid I've never seen one of those. I'm not familiar with that species."

Contradictory, Arbitrary Sequences

In this section are grouped a series of nine types of contradictory acts. The speaker contradicts himself, or violates logic in a variety of ways. The impact of these types of occurrences is to make a listener think: *I got it, but how can I deal with it?* He hears what the speaker says, but it contradicts what he heard before, or the speaker is violating the rules of logic and the listener is caught not knowing quite what to do about what he hears. The categories are:

CA1.   *Contradictory information*: Here are scored remarks which contradict earlier information and statements which are internally contradictory.

      "I've never seen a bat. . . Last summer a bat got in our cabin."

      (Tester: Tell me more about these *two women* you saw holding something and facing each other.) "Well, I just thought it might be *a person* looking in a mirror, getting ready to go out."

CA2.   *Incompatible alternatives and incompatible aspects of images*: The above item, CA1, scored contradictions between remarks; here are scored inconsistencies within the *image* the speaker's words create in the listener's mind.

      "That could be a broken *mirror* or a *bat*."

      "Two human beings standing on *each side of each other*."

CA3.   *Retractions and denials*: The speaker takes back or denies what he originally said.

      "Might be a crab on each side, legs on them, (In the inquiry:) I'll take that back. Crabs have feet twisted around, not shaped exactly like that."

CA4.   *Odd, tangential, inappropriate responses to questions or remarks:* Here are classed non sequitur *replies* to a preceding speaker.

      (Tester: What about the blot suggests a dog?) "What *kind* of a dog it reminds me of?" (Tester: No, what reminds you of a dog?)

      "Two little baby insects coming out." (Tester: I see.) "You mean you can't see it?"

CA5.   *Negativistic, temporary card rejection followed by a response*: The speaker says he sees nothing but goes on to give a response, or indicates in the midst of speaking that he is going to stop but goes on instead.

"Doesn't look like anything to me. I'd say a flying squirrel."

(Having given two responses, says:) "That's about all I would see in that, plus a bat."

CA6.   *Peculiar logic; illogical combinations of percepts*: The speaker pieces together images and concepts on the basis of contiguity.

Card III: "Two women. They're bending backwards to let a, to let a large butterfly pass through."

Card VIII: "Oh, now they look to me like two polar bears attached to a kite."

CA7.   *Non sequitur reasoning*: A variety of faulty reasoning is scored here.

"It's upside down, so it's an embryo."

"Well, they'd probably be actors because there're two of them."

CA8.   *Assigning meaning on the basis of nonessential attributes of the cards*: The speaker arbitrarily selects an attribute and reasons from it that things are similar or related because of the shared but not vital commonality.

"These are crabs, and there are other ones (center blue on Card X) because they are blue too."

"The North Pole, because it's at the top."

CA9.   *Contaminations*: Two ideas occur to the speaker, stemming from alternative meanings that he could assign. These ideas fuse into one and a single label is given that incorporates both. This item is a well-known Rorschach score.

Card V: "A rabbit rug." (The speaker saw a rabbit in the center and the rest of the card as a pelt, and the two ideas fused.)

Card IX: "A bear-grass skirt." (Bear, green, and grass were fused into one idea.)

Spouse and Family Rorschach Procedures

As we indicated earlier, this very abbreviated outline of the communication deviance manual for use with the individually administered Rorschach serves merely to convey the range and types of transactional deviances which are scored with this manual. We also apply these same general scoring criteria in our research using Spouse and Family Rorschach procedures.

First we shall describe the Spouse Rorschach procedure. For that task the husband and wife are asked to view Card I together, with the instructions to see how many ideas the two of them can agree the card looks like. The examiner then leaves the couple alone to work on the task and instructs them to ring a bell when they have finished. The entire procedure is tape recorded. The exchange usually runs about four or five minutes. Following this, each is given an actual size ink outline of the blot and asked to draw around the areas, and label carefully those things each thinks the two of them agreed upon. No talking is permitted during this process. A second card is given to them and the procedure repeated. Thus a total of about eight to ten minutes is used for this spouse interaction. Then the offspring are brought in and the whole family is given a card, with the instructions to see how many things the entire family can agree upon for the card. This is the Family Rorschach procedure in which all family members interact with one another over the task. (See Loveland, Singer and Wynne, 1963; Singer and Faunce, 1975; Singer, Glaser and Wynne, 1975; Wynne, 1970.)

The following is the total Spouse Rorschach transaction between the parents of a chronic schizophrenic young woman. The parents are viewing Card I together. Comments upon their transacting will be inserted after each spouse's speech without using our scoring code numbers so that reading is not disrupted by the numbers. We have a manual with specific examples from Spouse Rorschachs or Family Rorschachs for raters to use in scoring these interactions. Examples from two or more persons interchanging ideas need to be provided to show raters how to carry over the principles from the Individual Rorschach to the more complex exchanges in the Spouse and Family tasks. We find that while the general conversational faults occur across tasks, each conversational transaction has its own eliciting properties, and raters need specific examples of how the general types of deviances appear in group interactions. In the following spouse procedure, the examiner has given the standard instructions and has just left the room.

1. Father (Fa): Of course my opinions are always my own. I won't go by your opinions.

    This is a "transaction stopper." The father is baffling in his wording; nihilistic in his attitude; and resistive to participating and cooperating with his wife in the task. His impact upon what transpires is central. His opening gambit forecasts what he will permit to occur between himself and his wife, namely, no real sharing of a task. He simply pits himself against her. In this reaction, he really is covertly misconstruing the task. He is responding as if he were asked "to agree to her ideas." He is doing what we term "restructuring the task to himself without explicitly saying so."

2.   Mother (Mo): (interrupts) Well what do you see! What do you see!

The wife accepts his tacit redefinition of the task, which is actually a misinterpretation, and then repetitiously tries to get him to say what he will agree to say that *he* sees. She is caught in a bind, having accepted both his and the examiner's request, and not straightening out that he has misconstrued the request. The reader will recognize that this husband's opening gambit is a hard one to handle easily, because it is both bewildering and attacking. From the very start, this couple gets off on a tangential approach because the husband has misconstrued the task. Thus the wife can only try to get him "to say his opinion."

3.   Fa: I see the same thing I saw before; that looked like a bat to me.

He cites what he saw before in his individual Rorschach, again resisting the participation, and entrenching his negativistic stance. Also note he delays mentioning the content he saw by wording his remarks in a withholding, resistive way, keeping the idea of bat held far into his speech.

4.   Mo: Well, overall it's a bat. Ah, it could ah resemble a bat, but ah (sighs). See anything else? . . .

She agrees to his bat in a guarded way, but indicates her less than total acceptance. Again she asks him his idea.

5.   Fa: What do you see here?

His reply to her questions is another question.

6.   Mo: Well, it looks like little gnomes; heads up on the top (upper center detail) to me, and looks like little chickens opening their mouths, for food.

7.   Fa: Looks like a chicken?

Finally she states her two ideas, only to have her husband repeat her response back to her in a questioning, put-down manner. She tries again in speech 8.

8.   Mo: The little chickens up here (upper center detail).

9.   Fa: I see why we don't agree about things.

He sarcastically puts her down further, and diverts to life in general and beyond this task, thus leaving the task set. Further, his remark is a bit cryptic, but clearly demeaning in its intent.

10. Mo: And here's a little chicken's head with an eye in it.

11. Fa: (Mumbles to self) A little chicken's head. We're not "picken" that (half laugh), I'm not picking it apart. I'm seeing the pictures as I see it.

The mother once again in speech 10 tried to get him to look at her percept, only to have him respond by mumbling to himself, sarcastically repeat her remark, and chastise her approach to the blot, without making it explicit what he means. He really means he is looking at the whole blot and she at a little part. However, he never directly states this. Only because we as observers guess what he is alluding to, do we even know what the issue is. He thinks one is to look at only the whole blot. Yet he expresses this idea quite unintelligbly by insisting: "I'm seeing the picture as I see it." This is quite unfathomable without being bizarre. His covert notion that he and she are to view the entire blot and not view parts is never explicitly put into words between these two people. Also note his word play "chicken .. picken" which he follows with a half laugh. Word play is a diverting act. He however is so unclear in his ways that a second person merely feels puzzled about what transpires, almost unable to label what is going wrong in the conversation with this man.

12. Mo: Well then, that's all you agree on isn't it, that it looks like a bat, huh? You don't wanna agree on anything else, is that it?

13. Fa: No.

14. Mo: You don't wanna agree on anything else?

15. Fa: No, no, no.

Speeches 12 through 15 are a series of interchanges in which the wife reinforces the husband's negativistic stance. She is repetitive, he is repetitive.

16. Mo: Gnome's or little ducks with the mouth's open? All right, ring the bell.

The mother insistently repeats her "gnomes" heads, but changes from chickens to ducks.

17. Fa: You haven't made up your mind on what you see.

She obviously has made up her mind, has been persistent in repeating her notions. The husband's remark invalidates all that she has been repeatedly trying to get across. He creates the impression with his words that he has not heard what she has been saying.

18. Mo: Yeah, I said I see, I told you what I see. I see gnomes' heads and I agree uh, it has a bat ah overall, but I mean if you wanna analyze parts of it . . .

She repeats her gnomes' heads, agrees to his bat, and starts to bring out the issue between them about whether to look at the whole or parts of the blot, but words it rather unclearly, hesitates, and is interrupted by father:

19. Fa: (Interrupts) Well, you agree with me that it looks like a bat. Is that correct?

He repeats her agreement almost as if it had not been said to him. Thus twice in close proximity he has replied as if she had not said what she actually did say.

20. Mo: That's the only thing we agree on, you don't, you don't wanna agree on chicken's heads though?

She again agrees with "bat," but turns to eliciting further negativism from him by asking him in the negative form, "you don't wanna, you don't wanna," even restating the negative phrase twice. She has returned to labeling her percept "chickens" from the previous change to "ducks" in speech 16.

21. Fa: I don't see the little chicken's head.

22. Mo: Little mouths open with chickens?

Her word order is totally jumbled, but now father responds for the first time to paying attention to her ideas.

23. Fa: Where?

24. Mo: Right here.

25. Fa: Oh, you're taking one little part of it?

26. Mo: Little birds.

Speech 23 suggests he has at last paid attention, only to reveal in speech 25 he is back at the issue seen in speech 11, whether the whole or part of the blot is to be used. He implies criticism, asks her a question, to which she does not reply, but merely repeats her notion, now calling it "birds." The issue between them about how much of the blot to use has never been openly and clearly stated by either partner. We can infer that her repetition suggests she magically hopes that changing the label might change his reaction. She is doggedly hanging onto her notion, only shifting her labels in an unspecified way.

27. Fa: No. No. No. What do I . . . I don't see anything like that, that sure do-doesn't look like a bird to me.

28.   Mo: OK?

His phrasing is a bit disjointed; he strongly rejects her percept, but note she responds with an affirmative remark.

29.   Fa: Sometime this, when we get into the zoo, I'll point out birds to you.

30.   Mo: Birds with their mouths open, young birds have bigger mouths than anything else; that's all, they're all mouth.

31.   Fa: I know someone else (2 half laughs) that's got a mouth.

32.   Mo: All right, ring the bell, there's no use prolonging this.

In speech 29 he is sarcastic. Her reaction is to insistently repeat her ideas, he repeats his sarcasm in speech 31, this time laughing at her.

Thus in the end, no real consensus was achieved. In fact in their separate ways, neither parent really was able to try to participate in a consensus task between them. He was openly resistive, repetitive and unclear about the issues between them. She was unrelenting, repetitive, and as unchanging in her covert way as he was in his blatant way. The task itself was lost; the conflictual issues were never made explicit; the two partners by-passed each other. He acted as if he never heard what she said; that she should know what he meant even though what he said was not clear about the "area to be looked at" issue. Both partners were at a loss about how to talk together in this simple task. They engaged in an unrewarding, unproductive, repetitive exchange and disqualified each others ideas. At no point was any real focus of attention shared, not even about where to look; and no sharing of meaning occurred over a task which never was actually accomplished. From an interpersonal point of view these transactions reveal many psychological problems, ones of aggression, the roles each parent plays, their style of relating to one another, their self-concepts and so forth. However, in the context of this chapter we are concentrating on the information that can be obtained from a careful analysis of the communication deviances.

Perhaps a brief excerpt from a Spouse Rorschach from parents of the same upper middle social class (II, Hollingshead and Redlich, 1957) with two normal young adult daughters will serve to illustrate how well the following parents share attention and meaning and go about the task in contrast to the previous couple. They are also viewing Card I.

1.   Mo.: What do you see?

2.   Fa: Supposed to start?

3.   Mo: Uh Huh.

4.   Fa: A mask, two girls swinging, elephants.

5.   Mo: Well now, wait a minute. I see the elephants and the mask. Yeah, I see that.

6.   Fa: Or a cat, a big bug.

7.   Mo: A big bug, two girls' shapes.

8.   Fa: Yeah.

9.   Mo: One ah thin and one heavy?

10. Fa: Uh Huh.

11. Mo: Yeah, it looks like their feet are going the other way . . . Now we see the elephants facing us?

This couple settles right in to the task. When the father lists three ideas without pause, the mother tells him "wait a minute." Lets him know she sees two. He offers two more percepts, and she confirms one of them and finally cites his earlier "girls" shapes. Thus one can see these people are attending, listening to each other, trying to follow and grasp each other's ideas, and are task-oriented. The sheer quarrelsomeness of the first couple is not the crucial difference. Families of non-schizophrenic offspring can get into quarrels or be unpleasant to one another in public. However, they appear to experience sharing attention and meaning clearly and this is also conveyed to the reader. In contrast, the parents of the schizophrenic young woman in their Spouse Rorschach were unclear about each other's messages, the task per se, and where to even focus attention.

THE FAMILY RORSCHACH

The time actually consumed in the ordinary Spouse Rorschach is relatively brief for most couples. Following the Spouse Rorschach, the offspring are brought in to join the parents on the Family Rorschach procedure. Here the entire group is asked to see how many ideas the family as a group can agree upon together. The excerpts below are from the same parents, whose total Spouse Rorschach was presented, interacting with their twenty year old chronically schizophrenic daughter and mid-twenties normal daughter.

The examiner has instructed them and has just left the room. The father addresses the schizophrenic daughter:

1. Fa: What does this look like to you Betty?

2. Betty: A wolf.

3. Fa: A wolf! Yeah, it could be a wolf, I thought it looked like a bat.

   He repeats her remark in an exclamatory way, as he did with his wife, but catches himself and does not continue this as sarcasm, but accepts the daughter's idea tentatively, "could be" but affirms his idea as preferred.

4. Jane: I thought it looks like two bats carrying away a headless woman.

5. Mo: Is this the same, all the same card?

   The mother responds to a peculiar response from the older daughter with a peculiar response of her own, since the family is viewing the card.

6. Fa: Oh for heaven's sake. Carrying away a headless woman. Where do you get such a . . .

7. Jane: Well, here you have a woman. You see that figure right there?

8. Fa: Yeah.

9. Jane: That's a woman with no head. And there is two bats. And here's the woman with no head.

10. Mo: I don't see that.

    The mother who in the Spouse Rorschach seemed the victim of her husband's sarcasm, here and in the rest of the record acts as a disrupter. Each time the father and one or the other daughter gets an interchange of information going and agree to some idea, the mother stops the conversation, so to speak, by a repetitive entry in between the two about to share meaning, and breaks up the point they are sharing or about to share. Thus one sees a number of roles which shift about in the family when different members are seen interacting.

    As could be predicted, each parent then returns to pushing for acceptance of his or her own idea seen earlier in their Individual Rorschach's and which they attempted to get accepted in the Spouse Rorschach. In families of non-schizophrenics, while people do re-introduce ideas from their Individual Rorschach, they usually see new things in the present task and say so. Such spontaneity seems to permit more information, or a less fixed and doggedly held idea to enter the problem solving task of what they can agree to that the blot looks like.

The mother in the interim tries to get her gnome head from her Individual and Spouse Rorschach experience accepted. Father sarcastically repeats her remarks. Finally he turns to the schizophrenic daughter and asks her about her response which she gave way back in speech 2.

20.   Fa: What makes you think it's like a wolf, Betty?

21.   Mo: Just a minute. Let's each one discuss something. I'll tell you what I saw.

22.   Jane: All right, what else do you see besides there?

23.   Fa: You see lots of things.

24.   Mo: I see a gnome up on top there. Here is a . . .

25.   Fa: What does a gnome look like?

When father tried to draw Betty into the conversation, mother broke that up by implying she was going to introduce new ideas. Instead, she repeated what had been her speech 15. But now she treats it as if she has not said it before, which must be baffling to the family. The father's response of asking what a gnome looks like is odd, either as sarcasm, or as an adult asking such a question. The mother handles his stance equally puzzlingly by the following remark.

26.   Mo: I told you like a little dwarf with a hat on. See these two little things here? (Pointing to same area as she was using for the gnomes.) They look like little birds with their mouth open.

The fixity with which these parents hold onto ideas is clear, and the repetitiveness of patterns of interacting is also patently evident. The family transacting together here is in a pattern out of which they cannot emerge it seems.

For a number of exchanges father tried to align himself with Betty, and mother with Jane, but neither parent would actually accept or help with the ideas the girls were offering, nor would the girls join into a problem solving approach. It was merely two pairs of contending persons acting as if they were forming an alliance. The father and schizophrenic daughter were talking about his bat and her wolf and either a "line" or a "lion" which never became clear. Mother and Jane were locked into a no-win situation over whether they saw a poodle head or poodle tail in the same small area of the card. Finally the schizophrenic daughter inserted a long speech, which in its "mad way" alludes to the family having drifted from the task, and covertly implies how one "might list the animals," which was what the family was unable to do.*

76. Betty: Do you know that I had this paper, I had this paper in one of these puzzle books. Here's what is said. It said name how many animals can you think of that went into Noah's Ark, of each kind, what you think they were. To Noah's Ark. I wrote down what I thought, you know, and then it said how many, how many other animals there are, there are you picked out that were in Noah's Ark to be the . . .

77. Fa: Where did you read that?

Betty seemed to be alluding in her way to how one might solve the family dilemma, list the animals, all the animals. In other families, someone might have made use of the good part of her stance, instead father responds to only the most concrete thing possible, where had she read that. She responded by saying "in a paperback." The father returned to talking about his bat, Jane her two bats and mother the gnome. At speech 87 Betty abruptly rang the bell, signaling the family had concluded their work. Which in fact they had not, since they had not reached one agreement among them.

87. Betty: (Rings bell.) You happy now?

88. Mo: Delighted. Oh, I'm so overjoyed, I'm just tickled pink.

89. Fa: I think we did a good job with this, don't you Betty? I think Betty was closer than, Betty and I were the two closest.

The whole adventure ends on a note of madness. They have not done the task, no agreements were reached. When the girl precipitously ended the exchange by ringing the bell, no one commented on the fact that no agreements had been reached, and the mother responds with sarcasm, and the father who is usually the sarcastic

*Although there are many psychological studies of schizophrenic speech that no doubt have enriched our understanding of this disorder, it is our feeling that the present concentration on the conceptual framework we are offering here, brings an additional perspective for our understanding of the symptomatology characterizing these disorders (the schizophren*ias*, see Bleuler, 1911). Using the Rorschach procedures as outlined here appears especially promising for further exploration of the so-called "thinking disorders" of schizophrenic persons. Elsewhere we have offered the term "experience disorder" as a more appropriate term (Wynne and Singer, 1963). Schizophrenics have difficulties not only with communicating, but also with many aspects of experiencing, such as integrating feelings and maintaining major sets toward tasks. The so-called thought symptomatology is a convenient way of detecting and making inferences about the wider disorder.

one, aligns himself strongly with Betty, in an unreal and false way. His statement was as hard to fathom as any Betty made. The family had just done a disastrous job of not agreeing to anything, so how could he praise their efforts. Then he implicitly distorts the task that they had been attempting. His words imply they had been "guessing" or some such thing when he remarks about being "closer or closest." Additionally, there was a message at another level, the relationship level, that he and Betty were close. This had been one of the things the mother had been trying to break up throughout the task. At the end he openly hints at having accomplished what he intended and thereby aligns himself and Betty, in spite of mother's efforts.

This was a distracting, distracted and peculiar series of interchanges and the family group process was even more fragmented than the spouse interaction. Also note that the behavior of the schizophrenic young woman was not the source of the confusion. The group per se could not as the current saying goes "get it together." They were not able to focus their attention, share ideas and do a simple task together. We did not refer specifically to our various coding labels in the presentation of the Spouse or Family Rorschach procedures, but it was clear no doubt that the observed attentional and meaning problems are among those classed in the scoring system. Also many deviances which are scored were not illustrated by the excerpts shown.

Our purpose here was not to go into details of family processes, nor to present formulations about schizophrenia, but rather to illustrate our analysis of Rorschach communications within a transactional conceptualization. We have tried to demonstrate on the basis of earlier research how the Rorschach may be viewed as a means of exploring the psychological aspects of transactions among people. In the Rorschach procedure, more than in any other, attentional factors, sharing of meaning through language usage, reasoning, perceptual adequacy and other dimensions of conversational skills and cognitive processes can be studied as part of on-going interpersonal functioning.

BIBLIOGRAPHY

Bateson, G. *Steps to an ecology of mind*. New York: Ballantine Books, 1972.

Bertalanffy, Ludwig von. An outline of general system theory. *British Journal of the Philosophy of Science*, 1950, **1**, 134-165.

Bertalanffy, Ludwig von. General system theory - A critical review. *General Systems Yearbook*, 1962, **7**, 1-20.

Bleuler, E. *Dementia praecox or the group of schizophrenias*, (1911). Translated by Joseph Zinkin. New York: International Universities Press, 1950.

Hollingshead, A. B. and Redlich, F. C. *Social class and mental illness*. New York: John Wiley, 1957.

Jones, J. E. *Transactional style deviance in families of disturbed adolescents*. Unpublished dissertation, University of California, Los Angeles, 1974.

Jones, J. E. *Transactional style deviance in families of disturbed adolescents and parents of young adult schizophrenics*. In press, 1975b.

Loveland, N.T., Wynne, L. C., and Singer, M. T. The family Rorschach: A new method for studying family interaction. *Family Process*, 1963, **2**, 187-215.

Morris, G. O., and Wynne, L. C. Schizophrenic offspring and parental style of communication. *Psychiatry*, 1965, **28**, 19-44.

Ogden, C. K., and Richards I. A. *The meaning of meaning*. New York: Harcourt Brace, London, Routledge Paul, 1956.

Palombo, S. R., Merrifield, J., Weigert, W., Morris, G. O., and Wynne, L. C. Recognition of parents of schizophrenics from excerpts of family therapy interviews. *Psychiabry*, 1967, **30**, 405-412.

Rapaport, D. Cognitive structures. In J. Bruner (ed.), *Contemporary approaches to cognition*. Cambridge, Mass.: Harvard University Press, 1957.

Singer, M. T. A Rorschach view of the family. In D. Rosenthal (Ed.), *The Genain quadruplets: A case study and theoretical analysis of heredity and environment in schizophrenia*. New York: Basic Books, 1963, 315-325.

Singer, M. T. *Stylistic variables in family research*. Paper presented at symposium sponsored by Marquette University and Milwaukee Psychiatric Hospital, October, 1964.

Singer, M. T., and Wynne, L. C. Differentiating characteristics of parents of childhood schizophrenics, childhood neurotics and young adult schizophrenics. *American Journal of Psychiatry*, 1963, **120**, 234-243.

Singer, M. T., and Wynne, L. C. Thought disorder and family relations of schizophrenics: III. Methodology using projective techniques. *Archives of General Psychiatry*, 1965a, **12**, 187-220.

Singer, M. T., and Wynne, L. C. Thought disorder and family relations of schizophrenics: IV. Results and implications. *Archives of General Psychiatry*, 1965b, **12**, 201-212.

Singer, M. T., and Wynne, L. C. Principles for scoring communication defects and deviances in parents of schizophrenics: Rorschach and TAT scoring manuals. *Psychiatry*, 1966a, **29**, 260-288.

Singer, M. T., and Wynne, L. C. Communication styles in parents of normals, neurotics and schizophrenics: Some findings using a new Rorschach scoring manual. Washington, D.C.: *American Psychiatric Association Research Report*, 1966b, **20**, 25-38.

Singer, M. T. Family transactions and schizophrenia: I. Recent research findings. In J. Romano (Ed.), *The origins of schizophrenia*. Amsterdam: Excerpta Medica International Congress Series, No. 151, 1967, 147-164.

Singer, M. T. The consensus Rorschach and family transactions. *Journal of Projective Techniques and Personality Assessment*, 1968, **32**, 348-351.

Singer, M. T., Wynne, L. C., Levi, L. D., and Sojit, C. *Proverbs interpretation reconsidered: A transactional approach to schizophrenics and their families.* Presented at Symposium on Language and Thought in Schizophrenia, Newport Beach, California, 1968.

Singer, M. T. *Proverb scoring manual*, (Privately printed, 1969, 21 pp.)

Singer, M. T. *Scoring manual for communication deviances seen in individually administered Rorschachs.* Revision, 1973, (unpublished, 100 pp.).

Singer, M. T. *Impact versus diagnosis: A new approach to assessment techniques in family research and therapy.* Presented at the Nathan W. Ackerman Memorial Conference, Cumana, Venezuela, February, 1974.

Singer, M. T., and Faunce, E. *Spouse and family Rorschach manual* Privately printed, 1975.

Singer, M. T., Glaser, R. B. *Family, spouse and individual Rorschach responses of families with and without young adult schizophrenic offspring: Developmental level scoring.* Paper presented at the Western Psychological Association, Sacramento, California, April, 1975.

Watzlawick, P., Beavin, J. H., and Jackson, D. D. *Pragmatics of human communication.* New York: Norton and Company, 1967.

Wild, C., Singer, M. T., Rosman, B., Ricci, J., and Lidz, T. Measuring disordered styles of thinking. *Archives of General Psychiatry*, 1965, **13**, 471-476.

Wynne, L. C. The study of intrafamilial alignments and splits in exploratory family therapy. In N. Ackerman, F. L. Beatman, and S. N. Sherman (eds.), *Exploring the base for family therapy.* New York: Family Service Association of America, 1961.

Wynne, L. C. and Singer, M. T. Thought disorder and family relations of schizophrenics: I. A research strategy. *Archives of General Psychiatry*, 1963a, **9**, 191-198.

Wynne, L. C., and Singer, M. T. Thought disorder and family relations of schizophrenics: II. A classification of forms of thinking. *Archives of General Psychiatry*, 1963b, **9**, 199-206.

Wynne, L. C., and Singer, M. T. The transcultural study of schizophrenics and their families. Proceedings of Joint Meeting of the American Psychiatric Association and the Japanese Society of Psychiatry and Neurology. *Folia Psychiatrica et Neurologica Japonica*, 1963, Suppl. No. 7: 28-29.

Wynne, L. C., and Singer, M. T. *Schizophrenic impairment in sharing foci of attention: A conceptual basis for viewing schizophrenics and their families in research and therapy.* Presented as the Bertram H. Roberts' Memorial Lecture, Yale University, New Haven, Connecticut, 1966.

Wynne, L. C. Overview of the Conference Proceedings. *American Psychiatric Association Report*, No. 20, Washington, D. C.: American Psychiatric Association, 1966, 224-244;

Wynne, L. C. Family transactions and schizophrenia: II. Conceptual considerations for a research strategy. In J. Romano (Ed.), *The origins of schizophrenia.* Amsterdam: Excerpta Medica, International Congress Series 151, 1967, 165-178.

Wynne, L. C. Methodologic and conceptual issues in the study of schizophrenics and their families. *Journal of Psychiatric Research*, 1968 **6**, Suppl. 1, 185-199.

Wynne, L. C. Consensus Rorschach and related procedures for studying interpersonal patterns. *Journal of Projective Techniques and Personality Assessment*, 1968, **32**, 352-356.

Wynne, L. C. The family as a strategic focus in cross-cultural psychiatric studies. In W. Caudill and T. Lin (Eds.), *Mental health research in Asia and the Pacific.* Honolulu: East-West Center Press, 1969, 463-477.

Wynne, L. C. *Hearing a different drummer: Sources of schizophrenia in the family.* Presented as the Frieda Fromm-Reichmann Memorial Lecture, sponsored by the Washington School of Psychiatry, November, 1969.

Wynne, L. C. Communication disorders and the quest for relatedness in families of schizo-phrenics, *American Journal of Psychoanalysis*, 1970, **30**, 100-114.

Wynne, L. C., Singer, M. T., Bartko, J. J., and Toohey, M. L. *Schizophrenics and their families: Recent research on parental communication.* Mental Health Research Fund Lecture, London, 1968. In press, 1975.

THE
TEST
PATTERN

Then boldly stirs imagination's power,
And shapes these formless masses of the hour. *

JOHANN WOLFGANG GOETHE

14 | Roland Kuhn

SOME PROBLEMS CONCERNING THE PSYCHOLOGICAL IMPLICATIONS OF RORSCHACH'S FORM INTERPRETATION TEST

Since Hermann Rorschach's death, research on his form interpretation test has concentrated almost exclusively on statistical studies (1937). We should, however, understand clearly what can be achieved by statistical methods. They lead to the use of certain "signs,"[1] the meaning of which is either based on conventional procedure or has been derived from rather superficial relationships between indices. The validity of such signs may be established through the use of statistics, but statistical methods alone can never give us psychological understanding of inner relationships, nor the reason why a certain "sign" is considered indicative of a particular psychological characteristic. It is well known that Rorschach himself used and reported in addition to statistics quite different methods (1937, pp. 181-213), based chiefly on theoretical considerations. This kind of approach lends itself well to further development as demonstrated, e.g., by the research of Binder on chiaroscuro (1933)[2] and by that of the author on "mask" responses (Kuhn, 1954).

*Translated by J. C. Hüttner.
[1] The term sign is used here in the phenomenological sense of Edmund Husserl (1913, pp. 23-105).
[2] See Chapter 9.

Our ideas regarding the psychological nature of the Rorschach method will be presented in two parts. Part I will illustrate our testing procedure with the analysis of an individual case. Part II will attempt to throw new light upon the theoretical problems involved in the interpretation of certain test categories.

PART I

The method involves repeated spaced administration of the Rorschach by different examiners. This procedure has proved to be especially useful when the examiners were of different sexes. The theoretical underpinnings of results obtained by this method are too involved to be covered here. Neither does space allow us to take up possible objections that might be raised in regard to the technique itself. Our objective is merely to demonstrate on a single case how the method is to be applied and what kind of information it may yield. It is perhaps appropriate to mention here that we have been using this method for many years on a great number of cases and that our conclusions could be supported by numerous other examples.

The following summary of anamnesis is intended to provide background information regarding the subject's problems, past experiences, and the apparent interrelations between these experiences. The information has been gathered in the course of a prolonged psychiatric treatment, most of it by the patient's psychotherapist, a woman psychiatrist.

Summary of Anamnesis and Psychotherapy of W. E., born 1934 (compiled by Verena Gebhart, M.D.)

Family history. The patient comes from a middle-class family. The father has an economically secure position as clerk in a business firm. Both parents belong to the Methodist church. There are five children in the family, three brothers and two sisters. The patient is the second, and her sister is the youngest in birth order. On the paternal side of the family there were several cases of depression which, however, did not require hospitalization. The father is described as serious. All members of the family are said to be somewhat peculiar, the patient's younger brother being particularly poorly adjusted.

Personal history. The patient's intellectual level is above average. Her physical development was normal but her personality showed peculiar characteristics even in early childhood. As a small child she used to be excessively preoccupied with fairy tales and was hyperemotional in her reactions to the world around her. It is also reported that when the family went out for Sunday walks she used to walk behind the group, mumbling and talking to herself. She took no liking to work, yet once she started a task, she went about it in a slow but systematic and conscientious fashion. In grammar school she had no particular difficulties. Her performance was uneven: poor in arithmetic but above average in verbal facility. She always got along easily with her schoolmates and was well liked. While the patient was in the fourth and fifth grade, her mother had to take a job. During this period the children were cared for primarily by the grandmother, a person of extreme strictness and exactitude. Under her rule the patient became disorderly in her behavior and began to stay away from home after school. It was with great effort and after the second attempt only that she succeeded in being admitted to a secondary school. The subject in which she failed completely was arithmetic. In the secondary school she had good teachers and seemed to be getting along well; she enjoyed reciting poetry and showed signs of artistic talents, expecially in singing.

It was during her third year in secondary school when the first episode of depression occurred. This was, in all probability, precipitated by the sexual experiences she had with her father: for a period of several months, he used to come into her bedroom almost every night and, thinking she was asleep, he would touch her body. This stopped only when it was finally discovered by the patient's mother. In the same year she started to go out with a boy. Once she was beaten by her father for coming home very late at night where upon she locked herself into her room for two days and remained there until the door was forced open. From then on there were increasing difficulties and the patient wished to get away from home as soon as possible. She had two jobs as domestic help in the French part of Switzerland, one for three and the other for four months. In both places she did well in the beginning; her letters home were full of enthusiasm of how well off she was. Soon, however, she began to neglect her work, failed to get up in the morning, and became disgusted with everything, so that finally she had to be dismissed. The parents wanted the patient to return home and stay with them, but she expressed the wish to become an actress or receive training in voice. The parents did not consent to this. Finally it was agreed that the patient would go to Geneva to be trained as a baby nurse. The following year of studies and training-on-the-job is said to have gone quite well. She had to work rather hard, had little time to go out, and led a respectable life. In addition to this one-year training, she was required to complete two half-years of practicum. During this period she became acquainted with girls who liked to go out in the evenings. The patient joined them and went to dances where she met young men. She found pleasure in dancing, smoking, and being in male company. It was then that she had her first intimate relationships with men. At the end of her practicum year she went on a vacation trip with her boy friend, letting her parents believe that she had to stay on the job for a few more days.

The patient began her employment as a baby nurse in England. During her 18-month stay in that country she worked at three different places. Her first job, which she held for six months, she quit from one day to the other because she was not allowed to go out with her friend in the evening. Then she took a job in a hospital; here she enjoyed complete freedom after working hours and became rather promiscuous in her conduct. Toward the end of her stay in England, the patient did not work at all for several months. At that time she had many friends, was associated with so-called bohemian circles, and posed as a model. Finally, she became pregnant, had an abortion, and, a few days later, returned to her home in Switzerland. At home she felt tired and sick and did not get along anymore in her environment. For a while she worked as a substitute for vacationing personnel in a hospital. Later she took a job with a doctor who was an acquaintance of her parents. First she liked the job, but half a year later, after she had to be reprimanded because of unrestrained behavior and neglect of her duties, she resigned and returned home. There she fell into a dejected mood, complained of feelings of uselessness and of being a complete failure in life, and expressed guilt over her immoral conduct. She found no consolation in religion either, and felt desperate and helpless. It was then that she first attempted suicide. One night she hid a razor blade in her bed, intending to cut her wrist. The blade was discovered and taken away in time by her mother. The patient reacted to her mother's interference with a severe crying spell, insisting that she did not want to live any longer. From then on she felt very depressed and did not want to work. She quarreled with her sister and threw objects at her. Finally, she made a second suicidal attempt (two months after the first), this one by the use of gas. This attempt was almost successful and led to her hospitalization. It was in the hospital that we first met the patient. She gave the impression of a very sick person. Soon she was transferred to a mental institution. There she received psychotherapy and drug treatment, and by the end of 2½ months improved sufficiently to be discharged and sent home. Since then she has been working in a home for the crippled. There her condition keeps fluctuating between fair and severely depressed. Her spells of depression, which are particularly pronounced on days preceding the onset of the menstrual period, are characterized by complaints of difficulties in thinking, complete lack of motivation and, in the morning, a lack of desire to get up at all. During these depressed periods she sleeps poorly, dreams a lot, and also often simply takes off to meet one of her male acquaintances. Symptoms as severe as the ones just described occur, however, only when the patient is not under medication. Her work is said to be satisfactory although she has considerable difficulties in keeping things in order. Her neglect of order and neatness is most marked in her room, but it also shows in her dealings with the children. She is liked among her co-worders because of her friendly and cooperative attitude.

Themes from Psychotherapy

According to the patient, her mother has been very strict with her and has shown partiality in favor of her brothers. The patient reports having felt inferior to her brothers. She has no clear recollection of her childhood relationship to her father, in particular, during the period prior to his sexual advances to her. It seems that he actually showed little interest in the way his children were brought up. The patient always thought of him as a rather insignificant figure; nevertheless, she recalls that once, after having failed on an examination in the secondary school, she was depressed by the idea of having inflicted disgrace upon her father.

The patient states that, although as a small child she was very orderly and conscientious, she was still in her childhood when she became disorderly. She adds that she is simply unable to adjust to any rules or routine and that she cannot see the sense in adhering to order or in keeping within limits. She seems to relate this attitude to her artistic interests and to her tendency of indulging freely in esthetic experiences.

The patient complains of compulsive masturbation. Ever since she became sexually aroused by her father's nightly visits to her bedroom she sought satisfaction in masturbation now and again. Patient reports that her sexual relationships with men were not gratifying until she once experienced complete satisfaction in intercourse with a Negro. Perverse sexual practices she finds repulsive. Her esthetic orientation seems to play a considerable role in her sexual life, even though she insists that serving as a model had no sexual connotation for her. She has always found pleasure in looking at beautiful bodies and even in secondary school was fond of paintings of nudes. She also liked to observe herself nude in the mirror (this was said to have been the case before the occurrence of the sexually arousing episodes with her father) and liked to swim in the nude. She realizes that there is something wrong with her sense of shame. This was confirmed by her mother who noticed that the patient had been indulging, especially lately, in obscene talk about her sexual relations and about her abortion. Also, she is said to have remarked that she did not care about people's opinion of her.

Before we go into the interpretation of the three Rorschach records, a few things should be mentioned. The first protocol was obtained on the very first day of examination and treatment, i.e., immediately after the suicidal attempt, and in a state of depression. Protocols B and C originate from one and two months later respectively, and were taken while the patient was under treatment; they were obtained

The Rorschach Protocols

Protocol A   Date: April 9, 1956   Examiner: Dr. Verena Gebhart

Time 4:55 P.M.

I.	1.	"This is a bat, a distorted one . . ."	W	ChF+	A	P[3]
	2.	"Or a butterfly . . . , at any rate, it is a small animal."	W	F+	A	P
II.	1.	"This, too, could be an animal but I don't know what kind . . ."	W	F—	A	
III.	1.	"These are two people lifting something."	W	M+	H	P
IV.	1.	"Bear skin hung up, rug . . ."	W	F+	A	P
V.	1.	"This one could be a bat."	W	F+	A	P
VI.	1.	"This is a fish, disemboweled, or perhaps an eel, something of that sort. . . ."	W	F—	A	
VII.	1.	"Little Mickey-Mouse-like animals, two of them are horses or bunnies or something."	D	F+	A	
VIII.	1.	"Two sea lions climbing on rocks of some sort. . . ."	D	F+	A	P
IX.	1.	"This one is rather abstract, I can't make anything out of it. . . ."		Description Failure		
X.	1.	"Crystals."	W	ChF, CF+	N/Cryst.	

Time 5:06 P.M.

Protocol B   Date: May 2, 1956   Examiner: Dr. Verena Gebhart

Time 5:55 P.M.

I.	1.	"A butterfly."	W	F+	A	P
	2.	"It could also be a pattern produced by cutting folded paper. .[?] it doesn't represent much, it is only these corners here which are cut out so far."	W	F—	Obj.	
	3.	"It could also be an island. . . ."	W	F—	Geo.	
II.	1.	"My first guess would be—little animal. I don't know, there is again this division in the middle and the two sides are the same."	W	F—	A Symmetry	

[3] For explanation of scoring symbols, see Appendix, pp. 000 ff. [Editor].

The Rorschach Protocols (Continued)

Protocol B   Date: May 2, 1956   Examiner: Dr. Verena Gebhart

Time 5:55 P.M. *(Continued)*

III.	1.	"Two persons lifting something, they look exactly alike and the motions they go through are exactly the same."	W	M+	H	P
IV.	1.	"This could be the skin of a bear, as a rug, . . . spread out."	W	F+	A	P
V.	1.	"I see here a bat."	W	F+	A	P
	2.	"Could also be a bone, with flesh around it, the light parts are the bones. . . ."	W	ChF−	At	
VI.	1.	"Snake skin, may be the whole thing had been a snake."	W	F−	A	
VII.	1.	"Here I see two Mickey-Mouse figures."	D	F+	A	
	2.	"But it could also be a few snow-balls put together."	W	ChF−	N/Snow-ball	

[Interruption: examiner on the telephone for two minutes.]

VIII.	1.	"This, too, is an animal, a sea lion or something, the underwater world."	D	F+	A	P
	2.	"Crystals or something."	D	ChF, CF	Pl	
	3.	"Or animal in a jungle."	W	FCh−	A, N	
IX.	1.	"Ink wiper (i.e., a cloth that has been used for cleaning ink pens) [?], because of these colored blots neither of which seems to represent anything specific."	W	ChF, CF−	Obj.	
	2.	"This here strikes me as funny; it looks like a vein that connects something; one should think of some living creature but I don't see anything in here."	Dd	F−	At	
X.	1.	"Here are two caterpillars [middle green]."	D	F+	A	
	2.	"It could be also the inside of man, here the esophagus [middle grey] but I cannot remember well . . . , recollect any more how it looks inside. . . ."	D	F−	At	

Time 6:14 P.M.

The Rorschach Protocols (Continued)

Protocol C   Date: June 6, 1956   Examiner: Dr. Roland Kuhn

Time 5:24 P.M.

I.   1. "... I see it as a butterfly [turns   *W*   *F+*   *A*   *P*
        card repeatedly]."

II. > [Covers up lower half]...."I don't   Failure
        see anything in this one. Uh ..."

III. 1. "Here I imagine a human being who   *W*   *M+*   *H*   *P*
        is lifting something."

     > 2. "One could also imagine the ...   *Ws* *F−*   *Geo.*
        the white part as being the sea
        and the black ones islands ... and
        ... [And?] sort of inlets and fjords."

IV. 1. "Here I imagine a bear skin."   *W*   *F+*   *A*   *P*
V.   1. "Here I see a bat."   *W*   *F+*   *A*   *P*
VI.   "Uh ... [puts down card]...."

     1. "The top only [covers rest with   *D*   *F−*   *A*
        hand], I imagine, could be some
        type of fish."

     2. "Covering up this part here [lower   *Dd* *F−*   *A*
        part of upper lateral projections],
        I see some sort of a fowl, a type of
        pigeon [very unusual response, the
        head—the grey that surrounds furni-
        ture leg, the tail—remaining part of
        upper lateral projection]. I cannot
        make anything of the whole."

VII. 1. "Here I see a little Mickey-Mouse-   *D*   *F+*   *A*
        like animal, running away [right
        half of blot]."

VIII.   [Sighs]....

     > 1. "Here I see a polar bear or some-   *D*   *F+*   *A*   *P*
        thing of that sort."

     ∧ 2. "This here [center part] too, I   *Dd* *F−*   *At*
        noticed one could say a bone,
        well, I don't know, some sort of
        a ..., [Hm?] yes, a bone struc-
        ture, I don't know how should
        one say...."

     3. "Or it could be a caterpillar. This   *Dd* *F+*   *A*
        color combination I haven't noticed
        before ..., the orange fading into   Color Naming
        the red and the grey into the blue,

The Rorschach Protocols (Continued)

Protocol C   Date: June 6, 1956   Examiner: Dr. Roland Kuhn

Time: 5:24 P.M. *(Continued)*

IX.   I don't see anything" [rather quick   Failure
      reaction]. [Shakes head.]

X.   [Shakes head] "I don't see anything."   Failure

Time 5:46 P.M.

Note: Card III was seen as figures cut out of paper and set off against a white surface. The patient conveyed the impression that she saw more in the cards when previously tested by Dr. Verena Gebhart. She also remarked that in a previous session she did respond to the last card, but she felt her response was silly and therefore did not want to repeat it. As regards the test as a whole, the patient began to wonder whether the responses she gave in the previous sessions had been thought over carefully enough. She could give no definite answer to the examiner's question as to whether this time she felt more inhibited than during the previous testings. She did say, however, that this time she felt differently than in the previous sessions.

SUMMARY OF SCORES FOR PROTOCOLS
A, B, and C

	A	B	C
Total time, minutes	11	19	22
Time per response, seconds	66	63	120
Number of responses	10 (2)*	18 (7)*	11 (3)*
Failures	1	0	3

*Figures in parentheses refer to the number of responses on the last three cards [Editor].

Summary of Scores for Protocols A, B, and C (Continued)

Location	A	B	C		Determinants	A	B	C
W+	6	4	4		F+	5	6	6
W−	2	8	0		F−	2	6	4
Ws	0	0	1		M	1	1	1
D	2	5	3		FCh	0	1	0
Dd	0	1	3		ChF	1	2	0
					ChF, CF	1	2	0
	10	18	11		CF	0	0	0
						10	18	11

Content	A	B	C		Miscellaneous	A	B	C
A	8	9	8		Popular	6	5	5
H	1	1	1		Color naming	0	0	1
At	0	3	1		Description	1	0	0
Pl	0	1	0		Symmetry	0	1	0
N	1	1	0					
Geo.	0	1	1					
Obj.	0	2	0					
	10	18	11					

Quotients and Percentages	A	B	C
Experience balance	1:1	1:2	1:0
F+%	71	50	60
F%	70	67	91
A%	80	50	73

after a marked improvement in the patient's clinical condition had taken place. During the interval between the second and third testing, there was hardly any change in the clinical picture.

Our discussion of the test material will be oriented primarily toward a comparative analysis of the three records. This analysis is not planned to be exhaustive; we shall merely demonstrate with a few examples of how such a comparative analysis may be done. As background for the analysis it is pertinent to remember that the first and second protocols were taken by a female examiner whereas the third record was obtained by a male examiner.

Setting aside the first record produced while in a state of depression, we note that when the sex of the examiner differs from that of the subject the total number of responses goes down markedly and the number of responses on the last three cards diminishes to the extent of becoming suggestive of color shock. This finding is at variance with the norms at our institution based on a large number of cases. According to these data, the number of responses is lower when examiner and subject are of the same sex than when the sex differs. Particularly on the last three cards an increase in responses is to be expected. We have then a deviation from the norm here which, by itself, is already indicative of some disturbance in the patient regarding her relation to men.

Considering the content of the Rorschach responses, it is of interest to note that certain content categories tend to reoccur from record to record on cards different from the ones on which they occurred previously. One could, indeed, speak of certain individual content categories as having a tendency to shift from one card to another. Other contents, again, seem to be fixed to certain cards. The shifting of some contents as well as the card-bound behaviour of others are probably controlled in part, and in part only, by qualities of the particular ink blot; partly they appear also to be influenced by psychological factors. In the case of our patient, however, the role of the psychological factors cannot be readily investigated and demonstrated. Therefore, in this paper we have to content ourselves with merely mentioning the above phenomena as ones which deserve attention in the longitudinal study of Rorschach protocols.

Now let us discuss the individual content categories as they occur in the records of our patient. There is one human-movement response in each of the three protocols (on card III). Comparison of the verbal formulations of these responses reveals that: (a) in the first and second protocols, where patient and examiner were of the same sex, the response- is in terms of two figures, whereas in the third record, where patient and examiner were of different sexes, the response comprises one figure only; (b) in records A and B the patient speaks of "persons," whereas in record C she calls the figure "a human being." These differences, which could hardly be attributed to chance, found their parallels in some of the patient's animal responses. In the second protocol she saw two caterpillars on card X; in the third record a similar response was given to card VIII, but only one caterpillar was seen. To card VII both record A and record B contain the response of two Mickey-Mice; in record C, however, there is only one Mickey-Mouse and even this one is seen as running away. There is one response that does not fall in line with the aforementioned pattern: on card VIII, the two sea lions of the first protocol diminish to one already in the second record. Then, in the third record, the sea lion turns into a polar bear.

Also interesting is the disappearance of the "crystal" response in the last record after having occurred in both of the two preceding protocols. Similarly, all shading and color responses vanish in the third record; instead, a space response, not present in record A or B, makes its appearance in record C. The number of whole responses is lowest in the last protocol, i.e., even lower than in the first record which was produced in a state of depression. Furthermore, not until record C does a tendency towards small detail responses become clearly manifest. The first protocol does not contain any Dd responses at all; the second has one, and the third, in spite of a decrease in the number of responses as compared to recrod B, shows as many as three small detail responses. Finally, it merits notice that responses the content of which would fall under the category of inanimate objects appear in the second protocol only.

In order to gain more insight into the inner dynamics of the changes that occurred from one record to the other, one should also consider the patient's failure in responding to some of the cards. In record B, which was produced in a state of marked clinical improvement, there were no failures. Interestingly enough, in record C which, too, originates from a period characterized by improvement but was obtained by a male examiner, the patient failed to respond to as many as three of the cards. It is of particular interest to scrutinize the responses given in previous sessions to cards to which she failed to respond at the third testing. One may thus state that the patient displayed in her interpretations more freedom and spontaneity when the examiner was of the same sex, and that she experienced her task as different and more difficult when tested by a person of the opposite sex.

The question may be raised whether the differences between the records B and C, and in particular the signs of disturbance in record C, were not merely the result of the patient's trust and confidence in the first examiner who also was her therapist, and her unfamiliarity with the second examiner. The role of the factor of familiarity or unfamiliarity with the tester can hardly be doubted. It is to be emphasized, however, that to a certain extent the response patterns considered by us as the salient features of protocols obtained under same-sex conditions already made their appearance in the first record, i.e., before a relationship of trust and confidence had time to develop. We are referring here primarily to those human and animal responses discussed above which were featuring two figures each. These response patterns underwent significant modification in the third record where patient and tester were of different sexes. Thus it seems we are dealing here with a factor that is sex-determined.

This finding undoubtedly has not one but several possible diagnostic meanings. It is entirely conceivable, for instance, that because of her previous sexual experiences the patient is so inhibited in her associations with men that she no longer can conceive of a free interaction between a man and a woman and, consequently, tends to withdraw into herself. Thus, when confronted with a male examiner, she selectively perceives *one human creature* on the Rorschach, instead of seeing *people* in relationship and interaction with each other. Such an explanation of the dynamics would imply that the patient's Rorschach protocols are primarily determined by her life style and by specific past experiences. One may, however, go one step further and postulate behind both her Rorschach responses given to a male examiner and her deviant, promiscuous social conduct the same source, namely, a deep-seated disturbance in her relation to men.

This, again, may have been brought about by past experiences, especially by the patient's relationship to her father.

The Rorschach data by themselves will hardly enable one to decide in such a case which one of the several possible assumptions regarding the underlying dynamics is correct. The test findings will, however, be of invaluable service in pinpointing the crucial problem area which then can be probed into and clarified in the course of psychotherapy. Moreover, there is evidence that the Rorschach is apt to foster insight into problems that remain undisclosed for a considerable length of time even in intensive psychotherapy. The present case is a good example of how extremely difficult it is to penetrate by means of therapeutic interviews the inner layers of personality which hold the answers to questions regarding the underlying dynamics: psychotherapy of almost a year's duration has not yet succeeded in clarifying the psychodynamics of the patient's pathology. It has been revealed in the course of treatment that the patient believes herself to be suffering from a constitutionally determined disturbance which has led to her inability to become attached to a man for a substantial length of time. She is fully aware of her promiscuous tendencies and sees them as a consequence of her inability to establish genuine emotional relationships with men. A psychological explanation of her conduct and her disturbance in the interpersonal sphere could so far not be formulated.

PART II[4]

To gain a better understanding of the psychological problems involved in the Rorschach test, it is of primary importance to develop some definite and precise concepts. This constitutes an admittedly difficult task. Let us choose, for example, the whole (*W*) responses. By inspecting Rorschach's own writings (1937, p. 54) and those of some of his co-workers, a clear picture of the real meaning of whole responses may be obtained. According to Rorschach, whole re-

---

[4] The major part of the remainder of this chapter has been reprinted (revised and translated) from R. Kuhn, Grundlegende statistische und psychologische Aspekte des Rorschachschen Formdeutversuches, *Rorschachiana*, 1953, I, pp. 320-333.

sponses are related to "richness of associations," "marked availability of visual memory images," "active striving," "goal directed striving toward global comprehension," "tendency to combine details into a meaningful whole." Rorschach already noted that W responses must be further differentiated (1937, pp. 37-41). In keeping with these suggestions as well as with Furrer's research (1930), we currently classify the whole responses in the following way:

1. Simple whole responses of good form; also called "primary" or "abstract." The entire blot is taken in by one glance and simultaneously interpreted as a whole.

2. Combinatory whole responses of either good or poor form (in Rorschach's sense).

3. Primitive, undifferentiated whole responses ($W\ CF$ and $W\ ChF$).

4. Confabulatory whole responses (DW and DdW).

5. Other whole responses with poor form accuracy ($WF-$).

However, when attempting to apply these categories to the interpretation of an individual record, one may encounter certain difficulties. As an example, we might review the case of a hypomanic psychopath, who is an inventor, confidence man, and gambler. On the Rorschach he has 23 W out of 39 R. He does indeed show the expected comprehensive memory for visual images, specifically in the form of complex planning. Although his hypomanic temperament may be regarded as a form of lively activity, it would hardly be appropriate to speak here of goal-directed striving toward global comprehension since he lives merely for the moment at hand, displaying the most amazing skill in forgetting the burdensome problems of his swindler's career. Thus, he manages to sleep undisturbed despite his heavy debts and the constant threat of imprisonment for fraud. In trying to apply to this case the psychological meaning of combination of details into a whole, it turns out that this interpretation fits the builder and inventor aspects of his behavior very well, but fails in characterizing the swindler, who is completely incapable of relating and integrating his various activities. Still the inventor and swindler are united in this one person. Considering the distribution of his whole responses into 14 primitive undifferentiated W, 2 $W-$, 6 simple W, and 1 combinatory $W+$, one cannot help but wonder why his pathological lying is not expressed in the form of confabulatory responses.

Inspection of carefully examined and clinically thoroughly studied cases, such as the one briefly referred to above, reveals many unsolved problems concerning the interpretation of whole responses on the Rorschach. Although there is a good deal of validity in the standard interpretations of whole responses, our knowledge in this area is too schematic, and conceptually insufficiently clarified. Different, possibly more crucial, factors might well be obscured by our traditional categories and interpretations.

Any theory concerned with "wholes and parts," and this is what we are dealing with here, may be readily conceived of in terms of Plato's and Aristotle's ancient differentiation between "pan" versus "holon," "compositum" versus "totum," or the "sum" versus the "configuration." So far, the most significant contribution to these problems has been made by Husserl, who contrasted the sum as "a whole, consisting of independent parts," against the "genuine whole, consisting of dependent parts" (1913, pp. 223-293). This distinction may be illustrated by two responses to card I of the Rorschach test. The response "slag" (scored as W ChF) obviously refers to the subject's perceiving a whole with independent parts, similar to the ancient philosophers' notion of the gold nugget. Any given piece of slag may be divided, and each separate part will represent a complete whole just as the original one does. It is quite a different matter when a human face is perceived on that card. The parts of a human face, such as eyes, nose, mouth, can never represent the face in and of themselves; in other words, the whole response of a human face consists of (inter-) dependent parts.

Rather than simplifying, however, the problem of whole responses on the Rorschach test, the foregoing considerations appear at first to introduce further complications. For instance, the DW, DdW, and certain W $F-$ responses are probably much more complex than we thought. This, however, will not be discussed here. It may merely be suggested that once a whole response has been identified in the manner described above, Rorschach's "combination of details into a whole" may be further differentiated. In the case of a whole with clearly independent parts, such as the "slag" response cited earlier, we are dealing with a "striving toward totality" (*Totalisierungsbestreben*), tending to level and to simplify. Such an orientation may express itself in a number of ways, e.g., in the form of a generalized mood. Conversely, W with dependent parts suggest a tendency for structuring, a capacity to apprehend and follow the inherent laws of the given configurations (*Gestalten*). In the case of the inventor discussed above, the predominance of primitive whole responses, i.e., those with independent parts, suggests a tendency to make superficial judgments, sweeping generalizations, and purely visual combinations of parts, but also the ability to perceive parts by themselves—all of which brings us closer to a better understanding of the clinical picture.

There is a close relationship, statistically as well as psychologically, between whole responses with dependent parts, on the one hand, and movement responses, on the other. Both of them are determined not so much by the shape of the blot as by structuring from within.[5] Animated movement does not consist of a piecing together nor of a linking of independent parts. In effect each movement response constitutes a sequence, and thus includes both the movement immediately preceding it, and the one which follows. Goethe, impressed by a dancer's pose in a picture, wrote: "The beautiful fluidity of movement in transition which we admire in such artists has here been arrested for one moment, permitting us to visualize past, present, and future simultaneously and by this very experience we transcend earthy limitations"[6] (p. 378). Living motion, then, is also a whole, specifically one consisting of dependent parts, to the extent that its organization in time is experienced as the essential feature. Rorschach's *W M+* responses may thus be regarded as an intricately organized space-time entity, i.e., a whole consisting of interdependent parts. By reacting with this type of response, the subject reveals a rather specific capacity of the human mind.

To go a step further, the question arises as to the how and why of man's capacity for structuring perceptions in space and time. It appears that a cue to the problem may be found in man's experience of the temporal totality of human existence including death itself. Consistent with this reasoning is the increase of *W M+ H* responses during adolescence, a period when thoughts concerned with death seem to be quite common. Furthermore, there is some evidence that immediately following an encounter with death, children tend to produce many *W M+ H*.[7] To be sure, the awareness of the finality of

---

[5] These ideas were developed by A. Weber in "Ueber Bewegungsdeutungen," lecture given at meetings of Zurich Psychiatric Association, Summer 1941.

[6] Editor's translation.

[7] Personal communications by A. Friedman and A. Weber.

life may manifest itself in more than one way. For instance, profound inner and/or outer restlessness and discomfort may occur. In such cases, the production of *W M+ H* responses would be correspondingly reduced.

To throw further light upon this complex issue, it might be helpful to recall Rorschach's original definition of movement responses. According to Rorschach, as we know, a scoring of *M* is acceptable only if the movement is not just "associated," "seen," or "demonstrated"; rather it must be "sensed" (*erfühlt*) by the subject (1937, pp. 14-25). This was precisely the reason why Rorschach limited the use of the *M* score to responses involving humans and just those animals which are perceived in humanlike motion. It would only confuse matters if this definition of Rorschach's were ignored. Rorschach's "kinesthetic perception" occurs when the overt manifestation of a kinesthetic impulse is inhibited, a state of affairs for which Binswanger coined the felicitous expression "taming" (*Bändigung*) (1947, p. 24). The amount of active demonstrating made by a subject is therefore inversely related to the *M* quality of his interpretations; in extreme cases demonstrating or describing might actually replace the process of interpreting (Binder, 1933, p. 45 ff.). The restraining impact of fright or surprise upon spontaneous mobility is a common observation. It was left to Rorschach's genius, however, to highlight the phenomenon that during a state of being stunned or tamed, movement impulses set the perceptual world into motion, as it were; hence, the movement responses on the test. On the basis of these considerations, the relationship between *M* and creativity (*schöpferische Gestaltungskraft*) may be derived without difficulty, since "creating" (*gestalten*) actually means "bringing to life." Of course, this should not imply the idea that initially we are surrounded by dead objects, which are later set in motion by us through some kind of mysterious "psychic energy." Rather, the creative person at first glance perceives his environment as animated and moving. This experience he can direct either into artistic endeavor or into esthetic enjoyment. Such creativity is revealed by genuine movement responses on the Rorschach. The *M* responses do not by themselves, of course, provide a cue whether this form of creativity leads to artistic productivity or merely suggests the capacity for esthetic enjoyment. An interesting sidelight to the above considerations is the observation that people who produce

W M+ responses may under the impact of grief display increased creative activity. We cannot go into all the complicated ways which bring this about, and which may contribute to a person's awareness of the finiteness and totality of human existence. This awareness, in turn, has an inhibiting effect on free spontaneity. Such a person will not react with agitated unrest to experiences of the transitoriness of life. Some one who would react in that restless manner deprives himself of the possibility of perceiving the world in motion, and would, therefore, not see movement on the Rorschach plates.

Furthermore, a way of life which is governed by awareness of the finiteness and totality of human existence is also determined by developmental factors. If a subject with several genuine *W M+ H* responses on the test reports a happy childhood and gratitude to his parents for the many pleasant experiences provided for him, indicating that because of this he can meet any crisis with inner strength and comfort, he is in effect telling us of the high value he places on the past and on the sequential aspects of his existence. Such a value system appears to be closely related to *W M+ H* responses. Conversely, this kind of historic emphasis with respect to a person's life pattern (*Daseinsform*) may also give rise to neurotic developments. This observation is well in accord with the frequently voiced hypothesis regarding the intimate link between *M* responses and unconscious forces.

These examples were given to demonstrate the method here suggested for the interpretation of Rorschach protocols. It is in a true sense a psychological method. Its aim is to give an adequate description of experiences and their structural patterns, which, going beyond the experiences themselves, reveal the hidden interrelationships of these experiences. Such a method furthers the formulation of clearcut concepts. It relies, on the one hand, on experience analysis (*Erlebnisanalyse*) and, on the other hand, on empirically established material. A single case may be studied by comparing the test findings with psychological material that has been obtained from other sources. This cross validation results in an increasingly accurate personality picture of the individual. By studying a concrete case through such analysis, it becomes apparent how much closer we get to an understanding of the psychological foundations of the Rorschach test by this approach rather than by that of theoretical speculations, particularly since the latter involve coming to grips with some of the most complex philosophical writings. Nevertheless, the meaningful integration of statistical and psychological methods in Rorschach research ultimately depends on just such philosophical considerations. This was illustrated by our examples. As Rorschach had already observed, the M responses correlate positively with $W+$ responses (1937, p. 60). Although admittedly very incomplete, our attempts at elucidating the psychological significance of these two Rorschach factors make their statistical relationship appear plausible.

At this point it seems appropriate to take up Rorschach's usage of the term "introversion," which he closely relates to the M factor. This is a difficult task since Rorschach did not succeed in defining the concept unequivocally. A comparison of his discussions of this concept as given in different places reveals a rather vague, if not contradictory, picture. In addition to *Psychodiagnostics*, one should consult Rorschach's other publications, such as his article on reflex hallucinations (1912) and his studies on the behavior of sects (1927). One thing becomes fairly certain: Rorschach's concept of introversion has something to do with "inner life," "inner creativity," and an "orientation of interest toward intrapsychic life rather than the outer world" (Rorschach, 1937, p. 60 ff.). Furthermore, Rorschach does not conceive of introversion as a fixed state, but rather as a highly dynamic process. The latter point is brought out more specifically in his construct "experience type," where introversion is described as a shifting from the outer world to the inner, and "extratension," described as the reverse (Rorschach, 1937, pp. 69-83).

In line with the above discussion, the problem of introversion in the Rorschach test perhaps may be further clarified. If we follow Rorschach's ideas regarding the relationship between introversion and M responses, then introversion must also be related to the holistic longitudinal aspects in a person's existence. An interpretation of existence along these lines cannot depend, however, on merely traditional, inadequately understood "signs," nor on toying with arbitrary notions and vague concepts; in short, it cannot spring from commonplace "hearsay" from which so many derive their philosophy of life, or from their "psychodiagnostic" interpretations—with or without benefit of ink blots. Such an approach would obscure the test's intrinsic potential for revealing that aspect of living which cannot be understood in terms of the outer world, but which is concerned with the awareness of one's own existence. With his concept of introversion Rorschach attempted the difficult task of describing this particular aspect of human existence and thereby probably made his primary, most unique contribution. Only those individuals, however, will be able to follow Rorschach here who in their own life are capable of perceiving it in perspective and perhaps even of realizing the potentialities of their personal existence. In other words, the problems of the Rorschach test are closely linked with the existential problems of the person who does the testing and interpreting. Again and again the "hearsay" of everyday life tends to obscure and disguise the deeper awareness of one's own existence as manifested in the test. It is our responsibility to safeguard and, if possible, to advance further this kind of awareness, which has provided the access to Rorschach's most fundamental discoveries. This requires constant vigilance on the part of all serious Rorschach workers, who are called upon to join in the fight against the ever-present obfuscations of convenient, commonplace talk.

In conclusion, a further example may illustrate our approach to the interpretation of M responses. A young thief's Rorschach protocol of 21 responses shows 5 $W+$, no $W-$, no DW. The experience type is 4 $M: O C$. The $F+$ is 87%, and the animal percentage is 57. The content of the M responses is as follows: card II—(1) "Two clowns"; card III—(1) "Again two men"; card X—(2) "Here two human figures with heads" [red and grey]; card X—(3) "Here again, shaking hands" [central blue]. In order to arrive at a psychological interpretation of these M responses, the subject must be further questioned. Then it turns out, that the responses should actually read: card II—(1) "Two clowns with white, powdered faces, fooling around together"; card X—(2) "Two knights in iron helmets, their faces covered by visors, arms drawn up, jousting together"; card III—(1) "Two men, talking to each other, carrying two bags or baskets in their hands"; or, "Two women, who won't have anything to do with the skeleton, making a rejecting gesture."

Each of these three M responses are closely related to experiences and fantasies which are highly significant to the subject's "inner" life history. The youth has a severe corpse phobia. He is chiefly afraid of the corpse's pallor. In this connection there is pronounced fear of death. He tries to hide his anxiety from himself and from others through overt demonstrations of his masculine prowess in sports, and also through his fantasies. For instance, he imagines that he and the other young fellows of his village, masquerading in white sheets, will stage a "ghost patrol" or "wild chase" on horseback at night. Thus, by assuming the role of death, he is trying to frighten others. The white-faced clowns have the physiognomy of corpses; they are disguised, one cannot tell who or what they are. The helmeted knights are also fantasied as masked men, playing a game of life and death, similar to the game our subject plays in his sports contests and in individual fights. His fantasies always center around gaining or losing, the highest stake being life itself. His thefts too are such longitudinally multidetermined "games," which, psychiatrically speaking, have to be viewed as neurotic behavior.

Even from these brief sketches, it should become apparent how closely the *M* responses are related clinically to unconscious material and psychologically, to considerations of time perspective, particularly to the problem of finality of life which confronts every human being in one form or another. It is this struggle with his fate that makes man escape into illness or seek relief from anxiety in conventional life patterns, unless he accepts the alternative of facing the impenetrable forces of existence and thus attains maturity and independence.

BIBLIOGRAPHY

Binder, H. Die Helldunkeldeutungen im psychodiagnostischen Experiment von Rorschach. *Schweiz. Arch. Neurol. Psychiat.*, 1932-1933, **30**, 1-67, 233-286. Reprinted, Bern: Huber, 1959.
Binswanger, L., Der Fall Juerg Zuend. *Schweiz. Arch. Neurol. Psychiat.*, 1947, **58**, 1-43.
Furrer, A. *Der Auffassungsvorgang beim Rorschach'schen psychodiagnostischen Versuch.* Zurich: Buchdruckerei zur Alten Universität, 1930.
Goethe, J. W. Der Tänzerin Grab. *Collected works. Vol. 10.* Leipzig: Inselverlag.
Husserl, E. *Logische Untersuchungen. Vol. 2.* Halle: Niemeyer, 1913, part 1.
Kuhn, R. Grundlegende statistische und psychologische Aspecte des Rorschach'schen Formdeutversuches, *Rorschachiana*, 1953, **I**, 320-333.
Kuhn, R. *Maskendeutungen im Rorschach'schen Formdeutversuch.* Basel: S. Karger, 1954.
Rorschach, H. *Psychodiagnostik.* Bern: Huber, 1937, 3rd ed.
Rorschach, H. Ueber Reflexhalluzinationen. *Z. ges. Neur. Psychiat.*, 1912, **13**, 357-400.
Rorschach, H. Zwei schweizerische Sektenstifter. *Imago*, 1927, **13**, Sonderheft, 395-441 (posthumous).

The language I speak must be ambiguous, must have two meanings in order to be fair to the dual aspect of our nature. I strive quite consciously and deliberately for ambiguity of expression, because it is superior to unequivocality and reflects the nature of life ... I purposely allow all the overtones and undertones to be heard, partly because they give a fuller picture of reality. Unequivocality makes sense only in establishing facts but not in interpreting them.

C. G. JUNG

15 | *Robert S. McCully*

JUNG'S DEPTH PSYCHOLOGY
AND RORSCHACH PATTERNING [1]

In 1906 Dr. Jung initiated modern scientific interest in projective stimuli with the publication of his first experimental researches on the word association technique. Both Bruno Klopfer and Henry A. Murray, pioneers in the development of ambiguous stimuli as a means of exploring personality structure, have acknowledged their debt to Jung in developing their approaches to projective techniques.

In a recent appraisal of Jung's work, British analyst Gerhard Adler (1971) wrote:

Jung's acceptance of ambiguity led him to conclusions very different from Freud's. He came to understand the irrational nightside of the psyche as the matrix of the conscious mind, pregnant with creative and prospective potentialities. To him the unconscious is "the hidden treasure upon which mankind ever and anon has drawn and from which it has raised ... all those potent and mighty thoughts without which man ceases to be man..." The "hidden treasure" is the wealth of the eternal archetypal images which compensate

[1] Some of the material in this chapter has been reprinted from an article that appeared in the *Journal of Projective Techniques and Personality Assessment* (1965).

513

the one-sidedness of the conscious mind with the exclusive emphasis on reason. The compensatory relationship between conscious and unconscious shows that the psyche is a self-regulating system. This discovery seems to me one of the most creative contributions to modern psychology although its significance is still largely overlooked.

Perhaps Jung's model of the structure of the psyche has generated the greatest distinction between his thought and that of other pioneers. In separating symbol from symptom and in systematically investigating the sources of creative experiences, Jung may stand beside Plato in the history of man, since each achieved perhaps the most complete synthesis of human knowledge available in the times each lived. In the words of Edward F. Edinger (1972), Jung "penetrated to the root source of all religion and culture and thus has discovered the basis for a new organic syncretism of human knowledge and experience." That Jung's work is tantamount to such a synthesis is as yet little understood or grasped. A major reason for the neglect of Jung's work may be contained in the epigraph that heads this chapter. We do not live in a time that easily tolerates ambiguity. We require precision and lie vulnerable to any mode that shortcuts experience into the illusion of single, definitive conclusions. Perhaps the major lesson to be extracted from Jung's work is that the echoes of psychic activity ramify and mesh into various levels of meaning and application.

While his model is a theoretical one, Jung, unlike Freud, made no major effort to systematize his concepts and discoveries into a unified theory. Since Freud's libido theory was readily intelligible and had immediate clinical application, it has been widely used as a framework for understanding Rorschach material. This has led to the fairly general assumption that the mechanisms and dynamics that Freud described explain the functions of the Rorschach method. Our position is that such a view is incomplete. Various concepts proposed by Jung may enable us to expand theory concerning the complexities of Rorschach perception.

Hermann Rorschach is known to have attended seminars presented by Jung when Rorschach was a medical student at the University of Zurich in 1907-1908. Jung's influence on Rorschach shows itself in various of Rorschach's publications (1921, 1927), including his studies of certain Swiss religious sects. Rorschach applied Jung's concepts of "introversion" and "extraversion" as a means of organizing and explaining aspects of Rorschach data. Rorschach was careful to state that he used those terms rather differently from Jung, but the inspiration is there. While Jung coined the terms "introversion" and "extraversion" and developed them as concepts, Hermann Rorschach appeared to grasp distinctions about introversion and extraversion which do not seem implicit in Jung's first publication of *Psychological Types* in 1921. Rorschach published the *Psychodiagnostik* the same year. McCully (1971) suggested that Jung's viewpoint about his own concepts broadened with time, and that the two pioneers may not have been as far apart as they may have thought in 1921. In any event, some impressive controversies have developed about the differences in opinion between the two pioneers on the subject. Bash (1955) has thrown considerable light on the issues involved, and Brawer and Spiegleman (1964) carefully reviewed the significance of these issues more recently. These authors note that Rorschach was among those who felt considerable pique with Jung for his abrupt departure from psychoanalytic circles. George Roemer (1948) has published excerpts from letters he received from Hermann Rorschach. Shortly before his death in 1922, Rorschach wrote to Roemer, confiding that he was "drawing nearer to Jung" in certain questions. In any event, the Rorschach method remains an important research modality for extending our knowledge about the nature of introversion and extraversion, a matter of considerable neglect in recent times. The nonprojective scales that purport to measure these variables leave out important qualities that the Rorschach method supplies.

Additionally, Jung had a pioneering role in influencing existential psychology, notably through having trained several leaders in that area, including Ludwig Binswanger and Medart Boss. Nevertheless, Jung's work has had little impact on the mainstream of thought in psychology in the United States. There are indications that this situation is changing, particularly among graduate students who have access to new publications about Jung's thought. Until recently an appraisal of Jung's contribution to thought in projective techniques rested with a series of articles published by the *Journal of Projective Techniques* (1955) in an issue which Bruno Klopfer dedicated to Jung on his eightieth birthday. Several important European publications have reflected Jung's influence on Rorschach theory and personality assessment through the years. Some of these significant works include papers by the Swiss psychologist K. W. Bash (1952, 1956, 1972), David Kadinsky's (1963) book *Strukturelemente der Persoenlichkeit*, and works by Merei (1953), Binder (1959), and Mohr (1941, 1947).

Through clinical experience and observation, we have seen that the Rorschach inkplates seem to represent a coordinate system which corresponds in important ways to the structure of personality. To the extent that any personality theory has validity, the valid aspects of the theory evoke counterparts in Rorschach behavior. Holding this viewpoint, the present writer (1971) has applied Jung's theory of archetypes to the Rorschach method. *Rorschach Theory and Symbolism* is a systematic effort to correlate the validity of Jung's concepts with Rorschach phenomena, or, to complete our metaphor, to graph certain aspects of Jung's theory on the axes of Rorschach's coordinate system. The main thesis of this book is that Rorschach's plates correspond in important ways to the structure of personality because aspects of Rorschach's plates are inclusive enough to provide visual stimuli with the power to activate archetypal energy. Jung (1959) defined archetypes through their power to influence perception. Our position has been that symbol formation in Rorschach phenomena is partly a function of archetypal energy's facility to influence perception. Our effort to isolate and illustrate how archetypal energy potentiates structures in the internal matrix of Rorschach's blots, though subject to human error, is neither arbitrary nor eccentric, but strongly governed by Jung's theory of archetypal psychology. However, Jung's theory of archetypal psychology is not easy to grasp or to put into practice; the chief reason is that one must learn to recognize and decipher the hallmarks of *archetypal language*. This language applies to dream symbolism, and the student of Jung's approach must be trained in the art of applying objectivity to the vast range of complex subjective images and experiences.

Another feature in Jung's approach to psychic material which compounds difficulties in grasping Jung's theory pertains to his manner of viewing the products of conscious thought as due to different variables than subjective experience (which is not produced

by conscious intent) such as symbol formation. In offering a theory
of the paranormal, LeShan (1969) postulated two levels of reality:
One pertains to ordinary consciousness (on which most psychological
research is based); the second conforms to the world as envisioned
by modern physics. Some of Jung's concepts pertain more to rather
unfamiliar structuring evident in physicists' view of events in space
and time than to ordinary representations of cause and effect. The
Society of Personality Assessment recently published a monograph,
Toward a Discovery of the Person, edited by Dr. Robert W. Davis,
which includes a Carl G. Jung centennial symposium entitled "Personality Interpretation and Physical Models: A Jungian Viewpoint,"
which takes up these complex issues in some detail. A paper by this
author (1974) is included in the symposium, and attempts to hy-
pothesize about the relation between Rorschach processes and
physical theory.

It is also true that the *set* produced by a widespread application
of Freud's approach to symbolism (which we view as useful but incomplete) is hard to overcome, if we would look at the variables
which give birth to Rorschach symbols in a different fashion. As we
mentioned, in order to explore Rorschach symbols in a more directly
Jungian fashion, one must learn to deal with *archetypal language*.
This learning is not easy to come by because Jung's position, unlike
Freud's, contains no ready-made givens; it is, nevertheless, an approach with far more personal challenge. In comparing symbol
formation in the Rorschach with the symbolism of Tantric Buddhist
art forms, the author (1974) has discussed aspects of learning archetypal language in some detail. In another paper, McCully (1972) has
illustrated how archetypal language may be useful in deciphering
the psychology associated with the art forms of prehistory. Other
sources helpful to the reader in that regard include H. Zimmer's
(1948) *The King and the Corpse* and Jung's (1968) *Analytical
Psychology: Its Theory and Practice*. It is perhaps important to
note here, however, that an archetypal image is not equivalent to
a so-called universal image. An image qualifies as an "archetype"
insofar as it has an intrinsic quality which can be isolated and which
can, under certain conditions, activate (but not necessitate) a psychological response which is common to the human condition. The
moon, for example, may be an image-substitute or archetypal carrier

for feminine psychology, since we ordinarily project female qualities onto it. There are exceptions, since isolated cultures have projected something different onto the moon, but the archetypal aspect of the moon-as-female-symbol pertains to its attracting a feminine psychology *most* of the time. Thus, exceptions do not render the moon less susceptible to "standing-for" experiences which are generally associated with the feminine side of life. The most basic connection between woman and moon rests on the cyclic life of both. This is the stuff of which archetypes are built—not obscure phenomena, but repeated human experience which itself gives energy to the object. Archetypes are the most suitable and psychologically convenient image-vehicles for our projections. The Zodiac is perhaps an example of a no longer viable vehicle for human projection. As images, the signs of the Zodiac are obsolete archetypes. That they still attract us is variously interpreted, but that they do indeed shows that all of the psychological energy projected onto the idea of them is not completely drained. The Zodiac also illustrates the viability of projected psychology over great stretches of time. The *experience-response* is archetypal, not the object itself. Hence, an archetypal symbol or *substitute-image* is evocative only insofar as it stimulates a response common in human experience.

In her introduction to this book, Rickers-Ovsiankina emphasizes that Rorschach himself was primarily interested in *how*, rather than *what*, the Rorschach subject experiences. A failure to note this important distinction decreases the significance of the numerous validity and reliability studies that abound in Rorschach literature. We would like to emphasize that neither degree of conformity among judges of different persuasions nor *interpretation* (the "what" side of a subject's experience) of Rorschach data itself—no matter how clinically useful such interpretations may be—tells us anything about the mechanisms of emergence of Rorschach images (the "how" side of a subject's experience). We must learn more about the mechanisms that produce Rorschach data and not simply be satisfied with the essentially descriptive observation that the data are produced by personality dynamics. In addition to personality dynamics, there are probably intervening variables which are generally overlooked.

Perhaps insistence on consistency in interpretation and on ways to ensure replication by others—no matter how necessary to the dictates of scientific precision—is not itself precise, since much about the mediation of Rorschach data is unknown. The variability in analyses of interpretive data has confirmed the elusive nature of subjective affairs, but this indicts not the method but our unsure grasp of the complex issues involved. The manifold attempts to objectify subjective phenomena, despite their apparent logic, do not hold the final answer. It is perhaps scientifically unsound to fit data which are subject to a unique set of forces into the molds of conscious logic. Attempts in that regard work well for techniques like the MMPI because the data pertain mostly to conscious contents and processes. When Rorschach theory is satisfactorily extended, more inclusive research tools will be devised. By "Rorschach theory" we mean an exploration of the nature of those processes in Rorschach experience that produce the data. This means exploration beyond descriptions about the *effects* of those processes, such as labeling certain symbolic material "primary process materials" as if that designation were explanatory. In this regard, we agree with Piotrowski's (1972) recent observation that the Rorschach suffers from a general lack of differentiation between the theory of the technique itself and the theory of personality. Because the impact of negative findings associated with validation work has been so widespread, the necessity for distinction between Rorschach theory and personality theory cannot be overemphasized. Recent research has been directed far more to the product than to the source. Negative findings tell us that the personality theories applied in interpretation are not inclusive enough, that there are complex difficulties inherent in translating the non-rational into the rational, but not much about the Rorschach theory itself. One cannot rely on interpretation to measure validity as long as so much is unknown about the nature of sources and processes which produce a Rorschach pattern. Writing recently, Margaret Mead (1974) recalled how the Rorschach was a poor predictor of performance when it was used by the U.S. Armed Services during World War II. She remarked that one suggestion to account for its poor performance was that perhaps there were some individuals that the Rorschach did not test at all. No Rorschach clinician today would entertain such a thought, although it may have seemed a logical deduction at the time. The Rorschach is not a panacea, and we have better techniques for predicting the consequences of purely conscious events. Mead (1974) reviewed the complexities involved in using the Rorschach method in cross-cultural investigation. Yet, her long experience has suggested to her that the Rorschach does provide a means through which a kind of "cross-cultural intelligibility" accrues. She remarks: "This cross-cultural intelligibility is, I think, one of the ways of describing archetypal character. . . Beneath the various culturally specific evocations of culturally loaded symbolism, there seems to lie, in some relationship between subject and card, or interpreter and response, a deeper layer." Our view of this layer is that it reflects an archetypal ground in the psyche. It is the source of energy which creates a symbol-product, and the Rorschach enables us to examine how these ideas or symbols come into being, as well as the dynamics of the subject and his cultural tradition. Marcos E. Simón (1973), a Spanish psychologist, reported an interesting finding in a normative study of an African population. A worker came across a subculture of Africans who rejected all Rorschach plates *en masse*. This remarkable finding was apparently due to the Rorschach plates' too closely resembling a technique employed by the community's witch doctor, in which he used cloud figures to predict the present and future for his clients. The shaman had hit upon a viable means for stimulating human projection; hence, the foreign (Rorschach) blots' parallel with the local (African) method serves to affirm the projective hypothesis. At least in part, we see these methods as evocative through activating archetypal response patterns. Rorschach himself thought that his method included a key for understanding projections in the art forms of remote cultures. Indian physicist D. V. N. Sarma (1974) recently offered evidence that the author of the *Brihadaranyaka Upanishad* (c. 500 B.C.) was aware of the significance of the projective hypothesis.

Several years ago Scottish physicist Lancelot Law Whyte (1964) wrote:

> Knowledge remains alive by advancing. And today this means ceasing to rely on deceptively clear abstract models, and considering how the idea, the symbol, or the form of order came into existence, either in external nature or in the human mind. The genuine theoretical basis of knowledge may not be formal or abstract, but identical with the story of the historical origins of knowledge.

The Rorschach provides an arena in which to study how symbols come into being and a means for investigating aspects of the origins of psychic experience associated with the archetypal phenomena that may underlie certain historical origins of knowledge.

One of Jung's greatest contributions was to separate *symbol* from *symptom*, whereas Freud had linked them. Jung's view of a symbol was rather like that of George Boas (1967), who wrote, "The beauty of myth and symbol lies in their synthetic power; they can combine in one presentation disparate elements which would be self-contradictory if put into a declarative sentence." The word "symbol" in its original Greek meant "draws together." Our view of the symbol is that it is not the product of disguise, but a communication couched in archetypal language. Florence Miale's chapter in this book, as well as our own *Rorschach Theory and Symbolism* (1971), offers a wider treatment of a Jungian view of symbolism for the interested reader. In separating symbol from symptom, Jung removed the theory and practice of psychotherapy from the exclusive realm of pathology and related it to the whole history of the evolution of the human psyche in all its cultural manifestations.

Jung (1956) distinguished between imagination and fantasy, or "directed thinking" and "fantasy thinking." He stated that imagination involves the deliberate manipulation of concepts which are not necessarily unrealistic but characterized by novelty. Fantasy was described as a passive attitude toward occurrences of unrealistic images in one's mental life. He remarked that imagination produces innovations and adaptations; it reflects reality and tries to act upon it. Fantasy turns away from reality, sets free subjective tendencies, and, as regards adaptation, is more passive and less directly geared to action.

The Rorschach experience provides a subject with an opportunity to *place* thought into an imaginative frame and *allow* fantasy to come into play. Along the second mode symbols may emerge, depending on the openness of the subject to such events. Symbols appear apart from any conscious attempt to produce them. Hence, the Rorschach provides a unique advantage in allowing discovery to take place *without* the direction of thought.

One may say that the Rorschach provides conditions associated with *objective consciousness*, whose images consist of conscious ideas which correspond to blot areas, and *subjective consciousness*, whose images arise to consciousness around blot areas as a function of nonconscious processes. McCully (1965) has suggested a schema against which one may sort out images due to either of these processes. This gives us a way of looking at what is happening as Rorschach data form; *process*, an important dimension associated with Rorschach patterning, is what links happenings and patterns in this regard. Neither scores nor content, alone or combined, provides us with sufficient grasp of the *sources* associated with Rorschach events. We have called this manner of investigating Rorschach patterning "process analysis."

In the Rorschach we have the advantage of watching the products of spontaneous inner events form. The examiner is careful not to give a subject any pushes in directing his consciousness. Conscious judgment about the images which appear to subjective consciousness occurs *after* the subject becomes aware of their presence. As any examiner knows, a subject's own images frequently surprise him, and it is just at this point, the confluence between image formation and conscious reaction, that we get information about the *process* of interaction between subject and image. An analysis of this confluence informs us about the relation between the objective and subjective (conscious and nonconscious) worlds belonging to the subject. Knowledge of a subject's relationship to his nonconscious side has relevance to therapy. These matters make clear how, in Rorschach performance, we are dealing with complicated dimensions of psychic processes which are seldom involved in most other means of gathering psychological data. Qualitative differences in the kind of data the Rorschach provides make it elusive for research. Neglect of this knowledge may lead to misunderstanding concerning a diagnosis arrived at by other means. In many instances overt, observable behavior does not correspond with easily quantifiable Rorschach behavior in the usual sense of standard scores. This indicates less that the Rorschach "failed" than failure in our grasp of the data's significance. It shows how we often apply to Rorschach tasks research designs which are not broad or inclusive enough to evaluate two distinctly different kinds of data. One set of data is associated with the objective processes of consciousness and the other with subjective processes, themselves subject to different natural forces.

Process analysis is a particular kind of focus in the analysis of sequence. It is an analysis of the linking conditions that contribute to the nature of the sequence. Designating *sources* for 'subjective data aids us in analyzing them. It is an attempt to isolate and evaluate the process the subject unconsciously uses in structuring whatever emerges or becomes part of conscious awareness. To accomplish this, one must make defenses, dynamics, and other ordinary foci in Rorschach interpretation peripheral for the moment. Distinctions of this nature may sharpen our attitude toward Rorschach research. We must change our usual sets, since they may obscure identification of the process itself. We focus on what an individual is doing at any one time and its relation to the whole, a subtle use of interpretation of interaction between the subject and his image. Thus, a symbol, instead of a purely visual encounter, may be inherent in the nature of a particular process. Gammon (1974) has given us a provocative account of symmetry in the Rorschach as symbolic of processes which are related to some of the natural laws discovered by physics.

The schema we have developed may be useful in examining Rorschach processes in more depth than ordinary scoring procedures provide. This approach is not meant to serve as another form of scoring, but to add another dimension to Rorschach analysis. The schema offers us a means of examining patterns of responses against possible sources of data. In this manner one may identify processes related to psychic disturbance alongside those associated with adaptation. Various refinements and additions could be added to the schema by those interested in applying the approach to research design or by those clinicians interested in broadening the range of interpretation.

One may conceive two planes, one horizontal and the other vertical (see figure 1). This figure grew from a comparison we made between the Rorschach material and qualities in the handwriting of a particularly open, borderline patient. Readers familiar with graphology will recognize the frame as a basic one in that dicipline. On the left side of the horizontal plane at "A," we designate withdrawal, and on its right side at "B," we designate adaptation. Axis "AB" designates a movement zone reflecting the degree of formal adaptiveness. Vertically at "C," we designate objective consciousness (responses or processes due to conscious thought or intent) and at "D," we assign subjective consciousness (products of processes not

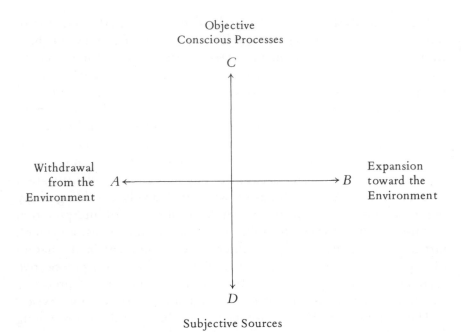

Fig. 15-1 *AB* axis designates a movement sphere reflecting the degree of formal adaptiveness. *CD* axis designates a sphere of movement between conscious awareness and symbol formation.

subject to conscious thought or intent). Although we view subjective consciousness as a function of nonconscious events, we have not designated point "D" as referring to unconscious material, that global concept which so imprecisely lumps together disparately determined events. The image assigned to point "D" is due to nonconscious events, but it now resides inside conscious awareness. We think this sort of distinction is important, and failure to draw it leads to confusion, especially apropos research. The "CD" axis is a continuum (as is "AB") providing for locating patterns of processes, sometimes with degrees or mixtures of the designations at eigher end.

Movement of all degrees and levels of adaptive processes may occur anywhere along these axes; they may vary from one moment to another or they may cluster in certain areas. A sample of Rorschach material may illustrate how we use our schema:

PLATE I

Responses	Inquiry
It looks like it could be one animal combined together. It could be Siamese twins. It could be a bat, but I don't think so.	It just looks like two animals born together. I wouldn't know what kind. Well, it sort of looked like a bat because of the little wings up here (means usual hands, central projections). Q-What about this part?—meaning the outer large *Ds* or usual bat wings—I haven't the slightest idea, they could be wings for all I know. It's possible that each one is a bat (each half of the card); it's very possible they could be having intercourse, but I doubt it. Q-Could this whole thing be a bat? I doubt it, because the wings are too far apart.

PLATE II

Responses	Inquiry
Two animals combined together with their beaks. They could possibly be having intercourse. Don't know what this is (top red).	Q-What makes them look like that? Well, the connections here (above) and here (below). Wouldn't know what kind.

PLATE III

Responses	Inquiry
This could be a man and a woman. I doubt if this would be the breast (center red). Or it could be two animals, but they're exactly the same. It's possible they could be having a relation.	Well, a man and woman that way. Q-Top red? Don't know. Q-Having a relation? The connection down here, but the faces are too far apart. Q-Center red? Breasts or could be a bow tie. It's impossible to tell if it's a man or woman.

Plate I provides the stimulus for an easily perceived popular image. The subject experiences the blot in terms of combination and separation. This appears to indicate an inner state in which she cannot separate conscious sources from unconscious ones. This psychological state defines the borderline condition in which consciousness is intruded upon by images and ideas which appear suddenly in awareness. The ego has lost some of its judgmental power. Lack of differentiation *within* determines lack of differentiation *without*. The image is that of separate figures that are fused. The source materials for the responses to Plate I center within the angle formed by "AD" on our schema. The strength of these processes is shown by the subject's spontaneous rejection of a more rational and far more conventional image, a bat. Inner movement comes from subjective consciousness, which tends to determine or influence objective consciousness. She is not unaware of the obvious (bat), but she rejects both the image and her thoughts about taking it at face value. She actually tells us why it is not a bat to her, and her reasoning is influenced by inner processes, *not* by the nature of the content of the image. This emphasizes the importance of attending to those processes involved. Forces that would not occur outside this kind of stimulus (in this instance, the Rorschach plate) determine her experience. When she actually tries to separate her image into parts ("could be two bats"), her judgment evaporates and she gets confused about what could be and what could not be the wings of the bat or bats. The process of trying to separate things throws her judgment askew. It becomes so strong that, when she is asked to respond to the obvious (large wings, side *Ds*),[1] she fails to recognize the bat. Some quality that is archetypal in its strength of energy emerges around separateness and combination as symbols inside the process. When asked, she rejects the notion that the whole card could be a bat. It is important to note that this patient is a borderline one, with a foot in each of two psychic worlds.

We have purposely omitted any consideration of the sexual comments the subject made. An interpretation for "bats having intercourse" is rather easy in isolation; however, by looking at the symbol inherent in the *process* of what happens, we may give interpretation more scope. There is no question that the patient has a "complex" associated with sexual differentiation. However, the symbol that emerges is itself centered around separation and combination as determiners of the *quality* of her perception. Intercourse between the bats is not itself a symbol; that is a conscious deduction she made about two bats that look physically joined together. Sexual differentiation is shown against a larger problem of general differentiation between conscious and nonconscious worlds.

[1] For explanation of scoring symbols, see Appendix, pp. 609 ff. [Editor].

No movement of processes occurs that suggests any social concern or interest in outward adaptation. In substance, Plate I has provided us with the information that the patient is highly sensitive to a process related to things being combined and separated, that an image (Siamese) formed which contained an aspect of those forces in it, and that those features within her are more predominant than her adaptive qualities connected with conscious judgments. One may conclude that this is the kind of borderline patient whose sexual preoccupations (or acts) are her last links with reality or relatedness, while the larger scope of the symbolism involved inside the process itself shows why her psychic stance here is unlikely to work.

Her response to Plate II shows us that the symbolization inside the process we isolated from Plate I continues to manifest itself. The blot contours are quite different, but we get much the same image as before, refitted to this blot. Bright color is present, and this can act as an emotional challenge allowing expression of concern or moving out to others, as well as the opposite, but the subject does not involve herself with it. The symbolism inside the process itself (image of how things are joined) continues along the lines of connection and fusion. Her consciousness lacks freedom to tolerate separation. We may assume that separating the two sides of the blot is blocked by nonconscious forces, and this determines the nature of the image. She is particularly sensitive to how her image is fused. When she reports "two animals," she gives us a popular image which would fall inside the "CB" angle on our schema, but qualities from the "AD" side contaminates what could be adaptive. Neither the animals' position nor their activity is conventional. Sexual qualities again are not themselves the symbol that forms; they are attributed to the figures (through "AD" area sources) because of the position observed (literal objective connectedness). Absence of separation means something sexual to the patient, but the symbolic vehicle is that of perceiving something connected, and this touches off an archetypal source (quite possibly symmetry) that is shunted through the personal dynamics of a sexual complex. A lack of inner separation or differentiation between conscious and nonconscious becomes vested with sexual channeling.

Her responses to Plate III show us that the processes taking place in the subject are much more powerful for her than blot contours or her percepts. Experiences related to differences and likenesses, separateness and connections, have become symbols for her. The strength of inner needs associated with those symbols infuses her images and logic. As with Plate II, she provides us with a popular image, people, but there are few other signs of "CB" area (adaptive) activity. She makes a conscious effort to make the two sides of the blot stimulus different (one male, one female), but this attempt distorts the stimulus since both sides are indeed exactly alike. The symbol message is that she is psychologically troubled by an *awareness* that the two sides look exactly alike. While we might see in this a homosexual element, that too is based on underlying lack of inner differentiation. This time she does question her own response. Consciousnesss makes a weak attempt to assert itself through judgment, but when this happens, almost at once her judgment becomes highly unrealistic (showing the much greater source-influence from "AD"), leading her to comment that the red center detail could be "a breast." That area is physically *separate* from the rest of the blot. Actually separating something from her image succeeds in separating the patient from realistic, conscious judgments. Red color, as a potential for a feeling response, might be experienced adaptively (bow tie), except archetypal influences alter the reality of her *perception*, leaving her with an image of breast. This shows the power of archetypal energy in influencing Rorschach perception and the way such power transcends conscious logic as an influence. We are saying that attributing this event in perception to sexual dynamics is not sufficient if we wish to understand the theory of Rorschach perception, since the way sexual dynamics influence *altered* perception may be assumed to operate through an archetypal route, and that route involves *synchronicity*, a psychic ordering of perception subject to forces apart from those of conscious logic. Jung speaks of synchronicity, when two events which have not been willed by conscious thought occur simultaneously, as being due to causeless order. We would say that the "causeless" aspect merely refers to an absence of the usual cause familiar to the laws of conscious acts and that it is due to other forces which bring the event into awareness through subjective consciousness. A more detailed description and hypotheses about the relation between Jung's concept of synchronicity and Rorschach symbol formation may be found in this author's (1974) paper, "The Rorschach, Synchronicity and Relativity," published in the Jung centennial symposium mentioned earlier.

Experiencing the two sides of the blot on Plate III as identical is of such troubling symbolic significance for this patient that she is unsure about reporting a popular image (bat), even though the idea of the popular image occurred to her. The nature of the process in her Rorschach responses plays out the extent of a generalized lack of differentiation. This takes place not simply because she has a sexual complex; indeed, the sexual complex has developed as a consequence of the differentiation problem. At this point, the patient is in danger of losing ego control, and the larger concern for her is separating what is conscious and connected with her complex on the one hand, and her negative influences from archetypal sources on the other. She is not separated from instinctual pressures and her Rorschach responses reflect this inner state. Animal figures carry the symbol of her fused or undifferentiated life within, which is the root substance of her dilemma. Separation and connectedness as symbol experiences touch off processes in the patient.

What happens in this patient between a percept of "bow tie" and "breast" for the same area illustrates what we mean by the power of archetypal energy. This power manifests itself in functioning to influence or alter perception. Phenomena of this order must surely have relevance to some of the vagaries in perception that interested Gestalt theorists. For example, Josef Ternus (1926; reprinted, 1967) investigated subjective factors associated with the problem of phenomenal identity. He noted that subjectively induced changes of unitary constellations usually involve new identity relations among segments of configurations. Alterations in subjectively induced patterns of cortical excitation were assumed to account for alterations in perception which we here suggest may be a function of archetypal energy. It may be that through those forces described by Ternus (the sudden appearance of a new configuration) the individual dynamics of a Rorschach observer find expression in the image of a symbol-substitute. Our position is that archetypal energy mediates the transaction. K. W. Bash (1946) considered some of the issues linking symbol, gestalt, and archetype some twenty years ago. In any event, mediating forces that influence subjective events have been neglected by experimental psychology. The Rorschach activates richer and more complicated imagery than did the geometric designs which intrigued the Gestalt theorists. We must assume that nothing magical is at work when a subject reports a remarkable perception such as a sexual reversal in Rorschach imagery. Even though the perceptual product may be (in part) a function of a particular dynamic, the reality of perceptual alteration remains to be explained in perceptual, not dynamic terms. Some form of energy must underwrite the remarkable instance of drastic perceptual alterations. An important aspect necessary to understand the processes of the patient we are considering include her "doubting" that the center detail could be breasts. We must grasp the implication of that if we would discern something fundamental about the Rorschach experience. First, the image of a breast forced itself; this happened totally *outside* any conscious intent on the part of the subject. After the image of breast occurred, consciousness of the event led her to report the symbol-image of breasts. Then she immediately doubted its existence. A subjective process constellated an image through forces that consciousness did not control; the image emerged despite any efforts to suppress it. The image did not remain "latent;" it happened. What ensued was a fascinating process that owes its existence to relationships separate from those applicable to conscious logic. In the first place, there are perfectly acceptable, realistic breasts on the figures of the blot, attached in an appropriate manner. We hold that a particularly important stimulus quality in Rorschach's plates lies in the variety of sexually toned contours, and those inappropriately attached to the human form may especially stir up responses involving archetypal energy, while organs appropriately attached (as in Plate III) do not. This issue is discussed in detail in *Rorschach Theory and Symbolism* (1971). With this particular patient, we may see a remarkable example of the archetypal significance of "detached" body parts. Their property of detachment from a body alters their meaning, sometimes widening the significance from the specifically sexual (for example) to generative qualities. Perception in this subject must be assumed to have been influenced by archetypal energy. We must take what the patient sees at face value. The properly attached breasts on the figures of Plate III were excluded to visual awareness while the separate center red detail became the visual carrier of the percept "breast," the matter being visually displaced. This is a rather remarkable visual gymnastic. The subject was not able consciously to tolerate a perception that the two figures were identical (either two females or two males). We would say that archetypal energy activated a subjective reaction, that of excluded awareness. When these conditions pertain, the *essential ingredients of symbol-formation* become manifest. This shows how careful attention to Rorschach processes enables us to widen our understanding about the nature of symbol-formation.

Not only does the stimulus plate provide for a percept of breasts appropriately placed on human figures, the subject told us that she recognized the central red detail conventionally as a "bow tie." *Despite* both of these clearcut perceptual vehicles, the subject's visual experience became nonlogical, and a source apart from conscious thought ordered her percept differently. It was as if perceptual lines for the bow tie dissolved and momentarily an image of a breast replaced it. The patient's need to see two figures that are objectively alike in form as different from each other (male and female) was powerful indeed. In our opinion, what happened perceptually was not a function of thinking the matter through (which does happen many times in the Rorschach performance), but was something that simply *happened* to the subject, mediated by the intrinsic structure of the blot and its power to activate subjective forces. Through the nature of this subject's dynamics, an archetypal source within flashed her an image of "breast." The image was a communication that appeared inside subjective consciousness because of the nature of the forces that came into play. The event was not mystical, but a function of subjective forces. We would have to decipher the meaning of the symbol of breast, an image with archetypal elements, inside the context of what is known about this patient's psychology. The archetypal element here is probably nurture. How much nurture can she give others as a woman and what effect did the presence or absence of nurture have on her as a child? Her sexual complex as an adult must connect directly with these questions.

Something of the same process had happened before on Plate I. When the subject consciously attempted to separate the whole into parts ("could be two bats"), and when she was asked if usual wing areas for a papular bat could be wings, some *process* separated her from logic associated with objective consciousness and drew her into a different frame which itself influenced the nature of her perception.

When this subject had been interviewed by another examiner with a goal of establishing a diagnosis and discovering complexes and dynamics, the interviewer got the impression that she was disturbed but not psychotic. She made appropriate responses to questions, although it was not clear to what extent her adaptiveness was impaired. Rorschach samples taken from her subjective state have aided us in grasping more about her through looking at subjective processes. The subject was actually in a quite precarious state. Her logic was not providing her with the structure to sustain adaptivity. She had a vulnerability for psychotic thinking under certain conditions. A struggle was ongoing and she exerted much energy toward trying to separate the products of her own conscious activity from functions of what happened below the level of consciousness.

Our schema may be useful for judging more global aspects of Rorschach data. It is, however, very general, and we must not leave out the possibility that any perceptual material may have a positive or negative influence on a given person. Some individuals may show "AD" (subjective sources) process activity and not be subject to either symptoms or potential disturbance. Others may show "CB" (conscious adaptation) activity and yet be subject to psychological collapse. The defenses of an overly adapted person may capsize in a storm due to over-reliance on facade and too little experience with powerful, temporary elements. So long as we keep an open attitude about what such experiences can mean for a person and we seek to identify as much about it as we can, we move on in understanding ourselves and others.

In closing, we would like to reemphasize our position that Rorschach's inkplates seem to represent a coordinate system which corresponds in important ways to the structure of personality. Freudian, existential, and other schools of thought have been seminal in the impetus they have provided for understanding meanings inside Rorschach data. Our goal has been to point out how certain of Jung's concepts may augment and extend our understanding of Rorschach theory. Jung's thought offers a different frame, since it enables us to examine sources and processes in a fashion apart from interpretation per se. We have proposed that certain Rorschach images are influenced by archetypal energy, an ingredient that we feel plays a role in symbol-formation, and perhaps in many forms of creativity.

While symptom and symbol are most surely related to personality dynamics, in separating symbol from symptom, Jung has provided the means for a wider understanding of the nature of the symbol itself, in its own right. To the extent that any personality theory has validity, the valid aspects of the theory evoke counterparts in Rorschach behavior. Hence, we see the studies of Rorschach processes as an important aspect of the future of the Rorschach method. It provides us with a laboratory for the study of creativity as well as a means of understanding disturbance. As Jung has cautioned, we must not look for unequivocality, but attend to overtones and undertones, if we would extend our theories.

BIBLIOGRAPHY

Adler, G. C. G. Jung after ten years. *Psychological Perspectives*, 1971, **2**, 91-96.

Bash, K. W. Gestalt, symbol und archetypus. *Schweizerische Zeitschrift für Psychologie und ihre Anwendungen*, 1946, 127-138.

Bash, K. W. Zur experimentellen Grundlegung der Jung'schen Traumanalyse. *Schweizerische Zeitschrift für Psychologie und ihre Anwendungen*, 1952, **11**, 282-295.

Bash, K. W. Einstellungstypus and erlebnistypus: C. G. Jung and Hermann Rorschach. *Journal of Projective Techniques*, 1955, **19**, 236-242.

Bash, K. W. Zur Inhaltsdeutung im Rorschach-Versuch. *Psyche* (Heidelberg), 1956, **9**, 584-602.

Bash, K. W. The soul image: Anima and animus as projected in the Rorschach test. *Journal of Personality Assessment*, 1972, **36**, 340-348.

Binder, H. *Die Helldunkeldeutungen im Psychodiagnostischen Experiment von Rorschach*. Bern: Hans Huber, 1959.

Boas, G. Preface to *Myth, Religion and Mother Right* (Johann Bachofen, 1885). Princeton: Princeton University Press, 1967.

Brawer, F., and Spiegleman, M. Rorschach and Jung. *Journal of Analytical Psychology*, 1964, **9**, 137-149.

Edinger, E. F. *Ego and Archetype*. New York: G. P. Putnam's Sons, 1972.

Gammon, M. The Rorschach mirror. In R. W. Davis, ed., *Toward a Discovery of the Person*. Society for Personality Assessment monograph, 1974. Pp. 46-50.

Jung, C. G. *Symbols of Transformation*. New York: Pantheon, 1956.

Jung, C. G. *The Structure and Dynamics of the Psyche*. New York: Pantheon (Bollingen Series XX), 1959. Pp. 229-231.

Jung, C. G. *Analytical Psychology, Its Theory and Practice*. New York: Pantheon, 1968.

Kadinsky, D. *Strukturelemente der Persoenlichkeit*. Bern: Hans Huber, 1963.

Klopfer, B., ed. C. G. Jung's birthday issue. *Journal of Projective Techniques*, **19**, 1955.

LeShan, L. Toward a general theory of the paranormal. *Parapsychological Monographs*, **9**, 1969.

McCully, R. S. Process analysis: A tool in understanding ambiguity in diagnostic problems in Rorschach. *Journal of Projective Techniques and Personality Assessment*, 1965, **29**, 436-444.

McCully, R. S. *Rorschach Theory and Symbolism*. Baltimore: Williams & Wilkins, 1971.

McCully, R. S. A psychologist looks at prehistoric art. *Art International* (lugano), 1972, **XIV**, 63-66.

McCully, R. S. Tantric art and Rorschach perception. *Rorschachiana Japonica*, 1974, **XV & XVI**, 123-134.

McCully, R. S. The Rorschach, synchronicity, and relativity. In R. W. Davis, ed., *Toward a Discovery of the Person*. Society for Personality Assessment monograph, 1974, Pp. 33-45, 74-78.

Mead, M. A note on the evocative character of the Rorschach test. In R. W. Davis, ed., *Toward a Discovery of the Person*. Society for Personality Assessment monograph, 1974, Pp. 62-67.

Merei, F. *Der Aufforderungscharakter der Rorschach-Tafeln* (trans. by S. Neiger from the Hungarian: A Rorschach-tablak felszolito jellege, *Szemle*, **3-4**, 1947). Innsbruck: University of Innsbruck Press, 1953.

Mohr, P. Die Inhalte der Deutungen beim Rorschach'schen Formdeutversuch und ihre Beziehungen zur Versuchsperson. *Schweizerische Archiv fuer Neurologie und Psychiatrie*, 1941, **47**, 237-270.

Mohr, P. Die schwarze und dunkle Farbe der Rorschach-Tafeln. In *Rorschachiana II*. Bern: Hans Huber, 1947, Pp. 24-36.

Piotrowski, Z. From inkblots to dreams: Perceptanalysis generalized. *Rorschachiana Japonica*, 1972, **XIV**, 1-10.

Roemer, G. Hermann Rorschach und die Forschungsergebnisse seiner beiden letzten Jahre. *Psyche* (Heidelbert), 1948, **1**, 523-542.

Rorschach, H. *Psychodiagnostics*. Bern: Hans Huber, 1942 (1921).

Rorschach, H. Zwei schweizerische Sektenstifter (Binggeli und Unternaher). (Two Swiss founders of sects). *Imago*, **13**, 395-441, 1927 (posthumous).

Sarma, D. V. N. Letter to the editor. *Journal of Personality Assessment*, 1974, **38**, 166.

Simón, M. E. Problemas transculturales en la unilización del test de Rorschach. In *Rorschachiana X*. Bern: Hans Huber, 1973, Pp. 438-443.

Ternus, J. Experimentelle Untersuchung über phänomenale Identität (trans. from the German: *Psychol. Forsch*, **7**, 81-136, 1926). In E. D. Willis, ed., *A Source Book of Gestalt Psychology*. New York: Humanities Press, 1967, Pp. 149-160.

Whyte, L. L. The growth of ideas. In Joseph Campbell, ed., *Man and Transformation*. New York: Pantheon, 1964, Pp. 250-270.

Zimmer, J. *The King and the Corpse*. New York: Pantheon, 1948.

Each thinker, however, has dominant habits of attention; and these practically elect from among the various worlds some one to be for him the world of ultimate realities.

WILLIAM JAMES

16 | *Lois and Gardner Murphy*

HERMANN RORSCHACH
AND PERSONALITY RESEARCH

I

The intimate relation between Hermann Rorschach's personality and the test which bears his name has often been forgotten in our attempt to devise a modern comprehensive test program based upon the utilization of ink blots. Even in the case of Alfred Binet's ingenious development of intelligence tests, much depends upon Binet's time, place, and culture, and much upon his own personality; but in the fifty years which have passed since his first tests, psychometrics has become almost an impersonal endeavor, a general branch of psychological science. Nothing of the sort has yet occurred in the domain of personality testing. The unique genius of Murray (1938) is evident in the Thematic Apperception Test; the Picture Frustration Test (Rosenzweig, 1935) eloquently bespeaks some of Saul Rosenzweig's insights; the Draw-A-Person of Karen Machover (1949), the Lowenfeld Mosaic (1954), and the Szondi (1952) tests are still essentially "sonnets" or "essays" in the literary style of individual psychologists. The Rorschach, because of its power, range, depth, and subtlety is to a still greater degree an expression of the man who made it.

This point can easily be forgotten, as one attempts to square Rorschach findings with those from psychoanalysis. For Rorschach, though an analyst, was working primarily within the European conception of the biological and psychological structure of personality as it obtained in the scientific and literary expressions of the 19th century, as Henri Ellenberger's beautiful little biographical sketch (1954) makes clear. Rorschach had been preoccupied through all his medical training and his early years of institutional and private practice with problems of personality dynamics which had been widely recognized by philosophers and medical men long before the dawn of psychoanalysis; he was concerned as much with the deeper creative aspects of personality as with those of immediate clinical import. He thought of himself as striving to cut through a forest of difficulties to the achievement of a brief, yet subtle representation of personality structure, as given to a very large degree by constitutionally grounded trends of development. At the same time he saw, as few were capable of seeing in his day, that this biological continuity is a biosocial continuity as well, and that the cultural world of the individual makes its permanent mark upon the developmental pattern. He had, then, a biosocial definition of personality in which psychoanalytic dynamics was one, but only one, of a number of contributing viewpoints.

It is also important to remember that he worked alone, having few friends or colleagues, and almost no intellectual stimulation in the world in which he moved. He had indeed a few intimate professional friends, such as Dr. Emil Oberholzer, who worked on Rorschach's "posthumous case" and presented it to the world, and who made himself for many years the primary avenue of information concerning the nature of Rorschach's life and work. There were his students, especially Dr. Behn, from whom Rorschach derived much inspiration, essentially along lines which he had himself laid down, but had not had the capacity to follow through until this response of a junior colleague gave him inspiration and direction. With these notable exceptions, Rorschach lived his brief life largely in his own intellectual world, deriving his inspiration from books and, above all, from reflection. How utterly out of line he was with the cultural atmosphere of the day is shown by the fact that almost no copies of the book were sold in the first few years, the publisher having bitterly reproached himself for taking on such a hopeless venture, and Rorschach in his last months having no comfort whatever from the sense of any intellectual response to his work. The impact of Rorschach's own personality is realized in such a context to be a major factor in the unique way in which unstructured visual materials were first used as personality test materials, a full fifteen years or more before Sanford (1936) and others realized the possibilities of these unstructured materials for what came soon to be called "projective testing" (Frank, 1939).

This solitary position of Rorschach and the fact that he saw so much more than his contemporaries will serve in some degree to explain the extreme tentativeness and modesty of his formulations. He had something very concrete to offer, knowing that it was the concrete that might possibly win some ultimate acceptance and that he could not in any sense enforce his broad philosophical scheme upon his contemporaries.

II

This situation, together with his biosocial orientation, made him eager to make clear at every point what the specific determining circumstances of the test response might be. Thus, some aspects of the test are most likely to vary in response to specific influences, for instance, the conscious effort of the individual who is being tested. Rorschach (1949) noted that many *W* imply affect and volition beside associative engrams, i.e., will; this might be a conscious or an unconscious will to produce.[1] *W* can be increased only when conscious willing is abetted by individual dispositional tendency (1949, p. 66). One could hardly ask for a more comprehensive conception of the way in which constitutional factors, long-range developmental factors, and immediate situational factors interact in the production of a response. In contrast, he noted responses over which the will had little control. For example, the reduction of the animal per cent, the increase of originals and of human movements could not be effected by an effort of the will, unless the dispositional tendency towards such pattern of responses was already present. On the other hand, the *F+%* and the clarity of perceptions and of associative processes, the ability to control and discipline the logical function

---

[1] For explanation of scoring symbols, see Appendix, pp. 609 ff. [Editor].

(sequence and apperceptive type), and the ability to form stereotyped associative sets (revealed in animal per cent) did respond, he
noted, to conscious volition (Rorschach, 1949, p. 66 ff.). Here again,
however, one is immediately reminded of "wide individual variations,"
the fact that, even in their most explicit and thoroughly understood
forms, the general principles of personality development did not
yet suffice for the specification of the quantitative variations from
person to person. There still remained unexplained "individual
variations" (Rorschach, 1949, p. 66).

From these passages follows a discussion of the general role of
learning in the environment as contrasted with constitutional talents;
the factors just mentioned show a prominent contribution from learning, while percentages of whole, movement, or original responses are
mainly the expression of abilities inherent in the disposition of the
individual. Conscious effort may indeed produce modifications in
percentages of these attributes primarily conceived to be inborn,
yet the effect of effort or set, although at first sight appearing to be
successful, may actually injure the function which is being expressed.
Human movement, for example, may be increased, but at the expense
of injury to the response, the reason lying simply in the fact that it
is unconscious emotional energy rather than conscious effort that
is normally expressed through these responses (Rorschach, 1949,
p. 65).

Similarly, the effort to "improve" performance, such as the tendency to good form, may indeed produce a measurable increase in
$F+\%$, but will at the same time produce a reduction in human
movement and whole responses, and a loss of quality in the apperception type. Together with this will go an increase in the number of
animal responses and a decrease in original and color responses,
again with "large individual variations" (Rorschach, 1949, p. 66).
In other words, Rorschach observed that changes in responses in one
area involved related or balancing changes in other areas; no dimension
could be changed without affecting other dimensions. The intensely
empirical character of the work is evident here as elsewhere. This
matter of interdependence of personality aspects came generally
to be recognized in the 1930's under gestalt-theoretical influence,
but, for Rorschach at his time, it was an empirically evident proposition which burst upon him and demanded emphasis. Even with

the best sophistication of 1975, we are still bewildered by this conception that nothing can be changed without changing everything else at the same time. It is basically alien to the thought forms which have come down from 17th century mechanics and a 17th century geometry appropriate for its own period, but today are out of line with biological and, especially, with psychosocial modes of analysis. Rorschach's thinking is still far ahead of our contemporary capacity for conceptualization. We have not yet found suitable quantitative techniques for the study of dynamic phenomena which, in this manner, resolutely refuse to display that atomic isolation and simplicity of character which would be so convenient for our traditional modes of quantitative thinking.

Another large area of contemporary psychology concerned with perceptual and cognitive functions to which Rorschach early gave much attention was the factors of temporary mood, set, or attitude, the factors which could be classed neither with sheer constitution, on the one hand, nor past learning, on the other hand. Of course, mood has its own biosocial history, but often it has to be dealt with as it appears, and its effects have to be traced out, even though we may have the gravest difficulties in defining its origins. For Rorschach nothing was more important than to note the difference between stable characteristics in the person and those which varied with mood or attitude, often side by side with consciously directed attention or will, as already noted.

Mood may, for example, exert a prominent effect upon form perception, sequence, human movement, and color (Rorschach, 1949, p. 93 ff.). Depressed moods typically tend, for example, to improve form perception and to increase rigidity of sequence. At the same time, whole responses may become less frequent and apperception type poorer; variability may decline; there may be fewer originals, but more animal responses; color may disappear altogether and human movement be reduced. In depressed moods, moreover, factors determined by an increase in control of associations are most accentuated. Those factors which depend on emotionally charged energy of associative activity and on freedom of association are reduced. On the other hand, elation and similar moods may likewise be defined in relation to a wide variety of characteristic responses. The moods themselves require analysis and their own vocabulary. There is, for example, a distinction to be made between the manic, the hypomanic, the elated, and a mood of sheer "good humor."

Of special philosophical importance in grasping the nature of personality is Rorschach's conception of variability *within* one's own characteristic mode of response, as well as variability from person to person. The tendency to vary from one's own norm and from one's own way is as basic to personality as is the maintenance of a special position or stance in comparison with other persons. There are different *ranges within which different individuals might vary*. Such variability is related, of course, to the extent of operation of both volition and mood, as already considered. Volition and mood are themselves expressions of varying positions on a curve of variability within one's own characteristic or normal response. Yet each person may vary more in one area of expression than in another, depending to some degree upon the anchorage or limiting effect of constitutional factors, certain capacities being conceived to be more definitely fixed by constitution than others.

III

From all these considerations it is evident that it was very far indeed from Rorschach's thought to believe that a single Rorschach test told the whole story of individual make-up, or that it defined the person's capacity to move in one direction or another from an exhibited norm, or that it revealed in a sort of X-ray fashion the basic constitutional make-up, or that it displayed simply the attitude, set, or learning processes operating within the person; or indeed that it manifested any of the other clichés which have been attributed to the Rorschach test. As we reread his work, what we observe is a thoughtful, imaginative, subtle craftsman, sensitive to human beings, a poet and philosopher concerned with the reaches and depths of individuality, a psychoanalyst, a practical hospital doctor, and a traveler; we also see a man of the world living in a little out-of-the-way institution where he either worked or dreamed as he saw fit, now plodding with difficulty, now bursting forth with seven-league boots, mastering a conception of the richness of human individuality and, in the span of a few years, creating an amazingly subtle, yet incomplete and unsystematic, sketch for the development of a study of the ways in which individuality is reflected in the structuring of semi-structured visual materials. ˙

There are, therefore, two ways of responding to his challenge. One is to revere him, read him, love him, and use him as one would Shakespeare, Goethe, Whitman, or Emerson, adapting him freshly day-to-day to new tasks, and never dreaming of any disloyalty in re-making and passing beyond the instrument which he left to the world. The other is to standardize him, codify him, make him basic, fixed, eternal, hallowed, a foreign body from 1921 stuck in the moving tissues of today's development. Both methods are all too human, and both will certainly continue to be tried. A third possibility would be to develop from his original conception new methods of testing which embody his rich awareness of the dimensions of personality to be tested through visual perception of unstructured forms, utilizing along with his experience that of the years which have followed since the time of his first publication. In doing this, one would regard as the permanent thing about Rorschach's contribution its embodiment of a conception of personality, its empirical spirit, its objective and quantitative aspects integrated with a subtle in-tuition, and its conception that, through many approaches made at the same time, one may begin, but only begin, to get some glimpse of the total structure of personality. It is by using Rorschach in this tentative way, by studying and applying his conception of human individuality, its levels, its interrelations, its dependence upon culture, the situation, and the mood and will of the individual that the Rorschach worker of today may best enrich the personality con-ceptions of classroom and clinic. It is not because Rorschach devised a test that his position will remain revered in psychology; it is because his test is the embodiment of a sensitive, exploratory, original view of human individuality, unfinished but capable nevertheless of being measured, the measures interrelated, moment by moment, as the demands of life change. It is because the Rorschach test is the expression of a profound conception of personality that it is im-portant in psychology today.

But the Rorschach is not only a clinical test but also a basic instru-ment in personality research. The assessment of personality necessi-tates (a) clear conceptualization of the tendencies within a person and the ways in which they may be interrelated; (*b*) the development of instruments to detect and, if possible, measure these tendencies and their interrelations. Whether we regard personality as a self-sufficient ordered whole with internal structure which can somehow be tapped by an instrument applied to the periphery, or whether we regard personality as an interaction of organism and environment in which our task is to observe the back-and-forth flow between inner and outer, the first task is to conceptualize what the processes are that can be reached through assessment instruments. This necessitates some sort of working conception of what are meant by personality tendencies and the mode in which such tendencies are interrelated.

In terms of that unique interaction of biological growth and individual learning processes which gives the developmental picture of a person, we seem driven to a conception of *levels*. The following are some of the more influential of the doctrines of levels that have guided modern work upon personality structure:

1.   The evolutionary view pictures human individuality as dependent upon a very broad base of biological continuity derived from those common organic processes which we share with all living things, processes which have to do with growth, differentiation, integration, and adaptation. From such a point of view, one retains the older basic primordial functions along with those which arrive in differentiated form at each new level. There is, for example, a superposition of central nervous functions upon the older biochemical forms of communication within the living system. When the differentiated central nervous system is capable at last of developing symbolic functions, the more primitive reflex functions still remain. There is thus an ever-developing proliferation of new functions superposed upon the old, but never replacing them. This will make especially useful for us Hughlings Jackson's conception that the most *recently arrived* and the most *complex* evolutionary functions are the most *individuated* and the most sensitive and, therefore, the most *vulnerable* to stress or pathology.

2.   A somewhat similar conception is that of Heinz Werner (1948) who asks us to imagine, in both race history and individual life history, a development from (*a*) a diffuse or global stage through (*b*) a differentiated or individuated stage into (*c*) an integrated stage in

which the individuated parts now find new structure. Werner's conception can legitimately be grafted upon the Hughlings Jackson conception as it relates to individual development. It may be applied to each specific system of functions within the individual—perceptual, motivational, motor, etc.—and it may, moreover, be applied to the development of fresh contacts with new features in the environment which we learn to perceive or to cope with; new adjustment processes may be conceived to pass through the same stages from global to individuated to integrated.

3. A third conception, that of Kurt Lewin (1935), having much in common both with the Jackson system and the Werner system, uses spatial representation in which life space as a whole undergoes differentiation here and there, until differentiated parts are capable of interacting in a total. But instead of emphasizing the phylogenetic or ontogenetic problems as central issues, it prefers in general an "ahistorical" approach, dealing with short time spans rather than long ones, making it relatively easy to take account of momentary regressions or returns from higher to lower levels and that process of "de-differentiation" in which there is a loss of the integrated in favor of the individuated (stage 2 noted above), or a loss of the individuated in favor of the earlier global patterns.

All these ways of thinking make it possible for us to regard personality structure more or less in pyramidal terms, as involving a broad base, consisting of the primitive raw stuff of human nature with its phylogenetic built-in basis in organ systems and their ingrained tendencies to respond in specific ways (all this remains as a base while differentiated functions develop), and through the later interaction of these differentiated processes, integrated wholes may be observed. As already noted, the learning process assists in both differentiation and integration, so that the three-level system may be applied as well to learning sequences as to growth sequences; the typical individual history comprises an intimate mingling of growth and learning, or, indeed, a single process from which learning and growth may conveniently be abstracted for analysis. Following Werner, we may likewise conceive of structures within structures, so that different functions, such as form perception, rhythm perception, language, locomotion, can all be conceived to go through their own cycles of development while still remaining very dependent upon one another and upon the basic rhythms of life as a whole. With all its inadequacies, then, the conception of levels gives a schema with both spatial and temporal attributes and very suggestive clues to functional

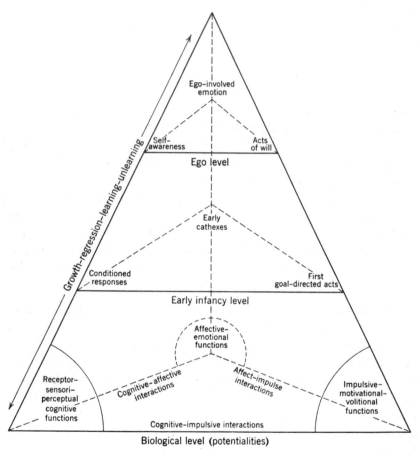

Fig. 16.1   A Personality Schema.

interdependence, which may be used to guide us in developing instruments to make contact with the various functions and their modes of interrelation within the person and within the organism-environment interaction processes which constitute his personality.

Implicit in the doctrine of levels is the conception that every kind of organ can be viewed in developmental terms and that every psychological process likewise undergoes development. It would follow, therefore, that the phenomena of perception, of motivation, or of learning are to be found at all levels in the developmental structure, and that there are, so to speak, horizontal relationships between the various psychological functions at each level. There is, for example, a relation between perception and motivation at the lowest level, and there is likewise a relation of perception and motivation at the highest level. (Fig. 16.1.) If we proceed, therefore, to slice horizontally at a given level, we have a system of interrelationships which will undergo transformation, but not disappear, as we move up the pyramid.

IV

This rough schema may be used as a sort of scaffolding for the preliminary classification and organization of findings about personality. It emphasizes (a) levels, and (b) the interdependence of functions. What now are the implications for the development of a suitable personality test? It would certainly seem that in any complete study of personality we need at each moment to sample all processes at all levels. We need, for example, to have some knowledge about perceptual, imaginative, memorial, motivational, and volitional phenomena, as they exist in their undifferentiated or primitive form, and also knowledge regarding all these variables as they appear at higher levels. For example, at the adult perceptual level, we need to know the residues of the more primitive perceptual functions, the mode of development of individuated perceptual responses, and the present functioning level of the person in terms of integral perceptual responses.

It will hardly be necessary to explain to the reader of this book that Rorschach's test is redolent with the problem of levels and, likewise, with the problem of interdependence; but a few examples may be useful. The Rorschach test distinguishes between levels two and three, in which the "large detail" is typically a response to a component already analyzed out from its context in what we have called "stage-two behavior," and the integral response often appears in highly structured interpretations ordinarily classed as "wholes."

The concept of global or *undifferentiated* response is, of course, not fully developed by the Rorschach method, though some "poor" wholes may give us a suggestion of this, and many color responses representing the flow of affect, with no use for either form or movement, may also come close to the stage-one process. The concept of differentiation and integration is particularly well brought out in the form-color category, and the concept of sequences through the three stages is frequently almost exactly what is involved in some of the succession patterns, such as *W* to *D* to *d* when followed by a new whole at a higher (articulated) level.

It is remarkable that the conception of fundamental personality regions (cognitive, affective, impulsive) and their interrelations should have been so fully developed at a time when perception was generally thought of almost solely in terms of a knowledge function rather than an affective and impulse function. Rorschach understood that perception might give clues to these other psychological dimensions. The phenomena of impulse control and many of the motor phenomena so essential for the understanding of refined adaptation to the environment are not fully grasped in the Rorschach scheme; but he *did* understand that one function could be used as a clue to all others related to it, just as he understood the developmental sequences and hierarchical structure of personality organization. And there can be no doubt that these ways of thinking, built into the Rorschach test, have contributed powerfully, through clinical and research work, to the development of modern personality theory. The Rorschach is the constant and eloquent reminder of *levels* and of *interdependence* in a visible and commanding form too cogent to allow either rejection or evasion.

V

We come now to the question of sampling the tendencies of personality. This is a question that must be answered if a test is to be expected to tap the aspects of an individual's personality in such a way as to give a sound over-all picture. The problem is immensely difficult. If we allow ourselves to tap the residues from, let us say, only three developmental levels, not taking into account the co-existence of separate functions which move at different rates, undergo stoppage and fresh accelerated movement at different times, and even if we allow ourselves only ten different personality functions to be sampled at each level, we shall need at least thirty scores to be derived from one testing instrument. But if the reliability of each score is not unity, and a single test item cannot give us a pure representation of the function, uncontaminated and free from all possibility of misinterpretation, we shall need many more. This is a formidable order. Can we perhaps determine the more important components and leave the rest out of the picture, hoping that by seeing the more important components and concentrating on the relation between them, we may somehow get the major structural outline of the personality? On all these questions of sampling personality functions through tests, clinical and experimental research has been focused from time to time, as in the work of Rapaport (1945), Witkin (1954), and others; but it can hardly be asserted that we have any test elements with the desired reliability of scoring, or that we understand the interrelations between observed test responses well enough to be able to sample this whole universe of personality dispositions.

This is one of the reasons why there is grave doubt as to the soundness of the many statements we currently hear about a test which is to reveal the "total personality." In terms of sampling of personality attributes, the problem appears to be insoluble. Of course, if it can ever be demonstrated that there really are a few cardinal attributes which pool their contributions in some definable way, it may be possible to derive a fairly good prediction regarding those attributes which depend upon these major components or their most important interactions. But even this more modest objective is very far from realization.

We fall back, therefore, necessarily to another line of defense and ask ourselves whether it is possible, by ignoring developmental levels, to invent devices which will, in fact, sample personality *at the present time*. If we use three test items to tap a function, fifteen responses would give us fairly uncontaminated information about five functions. If we could get twice or three times this number, we might get some rough preliminary picture of those functions which are ready, so to speak, to push themselves forward into our field of observation and have no need to hide from us.

But here we might have a brainstorm and grasp a new possibility. We might contrive methods by which a single response to our procedure will give us information about *several* kinds of things, several levels, several functions, at once. It seems altogether remarkable that, in point of fact, Hermann Rorschach had this brainstorm and grasped this technical point in the logic of personality analysis forty years ago. Just as he grasped the requirement set by the theory of levels and the theory of the interpretation of personal characteristics, Rorschach saw that by using ten cards, allowing multiple response, and scoring in three columns, he could extract an extraordinary amount of sampling information about personality functions and their interrelations. Twenty responses can give enormously more information than twenty items passed or failed on a linear measure of some simple cognitive skill. The strength of the test was chiefly in its applicability for effectively understanding the problem of sampling the many functions which enter into the personality structure. Hand in hand went the understanding that the time pattern, the sequences, the response emerging only at the time of the inquiry, and the ratios of frequency of one kind of response to frequency of another kind of response gave a rich network of facts about interrelationships of function, in that the number of items of information was far greater than the number of responses made.

VI

At the same time, this attempt to do so much involved a weakness in terms of the ultimate understanding of the basic dimensions being measured, by virtue of the very fact that by sampling so much with so little one gets involved in contamination, in problems of low reliabilities which cannot be explained away nor fully understood without cleaner measures of the separate functions. It became evident even in the 1930's that it would be worth while to separate out the various functions which enter into a Rorschach response in terms somewhat different from those which Rorschach had himself conceptualized. One can, for example, empirically analyze movement responses and their relations to other kinds of responses without assuming that movement is a pure or even a fairly safe clue to introversiveness or a rich inner life. One may study movement in its relation to various other Rorschach categories and in relation to many other types of clinically significant functions, as known through other approaches (see Chapter 10). In the same way, one may disentangle for study in the perception laboratory a great many of the components formulated by Rorschach, conceptualizing them or factoring them, ad lib.

The next step beyond this series of manipulations carried out with responses to the original Rorschach cards, or the Behn (Zulliger, 1952), Harrower (1945), or Levy (Zubin and Young, 1948) or other (Barron, 1955; Zulliger, 1948; Zulliger, 1954) series of cards, is to invent one's own semistructured visual materials, deliberately choosing the materials so as to get a relatively simple or even, if possible, one-dimensional range of responses. This would permit measurement in the sense in which a psychometric examination involves measurement, and, at an ideal level, it might permit a disentangling of basic personality dimensions comparable to the disentangling involved in the Thurstone Primary Mental Abilities Test (1938) as an approach to basic capacities.[2]

It is not a function of this chapter to describe the directions in which such investigations may move. It is evident by now that the original Rorschach test was successful largely because, in its time and place, it did an extraordinary variety of rich, interesting, challenging, and valuable things for clinicians, some of which they were ready to do and some of which they only learned to do a decade or more after Rorschach's death. His wisdom and imaginativeness established a high level which other workers have seldom again climbed. As in so many brilliant creative expressions of genius, much was left in poorly defined form. A foothold was nevertheless provided for any great successor to climb to a new height.

We might, in a certain sense, lament the fact that the Rorschach method became a standard procedure some 25 years ago, just as one might regret that the Stanford-Binet and later the Wechsler

[2] Wayne H. Holtzman (1959), for example, has extended the test so that there are 40 ink blots, indeed two parallel forms each using 40 ink blots, sacrificing number of responses and certain sequential variables in order to gain greater psychometric precision with regard to all the remaining variables. This is done by having the subject give one, and only one, response per card. Results are promising with respect to the preservation of the original meaning of the variables, at the same time increasing the reliability to about .90.

became standard, standardizing the imperfections along with the positive contributions. Those refinements which preserve what Rorschach was aiming to do, those improvements which make it possible to assess the dimensions which he saw in personality and to do a more consistent and reliable job, will certainly be used more and more in the next decade or two, and all this is to be welcomed.

What is, however, to be feared is that the technical skills may overwhelm and becloud the original vision. We have been surfeited in the last decade by refinements aimed primarily at doing highly specialized jobs with highly specialized groups of patients for highly specialized purposes. The basic conception of a way of sampling the rich fluid and growing structures of personality can hardly be said to have benefited by this. Seldom has the Rorschach test been used as a way of throwing light upon the fundamental conceptualization of personality. Seldom has any well-thought-out theory of personality been systematically tested by the use of Rorschach material. *Seldom, indeed, has the Rorschach been used as a personality research instrument in the serious sense.*

This seems altogether extraordinary. There has never been a time in the history of psychology when perception research has been as eager, as vivid, as far-ranging as it has in the period since World War II. If one thinks of the amazing developments from Innsbruck with reference to form perception (Kohler, 1955), the extraordinary development and influence of the work of Ames (1955), the rich proliferation of understanding with regard to the biology of perception, especially the cortical projection functions involved in visual perceiving, or if one looks at the developmental studies having to do with animal and human perceptual functions at various stages and in various kinds of environments, or at the interrelations between perception, on the one hand, and motor and affective phenomena, on the other hand—as shown in sensory-tonic theory (Werner, 1948), in need theory, or in any of the thirteen major theories of perception reviewed in the recent book by Allport (1955)—one is amazed to see the Rorschach work progress like a side stream, unaware of the mighty current of a new river flowing nearby. Here and there, as reported in some of the other chapters of this book, one may note comparisons of Rorschach functions with those of perceptual functions derived by other methods, particularly those of the laboratory. For the most part, however, the clinicians appear to go on refining their procedures rather than seeing the broader implications of the study of perception for the understanding of personality. The younger generation of clinicians who know their clinical as well as their experimental methodology may manage to prepare the great canal which will enable these streams to meet, and we shall have a psychology of perception which is big enough to do the huge job waiting to be done.

While they are doing this, they will add to our knowledge about the relations of perception to personality structure. For example, whether *perception*, rich as it is, *is* a big enough portion of the individual to reveal what personality assessment calls for is still not clear. It is conceivable that from the Rorschach a projective test can gradually be made, not too long nor too complex for everyday clinical practice, which will give us purified representations of the various personality dimensions which can be caught by such a procedure, and which, at the same time, will give a picture of memory and imagination, volition and impulse control, values and value conflicts, rhythms, styles, vortices and cadences, aspirations and despairs, consummations and frustrations, broad enough to pass reasonably as a picture of a person. The Rorschach test is still the best effort we have in this direction.

BIBLIOGRAPHY

Allport, F. H. *Theories of perception and the concept of structure.* New York: John Wiley, 1955.

Ames, A. *An interpretive manual for the demonstrations in the Psychology Research Center, Princeton University.* Princeton: Princeton University Press, 1955.

Barron, F. Threshold for the perception of human movement in inkblots. *J. consult. Psychol.,* 1955, **19**, 33-38.

Ellenberger, H. The life and work of Hermann Rorschach (1844-1922). *Bull. Menn. Clin.,* 1954, **18**, 173-219.

Frank, L. K. Projective methods for the study of personality. *J. Psychol.,* 1939, **8**, 389-413.

Harrower, M. R. (Harrower-Erickson), and Steiner, M. E. *A manual for psychodiagnostic inkblots.* (A series parallel to the Rorschach blots, with accompanying psychodiagnostic inkblots.) New York: Grune and Stratton, 1945.

Holtzman, W. H. Objective scoring of projective techniques. In: Bass, B. M., and Berg, I. A. (eds.), *Objective approaches to personality assessment.* Princeton: D. Van Nostrand Co., 1959.

Kohler, I. Experiments with prolonged optical distortions. *Proc. XIV intern. Cong. Psychol.,* Montreal, June 1954. Amsterdam: North Holland Publ. Co., 1955.

Lewin, K. *A dynamic theory of personality*. New York: McGraw-Hill, 1935.

Lowenfeld, M. *The Lowenfeld Mosaic Test*. London: Newman Neame, 1954.

Machover, K. A. *Personality projection in the drawing of the human figure: a method of personality investigation*. Springfield: C. C. Thomas, 1949.

Murray, H. A. *Explorations in personality*. New York: Oxford, 1938.

Rapaport, D., Gill, M., and Schafer, R. *Diagnostic psychological testing* (two volumes). Chicago: Year Book Publishers, 1945.

Rorschach, H. *Psychodiagnostics*, 4th ed. New York: Grune and Stratton, 1949.

Rosenzweig, S. A test for types of reaction to frustration. *Amer. J. Orthopsychiat.*, 1935, **4**, 395-403.

Sanford, R. N. The effects of abstinence from food upon imaginal processes: a preliminary experiment. *J. Psychol.*, 1936, **2**, 129-136.

Szondi, L. *Experimental diagnostics of drives*. New York: Grune and Stratton, 1952.

Thurstone, L. L. Primary mental abilities. *Psychomet. Monogr.*, No. 1, 1938.

Werner, H. *Comparative psychology of mental development* (rev. ed.). Chicago: Follett, 1948.

Witkin, H. A., et al. *Personality through perception*. New York: Harper, 1954.

Zubin, J., and Young, K. M. *Manual of projective and cognate techniques*. Madison: College Typing Co., 1948 (Levy blots).

Zulliger, H. *Der Diapositiv-Z-Test. Ein Verfahren zur psychologischen Untersuchung von Gruppen*. Bern: Hans Huber, 1948.

Zulliger, H. *Der Behn-Rorschach Test*. Vol. I—text, Vol. II—tables. Bern: Hans Huber, 1952.

Zulliger, H. *Der Tafeln Z-Test. Ein abgekürztes Rorschach-Verfahren für individuelle psychologische Prüfungen*. Bern: Hans Huber, 1954.

METHODOLOGICAL CONSIDERATIONS

17

Jules D. Holzberg

RELIABILITY
RE-EXAMINED

Assessing Rorschach reliability is a long-standing problem that has been perplexing and challenging to the clinician as much as to the experimentalist. In spite of much serious research directed toward determining the reliability of the Rorschach, the problem is by no means resolved, although it is the author's conviction that significant strides are being made in moving toward a resolution. It is a strange irony that the most significant contributions to the resolution of this problem have not emerged from research systematically designed to test the reliability of the Rorschach, but rather from research designed for other purposes, particularly validational studies.

There exist wide divergences in attitudes among psychologists toward the problem of Rorschach reliability. To some clinicians as well as to the bulk of experimental psychologists, the insistence is that the Rorschach must be considered like every other method of personality assessment and, therefore, must meet the *same* criteria of reliability according to traditional methods that are imposed on other instruments. A second group of psychologists, and they represent a fairly substantial number, insist that the problem of assessing reliability of the Rorschach is quite inappropriate for the purposes for which the Rorschach is being used in clinical practice and research. Thus, Symonds (1949) has stressed that the concept of reliability loses importance when the purpose of the technique of personality assessment is not so much to measure as it is to describe. Vernon

(1935), in a similar vein, argues that the Rorschach is analogous to a play technique in that it is not a test in the usual sense of the word but a means of obtaining insight into the personality. Some have stressed that the variable errors which psychometric reliability disregards may, from the point of view of personality diagnosis, be of great significance interpretively (Munroe, R. L., 1948, Mursell, J. L., 1953). Thus, from this vantage point, the issue of reliability is not a major concern.

A third attitude would ignore reliability *per se* and would stress validity of the Rorschach as the major concern, on the assumption that validity implies the presence of fundamental reliability. This position has been stressed by Piotrowski (1937) who stated, ". . . the Rorschach method can be subjected to measures of reliability only after its validity has been established." McClelland (1957) has emphasized that reliability has been overstressed in American psychology. His orientation is that the culture out of which American psychology has grown and developed is one which has emphasized traits such as regularity and dependability in the personality of its individuals, and this cultural emphasis has led to the stress in psychology on the concept of reliability of psychological instruments. He too would prefer to see reliability pursued through validational research. This emphasis on the search for evidence of validity as *prima facie* evidence of reliability has been challenged by Hertz (1941). She states that the validity of an instrument may be greater than its reliability and observes that a high degree of validity may be demonstrated by comparing Rorschach interpretations of an individual with outside clinical data, yet the reliability of these interpretations when compared with each other may not be high because different aspects of the personality may be emphasized by different interpretations.

A fourth attitude, and one with which the author is identified, stresses the fact that the Rorschach must, indeed, meet the criteria of reliability that are imposed on other measuring instruments, but that the methods for assessing reliability must be specifically adapted to the peculiarities of this unusual technique of personality study. Sargent has stated: "Questions of reliability and validity cannot be casually dismissed simply because the statistical treatment which serves for the simpler, more rigid measures of mental and emotional traits are unsuitable" (1948, p. 435).

If one agrees that the Rorschach should meet reliability criteria, the problem of the degree of reliability is posed. Jahoda et al. have offered their solution:

> There is no simple answer to the question of what is a satisfactory reliability. It depends upon one's purpose. If one wishes to distinguish precisely among a group of people who are similar in the characteristic being measured or if one hopes to find close relationships between variables, it is necessary to have highly reliable measuring instruments. If one wishes only to distinguish between people at the extremes or to determine whether a relationship exists, high reliability in the measures is not so necessary (1951).

THE HOLISTIC NATURE OF THE RORSCHACH

The special peculiarity of the Rorschach, which distinguishes it from psychometric methods of personality assessment, is its holistic nature. As Munroe has stated, ". . . the Rorschach is the first really extensive effort to apply 'objectively' in diagnosis and in research those holistic principles to which psychology at large does at least give lip service today. The familiar methodologies of psychology, especially of psychometrics, date from a more 'atomistic' era" (1945, p. 37). This peculiarity of the Rorschach presents a problem not merely for those interested in the study of reliability but for all research with the Rorschach. Here is a psychological assessment instrument that yields no single total score which is characteristic of methods in the field of psychometrics. Instead, there emerges as the end result of the use of this method a nonquantitative protocol diagnosing an individual personality. The problem posed is that of how to study the personality synthesis that emerges as the end product of the Rorschach method rather than to study a conglomeration of isolated parts which has been the frequent practice in much of the research in the field of reliability as well as with other research involving the Rorschach. To those who have been interested in a psychology that has meaning for the study of the individual human being, there has been an inclination to disregard such problems of reliability out of the recognition that these problems were being studied on a meaningless level, unrelated to the holistic nature of the Rorschach. Their attitude has been that conventional statistical comparisons of isolated test items have destroyed the total pattern on which the individual diagnosis of personality is based.

It has been on this peculiar facet of the Rorschach that much of the research pertaining to reliability has floundered. Hertz has, however, insisted that there is a need to study the consistency of parts of the Rorschach on the assumption that the establishment of the reliability at this level yields evidence that has significance for the instrument as a whole. However, this is subject to serious question, since it is evident that subparts of a test such as the Wechsler-Bellevue Intelligence Scale possess low reliabilities and yet the total test has acceptable reliability.

A number of methods have been developed to cope with this peculiar facet of the Rorschach, among these being the use of the psychogram, rating scales, and matching techniques (Macfarlane, J. W. and Tuddenham, R. D., 1951). The psychogram, which contains the quantitative statement of the major scoring categories in the Rorschach, has become the basis for a number of research studies which have been reluctant to utilize individual Rorschach variables in isolation. This is obviously an improvement over the use of individual scores, but even this has serious limitations. Much that goes on in the examining situation is grist for the mill of the clinician concerned with personality study. He observes many cues which cannot be written down explicitly and, consequently, do not appear in the psychogram. Thus, such factors as perseveration of content, the subject's style of speech, his manner of examination of each blot, etc., do not become recorded in the psychogram.

The second method that has been introduced into research with the Rorschach in order to take into account its holistic quality has been the use of rating scales of selected parts of the record, i.e., capacity for acting-out behavior, potentiality for therapeutic involvement, etc. Although the rating method has not been used primarily in reliability studies, a vast number of studies utilizing the Rorschach as a measuring instrument have used rating scales of specific variables and have demonstrated successful reliability for these ratings.

The most significant research development, and one which has been applied with some success in the study of reliability, has been the use of the matching technique. The matching method has been defined by Vernon as "... a method for establishing quantitative relationships between qualitative aspects of personality" (1936,

p. 149). He has stressed this method as a means of comparing whole Rorschach records in contradistinction to correlational methods which are usually applied to the comparison of isolated Rorschach variables. Matching can be used at several levels: matching two sets of protocols from the same subjects, matching the protocols with their interpretations, or matching interpretations of the same subjects made by different examiners. Although this is clearly a less artificial method for capturing the holistic quality of the Rorschach, there are a number of problems related to the use of this research tool. These are:

1. The complexity of the material to be matched is an important condition affecting results. The number of elements that are involved in the Rorschach are so numerous and varied that it becomes a difficult task for the judge to be able to grasp the total Rorschachs of different individuals in order to relate them to their mates.

2. The experience and skill of the judges comprise a second condition affecting the results of matching. Clearly, differing results will be obtained from individuals who are less experienced with the Rorschach than those with greater experience. This introduces the problem of the confusion between the role of the judge and the role of the test in the reliability findings.

3. Another factor determining the success of matchings is the length of time spent in the study of records. This is in part related to the complexity of the Rorschach but, unless there is sufficient time to comprehend the totality of the Rorschach protocol, there is likely to be greater unreliability introduced into the matching experiment.

4. The heterogeneity of the Rorschach protocols is another condition affecting success in matching. As the Rorschachs of the subjects involved are less unlike one another, the more difficult the task of matching becomes and the greater the degree of unreliability.

THE MEANING OF RORSCHACH RELIABILITY

When one talks of reliability as it pertains to the Rorschach, there is need to clarify more precisely what is meant. Is it the consistency between different judges in their *scoring* of the same protocols? Is it the consistency of the subject's *responses* to two or more Rorschach examinations? Is it the consistency between different judges in their *interpretations* of the same Rorschachs? Is it the consistency of one judge in his *scorings and/or interpretations of the same Rorschachs on two or more occasions?*

If our concern is with the consistency of the subject's responses to the Rorschach, do we refer to *temporal consistency* (test-retest), *consistency of performance on two forms of the test* (equivalency), or do we refer to the subject's *internal consistency* on a single administration of the Rorschach (split-half)? Each of these clearly have different psychological meanings.

It is evident that the practice of applying the single term "reliability" to all of these issues is indefensible, and it is our purpose in the remainder of this chapter to focus on the specific types of reliability enumerated above. In doing so, it should be noted that there will still remain considerable ambiguity, for it is evident that reliability, of whatever kind, cannot be generalized too freely for there is lack of information on relative reliabilities for groups differing in age, diagnosis, social background, etc. This is true not alone for the Rorschach but also for almost all psychological tests, psychometric as well as projective.

CONSISTENCY OF SCORING

This aspect of reliability of the Rorschach has received minimal treatment to date. It is evident that the similarity of scores, training, and ideological identifications with Rorschach authority determines how two judges will score. What little research is available suggests that, as individuals are oriented to the same scoring system, there will be higher consistency in their scoring. Sicha and Sicha (1936) had 300 responses scored by five Rorschach investigators and the results showed a high percentage of agreement (70 to 82%). This occurred despite the fact that there were differing criteria that were undoubtedly applied in determining the scores, inasmuch as the individuals doing the scoring were identified with different systems of scoring. Hertz, as reported by Vernon (1935), reports that there was 93% agreement between two scorers in the scoring of 11,000 responses.

In this instance, there had been prior agreement on scoring between the scorers. These results suggest that, as such prior agreement occurs, the reliability is increased.

CONSISTENCY IN SUBJECT RESPONSES[1]

Temporal Consistency (Test-Retest)

A number of investigations have studied the temporal consistency of subjects on the Rorschach, but here, as with other areas that will be reported, there are conflicting results. Typical of these are the studies by Ford, Swift, and Kerr who studied relatively young children in terms of test-retest reliability. Ford (1946) reports reliabilities of the determinants ranging from +.38 to +.86 based on a one-month interval of retesting. It was the author's conclusion that, since the reliabilities of tests at the preschool level tend to be lower than the reliabilities of these same tests when used with older subjects, the results with the Rorschach are striking. On the other hand, Swift (1944) in her analysis of the test-retest reliability of the Rorschach with children found that reliability of individual-scored items in retests after a short interval of time was only fairly satisfactory and, after a longer period of time (10 months), was quite unsatisfactory. Swift identifies a number of factors working against reliability, i.e., the small number of total responses, the low frequency of responses in many scoring categories, and the variability in the attention span and interest of her subjects during the retest situation. Kerr (1936), similarly, found low reliabilities after one year of retest with children. Here, as with a number of other studies, there is the question as to how much of the changes were due to real personality changes occurring in the children and how much to the unreliability of the method. Troup (1938), utilizing a matching technique, presented

[1] The attempt here is not so much to survey completely the research done in the area of Rorschach reliability but primarily to focus on the limitations of methodology employed in the various aspects of the study of reliability. A number of historically significant studies and reports will not be reviewed because, although they are of some *relevance* to the reliability problem, they are not *pertinent* to it, because they usually involve a second administration (Fosberg, I. E., 1941; Fosberg, I. E., 1938; Kimble, G. A., 1945; Rabin, A. L., and Sanderson, M. H., 1947) or they are not supported by statistical evidence for claims made (Brosin, H. W., and Fromm, E., 1942; Wertham, F. and Bleuler, M., 1939).

six judges with the task of matching the psychograms with their retest mates. A coefficient of contingency of +.94 is reported. Holzberg and Wexler (1950), in order to force unreliability, used an "unpredictable" population (schizophrenics) and found fairly good reliabilities for individual Rorschach variables on test-retest. In addition, there was excellent agreement in matching the psychograms of both testings.

A number of conditions which are required for the use of test-retest reliability cannot be said to be present when applied to the Rorschach.

1. It cannot be assumed that personality data can be reproduced exactly from one testing session to another. There is evidence to support the thesis that changes in the set of the subject will affect certain aspects of his Rorschach performance (Gibby, R. G., 1951; Schachtel, E. G., 1945; Schafer, R., 1954); changes in the nature of the testing situation, similarly, can produce changes in Rorschach performance (Kimble, G. A., 1945; Luchins, A. S., 1947); and, where different examiners are utilized, there is the problem of the effect of examiner personality and other characteristics on the Rorschach performance of the subject (Lord, E., 1950).

The giving of changed content on a retest does not necessarily reflect the unreliability of the Rorschach. The individual Rorschach examination, in a sense, has built within it a test-retest situation in that the initial part of the test is a free association (the test) whereas the conclusion of the examination consists of an inquiry (the retest). It is not unusual that, during this inquiry, different or additional responses will occur. The coming about of different or additional responses from test to retest may well have the same significance as the production of different or additional responses in the inquiry; i.e., as the subject becomes more familiar with the blots and with the total Rorschach situation, certain integrations of perceptions and associations may occur that would ordinarily not occur during the initial contact with the cards.

2. It cannot be assumed that the object of study, the personality of a subject, is unchanging. Significant aspects of the personality change through time in response to internal and external factors. This issue is particularly related to the ages at which testing occurs

and the length of time between testings. The younger the age at which test-retesting occurs, the greater is the expectation of change. Similarly, the longer the time interval between testings, the more change may be anticipated. Macfarlane and Tuddenham have stated it this way: "Although a subject's test performances at different times should be congruent with each other in the sense that they reveal the more central and enduring dimensions of personality, they should not be expected to show statistical reliability because the subject himself may have changed" (1951, p. 39). Swift has stated that, "Once the ambiguous material has been organized in a certain way, there is a tendency for this organization to interfere with subsequent attempts at reorganization, even when the factor of pure repetition is not present (that is, where the individual does not try consciously to repeat what he said before)" (1944, p. 209). This has been described even more succinctly by Kelley: ". . . if at the time of the second test there is any memory, conscious or sub-conscious, of the earlier responses, then certainly the mental operations being performed at the second taking are not the same or even similar in kind to those performed at the first taking" (1942, p. 80). Swift (1944) found that an average of 47% of the responses given to the first testing were remembered by her preschool children after 30 days, and presumably this percentage would even be higher in the case of adult subjects.

This does not merely mean that memory for the first testing will bring about the same responses. For certain individuals, the memory of the first testing may bring with it a desire to change responses in order to be "different" at the time of the second testing.

A number of ingenious attempts have been made to avoid the pitfall of the memory factor in test-retest reliability. Kelley, Margulies, and Barrera (1941) utilized a series of subjects who had received electroshock therapy and had developed complete amnesia for the first testing. These patients were free from confusion resulting from shock when they were readministered the Rorschach some two hours later. For the most part, the psychograms remained unchanged and the diagnostic impressions were the same. Griffith (1951) tested several patients with Korsakoff's syndrome, a disorder characterized by severe memory defect. These patients seemed to have a complete lack of recall for the first Rorschach testing that occurred 22 hours previously. The findings here were that the test-retest protocols were very similar, the original autistic content remained, and the reaction times were not significantly altered.

Equivalence Reliability (Equivalent Forms)

The use of equivalent forms of a test to determine the consistency of performance of subjects has long been a standard approach to the establishment of reliability in psychometrics. This method has been utilized with regard to the Rorschach, even though there has been considerable difficulty in developing a truly comparable or equivalent set of ink blots. A number of attempts to create such sets have been made, and the comparison of results on these as compared to the Rorschach has shown the same variable results as were found with the test-retest method.

Swift (1944) utilized a form of the Rorschach devised by Behn (the Behn-Rorschach) for retest after an interval of one week in her study with preschool children. Most of the scoring categories showed high reliability coefficients, but a number were strikingly low. Her conclusion was that the differences in the two sets made the Behn form *not* a completely equivalent set to be used in clinical practice. Singer, again utilizing the Behn, found that the ". . . group profile on the Behn would be almost identical with that on the Rorschach . . . the two tests seemed in this study to elicit in general the same number and type of responses" (1952, p. 241). McFarland (1954) showed that his modification of the Rorschach and his modification of the Behn correlated significantly with one another on all of the six variables that he considered. Similar findings were reported by Buckle and Holt who state: "The resulting similarity is not only one of similarity in scoring category, but is often a complete identity between actual responses given to the two blots" (1951, p. 491). Eichler, again comparing performance on the Behn and on the Rorschach, found that: "In general, the Behn showed substantial agreement with the measures obtained by the standard Rorschach" (1951, p. 187). However, on further analysis, he was able to show that the Behn tended to encourage the production of certain responses that did not occur as frequently on the regular Rorschach.

In general, findings relating performance on the Rorschach and the Behn series of ink blots support the general thesis of similarity of response, although there are sufficient differences as to arouse concern about this measure of reliability of the Rorschach.

Can the method of equivalence be considered appropriate when applied to a technique like the Rorschach? Clearly, the method of equivalence is less affected by memory and practive than is the method of test-retest but it is a questionable assumption that a subject taking the second form of the test is not in some way affected by the first form. In a task like the Rorschach, its novelty is a factor in affecting responses. Repetition, even with a second set of blots, destroys this novelty. Perhaps of greater significance is the assumption that the two forms are equivalent.

> A psychometrician constructing a true-false achievement test can be reasonably sure of achieving equivalence between its alternate forms, because all subjects are set to respond to the same aspect of each item [that is, to its correctness] and because the items in each form can be rendered comparable with respect to difficulty and content. In an unstructured projective test, different subjects are free to respond selectively to different qualities of the stimulus material. The projectivist may not always be able to specify all the aspects of his test to which a subject might conceivably respond (Macfarlane, J. W. and Tuddenham, R. D., 1951, p. 40).

Another issue posed by Buckle and Holt pertains to the problem of developing equivalent sets which, if they become truly equivalent, may well end up being the same set.

> The logical implication of endeavors to provide closer equivalence in the alternative form by figural similarity, leads in the end, to an exact reproduction of the original form. As complete equivalence is approached, the validity of the alternative form for retest is therby weakened. When a subject is re-tested with an alternative form of the test the same responses are likely to occur, both because the subject "recalls" them from the first test, and also because the similarity of the visual perceptual field tends to induce similar mental sets (Buckle, D. and Holt, N., 1951, p. 492).

Internal Consistency (Split-Half)

The split-half technique, long used in psychometric testing to establish one form of reliability, i.e., internal consistency, has also been used in the study of the Rorschach with, again, conflicting results. Thornton and Guilford (1936) report contradictory findings in their split-half study. Vernon (1933) found low split-half reliabilities for all of the Rorschach variables except the number of responses. He suggested the need of control for the number of responses if one was to utilize this method appropriately, based on his observation that reliabilities were higher for records of more than 30 responses. A major research effort, which contradicted the results of Vernon, is that of Hertz (1934) who—although she presently rejects the split-half method as applied to the Rorschach (1951)—did utilize it successfully and demonstrated that the odd-even cards in 100 records of junior high school students produced split-half correlations for Rorschach variables which range from .66 to .97 with an average of .83. More recently, Ford (1946), in her study of young children, found that her split-half reliabilities were comparable to those of Hertz. Wirt and McReynolds (1953) found an average correlation of .85 for the three groups they studied.

Clearly, the split-half technique eliminates the disadvantages of the other two methods of reliability insofar as it has no practice effects and makes no assumptions regarding changes in personality over the course of time. However, it does make the significant assumption that the Rorschach can in some way be divided into two equal halves, which is the basic condition involved in the split-half technique. Clearly, this condition cannot be met with the Rorschach where the blots vary in formal configuration, color, shading, etc. It is apparent that some cards in the Rorschach are more suggestive of certain content, such as humans as opposed to animals. Other cards are organizable in a particular perceptual mode such as wholes as opposed to details. Some cards have a "pull" for both humans and wholes, or animals and details, or some combination of these four variables, and these are only four of a much larger number of variables on the Rorschach. It is not probable that the ten ink blots can be separated into two equal halves such that there will be represented in each half the same opportunity to "pull" for all the Rorschach variables. Furthermore, the fact that the cards consist of five grey and five color cards requires that any splitting of the Rorschach into two halves would end up in unequal distribution with regard to this variable. However, this position with regard to split-half technique on the Rorschach is challenged by Orange who states:

Contrary to the contention . . . that the factor of differential stimulus-import on the Rorschach renders employment of split-half techniques theoretically impracticable, the establishment of extensive reliabilities in this study precipitates the challenging conclusion that organizational functions in perceptual behavior are self-assertive despite changing stimulus-configurations (1953, p. 228).

Another condition for the appropriate utilization of the split-half technique is that the test must be of sufficient length so that when it is split, there will not be an inadequate sampling of behavior. This condition cannot be met in the case of the Rorschach because of the low incidence of certain categories which, when split, would contribute to low reliabilities, and this inadequate sampling of many factors in the Rorschach cannot be compensated for by statistical operations to correct for its length. Unlike psychometric tests to which the split-half technique has been applied, the number of responses in the Rorschach is not determined by the examiner who brings with him a list of test items. Rather, the number of responses is determined exclusively by the subject. From a statistical point of view, this criterion applies equally to reliabilities of the test-retest or equivalent-form type.

CONSISTENCY OF RORSCHACH INTERPRETATION

Although the question of whether the Rorschach consistently elicits similar responses from the same individuals has been subjected to considerable research, as described in the previous sections, the question of the extent to which independent analysts agree with each other in the interpretation of the same Rorschachs has received only minimal treatment. To some Rorschach workers this has been the most critical reliability problem since it is the interpretation of the Rorschach that is used clinically. However, it is here that one deals with the most difficult aspect of the reliability problem inasmuch as the basic data are the nonquantitative personality descriptions prepared by the psychologist.

One of the classic attempts to study the degree of agreement between independent Rorschach workers in their interpretation of the same case was conducted by Hertz and Rubenstein (1939) who claim reliability for the test as a whole. Hertz, Beck, and Klopfer did blind interpretations of the same Rorschach record. A comparison of the three interpretations obtained showed a high degree of agreement among the Rorschach experts. This is based, however, on only a single case and is far from a crucial test of the reliability of Rorschach interpretation. Of concern here would be whether the same degree of agreement could have been obtained by individuals with less experience with the Rorschach. A close examination of the three interpretations did show a number of disagreements, which disagreements were nevertheless all valid. In the case of one instance, the emphasis was on the depressive features of the case; in the second, the excitable and extrovertive features were stressed; and in the third, emphasis was put on the conflict with regard to the feminine role. All of these emphases were checked against other clinical data and were verified. This poses one of the genuine problems in the study of the reliability of interpretations, since it is possible for judges to emphasize different aspects of the record, and yet all of these aspects may be valid.

The really crucial investigation on the reliability of interpretations was that done by Krugman (1942). Independent interpretations of 20 Rorschach records were prepared by two Rorschach workers. These were presented to three judges in four groups of five pairs. All identifying references were removed. The three judges made a perfect score in matching, showing that two Rorschach workers are able to interpret a record very similarly. The same judges also rated the degree of agreement between the two interpretations. Essential agreement was shown in 89.6% of the interpretations, fair agreement in 10%, and approximately equal amounts of agreement and disagreement in .4%. Krugman further studied the reliability of the Rorschach by securing matchings of 25 scored Rorschach records with their interpretations. Six judges achieved an average coefficient of contingency of .872. Clearly, these are impressive results, supporting the thesis that interpretations of Rorschachs can be very reliable. However, there is need for further research that will attempt to replicate this experiment in order that there may be greater confidence in the findings.

There are a number of special problems concerned with the study of the reliability of interpretations of the Rorschach. Clearly, one issue is that no single authentic interpretation of the Rorschach is possible. In the study by Hertz and Rubenstein, referred to above, three outstanding Rorschach workers, although agreeing in essentials, disagreed in certain features, and yet each was valid. Clinicians may devote attention to different phases of the Rorschach in their interpretations, partly as a function of their training, partly as a function of the purpose for psychological referral, and yet the analyses, although differing, may nevertheless be valid.

Perhaps this is another way of saying that there can never be a complete interpretation of the Rorschach, since an interpretation of a personality is the function, in part, of the background, training, competence, and psychological understanding of the interpreter. It is here that we must emphasize that unlike psychometric instruments, the Rorschach method cannot be isolated from the interpreter, the Rorschach and the psychologist being one integral methodology. To be sure, this has led some to complain that one confounds the interpreter with the test, but there is much feeling that it is this aspect that represents the great strength of the Rorschach as a personality assessment instrument (Munroe, R. L., 1948).

It should be stressed that differences in interpretation may also be a function of the conceptual scheme in which one operates with the Rorschach. Thus, there are psychologists who are essentially "sign oriented," whereas others develop their personality analyses on the bases of hypotheses that are formulated, tested, and then refined in the light of data as they emerge in the analysis of the Rorschach. Such differences of approach may well lead to different emphases in the interpretive write-up of the case (Holzberg, J. D., 1957).

One aspect of consistency of interpretation that has not been subjected to any systematic scrutiny has been that of the consistency of the same Rorschach worker in his interpretations of the same Rorschachs. Here, of course, we are dealing again with problems of memory which would mean that the interpretations would have to occur at significant intervals of time. With the recognition of the importance of the background and psychological sophistication of the psychologist as a factor in the interpretive process with the Rorschach, it is quite likely that self-consistency or reliability of interpretation may yield low correlations principally because of the maturing process of the psychologist as a function of his experience.

This by no means is a reflection on the instrument, but merely is a recognition that the deepening of one's understanding of personality, dynamics and psychopathology will be reflected in more penetrating interpretations of techniques such as the Rorschach.

PERCEPTUAL AND CONCEPTUAL CONSISTENCY AND RORSCHACH RELIABILITY

In a recent provocative paper, Dorken (1956) has suggested that much recent research, which has varied the stimulus properties of the blots only to find remarkable consistency of the subjects in their performances on the regular and altered blots, far from yielding data which invalidate the Rorschach offers evidence of the basic perceptual consistency of the subject. His thesis, extended, is that the Rorschach is reliable inasmuch as alterations in its perceptual qualities do not alter the responses of subjects: "The strength of the individual's characteristic mode of perception, whether he is normal or mentally disordered, permits a surprising degree of variance in the formal aspects of the test material before response is significantly altered" (p. 101). This thesis has been emphasized by others such as Brosin and Fromm who similarly state that a considerable degree of variation in the field ". . . will still elicit similar responses [since there is] a wide range of possibility for recognition of similar configurations" (1942, p. 5). In his thesis, Dorken does not deny that each blot of the Rorschach has stimulus value that has some influence on response, but "This influence, however, must be relatively less than that of the individual personality structure, otherwise there would be insufficient divergence of response between individuals to provide any basis for the differential evaluation of personality" (p. 103). Baughman similarly suggests this same approach in his analysis of his research:

> Many of the measures that we make of perceptual behavior in the Rorschach test appear to be primarily dependent upon processes inherent in the perceiver . . . rather than upon properties of the stimulus (1954, p. 163).

> The data are clear and impressive in their demonstration that the major dimensions of perceptual behavior in the Rorschach task remain remarkably constant even though marked alterations are made in the stimulus attributes.

... The fact that perceptual behavior is so minimally affected by major changes in stimulus characteristics should make us feel more secure in our use of such techniques for personality evaluation (1954, pp. 161, 163).

These attitudes, it seems to the author, are not wholly satisfactory. To the extent that color, shading, figure-ground qualities, etc., are variables that are used in the interpretation of the Rorschach, failure to show alterations in responses while varying these stimulus conditions poses a serious problem for the validity of these interpretations. Furthermore, this hardly seems to be an answer to the problem of reliability. This becomes the earlier argument in reverse, i.e., instead of validity presuming reliability, the absence of validity presumes reliability. This argument is not particularly impressive.

I do believe that it is possible to extend Dorken's argument one step further, and stress that perceptual and conceptual consistency in *differing* tasks does hold out hope of providing a more reasonable basis for assessing the reliability of the Rorschach. In a study done by McFarland (1954), he was concerned with the consistency of verbal responses to a series of differing perceptual and conceptual tasks. Using four tasks, i.e., a modified Rorschach, a modified Behn, a picture title test, and an object recognition test, McFarland was able to demonstrate that subjects respond consistently to all of these tasks in terms of the number of responses, the range of interpretations, and the frequency with which responses are given to different stimuli. McFarland here demonstrated certain consistencies in perceptual and conceptual behavior between the Rorschach and these other tasks. If we look upon the other tasks as being forms of perceptual and conceptual tasks which are alternate to the Rorschach, it is the author's thesis that research of this type can become the basis for demonstrating the essential reliability of the Rorschach.

Another study in this same vein which the author believes is a demonstration of the reliability of the Rorschach is that of Holzberg and Schleifer (1955) who related the performance of subjects on the color-versus-noncolor cards of the Rorschach to their performance on a number of perceptual and conceptual tasks in which color was introduced as a variable. In this research, they were able to demonstrate a significant degree of consistency in behavior insofar as the subjects' responses to color are concerned. This would be another demonstration of the use of other perceptual and conceptual tasks as alternate forms for purposes of determining the consistency of subjects' performances on the Rorschach and in other perceptual and conceptual operations.

CONCLUSIONS

The problem of the reliability of the Rorschach is a many-faceted problem. This chapter has stressed that the Rorschach must, like all instruments of study, demonstrate its reliability, but that it should demonstrate it through methods which take into consideration the peculiar characteristics of the Rorschach. It has furthermore been stressed that the concept of "reliability" has multiple meanings, and that there are a number of reliability problems as they pertain to the Rorschach as there are with all instruments of personality study. It has also been emphasized that the traditional methods of assessing psychometric reliability are inappropriate to the Rorschach, and it is felt that the most fruitful approach to the reliability problem is through the study of perceptual and conceptual consistency, and comparing performance on the Rorschach with other perceptual and conceptual tasks, with these other perceptual and conceptual tasks being looked upon as alternate forms.

While such research on the ultimate reliability of the Rorschach proceeds, the Rorschach will continue to be used by trained clinicians who recognize its unsettled reliability status. Such ambiguity that does exist will encourage the clinician to utilize complementary sources of data from test batteries, case histories, and interactional data from the clinical testing situation. He will continue to think in terms of probabilities rather than certainties in his formulations of personality from the Rorschach (Holzberg, J., 1957).

BIBLIOGRAPHY

Baughman, E. A comparative analysis of Rorschach forms with altered stimulus character-
istics. *J. proj. Tech.*, 1954, **18**, 151-164.
Brosin, H. W., and Fromm, E. Some principles of gestalt psychology in the Rorschach
experiment. *Rorschach Res. Exch.*, 1942, **6**, 1-15.
Buckle, D., and Holt, N. Comparison of Rorschach and Behn inkblots. *J. proj. Tech.*, 1951,
15, 486-493.
Dorken, H. Psychological structure as the governing principle of projective technique:
Rorschach theory. *Canad. J. Psychol.*, 1956, **10**, 101-106.

Eichler, R. A comparison of the Rorschach and Behn-Rorschach inkblot tests. *J. consult. Psychol.*, 1951, **15**, 185-189.

Ford, M. The application of the Rorschach test to young children. *Univ. Minn. Inst. Child Welf. Monogr.*, 1946, No. 23.

Fosberg, I. A. An experimental study of the reliability of the Rorschach psychodiagnostic technique. *Rorschach Res. Exch.*, 1941, **5**, 72-84.

Fosberg, I. A. Rorschach reactions under varied instructions. *Rorschach Res. Exch.*, 1938, **3**, 12-38.

Gibby, R. G. The stability of certain Rorschach variables under conditions of experimentally induced sets: I. The intellectual variables. *J. proj. Tech.*, 1951, **15**, 3-26.

Griffith, R. M. The test-retest similarities of the Rorschachs of patients without retention, Korsakoff. *J. proj. Tech.*, 1951, **15**, 516-525.

Hertz, M. R. Current problems in Rorschach theory and technique. *J. proj. Tech.*, 1951, **15**, 307-338.

Hertz, M. R. The reliability of the Rorschach ink-blot test. *J. appl. Psychol.*, 1934, **18**, 461-477.

Hertz, M. R. Rorschach: Twenty years after. *Rorschach Res. Exch.*, 1941, **5**, 90-129.

Hertz, M. R., and Rubenstein, B. B. A comparison of three "blind" Rorschach analyses. *Amer. J. Orthopsychiat.*, 1939, **9**, 295-314.

Holzberg, J. D. The clinical and scientific methods: synthesis or antithesis? *J. proj. Tech.*, 1957, **21**, 227-242.

Holzberg, J. D., and Schleifer, M. J. An experimental test of the Rorschach assumption of the impact of color on perceptual and associative processes. *J. proj. Tech.*, 1955, **19**, 130-137.

Holzberg, J. D., and Wexler, M. The predictability of schizophrenic performance on the Rorschach test. *J. consult. Psychol.*, 1950, **14**, 395-399.

Jahoda, M., Deutsch, M., and Cook, S. W. *Research methods in social relations.* New York: Dryden, 1951.

Kelley, D. M., Margulies, H., and Barrera, S. E. The stability of the Rorschach method as demonstrated in electric convulsive therapy cases. *Rorschach Res. Exch.*, 1941, **5**, 35-43.

Kelley, T. L. The reliability coefficient. *Psychometrika*, 1942, **7**, 75-83.

Kerr, M. Temperamental differences in twins. *Brit. J. Psychol.*, 1936, **27**, 51-59.

Kimble, G. A. Social influence on Rorschach records. *J. abnorm. soc. Psychol.*, 1945, **40**, 89-93.

Krugman, J. E. A clinical validation of the Rorschach with problem children. *Rorschach Res. Exch.*, 1942, **6**, 61-70.

Lord, E. Experimentally induced variations in Rorschach performance. *Psychol. Monogr.*, 1950, No 64.

Luchins, A. S. Situational and attitudinal influences on Rorschach responses. *Amer. J. Psychiat.*, 1947, **103**, 780-784.

Macfarlane, J. W., and Tuddenham, R. D. Problems in the validation of projective techniques. In: Anderson and Anderson (eds.)., *An introduction to projective techniques and other devices for understanding the dynamics of human behavior.* New York: Prentice-Hall, 1951.

McClelland, D. C. Toward a science of personality psychology. In: David and von Bracken (eds.), *Perspectives in personality theory.* London: Tavistock, 1957.

McFarland, R. Perceptual consistency in Rorschach-like projective tests. *J. proj. Tech.*, 1954, **18**, 368-378.

Munroe, R. L. Considerations on the place of the Rorschach in the field of general psychology. *Rorschach Res. Exch.*, 1945, **9**, 30-40.

Munroe, R. L. The use of projective methods in group testing. *J. consult. Psychol.*, 1948, **12**, 8-15.

Mursell, J. L. *Psychological testing.* New York: Longmans, Green, 1949.

Orange, A. Perceptual consistency as measured by the Rorschach. *J. proj. Tech.*, 1953, **17**, 224-228.

Piotrowski, Z. A. The reliability of Rorschach's Erlebnistypus. *J. abnorm. soc. Psychol.*, 1937, **32**, 439-445.

Rabin, A. I., and Sanderson, M. H. An experimental inquiry into some Rorschach procedures. *J. clin. Psychol.*, 1947, **3**, 216-225.

Sargent, H. Projective methods. In: Pennington and Berg (eds.), *An introduction to clinical psychology.* New York: Ronald, 1948.

Schachtel, E. G. Subjective definitions of the Rorschach test situation and their effect on test performance. *Psychiatry*, 1945, **8**, 419-448.

Schafer, R. *Psychoanalytic interpretation in Rorschach testing.* New York: Grune and Stratton, 1954.

Sicha, K., and Sicha, M. A step towards the standardization of the scoring of the Rorschach test. *Rorschach Res. Exch.*, 1936, **1**, 95-101.

Singer, J. The Behn-Rorschach inkblots: a preliminary comparison with the original Rorschach series. *J. proj. Tech.*, 1952, **16**, 238-245.

Swift, J. W. Reliability of Rorschach scoring categories with preschool children. *Child Developm.*, 1944, **15**, 207-216.

Symonds, M. *Adolescent fantasy.* New York: Columbia University Press, 1949.

Thornton, G. R., and Guilford, J. P. The reliability and meaning of Erlebnistypus scores in the Rorschach test. *J. abnorm. soc. Psychol.*, 1936, **31**, 324-330.

Troup, E. A comparative study by means of the Rorschach method of personality development in twenty pairs of identical twins. *Genet. Psychol. Monogr.*, 1938, **20**, 461-556.

Vernon, P. E. The matching method applied to investigations of personality. *Psychol. Bull.*, 1936, **33**, 149-177.

Vernon, P. E. Recent work on the Rorschach test. *J. ment. Sci.*, 1935, **81**, 1-27.

Vernon, P. E. The Rorschach ink-blot test. II. *Brit. J. med. Psychol.*, 1933, **13**, 179-205.

Wertham, F., and Bleuler, M. Inconstancy of the formal structure of the personality: experimental study of the influence of mescaline on the Rorschach test. *Arch. Neurol. Psychiat.*, 1932, **28**, 52-70.

Wirt, R., and McReynolds, P. The reliability of Rorschach number of responses. *J. proj. Tech.*, 1953, **17**, 493-494.

The probability is that when we learn to put the question rightly, the answer will come.

J. ARTHUR THOMSON

18 | *Irving B. Weiner*

APPROACHES TO
RORSCHACH VALIDATION

Over many years in which clinicians have struggled with issues of Rorschach validity, three types of opinion have emerged concerning the psychometric status of the instrument. As one opinion, some psychologists have concluded from their reading of a seemingly mixed and inconclusive literature that the Rorschach's failure to demonstrate its validity despite literally thousands of research studies, strips it of any rightful place among assessment procedures employed by informed behavioral scientists.

A second opinion, bred to divert the psychometric attack of researchers who found the Rorschach wanting and urged its being laid quickly to rest, holds that Rorschach's test is not really a test at all. Rather, argue proponents of this view, the Rorschach is a special kind of clinical interaction that owes its utility to the skills and sensitivities of the examiner rather than to any psychometric properties of the instrument. Hence, the argument continues, research studies of statistical validity are inappropriate to the nature of the Rorschach, and the results of such studies have no bearing on its merit as a clinical tool.

Although proponents of this second view have accurately called attention to difficulties in designing validity studies that adequately reflect clinical applications of the Rorschach method, they have also tended to create an unfortunate Rorschach cult. This cult comprises a closed circle of believers who reaffirm each other's devotion to the Rorschach by sharing their positive personal regard for it and ignoring any voices that are raised out of tune with their faith. Such cultishness is unfortunate because it isolates the Rorschach from the mainstream of behavioral science and justifies skeptical researchers in their depreciation of it.

Representing a third point of view, some psychologists have been determined to maintain their scientist's respect for objective data without sacrificing the richness and utility of the Rorschach in which they had come to believe as clinicians. This determination has engendered thoughtful criticism of previous validity studies and proposals for new approaches to Rorschach validation that combine sophisticated research design with adequate attention to the nuances of clinical practice.

It is from this third point of view that the present chapter is written. It neither belabors the Rorschach with the voluminous research data often presumed to document its uselessness, nor does it deny the importance of such data for assessing the merits of the instrument. Rather, it attempts to provide some perspectives on Rorschach validation by which the adequacy of previous research can be judged, the current status of the evidence can be weighed, and appropriate designs for future research can be identified.

To review substantive and methodological issues in Rorschach validation, it is instructive to consider in detail the evolution of four approaches to using and evaluating the Rorschach: the *empirical sign* approach, the *cluster and configuration* approach, the *global impression* approach, and the *conceptual* approach. Following the discussion of these approaches to applying and validating the Rorschach, attention is given to the importance in clinical and research work of distinguishing between *representative* and *symbolic* interpretations of Rorschach data.

THE EMPIRICAL SIGN APPROACH

The empirical sign approach to Rorschach data originated with Hermann Rorschach's examination of the responses given to his inkblots by previously identified groups of schizophrenic, manic-depressive, psychotic, mentally retarded, brain damaged, and normal subjects. As summarized in his *Psychodiagnostics* (1921), comparisons among these groups suggested that certain Rorschach "signs" occurred more frequently in some groups than in others and could therefore be used to facilitate differential diagnosis among them.

When research with the Rorschach took hold in the United States in the 1930's, the prevailing pattern for developing applications of the test consisted of similar inspection techniques for deriving empirical signs. Without benefit of sophisticated data analysis or hypothesis testing, protocol comparisons were used to identify differences in response patterns among known groups, and these differences were then adopted as diagnostic signs for clinical purposes. In this way, for example, signs were developed for schizophrenia by Beck (1938) and Rickers-Ovsiankina (1938), for organicity by Piotrowski (1937), and for neurosis by Miale and Harrower-Erickson (1940).

The empirical sign approach culminated in the early textbook by Klopfer and Kelley (1942), which provided lists of signs for making various clinical diagnoses, and in the extensive psychodiagnostic research study conducted at the Menninger Foundation by Rapaport, Gill, and Schafer (1946). The Menninger study compared subjects representing a wide range of diagnostic categories on each of the Rorschach variables in the detailed Rapaport scoring system. The salient results of this investigation were subsequently summarized by Schafer (1948) in his *Clinical Application of Psychological Tests*. Despite Schafer's efforts to provide a rationale for the diagnostic guidelines he proposed, his influential book became best known and most widely used as a manual of diagnostic sign lists.

Limitations of the Empirical Sign Approach

The empirical sign approach on which early applications of the Rorschach were based had three serious limitations that undermined

both the utility of the instrument and its prospects for being validated. First, in much of this work signs were based on just a single
comparison study without regard for the *shrinkage* that ineviatably
accompanies empirical derivation of diagnostic indices. *Shrinkage*
refers to the fact that any test score identified by inspection to
differentiate among known groups with a certain degree of accuracy
can be expected to demonstrate somewhat less accuracy on re-
examination with another sample, and any newly identified list of
differentiating test scores will include some that hold up better than
others on such re-examination.

To derive a sign list with reasonable likelihood of stability in subsequent applications, it is necessary first to winnow and refine it
through as many subject samples as it takes to reduce shrinkage
within the range of acceptable error variance. In striking contrast to
this requirement for adequate empirical derivation of differential
test indices, and as a reasonably representative sample of the early
Rorschach sign approach, the Miale and Harrower-Erickson neurotic
signs were based on a single comparison study in which score differences were identified in the records of 43 diagnosed neurotic and 20
"normal" subjects.

Second, many frequently used Rorschach sign lists were derived
from the test scores of *nonrepresentative criterion groups*. To be useful for some differential purpose, a test score must be standardized
among the same kinds of subjects with whom it is to be used for
that purpose. Yet the early sign approach was grounded primarily in
comparisons between disparate subject groups that did not adequately represent subjects seen in actual practice.

For example, the Beck and Rickers-Ovsiankina signs for schizophrenia were based on differences observed between clearly schizophrenic and apparently normal subjects. Whereas comparisons
between clearly schizophrenic and apparently normal subjects may
contribute to understanding the nature of schizophrenia, they are
unlikely to yield differential indices that can be successfully applied
in clinical practice. In practice the task is rarely to distinguish obvious
schizophrenia from apparent normality. Rather, the psychodiagnos-
tician is likely to be called on to help differentiate subtle shades of
schizophrenic and nonschizophrenic disturbance in emotionally
troubled patients who are neither obviously schizophrenic nor appar-

ently normal. Because of the nonrepresentative nature of the criterion groups they represent, then, there is little reason to expect such diagnostic indices as those extracted by Beck and Rickers-Ovsiankina from comparisons between widely disparate subjects to contribute significantly to differential diagnosis among patients of ambiguous and uncertain status referred for examination in clinical practice.

Third, because much of the early Rorschach research utilized grossly identified subject groups for deriving diagnostic signs, it failed to take account of the *heterogeneity of diagnostic categories*. Schizophrenia, for example, is known to occur in a number of forms (acute/chronic), patterns (paranoid/nonparanoid), and phases (incipient/remitting), each of which has different implications for overt behavior and for psychodiagnostic indices of this behavior (see Weiner, 1966, Chapters 13-15). "Neurosis" and "organicity" likewise embrace broad variations in personality style and cognitive impairment, as illustrated by the considerable differences between obsessive-compulsive and hysterical personality styles (see Shapiro, 1965, Chapters 2 and 4) and by the differential impairments associated with specific kinds and localizations of brain damage (see Reitan, 1962; Russell, Neuringer, and Goldstein, 1970).

There is consequently little basis for anticipating that diagnostic indices derived from comparisons among unspecified groups of schizophrenic, neurotic, and organic subjects will subsequently prove useful in differentiating these groups. In replication studies the heterogeneity of such gross diagnostic categories is bound to generate enough overlap and within-group variance to cancel out all but the most extreme and obvious differences between them.

Validation Research on the Empirical Sign Approach

Given the limitations imposed by shrinkage, nonrepresentative criterion groups, and heterogeneous diagnostic categories, it was preordained that efforts to validate such empirically derived Rorschach signs would provide disappointment for psychologists who had grown fond of the test, disenchantment for those who had begun to flirt with it, and ample ammunition for those who wished to shoot it down. Over time, replication studies inevitably produced an extensive literature in which most of the early

Rorschach signs displayed spotty utility and some lost all claim to serious consideration. However, not only did validation research on empirical signs tap into a flawed approach to using the Rorschach, and thus have few prospects for success to begin with, but it also embraced ill-conceived research designs that aborted even further the possibilities for positive outcome.

In the first place, most studies concerned with the diagnostic validity of Rorschach signs have relied on recorded psychiatric diagnosis to identify comparison groups. Unfortunately, ample evidence indicates that psychiatric diagnosis is not a particularly reliable procedure (Frank, 1969; Zubin, 1967). Because the degree to which two indices can correlate is statistically limited by how reliable they are, the unreliability of recorded psychiatric diagnosis has fairly regularly served to attenuate the extent to which Rorschach signs could correlate with them and thereby demonstrate their validity.

Second, research evaluating the empirical sign approach has often been extended beyond specific sign lists to include a smorgasbord of signs or simply a roster of traditional summary scores. In assessing the diagnostic validity of the Rorschach for schizophrenia, for example, Rieman (1953) compared schizophrenic and control subjects on an 86-item "Rorschach Element List," and Knopf (1956), Sherman (1952), and Vinson (1960) reported similar comparisons for Rorschach summary scores. Such indiscriminate assembling of signs, independently of any a priori reason to consider them related to schizophrenia and without regard for the strength of previous evidence concerning them, produces a sign list bulky with chaff, that is, a list weighted down with items that have no reasonable expectation of contributing to the differential diagnosis under study.

The statistical implications of such research designs, which require a large number of significance tests to be conducted, are very serious. Should there be just a few signs in the bulky list that in fact contribute to an accurate diagnosis of schizophrenia, they will be far outnumbered by signs that do not. The impression will then be conveyed that, because only a small percentage of the statistical tests conducted yielded differences significant at or beyond the .05 level, the Rorschach is not valid for the diagnosis of schizophrenia.

Any researcher who wishes to report a presumably negative validity study of the Rorschach can be guaranteed of "success" if he proceeds as follows: let him take any reasonably discrete personality variable, whether schizophrenia, depression, hysterical character, homosexual concern, or whatever, and compare individuals demonstrating this condition with some appropriate control group across all Rorschach summary scores. He is almost certain to find that some Rorschach scores are associated with the condition but most are not, and he can then publish one more "failure" of the Rorschach to demonstrate validity as a diagnostic instrument. But the informed reader of his paper should have no doubt about the inappropriateness of this researcher's procedures and the irrelevance of his findings: a routine scanning and equal weighing of Rorschach summary scores as isomorphic indices of some human condition neither is nor should be the way in which psychologists apply the Rorschach for clinical and research purposes.

Implicit in this illustration is a third weakness of the research designed to assess the empirical sign approach, namely, a failure to reflect the manner in which clinicians actually use the test, particularly with respect to *scoring refinements* and the *interrelationship of variables*. Inadequate attention to scoring refinements is exemplified by the reported failure of the Rorschach Whole response (W)[1] to mean what it is supposed to mean. Whereas Rorschach (1921, p. 40) regarded Whole responses as indicating a "freedom and wealth of associations" that is associated with intelligence, neither the number nor percentage of W responses in a record has been found to correlate significantly with measured intelligence. At first blush it might therefore seem that the Rorschach cannot provide a valid assessment of intellectual functioning and that the foundation of Rorschach's hypotheses about location choice rests on shaky ground—or on quicksand, depending on how eager one is to see the Rorschach sink from sight.

Yet all clinicians experienced with the Rorschach know that W responses differ along several dimensions. Some involve articulated forms and some are vague or amorphous, without discrete form; among those that are articulated, some are of good form quality

---

[1] For explanation of scoring symbols, see Appendix, p. 609 [Editor].

and others are inaccurately perceived; and of those that are of good form quality, some involve a complex integration of the blot ("Two witches dancing around a maypole" on Card I) and others reflect little such integrative activity ("Butterfly" on Card I). In seeking to assess a subject's intellectual functioning and integrative capacity, it is to the number and percent of such accurately perceived and ambitiously organized W's in a record that the clinician attends.

These scoring refinements have been examined in Rorschach studies of intellectual functioning by Blatt and Allison (1963), Allison and Blatt (1964), and Marsden (1970). In contrast to the negative findings obtained when all W responses are lumped together, these investigators found that, with W's more precisely scored to reflect variations among them, the percent of accurate, integrated Whole responses in a record correlates significantly with problem-solving efficiency and with WAIS and WISC I.Q. scores.

The interrelationship of variables refers to the fact that sophisticated Rorschach examiners base their inferences on multiple checks and balances among test indices. The Human Movement response (M), for example, does not have the same meaning when it is a perceptually accurate response to a common detail involving human content ($DM+H$) as when it represents a dehumanized, inaccurately perceived response to an unusual detail ($DdM-(H)$). Similarly, the implications of virtually every Rorschach score are enhanced or attenuated in respect to certain other scores. Thus the implications of a certain number of M for an introversive or extratensive Experience Balance depend on the number and nature of chromatic color responses given, and the implications of a low $F+\%$ for impaired reality testing depend on the length of the record in which it occurs. Despite the obvious role such interrelationships play in the clinician's actual use of Rorschach signs, they have for the most part been overlooked or ignored in validity studies of the empirical sign approach.

This critique of the manner in which empirical signs were derived and evaluated in the early Rorschach literature, extending through the 1950's, is not meant to negate the possibility of extracting signs valid for some useful purpose on an empirical basis. To incorporate adequate research design, however, empirical derivation of Rorschach signs must proceed through several cross-validating studies with reasonable homogenous subject samples closely representative of the subjects with whom the signs are eventually to be employed for clinical or research purposes. In view of how rarely Rorschach signs have been derived in this way and how frequently they have been put to ill-conceived tests of their validity, the striking feature of the work in this area is not the preponderantly negative tenor of the findings, but the fact that many Rorschach signs have consistently achieved the differentiations asked of them.

Poor form-level, for example, which both Beck and Rickers-Ovsiankina included among their signs for schizophrenia, has proved extremely robust in differentiating schizophrenic from nonschizophrenic subjects, despite the attenuating effects of unreliable diagnosis, unrefined scoring, and inattention to interrelated Rorschach variables in the validating studies (see Weiner, 1966, pp. 109-110). As another example, a checklist of 20 signs compiled by Wheeler (1949) for identifying homosexual concerns has proved capable of distinquishing homosexual from nonhomosexual groups, delusional from nondelusional psychotics, and obsessive-compulsive from undifferentiated neurotics, despite the fact that several of its individual signs are of questionable validity (Goldfried, Stricker, and Weiner, 1971, Chapter 7).

Occasional interest in the empirical sign approach continued into the 1960's, and the more recent studies happily reflect some improvements in methodology. Evans and Marmorston (1963, 1964), for example, used repetitive screening procedures with fairly representative subject groups to select and weigh a 10-item Rorschach checklist for organicity. Proceeding with equal care, Appelbaum and Holzman (1962; see also Appelbaum and Colson, 1968) developed a color-shading sign for suicidal behavior from observing the responses of several successive samples of suicidal and non-suicidal subjects. Largely because of the complexity of assessing organicity and suicidal potential, however, neither of these careful empirical approaches has produced much advantage over earlier, less systematically derived sign lists proposed for assessing them (see Goldfried et al., 1971, Chapters 8 and 11).

As a general trend, moreover, Rorschach workers gradually discarded the empirical sign approach as they became acquainted with its limitations. In its place, attention shifted toward the possibility of combining Rorschach scores into clusters and configurations that would be more powerful than individual signs in making replicable and valid differentiations.

THE CLUSTER AND CONFIGURATION APPROACH

The effort to improve on the empirical sign approach to using and evaluating the Rorschach by employing clusters and configurations of scores resulted in numerous Rorschach indices created to serve some specific purpose. With respect to schizophrenia, for example, Watkins and Stauffacher (1952) assigned scoring weights to 15 signs of pathological thinking proposed by Rapaport, such as contamination and fabulized combination, and used them to calculate a "Delta Index" for schizophrenic disturbance; Thiesen (1952) used comparisons between normal and schizophrenic subjects to identify five "Patterns" indicative of schizophrenia, each of which involves a relationship between two or more traditional scores; and Weiner (1961, 1964, 1965a) examined repetitive samples of patients referred for psychological examination to extract a "Color Stress" index, based on several characteristics of chromatic color use that appeared associated with schizophrenia. Because the assessment of schizophrenia has played a very large role in the history of Rorschach validity research (see Weiner, 1970), these three indices can be used to illustrate some basic limitations of the cluster and configuration approach and the inadequacy of most evaluation studies employing it.

Limitations of the Cluster and Configuration Approach

The recourse to clusters and configurations overcame many of the previously noted disadvantages of the earlier sign approach to using the Rorschach. In particular, indices could be and were constructed to reflect whatever scoring refinements and interrelationships of variables were known to be employed by experienced clinicians in their use of the test. Thiesen's Pattern B for schizophrenia, for example, is determined jointly from poor form level ($F+\%$ less than 69) and minimal organizational activity (Z less than 8.0).

Additionally, the specificity provided by a signle cluster or configuration designed for some purpose avoids the pitfall of sign lists weighted down with individual scores having no expected or demonstrated bearing on the purpose to be served. Each individual component of the Delta Index, for example, is presumed to relate to schizophrenic thought disorders, and diagnosing schizophrenia with Delta is therefore freer from avoidable sources of error variance than using an unselected list of scores to make the diagnosis.

Nevertheless, as an empirical procedure for deriving differential indices, the cluster and configuration approach faced many of the same methodological challenges as the sign approach, and it met them with only indifferent success. Still common as the basis for extracting new indices were one-shot comparisons among disparate groups, and glowing portents were reported for these indices before there had been adequate cross-validation to minimize shrinkage and guarantee the   representativeness of criterion groups. Weiner in developing his Color Stress index attempted to avoid these errors by using repeated samples of referred patients from case files. In this way he was able to allow for shrinkage and also to promote the likelihood that his index would identify schizophrenia in actual clinical practice among referred patients with uncertain diagnosis. Unfortunately, however, any such routine effort to identify or validate diagnostic indicators from case files encounters another limitation of empirical research, namely, contamination of the independent and dependent variables.

Contamination of variables in psychodiagnostic validity research ensues whenever the test indices being evaluated may have played a role in determining the subjects' recorded diagnosis. For example, congruence between poor form-level on the Rorschach and a recorded diagnosis of schizophrenia may mean that the former is a valid index of the latter, but it can also occur if the examining psychologist *believes* that poor form-level indicates schizophrenia and is in a position to influence the patient's diagnosis on the basis of this belief. To the extent that a recorded diagnosis has been influenced by the Rorschach indices being assessed in a validity study, the independent variables (diagnostic status of the subjects) and dependent variables (Rorschach indices) in the study will be contaminated. Consequently, any significant relationship observed between them may represent an illusory correlation rather than concurrent validity of the Rorschach indices.

There are ways out of this apparent dilemma, other than turning back to disparate, nonrepresentative criterion groups whose diagnosis can be clearly established without testing. For example, contamination of variables can be eliminated by witholding test results on patients referred for psychological examination in a clinical setting until diagnostic judgments are made on other grounds. Where such withholding of information is deemed contrary to the best interests of the patient or to the responsible participation of the psychologist in treatment planning, procedures independent of the actual clinical evaluation can be used to select criterion groups for research purposes. Such procedures include patient behavior ratings (e.g., Lorr et al., 1966) and structured diagnostic interviews (e.g., Burdock and Hardesty, 1969; Spitzer et al., 1970), both of which can be conducted without interfering with standard diagnostic procedures and without prior knowledge of either the Rorschach data or the recorded diagnosis. However, these methods represent relatively recent advances in research designs, and they have rarely been utilized in the empirical derivation of Rorschach clusters and configurations.

In addition to sharing with empirical signs the limitations imposed by the manner in which they were derived, clusters and configurations have suffered from several unique handicaps that have discouraged their clinical use and complicated their validation. First, because Rorschach configurations are intended to summarize and integrate a set of Rorschach scores, many of them involve a cumbersome scoring system that examiners have seldom been interested in learning and applying. The Delta Index, for example, although it can be reliably scored, requires scoring each response for the extent of pathological thinking it contains on a scale from 0.00 to 1.00 and then expressing the sum of weighted scores as a percentage of total R. There is little indication that clinicians have been inclined to add such detailed scoring procedures to their usual means of evaluating a Rorschach protocol.

Second, some configurations have proved to be so selectively constructed for their intended purpose that they rarely occur even in the records of a representative criterion group. Thiesen's configurations, for example, which have the advantage of being easily identifiable from a brief inspection of traditional summary scores and which appear more frequently in the records of schizophrenic than normal subjects, are infrequent *even* in the records of schizophrenics. Hence their utility in contributing to diagnostic judgments in clinical practice is restricted to a few rare instances in which they occur, and their evaluation in research studies is made unwieldy by the   large number of protocols that must be obtained to generate a sufficient frequency of occurence to allow reliable statistical analysis.

Third, some configurations represent a mechanistic, narrowband approach to personality assessment that serves its purpose when it works but provides no information when it does not. The Delta Index and the Thiesen Patterns escape this limitation to some extent because they draw on scores (e.g., $F+\%$) and verbalizations (e.g., fabulized combination) for which many interpretive meanings are suggested in the literature. The Color Stress index, on the other hand, because it was derived on a purely empirical basis without prior concern with the significance of its component scores, has no established or even postulated meaning other than what may be hypothesized for it on an after-the-fact basis. Like any empirically derived sign or configuration that has not been extensively studied in its own right, the Color Stress index is useful when it accomplishes its purpose, which is to identify schizophrenia, but provides no basis for understanding why it accomplishes its purpose or for learning anything about the nature of the condition it identifies.

Validation Research on the Cluster and Configuration Approach

Given the general and specific limitations of the cluster and configuration approach to using the Rorschach, its prospects for finding strong support in validation research were equally grim as those for the empirical sign approach. Although the use of clusters and configurations meant that research could now be based on refined indices intended to serve some particular purpose, inadequacies in the derivation of these indices were compounded by the continuing use of inappropriate or unreliably categorized criterion groups in validity studies. The validation research on clusters and configurations was further compromised by two other methodological vagaries that interfered with systematic accumulation of meaningful data.

First, the nature of Rorschach clusters and configurations encouraged so much "tinkering" that true replication studies of the original indices were rarely done. In assessing the Delta Index, for example, Powers and Hamlin (1955) recommended a different cutting score for identifying schizophrenia from the one Watkins and Stauffacher used, and Pope and Jensen (1957) employed a modified table of scoring weights for arriving at Delta. In studying Color Stress, Klinger and Roth (1964) and Orme (1964) examined only the individual validity of the component scores of the index rather than the combinations of these scores suggested by Weiner as having diagnostic utility (see Weiner, 1965b).

Second, configurations known to occur infrequently, such as the Thiesen patterns, were assessed with subject samples too small to permit them a reasonable frequency of occurence. Aside from the question of whether a diagnostic index occurs with sufficient frequency to be useful, its validity is as much a function of whether its presence identifies some condition as of whether its absence rules the condition out. Many Rorschach configurations used for purposes of clinical diagnosis are expected to increase the likelihood of some diagnostic category when they occur in the record but *not* to rule it out when they do not occur. Thiesen's patterns, for example, suggest schizophrenia in those occasional instances when they occur but have no implications for the presence or absence of schizophrenia when they do not occur.

Unfortunately for the fate of these kinds of configuration, research with them commonly employed a Chi-square design for statistical analysis, in which the association of non-occurrences weighs equally with the association of occurrences in determining size of the statistic. However, continuing with the example of the Thiesen patterns, it is to be expected that their non-occurrence will be spread almost randomly over schizophrenic and control groups. Occurrence of the patterns, on the other hand, which should be limited mainly to the schizophrenic group, will account for only a small percentage of the numbers entered in the table and hence, exert a relatively small influence on the size of the statistic computed from it.

This problem in data analysis can be avoided if the total sample is selected to include equal frequencies of occurrence and non-occurrence for the Thiesen patterns, but such procedures have rarely been followed. Rather, in the absence of balanced marginal frequencies, the type of data analysis typically conducted in studies of Rorschach configurations that occur infrequently and have diagnostic significance only when they occur has served more to conceal than to reflect their validity.

Despite all of these obstacles to their success, the Delta, Thiesen, and Color Stress indices for schizophrenia have managed to demonstrate reasonably good diagnostic validity (see Goldfried et al., 1971, Chapter 10). However, this particular impression of this particular body of research is not very important. Other readers of the literature may be less impressed with the validity data on these three configurations, future research may yet generate an abundance of negative findings for all three of them, and many other Rorschach configurations can be cited on which the validity data range from mixed to consistently negative.

What is important to stress is that neither the derivation of Rorschach clusters and configurations nor the research addressed to validating them represented much improvement in psychometric sophistication over the empirical sign approach. Empirical configurations do not begin to tap the richness of the Rorschach as a measure for assessing personality functioning, nor does the research concerning them begin to speak meaningfully to the question of whether the Rorschach can find valid applications in clinical and research activities.

THE GLOBAL IMPRESSION APPROACH

Because of the weaknesses inherent in the empirical sign and configuration approaches to Rorschach applications, and because of the methodological shortcomings in much of the research designed to assess them, critics of the Rorschach have had abundant data with which to document reservations about its validity. As the preceding discussion indicates, adequate validating research on Rorschach signs and configurations is difficult to design, whereas studies that are destined to yield negative results can be cranked out with relative ease. Hence any reviewer who tabulates "successes" and "failures" of the Rorschach inevitably comes to the conclusion that the instrument has little to offer to practice and research in clinical psychology. As cases in point, Dana, Eron, and Jensen report in the sixth edition of Buros' *Mental Measurements Yearbook* (1965) that the "grim picture" of Rorschach validity has brought us to "the end of an era," and that "the rate of scientific progress in clinical psychology might well be measured by the speed and thoroughness with which it gets over the Rorschach" (pp. 492-509).

Such intemperate outbursts reflect at best either a lack of familiarity with the Rorschach literature or failure to recognize the conceptual and methodological limitations of much of the research it includes. At worst, they reflect cavalier assassination of an assessment technique that has considerable potential for contributing to the understanding of personality functioning and the planning of differential treatment for people in need of psychological help. The potential of the Rorschach is elaborated in the next section on conceptual approaches to its use. To follow the historical evolution of approaches to using and evaluating the Rorschach, however, consideration of conceptual approaches must be preceded with some discussion of the global impression approach.

The global impression approach was adopted by Rorschach workers who were discouraged by the largely negative results emerging from studies of Rorschach signs and configurations but who nevertheless wanted to retain the instrument as a clinical tool. In the global impression approach no specific Rorschach scores or configurations are used to make inferences or are evaluated in research studies. Instead, the examiner's interpretations of the test responses and his conclusions about the status of the subject provide the basis for applying the test and attempting to validate it. In this respect the global impression approach to the Rorschach exemplifies the general view advanced by Hunt (1959) that in all diagnostic situations it is the examiner rather than his tests that constitutes the crucial clinical instrument.

The use of the Rorschach as an aid in making clinical judgments, rather than as a psychometric instrument in its own right, was stimulated primarily by the work of Zubin and his colleagues (Zubin,

1954; Zubin, Eron, and Schumer, 1965). Earlier papers by Bialick and Hamlin (1954), Garfield (1947), Palmer (1951), and others had suggested that the impressions of the examiner were more accurate than sign lists in making clinical judgments, and Zubin argued convincingly that Rorschach examiners should accordingly abandon their "atomistic" concern with traditional scoring categories and capitalize instead on the apparent potential of the test to facilitate valid global impressions.

The use of the Rorschach as a basis for examiner judgments, rather than as a test comprised of scores and indices, continues to the present to influence its clinical and research applications. In regard to specific validation studies, for example, Long and Karon (1969) have confirmed the ability of experienced Rorschach examiners to make accurate judgments about the relative adjustment level of subjects even within such a narrow population as hospitalized schizophrenic patients. In more general terms, Potkay (1971) devotes a monograph on *The Rorschach Clinician* to arguing that "the critical influence in Rorschach interpretation may not be Rorschach's test per se but the professional worker who puts the instrument to use" (p. 15). In support of his position, Potkay reports a survey in which experienced clinicians were found to draw more on qualitative than on quantitative sources of information in arriving at their Rorschach interpretations.

Problems of Separating the Examiner from his Instrument

As useful as the Rorschach may be in facilitating accurate clinical judgments, and regardless of how many clinicians prefer to consider the Rorschach a qualitative rather than a quantitative measure of personality, the global impression approach opened up a host of new problems for validity research. First, because the accuracy of global impressions depends on the clinician's ability to interpret a Rorschach protocol, the outcome of validating studies is influenced significantly by the examiners' level of training and experience. If the examiners in a study are not well-trained and experienced in the Rorschach, attempts to validate the inferences they draw from it are likely to produce negative findings that fuel criticisms of the Rorschach but, in fact, say more about the ineptness of the examiners than about any fault with the instrument.

This problem may seem easily remedied by using only experienced and well-trained examiners in attempts to validate global impressions based on the Rorschach. However, although training and experience can be expected to improve Rorschach skills, there is no necessary uniformity of skill among well-trained and experienced examiners. Such variation in skill is illustrated in two frequently cited studies of clinical judgments based on the Rorschach, one reporting positive results and the other negative results.

In one of these studies Chambers and Hamlin (1957) found that 20 experienced examiners asked to assign Rorschach protocols to diagnostic categories were able as a group to match independently made diagnoses with greater than chance accuracy. As individuals, however, the judges were found to differ significantly in their accuracy, with some judges making frequent errors and five of the judges making no diagnostic errors at all. In the other study, Little and Shneidman (1959) asked 12 Rorschach "experts" to provide diagnostic labels and adjustment ratings for Rorschach protocols that had been independently rated from case history data. The concordance between judgments based on the Rorschach and inferences drawn from the case history was spotty, and Little and Shneidman concluded that their results cast doubt on the utility of the Rorschach as a diagnostic instrument. Like Chambers and Hamlin, however, they also noted that their Rorschach judges, although agreeing with each other beyond chance levels, nevertheless varied enormously in the judgments they made.

Leaving aside all other possible methodological limitations in these and other studies of clinical judgments based on the Rorschach, the question remains whether failure to achieve positive results is due to inadequacies of the test or inadequacies of the examiner. Even with groups of well-trained and experienced examiners, as in the Chambers and Hamlin and the Little and Shneidman studies, there are likely to be differences in skill. This is not to argue that when the Rorschach works it is because the test is good and when it does not work it is because the examiner is inept. Rather, the point is that the instrument and the examiner cannot be separated when the global impression approach is employed. When validating studies with this approach yield positive results, both the instrument and the examiner's judgments are proved useful. When negative results emerge, there is no way of determining whether the fault lies with weaknesses in the instrument or shortcomings of the examiner.

Problems of Prediction

As a second source of problems for validity research, the global impression approach to using the Rorschach generated a wave of prediction studies, most of which had dim prospects for yielding positive results. Prediction of behavior from the Rorschach is of course not tied to the global impression approach, since predictions can be based on scores and configurations as well as on examiner judgments. However, because the global impression approach fostered enormous confidence in how powerful the Rorschach could be in the hands of a skilled examiner, it encouraged clinicians to believe that its applications were virtually unlimited not only in making diagnostic judgments but also in predicting all mannner of variations in human behavior.

Such expectations are justified neither by the nature of the Rorschach nor by the factors that determine behavior. As the author has stressed elsewhere (Weiner, 1972), the Rorschach is a method of appraising personality processes, and behavior is determined by a complex interaction between an individual's personality processes and whatever situational factors are impinging on him. Lewin's postulate in this regard, that behavior is a function of the person and the environment, has never been seriously challenged. In common with other measures of personality, then, the Rorschach cannot and should not be expected to predict behavior except in circumstances where personality variables have been demonstrated to measure and are in turn known to account for the behavior to be predicted, and where the influence of unmeasured situational variables is accordingly minimal.

For example, Rorschach responsivity (R) appears to be a fairly good predictor of being able to participate effectively in verbal psychotherapy (Endicott & Endicott, 1963, 1964), whereas Rorschach indices alone are of limited utility in predicting prospects for social restitution among hospitalized schizophrenics (see Weiner, 1966, pp. 250-254). In the first case, ideational expressiveness as measured by R relates closely to the patient's task in psychotherapy; in the second case, prognosis in schizophrenia is influenced by a number of treatment and sociocultural factors that have little to do with the patient's personality characteristics.

The matter of deciding when the Rorschach should be expected to predict behavior is considered further in the next section on conceptual approaches to its use. It should be noted in the present context, however, that many unfortunate aspersions on Rorschach validity have been cast by predictive studies that extended far beyond the boundaries of reasonable expectation. Most noteworthy in this regard are the frequently cited failures of Kelly and Fiske (1951) to predict performance among clinical psychology graduate students and of Holtzman and Sells (1954) to predict success among aviation cadets. Because of the extent to which such complex behaviors as performance in graduate school and flight training are influenced by situational factors unrelated to variations in individual personality, there is little reason to expect them to be predictable from the Rorschach or from any other personality measure. Negative studies of Rorschach validity can be generated almost at will by attempting to predict broad and complex behavioral criteria of this kind, but the results of such studies have negligible bearing on the validity of the Rorschach for measuring personality processes.

Problems of Contributing to Knowledge

To return specifically to the global impression approach of using and evaluating the Rorschach, it should finally be pointed out that its role in advancing knowledge of the instrument is minimal, regardless of the results it achieves in validity studies. To document this point, suppose a Rorschach examiner who has proved capable of arriving at accurate global impressions of some personality variable is asked to specify how he arrived at his impressions. If he cannot do so, there will be no way to determine if and how the Rorschach contributed to his diagnostic accuracy. Moreover, the skillful examiner who cannot specify the basis of his judgments cannot share or pass on his skills to others. A skill that cannot be taught may be valuable in the hands of whoever happens to possess it, but it makes no cumulative contribution to progress either in research efforts or clinical practice.

Suppose, on the other hand, that a skilled examiner who has

made an accurate clinical judgment from the Rorschach *is* able to specify the basis of his impressions. Since these specifications will refer to some features of how the subject responded to the inkblots, they will all be translatable into location, determinant, content, and verbalization scores and configurations. In other words, then, the global impression approach is either irrelevant to learning about the Rorschach, as it is when the examiner cannot specify the basis of his impressions, or it consists of the examiner's particular way of using scores and configurations, when he can specify how he has arrived at his impressions. For this reason the global impression approach, while useful for validating the activity of the clinician, does not add any new dimensions to validating the Rorschach as an assessment procedure.

THE CONCEPTUAL APPROACH

The conceptual approach to using and evaluating the Rorschach emerged from the gradual recognition that the basic purpose of the instrument is to assess personality processes. In the conceptual approach personality processes provide a bridge between Rorschach data and whatever condition is to be evaluated or behavior to be predicted. Viewed in this frame of reference, the Rorschach successfully identifies the presence of some condition or predicts some aspect of behavior only when the instrument accurately measures personality variables that in turn account in substantial part for the condition or the behavior.

In using the Rorschach conceptually, the examiner poses two questions for himself. First, what personality variables account for the condition or behavior he wishes to assess? Second, what features of a Rorschach protocol measure these personality variables? If the condition or behavior to be assessed does not depend primarily on personality variables, or if the personality variables on which it depends are not particularly well measured by the Rorschach, then the Rorschach is not an appropriate instrument to be used. If on the other hand the condition or behavior does relate to personality variables that the Rorschach measures, the Rorschach variables that measure it should be expected to yield a valid assessment or predicition.

These basic considerations in a conceptual approach to using and evaluating the Rorschach can be illustrated by referring again to some basic lines of research with the instrument. With respect to assessing schizophrenia, for example, it is generally acknowledged that one of the defining personality characteristics of this disorder is impaired reality testing, which consists largely of inaccurate perceptual functioning, and inaccurate perceptual functioning is directly measured on the Rorschach by poor form level, expressed in a low $F+\%$ or $R+\%$ (see Bellak, 1958, 1969; Weiner, 1966, Chap. 7). Hence, because inaccurate perceptual functioning provides a conceptual link between the presence of schizophrenia and poor form level, low $F+\%$ and $R+\%$ should be expected to contribute to the diagnosis of this condition—as they have been demonstrated to do.

In contrast, there is no set of personality variables generally recognized to account for success in aviation school, and hence no basis for using or expecting the Rorschach to predict it. Regarding organic brain dysfunction, on the other hand, which is generally acknowledged to consist in part of impaired attention, memory, and perceptual-motor coordination, personality variables should provide a good diagnostic index, assuming that such cognitive functions as attention, memory, and perceptual-motor coordination are considered features of personality. Yet these features of personality are measured peripherally if at all on the Rorschach, and many other diagnostic instruments are more suitable than the Rorschach for measuring them. Hence the Rorschach should not be used to help identify the presence of organic brain dysfunction (although it may indicate important aspects of how the brain-damaged individual is attempting to cope with his loss of function), nor should it be expected to yield valid indices of organicity (although as noted earlier some minimal success has been achieved in this regard).

Implications of the Conceptual Approach for Validity Studies

In contrast to the sign, configuration, and global impression approaches to using and evaluating the Rorschach, the conceptual approach addresses *construct* validity rather than *criterion-related* validity. Whereas criterion-related validity for the Rorschach consists of the extent to which its scores correlate with some concurrent condition of the subject or some predicted aspect of his behavior, construct validity consists of the extent to which a theoretical formulation can account for relationships between a Rorschach protocol and some condition or behavior. Although evaluations of construct validity include attention to criterion-related correlations, they are not limited to assessing the validity of a test for some particular purpose. Rather, positive outcomes in construct validity studies of personality measures simultaneously validate both the theoretical formulations concerning certain personality variables and the tests used for measuring these variables.

The challenge in designing construct validity studies, then, is to formulate theoretical relationships that adequately link the personality characteristics being measured with the condition being assessed or the behavior being predicted. These theoretical relationships can then guide appropriate clinical and research applications of the Rorschach, and, as an advantage for validity studies, they can be examined for the extent to which the bridge they provide between a Rorschach protocol and some aspect of behavior is firmly anchored at both ends.

This advantage of the conceptual approach for Rorschach validation can be illustrated by continuing with the example of the link between poor form level and schizophrenia that is provided by the construct of inaccurate perceptual functioning. On the measurement side, it is possible to determine the relationship between inaccurate perception and low $F+\%$ independently of schizophrenia, by examing correlations between $F+\%$ and performance on numerous other measures of perceptual accuracy. On the behavioral side, it is possible to determine the relationship between inaccurate perception and schizophrenia independently of the Rorschach, by examining the performance of schizophrenic subjects on other measures of perceptual accuracy. Because of the dimensionality of this approach, any failures to validate poor form level as an index of schizophrenia could be traced to their origin, whether in the failure of low $F+\%$ to measure perceptual accuracy, or in the irrelevance of inaccurate perception to the schizophrenic condition, or both.

Even more importantly, if the contribution of low $F+\%$ to diagnosing schizophrenia is validated in the above manner, it no longer exists as an isolated phenomenon idiosyncratic to the workings of the Rorschach. Rather, is stands broadly related to other sources of knowledge about perceptual functioning and about schizophrenic disturbance. Thus a conceptual approach to its use and evaluation allows the Rorschach to shed any lingering trappings of a private art divorced from behavioral science, and instead to be fully integrated with the general psychology of normal and abnormal personality functioning.

It is furthermore within the context of a conceptual approach that the Rorschach can be most clearly identified as an instrument for assessing personality processes, which it is, rather than as a test for diagnosing or predicting behavior, which it is not. Information gleaned from the Rorschach reveals to the knowledgeable examiner aspects of the subject's personality functioning. Whether or not he can use this knowledge to make accurate diagnostic judgments or behavioral predictions will, as previously noted, depend on the extent to which he can account for the diagnosis or prediction in terms of the personality variables he has assessed.

Utility of the Conceptual Approach

Because of the advantages it represents, the conceptual approach to the Rorschach has demonstrated considerable utility both for accomplishing clinical and research purposes and for generating favorable validity studies. This utility is attested in part by the results achieved with several widely used conceptually derived scoring indices, including Friedman's Developmental Level scoring, Holt's Primary Process scoring, and Klopfer's Prognostic Rating Scale.

Developmental Level (DL) scoring emerged from Friedman's (1953) use of Werner's theories of perceptual development to link Rorschach responses with aspects of behavior related to perceptual maturation and regression. Friedman based DL scoring on the extent to which the subject's use of Rorschach locations reflects capacity for perceptual differentiation and integration, and he proposed applying DL scores in the evaluation of conditions believed to be influenced by these perceptual capacities. Consistently with expectations derived from personality theory, maturity of perceptual functioning as measured by Rorschach DL has been found to differentiate among children at different chronological age levels, among mental defectives at different mental age levels, and among schizophrenics at different levels of disturbance (see Goldfried et al., 1971, Chapter 2). In addition, *DL* scores have proved capable of discriminating among neurotic, schizophrenic, brain-damaged, and normal adults and of predicting amount of social participation and length of stay among hospitalized schizophrenic patients. (see also Chapter 3 in this volume).

The Primary Process (*PP*) scoring developed by Holt (1966, and Chapter 2 in this volume) draws on certain traditional scores, content categories, and indications of cognitive control to arrive at indices of adaptive and maladaptive regression, and it has proved successful in evaluating a wide range of behavior conceptually related to adaptive and maladaptive regression. With respect to openness to experience, for example, the *PP* index has been found to correlate significantly with experiences of religious conversion among theology students, with empathic capacity among psychotherapists, with tolerance for unrealistic experiences, and with vividness of both dreaming and waking imagery (see Holt, 1970, and Chapter 1 in this volume). With respect to psychological adjustment, adaptive regression as measured by *PP* scores is related to flexibility of autonomic nervous system functioning and can differentiate schizophrenic from normal subjects and poorly-organized from well-organized college students. There is also preliminary evidence to suggest that *PP* scores can predict outcome in psychotherapy and can be used effectively to measure changes occurring during the course of such treatment (Fishman, 1973).

Klopfer et al. (1951) developed the Rorschach Prognostic Rating Scale (*PRS*) specifically to aid predictions of response to psychotherapy. The *PRS* is based on a weighted scoring system for various aspects of human movement, animal movement, inanimate movement, shading, color, and form level that were selected to provide an index of ego strength. To the extent that good ego strength contributes to favorable outcomes in psychotherapy, then, it was expected that the *PRS* index would provide a valid and useful predictor of treatment response. Considerable evidence confirms that the *PRS* can in fact predict overt behavior change among clinic and hospital patients, due either to treatment or "spontaneous remission," and can also predict capacity to adjust to new and difficult situations (see Goldfried et al., 1971, Chapter 12). Recent evidence suggests further that the capacity of the *PRS* to predict response to psychotherapy extends beyond insight-oriented therapy to include rational-emotive therapy and behavior modification as well (Newmark et al., 1973, 1974).

Separately from these formal scoring systems, an accumulating body of research employing a conceptual framework is yielding positive results bearing on Rorschach validity. Mayman (1967), for example, postulating that vivid internalized images of others contribute to the potential for good interpersonal relatedness, found a significant relationship between Rorschach content indices of object representations and independently assessed level of psychopathology. Weiss and Masling (1970), drawing on psychoanalytic notions relating early oral difficulties to a variety of adult disturbances, found more oral dependent responses in the Rorschach protocols of subjects with problems of obesity, stuttering, ulcer, and alcoholism than in protocols of control subjects. Ostrov et al. (1972) relied on the construct of impulsivity to demonstrate a relationship between a Rorschach index of impulsivity, based on three measures of reaction to color cards, and a history of greater and more frequent delinquency among adolescent boys and girls. Glatt and Karon (1974), studying ego regression among schizophrenic patients, found that Rorschach indices of ego regression accurately monitored changes in the status of the patients' pathogenic process over a 20-month period during which they were examined on four occasions.

Although these four studies are mentioned for illustrative purposes, rather than to introduce an exhaustive survey of the literature, it is correct to say that, the more adequately validation research has been designed to reflect conceptual approaches to the Rorschach, the more consistently it has yielded positive findings. Earlier surveys of the research literature by Klinger and Roth (1965) and Levy and Orr (1959) are still relevant in this regard. Klinger and Roth found a direct relationship between how closely investigators approximated actual clinical use of the Rorschach and the frequency with which positive validating data emerged from their research. Levy and Orr, comparing the outcomes of construct validity and criterion validity studies with the Rorschach, found that studies of the construct type were more than twice as likely as studies of the criterion type to yield positive results. As further support for these affirmations of the Rorschach's demonstrable validity when it is used and evaluated within a carefully delineated conceptual frame of reference, it is almost impossible to find in the recent literature a report of construct validation in which the Rorschach has failed to achieve what could reasonably be expected of it.

Hence it is not surprising that the most recent edition of Buros' *Mental Measurements Yearbook*, published in 1972, contains far different comments on the Rorschach from the grim aspersions cast on it in the 1965 edition. Reviews by Burstein, Knutson, McArthur, Rabin, and Reznikoff (Buros, 1972, pp. 432-439) include the following comments: "It is a tribute to the vigor of the core notion that it has survived;" "It remains a clinically vigorous technique;" "There is a good deal of evidence that the vitality of the Rorschach as a clinical and research instrument has not diminished tremendously;" "Six years have passed and psychology has not gotten over the Rorschach;" and finally, "The rich sample of patterned interactions among a man's perceptual, cognitive, emotional, and social sides that appears in even one Rorschach response is neither matched nor approximated by any other psychological tool."

REPRESENTATIVE AND SYMBOLIC INTERPRETATIONS OF THE RORSCHACH

In concluding this discussion of approaches to Rorschach validity, it is relevant to comment on the distinction between representative and symbolic interpretations of Rorschach data. Representative interpretations utilize Rorschach behavior as direct representations of the actual behavior the examiner is attempting to assess or predict, whereas symbolic interpretations use Rorschach responses as symbolic clues to the behavior under study. The following paragraphs elaborate the distinction between these two types of interpretation and identify the differing implications they have for Rorschach validation.

Distinctions between
Representative and Symbolic Interpretations

Representative interpretations of Rorschach data define the Rorschach as a *perceptual-cognitive task* in which the subject is called on to impose some structure and organization on a variegated stimulus field. The perceptual-cognitive abilities and preferences the subject exercises in performing this task are presumed to constitute a representative sample of his perceptual-cognitive abilities and preferences, and his Rorschach behavior is accordingly presumed to reflect directly his behavior in other situations that are determined by perceptual organization and cognitive style.

For example, a subject who selects a large number of unusual details (*Dd*) and tends to ignore obvious details (*D*) in responding to the Rorschach is demonstrating an inordinate preoccupation with detail. It is reasonable to expect that such a person becomes similarly preoccupied with details in other situations that call for selective perceptual attention, so that he is the kind of person who loses sight of the forest for the trees. Hence a high *Dd*% on the Rorschach, because it represents preoccupation with detail, should provide a valid index of preoccupation with detail as a general personality characteristic, and it should aid in identifying conditions in which this characteristic is prominent, such as obsessive-compulsive neurosis. Many different aspects of a subject's perceptual-cognitive style in responding to the Rorschach similarly provide direct representations of personality characteristics that in turn relate to the understanding and prediction of various kinds of behavior.

Another central feature of representative interpretations of Rorschach data is the attention they call to the *structure* of the subject's responses. Perceptual-cognitive preferences and abilities are represented in Rorschach responses by the parts of the inkblots the subject selects to respond to and the way he organizes them, by the properties of the inkblots he draws on in forming his percepts, by the kinds of things he sees in the inkblots, and by the manner in which he expresses himself. In other words, representative Rorschach behavior is measured by formal scoring for aspects of location choice, determinant use, content categories, and verbalization. It is in these structural aspects of a Rorschach record that the subject provides representative samples of his behavior in situations that require him to exercise his perceptual-cognitive abilities and preferences.

Symbolic interpretations, on the other hand, define the Rorschach as a *stimulus to fantasy*, in which the subject's responses are important not for how he formulates or verbalizes his responses, but for what he sees in the inkblots and how he elaborates his impressions. In symbolic interpretations it is the *content* of a Rorschach protocol and not its structure that provides the most important sources of inferences about the subject's personality. Rorschach content is used not as representative of any overt behavior, but rather as thematic material that provides clues to underlying feelings and attitudes of the individual.

For example, it can be hypothesized that a male subject who reports seeing "a naked man with his back toward me with his buttocks here" has some underlying homosexual inclinations or concerns. The basis for such an interpretation is not representative, since it is unlikely that the subject in his daily life is characteristically forming images of naked male buttocks from his perceptual field, unless he happens to be hallucinatory. Rather, the interpretation devolves from a chain of inferences, such as the following: male homosexuals tend to be concerned with approach from the rear and therefore to be interested in the appearance of other men's buttocks; this subject appears to be interested in the appearance of men's buttocks; since this subject shares some interests in common with male homosexuals, he may well have some homosexual inclinations or concerns.

Obviously this chain of inference, like all inferential sequences underlying interpretations of symbolic material, admits of exceptions. Some male homosexuals may not be interested in approach from the rear, for example, or the subject may be interested in buttocks for reasons that have nothing to do with homosexuality, or the subject may share some interests with homosexuals without himself having any concerns in this regard. Despite these possible exceptions, however, "buttocks" responses appear to have good validity as an index of homosexual concern in male subjects (see Goldfried et al., 1971, p. 196), which means that the logic behind this particular interpretation has some general applicability. Yet the point remains that a Rorschach interpretation based on multiple sequential inferences is subject to error at each step in the inferential process. The more such steps that are taken in arriving at an inter-pretation and the more highly inferential these steps are, the more the interpretation embodies possible sources of error and the less promising are its prospects for being broadly validated.

Implications for Using
and Evaluating the Rorschach

These differences between representative and symbolic interpre-tations have important implications for Rorschach use and evaluation. Representative interpretations involve few inferences beyond the presumption of some continuity in perceptual-cognitive behavior from one situation to the next. These interpretations are based primarily on the structure of the protocol and are in turn addressed to structural aspects of the subject's personality, such as the extent of his imaginal capacity, the logic of his reasoning, and the nature of his defensive style. Symbolic interpretations, on the other hand, involve levels of inference in which the content of the protocol is used to formulate hypotheses about the subject's personality dynam-ics, including his underlying needs, attitudes, and sources of concern. Whereas validity for a representative interpretation requires only that the expected similarity between some Rorschach behavior (e.g., a high $Dd\%$) and some real-life behavior (e.g., preoccupation with details) has been accurately conceptualized, validity for a symbolic interpretation requires accurate inference at each step in the inferential chain that supports it.

Symbolic interpretations are consequently much more difficult to validate than representative interpretations. Indeed, some symbolic interpretations may embrace so many exceptions at various points in their inferential chain that they cannot be validated in any general sense, even though they prove highly accurate and very helpful in understanding certain individual subjects. For example, the upper side details of Card IV seen as "a limp rope just hanging there" is very likely to suggest concerns about impotence in a male subject. However, in some male subjects such a response may reflect a feeling of weakness rather than more specifically of impotence, and in a female subject it may reflect something entirely different, such as a feeling of scorn for men or a need to depreciate them. In contrast, low $F+\%$ represents inaccurate perceptual functioning for all subjects, regardless of their sex or any other individual differences among them.

For this reason symbolic interpretations that may be quite accurate in specific circumstances will frequently produce negative validity findings when they are assessed under more general circumstances. This point is important to keep in mind, because many presumably negative validity studies with the Rorschach have addressed the generality of symbolic interpretations, and critics of the Rorschach have typically focused on symbolic interpretations in arguing that the instrument can neither be validated nor given credence by serious behavioral scientists. However, careful attention to interpretations that construe the Rorschach as a representative sample of behavior reveals an impressive weight of positive outcomes in validity studies, and the findings for representative interpretations provide clear evidence that Rorschach examiners can accomplish as much as other behavioral scientists when they stick close to their data.

For the practicing clinician this distinction between representative and symbolic interpretations of the Rorschach cautions him to keep track of the levels of inference at which he is working. In assessing personality processes with the Rorschach, there is clearly a need to formulate hypotheses about both personality structure and personality dynamics and to draw on both the structure and content of a Rorschach protocol in doing so. However, it is when the examiner is utilizing the formal structure of Rorschach responses to formulate hypotheses about personality structure that he is operating close to his data and drawing inferences that are likely to be generally valid. When he is utilizing content elaborations to formulate hypotheses about personality dynamics, on the other hand, he is employing levels of inference that remove him from representative aspects of the data and are less likely to be uniformly valid.

In reporting on his findings, the examiner should accordingly express his representative interpretations as reasonable certainties about the subject and couch his symbolic interpretations more in the language of conjecture. Used in this way, the Rorschach rests on solid empirical ground and helps the clinician avoid either underestimating the import of reliable findings or overselling the significance of tenuous ones.

BIBLIOGRAPHY

Allison, J., and Blatt, S. J. The relationship of Rorschach whole responses to intelligence. *Journal of Projective Techniques & Personality Assessment*, 1964, **28**, 255-260.

Appelbaum, S. A., and Colson, D. B. A reexamination of the color-shading Rorschach test response. *Journal of Projective Techniques and Personality Assessment*, 1968, **32**, 160-164.

Appelbaum, S. A., and Holzman, P. S. The color-shading response and suicide. *Journal of Projective Techniques*, 1962, **26**, 155-161.

Beck, S. J. *Personality structure in schizophrenia: A Rorschach investigation of eighty-one patients and sixty-four controls*. New York: Nervous and Mental Disease Monograph, 1938.

Bellak, L. The schizophrenic syndrome: A further elaboration of the unified theory of schizophrenia. In L. Bellak (Ed.), *Schizophrenia: A review of the syndrome*. New York: Logos Press, 1958. Pp. 3-63.

Bellak, L. Research on ego function patterns: A progress report. In L. Bellak and L. Loeb (Eds.), *The schizophrenic syndrome*. New York: Grune & Stratton, 1969. Pp. 11-65.

Bialick, I., and Hamlin, R. M. The clinician as judge: Details of procedure in judging projective material. *Journal of Consulting Psychology*, 1954, **18**, 239-242.

Blatt, S. J., and Allison, J. Methodological considerations in Rorschach research: The *W* response as an expression of abstractive and integrative strivings. *Journal of Projective Techniques*, 1963, **27**, 267-278.

Burdock, E. I., and Hardesty, A. S. *Structured clinical interview manual*. New York: Springer, 1969.

Buros, O. K. (Ed.) *The sixth mental measurements yearbook*. Highland Park, N.J.: Gryphon Press, 1965.

Buros, O. K. (Ed.) *The seventh mental measurements yearbook*. Highland Park, N.J.: Gryphon Press, 1972.

Chambers, G. S., and Hamlin, R. M. The validity of judgments based on "blind" Rorschach records. *Journal of Consulting Psychology*, 1957, **21**, 105-109.

Endicott, N. A., and Endicott, J. "Improvement" in untreated psychiatric patients. *Archives of General Psychiatry*, 1963, **9**, 575-585.

Endicott, N. A., and Endicott, J. Prediction of improvement in treated and untreated patients using the Rorschach Prognostic Rating Scale. *Journal of Consulting Psychology*, 1964, **28**, 342-348.

Evans, R. B., and Marmorston, J. Psychological test signs of brain damage in cerebral thrombosis. *Psychological Reports*, 1963, **12**, 915-930.

Evans, R. B., & Marmorston, J. Rorschach signs of brain damage in cerebral thrombosis. *Perceptual and Motor Skills*, 1964, **18**, 977-988.

Fishman, D. B. Rorschach adaptive regression and change in psychotherapy. *Journal of Personality Assessment*, 1973, **37**, 218-224.

Frank, G. H. Psychiatric diagnosis: A review of research. *Journal of General Psychology*, 1969, **81**, 157-176.

Friedman, H. Perceptual regression in schizophrenia: An hypothesis suggested by the use of the Rorschach test. *Journal of Projective Techniques*, 1953, **17**, 171-185.

Garfield, S. L. The Rorschach test in clinical diagnosis. *Journal of Clinical Psychology*, 1947, **3**, 375-381.

Glatt, C. T., and Karon, B. P. A Rorschach validation study of the ego regression theory of psychopathology. *Journal of Consulting and Clinical Psychology*, 1974, **42**, 569-576.

Goldfried, M. R., Stricker, G., and Weiner, I. B. *Rorschach handbook of clinical and research applications*. Englewood Cliffs, N.J.: Prentice-Hall, 1971.

Holt, R. R. Measuring libidinal and agressive motives and their controls by means of the Rorschach test. In D. Levine (Ed.), *Nebraska symposium on motivation*. Lincoln, Neb.: University of Nebraska Press, 1966. Pp. 1-47.

Holt, R. R. Artistic creativity and Rorschach measures of adaptive regression. In B. Klopfer, M. M. Meyer, and F. B. Brawer (Eds.), *Developments in the Rorschach technique.* Vol. III. New York: Harcourt Brace Jovanovich, 1970, Pp. 263-320.

Holtzman, W. H., and Sells, S. B. Predictions of flying success by clinical analysis of test protocols. *Journal of Abnormal and Social Psychology*, 1954, **49**, 485-498.

Hunt, W. A. An actuarial approach to clinical judgment. In B. M. Bass and I. A. Berg (eds.), *Objective approaches to personality assessment.* Princeton, N.J.: Van Nostrand, 1959. Pp. 169-191.

Kelly, E. L., and Fiske, D. W. *The prediction of performance in clinical psychology.* Ann Arbor, Mich: University of Michigan Press, 1951.

Klinger, E., and Roth, I. Diagnosing schizophrenia with Rorschach color responses. *Journal of Clinical Psychology*, 1964, **20**, 386-388.

Klinger, E., and Roth, I. Diagnosis of schizophrenia by Rorschach patterns. *Journal of Projective Techniques & Personality Assessment*, 1965, **29**, 323-335.

Klopfer, B., and Kelley, D. M. *The Rorschach technique.* Yonkers-on-Hudson: World Book, 1942.

Klopfer, B., Kirkner, F. J., Wisham, W., and Baker, G. Rorschach prognostic rating scale. *Journal of Projective Techniques*, 1951, **15**, 425-428.

Knopf, I. J. Rorschach summary scores in differential diagnosis. *Journal of Consulting Psychology*, 1956, **20**, 99-104.

Levy, L. H., and Orr, T. B. The social psychology of Rorschach research. *Journal of Abnormal and Social Psychology*, 1959, **58**, 79-83.

Little, K. B., and Shneidman, E. S. Congruencies among interpretations of psychological test and anamnestic data. *Psychological Monographs*, 1959, **73**, Whole No. 476.

Long, F. J., and Karon, B. P. Rorschach validity as measured by the identification of individual patients. *Journal of Projective Techniques & Personality Assessment*, 1969, **33**, 20-24.

Lorr, M., Klett, J. C., McNair, D. M., and Lasky, J. J. *Inpatient multidimensional psychiatric rating scale.* Palo Alto, Cal.: Consulting Psychologists Press, 1966.

Marsden, G. Intelligence and the Rorschach Whole response. *Journal of Projective Techniques & Personality Assessment*, 1970, **34**, 470-476.

Mayman, M. Object-representations and object-relationships in Rorschach responses. *Journal of Projective Techniques and Personality Assessment*, 1967, **31**, 17-24.

Miale, F. R., and Harrower-Erickson, M. R. Personality structure in the psychoneuroses. *Rorschach Research Exchange*, 1940, **4**, 71-74.

Newmark, C. S., Finkelstein, M., and Frerking, R. A. Comparison of the predictive validity of two measures of psychotherapy prognosis. *Journal of Personality Assessment*, 1974, **38**, 144-148.

Newmark, C. S. Hetzel, W., Walker, L., Holstein, S., and Finkelstein, M. Predictive validity of the Rorschach Prognostic Rating Scale with behavior modification techniques. *Journal of Clinical Psychology*, 1973, **29**, 246-248.

Orme, J. D. *A study of Weiner's Rorschach schizophrenic indicators.* Journal of Clinical Psychology, 1964, **20**, 531-532.

Ostrov, E., Offer, D., Marohn, R. C., and Rosenwein, T. The "impulsivity indes": Its application to juvenile delinquency. *Journal of Youth and Adolescence*, 1972, **1**, 179-206.

Palmer, J. O. A dual approach to Rorschach validation: Methodological study. *Psychological Monographs*, 1951, **65**, Whole No. 325.

Pope, B., and Jensen, A. R. The Rorschach as an index of pathological thinking. *Journal of Projective Techniques*, 1957, **21**, 54-62.

Potkay, C. R. *The Rorschach clinician.* New York: Grune and Stratton, 1971.

Powers, W. T., and Hamlin, R. M. Relationship between diagnostic category and deviant verbalizations on the Rorschach. *Journal of Consulting Psychology*, 1955, **19**, 120-125.

Rapaport, D., Gill, M., and Schafer, M. *Diagnostic psychological testing.* Vol. II. Chicago: Year Book Publishers, 1946.

Reitan, R. M. Psychological deficit. *Annual Review of Psychology*, 1962, **13**, 415-444.

Rickers-Ovsiankina, M. A. The Rorschach test as applied to normal and schizophrenic subjects. *British Journal of Medical Psychology*, 1938, **17**, 227-257.

Rieman, G. W. The effectiveness of Rorschach elements in the discrimination between neurotic and ambulatory schizophrenic subjects. *Journal of Consulting Psychology*, 1953, **17**, 25-31.

Rorschach, H. (1921) *Psychodiagnostics*. Berne: Hans Huber, 1942.

Russell, E. W., Neuringer, C., and Goldstein, G. *Assessment of brain damage: A neuropsychological key approach*. New York: Wiley, 1970.

Schafer, R. *Clinical application of psychological tests*. New York: International Universities Press, 1948.

Shapiro, D. *Neurotic styles*. New York: Basic Books, 1965.

Sherman, M. H. A comparison of formal and content factors in the diagnostic testing of schizophrenia. *Genetic Psychology Monographs*, 1952, **46**, 183-234.

Spitzer, R. L., Endicott, J., Fleiss, J. L., and Cohen, J. The Psychiatric Status Schedule: A technique for evaluating psychopathology and impairment in role functioning. *Archives of General Psychiatry*, 1970, **23**, 41-55.

Thiesen, J. W. A pattern analysis of structural characteristics of the Rorschach test in schizophrenia. *Journal of Consulting Psychology*, 1952, **16**, 365-370.

Vinson, D. B. Responses to the Rorschach test that identify schizophrenic thinking, feeling, and behavior. *Journal of Clinical & Experimental Psychopathology*, 1960, **21**, 34-40.

Watkins, J. G., and Stauffacher, J. C. An index of pathological thinking in the Rorschach. *Journal of Projective Techniques*, 1952, **16**, 276-286.

Weiner, I. B. Three Rorschach scores indicative of schizophrenia. *Journal of Consulting Psychology*, 1961, **25**, 436-439.

Weiner, I. B. Pure C and color stress as Rorschach indicators of schizophrenia. *Perceptual & Motor Skills*, 1964, **18**, 484.

Weiner, I. B. Follow-up validation of Rorschach tempo and color use indicators of schizophrenia. *Journal of Projective Techniques & Personality Assessment*, 1965, **29**, 387-391. (a)

Weiner, I. B. Rorschach Color Stress as a schizophrenic indicator: A reply. *Journal of Clinical Psychology*, 1965, **21**, 313-314. (b)

Weiner, I. B. *Psychodiagnosis in schizophrenia*. New York: Wiley, 1966.

Weiner, I. B. Rorschach diagnosis of schizophrenia: Empirical validation *Proceedings of the VIIth International Congress of Rorschach and other Projective Techniques*. Berne: Hans Huber, 1970. Pp. 913-920.

Weiner, I. B. Does psychodiagnosis have a future? *Journal of Personality Assessment*, 1972, **36**, 534-546.

Weiss, L., and Masling, J. Further validation of a Rorschach measure of oral imagery: A study of six clinical groups. *Journal of Abnormal Psychology*, 1970, **76**, 83-87.

Wheeler, W. M. An analysis of Rorschach indices of male homosexuality. *Rorschach Research Exchange and Journal of Projective Techniques*, 1949, **13**, 97-126.

Zubin, J. Failures of the Rorschach technique. *Journal of Projective Techniques*, 1954, **18**, 303-315.

Zubin, J. Classification of the behavior disorders. *Annual Review of Psychology*, 1967, **18**, 373-401.

Zubin, J., Eron, L. D., and Schumer, F. *An experimental approach to projective techniques*. New York: Wiley, 1965.

APPENDIX | *Laura C. Toomey and*
Maria A. Rickers-Ovsiankina

TABULAR COMPARISON OF
SCORING SYSTEMS

These tables represent a comparison of the basic features of several of the scoring systems that are relatively frequently used in English language writings.

The tables have been prepared to provide the following information:

1. To give the major scoring categories of each system in compact form for quick reference.

2. To show graphically what score in one system corresponds to what score in another system, and to what extent.

3. To demonstrate the general approach of each scoring system in terms of such practical considerations as relative inclusiveness, refinement, clarity, and communicability.

The systems of the following people have been included: Rorschach, Binder, Rapaport and Schafer, Beck, Piotrowski, Hertz, and Klopfer. Binder's scoring is identical with that of Rorschach, except for shading, and with that exception the two systems have been listed as one. The order of presentation is as given above, except in Tables A.2A (Chiaroscuro) and A.4 (Popular-Original), where special features of certain systems made different grouping more logical.

The scores of each system and their definitions are presented in a vertical column, with equivalent scores on the same horizontal level. Where a score is common to two or more systems, the definition extends across the corresponding columns. In general, where vertical lines separate columns, there are significant differences between the systems involved, in categories, in the details of the definitions, or both. Where a score is basically the same for two systems, but minor differences in definition exist, or the notation for the score is not the same, an incomplete vertical line separates only that part of the material that is not common to the two (e.g., in Table A.2, the *FM* of Piotrowski, Hertz, and Klopfer). Explanations and definitions, as far as possible, are each authors' own.

When an author has given a name to a scoring symbol, it has been included. Names have been assigned to nearly all the scores by everybody except Rapaport and Schafer, who in their writings refer to many of the scores by symbol only. A few "nonscorable" kinds of responses have been mentioned in the tables for reasons of completeness of comparison (in at least one other system, by contrast, they rate a score), and for these, of course, no symbol is given since none is used in actual scoring. For the most part, space limitations precluded illustrating the applications of scoring with actual responses, but in a few places where clarity seemed to demand it, examples have been given.

Table A.1 contains the principal location categories. No attempt has been made to cover the qualitative classifications, such as "fabulized combination" and "contamination," since they are not part of the formal scoring system in the same way as location.

Table A.2 contains the determinant categories other than shading, and Table A.2*A* covers shading categories. Shading was put into a separate table because the shading scores of one system cannot be compared with the corresponding scores of all the others as can such categories as form and movement.

Table A.3 compares form quality criteria, and Table A.4 covers the popular-original classification. Designation of response content has not been included in the tabulation, because content categories vary widely in range and inclusiveness, and because their names are generally self-explanatory. It is Hertz who has the most comprehensive list of content scores, and she also uses many content subdivisions in her quantitative analysis.

The tables outline the components of the basic scoring only, and no comparison has been made of the ways in which the different authors use summation scores or ratios (such as total number of responses or weighted color sum), or of the different approaches to organization.

Besides their rather obvious function as a convenient reference list, it is hoped that the tables may serve a somewhat broader purpose. For instance, comparison of the classificational criteria employed by different systems may foster insights into the logic underlying the categories, and in some cases might throw new light upon the implicit psychological nature of these categories.

The selection of a set of scores most suitable for a particular research project should be facilitated by viewing the specific features of each scoring system in the light of the problem under investigation. In fact, in certain cases, the availability of a scoring category might actually prompt a refinement or greater precision in the experimental design.

TABLE A.1. Locations

	RORSCHACH AND BINDER	RAPAPORT AND SCHAFER	BECK	PIOTROWSKI	HERTZ	KLOPFER
WHOLE RESPONSE	**DW** A single detail, more or less clearly perceived, is used as the basis for the interpretation of the whole. Detail used may also be rare or space detail. CONFABULATED RESPONSE			Interpretation applies well to particular detail, but not to whole blot.	Used only for confabulatory responses.	
	W WHOLE Response to the whole blot, with no part specifically omitted except white spaces.	The entire blot *must* be used.				(1) Entire blot used, or (2) Subject intends to respond to the whole, but inadvertently omits minor part(s).
				Exception: *M* on card III is *W* even when it covers only usual figures.	**w** CUT-OFF WHOLE One or two small parts omitted; subject intends to respond to whole.	**w** CUT-OFF WHOLE Subject uses at least 2/3 of blot and makes a point of omitting certain portions.
				Dr *D* plus some adjacent portions of the blot.		

611

TABLE A.1. Locations (Continued)

	RORSCHACH AND BINDER	RAPAPORT AND SCHAFER	BECK	PIOTROWSKI	HERTZ	KLOPFER
D Response to a portion which is relatively large, clearly set off, and/or frequently interpreted.						
LARGE or USUAL DETAIL	DETAIL "Can be deter-mined statisti-cally"; in practice becomes known through experience.	NORMAL DETAIL **Dd** Small but not tiny area, clearly set off from the bulk of the blot.	DETAIL Statistically deter-mined by fre-quency of each *D* in each card.	NORMAL DETAIL Frequently selected by healthy sub-jects.	NORMAL DETAIL "Frequently per-ceived" by normal subjects, statisti-cally determined.	LARGE USUAL DETAIL Large detail, clearly marked off from rest of blot. **d** SMALL USUAL DETAIL Small detail clearly marked off from rest of blot.
DETAIL	**Dd** SMALL DETAIL An unusual or small detail.	**Dr** Tiny area, or areas neither clearly set off nor frequently interpreted.	**Dd** RARE DETAIL Not frequently enough selected to be *D*.	**d** SMALL OR RARE DETAIL Area rarely selected.	**Dr** RARE DETAIL Detail which is rarely perceived, as statistically deter-mined.	**dd** TINY DETAIL Minute detail.

	Do OLIGOPHRENIC DETAIL Part of Human or animal usually seen complete.	**De** EDGE DETAIL Contour part.	**Hdx** **Adx** Same as Rorschach's *Do*; scored under Content.	**Do** (After Rorschach.)	**Df** (After Rorschach.)	**de** EDGE DETAIL: Outline only. **di** INSIDE DETAIL: Demarcated by shading differences. **dr** RARE DETAIL: Unusual detail or unusual combination of usual details.
SMALL or RARE		**Do** OLIGOPHRENIC DETAIL Part of any concept usually seen complete.				
WHITE SPACE	**S** SPACE DETAIL White intermediate figures rather than surrounding black or colored areas.	**S** A relatively large white area in or around the blot.	**Ds** MAJOR WHITE SPACE (1) White areas in cards II, VII, and IX which qualify as *D* on frequency basis; *or* (2) *D* with major or minor white space as unit.	**S** NORMAL SPACE DETAIL White space which is frequently selected by normal subjects.		**S** WHITE SPACE Reversal of figure and ground so that white space is used for principal part of response.
		s A relatively small white area.	**Dds** MINOR WHITE SPACE (1) White area not *Ds*; *or* (2) *Dd* with minor white space as unit.	RARE OR SMALL SPACE DETAIL		
				d	**s**	

TABLE A.2. Determinants (excluding shading)

RORSCHACH AND BINDER	RAPAPORT AND SCHAFER	BECK	PIOTROWSKI	HERTZ	KLOPFER
F FORM	Response determined solely by the outline or shape of the blot area.				
				FM ANIMAL MOVEMENT	→**FM** TENDENCY TO ANIMAL MOVEMENT
				Animal in non-humanlike movement or posture.	Animal movement acknowledged reluctantly, posture in drawing, etc., of animal; animal-like expression in animal; weak movement or weak posture in animal.
				Involves a feeling of change in muscular tension.	Includes parts of animals in animal-like motion.

FORM

MOVEMENT

M (Human movement)

(In rare cases, animals and inanimate objects in motion are scored **M**. Ordinarily a tendency to **M** is noted, but the response is still scored **F**.)

Inanimate movement informally noted as **m** but scored **F**.

INANIMATE MOVEMENT

(Sometimes scored **M**, but generally scored **F**, after Rorschach.)

m INANIMATE MOVEMENT

Response involving both (1) "feeling of change in muscular tension" and (2) inanimate object in movement or state in which movement is actively prevented.

Fm Inanimate object moving or being moved; response determined primarily by definite form. Includes natural forces and artificial happenings. | Includes unreal figures or masks, animal or human.

mF Inanimate object of indefinite form moving or being moved.

m Inanimate object moving or being moved; no form involved. Includes abstract forces, facial expressions, phallic forces.

Also animal falling.

→**M** TENDENCY TO HUMAN MOVEMENT

Human movement or posture conceded reluctantly; human posture in drawing, humanlike expression on animal; tiny human in landscape.

Includes part of human in motion.

FM

WEAK MOVEMENT TENDENCY

Probable *M*-impression admitted under leading questions; usual humans seen as animals in humanlike movement; large part of human in clear movement.

Includes part of human in motion.

Includes animal in humanlike movement.

Ms

Human-movement response using relatively small area.

Includes animal in humanlike movement.

TABLE A.2. Determinants (excluding shading) (Continued)

RORSCHACH AND BINDER	RAPAPORT AND SCHAFER	BECK	PIOTROWSKI	HERTZ	KLOPFER
MOVE-MENT			**M** HUMAN MOVEMENT		
	Human figure in movement or posture, involving feeling of muscular tension on the part of the subject.				
COLOR Color			**FC** FORM-COLOR		
	Interpretation determined primarily by form, secondarily by color.				
					Colored object of definite form, where color used is that of the object in its natural state.
	FC ARBITRARY ARBITRARY FORM-COLOR (Same as Klopfer.)			**FC ARBIT** ARBITRARY FORM-COLOR (Same as Klopfer.)	**F↔C** FORCED FORM-COLOR Form-color response where subject "forces" color not that of object naturally; makes some attempt to rationalize color.

F/C ARBITRARY FORM-COLOR

Color is used to demarcate areas where the specific color is irrelevant.

FC sym FORM-COLOR SYMBOLISM

Form-color response where color is used symbolically.

F/C ARTIFICIAL FORM-COLOR

Same as Rapaport and Schafer.

FC DENIAL FORM-COLOR DENIAL

Color is referred to, but denied or negated.

Cd COLOR DENIAL

Color which presumably was used is denied. ("Flowers, but not because of the colors.")

F/C

Form-color response where color is used artificially, as "a map of Norway."

FC̄ FORM-COLOR BY DENIAL

Form-color response where inappropriate color is specifically excluded. ("A bear but it's the wrong color.") Not included in calculation of experience balance.

617

TABLE A.2. Determinants (excluding shading) (Continued)

RORSCHACH AND BINDER	RAPAPORT AND SCHAFER	BECK	PIOTROWSKI	HERTZ	KLOPFER
	FC' Response determined primarily by form, secondarily by black, grey or white color.	**FY FLAT GREY** Response in which form is "dominant," shading as an element in the black-white series is secondary.	**Fc'** Response determined primarily by the form; refers clearly to the dark or black aspects of the blot.	**FCh''** Response determined primarily by form, secondarily by black or dark grey color.	**FC' FORM-ACHROMATIC COLOR** Response determined primarily by definite form, secondarily by black, grey or white color.
			FCw Response determined primarily by form, secondarily by white color.	**FCh'** Response determined primarily by form, secondarily by light grey or white color.	

FORM COLOR
Achromatic Color

618

Interpretation determined primarily by color, secondarily by form.

Colored object of vague or indefinite form, with color that of object in its natural state.

C↔F FORCED COLOR-FORM

Color-form response where subject "forces" color not that of the object naturally.

CF sym COLOR-FORM SYMBOLISM

Color-form response where color is used symbolically.

(Same as Klopfer.)

CF COLOR-FORM

FORM COLOR
Chromatic Color

TABLE A.2. Determinants (excluding shading) *(Continued)*

RORSCHACH AND BINDER	RAPAPORT AND SCHAFER	BECK	PIOTROWSKI	HERTZ	KLOPFER
	C/F Color-form response where color is used artificially, as "a colored map."			**C/F** ARBITRARY COLOR-FORM Same as Rapaport and Schafer.	
COLOR FORM Achromatic Color	**C'F** Response determined primarily by black, grey or white color, secondarily by form.	**YF** Response in which shading as values of grey is dominant, form is secondary.	(For practical reasons of simplification, c'F is omitted from this scoring scheme, and all potential c'F are scored as either Fc' or c'.)	**Ch''F** Response determined primarily by dark grey or black color, secondarily by form. **Ch'F** Response determined primarily by light grey or white color, secondarily by form.	**C'F** ACHROMATIC COLOR-FORM Response determined primarily by black, grey or white color, secondarily by form.

C PURE COLOR

Interpretation determined by color, no form being involved.

Scored only where a certain color signifies the same concept in several cards and no attempt is made to relate the concept to other responses in those cards. Ex.: "blood" in isolation, no "animal fighting," etc.

Scored only when subject intends as interpretation and gives no other response to same blot.

Cn COLOR NAMING Color is named, with no attempt at interpretation.

Scored and tabulated, but not included in sum C.

Scored only when subject intends as interpretation.

Scored as a response, since it is so intended, as an answer to "what could this be?"

621

TABLE A.2. Determinants (excluding shading) *(Continued)*

	RORSCHACH AND BINDER	RAPAPORT AND SCHAFER	BECK	PIOTROWSKI	HERTZ	KLOPFER
Color		COLOR DENOMINATION Not a scorable response and not so intended by the subject.			**C denom** COLOR DENOMINATION Color referred to specifically ("red as you see it in a spectrum"). Infrequently a scorable response.	
		COLOR DESCRIPTION Not a scorable response. Reference to beauty or colorfulness of blot.			**C des** COLOR DESCRIPTION Colors are described with no attempt at interpretation. Scored only when subject intends as interpretation.	
					C sym SYMBOLIC CRUDE COLOR Color stands for an abstract idea.	**C sym** COLOR SYMBOLISM

PURE COLOR

Chromatic	**C det** DETERIORATION CRUDE COLOR Pure color response with gory or "uncanny" impression or haphazard association like "urine" or "inflammation."	**C det** DETERIORATION CRUDE COLOR Pure color response involving deterioration, disintegration, disease, goriness, etc.	**C'** ACHROMATIC COLOR Response determined by black, grey, or white color, with no form.
Achromatic Color	**C'** Response determined entirely by black, grey or white color.	**Y** Response determined entirely by grey values; no form.	**c'** Interpretation of the very dard nuances of the blot, in which the form is disregarded and in which direct reference is made to the dark or black interpreted areas.
		Ch'' Response determined entirely by dark grey or black color.	
		Ch' Response determined entirely by light grey or white color.	

623

TABLE A.2.A. Chiarascuro (shading)

RORSCHACH	BINDER	RAPAPORT AND SCHAFER	PIOTROWSKI	HERTZ	KLOPFER	BECK
				Fc DIFFERENTIATED TEXTURE		**FT** FORM-TEXTURE
				Response determined primarily by form, secondarily by differentiated surface or texture.		
F(C)			**Fc**		Also: Rounded effect; surface reflection.	Rounded effect; surface reflection.
Response determined primarily by form, secondarily by light-dark nuances of separate shadings.		Shading used to define form within heavily shaded area.	Interpretation based primarily on form, enriched by light graded (differentiated) shading.	**F(C)** Response determined primarily by form, secondarily by light-dark nuances of separate shadings. Includes vista or perspective.	**FK** VISTA	**FV** VISTA
		FC(C)			Response involving differentiated depth: a 3-dimensional effect, stressing:	
Includes vista.		Shading used to elaborate an *FC* response.	Includes vista.		one object in front of another; form unimportant.	distance, height, or depth.
		FORM SHADING **FCh**		**FCh**	**Fk**	**FY** FLAT-GREY
		Response determined primarily by definite form, secondarily by diffuse total "shading impression" which is well integrated with form.		(Same as Rapaport and Schafer.)	3-dimensional expanse projected on a 2-dimensional plane.	Light-determined response, where form is dominant.

FORM SHADING

624

	Form is definite, but shading is undifferentiated.		
	TF TEXTURE-FORM	**cF** UNDIFFERENTIATED TEXTURE	
		Response determined primarily by surface texture and secondarily by form.	
	VF Depth or distance dominates form.	**KF** UNDIFFERENTIATED DIFFUSION	**(C)F**
		Response involving diffusion and vague form.	3-dimensional-effect; shading dominates form.
	YF Light-determined response, where shading is dominant, form is secondary.	**kF**	**ChF**
		3-dimensions projected on 2; undifferentiated shading and vague form.	(Same as Rapaport and Schafer, excluding texture.)

Includes texture.	SHADING FORM **ChF**	
	Response determined primarily by general diffuse shading impression with indistinctly perceived form.	(For practical reasons of simplification, cF is omitted from this scoring scheme, and all potential cF are scored as either Fc or c.)

SHADING FORM

TABLE A.2.A. Chiarascuro (Shading) (Continued)

RORSCHACH	BINDER	RAPAPORT AND SCHAFER	PIOTROWSKI	HERTZ	KLOPFER	BECK
		(C)F Response in which shading is used to define form rather than "as shading," but form is vague. Also: Shading used in nondefinitive response to a colored area.				

SHADING FORM (Cont.)

PURE TEXTURE

Response determined solely by undifferentiated surface texture, form disregarded.

	c	**K**	**T**
(C) 3-dimensional effect; shading; no form.	**c** Interpretations in which the form is disregarded, but which nevertheless point to a concrete object with a definite physical structure. (Example: "topographical maps," "fog," "summer clouds.") Explicitly excludes responses in which achromatic area is interpreted as dark or black.	**K** Diffusion; depth with no form, space-filling light.	**V** Formless depth distance.
Ch (Same as Rapaport and Schafer excluding texture.)		**k** 3-dimensional object projected on a 2-dimensional plane, with no form at all.	**Y** Response determined entirely by grey values, with no form.

Ch PURE SHADING

Response determined entirely by general diffuse "shading" impression, with no form at all.

SHADING

TABLE A.3. Form Quality

RORSCHACH AND BINDER	RAPAPORT AND SCHAFER	BECK	PIOTROWSKI	HERTZ	KLOPFER
		F+ GOOD FORM			
Form as good as or better than those "given frequently" by normals.	Form responses of acceptable or superior accuracy: (1) can be readily empathized with, or (2) are given frequently by normals.	Established by comparison with tables of responses frequently given by normal subjects and infrequently by mental patients.	Sharply perceived form, which fits blot as well as or better than the percepts of popular responses fit their respective areas.	In accordance with frequency tables based on: (1) Given frequently by normals, or (2) response resembling established $F+$, or (3) response quite unlike any in lists, but subjectively judged to fit the blot area.	Form responses above average in accuracy, organization, and/or elaboration.
	F± Basically acceptable ($F+$) response with some minor inaccuracy.	**F** Response to minute Dd, too infrequent to have established criteria.	**F±** Response referring to object which does not have permanent invariable shape, though not formless.		**F** Ordinary, popular, or vague form responses.
	F∓ Basically inaccurate ($F-$) form with				Recent publications prefer to use the finer gradations of the form level rating system.

628

some saving feature; form responses referring to object with vague shape (cloud, map, etc.).

F— POOR FORM

| Form less good than F+. | Form response of inferior accuracy; strikingly vague or arbitrarily organized response with content that in reality is well articulated. | Established by comparison with tables of responses infrequently given by normal subjects, and frequently by mental patients. | Image of an object with a definite shape, but which does *not* fit its area well; (i.e., less well than popular responses fit their respective areas). | According to frequency tables. Includes subjective criterion of "lack of fitness." | Form responses where there is marked discrepancy between form qualities of the concept and those of the blot. |

TABLE A.4. Popular–Original

	RORSCHACH AND BINDER	RAPAPORT AND SCHAFER	HERTZ	KLOPFER	BECK	PIOTROWSKI
P POPULAR						
POPULAR	Response given by at least one out of three subjects to that blot area.	Response given by at least one out of five subjects to that blot area, excluding responses which are vague in form.	Response given by at least one out of six normal subjects to that blot area.	One of the ten responses representative of the most frequently given, for the whole test.	Response that is *both*: (1) given at least three times as often as the next most frequent response to that location: *and* (2) given by at least 14% of normal subjects.	A list of 13, given by at least 27% of a group of 200 "normal" and "mildly neurotic" adults.
		(P) Response approximately but not exactly the same as a popular.	Popular form incorporated in a more elaborated response.	(Same as Rapaport and Schafer.)		
O ORIGINAL						
ORIGINAL	Response given by no more than one out of 100 subjects.				(Beck does not score original responses.)	(After Rorschach.)
		O+ involves good form O− involves poor form O involves no form				

630

BIBLIOGRAPHY

Beck, S. J. *Rorschach's test, Vol. I: Basic processes.* New York: Grune and Stratton, 1944 (3rd ed., Revised with A. G. Beck, E. E. Levitt and H. B. Molish, 1961).

Hertz, H. Binder's shading responses. *Rorschach Res. Exch.*, 1938, 2, 79-88.

Hertz, M. R. *Rorschach scoring symbols with definitions, scoring formulae, and qualitative notations.* Department of Psychology, Western Reserve University (mimeographed).

Hertz, M. R. *Frequency tables for scoring responses to the Rorschach inkblot test.* Cleveland: Case Western Reserve University Press, 1970.

Klopfer, B., and Kelley, D. *The Rorschach technique.* Yonkers: World Book Co., 1942.

Klopfer, B., Ainsworth, M. D., Klopfer, W. G., and Holt, R. R. *Developments in the Rorschach technique, Vol. I: Technique and theory.* Yonkers: World Book Co., 1954.

Klopfer, B. The shading responses. *Rorschach Res. Exch.*, 1938, 2, 76-78.

Piotrowski, Z. A. A comparative table of the main Rorschach symbols. *Psychiat. Quart.*, 1942, 16, 30-37.

Piotrowski, Z. A. A Rorschach compendium, revised and enlarged. In Brussel, J. A., Hitch, K. S., and Piotrowski, Z. A. *A Rorschach training manual.* Utica, N. Y.: State Hospital Press, 1950, pp. 33-86.

Piotrowski, Z. A. *Perceptanalysis.* Privately published 1974 (orig. publ. New York: MacMillan, 1957.)

Rapaport, D., Gill, M. and Schafer, R. *Diagnostic psychological testing* (Revised edition by R. R. Holt). New York: International Universities Press, 1968.

Rorschach, H. *Psychodiagnostics.* Bern: Hans Huber; New York: Grune & Stratton, 1951 (Orignally published 1921).

Schafer, R. *Psychoanalytic interpretation in Rorschach testing.* New York: Grune & Stratton, 1954.

NAME INDEX *

Abbey, D., 415, 420
Abeles, N., 348, 369
Abrahamsen, D., 218, 226
Ackerman, N., 484
Adler, G., 513 533
Ainsworth, M. D., 81, 179, 186, 304, 324, 328, 336, 337, 366, 424, 425, 453
Allison, J., 103, 106, 109, 172, 184, 411, 415 ff., 418, 582, 606
Allport, F. H., 550, 551
Allport, G., 145, 154
Ames, A., 550, 551
Ames, L. B., 104, 109, 257, 259, 300
Angel, E., 24
Angyal, A., 145, 147, 154
Antrobus, J. S., 348, 371
Appelbaum, S. A., 583, 606
Arnheim, R., 10, 24, 355, 366
Arnold, M., 15, 24
Aronow, E., 332, 366
Asch, S. E., 440, 453

Bachrach, H., 411, 415, 417, 418
Baker, G., 607
Baker, L. M., 179, 184
Bandura, A., 116, 119, 120, 123, 124, 126, 128, 137, 141, 154
Barrell, R. P., 346, 366
Barrera, S. E., 563, 573
Barron, F., 345, 350, 366, 366, 549, 551
Bartko, J. J., 456, 457, 460, 485
Bash, K. W., 11, 12, 24, 325, 354, 366, 515, 516, 529, 533

Bass, B. M., 551, 607
Bateson, G., 455, 483
Batt, H. V., 57, 79
Baughman, E. E., 120, 154, 570, 572
Beatman, F. L., 484
Beavin, J. H., 484
Beck, S. J., 30, 31, 32 ff., 47, 54 ff., 59 ff., 64, 79, 86, 154, 160, 161, 162, 165, 168, 170, 171, 184, 191, 226, 304, 323, 326, 337, 366, 371, 435, 453, 567, 577 ff., 583, 606
Becker, W. C., 31, 32, 80, 100, 104, 109
Behn, H., 536, 549, 564
Beizmann, C., 170, 184
Belden, A. W., 120, 154
Bellak, L., 162, 163, 184, 596, 606
Bene, E., 330, 358, 364, 366
Benfari, R. C., 412, 418
Berg, I. A., 551
Bergan, J. R., 415, 418
Bertalanffy, V. L., 455, 483
Bialick, I., 591, 606
Bibace, R., 101
Bieri, J., 338, 349, 366
Billig, O., 118, 154
Binder, H., 16, 17, 303 ff., 323, 489, 507, 511, 516, 533
Binet, A., 535
Binswanger, L., 507, 511
Blacker, E., 338, 349, 366
Blake, R. R., 34, 82
Blatt, S. J., 103, 106, 109, 172, 184, 416, 418, 582, 606

*Numbers in boldface refer to entries in the bibliography.

633

Blechner, J. E., 341, 366
Bleuler, E., 113, 144, 145, 154, 481, 483
Bleuler, M., 561, 574
Blewett, D., 332, 333, 367
Block, J., 331, 366
Boardman, W. K., 328, 359, 368
Boas, G., 521, 533
Bohm, E., 117, 154, 303–324, 319, 323
Boland, G. C., 177, 186
Booth, C. G., 210, 211, 226
Borgatta, E. F., 124, 134, 135, 143, 154
Boss, M., 117, 151, 154
Bowers, M. K., 215, 216, 226
Brackbill, G., 100, 109
Braun, E., 304, 323
Brawer, F. B., 186, 515, 533, 607
Brecher, S., 215, 216, 226
Bremer, A. H., 218, 226
Bricklin, B., 223, 226
Broekmann, N. C., 331, 366
Brosin, H. W., 8, 24, 561, 572
Brower, D., 330, 366
Brown, F., 424, 453
Brown, S. L., author, 325-372
Brozek, J., 174, 185
Bruner, J. S., 9, 24
Brunswik, E., 348, 367
Brussel, J. A., 631
Buckle, D., 564, 565, 572
Buhler, C., 118, 154
Buhler, K., 118, 154
Burdock, E. I., 586, 606
Buros, O. K., 590, 601, 606
Burstein, A. G., 601
Butler, S., 159
Bychowski, S., 226

Caldwell, M., 178, 185
Calogeras, R. C., 412, 418
Campbell, J., 534
Capone, T. A., 345, 368
Carlson, V. R., 180, 185

Carson, R. C., 138, 154
Caruth, E., 163, 186
Caston, J., 209, 226
Chambers, G. S., 592, 606
Claire, 347, 372
Clark, K. B., 185
Climes, S., 103, 105, 109
Cocking, R., 348, 367
Coff, P., 344, 371
Cohen, J. 608
Cohen, R., 347, 368
Colson, D. B., 583, 606
Cook, S. W., 557, 573
Cooper, L., 209, 226
Couch, A., 145, 154
Counts, R. M., 135, 154
Coyle, F. A. Jr., 173, 187
Crabbé-Decléve, G., 119, 123, 139, 154
Crandell, V. J., 85, 109

Dana, R. H., 346, 348, 367, 590
Davidson, H., 81, 178, 186
Davis, R. W., 534
Dawo, A., 332, 367
De Koninck, J. M., 119, 123, 139, 154
Derman, B. I., 415, 418
Descoudres, 256, 300, 301
Despert, J. L., 226
Deutsch, M., 557, 573
Dorken, H., 570, 572
Dudek, S. Z., 103, 106, 109, 223, 226, 352, 367
Dworetzki, G., 102, 259, 260, 300
Dyk, R. B., 337, 372

Eckhardt, W., 355, 367
Edinger, E. F., 514, 533
Efron, H. Y., 201, 226
Eichler, R., 332, 341, 367, 564, 572
Einsdorfer, C., 103, 105, 109
Eisenstein, V. W., 226
Ellenberger, H., 18, 24, 536, 551
Endacott, J. L., 118, 154
Endicott, J., 593, 606
Endicott, N. A., 593, 606

Erginel, A., 328, 367
Eriksen, C. W., 180, 185
Eron, L. D., 32, 82, 177, 187, 590, 608
Eschenbach, A. E., 124, 134, 135, 143, 154
Evans, R. B., 583, 606
Exner, J. E. Jr., 115, 126, 135, 154, 164, 185
Eysenck, H. J., 329, 355, 367

Faterson, H. F., 139, 156, 337, 372
Faunce, E., 464, 473, 484
Favorite, L., 344, 371
Feirstein, A., 415 ff., 418
Feldstein, S., 356, 367
Felzer, S. B., 332, 341, 367
Fenichel, O., 146, 154
Ferenczi, S., 238, 249
Fine, H. J., 100, 109
Finkelstein, M., 607
Finn, J. A., 119, 148, 154
Finney, B. C., 338, 367
Fishman, D. B., 417, 418, 599, 606
Fiske, D. W., 594, 607
Fister, W. P., 330, 370
Fleiss, J. L., 608
Fonda, C. P., author, 61, 81, 113–156, 116, 127, 136, 137, 138, 155
Ford, M., 30, 80, 257, 259, 300, 336, 337, 367, 561, 566, 573
Fortier, R. H., 328, 359, 367
Fosberg, I. A., 561, 573
Foster, A., 361, 367
Fowler, N., 100, 109
Fox, E., 149, 155
Framo, J. L., 95, 101, 109, 110
Frank, G. H., 580, 606
Frank, I. K., 92, 109
Frank, L. K., 422, 453, 537, 551
Frankle, A. H., 244, 249
Freed, E., 97, 109
Frerking, R. A., 607
Freud, S., 80, 85, 145, 155, 238, 249, 305, 323, 439, 453
Friedman, A., 506

Friedman, H., 31, 48, 80, 85, 89, 90, 103, 104, 106, 109, 171, 172, 185, 336, 356, 357, 367, 598, 606
Fromm, E., 8, 24, 561, 572
Fulkerson, S. C., 109
Furrer, A., 504, 511
Fuschillo, J., 347, 369

Gammon, M., 523, 533
Gardner, R. W., 173, 186, 338, 367, 404, 415, 419
Garfield, S. L., 591, 606
Gebhart, V., 490
Gediman, H. K., 163, 184
Gellerman, S., 347 ff., 368
George, C. E., 180, 187
Gibby, R. C., 177, 185, 349, 367, 562, 573
Gibson, J. J., 12, 24
Gill, M. M., 118, 156, 161, 166, 181, 186, 232, 249, 252, 270, 300, 552, 577, 607
Glass, H., 331, 339, 347, 368
Glatt, C. T., 600, 606
Glaser, R. B., 458, 473, 484
Goethe, J. W., 421, 489, 506, 511
Goldberg, L., 340, 367, 414, 415, 418
Goldberger, L., 237, 249, 414, 415, 418
Goldfarb, W., 56, 80, 118, 155, 330, 367
Goldfried, M. R., 32, 80, 103, 105, 109, 172, 185, 583, 589, 599, 600, 603, 606
Goldman, A. E., 367
Goldman, G. D., 236, 249, 347, 356, 371
Goldman, R., 179, 185
Goldstein, G. 579, 608
Goldstein, K., 10, 12, 24, 262, 300
Gombosi, P. G., 416, 418
Goodenough, D. R., 139, 156, 337, 372
Gottlieb, S. G., 223, 226

Govinda, A., Lama., 12, 24
Grace, N. B., 101, 109
Grassi, J., 8, 24
Gray, J. J., 410, 418
Griffin, D. P., 347, 367
Griffith, R. M., 563, 573
Grossman, C. 80
Guilford, J. P., 383, 566, 574
Guirdham, A., 30, 80

Hall, C. S., 439, 440, 453
Halpern, F., 257, 300
Hamlin, R. M., 588, 591, 592, 606, 607
Hammer, E. F., 194, 226
Hamilton, J., 332, 333, 367
Hanfmann, E., 260, 261, 262, 300
Hardesty, A. S., 586, 606
Harlow, H. F., 300
Harrington, R. L., 349, 367
Harris, J. S., 179, 184
Harrower-Erikson, M. R., 549, 551, 577, 578, 607
Hartmann, H., 180, 185, 363, 368, 377, 378, 418
Havel, J., 376, 392
Hay Associates, 220, 223, 224, 226
Hays, J. R., 328, 359, 368
Hays, W., 347 ff., 368
Heath, D. H., 416, 419
Heise, M. R., 212, 227
Hemmendinger, L., author, 31, 48, 80, 83–111, 89, 109, 172
Hendrick, I., 145, 155
Herman, J., 339, 344, 346, 347, 349, 368, 371
Herron, E. W., 81, 125, 155
Hersch, C., 101, 103, 106, 107, 110, 347, 368
Hertz, M. R., author, 29–82, 30, 31, 36, 37, 47, 49 ff., 64, 65, 67, 68, 71, 72, 80, 86, 160, 165, 168, 185, 556, 560, 566, 567, 568, 573
Hertzman, M., 180, 185, 241, 249, 330, 368

Hetzel, W., 607
Higgins, J., 332, 368
Hill, E. F., 125, 155
Hitch, K. S., 631
Hoch, P. H. 155, 226
Hollingshead, A. B., 477, 483
Holstein, S., 607
Holt, N., 564, 565, 572
Holt, R. R., author, 81, 173, 179, 185, 186, 237, 249, 304, 324, 343, 355, 368, 375–420, 377, 380, 382, 412, 413, 418, 419, 599, 606
Holtzman, W. H., 32, 48, 62, 81, 118, 125, 155, 338, 368, 410, 549, 551, 594, 607
Holzberg, J. D., 555–574, 569, 571, 573
Holzman, P. S., 583, 606
Honkavaara, S., 300
Hoover, T. O., 222, 227, 341, 372
Hunt, W. A., 590, 607
Hunter, M., 331, 368
Hurvich, M., 163, 184
Hurwitz, I., 101, 110
Husserl, E., 489, 505, 511
Hutt, M. L., 177, 185
Huxley, A., 263, 300

Ingram, W., 129, 155
Irizarry, R., 410, 419

Jacks, I., 194, 226
Jackson, D. D., 484
Jackson, H., 542, 543
Jahoda, M., 557, 573
James, W., 535
Janoff, I. Z., 30, 81
Jensen, A. R., 588, 590, 607
John, E. R., 416, 417, 419
Jolles, I., 35, 57, 59, 81
Jones, E., 375
Jones, J. E., 456, 483

Jung, C. G., 22, 325, 354, 355, 425, 426, 435, 436, 439, 453, 513, 514, 517, 521, 533

Kaden, S., 81, 103, 110
Kadinsky, D., 516, 533
Kahn, M. W., 173, 185, 331, 371
Kalter, N., 124, 155
Kantor, R., 105, 109
Karon, B. P., 591, 600, 606, 607
Karp, S. A., 139, 156, 337, 372
Kasanin, J., 260, 261, 300
Kass, W., 85, 110
Katz, D., 263, 267, 300, 310, 323
Kay, L., 178, 187
Kelley, D. M., 166, 171, 175, 176, 186, 563, 573, 577, 607
Kelley, T. L., 563, 573, 594, 607
Kelly, E. L., 244, 249, 607
Kendig, I., 347, 372
Keniston, K., 145, 154
Kennard, M. A., 330, 370
Kennedy, S., 67, 80
Kerr, M., 561, 573
Kimball, A. J., 162, 166, 167, 168, 185
Kimble, G. A., 561, 562, 573
King, G. F., 244, 249, 346, 368
Kirkner, F. J., 607
Kisker, G. W., 179, 185
Kissel, S., 103, 106, 110
Kjenaas, N. K., 174, 185
Klages, L., 311, 324
Klebanoff, S. G., 118, 155
Klee, P. 29
Klein, G. S., 334, 368, 415, 419
Kleinman, R. A., 332, 368
Klett, J. C., 607
Klinger, E., 588, 601, 607
Klopfer, B., 30, 48, 56, 81, 160, 166, 168, 169, 175, 176, 179, 185, 186, 235, 240, 249, 257, 300, 304, 324, 336, 337, 354, 368, 447, 453, 515, 533, 568, 577, 598, 599, 607

Klopfer, W. G., 81, 179, 186, 304, 324, 424, 428, 453
Knoph, I. J., 580, 607
Knutson, J. F., 601
Koehler, W., 14, 24
Koffka, K., 8, 12, 24, 83, 119, 155
Kohler, I., 550, 551
Korchin, S. J., author, 159–187, 339, 347, 356, 369
Kraemer, D., 337, 351, 368
Kretschmer, E., 314, 324, 329
Kris, E., 75, 76, 81, 180, 186, 343, 368, 377, 379, 413, 419
Krohn, A., 248, 249
Kronenburg, B., 156
Kropp, R. P., 34, 57, 62, 81, 85
Kruger, A., 100
Kruglov, L., 178, 185
Krugman, J. E., 568, 573
Kubie, L., 181
Külpe, O., 306, 324
Kuhn, R., author, 489–511, 511
Kupper, H. L., 350, 359, 368
Kurz, R. B., 345, 347, 368
Kushner, E. N., 415, 419

Lair, W. S., 357, 368
Lane, B. M., 347, 368
Larson, D. G., author, 159–187
Lasky, J. J., 607
Latif, I., 238, 249
Lazarus, R. S., 180, 185
Learned, J., 257, 300
Lederman, R. 351, 370
Lefever, D. W., 118, 154
Leiman, C. J., 334, 335, 368
Lemkau, P., 156
Lerner, B., 144, 155, 168, 186, 348, 356, 368
Le Shan, L., 517, 533
Leventhal, H., 81
Levi, J., 337, 351, 368
Levi, L. D., 456, 484
Levine, D., 103, 106, 110
Levine, K., 8, 24

Levine, M., 331, 339, 347, 368, 369
Levy, D. M., 145, 155, 549
Levy, L. H., 600, 607
Lewin, K., 3, 15, 24, 336, 369, 543, 552
Lidz, T., 456, 483, 484
Lindberg, B. J., 256, 300
Linn, L., 118, 155
Linton, H. B., 398, 419
Lipton, H., 103, 110
Little, K. B., 592, 607
Litwin, D., 342, 369
Loehrke, L. M., 49, 68, 72, 81
Lofchie, S. H., 110
Lohrenz, L. L., 173, 186
Lohrenz, L. J., 404, 419
Long, F. J., 591, 607
Lonstein, M., 60, 81
Lord, E., 135, 136, 155, 177, 186, 562, 573
Lorr, M., 586, 607
Loveland, N. T., 348, 369, 458, 473, 483
Lowenfeld, M., 535, 552
Luchins, A. S., 562, 573
Luborsky, I., 244, 249
Luria, A. P., 336, 369

Macfarlane, J. W., 558, 563, 565, 573
Machover, K., 535, 552
MacLeod, R. B., 17, 24
Mann, L., 338, 369
Margulies, H., 257, 300, 336, 337, 368, 563, 573
Marmorston, J., 583, 606
Marohn, R. C., 607
Marsden, G., 103, 106, 110, 124, 155, 582, 607
Marwit, S. J., 329, 371
Martin, F. B., 220
Masling, J., 600, 608
Maslow, A., 363, 369
Matarazzo, R. G., 335, 369
Maupin, E. W., 415, 419
May, R., 22, 24

Mayman, M., author, 160, 162, 171 ff., 186, 236, 237, 248, 229–250, 404, 410, 419, 600, 607
McArthur, C. R., 601
McCall, R. J., 137, 155
McCandless, B. R., 59, 81
McClelland, D. C., 556, 573
McCraven, V., 347, 361, 371
McCully, R. S., author, 423, 453, 513–534, 515, 517, 522, 528, 530, 533, 534
McFarland, R., 564, 571, 573
McMahon, J., 411, 419
McNair, D. M., 607
McReynolds, P., 566, 574
Mead, G. H., 357, 369
Mead, M., 520, 534
Meehl, P. E., 138, 155
Meer, B., 331, 371
Megargee, E. I., 218, 221, 226
Meili-Dworetzki, G., 30, 31, 67, 81
Meltzoff, J., 236, 249, 331, 339, 340, 342, 347, 356, 368, 369, 371
Melville, H., 113, 117, 155, 340
Mensh, I. H., 135, 154
Merei, F., 516, 534
Merrifield, J., 458, 483
Metraux, R. W., 257, 300
Metzger, W., 12, 15, 16, 24
Meyer, M. M., 163, 186, 607
Miale, F. R., author, 422, 421–454, 577, 578, 607
Milgram, S., 141, 155
Milton, E. O., 177, 185
Mindess, H., 355, 369, 423, 424, 436, 437, 441, 454
Mirin, B., 192, 193, 226
Misch, R. C., 99, 100, 110, 338, 369
Mitsunaga, A., 351, 369
Mohr, P., 319, 320, 324, 515, 534
Molish, H. B., 54, 55, 60, 81, 154, 178, 187, 337, 371
Morris, G. O., 458, 483
Mueller, W. J., 348, 369
Munroe, R. L., 556, 557, 569, 573

Murawski, B., 334, 347, 351, **369**
Murphy, G., *author*, 159, **186**, 535–552
Murphy, L., *author*, 535–552
Murray, D. C., 132, 133, 136, 140, 141, **155**
Murray, H. A., 535, **552**
Mursell, J. L., 556, **573**
Myers, T. I., 410, 415, **419**

Nasielski, S., 119, **155**
Neiger, S., 125, **156**
Nelson, W. D., 116, 121, 137, **155**
Neuringer, C., 119, 148, **154**, 579, **608**
Newmark, C. S., 600, **607**
Nickerson, E. T., 351, **369**

Oberholzer, E., 118, **156**, 421, 447, 454, 536
Oberlander, M. I., 412, 416, **419**
Offer, D., **607**
Ogden, C. K., 455, **483**
Opler, M. K., 345, 359, **369**, 371
Orange, A., 566, 567, **573**
Orgel, S., 103, 106, **109**
Orlansky, J., 330, **368**
Orme, J. D., 588, **607**
Orr, T. B., 600, **607**
Osgood, C. E., 328, 359, 360, **369**
Ostrov, E., 600, **607**
Otis, L. S., 59, **81**

Page, H. A., 347, 348, **369**
Palmer, J. O., 331, 333, 348, 350, 356, **369**, 591, **607**
Palombo, S. R., 458, **483**
Paolino, A. F., 49, 52, 53, 64, 65, 68, 71, **80**
Parker, R. S., 194, **226**, 346, **369**
Pearce, J., 241, **249**
Pêna, C. D., 92, **110**
Phillips, L., 31, 45, 48, 69, 81, 90, 101, 103, 104, 107, **110**, 424, **454**
Piaget, J., 336, **369**, 383
Pickering, W. D., 348, 349, **369**

Pine, F., 381, 413, **419**
Piotrowski, Z. A., *author*, 160, 161, 166, 170, 179, **186**, 189–227, 342, 343, 346, 362, **369**, 370, 519, **534**, 556, **574**, 577
Pious, W. L., 242, **249**
Podkomenyi, A., 410, **419**
Pope, B., 588, **607**
Potkay, C. R., 591, **607**
Pottharst, K., 177, **185**
Powers, W. T., 588, **607**
Prola, M., 340, **370**
Pryor, D. B., 173, **186**

Quirk, D. A., 125, **156**

Rabin, A. I., 117, **156**, 178, 184, 561, **574**, 601
Rabinovitch, M. S., 330, **370**
Rabkin, J., 412, **419**
Rapaport, D., 31, 45, 69, 81, 118, **156**, 160, 163, 166, 168, 171, 181, **186**, 230, 232, 236, **249**, 252, 253, 270, 300, 336, 356, 359, **370**, 377, 404, **420**, 422, **454**, 459, **483**, 547, **552**, 577, 584, **607**
Ray, J. B., 139, 140, **156**
Raychaudhuri, M., 332, **370**
Redlich, F. C., 477, **483**
Reichard, S., 85, **110**
Reik, T., 142, **156**
Reitan, R. M., 61, **81**, 579, **608**
Resnik, H. L. P., **226**
Revesz, G., 256, **300**
Reznikoff, M., 601
Ribot, T., 307, **324**
Ricci, J., 456, **484**
Ricciuti, H. N., **110**
Richards, I. A., 455, **483**
Richards, T. W., 351, **370**
Richter, R. H., 347, **370**
Rickers-Ovsiankina, M. A., *author*, 3–25, 11, **24**, 252, 275, **300**, 339, 343, 355, 359, **370**, 577, 578, 583, **608**

Rieman, G. W., 580, 608
Riesen, A. H., 264, 266, 301
Rimbaud, J. N. A., 251
Rioch, M. J., 343, 370
Roberts, R., 58, 82
Robinson, C., 389
Rochwarg, H., 101, 110
Rock, M. R., 224, 226
Roe, A., 107, 352, 353, 364, 366, 370
Roemer, G. A., 193, 194, 223, 227, 515, 534
Rorschach, H., 3, 13 ff., 18, 24, 29, 30, 81, 110, 113, 114, 156, 161, 165, 186, 189, 190, 191, 193, 221 ff., 227, 230, 231, 249, 300, 325 ff., 354, 370, 421, 435, 447, 454, 489, 503, 504, 507, 509, 511, 515, 534, 535 ff., 541, 545, 548, 552, 577, 608
Rosanes, M., 211, 227
Rosen, E., 151, 156
Rosen, M., 413, 416, 417, 420
Rosenberg, N., 138, 156
Rosenblatt, B., 100, 111
Rosenthal, D., 483
Rosenthal, M., 344, 370
Rosenzweig, S., 535, 552
Rosenwein, T., 607
Rosman, B., 456, 484
Roth, E., 122, 156
Roth, I., 588, 600, 607
Royal, R. E., 344, 370
Rubin, E., 113, 156
Rubin, H., 60, 81
Rubinstein, B. B., 567, 573
Russell, E. W., 579, 608
Rychlak, J. F., 177, 186

Safrin, R., 383, 420
Sanderson, M. H., 561, 574
Sanford, R. N., 537, 552
Sarason, E. K., 34, 57, 81
Sarason, S. B., 170, 177, 186
Sargent, H., 556, 574
Sarma, D. V. N., 520, 534

Schachtel, E. G., 12, 25, 151, 156, 163, 169, 170, 174, 177, 181, 186, 237, 244, 249, 252, 300, 353, 355, 359, 370, 562, 574
Schacter, M., 138, 156
Schafer, M., 577, 607
Schafer, R., 118, 156, 160, 161, 166, 168, 169, 177, 181, 186, 187, 232, 237, 249, 252, 284, 300, 376, 416, 420, 427, 436, 437, 454, 552, 562, 574
Scharmann, T., 122, 156
Scheerer, M., 262, 300
Scheler, M., 311, 324
Schilder, P., 229, 263, 267, 300
Schleifer, M. J., 571, 573
Schlesinger, H. J., 334, 368, 415, 419
Schmidt, B., 329, 370
Schmidt, H. O., 61, 81
Schoektel, E.
Schonbar, R., 347, 348, 371
Schreiber, M., 208, 225, 226, 342, 343, 370
Schultz, D., *author,* 103–111
Schumer, F., 32, 82, 177, 187, 334, 347, 349, 370, 591, 608
Seitz, C., 330, 368
Selzer, M., 443, 453
Sells, S. B., 594, 607
Senden, M., 255, 263 ff., 268, 273, 277, 286, 300
Shaffer, L. F., 129, 156
Shapiro, D., *author,* 12, 25, 119, 148, 156, 251–301, 349, 355, 359, 360, 370, 579, 608
Shatin, L., 347, 350, 358, 370
Shaw, G. B., 555
Sheerer, M., 14, 25
Sherif, M., 334
Sherman, M. H., 580, 608
Sherman, S. N., 484
Shneidman, E. S., 592, 607
Sicha, K., 560, 574
Sicha, M., 560, 574
Siegal, E. L., 31, 82, 92, 104

Siipola, E., 328, 337, 338, 360, 370
Silverman, L. H., 382, 420
Simón, M. E., 520, 534
Singer, D. G., 371
Singer, J. L., author, 236, 237, 325–
    372, 332, 334 ff., 338 ff., 344,
    346, 347 ff., 355, 356, 358, 359,
    361, 369, 370, 371, 564, 574
Singer, M. T., author, 455–485, 456,
    457, 458, 460, 464, 473, 483,
    484, 485
Sinnett, E. R., 58, 82
Sisson, B. D., 34, 58, 60, 82
Slemon, A. G., 125, 156
Sloan, W., 59, 82, 347 ff., 368
Smith, G. M., 185
Smith, J. G., 31, 45, 69, 81, 424, 454
Smith, S., 180, 187
Smith, W. H., 173, 187
Sojit, C., 456, 484
Solomon, P., 100, 111
Spiegelman, M., 102, 111, 515, 533
Spielberger, C. D., 226
Spitzer, R. L., 586, 608
Spivack, G., 347, 369
Spohn, H., 339, 346, 347, 371
Sprigle, H., 347, 371
Starzynski, S., 347, 368
Stauffacher, J. C., 584, 588, 608
Steele, N. M., 331, 371
Stein, H., 85, 102, 111
Stein, M. I., 122, 156, 161, 187, 259,
    300, 331, 371
Stein, M. L., 119, 141, 148, 156
Steiner, M. E., 551
Stern, W., 159, 187
Stotsky, B. A., 349, 367
Stromgen, E., 316, 324
Strange, J. R., 180, 185
Strauss, M. E., 329, 371
Stricker, G., 32, 80, 172, 185, 583,
    606
Suares, N., 117, 156
Suci, G. J., 328, 359, 360, 369
Sugarman, D., 348, 358, 371

Sullivan, D. J., 118, 154
Sullivan, H. S., 371
Swartz, J. D., 81, 125, 126, 155
Swift, J. W., 561, 563, 564, 574
Sydiaha, D., 332, 333, 367
Symonds, M., 555, 574
Szondi, L., 535, 552
Szymanski, J. S., 307, 324

Tamaus, J. C., 105, 109
Tannenbaum, P. H., 328, 359, 360, 369
Taulbee, E. S., 34, 58, 60, 82
Tavernier, A., 347, 369
Taylor, V., 337, 338, 360, 370
Teltscher, H. O., 341, 371
Temerlin, M. K., 349, 371
Ternus, J., 529, 534
Thetford, W. N., 35, 36, 58, 60, 82,
    178, 184, 187, 336, 337, 351,
    371
Thiesen, J. W., 82, 338, 344, 371, 584,
    587, 608
Thiesen, W. G., 35, 79, 184
Thomas, R. W., 349, 367
Thompson, J., 59, 82, 256, 300
Thomson, J. A., 575
Thornton, G. R., 566, 574
Thorpe, J. S., 32, 62, 82, 125, 126,
    155
Thurstone, L. L., 549, 552
Tomkins, S. S., 398, 403, 420
Toohey, M. L., 456, 457, 460, 485
Toomey, L. C., author, 609–631
Troup, E., 332, 372, 561, 574
Trubetskoi, E. N., 12, 25
Tuddenham, R. D., 558, 563, 565, 573

Ulett, G. A., 335, 369

Vakar, G., 12, 25
van Kaam, A. L., 22, 23, 25
Varvel, W. A., 35, 62, 67, 82
Vernier, C., 347, 372
Vernon, P. E., 30, 82, 555, 556, 558,
    561, 566, 574

Vinson, D. B., 580, 608
Volkelt, J., 311, 312, 324
Vorhaus, P., 178, 187
Voth, H. M., 236, 250

Wagner, E. E., 212, 222, 227, 341, 372
Waldman, M., 81, 101, 105, 110
Walker, L., 607
Walker, R. G., 166, 167, 187
Walker, R. N., 257, 300
Wapner, S., 10, 11, 25, 355, 356, 372
Ward, A. J., 342, 372
Warshawsky, F., 80
Watkins, J. G., 584, 588, 608
Watson, R. I., 335, 369
Watzlawick, P., 455, 484
Weber, A., 506
Weber, C. O., 336, 372
Wechsler, D., 383
Weigert, W., 458, 483
Weigl, E., 260, 261, 301
Weiner, D., 452
Weiner, I. B., author, 80, 160, 164, 170, 179, 185, 187, 575–608, 579, 583, 584, 585, 588, 593, 596, 606, 608
Weiss, L., 600, 608
Weiss, R., 415, 420
Weltman, R., 136, 156
Wenger, M. A., 329, 363, 372
Werner, H., 3, 10, 11, 25, 31, 82, 83, 84, 111, 172, 187, 231, 238, 250, 254, 256, 258, 301, 333 ff., 360, 372, 542, 543, 550, 552
Wertham, F., 561, 574
Wertheimer, M., 86, 102, 111

Wexler, M., 562, 573
Wheeler, W. M., 583, 608
White, R. W., 119, 148, 156
Whyte, L. L., 520, 534
Wild, C., 456, 484
Wilensky, H., 103, 106, 111, 347, 361, 371
Williams, M., 180, 187
Wilson, G. P., 34, 57, 82
Wilson, M. T., 101, 111
Wilson, P. D., 266, 301
Winter, W. D., 347, 370
Wirt, R., 566, 574
Wisham, W. 607
Wishner, J., 36, 57, 82
Witkin, H. A., 119, 139, 150, 156, 337, 372, 547, 552
Wittenborn, J. R., 328, 361, 372
Wittgenstein, L., 455
Wittkower, E., 351, 372
Wolfson, W., 136, 156
Wolman, B. B., 226
Wright, N. A., 415, 420
Wynne, L. C., 455 ff., 460, 473, 483, 484, 485

Young, K. M., 549, 552

Zimet, C. N., 100, 109
Zimmer, J., 517, 534
Zollinger, A., 303
Zubek, J. P., 415, 420
Zubin, J., 32, 48, 82, 155, 177, 187, 226, 354, 355, 372, 549, 552, 580, 590, 591, 608
Zulliger, H., 117, 156, 316, 324, 549, 552

SUBJECT INDEX

Abstract ability, 33, 63
Abstract attitude, 261-262
    and emotionality, 262
Action tendencies, 194
Actors, 222
Actuarial research, 123-124
Adults, 93-94
Age regression, hypnotic, 215 ff.
Aggression, 133-135
Alcohol, 218-219
Analytic psychology, 354
Anxiety, 318-319
Archetypal, character and cross cultural intelligibility, 520
    energy, 516, 529-531
    image, 517-518
    language, 516-517
Assasins, 217
Attentional level, 458
Autochthonous principle, 86
Autokinetic phenomena, 333-334
Autokinetic Test (Sherif's), 139-140
Autonomy drive, 129, 147-148
Aviation school, success in, 594, 596

Behn-Rorschach Test, 564
Binder's scoring system, 312-318
Binder's theory, 304-312
Blocking, 400
Brain damage, 92, 100, 231, 260-261, 596

Categories of analysis, 5-6
Chiaroscuro responses, 303-323
    scoring, 312 f.
    see also Shading

Children, 89, 93, 255-260
Cognitive differentiation, 149-150
Color, 11, 14-15
Color avoidance, 276-277
Color experience, 252-254
Color-form response, 277 ff., 310
Color naming, 258-259
Color perception,
    in brain damage, 260-261
    in children, 255 ff.
    in formerly blind subjects, 255, 263-265
    in hypomanic patients, 283-284
    in hysteria, 277-278, 281 ff.
    in form perception, 264 ff., 268-269
Color response,
    absence of, 274-276
    and emotion, 274
    artificial, 283-285
    pure (C), 270-277
    understanding of, 270 f.
Color stress index, 584-587
Combination, fabulized, 45
    see also Fabulized response
Communication, deviances, 464-478
    in commitment, 464-466
    in disruption, 469-470
    in language, 467-469
    in referents, 466-467
    in sequences, 471-472
Communication, process of, 455
    impact of, 456-457
    samples of, 459
Communication styles,
    family, 457-458, 472, 478-482
    spouse, 472-478

Communication, verbal, 20
Compatability scale, marital, 223
Condensation, 393-394
Configuration approach, 79
Consciousness, objective, 521-522, 526
    subjective, 521-522, 526
Construct validity, 596
Contamination, 46
Content, 5, 18
    aggressive, 390-392
    libidinal, 384-385, 389-390
Content analysis, 423-453
    and scoring categories, 447-453
Context, 399-400
Contradiction, 395-
Creativity, 106-107, 403, 507-508

Dark shock, 318-320
Defense, 397-403
    mechanisms, 151-152, 174-178
Delay, 400
Delayed response, 161
Delta index, 584, 586-587
Depression, 313, 318-319, 437
Determinants, 6, 8-9
Developmental levels, 542-545
    scoring, 104, 598-599
    (Werner), 172
Developmental theory, 7, 84-85, 254
Deviance manual, 460-464
Diagnosis, psychiatric, 580
Differentiation, 543
Displacement, 394-395
Downey's Motor Inhibition Test, 361
Downey's Will Temperament Scale, 340
Draw-a-Person Test, 535
Dreams, 144, 191-192, 392-395, 435-
    436

Ego, 304-305
Ego functioning, 159-160, 182-183
Electroencephalogram, 330-356
Emotion, 308-311
Empathy, 244 ff., 311-312
Epilepsy, 316

Examiner, sex of, 500
Executives, 223-224
Existence, 506 ff.
Existentialism, 22
Experience balance,
    and autokinetic phenomena, 333-
        334
    and constitutional factors, 329-333
    and environmental responsiveness,
        336-344
    and fantasy, 344-353
    and imagination, 344-353
    and motor activity, 336-344
    and perceptual correlates, 333-336
    and space response, 115
    and theory, 353-366
    and thinking, 344-353
    see also experience type
Experience type, 17-18
    behavioral correlates of, 326-353
    physiological correlates of, 329-333
Extratension, 509
    see also Introversion-extratension

Fabulized combination, 45
Fabulized response, 235-237
Family communication styles, 457-
        458, 472, 478-482
Fantasy, 234-237, 344-353
    vs. imagination, 521
Feelings, characteristics of, 305
    categories of, 305-307
Figure-ground, 48
Figure-ground reversal, 7-8, 117, 120
Form, 9-10, 13-14
Form appropriateness (FA), 32, 62
Form-color response (FC), 287-299,
        310
    inadequate (F/C) 292 ff.
Form definiteness (FD), 32, 62
Form-level, 583, 596-598
Form-level,
    and clinical groups, 178-179
    and defense, 174-175
    and integration ability, 175-176

and motivation, 176
and needs, 174
and psychological health, 180 ff.
and stress, 179-180
Form-level rating, 30 f., 48, 172-173
scoring, 168-170
Form perception *(F+)*, 159-184
Formerly blind subjects, 255, 263-265

g (Vernon), 30
g (Hertz), 30, 36-40, 62-73
and clinical groups, 67-73
and intelligence, 65-67
interpretation of, 72 ff.
norms of, 48-53
(g) reliability of 53-54
(g) validity of, 73
Gestalt theory, 231, 529-530, 538
principles of, 8
Graphology, 423

Holistic nature of the Rorschach, 557-559
Holtzman Inkblot Technique, 106, 118, 125, 410
Homosexuals, 583
Hostility, 135-136
Humor, 379
Hypomanics, 283-284
Hysterics, 277-278, 280 ff.

Identification, 244 ff.
Identity, 238, 243, 433
Imagination, 344-353
vs. fantasy, 521
Individuality, 541
Integration, 32, 48, 62, 97
Intelligence, 106
and *g*, 65-67
and *Z*, 54-62
Intelligence Scale, Wechsler-Bellevue, 56 f., 383, 558
Interaction, principles of, 4

Interdependence,
of functions,538-545
Interference phenomenon, 319
Interpretation,
consistency of, 567-570
dream, 435-436
representational, 453, 601-605
symbolic, 20, 423 ff., 601-605
Interrelationship,
of variables, 582-584
Introversion-extratension, 327 ff., 509-510
Introversion-extraversion, 514-515

Katona Match Stick Test, 344
Kinesthesia, 237-241, 327 ff.
Kinesthetic,
memory, 237-238
response, *see* Movement

Location, 5, 6-8
Location score, 83
Lowenfeld Mosaic Test, 535

Mastery striving, 145-146, 151
Matching technique, 558 559
Mayman's *FL* system, 403-404
Mechanisms of defense, 151 ff., 174-175
see also Defense mechanisms
Mental deficiency, 49, 100
Miller Analogies Test, 346
Minnesota Multiphasic Personality Inventory, 151, 350
Mood, 307-308, 322, 539-540
Motivation, 176 ff.
Movement, 9, 10-11
Movement response, 506-507
and empathy, 244-248
and fantasy, 234-237
and gestalt theory, 230 ff.
and interpersonal relationships, 222, 241-244
and kinesthesia, 237-241

Movement response—*Cont.*
   and motor inhibition, 191 f., 236-237
   and perceptual imbalance, 231
   and psychotherapy, 224-225, 241 ff.
   and the unconscious, 243
   axial vs. lateral, 210-211
Movement response, animal
   and age regression, 215 ff.
   and alcohol, 218-219
   and psychotherapy, 223
Movement response, human
   and army life, 195 ff.
   and intoxication, 218-219
   and multiple personality, 212 ff.
   and suicide, 203 ff.
   of actors, 221-222
   of executives, 223-224
   of killers, 217-218
   of pedophiles, 194
   of rapists, 194
   of schizophrenics, 194, 198, 200 ff.
   of strippers, 221-222
Movement response, inanimate, 224-225, 240
Movement types, human
   ambivalent, 222
   and overt behavior, 207
   and psychotherapy changes, 208
   exhibitionistic, 222
Mp [movement projection], 222

Needs, 174
Negativism, 113-114, 132-133, 144-145
Neurosis, 578
Neurotics, 222, 278 f., 315, 318-319
Norms, for *g* score, 48-53
   for *Z* score, 35-36

Object-sorting test, 255-256, 259-260, 268, 456
Ontogenetic principle, 90
Oppositional tendency, *see* Negativism
Organicity, 583, 596
Organization, ability of, 30 ff.

Original response, *see* Popularity-originality,

PAR (Computer Rorschach), 220-221
Pathology, visual, 263-265
Perception, 308-310
   distortion of, 396-397
   research, 550-551
Perceptual-cognitive theory, 63
Perceptual passivity, 253-254, 266
   processes, 9
Personality, definition of,
   biosocial, 536-537
   evolutionary, 542
   functions, 547-548
   multiple, 212 ff.
   research, 541
   structure, 22, 542-544
   tendencies, 546-548
Personology, interest in, 193
Phenomenological psychology, 16, 304
Phenomenology, 16, 489
Picture Frustration Test, 137
Popularity-originality, 6
Porteus Maze Test, 345, 361
Prägnanz, 119
Prediction, 593-594
   and army life adjustment, 196
   and effect of alcohol, 218-219
   and personality, multiple, 212 ff.
   of Rorschach performance, 223
   of schizophrenia course, 194
Primary Mental Abilities Test (Thurston's), 549
Primary process, scoring, 598-599
Primary-secondary process, 375-418
Process, analysis, 523
Process, non-conscious, 521-522, 524
Prognostic scale, long term, 200-201
   Whitman's, 100
Prognostic Rating Scale *(PRS)*, 599-600
Projection, hypothesis,
   self reference of, 425 ff.
Proverb Interpretation Test, 456
Psychoanalysis, 376
Psychodiagnosis, 421-422, 456-457

Psychological health, 180 ff.
Psychometrics, 23, 564-567, 535
Psychopathology, 105-106
Psychopaths, 315, 318-319, 320-321, 421
Psychosomatic, 105
Psychotherapy, and Rorschach findings, 208, 223 f., 241-242, 502-503

Rapid eye movement, 356
Reality testing, 162 ff., 169-170, 596
Regression, 105
  in the service of the ego, 379, 413-414
  perceptual, 92, 100
Relationships, interpersonal, 222, 241-243
Reliability, 23, 411-412
  consistency of interpretation, 567-570
  equivalent forms, 564-565
  of g and Z, 53-54
  split-half, 565-567
  test-retest, 561-564
Research, clinical, 107
Ring test, 256

Schizophrenia, 92, 93, 194, 198, 201-202, 209, 222, 255, 260-261, 274, 278, 438, 577-579, 583, 584-589, 596-599
  chronic, 462-464
  process-reactive, 100, 106
Scoring, form-level, 167 ff.
  Handbook of (Beizman's), 170
Secondary process, 375-418
Self-esteem, 136-137
Sensory deprivation, 414
Sensory-tonic theory, 7
Serendipities, 143
Sex of M figures, 194
Shading, 12, 15-16
  see also chiaroscuro
Shading response,
  fine shading F(C), 312 ff.

form-shading (FCh), 315 ff.
  proper (Ch), 315
  shading-form [ChF], 316-317
Shrinkage of data, 578
Sign approach, 577-583
Social intelligence, 143
Sophropsyche, 304
Sophropsychic control, 304-305

Space response, 113 ff.
  and aggression, 133-135
  and cognitive differentiation, 149-150
  and disobedience, 141-142
  and dream analysis, 144
  and experience balance, 114-115
  and hostility, 135-136
  and indecisiveness, 137-138
  and independence, 139-141
  and mechanisms of defense, 151-153
  and psychiatric nosology, 150-151
  and psychological differentiation, 138-139
  and self-esteem, 136-137
  and serendipities, 143-144
  and social intelligence, 143
  clinical considerations of, 148-153
  correlates of, 128 144
  primary, 113-115
  reliability of, 126-128
  secondary, 115-117, 121-122

Street gestalt test, 334-335
Stress, 178-180
Subject-environment relation, 10, 11, 12, 13, 15, 17
Suicide, 203, 583
Suicide scale, 206
Symbol, formation, 531
Symbol vs symptom, 521, 533
Symbolism, 395, 601 f.
Symbols,
  metaphoric character of, 439-447
  reference of, 424-439
Synchronicity, 528-529
Szondi test, 535

Tachistoscopic experiment, 259
Test pattern, 20-22
Testing, group vs. individual, 195-196
Thematic Apperception Test (*TAT*),
    340, 347-348, 358, 456, 535
Thinking, 344-353
Thought, distortion of, 396-397
Time perspective, 510-511

Unconscious, 508, 511

Validity, 23, 128-129, 411, 412-418,
    556
  and cluster approach, 584-589
  and concept approach, 595-601
  and configuration approach, 584-
    589
  and empirical sign approach, 577-
    584
  and global impression approach,
    589-595
  and negative studies, 581
  and sign approach, 577-584

of *g*, 72-73
Verbalization, 396
  pathognomic (*V*), 32
  relationship, 45
Vigotsky Test, 260, 261, 262
Violence, impulsive vs. calculated,
    194, 218-220
Visual pathology, 263-265

Wechsler-Bellevue Intelligence Scale,
    558
White space as color, 117
White space *see* space response
Whole responses (*W*), 29 ff., 503-507,
    581

Z score (Beck's), 30, 33-36, 171
  and clinical groups, 55 f.
  and intelligence, 54 ff.
  and intellectual energy, 55
  norms of, 35-36
  reliability of, 53-54
  weighted values, 33

ACKNOWLEDGMENTS

Thanks are due to the following authors and publishers for use of the materials indicated:

Adler, G., "C. G. Jung after ten years," *Psychological perspectives Journal,* 2, 1971. Used in Chapter 15.

Ainsworth, M. D., "Illustrative case study." In B. Klopfer, M. D. Ainsworth, W. G. Klopfer and R. R. Holt, *Developments in the Rorschach Technique,* Vol. I, World Book Company, 1954. Used in Chapter 12.

Allison, J., "Adaptive regression and intense religious experience," *Journal of nervous and mental Disease,* 145, 1967. Used in Chapter 11.

Angyal, A., *Neurosis and treatment: a holistic theory,* Wiley, 1965. Used in Chapter 4.

Arnheim, R., *Art and visual perception,* University of California Press, 1969. Used in Chapter 1.

"Artistic symbols—Freudian and otherwise," *Journal of aesthetics and art Criticism,* 12, 1953. Used in Chapter 12.

Asch, S. E., "On the use of metaphor in the description of persons." In H. Werner (Ed.), *On expressive language,* Clark University Press, 1955. Used in Chapter 12.

Bandura, A., "The Rorschach white space response and perceptual reversal," *Journal of experimental Psychology,* 1954.

Beck, S. J., "Emotions and understanding", *International psychiatry Clinics,* 3, 1966. Used in Chapter 5.

Rorschachs test, Vol. I. Basic processes (2nd ed., revised), Grune and Stratton, 1949.

Rorschach's test, Vol. II. A variety of personality pictures, Grune and Stratton, 1945. Used in Chapter 2.

Rorschach's test, Vol. III. Advances in interpretation, Grune and Stratton, 1952. Used in Chapter 2.

Becker, W. C., "A genetic approach to the interpretation and evaluation of the process-reactive distinction of schizophrenia," *Journal of abnormal social Psychology,* 53, 1956. Used in Chapter 3.

Bellak, L., Hurvich, M. and Gediman, H. K., *Ego functions in schizophrenics, neurotics, and normals: a systematic study of conceptual, and therapeutic aspects,* Wiley, 1973. Used in Chapter 5.

Benfari, R. C., and Calogeras, R. C., "Levels of cognition and conscience typologies," *Journal of projective techniques and personality Assessment,* 32, 1968. Used in Chapter 11.

Bleuler, E., "The theory of schizophrenic negativism, *Nervous and mental disease Monographs,* N. 11, 1912. Used in Chapter 4.

Boas, G., Preface to *Myth, religion and mother right* (Johann Bachofen, 1885), Princeton University Press, 1967. Used in Chapter 15.

Bohm, E., "Das Binder'sche Helldunkelsystem," *Rorschachiana,* Vol. V, Hans Huber, 1959.

Borgatta, E. F., and Eschenbach, A. E., "Factor analysis of Rorschach variables and behavioral observation," *Psychological Reports, 1,* 1955. Used in Chapter 4.

Boss, M., "Psychologisch-charkterlogische Untersuchungen bei antisozialen mit Hilfe des Rorschachschen Formdeuteversuches," *Zeitschrift für gesamte Neurologie und Psychiatrie, 133,* 1931. Used in Chapter 4.;

Bowers, M. K., and Brecher, S., "The emergence of multiple personalities in the course of hypnotic investigation," *J. clinical and experimental Hypnosis, 3,* 1955. Used in Chapter 6.

Brown, F., "An exploratory study of dynamic factors in the content of the Rorschach protocol," *Journal of projective Techniques, 17,* 1953. Used in Chapter 12.

Bühler, C., Bühler, K. and Lefever, D. W., *Development of the basic Rorschach score with manual of directions* (Rev.), Rorschach Standardization Studies, No. 1, 1949. Used in Chapter 4.

Buros, O. K. (Ed.), *The sixth mental measurements yearbook,* Gryphon Press, 1965. Used in Chapter 18.
The seventh mental measurement yearbook, Gryphon Press, 1972. Used in chapter 18.

Edinger, E. F., *Ego and archetype,* G. P. Putnam's Sons, 1972. Used in Chapter 15.

Exner, J. E., Jr., *The Rorschach: A comprehensive system,* Wiley, 1974. Used in Chapter 4.

Fenichel, O., The psychoanalytic theory of neurosis, Norton, 1945. Used in Chapter 4.

Fonda, C. P., "the nature and meaning of the Rorschach white space response," *Journal of abnormal and social Psychology, 46,* 1951. Used in Chapter 4.

Goldstein, K., *The organism,* American Book Company, 1963. Used in Chapter 1.

Hall, C. S., *The meaning of dreams,* Harper, 1952. Used in Chapter 12.

Hendrick, I., "Instinct and the ego during infancy" and "The discussion of the 'instinct to master'," *Psychoanalytic Quarterly, 12,* 1943. Used in Chapter 4.

Hertz, M. R., and Paolino, A. F., "Rorschach indices of perceptual and conceptual disorganization," *Journal of projective Techniques,* 24, 1960. Used in Chapter 2.

Hollingshead, A. B. and Redlich, F. C., Social class and mental illness, John Wiley, 1957. Used in Chapter 13.

Holt, R. R., "Artistic creativity and Rorschach measure of adaptive regression." In B. Klopfer, M. M. Meyer and F. B. Brawer (eds.), *Developments in the Rorschach technique, Vol. III: Aspects of personality structure,* Harcourt Brace Jovanovich, 1970. Used in Chapter 11.

"Gauging primary and secondary processes in Rorschach responses," *Journal of Projective Techniques,* 20, 1956.

Holtzman, W. H., Personal communication, November, 1974. Used in Chapter 4.

Ingram, W., "Prediction of aggression from the Rorschach," *Journal of consulting psychology,* 18, 1954. Used in Chapter 4.

Jung, C. G., *The practice of psychotherapy,* Pantheon, 1954. Used in Chapter 12.

Psychological types, 1921. Used in Chapter 15.

Symbols of transformation, Pantheon, 1956. Used in Chapter 15.

Two essays on analytical psychology, Pantheon, 1953. Used in Chapter 12.

Ueber die Energetik der Seele und andere psychologische Abhandlungen, Rascher, 1928. Used in Chapter 12.

Kimball, A. J., *Evaluation of form-level in the Rorschach.* Doctoral dissertation, University of California, Berkley, 1948. Used in Chapter 5.

Klopfer, B., "Technique and theory". In B. Klopfer, M. D. Ainsworth, W. G. Klopfer and R. R. Holt, *Developments in the Rorschach Technique,* Vol. I, World Book Company, 1954. Used in Chapters 5 and 12.

Klopfer, B. and Kelley, D. M., *The Rorschach technique,* World Book Company, 1942. Used in Chapter 7.

Klopfer, W. G., "Interpretative hypotheses derived from analysis of content." In B. Klopfer, M. D. Ainsworth, W. G. Klopfer, R. R. Holt, *Developments in the Rorschach technique,* Vol. I, World Book Company. Used in Chapter 12.

Kris, E., *Psychoanalytic explorations in art,* International Universities Press, 1952. Used in Chapters 2 and 11.

Kuhn, R., "Grundlegende statistische und psychologische Aspekte des Rorschachschen Formdeutversuches," *Zeitschrift fur diagnostische Psychologie,* 1. Jahrgang, Heft 4, Hans Huber, 1953.

Lerner, B., "A new method of summarizing perceptual accuracy on the Rorschach," *Journal of projective techniques and personality Assessment,* 32, 1968. Used in Chapter 5.

"Rorschach movement and dreams: a validation study using drug-induced dream deprivation," *Journal of abnormal Psychology,* 71, 1966. Used in Chapter 4.

Levy, D. M., "Oppositional syndromes and oppositional behavior," In *Psychopathology of childhood,* P. H. Hoch and J. Zubin (Eds.), Grune and Stratton, 1955. Used in Chapter 4.

Mayman, M., "Reality contact, defense effectiveness, and psychopathology in Rorschach form-level scores." In B. Klopfer, N. M. Meyer, F. B. Brawer and W. G. Klopfer (Eds), *Developments in the Rorschach technique, Vol. III. Aspects of personality structure,* Harcourt Brace Jovanovich, Inc., 1970. Used in Chapter 5.

McCully, R. S., *Rorschach theory and symbolism: a Jungian approach to clincial material,* The Williams and Wilkins Company, 1971. Used in Chapter 12.

McMahon, J., *The relationship between "over-inclusive" and primary process thought in a normal and a schizophrenic population.* Unpublished doctoral dissertation, New York University, 1964. Used in Chapter 11.

Mead, M., "A note on the evocative character of the Rorschach test." In R. W. Davis (Ed.), *Toward a discovery of the person,* Society for Personality Assessment Monograph, 1974. Used in Chapter 15.

Meehl, P. E., "Comments on the invasion of privacy issue." In J. N. Butcher (Ed.), *MMPI: research developments and clinical application,* McGraw Hill, 1969. Used in Chapter 4.

Megargee, E. I., "The prediction of violence with psychological tests." In C. D. Spielberger (Ed.), *Current topics in clinical and community psychology,* Academic Press, 1970. Used in Chapter 6.

Mindess, H., "Analytical psychology and the Rorschach test," *Journal of projective Technique,* 19, 1955. Used in Chapter 12.

Morris, C. W., *Foundations of the theory signs,* University of Chicago Press, 1955.

Murray, D. C., "An investigation of the Rorschach white space response in an extratensive experience balance as a measure of outwardly directed opposition, *Journal of projective Techniques,* 21, 1957. Used in Chapter 4.

Oberlander, M. I., *Pupillary reaction correlates of adaptive regression.* Unpublished doctoral dissertation, University of Chicago, 1967. Used in Chapter 11.

Phillips, L. and Smith, J. G., *Rorschach interpretation: advanced technique,* Grune and Stratton, 1953. Used in Chapter 12.

Piotrowski, Z. A. *Perceptanalysis,* Macmillan Company, 1957. *Perceptanalysis: a fundamentally reworked, expanded and systematized Rorschach method,* 3rd print, Ex Libris, 1974. Used in Chapter 6.
"The M, FM and m responses as indicators of changes in personality," (Rorschach research Exch., 1, 1937. Used in Chapter 6.

Potkay, C. R., *The Rorschach clinician,* Grune and Stratton, 1971. Used in Chapter 18.

Rabkin, J., *Psychoanalytic assessment of change in organization of thought after psychotherapy.* Unpublished doctoral dissertation, New York University, 1967. Used in Chapter 11.

Rapaport et al., *Diagnostic psychological testing,* Year Book Publishers, 1946.

Reik, T., *The search within,* Aronson, 1974. Used in Chapter 4.

Rorschach, H., *Psychodiagnostics, a diagnostic test based on perception,* Translated by P. Lemkau and B. Kronenburg. Hans Huber, 1942. Used in Chapter 4.

Schachtel, E. G., *Experiential foundations of the Rorschach test,* Basic Books, 1966. Used in Chapter 5.

Shapiro, David, Reply to Jerome L. Singer's question in Chapter 10.

Singer, M. T., *Scoring manual for communication deviances seen in individually administered Rorschachs,* revision, 1973. Unpublished. Used in Chapter 13.

Wagner, E. E., and Heise, M. R., "A comparison of Rorschach records of three multiple personalities," *Journal of projective Techniques,* 38, 1974. Used in Chapter 6.

Werner, H. and Wapner, S., "Sensory-tonic field theory of perception." *J. Personal.,* 18, 1949.

Whyte, L. L., "The growth of ideas." In Joseph Campbell (Ed.), *Man and transformation,* Pantheon, 1964. Used in Chapter 15.

Zollinger, A., One poem from a collection of Swiss poetry. Hans Huber.